ORGANIZATIONAL BEHAVIOR

Managing People and Organizations

TWELFTH EDITION

Ricky W. Griffin
Texas A&M University

Jean M. Phillips
Pennsylvania State University

Stanley M. Gully
Pennsylvania State University

Australia • Brazil • Japan • Korea • Mexico • Singapore • Spain • United Kingdom • United States

Organizational Behavior: Managing People and Organizations, Twelfth Edition
Ricky W. Griffin, Jean M. Phillips, Stanley M. Gully

Vice President, General Manager, Social Science & Qualitative Business: Erin Joyner

Product Director: Jason Fremder

Senior Product Manager: Scott Person

Senior Content Developer: Julia Chase

Product Assistant: Brian Pierce

Marketing Director: Kristen Hurd

Marketing Manager: Emily Horowitz

Marketing Coordinator: Christopher Walz

Manufacturing Planner: Ron Montgomery

Art and Cover Direction, Production Management, and Composition: Cenveo Publisher Services

Cover Image(s): ©Rawpixel/Shutterstock.com

Intellectual Property

Analyst: Diane Garrity

Project Manager: Sarah Shainwald

Library of Congress Control Number: 2015950160

ISBN: 978-1-305-50139-3

Cengage Learning
20 Channel Center Street
Boston, MA 02210
USA

Cengage Learning is a leading provider of customized learning solutions with office locations around the globe, including Singapore, the United Kingdom, Australia, Mexico, Brazil, and Japan. Locate your local office at: **www.cengage.com/global**

Cengage Learning products are represented in Canada by Nelson Education, Ltd.

To learn more about Cengage Learning Solutions, visit **www.cengage.com**

Purchase any of our products at your local college store or at our preferred online store **www.cengagebrain.com**

Printed in the United States of America
Print Number: 06 Print Year: 2018

ABOUT THE AUTHORS

Ricky W. Griffin

Ricky W. Griffin holds the Blocker Chair in Business and is University Distinguished Professor of Management in the Mays Business School at Texas A&M University. He has also served as Head of the Department of Management, Executive Associate Dean, and Interim Dean at Mays.

Ricky is both a member and Fellow of the Academy of Management and has served as program chair and division chair of the organization's Organizational Behavior division. He also served as editor of the *Journal of Management*. Ricky's research has appeared in *Administrative Science Quarterly*, *Academy of Management Review*, *Academy of Management Journal*, *Journal of Management*, and several other journals. He has also edited several scholarly books, most recently *The Dark Side of Organizational Behavior*.

He has authored or co-authored several leading textbooks, most of which have been revised across multiple editions. His books have also been translated or adapted for use in over a dozen other countries. Ricky teaches international management, organizational behavior, human resource management, and general management. He has taught both undergraduate and graduate students, participated in numerous executive training programs, and has lectured in London, Paris, Warsaw, Geneva, Berlin, Johannesburg, Tokyo, Hong Kong, and Sydney.

Jean M. Phillips

Jean Phillips is a Professor of Human Resource Management in the School of Labor and Employment Relations at Penn State University. Jean earned her Ph.D. from Michigan State University in Business Management and Organizational Behavior. Her interests focus on leadership and team effectiveness, recruitment and staffing, and the processes that lead to employee and organizational success.

Jean was among the top 5 percent of published authors in the *Journal of Applied Psychology* and *Personnel Psychology* during the 1990s and she received the 2004 Cummings Scholar Award from the Organizational Behavior Division of the Academy of Management. She has published over thirty research articles and nine books, including *Strategic Staffing* (3e, 2014), *Organizational Behavior* (2e, 2013), *Human Resource Management* (2013), *Managing Now* (2008), and the five-book *Staffing Strategically* (2012) series for the Society for Human Resource Management. Jean was also the founding co-editor of the Organizational Behavior/Human Resource Management series for Business Expert Press.

Her applied work includes leveraging employee surveys to enhance strategic execution and business performance, developing leadership and teamwork skills, and creating and evaluating strategic recruitment and staffing programs. Jean has taught online and traditional courses in Human Resource Management and Organizational behavior in the U.S., Iceland, and Singapore.

Stan M. Gully

Stan Gully is a Professor of Human Resource Management in the School of Labor and Employment Relations at Penn State University. Stan holds M.A. and Ph.D. degrees in Industrial/Organizational Psychology from Michigan State University and he is a Fellow of the Society for Industrial and Organizational Psychology.

Stan has authored, co-authored, edited, or presented numerous papers, books, and book chapters on a variety of topics, including leadership, team effectiveness, motivation, training, staffing, and recruitment. He is a founding co-editor of the Organizational Behavior/Human Resource collection of Business Expert Press. Stan is ranked in the top fifty of the most influential scholars who received their degrees since 1991 based on impact inside and outside of the Academy of Management and he has won awards for his teaching, research, and service.

Stan has taught courses at the undergraduate, master's, executive, and Ph.D. levels covering a wide range of topics including team effectiveness, leadership, organizational learning and innovation, staffing, human resource management, training, and statistics. He has taught using traditional and hybrid technologies in the United States, Iceland, Singapore, and Indonesia. His applied work includes, but is not limited to, management at UPS, design of leadership training programs, implementation of team communication interventions, and implementation of a multi-source feedback system.

BRIEF CONTENTS

CONTENTS

PART 2
INDIVIDUAL BEHAVIORS AND PROCESSES IN ORGANIZATIONS

CHAPTER 3
Individual Characteristics 86

PART 3
SOCIAL AND GROUP PROCESSES IN ORGANIZATIONS

PREFACE

Welcome to the 12th edition of *Organizational Behavior*. Or is it the 3rd edition? Or even the 1st edition? In some ways any of these edition numbers might be correct. How is this possible? Let's explain. …

Ricky Griffin and Greg Moorhead published a textbook entitled *Organizational Behavior* in 1986. The book was very successful and underwent regular revisions every few years. The hallmark of *Organizational Behavior* has long been comprehensive content based on sound academic research brought to life through examples and case studies. Since its very first edition the book has been a market leader. A few years ago Greg retired from teaching after a long and distinguished career but continued to work with Ricky on multiple editions of *Organizational Behavior*. However, he finally decided to give up this work as well, and the 11th edition was his last.

Meanwhile, Jean Phillips and Stan Gully published the first edition of their own *Organizational Behavior* textbook in 2012 and revised it in 2014. Jean and Stan's book also had strong content, of course, but it truly set new standards of excellence with its outstanding array of features, learning aids, digital support material, and video programs. In 2014, Ricky, Jean, and Stan met in Philadelphia during the Academy of Management meeting and came up with the idea of combining our books. We saw this as a true win-win opportunity to create a new book that would merge the historically strong content of the older book with the contemporary content and cutting-edge support materials of the newer book.

Development Process

We started our work by carefully reviewing each of the two existing books, new and current developments in the field of organizational behavior, and reviewer feedback about the strengths of each book. We then carefully developed a new outline of sixteen chapters. In our judgment, this structure provides thorough and comprehensive coverage of the major topics within the field of organizational behavior while also providing a framework that can be effectively covered in a single semester.

We also developed an integrated learning model that demonstrates how all of the topics within the book relate to one another. This model is developed in Chapter 1. It is then revisited at the beginning of each part. The reader is reminded of how earlier chapters led them to the current discussion and where the discussion is headed next. Last but not least, we included most of the features that Jean and Stan had so carefully created.

Our goals are to make you more successful in your life and career by helping you understand yourself, understand organizations, and understand the role of organizational behavior (OB) in your personal career success. We also want to cultivate an understanding of and ability to apply knowledge about individual and group behavior in organizations and to appreciate how the entire organizational system operates. This will enhance your understanding of how to flexibly apply the OB concepts that are appropriate for different problems or situations. Finally, we want to ensure that you have a complete understanding of the modern OB context, including ethics, diversity, competitive advantage, technology, and the global context.

Features

Our new book contains several features designed to reinforce the themes of the book and further develop your OB skills.

Real World Challenge To help you recognize OB-relevant issues in organizations, each chapter begins with a *Real World Challenge* that describes a real challenge or problem faced by a person or organization that relates to that chapter's content. The chapter then concludes with a description of how the company or individual addressed the challenge.

Global Issues A *Global Issues* feature in each chapter highlights the global implications of some of the chapter's content.

Case Study A *Case Study* in each chapter reinforces some of each chapter's material and gives you the opportunity to apply what you learn in the chapter to a real organizational situation.

Understand Yourself To help you better understand your own characteristics, an *Understand Yourself feature* in each chapter gives you the chance to assess yourself on a variety of topics relevant to OB. This feature will help you better understand what motivates you, how you view money, your leadership style, your emotional intelligence, and your diversity awareness, among other things.

Improve Your Skills Each chapter also contains an *Improve Your Skills* box to help you become more effective in different areas including dealing with challenging managerial behaviors, interviewing, managing stress, negotiating, and assessing an organization's culture and political environment.

Group Exercises Each chapter also includes a group-based experiential exercise. This exercise will help both further your understanding of basic concepts of organizational behavior while simultaneously helping you improve your skills in working with others.

Now What? Video Cases Captivating *Now What*? decision-making videos put you in the manager's chair. Four videos are included for each chapter, with the first video presenting a business challenge, and three shorter videos providing "correct" and "incorrect" responses to the challenge. A short synopsis and discussion questions to accompany each video are included at the end of the chapter.

Video Exercises Also included with each chapter are separate stand-alone videos featuring real-world companies to show managerial challenges. These exercises and discussion questions appear at the end of each chapter.

Instructor Support Materials

- Instructor Companion Website: Instructors can find course support materials, including Instructor's Resource Manual, Test Bank files, PowerPoint® slides, and DVD guide.

- On the Job DVD: "On the Job" videos provide behind-the-scene insights into management concepts at work within actual small and large businesses. Corresponding support material can be found in the DVD guide.
- Cengage Learning Testing, powered by Cognero® Instant Access: Cengage Learning Testing powered by Cognero® is a flexible, online system that allows you to: import, edit, and manipulate content from the text's test bank or elsewhere, including your own favorite test questions; create multiple test versions in an instant; and deliver tests from your LMS, your classroom, or wherever you want.

Student Support Materials

- MindTap® Management is the digital learning solution that helps instructors engage students and help them relate management concepts to their lives. Through interactive assignments students connect management concepts to real-world organizations and say how managers should perform in given situations. Finally, all activities are designed to teach students to problem-solve and think like management leaders. Through these activities and real-time course analytics, and an accessible reader, MindTap helps you turn cookie cutter into cutting edge, apathy into engagement, and memorizers into higher-level thinkers.

  Our adaptive learning solution provides customized questions, text, and video resources based on student proficiency. Priced to please students and administrators, this solution will help you develop the next generation of managers.
- The **learning path** is based on our **Engage**, **Connect**, **Perform**, and **Lead** model. Students are drawn into the material with self-assessments. Quizzes and homework assignments help students connect concepts with the real world, and higher level homework assignments ask students to analyze and manage complex situations.
  - **Self-Assessments** engage students by helping them make personal connections to the content presented in the chapter.
  - **Reading Quizzes** assess students' basic comprehension of the reading material to help you gauge their level of engagement and understanding of the content. Students are able to see compare their responses against others in their class, school and everyone one who's previously taken the self-assessment.
  - **Assignments** for each chapter elevate thinking challenging students to think critically and begin to think like managers.
  - **Concept Videos** present short enrichment clips of information on topics students typically struggle with.
  - **Video Case Activities** engage students by presenting everyday businesses facing managerial challenges, placing concepts in real-world context and making for great points of discussion.
  - **Experiential Exercises powered by YouSeeU** include role play and group projects challenge students to work in teams in our one-of-a-kind collaborative environment to solve real-world managerial problems, develop skills and begin to experience firsthand what it's like to work in management.
  - **Branching Activities** challenge students to evaluate work situations and decide what actions they might take as managers. Then students

use their knowledge of management to identify the advantages and disadvantages of different managerial approaches.

- **Adaptive Study Centers powered by Knewton** are provided at the unit level and the exam level to help students work toward mastery of course content. Material presented is customized to students' specific needs and serves up questions, feedback, remediation, and instructional content according to how they progress.
- **Writing Activities powered by Write Experience** offers students the opportunity to improve their writing and analytical skills without adding to your workload. Offered through an exclusive agreement with Vantage Learning, creator of the software used for GMAT essay grading, Write Experience evaluates students' answers to a select set of assignments for writing for voice, style, format, and originality.

ACKNOWLEDGMENTS

Although this book bears our three names, many other people have also contributed to it. Through the years we have had the good fortune to work with many fine professionals who helped us to sharpen our thinking about this complex field and to develop new and more effective ways of discussing it. Over the course of multiple editions of two different books literally dozens of reviewers have helped us develop and refine our materials. Their contributions were also essential to the development of this edition. Any and all errors of omission, interpretation, and emphasis remain the responsibility of the authors.

The 12th edition could never have been completed without the support of Texas A&M University, Rutgers University, and Penn State University. We would also like to acknowledge the outstanding team of professionals at Cengage Learning who helped us prepare this book. Julia Chase has been steadfast in her commitment to quality and her charge to us to raise quality throughout the book. Scott Person, Carol Moore, Mike Schenk, Jason Fremder, Brian Pierce, and Erin Joyner were also instrumental to our work. Jennifer Ziegler, Rajachitra Suresh, Sarah Shainwald, and Diane Garrity were also key players in the creation of this text and support program. We would also like to acknowledge the decades-long contributions that Greg Moorhead made to this book. His friendship and professionalism will always be remembered. We would like to thank the iTV studio team as well as the entire cast and crew for helping us to create engaging and interesting videos that bring the book concepts to life. We wish to highlight the efforts of J. Allen Sudeth, Pete Troost, John Keller, and Hebert Peck for making the videos possible.

Finally, we would like to acknowledge importance of our families. For Ricky, he was reminded many times during the work on this book about the central role of family and the fragility of life. He sends special appreciation to Glenda, Dustin, Ashley, Matt, and Lura. For Jean and Stan, Ryan, Tyler, Murphy (the dog), and Mooch (the cat), provided love and laughs to motivate them and to help them to keep things in perspective.

DEDICATION

For the next generation—Griffin, Sutton, and Andrew (RWG)

To Ryan and Tyler, who make our lives complete (JMP & SMG)

PART 1 INTRODUCTION TO ORGANIZATIONAL BEHAVIOR

Managers strive to make their organizations as effective and successful as possible. To do this they rely on assets such as financial reserves and earnings, technology and equipment, raw materials, information, and operating systems and processes. At the center of everything are the employees who work for the organization. It is usually their talent, effort, skill, and ability that differentiates effective from less effective organizations. It is critical, then, that managers understand how the behaviors of their employees impact organizational effectiveness.

In general, managers work to enhance employee performance behaviors, commitment and engagement, and citizenship behaviors and to minimize various dysfunctional behaviors. A number of environmental, individual, group and team, leadership, and organizational characteristics can make the manager's work easier or more difficult depending on how well they understand organizational behavior. This model will be more fully developed in Chapter 1 and will serve as a roadmap for your study of organizational behavior throughout this book.

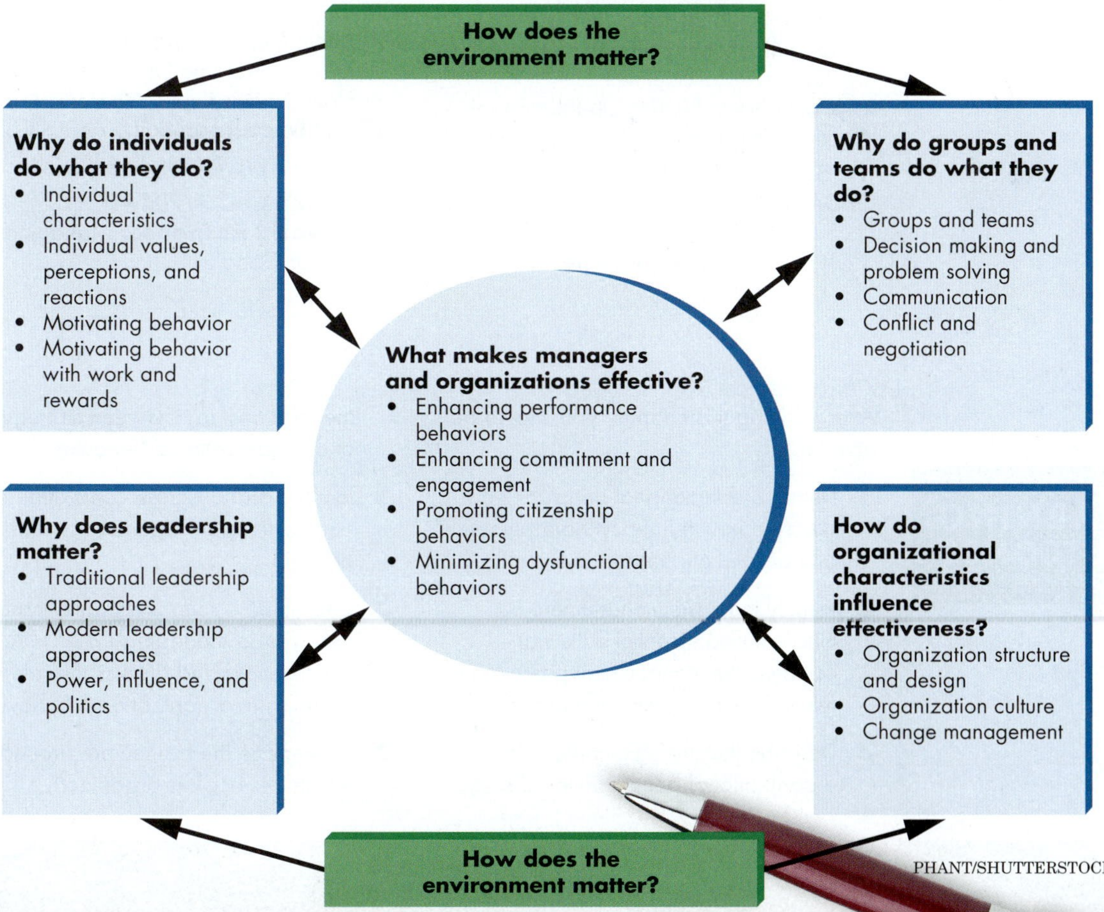

LOSKUTNIKOV/SHUTTERSTOCK.COM

CHAPTER 1

AN OVERVIEW OF ORGANIZATIONAL BEHAVIOR

CHAPTER OUTLINE

LEARNING OUTCOMES

After studying this chapter, you should be able to:

1. Define organizational behavior and describe how it impacts both personal and organizational success.
2. Identify the basic management functions and essential skills that comprise the management process and relate them to organizational behavior.
3. Describe the strategic context of organizational behavior and discuss the relationships between strategy and organizational behavior.
4. Identify and describe contextual perspectives on organizational behavior.
5. Describe the role of organizational behavior in managing for effectiveness and discuss the role of research in organizational behavior.
6. Summarize the framework around which this book is organized.

LOSKUTNIKOV/SHUTTERSTOCK.COM

REAL WORLD CHALLENGE

MANAGING GROWTH AT GOOGLE

Google's popular search engine was created in 1998 when founders Larry Page and Sergey Brin cofounded the firm with the goal of making the world's information available to everyone.[1] Being a startup, Google's founders were understandably concerned about inspiring and retaining the innovative talent that would make or break the company's future success.

Page and Brin realized that Google's explosive growth needed to be closely monitored, and that its employees needed to continue feeling like an important part of the team.[2] The founders wanted to make Google an engaging place to work and set out to design the organization and its culture in a way that would appeal to its current and future employees. Imagine that Google's founders asked you for advice during the early days of Google. What advice would you give them about the role of its people in its future success and how to set up the company to maximize employee innovation, trust, and loyalty?

AP IMAGES/DYCJ

LUCKY BUSINESS/SHUTTERSTOCK.COM

PRESSMASTER/SHUTTERSTOCK.COM

The success of any organization is often determined by how effectively managers can enhance the performance behaviors of their employees, enhance their commitment to and engagement with the organization, promote citizenship behaviors, and minimize dysfunctional behaviors.

Regardless of their size, scope, or location, all organizations have at least one thing in common—they are comprised of people. It is these people who make decisions about the strategic direction of a firm, it is they who acquire the resources the firm uses to create new products, and it is they who sell those products. People manage a firm's corporate headquarters, its warehouses, and its information technology, and it is people who clean up at the end of the day. No matter how effective a manager might be, all organizational successes—and failures—are the result of the behaviors of many people. Indeed, no manager can succeed without the assistance of others.

Thus, any manager—whether responsible for a big business such as Google, Abercrombie & Fitch, General Electric, Apple, Starbucks, or British Airways; for a niche business such as the Boston Celtics basketball team or a Mayo Clinic facility; or for a local Pizza Hut restaurant or neighborhood dry cleaning establishment—must strive to understand the people who work in the organization. This book is about those people. It is also about the organization itself and the managers who operate it. Together, the study of organizations and the study of the people who work in them constitute the field of organizational behavior. Our starting point in exploring this field begins with a more detailed discussion of its meaning and its importance to employees, business owners, and managers.

WHAT IS ORGANIZATIONAL BEHAVIOR?

What exactly is meant by the term "organizational behavior"? And why should it be studied? Answers to these two fundamental questions will both help establish our foundation for discussion and analysis and help you better appreciate the rationale as to how and why understanding the field can be of value to you in the future.

The Meaning of Organizational Behavior

organizational behavior
The study of human behavior in organizational settings, the interface between human behavior and the organization, and the organization itself.

Organizational behavior (OB) is the study of human behavior in organizational settings, of the interface between human behavior and the organization, and of the organization itself.[3] Although we can focus on any one of these three areas, we must also remember that all three are ultimately necessary for a comprehensive understanding of organizational behavior. For example, we can study individual behavior without explicitly considering the organization. But because the organization influences and is influenced by the individual, we cannot fully understand the individual's behavior without learning something about the organization. Similarly, we can study organizations without focusing

Managers at businesses like The Home Depot need to understand individual employee behavior, characteristics of the organization itself, and the interface between individual behavior and the organization.

ISTOCKPHOTO.COM/LOKIBAHO

explicitly on the people within them. But again, we are looking at only a portion of the puzzle. Eventually we must consider the other pieces, as well as the whole. Essentially, then, OB helps explain and predict how people and groups interpret events, react, and behave in organizations and describes the role of organizational systems, structures, and process in shaping behavior.

Figure 1.1 illustrates this view of organizational behavior. It shows the linkages among human behavior in organizational settings, the individual–organization interface, the organization itself, and the environment surrounding the organization. Each individual brings to an organization a unique set of personal characteristics and a unique personal background and set of experiences from other organizations. Therefore, in considering the people who work in their organizations, managers must look at the unique perspective each individual brings to the work setting. For example, suppose managers at The Home Depot review data showing that employee turnover within the firm is gradually but consistently increasing. Further suppose that they hire a consultant to help them better understand the problem. As a starting point, the consultant might analyze the types of people the company usually hires. The goal would be to learn as much as possible about the nature of the company's workforce as individuals—their expectations, their personal goals, and so forth.

Figure 1.1

The Nature of Organizational Behavior

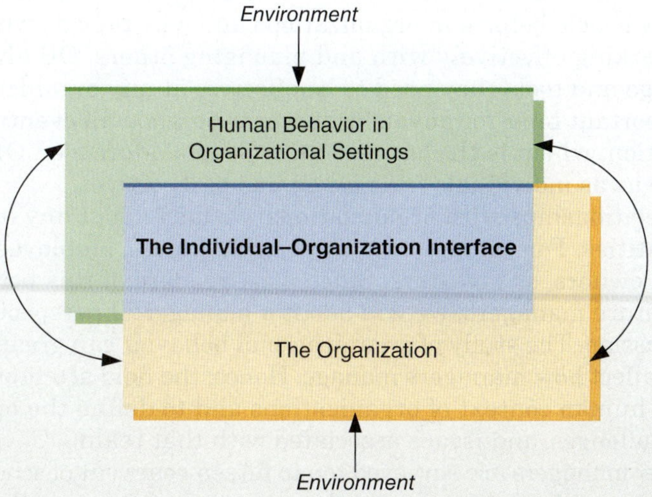

The field of organizational behavior attempts to understand human behavior in organizational settings, the organization itself, and the individual–organization interface. As illustrated here, these areas are highly interrelated. Thus, although it is possible to focus on only one of these areas at a time, a complete understanding of organizational behavior requires knowledge of all three areas.

But individuals do not work in isolation. They come in contact with other people and with the organization in a variety of ways. Points of contact include managers, coworkers, the formal policies and procedures of the organization, and various changes implemented by the organization. In addition, over time, individuals change, as a function of personal experiences and maturity as well as through work experiences and organizational developments. The organization, in turn, is affected by the presence and eventual absence of the individual. Clearly, then, managers must also consider how the individual and the organization interact. Thus, the consultant studying turnover at The Home Depot might next look at the orientation procedures and initial training for newcomers to the organization. The goal of this phase of the study would be to understand some of the dynamics of how incoming individuals are introduced to and interact with the broader organizational context.

An organization, of course, exists before a particular person joins it and continues to exist after he or she leaves. Thus, the organization itself represents a crucial third perspective from which to view organizational behavior. For instance, the consultant studying turnover would also need to study the structure and culture of The Home Depot. An understanding of factors such as a firm's performance evaluation and reward systems, its decision-making and communication patterns, and the structure of the firm itself can provide added insight into why some people choose to leave a company and others elect to stay.

Clearly, then, the field of organizational behavior is both exciting and complex. Myriad variables and concepts accompany the interactions just described, and together these factors greatly complicate the manager's ability to understand, appreciate, and manage others in the organization. They also provide unique and important opportunities to enhance personal and organizational effectiveness.

How Organizational Behavior Impacts Personal Success

You may be wondering about the relevance of OB to your current major or career path. You might be thinking, "I don't know any organizational behaviorists. Why is this topic important?" We field this question all the time from people unfamiliar with OB. The core of OB is being effective at work. Understanding how people behave in organizations and why they do what they do is critical to working effectively with and managing others. OB gives everyone the knowledge and tools they need to be effective at any organizational level. OB is an important topic for anyone who works or who will eventually work in an organization, which is the case for most people. Moreover, OB is actually important to us as individuals from numerous perspectives.

In our relationships with organizations, we may adopt any one of several roles or identities. For example, we can be consumers, employees, suppliers, competitors, owners, or investors. Since most readers of this book are either present or future managers, we will adopt a managerial perspective throughout our discussion. The study of organizational behavior can greatly clarify the factors that affect how managers manage. Hence, the field attempts to describe the complex human context of organizations and to define the opportunities, problems, challenges, and issues associated with that realm.

Whenever managers are surveyed ten to fifteen years out of school and asked to identify the most important classes they ever took, OB is usually one of them.

This is not because it made them technically better in their area of specialty, but because it made them more effective employees and better managers. As one expert has put it, "It is puzzling that we seek expert advice on our golf game but avoid professional advice on how we can deal with other people."[4] Using your knowledge of OB can help you to succeed faster in any organization or career.

UNDERSTAND YOURSELF

GLOBAL MINDSET

A global mindset reflects your ability to influence people, groups, and organizations from a variety of backgrounds and cultures. Multinational companies' ability to create globally integrated systems depends on their ability to get employees, managers, and executives to understand and adapt to the realities of a globalized economy. The ability to integrate talent from many parts of the world faster and more effectively than other companies is a source of a firm's competitive advantage[5] as well as your own personal competitive advantage.

Please use the following scale in responding to the ten questions below. When you are finished, follow the scoring instructions at the bottom to calculate your score. Then read more about what your score means, and how you can improve your global mindset.

___ 1. In interacting with others, I assign equal status to people regardless of their national origin.

___ 2. I consider myself as equally open to ideas from other countries and cultures as I am to ideas from my own country and culture of origin.

___ 3. Finding myself in a new cultural setting is exciting.

___ 4. I see the world as one big marketplace.

___ 5. When I interact with people from other cultures, it is important to me to understand them as individuals.

___ 6. I regard my values to be a hybrid of values acquired from multiple cultures as opposed to just one culture.

___ 7. I get very curious when I meet someone from another country.

___ 8. I enjoy trying food from other countries.

___ 9. In this interlinked world of ours, national boundaries are meaningless.

___ 10. I believe I can live a fulfilling life in another culture.

Scoring: Add up your responses to identify your global mindset score.

Interpretation: Because experiences influence global mindset in a positive or negative manner,[6] you can take steps to improve your global mindset. Based on your score, you might consider some of the personal development activities identified below, or you might come up with others.

If your score is *between 10 and 20*, you have a relatively low global mindset. Formal training/educational programs, self-study courses, university courses, or in-company seminars or management development programs can help you to increase your global mindset.

If your score is *between 21 and 35*, you have a moderate global mindset. You do not exhibit extremely high parochialism, but at the same time you are not as open to people from other cultures as you could be. In addition to the self-development activities listed above, you might consider joining some culturally diverse student organizations and making a point of befriending some people from other cultures to gain more experience and become more comfortable with people from other cultures.

If your score is *between 36 and 50*, you have a high global mindset. This means that you are open to meeting people from a variety of cultures, and are comfortable with global diversity. This does not mean you cannot improve further! Joining international student organizations, working with international volunteer organizations, and befriending people from a variety of cultures will further develop your global mindset.

Source: Adapted from Gupta, A.K., & Govindarajan, V. (2002). Cultivating a global mindset. *Academy of Management Executive, 16*(1), 116–126; Kefalas, A. G., & Neuland, E. W. (1997). Global mindsets: an exploratory study. Paper presented at the Annual Conference of the Academy of International Business, Moneterrey, Mexico, 4–7 October; Nummela, N., Saarenketo, S., & Puumalainen, K. (2004). Global mindset—a prerequisite for successful internationalisation? *Canadian Journal of Administrative Sciences, 21*(1), 51–64.

JEROME FAVRE/BLOOMBERG/GETTY IMAGES

HSBC, an global financial services business, routinely sends its most promising young managers on international assignments. The purpose of this approach is to build a cohort of future top managers and leaders who have extensive international experience.

We will discuss diversity and the importance of flexibly applying OB concepts to different people throughout the book. This chapter's *Understand Yourself* feature gives you the opportunity to better understand your global mindset, or set of individual attributes that enable you to influence individuals, groups, and organizations from diverse socio/cultural/institutional systems.[7] Global mindset combines cultural intelligence and a global business orientation.[8] Most chief executives of large multinational organizations believe that having a strong cadre of globally minded leaders would strengthen their organization's competitiveness.[9]

Because global mindset is learned, experiences can influence it in a positive or negative manner.[10] Every year, the financial services giant HSBC sends promising new hires and managers into long-term business experiences abroad to build a cohort of international officers. Locations include western countries as well as Saudi Arabia, Indonesia, and Mexico. To make a career at HSBC, managers must perform these international missions. This enables HSBC to develop a continuous supply of globally minded managers capable of cross-border learning. Similar approaches are pursued by other multinationals to enable them to transfer expertise and know-how across geographical, cultural, and political divides.[11]

How Organizational Behavior Impacts Organizational Success

Organizations as a whole also benefit from OB. Imagine the difference between a company with motivated, engaged employees with clear goals aligned with the business strategy and one with unhappy employees, a lot of conflict, weak leadership, and a lack of direction. Effectively implementing OB concepts and models is what creates effective and successful companies. OB is clearly important to organizations. By appropriately applying OB knowledge about individuals, groups, and the effect of organizational structure on worker behavior, the conditions can be created that make organizations most effective.

OB also helps companies perform well. A mounting body of evidence shows that an emphasis on the softer side of business positively influences bottom line results. By listening to employees, recognizing their work, building trust, and behaving ethically, managers have boosted such performance measures as operating earnings, return on investment, and stock price.[12] In addition to financial performance and job satisfaction, OB also influences absenteeism and turnover. Reducing absenteeism and turnover can be worth millions of dollars to organizations through increased productivity and customer service and decreased staffing costs. This chapter's *Case Study* highlights The J.M. Smucker Company's attention to OB principles including ethics, organizational culture, and values.

CASE STUDY The J.M. Smucker Company

From its founding in 1897, when Jerome Monroe Smucker sold apple butter from the back of a horse-drawn wagon, the J.M. Smucker Company has recognized that acting ethically is a key element of its success. The Orrville, Ohio, manufacturer wants to ensure that its signature comfort foods—fruit spreads, frostings, juices, and beverages—remain American staples, and that its daily operations are guided by honesty, respect, trust, responsibility, and fairness.

Ensuring that the company meets the highest ethical standards starts with hiring people who already have a strong personal value system. To do this, Smucker steeps job candidates in its ethical standards and refers frequently to how company values relate to the particular position a job candidate is seeking. The company also engages in rigorous reference checks. Once hired, the ethics emphasis intensifies. Each new hire attends a day-long training seminar that includes presentations by company officials, videos, and breakout sessions on moral awareness, moral courage, and values.

The discussions go much deeper than a superficial review of how to be a good person. One session concentrates on three ways to make a decision when faced with a dilemma. One option is seeking to do the greatest good for the greatest number of people. The second is a rules-based approach in which the decision will set a standard that everyone else follows. The final alternative is to use the Golden Rule: "treat others as you would like to be treated."

The sessions also explore the complexity of ethics. Employees are rarely in a clear-cut situation where right and wrong are obvious. Ethical decisions often involve a nuanced balance between right and right. For example, the choice an employee has to make may involve questions related to the pulls between truth and loyalty, the individual versus the community, and short-term versus long-term approaches to business decisions. Smucker communicates that it wants its employees to act with truth over loyalty, community over the individual, and long-term over short-term company interests. All employees go through the ethics program again every three to five years, and sign a detailed nine-page ethics statement annually to ensure that they truly understand the level of performance Smucker expects from them.

Smucker also strongly believes in environmental sustainability, including utilizing renewable energy, improving wastewater management, using sustainable raw materials, and reusing resources rather than consuming new ones. Smucker promotes social sustainability in the communities in which it operates, promoting initiatives and programs that support and enhance the quality of life. The J.M. Smucker Company has consistently appeared on *Fortune Magazine*'s "100 Best Places to Work For" list, which it attributes in part to its strong culture.

Questions:

1. Why would ethics be important to a company like J.M. Smucker? How can its focus on values and ethics improve its business performance?
2. Appearing on "best places to work" lists can increase an employer's popularity, even among lower-qualified applicants. The increased volume of applicants can be costly and time-consuming. What do you feel are the benefits and drawbacks to being on this type of list? Do you think that it is generally beneficial to be publicly recognized as a good employer? Why or why not?
3. Do J.M. Smucker's values and culture appeal to you as a potential employee? Why or why not?

Source: J.M. Smucker. (2014). J.M. Smucker 2014 Annual Report. Retrieved from http://static1.squarespace.com/static/53650b18e4b08e20f53d167b/t/539ee6cee4b06b36446ac3f1/1402922702613/Smucker%27s+2014+Annual Report_embed.pdf; Smucker Gift Will Establish Business Leadership Institute (2012). The University of Akron, April 23. Available online: http://www.uakron.edu/im/online-newsroom/news_details.dot?newsId=d24e5be1-b6fc-431b-871c-164ada224a69&crumbTitle=Smucker%20gift%20will%20establish%20business%20leadership%20institute; Harrington, A. (2005). Institute for Global Ethics Expands Focus on Business Practices with Center for Corporate Ethics, CSRWire, January 27. Available online at: http://www.csrwire.com/News/3473.html; Schoeff, M. (2006). Workforce Management, March 13, p. 19; "Award-Winning Company," smuckers.com. Available online at: http://www.smuckers.com/family_company/join_our_company/award_winning_company.aspx; "Sustainability," smuckers.com. Available online at: http://www.smuckers.com/family_company/join_our_company/sustainability.aspx.

One central value of organizational behavior is that it isolates important aspects of the manager's job and offers specific perspectives on the human side of management: people as organizations, people as resources, and people as people. To further underscore the importance of organizational behavior to managers, we should consider this simple fact: Year in and year out, most of the firms on *Fortune*'s list of the world's most admired companies have impeccable reputations for valuing and respecting the people who work for them.[13] Similarly, as the use of technology steadily increases, virtual teams become more common. The success of virtual teams, in turn, often depends on the type of leadership exhibited by managers. Organizational behavior allows us to understand that as a leader of a virtual team, one must foster trust, encourage open dialogue, and clarify guidelines. Clearly, then, an understanding of organizational behavior can play a vital role in managerial work. To most effectively use the knowledge provided by this field, managers must thoroughly understand its various concepts, assumptions, and premises. To provide this foundation, we next tie organizational behavior even more explicitly to management and then turn to a more detailed examination of the manager's job itself.

THE MANAGERIAL CONTEXT OF ORGANIZATIONAL BEHAVIOR

Virtually all organizations have managers with titles such as chief financial officer, marketing manager, director of public relations, vice president for human resources, and plant manager. But probably no organization has a position called "organizational behavior manager." The reason for this is simple: Organizational behavior is not a defined business function or area of responsibility similar to finance or marketing. Rather, an understanding of OB provides a set of insights and tools that all managers can use to carry out their jobs more effectively. The managerial context of OB can viewed from the perspective of basic management functions, critical management skills, and overall human resource management.

Basic Management Functions and Organizational Behavior

Managerial work is fraught with complexity and unpredictability and enriched with opportunity and excitement. However, in characterizing managerial work, most educators and other experts find it useful to conceptualize the activities performed by managers as reflecting one or more of four basic functions. These functions are generally referred to as planning, organizing, leading, and controlling. While these functions are often described in a sequential manner, in reality, of course, most managerial work involves all four functions simultaneously.

Similarly, organizations use many different resources in the pursuit of their goals and objectives. As with management functions, though, these resources can also generally be classified into four groups: human, financial, physical, and/or information resources. As illustrated in Figure 1.2, managers combine these resources through the four basic functions, with the ultimate purpose of efficiently and effectively attaining the goals of the organization.

Figure 1.2

Basic Managerial Functions

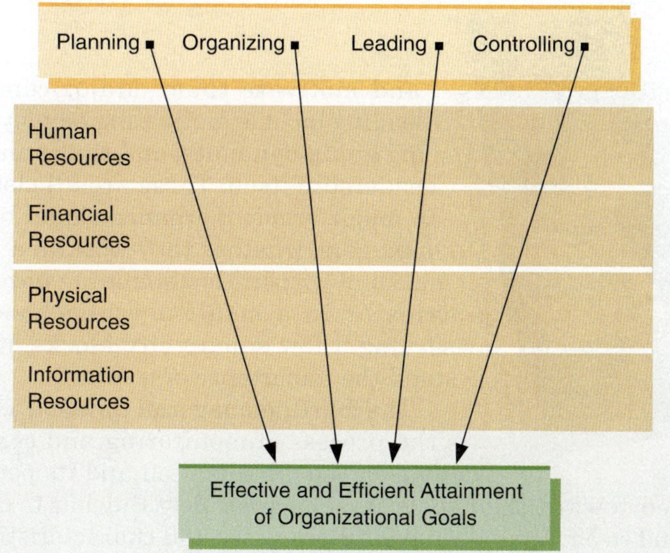

Managers engage in the four basic functions of planning, organizing, leading, and controlling. These functions are applied to human, financial, physical, and information resources with the ultimate purpose of efficiently and effectively attaining organizational goals.

That is, the figure shows how managers apply the basic functions across resources to advance the organization toward its goals.

Planning, the first managerial function, is the process of determining the organization's desired future position and deciding how best to get there. The planning process at Urban Outfitters, for example, includes studying and analyzing the environment, deciding on appropriate goals, outlining strategies for achieving those goals, and developing tactics to help execute the strategies. OB processes and characteristics pervade each of these activities. Perception, for instance, plays a major role in environmental scanning, and creativity and motivation influence how managers set goals, strategies, and tactics for their organization. Larger corporations such as Walmart and Starbucks usually rely on their top management teams to handle most planning activities. In smaller firms, the owner usually takes care of planning.

planning
The process of determining an organization's desired future position and the best means of getting there

The second managerial function is ***organizing***—the process of designing jobs, grouping jobs into manageable units, and establishing patterns of authority among jobs and groups of jobs. This process produces the basic structure, or framework, of the organization. For large organizations such as Apple and Toyota, that structure can be incredibly complex. The structure includes several hierarchical layers and spans myriad activities and areas of responsibility. Smaller firms can often function with a relatively simple and straightforward form of organization. As noted earlier, the processes and characteristics of the organization itself are a major theme of organizational behavior.

organizing
The process of designing jobs, grouping jobs into units, and establishing patterns of authority between jobs and units

Leading, the third major managerial function, is the process of motivating members of the organization to work together toward the organization's goals. An Old Navy store manager, for example, must hire people, train them,

leading
The process of getting the organization's members to work together toward the organization's goals

WAVEBREAKMEDIA/SHUTTERSTOCK.COM

Leading is a major part of the jobs of most managers. This manager is presenting information to his team in an effort to lead them to perform at a higher level.

and motivate them. Major components of leading include motivating employees, managing group dynamics, and the actual process of leadership itself. These are all closely related to major areas of organizational behavior. All managers, whether they work in a huge multinational corporation spanning dozens of countries or in a small neighborhood business serving a few square city blocks, must understand the importance of leading.

The fourth managerial function, ***controlling***, is the process of monitoring and correcting the actions of the organization and its people to keep them headed toward their goals. A manager at Best Buy has to control costs, inventory, and so on. Again, behavioral processes and characteristics are a key part of this function. Performance evaluation and reward systems, for example, both apply to control. Control is of vital importance to all businesses, but it may be especially critical to smaller ones. Target, for example, can withstand with relative ease a loss of several thousand dollars due to poor control, but an equivalent loss may be devastating to a small firm.

controlling
The process of monitoring and correcting the actions of the organization and its members to keep them directed toward their goals

technical skills
The skills necessary to accomplish specific tasks within the organization

Critical Management Skills and Organizational Behavior

Another important element of managerial work is mastery of the skills necessary to carry out basic functions and fill fundamental roles. In general, most successful managers have a strong combination of technical, interpersonal, conceptual, and diagnostic skills.[14]

Technical skills are skills necessary to accomplish specific tasks within the organization. Designing a new mobile game app for Rovio, the company that created Angry Birds, developing a new weight loss supplement for Advocare, or writing a press release for Halliburton about the firm's new drilling technologies all require technical skills. Hence, these skills are generally associated with the operations employed by the

ECHO/GETTY IMAGES

Technical skills are the skills needed to perform specific tasks. This retail manager is teaching a new sales clerk how to operate the store's payment system. He has to have the the technical skills needed for this task in order to teach others.

Ursula Burns, Chairman and CEO of Xerox Corporation, started her career as a mechanical engineer. She subsequently moved into management and now leads a major corporation.

WENN LTD / ALAMY

organization in its production processes. For example, the Chairman and CEO of Xerox Corporation, Ursula Burns, began her career with the company as a mechanical engineering intern. Other examples of managers with strong technical skills include Rex Tillerson (CEO of ExxonMobil, who began his career as a production engineer) and Andrew Taylor (former CEO of Enterprise Holdings, who began his career washing cars on Rent-A-Car lots when he was 16 years of age). The CEOs of the Big Four accounting firms also began their careers as accountants.

Managers use ***interpersonal skills*** to communicate with, understand, and motivate individuals and groups. As we have noted, managers spend a large portion of their time interacting with others, so it is clearly important that they get along well with other people. For instance, Howard Schultz is the CEO of Starbucks. Schultz is able to relate to employees by demonstrating respect and dignity. Schultz remains committed to providing health benefits despite rising healthcare costs and has created educational opportunities for Starbucks partners to finish school. Schultz has been recognized for his passion and leadership. These qualities inspire others throughout the organization and motivate them to work hard to help Starbucks reach its goals.

interpersonal skills
The ability to effectively communicate with, understand, and motivate individuals and groups

Conceptual skills are the manager's ability to think in the abstract. A manager with strong conceptual skills is able to see the "big picture." That is, she or he can see opportunity where others see roadblocks or problems. For example, after Steve Wozniak and Steve Jobs built a small computer of their own design in a garage, Wozniak essentially saw a new toy that could be tinkered with. Jobs, however, saw far more and convinced his partner that they should start a company to make and sell the computers. The result? Apple Computer. In subsequent years, Jobs also used his conceptual skills to identify the potential in digital media technologies, leading to the introduction of such products as the iPod, the iPhone, iTunes, and the iPad as well as his overseeing the creation of Pixar Animation Studios. When he died in 2011 Jobs was hailed as one of the most innovative managers of all time.

conceptual skills
The ability think in the abstract

Most successful managers also bring diagnostic skills to the organization. ***Diagnostic skills*** allow managers to better understand cause-and-effect relationships and to recognize the optimal solutions to problems. For instance, when Ed Whitacre was chairman and CEO of SBC Communications, he recognized that, though his firm was performing well in the consumer market, it lacked strong brand identification in the business environment. He first carefully identified and then implemented an action to remedy the firm's shortcoming—SBC would buy AT&T (for $16 billion), acquiring in the process the very name recognition that his company needed. After the acquisition was completed, the firm changed its corporate name from SBC to AT&T. And it was

diagnostic skills
The ability to understand cause-and-effect relationships and to recognize the optimal solutions to problems

Whitacre's diagnostic skills that pulled it all together.[15] Indeed, his legacy of strong diagnostic skills led to his being asked to lead the corporate turnaround at General Motors in 2009.

Organizational Behavior and Human Resource Management

human resource management (HRM)
The set of organizational activities directed at attracting, developing, and maintaining an effective workforce

We noted earlier than OB is generally related to all areas of an organization. It is especially relevant, though, to human resource management. ***Human resource management (HRM)*** is the set of organizational activities directed at attracting, developing, and maintaining an effective workforce. More precisely, HR managers select new employees, develop rewards and incentives to motivate and retain employees, and create programs for training and developing employees. But how do they know which applicants to hire? And how do they know which rewards will be more motivating than others? The answers to these and related questions are generally drawn from the field of OB. For example, personality traits (covered in Chapter 3) are frequently used in selection decisions. Likewise, motivation theories (as discussed in Chapters 5 and 6) help managers understand how to most effectively reward and retain employees. This chapter's *Improve Your Skills* feature highlights some common job interview questions that you should be prepared to answer before interviewing for your next job. These questions and your answers to them all involve OB concepts.

Consider, for example, a recent announcement made by Walmart. In early 2015 the giant retailer began giving pay raises to 500,000 U.S. workers. At the same time, the company indicated that it was changing the methods it uses to hire and train new employees.[16] Clearly, Walmart did not make the decision to raise its labor costs lightly. Instead, its managers expect that the higher wages and new HR practices will enable the company to better recruit new employees and retain its existing ones. Hence, this significant—and expensive—decision by Walmart managers had its origins in theories and research from OB and will be implemented in the firm through human resource management.

IMPROVE YOUR SKILLS

OB RELATED JOB INTERVIEW QUESTIONS

1. What do you think is the most important thing that a manager does?
2. What was the most ethical decision you've had to make at work?
3. Tell me about a conflict you've experienced at work and how you handled it.
4. Tell me about a challenging team experience you have had and how you handled it.
5. How would you manage an employee who misses performance goals?
6. How would you describe your leadership style?
7. How do you deal with stressful deadlines at work?
8. Have you ever dealt with a difficult boss? If so, how did you manage the situation? If not, what would you do if you found yourself in this situation?
9. What types of innovative problem-solving or decision-making techniques do you use at work?
10. What type of organizational culture would be the best fit for you? Why?

Walmart recently announced plans to raise the hourly pay rates for 500,000 of its U.S. employees. The retailer expects its higher wages to make it easier to hire new employees and retain existing ones.

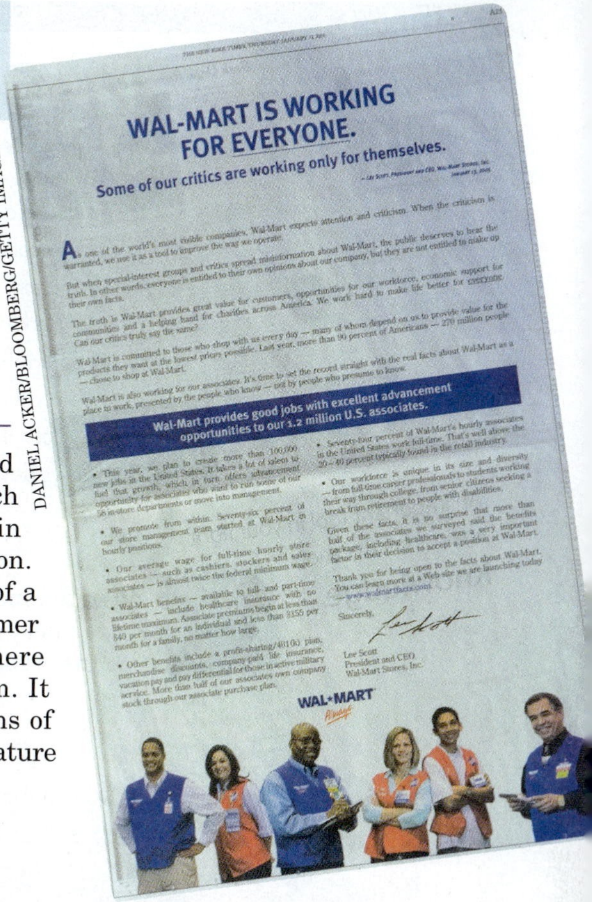

DANIEL ACKER/BLOOMBERG/GETTY IMAGES

The Walmart example also provides a preview of the strategic context of OB, explored in our next section.

THE STRATEGIC CONTEXT OF ORGANIZATIONAL BEHAVIOR

Successful business strategies are grounded in creating and maintaining a sustainable ***competitive advantage***, which exists any time an organization has an edge over rivals in attracting customers and defending itself against competition. The effective management of people is key to the creation of a competitive advantage and business strategy execution. As former General Electric CEO Jack Welch said, "We now know where productivity—real and limitless productivity—comes from. It comes from challenged, empowered, excited, rewarded teams of people."[17] We now turn our attention more specifically to the nature of management and is relationship to OB.

Sources of Competitive Advantage

competitive advantage
Anything that gives a firm an edge over rivals in attracting customers and defending itself against competition

How does an organization gain a competitive advantage? Michael Treacy and Fred Wiersma have identified many sources of competitive advantage including having the best-made or cheapest product, providing the best customer service, being more convenient to buy from, having shorter product development times, and having a well-known brand name.[18] Because it is an organization's people who are responsible for gaining and keeping any competitive advantage, effective management is critical to business success.[19]

Warehouse retailer Costco's strong and loyal customer base, access to a broad range of high-quality products for a low price, and committed employees give it a competitive advantage over smaller and lesser-known retailers. Although Costco pays its employees substantially more than its closest competitor, Sam's Club, it has similar financial returns on its labor costs due to lower turnover and higher levels of employee productivity.[20] This, in turn, results in a higher-quality customer experience.

According to Michael Porter, to have a competitive advantage a company must ultimately be able to give customers superior value for their money (a combination of quality, service, and acceptable price)—either a better product that is worth a premium price or a good product at a lower price can be a source of competitive advantage.[21] Table 1.1 lists some possible sources of competitive advantage. You should note that an organization's talent is the key to securing each of these.

Table 1.1

Businesses can choose to pursue competitive advantage by using an array of different sources.

- *Innovation:* developing new products, services, and markets and improving current ones
- *Distribution:* dominating distribution channels to block competition
- *Speed:* excelling at getting your product or service to consumers quickly
- *Convenience:* being the easiest for customers to do business with
- *First to market:* introducing products and services before competitors
- *Cost:* being the lowest-cost provider
- *Service:* providing the best customer support before, during, or after the sale
- *Quality:* providing the highest-quality product or service
- *Branding:* developing the most positive image

One of the most important things managers do is execute a firm's business strategy. We next discuss business strategy in more detail, as well as how OB can reinforce the organization's overall business strategy and support its execution.

DANIEL ACKER/BLOOMBERG/GETTY IMAGES

ALASTAIR WALLACE/SHUTTERSTOCK.COM

Sam's Club and Costco are major competitors but have very different approaches to competitive advantage. Sam's Club pays its workers relatively lower wages in order to keep its costs and prices lower. Costco pays higher wages, though, in order to hire more more experienced employees and provide better customer service.

Types of Business Strategies

A company may create value based on price, technological leadership, customer service, or some combination of these and other factors. Business strategy involves the issue of how to compete, but also encompasses:

- The strategies of different functional areas in the firm
- How changing industry conditions such as deregulation, product market maturity, and changing customer demographics will be addressed
- How the firm as a whole will address the range of strategic issues and choices it faces

Business strategies are partially planned, and partially reactive to changing circumstances. A large number of possible strategies exist for any organization, and an organization may pursue different strategies in different business units. Companies may also pursue more than one strategy at a particular time. According to Michael Porter, businesses can compete successfully by being the cheapest producer, by making unique products valued by consumers, or by applying their expertise in a narrow market segment to meet that segment's particular product or service needs.[22] These three primary business strategies are:

1. Cost leadership
2. Differentiation
3. Specialization

Another strategic choice is whether to grow the business, and if so how to do it. We next discuss each of these strategies and their implications for OB.

Cost Leadership Strategy

Firms pursuing a ***cost leadership strategy*** strive to be the lowest-cost producer in an industry for a particular level of product quality. These businesses are typically good at designing products that can be efficiently manufactured (e.g., designing products with a minimum number of parts needing assembly) and engineering efficient manufacturing processes to keep production costs and customer prices low. Walmart is a good example of a firm that uses a cost leadership strategy.

cost leadership strategy
Striving to be the lowest-cost producer for a particular level of product quality

Organizations pursuing a strategy of keeping costs and prices low try to develop a competitive advantage in ***operational excellence***. Employees in these firms need to identify and follow efficient processes and engage in continuous improvement. Manufacturing and transportation companies frequently adopt this approach. These organizations continually look for ways to modify their operational systems in order to reduce costs and lower prices while offering a desirable product that competes successfully with competitors' products. Dell Computers, Federal Express, and Walmart are good examples of companies whose competitive advantage is based on operational excellence.

operational excellence
Maximizing the efficiency of the manufacturing or product development process to minimize costs

Most operationally excellent firms require managers to hire and train flexible employees who are able to focus on shorter-term production objectives, who avoid waste, and who are concerned about minimizing production costs.[23] Operationally excellent organizations function with tight margins and rely more on teamwork than individual performance.

differentiation strategy
Developing a product or service that has unique characteristics valued by customers

Differentiation Strategy

A ***differentiation strategy*** calls for the development of a product or service with unique characteristics valued by customers. The value added by the product's uniqueness may enable the business to charge a premium price for it. The dimensions along which a firm can differentiate include image (Coca-Cola), product durability (Wrangler clothing), quality (Lexus), safety (Volvo), and usability (Apple Computer). Some companies, such as Southwest Airlines, differentiate themselves from their competitors by pursuing a strategy based on only providing no-frills, basic products and services at a low cost. Companies can pursue more than one strategy at a time. In this case, Southwest Airlines is both a cost leader and a differentiator.

OLGA BESNARD/SHUTTERSTOCK.COM

Lexus uses a differentiation strategy. It promotes its automobiles as being higher in quality than those sold by competitors. This differentiation, in turn, allows Lexus to sell its automobiles for premium prices.

product innovation
Developing new products or services

Organizations pursuing a differentiation strategy often try to develop a competitive advantage based on ***product innovation***. This requires employees to continually develop new products and services to create an advantage in the market. These companies create and maintain a culture that encourages employees to bring new ideas into the company. These companies then listen to and consider these ideas, however unconventional they might be. For these companies, the frequent introduction of new products is key to staying competitive. This strategy is common in technology and pharmaceutical companies. Johnson & Johnson, Nike, and 3M are good examples of organizations whose competitive advantage is based on product innovation.

Product innovators must protect their entrepreneurial environment. To that end, managers develop and reinforce an innovative culture. Instead of selecting job candidates based only on their related experience, they also assess whether a candidate can work cooperatively in teams and whether the candidate is open-minded and creative.[24] An organization with a product innovation competitive advantage would likely seek a core workforce of research and development employees who have an entrepreneurial mindset, long-term focus, high tolerance for ambiguity, and an interest in learning and discovery. Employees who need stability and predictability would not fit as well. Managers in innovative companies also need to motivate and empower employees.[25]

Specialization Strategy

specialization strategy
Focusing on a narrow market segment or niche and pursuing either a differentiation or cost leadership strategy within that market segment

Businesses pursuing a ***specialization strategy*** focus on a narrow market segment or niche—a single product, a particular end use, or buyers with special needs—and pursue either a differentiation or cost leadership strategy within that market segment. Successful businesses following a specialist strategy know their market segment very well, and often enjoy a high degree of customer loyalty. This strategy can be successful if it results in either lower costs than competitors serving the same niche, or an ability to offer customers something other competitors do not (e.g., manufacturing nonstandard parts). Chuck E. Cheese, Dunkin' Donuts, and Starbucks are examples of companies that use a specialization strategy.

customer intimacy
Delivering unique and customizable products or services to meet customers' needs and increase customer loyalty

Organizations pursuing a specialization strategy often try to develop a competitive advantage based on ***customer intimacy*** and try to deliver unique and customizable products or services to meet their customers' needs and increase customer loyalty. This approach involves dividing markets into segments or niches and then tailoring the company's offerings to meet the demands of those niches. Creating customer loyalty requires employees to combine detailed knowledge about their customers with operational flexibility so they can respond quickly to almost any customer need, from customizing a product to fulfilling special requests. Consulting, retail, and banking organizations often adopt this approach.

Most service-quality experts say that talent is the most critical element in building a customer-oriented company.[26] Hiring active learners with good customer relations skills and emotional resilience under pressure would complement a customer intimacy competitive advantage, and help ensure that the organization continually enhances its ability to deliver on promises to customers.[27] Because employee cooperation and collaboration are important to developing customer intimacy, managers should also focus on building effective teams and creating effective communication channels.

Companies such as Starbucks are able to get a high price for their products because of their focus on customer relationships. Imagine if Starbucks began to hire cheaper labor, including people with weak communication skills, and cut back on its investments in employee training and satisfaction. Starbucks' competitive advantage would quickly erode, and the company would have to reduce the price of its coffee to keep customers coming back. This could eventually result in Starbucks pursuing a cost leadership strategy rather than a specialization strategy because they failed to attract, motivate, and retain the right types of employees.

Growth Strategy

Another strategic choice is whether to expand the company and seek to increase business. Companies often pursue a ***growth strategy*** in response to investor preferences for rising earnings per share, and the required business expansion generally requires the acquisition of additional talent. For example, growth-oriented chains such as Chipotle Mexican Grill regularly open new stores that require additional management, employees, and even product distribution staff.

growth strategy
Company expansion organically or through acquisitions

The success of a growth strategy depends on the firm's ability to find and retain the right number and types of employees to sustain its intended growth. Growth can be organic, happening as the organization expands from within by opening new factories or stores. If it is, it requires an investment in recruiting, selecting, and training the right people to expand the company's operations. Firms can also pursue growth strategies through mergers and acquisitions. Mergers and acquisitions have been a common way for organizations to achieve growth, expand internationally, and respond to industry deregulation. In addition to expanding the organization's business, mergers and acquisitions can also be a way for an organization to acquire the quality and amount of talent it needs to execute its business strategy.

When using mergers and acquisitions as a way to implement a growth strategy, it is important to consider the match between the two organizations' cultures, values, and organizational structures. Mismatches between merged or acquired organizations can result in underperformance and the loss of talented employees. Mergers and acquisitions often fail because of culture issues rather than technical or financial issues.[28] The failed DaimlerChrysler, HP and Compaq, and AOL-Time Warner mergers are just a few prominent examples.

Connecting Business Strategy to Organizational Behavior

There are a number of significant linkages that connect business strategy and OB. For instance, a firm that relies on a cost leadership strategy will usually need to keep all of its expenses as low as possible. Therefore, this strategy might dictate relying on low-wage employees and trying to automate as many jobs as possible. These actions, in turn, clearly relate to employee motivation and the design of work. Likewise, a company using a differentiation strategy might want to emphasize exemplary customer service. As a result, it needs employees who are motivated to provide high levels of service, leaders who can help develop a customer service culture, and a reward structure tied to customer service. A specialization strategy often requires employees with specialized skills and abilities.

Strategy implementation and strategic change require also require large-scale organizational changes; two of the largest may be the new organizational culture and new behaviors required of employees. Depending on the nature of a strategic change, some employees are likely to lack the willingness or even the ability to support the new strategy. Targeting management efforts to coach, motivate, and influence the people who are critical to implementing a new strategy may help it to take hold and ultimately influence the strategy's effectiveness.

Imagine an organization currently manufacturing semiconductor chips. The competitive environment is such that the organization must compete on cost. The organization is focused on operational efficiencies to control expenses. Its focus is on keeping costs contained, and the culture reinforces strict adherence to operating rules to help achieve these goals. Now consider what would change if the organization were to identify a better competitive position by specializing in designing new and innovative computer chips and outsourcing their production. The organization's focus would now be on innovation, problem solving, and teamwork. Managers would need to do less rule enforcement and more leading, motivating, and communicating. Employee involvement in decision making might also increase. Intel went through this type of transformation in the early 1970s when it moved from being a producer of semiconductor memory chips to programmable microprocessor chips.

The previous discussion should help you to understand the role of OB in executing a variety of business strategies. Effective managers understand what needs to be done to execute a company's business strategy, then they plan, organize, direct, and control the activities of employees to get it done. It is important to note that managers do not accomplish organizational objectives by themselves—they get work done through others. Flexibly applying OB principles will help you to do that most effectively.

CONTEXTUAL PERSPECTIVES ON ORGANIZATIONAL BEHAVIOR

Several contextual perspectives—most notably the systems and contingency perspectives and the interactional view—also influence our understanding of organizational behavior. Many of the concepts and theories discussed in the chapters that follow reflect these perspectives; they represent basic points of view that influence much of our contemporary thinking about behavior in organizations. In addition, they allow us to see more clearly how managers use behavioral processes as they strive for organizational effectiveness. Before examining these perspectives, though, let's first take a detour to explain how the field of OB has developed.

Where Does Organizational Behavior Come From?

OB could date back to prehistoric times, when people first started trying to understand, motivate, and lead others. The Greek philosopher Plato contemplated the essence of leadership, and Aristotle discussed persuasive communication. The foundation of organizational power and politics can be found in the more than 2,300-year-old writings of Sun-Tzu and those of 16th-century Italian philosopher Machiavelli. Charismatic leadership was later discussed by German sociologist Max Weber. OB topics have clearly been of interest to many people for a long time. Let's briefly review some history to better understand the origins of the scientific study of OB.

Frederick Winslow Taylor was one of the pioneers of scientific management. He advocated that managers should study the jobs of workers, break those jobs down into small tasks, train workers in the "one best way" of doing their jobs, and then pay workers based on the number of units they produced.

ULLSTEIN BILD/GETTY IMAGES

Formal study of OB began in the 1890s, following the industrial relations movement spawned by Adam Smith's introduction of the division of labor. In the 1890s, Frank and Lillian Gilbreth and Frederick Winslow Taylor identified the positive effects of precise instructions, goal setting, and rewards on motivation. Their ideas became known as ***scientific management***, and are often considered the beginning of the formal study of OB.

Scientific management is based on the belief that productivity is maximized when organizations are rationalized with precise sets of instructions based on time-and-motion studies. The four principles of Taylor's scientific management are:[29]

1. Replace rule-of-thumb work methods with methods based on scientifically studying the tasks using time-and-motion studies.
2. Scientifically select, train, and develop all workers rather than leaving them to passively train themselves.
3. Managers provide detailed instructions and supervision to workers to ensure that they are following the scientifically developed methods.
4. Divide work nearly equally between workers and managers. Managers should apply scientific management principles to planning the work, and workers should actually perform the tasks.

scientific management
Based on the belief that productivity is maximized when organizations are rationalized with precise sets of instructions based on time-and-motion studies

Although scientific management improved productivity, it also increased the monotony of work. Scientific management left no room for individual preferences or initiative, and was not always accepted by workers. At one point, complaints that it was dehumanizing led to a congressional investigation.[30] After World War I, attention shifted to understanding the role of human factors and psychology in organizations. This interest was spawned by the discovery of the ***Hawthorne effect*** in the 1920s and 1930s. The Hawthorne effect occurs when people improve some aspect of their behavior or performance simply because they know they are being assessed. This effect was first identified when a series of experiments that came to be known as the Hawthorne studies were conducted on Western Electric plant workers in Hawthorne, just outside of Chicago, to see the effects of a variety of factors, including individual versus group pay, incentive pay, breaks, and snacks, on productivity.

Hawthorne effect
When people improve some aspect of their behavior or performance simply because they are being assessed

One of the working conditions tested at the Hawthorne plant was lighting. When they tested brighter lights, production increased. When they tested dimmer lights, production also increased! Researchers observed that productivity almost always improved after a lighting change—any change—but eventually returned to normal levels. Workers appeared to try harder when the lights were dimmed just because they knew they were being evaluated. George Elton Mayo, founder of the human relations movement initiated by the Hawthorne studies, explained this finding by saying that the workers tried harder because of the sympathy and interest of the observers. Mayo stated that the reason workers are more strongly motivated by informal things is that individuals have a deep psychological need to believe that their organization cares about them.[31] Essentially, workers are more motivated when they believe their organization is open, concerned, and willing to listen.

The Hawthorne studies prompted further investigation into the effects of social relations, motivation, communication, and employee satisfaction on factory productivity. Rather than viewing workers as interchangeable parts in mechanical organizations as the scientific management movement had done, the ***human relations movement*** viewed organizations as cooperative systems and treated workers' orientations, values, and feelings as important parts of organizational dynamics and performance. The human relations movement stressed that the human dimensions of work, including group relations, can supersede organizational norms and even an individual's self-interests.

human relations movement
Views organizations as cooperative systems and treats workers' orientations, values, and feelings as important parts of organizational dynamics and performance

Unsophisticated research methods did render some of the conclusions of human relations researchers incorrect.[32] For example, the relationship between employee satisfaction and performance is more complex than researchers initially thought. Nonetheless, the movement ushered in a new era of more humane, employee-centered management by recognizing employees' social needs, and highlighted the importance of people to organizational success.

Harvard social work professor and management consultant Mary Parker Follett was known as a "prophet of management" because her ideas were ahead of her time. Follett discovered a variety of phenomena, including creativity exercises such as brainstorming, the "groupthink" effect in meetings (in which faulty decisions are made because group members try to minimize conflict and reach consensus by neglecting to critically analyze and test ideas), and what later became known as "management by objectives" and "total quality management." Follett also advocated for power-sharing arrangements in organizations. In the 1950s, Japanese managers discovered her writings. They credit her ideas, along with those of W. Edwards Deming, in revitalizing their industrial base.

W. Edwards Deming is known as the "guru of quality management." In postwar Japan, Deming taught Japanese industrialists statistical process control and quality concepts. His classic 1986 book[33] describes how to do high-quality, productive, and satisfying work. Deming's plan-do-check-act cycle of continuous improvement promoted the adoption of fourteen principles to make any organization efficient and capable of solving almost any problem. Deming believed that removing fear from the workplace gives employees pride in their workmanship, which increases production. Deming also felt that when things go wrong, there is a 94 percent chance that the system (elements under managerial control including machinery and rules) rather than the worker is the cause.[34] He believed that making changes in response to normal variations was unwise, and that a proper understanding of variation includes the mathematical certainty that variation will normally occur within a certain range. The total quality management movement initiated by Deming again highlights the importance of people, teamwork, and communication in an organization's success. You will read much more about the evolution of OB throughout this book, but this brief history helps to set the stage for how we got this far. We now turn our attention to other important contextual perspectives that help us understand both organizations and the behaviors of individuals that comprise them.

Organizations as Open Systems

The systems perspective, or the theory of systems, was first developed in the physical sciences, but it has been extended to other areas, such as

Figure 1.3

The Systems Approach to Organizations

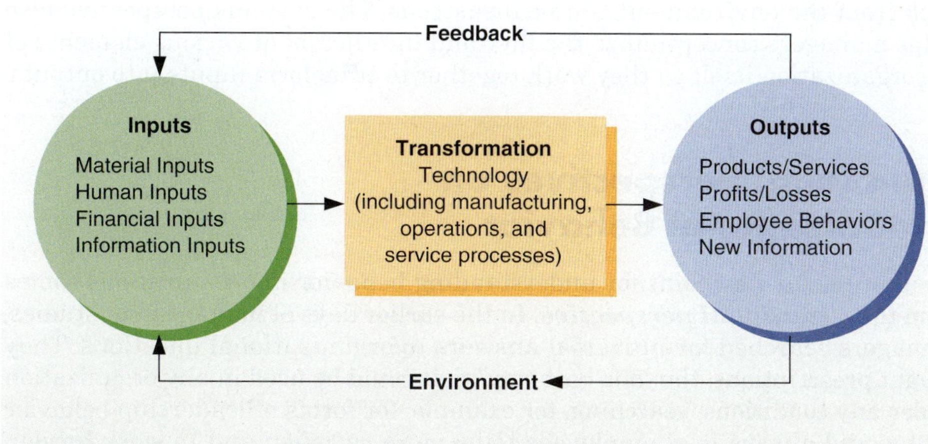

The systems approach to organizations provides a useful framework for understanding how the elements of an organization interact among themselves and with their environment. Various inputs are transformed into different outputs, with important feedback from the environment. If managers do not understand these interrelations, they may tend to ignore their environment or overlook important interrelationships within their organizations.

management.[35] A ***system*** is an interrelated set of elements that function as a whole. Figure 1.3 shows a general framework for viewing organizations as systems.

system
A set of interrelated elements functioning as a whole

According to this perspective, an organizational system receives four kinds of inputs from its environment: material, human, financial, and informational (note that this is consistent with our earlier description of management functions). The organization's managers then combine and transform these inputs and return them to the environment in the form of products or services, employee behaviors, profits or losses, and additional information. Then the system receives feedback from the environment regarding these outputs.

As an example, we can apply systems theory to the Shell Oil Company. Material inputs include pipelines, crude oil, and the machinery used to refine petroleum. Human inputs are oil field workers, refinery workers, office staff, and other people employed by the company. Financial inputs take the form of money received from oil and gas sales, stockholder investment, and so forth. Finally, the company receives information inputs from forecasts about future oil supplies, geological surveys on potential drilling sites, sales projections, and similar analyses.

Through complex refining and other processes, these inputs are combined and transformed to create products such as gasoline and motor oil. As outputs, these products are sold to the consuming public. Profits from operations are fed back into the environment through taxes, investments, and dividends; losses, when they occur, hit the environment by reducing stockholders' incomes. In addition to having on-the-job contacts with customers and suppliers, employees live in the community and participate in a variety of activities away from the workplace, and their behavior is influenced in part by their experiences as Shell workers. Finally, information about the company and its operations is also released into the environment. The environment, in turn, responds to these outputs and influences future inputs. For example, consumers may buy more or less gasoline depending on the quality and price of Shell's product, and banks may be more or less willing to lend Shell money based on financial information released about the company.

The systems perspective is valuable to managers for a variety of reasons. First, it underscores the importance of an organization's environment. For instance, failing to acquire the appropriate resources and failing to heed feedback from the environment can be disastrous. The systems perspective also helps managers conceptualize the flow and interaction of various elements of the organization itself as they work together to transform inputs into outputs.

Situational Perspectives on Organizational Behavior

situational perspective
Suggests that in most organizations, situations and outcomes are influenced by other variables

Another useful viewpoint for understanding behavior in organizations comes from the ***situational perspective***. In the earlier days of management studies, managers searched for universal answers to organizational questions. They sought prescriptions, the "one best way" that could be used in any organization under any conditions, searching, for example, for forms of leadership behavior that would always lead employees to be more satisfied and to work harder. Eventually, however, researchers realized that the complexities of human behavior and organizational settings make universal conclusions virtually impossible. They discovered that in organizations, most situations and outcomes are contingent; that is, the precise relationship between any two variables is likely to be situational (i.e., dependent on other variables).[36]

Figure 1.4 distinguishes the universal and situational perspectives. The universal model, shown at the top of the figure, presumes a direct cause-and-effect linkage between variables. For example, it suggests that whenever a manager encounters a particular problem or situation (such as motivating employees to work harder), a universal approach exists (such as raising pay or increasing autonomy) that will lead to the desired outcome. The situational perspective, on the other hand, acknowledges that several other variables

Figure 1.4

Universal Versus Situational Approach

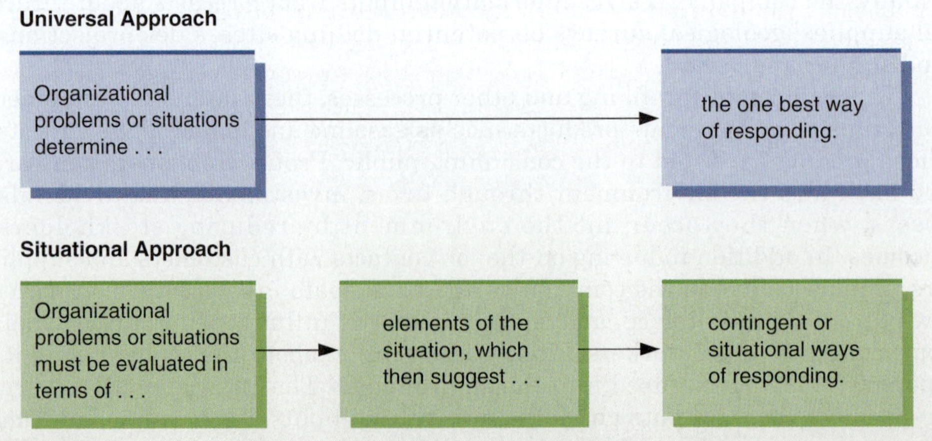
Universal Approach
Organizational problems or situations determine . . .
the one best way of responding.
Situational Approach
Organizational problems or situations must be evaluated in terms of . . .
elements of the situation, which then suggest . . .
contingent or situational ways of responding.

Managers once believed that they could identify the "one best way" of solving problems or reacting to situations. Here we illustrate a more realistic view, the situational approach. The situational approach suggests that approaches to problems and situations are contingent on elements of the situation.

alter the direct relationship. In other words, the appropriate managerial action or behavior in any given situation depends on elements of that situation. The field of organizational behavior has gradually shifted from a universal approach in the 1950s and early 1960s to a situational perspective. The situational perspective has been widely documented in the areas of motivation, job design, leadership, and organizational design, and it is becoming increasingly important throughout the entire field.

Interactionalism: People and Situations

Interactionalism is another useful perspective to help better understand behavior in organizational settings. First presented in terms of interactional psychology, this view assumes that individual behavior results from a continuous and multidirectional interaction between characteristics of the person and characteristics of the situation. More specifically, ***interactionalism*** attempts to explain how people select, interpret, and change various situations.[37] Note that the individual and the situation are presumed to interact continuously. This interaction is what determines the individual's behavior.

interactionalism
Suggests that individuals and situations interact continuously to determine individuals' behavior

The interactional view implies that simple cause-and-effect descriptions of organizational phenomena are not enough. For example, one set of research studies may suggest that job changes lead to improved employee attitudes. Other studies may propose that attitudes influence how people perceive their jobs in the first place. Both positions probably are incomplete: Employee attitudes may influence job perceptions, but these perceptions may in turn influence future attitudes. Because interactionalism is a fairly recent contribution to the field, it is less prominent in the chapters that follow than the systems and contingency theories. Nonetheless, the interactional view appears to offer many promising ideas for future development.

MANAGING FOR EFFECTIVENESS

Earlier in this chapter, we noted that managers work toward various goals. We are now in a position to elaborate on the nature of these goals in detail. Essentially, managers and leaders generally try to direct the behaviors of people in their organizations in ways that promote organizational effectiveness. They can do this by enhancing behaviors and attitudes, promoting citizenship, minimizing dysfunctional behaviors, and driving strategic execution. Of course, it may sometimes be necessary to make trade-offs among these different kinds of outcomes, but in general each is seen as a critical component of organizational effectiveness. The sections that follow elaborate on these and other points in more detail.

Enhancing Individual and Team Performance Behaviors

First, several individual behaviors result from a person's participation in an organization. One important behavior is productivity. A person's productivity is a relatively narrow indicator of his or her efficiency and is measured in terms of the products or services created per unit of input. For example, if Bill makes 100 units of a product in a day and Sara makes only 90 units in a day, then, assuming that the units are of the same quality and that Bill and Sara make the same wages, Bill is more productive than Sara.

Performance, another important individual-level outcome variable, is a somewhat broader concept and is made up of all work-related behaviors. For example, even though Bill is highly productive, it may also be that he refuses to work overtime, expresses negative opinions about the organization at every opportunity, will do nothing unless it falls precisely within the boundaries of his job, calls in sick frequently, and is often late. Sara, on the other hand, may always be willing to work overtime, is a positive representative of the organization, goes out of her way to make as many contributions to the organization as possible, and seldom misses work. Based on the full array of behaviors, then, we might conclude that Sara actually is the better performer.

Another set of outcomes exists at the group and team level. Some of these outcomes parallel the individual-level outcomes just discussed. For example, if an organization makes extensive use of work teams, team productivity and performance are important outcome variables. On the other hand, even if all the people in a group or team have the same or similar attitudes toward their jobs, the attitudes themselves are individual-level phenomena. Individuals, not groups, have attitudes. But groups or teams can also have unique outcomes that individuals do not share. For example, as we will discuss in Chapter 7, groups develop norms that govern the behavior of individual group members. Groups also develop different levels of cohesiveness. Thus, managers need to assess both common and unique outcomes when considering the individual and group levels.

Enhancing Employee Commitment and Engagement

Another set of individual-level outcomes influenced by managers consists of individual attitudes. Levels of job satisfaction or dissatisfaction, organizational commitment, and employee engagement all play an important role in organizational behavior. Extensive research conducted on job satisfaction has indicated that personal factors, such as an individual's needs and aspirations, determine this attitude, along with group and organizational factors, such as relationships with coworkers and supervisors, as well as working conditions, work policies, and compensation. A satisfied employee also tends to be absent less often, to make positive contributions, and to stay with the organization. In contrast, a dissatisfied employee may be absent more often, may experience and express stress that disrupts coworkers, and may be continually looking for another job. Contrary to what many managers believe, however, high levels of job satisfaction do not necessarily lead to higher levels of performance.

A person with a high level of commitment is likely to see herself as a true member of the organization (for example, referring to the organization in personal terms like "We make high-quality products"), to overlook minor sources of dissatisfaction with the organization, and to see herself remaining a member of the organization. In contrast, a person with less organizational commitment is more likely to see himself as an outsider (for example, referring to the organization in less personal terms like "They don't pay their employees very well"), to express more dissatisfaction about things, and to not see himself as a long-term member of the organization.

Promoting Organizational Citizenship Behaviors

Organizational citizenship is the behavior of individuals that makes a positive overall contribution to the organization.[38] Consider, for example, an employee who does work that is acceptable in terms of both quantity and quality. However, she refuses to work overtime, will not help newcomers learn the ropes, and is generally unwilling to make any contribution to the organization beyond the strict performance of her job. Although this person may be seen as a good performer, she is not likely to be seen as a good organizational citizen.

organizational citizenship *The behavior of individuals that makes a positive overall contribution to the organization*

Another employee may exhibit a comparable level of performance. In addition, however, he will always work late when the boss asks him to, take time to help newcomers learn their way around, and is perceived as being helpful and committed to the organization's success. Although his level of performance may be seen as equal to that of the first worker, he is also likely to be seen as a better organizational citizen.

The determinant of organizational citizenship behaviors is likely to be a complex mosaic of individual, social, and organizational variables. For example, the personality, attitudes, and needs of the individual will have to be consistent with citizenship behaviors. Similarly, the social context in which the individual works, or work group, will need to facilitate and promote such behaviors. And the organization itself, especially its culture, must be capable of promoting, recognizing, and rewarding these types of behaviors if they are to be maintained. Although the study of organizational citizenship is still in its infancy, preliminary research suggests that it may play a powerful role in organizational effectiveness.

Minimizing Dysfunctional Behaviors

Some work-related behaviors are dysfunctional in nature. ***Dysfunctional behaviors*** are those that detract from, rather than contribute to, organizational performance.[39] Two other important individual-level behaviors are absenteeism and turnover. Absenteeism is a measure of attendance. Although virtually everyone misses work occasionally, some people miss far more than others. Some look for excuses to miss work and call in sick regularly just for some time off; others miss work only when absolutely necessary. Turnover occurs when a person leaves the organization. If the individual who leaves is a good performer or if the organization has invested heavily in training the person, turnover can be costly.

dysfunctional behaviors *Those that detract from, rather than contribute to, organizational performance*

Other forms of dysfunctional behavior may be even more costly for an organization. Theft and sabotage, for example, result in direct financial costs for an organization. Sexual and racial harassment also cost an organization, both indirectly (by lowering morale, producing fear, and driving off valuable employees) and directly (through financial liability if the organization responds inappropriately). So, too, can politicized behavior, intentionally misleading others in the organization, spreading malicious rumors, and similar activities. Incivility and rudeness can result in conflict and damage to morale and the organization's culture.[40]

SHI YALI/SHUTTERSTOCK.COM

Dysfunctional behaviors in organizations generally include things like excessive absenteeism and incivility. Sometimes, though, employees turn violent. When this happens the workplace can turn into a crime scene.

Bullying and workplace violence are also growing concerns in many organizations. Violence by disgruntled workers or former workers results in dozens of deaths and injuries each year.[41] The factors that contribute to workplace violence—not to mention the factors involved in its increases and decreases—are difficult to pin down but of obvious importance to managers.

Driving Strategic Execution

Finally, another set of outcome variables exists at the organization level. These outcomes usually relate to strategic execution—how well managers and their employees understand and carry out the actions needed to achieve strategic goals. As before, some of these outcomes parallel those at the individual and group levels, but others are unique. For example, we can measure and compare organizational productivity. We can also develop organization-level indicators of absenteeism and turnover. But profitability is generally assessed only at the organizational level.

Organizations are also commonly assessed in terms of financial performance: stock price, return on investment, growth rates, and so on. They are also evaluated in terms of their ability to survive and the extent to which they satisfy important stakeholders such as investors, government regulators, employees, and unions.

Clearly, then, the manager must balance different outcomes across all three levels of analysis. In many cases, these outcomes appear to contradict one another. For example, paying workers high salaries can enhance satisfaction and reduce turnover, but it also may detract from bottom-line performance. Similarly, exerting strong pressure to increase individual performance may boost short-term profitability but increase turnover and job stress. Thus, the manager must look at the full array of outcomes and attempt to balance them in an optimal fashion. The manager's ability to do this is a major determinant of the organization's success and how well it implements its business strategy.

How Do We Know What We Know?

Another important part of being an effective manager is understanding the quality of the information you use to make decisions. Not all information is accurate! Accordingly, it is important for you to understand the processes that have been used to establish our knowledge about OB, and why we know what we know. People sometimes believe that OB is simply a collection of common sense ideas because the theories can seem obvious. For example, everyone "knows" that having higher goals and confidence leads to better performance, more job satisfaction leads to greater productivity, greater group cohesion will lead to higher group performance, and valuing rewards leads to greater motivation, right? So if it is all common sense, why do we need OB research? And why do we need to study these theories?

The answer is that common sense isn't so common. People don't always agree. If ten different people see the same leadership interaction you may find ten different "common sense" perspectives on what leadership is and how it works. Even if you don't find ten different perspectives, you will certainly not find perfect agreement on the same phenomenon. Take two common sense statements: "Absence makes the heart grow fonder" and "When the cat is away the mice will play." Which one is correct? Why?

Another answer is that common sense is not always right. Findings may seem common sense after the research is done, but beforehand we don't really know what is going on. For example, in this book you will learn that each of the common sense statements made earlier is either false or conditional. Goals and confidence do not always work, satisfaction does not always lead to productivity, cohesion does not always enhance group performance, and having valued rewards sometimes doesn't motivate people. So it isn't just common sense. We need science and research because it is built on careful and systematic testing of assumptions and conclusions. This process allows us to evolve our understanding of how things work and it allows us to learn when goals, confidence, satisfaction, cohesion, and rewards affect outcomes and why it happens. That is why you need to learn the theories and why you can't just operate on common sense.

Intuition

Many people feel that they have a good understanding of other people from observing them all of their lives. When you want to persuade or motivate a friend or colleague to do something, for example, you likely use various techniques and tricks that have worked for you in the past. So why should you study OB?

Although we can certainly develop a good understanding of many of the norms, expectations, and behaviors of others by living and working with them, there are many things that are not well understood without more systematic study. Decades of research have both reinforced some of the things many people intuitively believe and identified common misunderstandings or misperceptions about OB. For example, when are different leadership approaches most effective? What are the advantages and disadvantages of different influence approaches? What goal level will best motivate someone? How important is employee satisfaction to job performance? Is stress always bad? The answers to some of these questions may surprise you, and will help make you a more successful manager.

We encourage you to read this book with an open mind, and to not assume that you know all there is to know about a topic before you have studied it. Our goal is to help you be as effective as possible in organizations, and to help you create successful organizations. Help us help you succeed by being open to challenging and replacing popular but incorrect notions you may have about OB.

The Scientific Method

Rather than relying on experience or intuition, or just assuming that ideas are correct because they seem to make sense, the ***scientific method*** relies on systematic studies that identify and replicate a result using a variety of methods, samples, and settings. Although he himself was not a distinguished scientist, Sir Francis Bacon developed the scientific method, shown in Figure 1.5, in the 1600s.[42]

scientific method
Method of knowledge generation that relies on systematic studies that identify and replicate a result using a variety of methods, samples, and settings

Figure 1.5

The scientific method is a useful approach to learning more about organizational behavior. Using theory to develop hypotheses and then collecting and studying relevant data can help generate new knowledge.

The Scientific Method

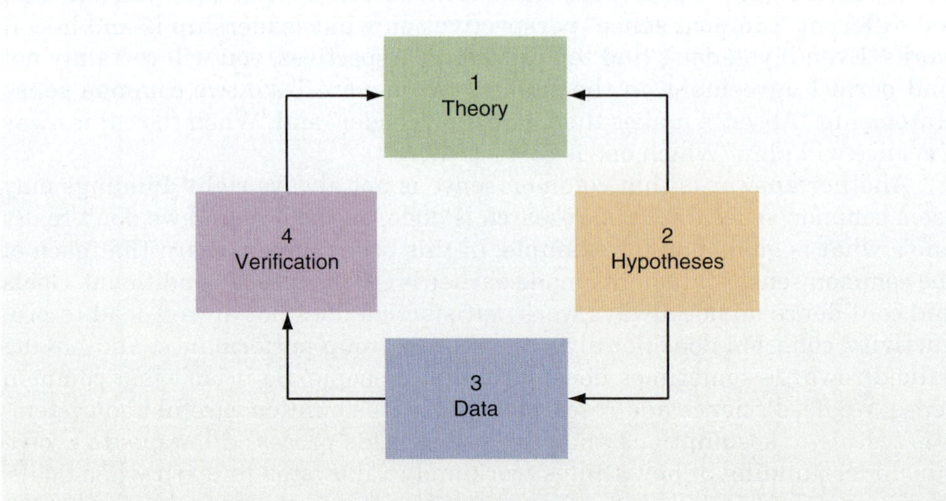

theory
A collection of verbal and symbolic assertions that specify how and why variables are related, and the conditions under which they should and should not relate

hypotheses
Written predictions specifying expected relationships between certain variables

independent variable
The variable that is predicted to affect something else

dependent variable
The variable predicted to be affected by something else

correlation
Reflects the size and strength of the statistical relationship between two variables; ranges from −1 to +1

The scientific method begins with ***theory***, which is a collection of verbal and symbolic assertions that specify how and why two or more variables are related, and the conditions under which they should and should not relate.[43] Theories describe the relationships that are proposed to exist among certain variables, when, and under what conditions. Until they are proven to be correct, theories are no guarantee of fact. It is important to systematically test any theory to verify that its predictions are accurate.

The second step in the scientific method is the development of ***hypotheses***, or written predictions specifying expected relationships between certain variables. "Setting a specific goal will be positively related to the number of products assembled" is an example of a hypothesis (and, in fact, it's true!). So how can you test this hypothesis?

Hypothesis testing can be done using a variety of research methods and statistical analyses. For our purposes, assume we collect data on our predictor, or ***independent variable***, and our criterion, or ***dependent variable***. In this hypothetical case, setting a specific, difficult, achievable goal is the independent variable, and the number of products assembled is our dependent variable. We identify a representative group of assemblers, and record their goals and their performance during a one-hour work period. We can then analyze the ***correlation***, abbreviated r, between the two variables to test our hypothesis. The correlation reflects the strength of the statistical relationship between two variables. Rather than answering a question with a "yes" or "no," the correlation answers with "how strong the relationship is."

The correlation ranges from −1 to +1, and can be positive or negative. A correlation of 0 means that there is no statistical relationship. We can also imagine a correlation as a graph. As you can see from Figure 1.6, in the context of our example, a correlation of 0 would mean that setting a goal has no effect on the number of products assembled, while a correlation of +1 means

Figure 1.6

Interpreting Correlations

Correlations between variables can range from −1 to +1. By studying correlations we can learn more about how two variable are related. Correlations of −1 or +1 are unusual, as is a correlation of 0. Fortunately, we can still learn a great deal from correlations that are statistically significant.

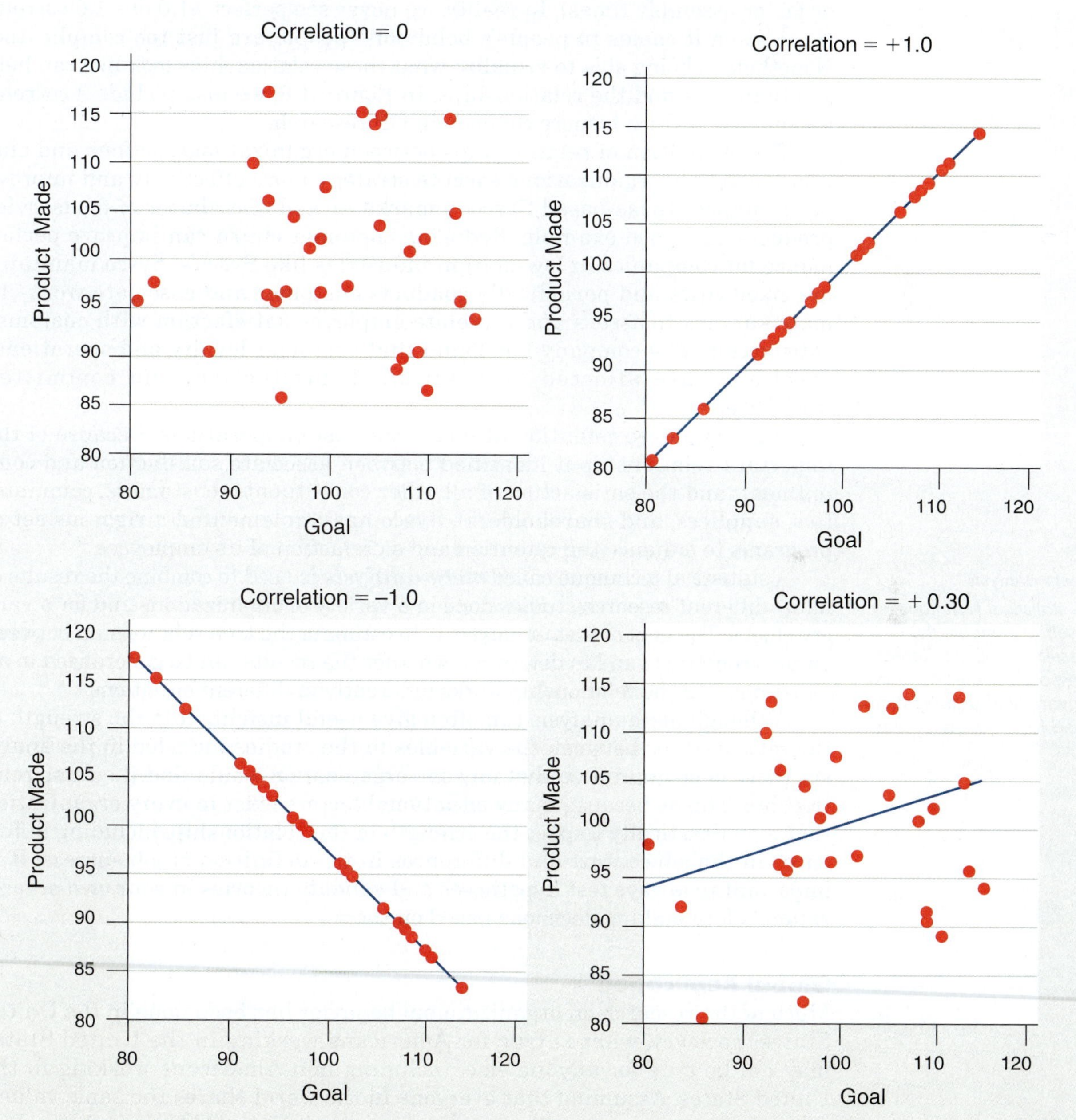

that there is a perfect positive relationship—the higher the goal, the more products assembled. A correlation of +1.0 is as strong a positive relationship as we can get, and shows that we can predict the number of products assembled perfectly from the level of the assembler's goals.

As you can also see from Figure 1.6, a correlation of −1.0 is as strong a negative relationship as we can get. It would indicate that the higher an assembler's goal, the lower her performance. A negative correlation is not necessarily bad. In this case, it would simply mean that to maximize assemblers' performance, the manager should set *lower* goals (perhaps goals for lower error rates or faster assembly times). In reality, we never see perfect +1.0 or −1.0 correlations when it comes to people's behavior—people are just too complicated. Nonetheless, being able to visualize what these relationships look like can help you to understand the relationships. In Figure 1.6, we also include a correlation of +0.30, which is more common in OB research.

The evaluation of relationships between organizational actions and outcomes can help organizations execute strategy more effectively and improve performance. Texas-based Sysco, a marketer and distributor of foodservice products, is a good example. Reducing customer churn can improve performance for companies in low-margin industries like Sysco's. Sysco maintains low fixed costs and periodically conducts customer and associate work-climate surveys to assess and correlate employee satisfaction with customer satisfaction. The company has found that customer loyalty and operational excellence are affected by a satisfied, productive, and committed workforce.[44]

High employee retention also cuts the cost of operations. Because of the important relationship it identified between associate satisfaction and commitment, and the satisfaction of all other constituents (customers, communities, suppliers, and shareholders), Sysco has implemented a rigorous set of programs to enhance the retention and satisfaction of its employees.[45]

meta-analysis
A statistical technique used to combine the results of many different research studies done in a variety of organizations and for a variety of jobs

A statistical technique called ***meta-analysis*** is used to combine the results of many different research studies done in a variety of organizations and for a variety of jobs. The goal of meta-analysis is to estimate the true relationship between various constructs and to determine whether the results can be generalized to all situations or if the relationship works differently in different situations.

Although meta-analysis can often give useful insights into the strength of the relationships between the variables in the studies included in the analysis, there is no guarantee that any one organization would find the same relationship. This is because many situational factors exist in every organization that may drastically impact the strength of the relationship, including differences in the job context and differences in the definition of job success. It is important to always test hypotheses and validate theories in your own organization before making decisions based on them.

Global Replication

Much of the research on organizational behavior has been done in the United States; however, what is true for Americans working in the United States may not be true for anyone else, including non-Americans working in the United States. Assuming that everyone in the world shares the same values, norms, and expectations about work is incorrect. National boundaries no longer limit many organizations, and many U.S. companies employ people from around the world.

GLOBAL ISSUES

MANAGING ACROSS CULTURES

Effective management requires flexibility and an appreciation that people's expectations and values differ. The U.S. workforce is already very diverse, and is expected to become even more diverse in coming years. The more comfortable you are in tailoring your motivation and leadership efforts to the people you want to lead, the more effective you will be as an employee and as a manager.

Although good pay and interesting work appear to be universally motivating,[46] people from different cultures have different traditions, are often motivated by different things, and communicate in different ways.[47] For example, some cultures communicate directly while others are more reserved. Some cultures put a high value on family life whereas others stress the importance of work. As one expert puts it, "to understand why people do what they do, we have to understand the cultural constructs by which they interpret the world."[48] Clearly, motivating employees in a multinational organization is challenging, particularly if managers adopt a "one-size-fits-all" motivation strategy.

Cultural differences also influence the effectiveness of different leadership behaviors.[49] Effective leadership behaviors are determined by the roles of expectations, norms, and traditions in the particular society. Managers supervising employees from different cultures must recognize these differences and adapt their behaviors and relationships accordingly. For example, societies such as the United States, Sweden, and Germany have small variation in the distribution of power across supervisors and employees, but others such as Japan and Mexico have a large power difference. If employees feel that large power differences are legitimate and appropriate, they may be uncomfortable if their supervisor tries to reduce the expected power difference by acting more friendly and accessible.

In this book, the *Global Issues* feature in each chapter will highlight global issues that are relevant to the concepts we discuss. In the Global Issues feature in this chapter, you will learn more about how effective motivation and leadership vary in different cultures.

THE FRAMEWORK OF THE BOOK

Figure 1.7 presents the framework around which our book is organized. As you can see, we suggest that organizations and the behaviors of the people who comprise them all function within an environment context. Both this chapter and Chapter 2 help establish the key elements of this context. At the center of the framework we also note several important factors that determine whether or not managers and organizations are effective. These factors, discussed earlier in this chapter, involve enhancing performance behaviors, enhancing commitment and engagement, promoting citizenship behaviors, and minimizing dysfunctional behaviors.

Operating between the environmental context and the indicators of effectiveness are four sets of factors. One set of factors relate to individuals and include individual characteristics, individual values, perceptions, and reactions, motivation concepts and models, and the role of work and reward in tapping those motivation concepts and models. The four chapters in Part 2 of the book discuss these factors in detail.

A second set of factors that determine effectiveness involves groups and teams. Special considerations here are the role of groups and how

Figure 1.7

Organizational Behavior Framework

An array of environmental, individual, group and team, leadership, and organizational characteristics impact organizational behavior. If managers understand these concepts and characteristics they can better promote organizational effectiveness.

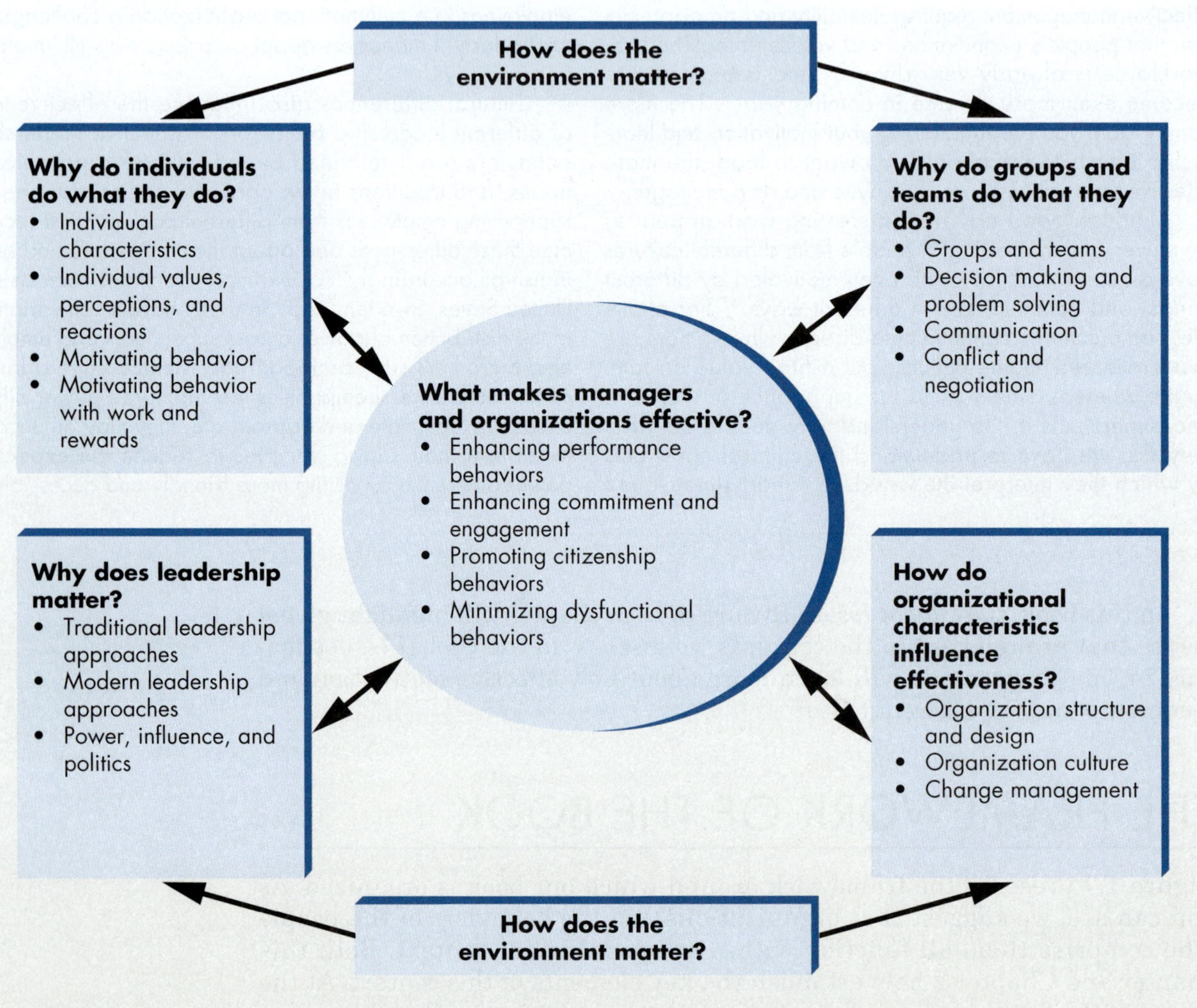

organizations use teams, decision-making and problem-solving processes, communication, and diversity. Part 3 includes four chapters that explore these factors.

Leadership is also of great importance in determining organizational effectiveness. Traditional leadership models; modern leadership approaches; power, influence, and politics; and conflict and negotiation are all important aspects of leadership and are covered in detail in Part 4.

Finally, several factors associated with the organization itself also impact effectiveness. Organization structure, design, and culture and how the organization manages change are the central elements of importance and are the subject of Part 5.

We believe that this framework will serve as a useful roadmap for you as you learn about organizational behavior. The framework will be reintroduced at the beginning of each part in the book. We will use it to both remind you of where our discussion has taken us and where we are headed next.

SUMMARY AND APPLICATION

Organizational behavior is the study of human behavior in organizational settings, the interface between human behavior and the organization, and the organization itself. The study of OB is important because organizations have a powerful influence on our lives. It also directly relates to management in organizations. Indeed, by its very nature, management requires an understanding of human behavior to help managers better comprehend behaviors at different organizational levels, at the same organizational level, in other organizations, and in themselves.

A manager's job can be characterized in terms of four functions. These basic managerial functions are planning, organizing, leading, and controlling. Planning is the process of determining the organizations' desired future position and deciding how best to get there. Organizing is the process of designing jobs, grouping jobs into manageable units, and establishing patterns of authority among jobs and groups of jobs. Leading is the process of motivating members of the organization to work together toward the organization's goals. Controlling is the process of monitoring and correcting the actions of the organization and its people to keep them headed toward their goals.

Why is it that some people rise in organizations despite being only average accountants, marketers, researchers, and so on? Often the answer is that those people know how to interact effectively with other people. Effective interaction with people is critical for advancement in organizations, and often for effective job performance. Being able to understand what people think and feel, knowing how to persuade and motivate others, and knowing how to resolve conflicts and forge cooperation are among the most important skills of successful leaders.[50] "People skills" are often what make the difference between an average and an excellent performer in almost any job.

This book can help you better understand yourself, understand organizations, understand the role of organizational behavior in your personal career success, and improve your OB skills. All we can do, however, is make these things possible: You need to make them happen. We encourage you to stay open-minded and receptive to new ideas and to information that disconfirms some of your current assumptions about people, organizations, and management. By studying the chapters and putting some thought into how you can use various the concepts in different situations, you will be taking an important step in advancing your career.

REAL WORLD RESPONSE

MANAGING GROWTH AT GOOGLE

Between 1998 and 2015 Google grew from a two-person startup to employing over 50,000 people[51] in more than 40 countries.[52] This rapid growth presented tremendous challenges in integrating new employees while motivating them to be innovative, productive, and loyal to the fast growing company. To maximize employee innovation, trust, and loyalty Google's founders researched other organizations that had histories of caring for their people, driving extraordinary innovation, and building great brands. Visiting with executives at the SAS Institute, frequently ranked as the best multinational company to work for by the Great Place to Work Institute, reinforced the founders' belief that people thrive in and are loyal to their jobs when they feel fully supported and authentically valued.[53] This understanding led to the development of a culture anchored by trust, transparency, and inclusion.

Google is now known for offering its employees a wide variety of perks the help its employees to be more effective at work, including free organic food and snacks, free fitness classes and gyms, and the ability to bring pets to work.[54] Google regularly surveys employees about their managers, using the information to publicly recognize the best ones and give the worst managers intensive coaching and support that helps 75 percent of them improve within three months.[55] Google also hires smart, ambitious people who share the company's goals and vision and maintains an open culture in which employees feel comfortable sharing opinions and ideas. In weekly meetings, Google employees can even ask questions directly to executives including founders Page and Brin about company issues.[56] Google's proactive efforts to be an engaging and inspiring place for its employees has both helped the company succeed and made it a staple on various "most desired employer" lists, including being named the #1 Best Place to Work honor from Glassdoor in 2015.[57]

DISCUSSION QUESTIONS

1. What do you think are the most important things a manager does? Is how a manager does these things also important? Why or why not?
2. Some people have suggested that understanding human behavior at work is the single most important requirement for managerial success. Do you agree or disagree with this statement? Why?
3. The chapter identifies four basic managerial functions. Based on your own experiences and observations, provide an example of each function.
4. Why will learning about OB help you to get a better job and a better career, and be a better manager?

5. Some people believe that individuals working in an organization have basic human rights to satisfaction with their work and to the opportunity to grow and develop. How would you defend this position? How would you argue against it?
6. Think of something that you believe leads to employee productivity based on intuition that may not prove to be true if tested systematically. Now apply the scientific method and describe how you might test your theory.

UNDERSTAND YOURSELF EXERCISE

Global Mindset

This chapter's *Understand Yourself* feature gives you the chance to self-assess your global mindset. Global mindset reflects how well we influence people, groups, and organizations from a variety of backgrounds and cultures. The ability to work effectively with people from many parts of the world will help you to perform well on the job and advance your career faster. After completing the self-assessment, answer the following questions:

1. Do you think that your score accurately reflects your global mindset? Why or why not? What, if anything, is missing from the assessment?
2. How do you think that having a higher global mindset will help you to be a better manager and leader? How can this characteristic help you succeed in your career?
3. What might you do in the next year to increase your global mindset? Identify and discuss three specific behaviors, activities, or other things that increase your global mindset.

GROUP EXERCISE

Managing A Successful Restaurant

Form groups of 3–5 students. Imagine that you are all managers in a local restaurant (your group can choose the name). There are many restaurants in town, making it a competitive business. Your food is good, but so is the food at many other dining options in town. You recognize that providing high quality, friendly service and having actively engaged employees is going to make the difference between your restaurant's success and failure.

Your management team decides to first address organizational citizenship and employee engagement as drivers of high quality customer service. After all, employees who are not engaged and who are unwilling to engage in citizenship behaviors are less likely to contribute to your desired culture of providing great customer service and a friendly atmosphere. First think independently about what your restaurant can do to enhance the engagement and citizenship behaviors of your employees. Then share your ideas with the group and identify your top three suggestions for the restaurant. Be ready to share your ideas with the class.

Your management team next decides that it will be important to minimize dysfunctional employee behaviors if the restaurant is to succeed. Behaviors including theft, harassment, rumor spreading, absenteeism, and high turnover will hurt the restaurant's finances, negatively affect morale, and weaken your team's ability to provide quality customer service. First think independently about what your restaurant can do to minimize the occurrence of these destructive behaviors. Then share your ideas with the group and identify your top three suggestions for the restaurant. Be ready to share them with the class.

VIDEO EXERCISE

Managing at Camp Bow Wow

Camp Bow Wow, a sort of combination day camp/B&B for dogs, was started in 2000 by a dog-loving entrepreneur named Heidi Ganahl. The business is a *franchise*, a form of ownership in which a franchiser grants a *franchisee* the right to use its brand name and processes and sell its products or services. Sue Ryan left the corporate world in 2004 take over a Camp Bow Wow franchise in Boulder, Colorado. To reduce the demands placed on her as the sole manager, Ryan developed other employees' managerial skills so that they could be promoted and share in the managerial responsibilities of the business.

As a class, watch "Camp Bow Wow" (5:57) and then individually consider the following questions. After you have come up with your own ideas, form groups of 4–5 people and discuss your insights. Be sure to nominate someone to serve as a spokesperson to share your ideas with the class.

1. How does Sue Ryan perform the three basic managerial roles—interpersonal, informational, and decision making—in her role at Camp Bow Wow?
2. How do Candace Stathis and Sue Ryan apply the four critical managerial skills—technical, interpersonal, conceptual, and diagnostic—in their roles at the company? Which of these skills do you think is most important skill for a manager at Camp Bow Wow and why?
3. How do Ryan and Stathis balance the three levels of business outcomes—individual, group and team, and organizational? How would each manager rank the importance of the three outcomes? Why are their rankings likely to be the same or different?

VIDEO CASE

Now What?

Imagine being a new manager at Happy Time Toys, a company that designs and manufactures novelty toys. While attending a group meeting with your boss and two coworkers, your boss asks for ways of better using the organization's talent to create a competitive advantage. *What do you say or do?* Go to this chapter's "Now What?" video, watch the challenge video, and choose the best response. Be sure to also view the outcomes of the two responses you didn't choose.

Discussion Questions

1. Which aspects of management and organizational behavior discussed in this chapter are illustrated in these videos? Explain your answer.
2. How could a company's talent strategy undermine its ability to create a competitive advantage?
3. How else might you answer the question of how Happy Time Toys can create a competitive advantage through its talent?

ENDNOTES

[1]Our History in Depth. Google.com. Available online: http://www.google.com/about/company/history/.

[2]Shontell, A. (2011, May 4). 13 Unusual Ways Sergey Brin and Larry Page Made Google the Company to Beat. *Business Insider*. Available online: http://www.businessinsider.com/history-sergey-brin-larry-page-and-google-strategy-2011-3#and-celebrated-tgif-12.

[3]For a classic discussion of the meaning of organizational behavior, see Cummings, L. (1978, January). Toward Organizational Behavior. *Academy of Management Review*, 90–98. See also Nicholson, N., Audia, P., & Pillutla M. (eds.) (2005). *The Blackwell Encyclopedia of Management: Organizational Behavior* (Vol. 11). London: Blackwell Publishing.

[4]Lubit, R. (2004, March/April). The Tyranny of Toxic Managers: Applying Emotional Intelligence to Deal with Difficult Personalities. *Ivey Business Journal*. Available online: http://iveybusinessjournal.com/publication/the-tyranny-of-toxic-managers-an-emotional-intelligence-approach-to-dealing-with-difficult-personalities/

[5]Javidan, M., Steers, R. M., & Hitt, M. A. (2007). *The Global Mindset, Advances in International Management* (Vol. 19). New York: Elsevier.

[6]Arora, A., Jaju, A., Kefalas, A. G., & Perenich, T. (2004). An Exploratory Analysis of Global Managerial Mindsets: A Case of U.S. Textile and Apparel Industry. *Journal of International Management,10*, 393–411.

[7]Javidan, M., Steers, R. M., & Hitt, M. A. (2007). *The Global Mindset, Advances in International Management* (Vol. 19). New York: Elsevier.

[8]Story, J. S. P. & Barbuto, J. E. (2011). Global Mindset: A Construct Clarification and Framework. *Journal of Leadership &Organizational Studies, 18*(3), 377–384.

[9]Dumaine, B. (1995, August). Don't Be an Ugly American Manager. *Fortune*, 225.

[10]Lane, H. W., Maznevski, M., & Dietz, J. (2009). *International Management Behavior: Leading with a Global Mindset* (6th ed.). Sussex, UK: John Wiley & Sons.

[11]Warren, K. (2009). *Developing Employee Talent to Perform*, eds. J. M. Phillips & S. M. Gully. New York: Business Expert Press.

[12]Pfeffer, J. (2003). *Business and the Spirit: Management Practices That Sustain Values, Handbook of Workplace Spirituality and Organizational Performance*, eds. R. A. Giacolone and C. L. Jurkiewicz (pp. 29–45). New York: M. E. Sharpe Press; Ulrich, D., & Smallwood, N. (2003). *Why the Bottom Line Isn't! How to Build Value through People and Organization*. New Jersey: John Wiley & Sons.

[13]The World's Most Admired Companies, (2015, March 16) *Fortune*, 135–140.

[14]Katz, R. L. (1987 September-October). The Skills of an Effective Administrator. *Harvard Business Review*, 90–102; see also Hansen, M., Ibarra, H., & Peyer, U. (2010, January-February). The Best-Performing CEOs in the World. *Harvard Business Review*, 104–113.

[15]SBC Chief Says Deal Preserves an "Icon." *USA Today* (2005, February 1), 1B, 2B.

[16]Walmart Says It's Giving 500,000 U.S. Workers Pay Raises. *Los Angeles Times* (2015, February 19)., 9B.

[17]Jack Welch speech to the Economic Club of New York, Detroit, May 16, 1994.

[18]Treacy, M., & Wiersema, F. (1997). *The Discipline of Market Leaders*. New York: Perseus Books.

[19]Lado, A. A., Boyd, N. G., & Wright, P. (1992). A Competency-Based Model of Sustainable Competitive Advantage: Toward a Conceptual Integration. *Journal of Management, 18*, 77–91.

[20]Worrell, D. (2011). Higher Salaries: Costco's Secret Weapon, Allbusiness.com. Available online: http://www.allbusiness.com/staffing-hr/16745820-1.html.

[21]Porter, M. E. (1985). *Competitive Advantage*. New York: Free Press.

[22]Porter, M. E. (1985). *Competitive Advantage*. New York: Free Press; Porter, M. E. (1998). *Competitive Strategy: Techniques for Analyzing Industries and Competitors*. New York: Free Press.

[23]Beatty, R. W., & Schneier, C. E. (1997). New HR Roles to Impact Organizational Performance: From "Partners" to "Players." *Human Resource Management, 36*, 29–37; Deloitte & Touche, LLP. (2002). *Creating Shareholder Value through People: The Human Capital ROI Study*. New York: Author; Treacy, M., & Wiersema, F. (1993). Customer Intimacy and Other Value Disciplines. *Harvard Business Review, 71*, 84–94.

[24]Beatty, R. W., & Schneier, C. E. (1997). New HR Roles to Impact Organizational Performance: From "Partners" to "Players." *Human Resource Management, 36*, 29–37; Deloitte & Touche, LLP. (2002). *Creating Shareholder Value through People: The Human Capital ROI Study*. New York: Author; Treacy, M., & Wiersema, F. (1993). Customer Intimacy and Other Value Disciplines. *Harvard Business Review, 71*, 84–94.

[25]Pieterse, A. N., van Knippenberg, D., Schippers, M., & Stam, D. (2010). Transformational and Transactional Leadership and Innovative Behavior: The Moderating Role of Psychological Empowerment. *Journal of Organizational Behavior, 31*, 609–623.

[26]Groth, M. & Goodwin, R. E. (2011). Customer Service. In *APA Handbook of Industrial and Organizational Psychology: Maintaining, Expanding, and Contracting the Organization*, ed. S. Zedeck (Vol. 3, pp. 329–357). Washington, DC: American Psychological Association.

[27]Beatty, R. W., & Schneier, C. E. (1997). New HR Roles to Impact Organizational Performance: From "Partners" to "Players." *Human Resource Management, 36*, 29–37; Deloitte & Touche, LLP. (2002). *Creating Shareholder Value through People: The Human Capital ROI Study*. New York: Author; Treacy, M., & Wiersema, F. (1993). Customer Intimacy and Other Value Disciplines. *Harvard Business Review, 71*, 84–94.

[28]Weber, Y. & Fried, Y. (2011), Guest Editors' Note: The Role of HR Practices in Managing Culture Clash During the Post-merger Integration Process. *Human Resource Management, 50*, 565–570.

[29]Taylor, F. W. (1911). *The Principles of Scientific Management*. New York: Harper & Brothers.

[30]Spender, J. C., & Kijne, H. (1996). *Scientific Management: Frederick Winslow Taylor's Gift to the World?* Boston: Kluwer.

[31]Mayo, E. (1945). *The Social Problems of an Industrial Civilization*. Boston: Harvard University Press.

[32]Organ, D. W. (2002, March–April). Elusive Phenomena. *Business Horizons*, 1–2.

[33]Deming, W. E. (1986). *Out of the Crisis*. Boston: Massachusetts Institute of Technology.

[34]Deming, W. E. (1986). *Out of the Crisis*. Boston: Massachusetts Institute of Technology, p. 315.

[35]Kast, F., & Rosenzweig, J. (1972, December). General Systems Theory: Applications for Organization and Management. *Academy of Management Journal*, 447–465.

[36]For a classic overview and introduction, see Kast, F., & Rozenzweig, J. (eds.). (1973). *Contingency Views of Organization and Management*. Chicago: Science Research Associates.

[37]Terborg, J. (1981, October). Interactional Psychology and Research on Human Behavior in Organizations. *Academy of Management Review*, 569–576; Schneider, B. (1983) Interactional Psychology and Organizational Behavior. In *Research in Organizational Behavior*, eds. L. Cummings & B. Staw (Vol. 5, pp. 1–32). Greenwich, CT: JAI Press; Turban, D. B., & Keon, T. L. (1993). Organizational Attractiveness: An Interactionist Perspective. *Journal of Applied Psychology*, *78*(2), 184–193.

[38]For recent findings regarding this behavior, see Podsakoff, P. M., MacKenzie, S. B., Paine, J. B., & Bacharah, D. G. G. (2000) Organizational Citizenship Behaviors: A Critical Review of the Theoretical and Empirical Literature and Suggestions for Future Research. *Journal of Management*, *26*(3), 513–563; see also Organ, D. W., Podsakoff, P. M., & Podsakoff, N. P. (2010). Expanding the Criterion Domain to Include Organizational Citizenship Behavior: Implications for Employee Selection. In *Handbook of Industrial and Organizational Psychology: Selecting and Developing Members for the Organization*, ed. S. Zedeck (Vol. 2, pp. 281–323). Washington, DC: American Psychological Association.

[39]Griffin, R., & Lopez, Y. (2005) "Bad Behavior" in Organization: A Review and Typology for Future Research. *Journal of Management*, *31*(6), 988–1005.

[40]For an illustration, see Lim, S., Cortina, L. M., & Magley, V. J. (2008). Personal and Workgroup Incivility: Impact on Work and Health Outcomes. *Journal of Applied Psychology*, *93*(1), 95–107.

[41]See O'Leary-Kelly, A., Griffin, R. W., & Glew, D. J. (1996, January). Organization-Motivated Aggression: A Research Framework. *Academy of Management Review*, 225–253. See also Douglas, S. C., Kiewitz, C., Martinko, M.J., Harvey, P., Kim, Y., & Chun, J. U. (2008). Cognitions, Emotions, and Evaluations: An Elaboration Likelihood Model for Workplace Aggression. *Academy of Management Review*, *33*(2), 425–451; and Barclay, L. J., & Aquino, K. (2010). Workplace Aggression and Violence. In *Handbook of Industrial and Organizational Psychology: Maintaining, Expanding, and Contracting the Organization*, ed. S. Zedeck (Vol. 3, pp. 615–640). Washington, DC: American Psychological Association.

[42]Bacon, F., Silverthorne, M., & Jardine, L. (2000). *The New Organon*. Cambridge, UK: Cambridge University Press.

[43]Campbell, J. P. (1990). The Role of Theory in Industrial and Organizational Psychology. In *Handbook of Industrial and Organizational Psychology*, eds. M. D. Dunnette and L. M. Hough (Vol. 1, pp. 39–74). Palo Alto, CA: Consulting Psychologists Press.

[44]Carrig, K., & Wright, P. M. (2007, January). Building Profit through Building People. *Workforce Management*. Available online: http://www.workforce.com/section/09/feature/24/65/90/index.html.

[45]Carrig, K., & Wright, P. M. (2007, January). Building Profit through Building People. *Workforce Management*. Available online: http://www.workforce.com/section/09/feature/24/65/90/index.html.

[46]Festing, M., Engle, A. D. Sr., Dowling, P. J. & Sahakiants, I. (2012). Human Resource Management Activities: Pay and Rewards. In *Handbook of Research on Comparative Human Resource Management*, eds. C. Brewster & W. Mayrhofer (pp. 139–163). Northampton, MA: Edward Elgar Publishing.

[47]Forstenlechner, I., & Lettice, F. (2007). Cultural Differences in Motivating Global Knowledge Workers. *Equal Opportunities International, 26*(8), 823–833.

[48]D'Andrade, R. G., & Strauss, C. (1992). *Human Motives and Cultural Models* (p. 4). Cambridge, UK: Cambridge University Press.

[49]Ayman, R. & Korabik, K. (2010). Leadership: Why Gender and Culture Matter. *American Psychologist*, *65*, 157–170.

[50]Lubit, R. (2004, March/April). The Tyranny of Toxic Managers: Applying Emotional Intelligence to Deal with Difficult Personalities. *Ivey Business Journal*. Available online: http://www.iveybusinessjournal.com/view_article.asp?intArticle_ID=475.

[51]Number of full-time Google Employees from 2007 to 2014. (2015) *Statista*. Available online: http://www.statista.com/statistics/273744/number-of-full-time-google-employees/.

[52]Google Locations. Google. Available online at: https://www.google.com/about/company/facts/locations/.

[53]Crowley, M. C. (2013, March 21). Not a happy accident: How Google deliberately designs workplace satisfaction. *Fast Company*. Available online: http://www.fastcompany.com/3007268/where-are-they-now/not-happy-accident-how-google-deliberately-designs-workplace-satisfaction.

[54]D'Onfro, J. & Smith, K. (2014, July 1). Google Employees Reveal Their Favorite Perks About Working for the Company. *Business Insider*. Available online: http://www.businessinsider.com/google-employees-favorite-perks-2014-7?op=1.

[55]Google's Secrets of Innovation: Empowering Its Employees. (2013, March 29). *Forbes*. Available online: http://www.forbes.com/sites/laurahe/2013/03/29/googles-secrets-of-innovation-empowering-its-employees/.

[56]Our Culture. Google. Available online: http://www.google.com/about/company/facts/culture/.

[57]Glassdoor Employees' Choice Award Winners Revealed: Google #1 Best Place to Work in 2015. (2014, December 9). Glassdoor.com,. Available online: http://www.glassdoor.com/blog/glassdoor-employees-choice-award-winners-revealed-google-1-place-work-2015/.

LOSKUTNIKOV/SHUTTERSTOCK.COM

CHAPTER 2

THE CHANGING ENVIRONMENT OF ORGANIZATIONS

CHAPTER OUTLINE

LEARNING OUTCOMES

After studying this chapter, you should be able to:

1. Describe the nature of diversity in organizations.
2. Describe the different types of diversity and barriers to inclusion that exist in the workplace.
3. Discuss the emergence of globalization and cross-cultural differences and similarities.
4. Discuss the changing nature of technology and its impact on business.
5. Describe emerging perspectives on ethics and corporate governance.
6. Discuss the key issues in new employment relationships.

LOSKUTNIKOV/SHUTTERSTOCK.COM

REAL WORLD CHALLENGE

GLOBAL DIVERSITY AT COCA-COLA

With over 130,000 global employees, over 65,000 of them in in the U.S.,[1] beverage giant The Coca-Cola Company is a global business that operates in a multicultural world both in the workplace and in the marketplace. The company recognizes that its ability to thrive in a multicultural world is both critical to its financial performance and consistent with its values.[2] Accordingly, diversity is recognized by Coca-Cola as an important component of their vision for the company in 2020.[3] As The Coca-Cola Company's CEO Muhtar Kent said, "The real power of diversity is the incredible synergies that result when different people and cultures come together united behind a common goal of winning and creating shared value. Extraordinary things truly happen."[4]

The Coca-Cola Company understands that although it has been recognized as a diversity leader there is always more it can do. Imagine that the company's leaders ask you for advice on how to build a diverse and inclusive workforce that allows it to leverage the potential of its diverse employees to enhance the company's performance. After reading this chapter, what would you tell them?

ANTONY MCAULAY/SHUTTERSTOCK.COM

The environment of all organizations is changing at an unprecedented rate. People work in different ways and places than in the past, the workplace is increasingly diverse, ethical challenges are a constant issue, and globalization is commonplace. Indeed, in some industries, such as consumer electronics, popular entertainment, and information technology, the speed and magnitude of change are truly breathtaking. YouTube, for instance, uploads over 60 hours of new video footage every hour. And it's only been during the last decade or two that smartphone technologies, Facebook, and other forms of social networking have become commonplace.

Even industries characterized by what have been staid and predictable environments, such as traditional retail and heavy manufacturing, also face sweeping environmental changes today. Understanding and addressing the environment of a business has traditionally been the purview of top managers. But the effects of today's changing environment permeate the entire organization. Hence, to truly understand the behavior of people in organizational settings, it is also necessary to understand the changing environment of business.[5] This chapter is intended to provide the framework for such understanding. Specifically, as illustrated in Figure 2.1, we introduce and examine five of the

Figure 2.1

The Changing Environment of Business

The changing environment of business presents both opportunities and challenges for managers today. Five important environmental forces are globalization, diversity, technology, ethics and corporate governance, and new employment relationships.

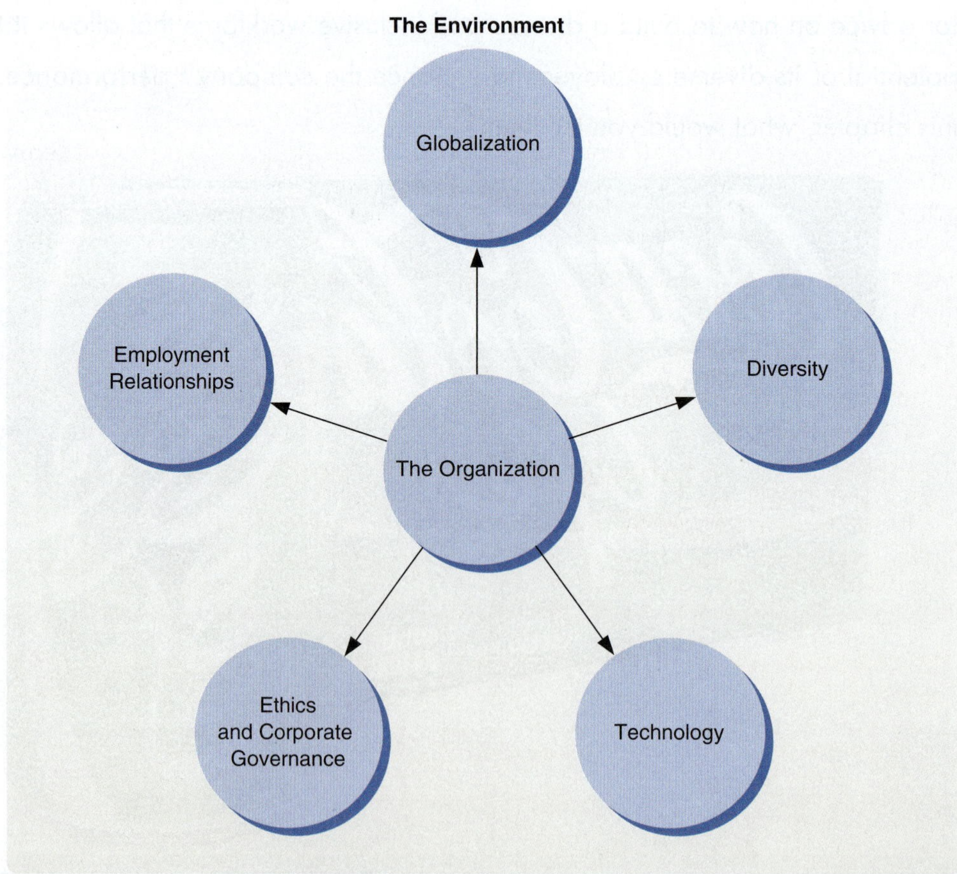

central environmental forces for change faced by today's organizations: diversity, globalization, technology, ethics and corporate governance, and new employment relationships. An understanding of these forces will then set the stage for our in-depth discussion of contemporary organizational behavior.

DIVERSITY AND BUSINESS

Diversity is a major part of the changing environment of business. ***Diversity*** refers to the variety of observable and unobservable similarities and differences among people. Some differences, such as gender, race, and age, are often the first diversity characteristics to come to mind. But diversity is much more than demographics and can reflect combinations of characteristics rather than a single attribute. Each individual also has a variety of characteristics, and combinations of them can result in diversity. We begin our discussion of diversity by examining some of the many types of diversity relevant to organizations.

diversity
The variety of observable and unobservable similarities and differences among people

TYPES OF DIVERSITY AND BARRIERS TO INCLUSION

Types of Diversity

Have you ever met someone, thought he or she was different from you, and then learned that the two of you actually had a lot in common? This reflects two types of diversity: surface-level diversity and deep-level diversity. ***Surface-level diversity*** refers to observable differences in people, including race, age, ethnicity, physical abilities, physical characteristics, and gender. Surface-level diversity reflects characteristics that are observable and known about people as soon as you see them.

surface-level diversity
Observable differences in people, including race, age, ethnicity, physical abilities, physical characteristics, and gender

Deep-level diversity refers to individual differences that cannot be seen directly, including goals, values, personalities, decision-making styles, knowledge, skills, abilities, and attitudes. These "invisible" characteristics in others take more time to learn about, but can have stronger effects on group and organizational performance than surface-level characteristics. Even pay differences[6] in a group and differences based on rank or power can affect group processes and performance.[7]

deep-level diversity
Individual differences that cannot be seen directly, including goals, values, personalities, decision-making styles, knowledge, skills, abilities, and attitudes

Two prominent diversity researchers, David Harrison and Katherine Klein, have identified

VGSTOCKSTUDIO/SHUTTERSTOCK.COM

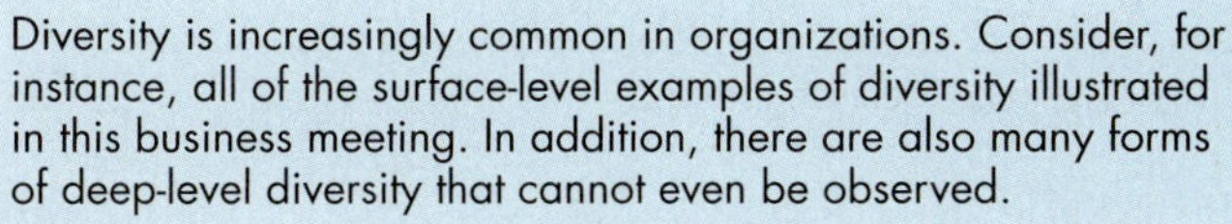

Diversity is increasingly common in organizations. Consider, for instance, all of the surface-level examples of diversity illustrated in this business meeting. In addition, there are also many forms of deep-level diversity that cannot even be observed.

The two people working in the top photo reflect several examples of surface-level diversity while the two individuals in the bottom photo would appear to be considerably less diverse. Of course, when we take into account deep-level diversity the two people in the top photo might be more similar than we think, and the two people in the bottom photo may be more different than we think.

RACORN/SHUTTERSTOCK.COM

POTSTOCK/SHUTTERSTOCK.COM

three other types of within-group diversity that reflect different types of deep-level diversity:[8] ***Separation diversity*** refers to differences in position or opinion among group members reflecting disagreement or opposition—dissimilarity in an attitude or value, for example, especially with regard to group goals or processes. ***Variety diversity*** exists when there are meaningful differences in a certain type or category, including group members' expertise, knowledge, or functional background. Finally, ***disparity diversity*** reflects differences in the concentration of valuable social assets or resources—dissimilarity in rank, pay, decision-making authority, or status, for instance.

To illustrate these three types of diversity, consider three six-member teams, each of which is responsible for generating a new product idea. Team Separation's diversity is in their attitudes toward the best approach to use. Half of the team prefers creative brainstorming while the other half prefers basing the product on objective, data-based customer analysis. Members of Team Variety vary in their functional areas of expertise. One is a marketing professional, one a materials specialist, and the others represent manufacturing, product safety, advertising, and law. Lastly, members of Team Disparity vary in their rank in the organization. One member of the team is a vice president, two are mid-level managers, and three are lower-level employees. The diversity in each team is obvious, yet you can imagine how the effects of the diversity will likely differ across each team. Table 2.1 summarizes these five types of diversity.

Table 2.1

Five Types of Diversity

1. *Surface-level diversity:* observable differences in people, including gender, race, age, ethnicity, and physical abilities
2. *Deep-level diversity:* individual differences that cannot be seen directly, including goals, values, personalities, decision-making styles, knowledge, and attitudes
3. *Separation:* differences in position or opinion among group members reflecting disagreement or opposition, especially with regard to group goals or processes—dissimilarity in an attitude or value, for example (a type of deep-level diversity)
4. *Variety:* differences in a certain type or category, including group members' expertise, knowledge, or functional background (a type of deep-level diversity)
5. *Disparity:* differences in the concentration of valuable social assets or resources—including dissimilarity in rank, pay, decision-making authority, or status (a type of deep-level diversity)

Trends in Diversity

As the great U.S. baseball manager Yogi Berra once observed, "It's tough to make predictions, especially about the future." Nonetheless, some short-term demographic trends are strong enough to suggest that the changing demographic mix in the workforce will continue to increase the importance of understanding and leveraging diversity. For example, the ethnic and cultural mix of the U.S. workforce is changing in fairly predictable ways. The Census Bureau projects that by 2020 the U.S. workforce will consist of 62.3 percent White non-Hispanics, 18.6 percent Hispanics, 12 percent Blacks, and 5.7 percent Asians. Longer-term U.S. demographic projections further highlight the increasingly diverse character of the United States:[9]

separation diversity
Differences in position or opinion among group members reflecting disagreement or opposition—dissimilarity in an attitude or value, for example, especially with regard to group goals or processes

variety diversity
Differences in a certain type or category, including group members' expertise, knowledge, or functional background

disparity diversity
Differences in the concentration of valuable social assets or resources—dissimilarity in rank, pay, decision-making authority, or status, for example

- The population is projected to become older. By 2030, about one in five people will be sixty-five or over (we discuss age diversity in our next section).
- By 2050, the total population is forecasted to grow from 282.1 million in 2000 to 419.9 million, a 49 percent increase. (This is in sharp contrast to most European countries, whose populations are expected to decline by 2050.)
- Non-Hispanic Whites are expected to decrease from the current 69.4 percent of the total population to 50.1 percent by 2050.
- People of Hispanic origin (of any race) are projected to increase from 35.6 million in 2002 to 102.6 million in 2050, an increase of 188 percent. This would nearly double the Hispanic share of the nation's population, from 12.6 percent to 24.4 percent.
- The Black population is projected to rise from 35.8 million in 2000 to 61.4 million in 2050, an increase of about 26 million or 71 percent. This would increase the Black share of the population to 14.6 percent from 12.7 percent.
- The Asian population is forecasted to grow 213 percent, from 10.7 million in 2000 to 33.4 million in 2050. This would double the Asian share of the population from 3.8 percent to 8 percent.

Non-Whites are expected to make up half of the working-age population in 2039 and more than 55 percent in 2050—up from 34 percent today. On the other hand, although the Bureau of Labor Statistics reported as early as 1996 that almost half of all management positions in the United States were held by White men, diversity remains elusive in the top jobs. In 2014, only 23 of the Fortune 500 CEOs were minorities, and White people held 87% of total seats on corporate boards of directors.[10]

Many countries and regions face talent shortages at all levels, and those gaps are expected to worsen. By 2040, Europe is forecast to have a shortfall of 24 million workers aged fifteen to sixty-five; raising the proportion of women in the workplace to that of men would cut the gap to 3 million. In the United States, the retirement of the baby boomer generation will probably mean the loss of large numbers of senior-level employees in a short period of time—nearly one-fifth of the working-age population (sixteen and older) of the United States will be at least sixty-five by 2016.[11]

Talent shortages are forecast to rise globally. In the United Kingdom, male-dominated sectors with a shortage of workers include engineering, IT, and skilled trades—yet 70 percent of women with science, engineering, or technology qualifications are not working in these fields.[12] Pursuing diversity can allow firms to attract and retain scarce talent as well as reach other business goals. One European Commission study showed that 58 percent of

As the U.S. workforce continues to age, generational differences in the workplace are becoming increasingly common. These differences, in turn, pose new challenges and opportunities for organizations and their managers.

companies with diversity programs reported higher productivity, improved employee motivation, and greater efficiency; and 62 percent said that the programs helped to attract and retain top talent.[13] Indeed, today's war for talent is global, making recruiting and retaining a diverse workforce a more competitive business issue than ever.

Generational Differences

As noted above, age-based diversity is a major issue facing many organizations today. Figure 2.2 provides a clear indicator of why this is true. Specifically, the U.S. Bureau of Labor Statistics projects a dramatic increase in workers age sixty-five and older during the next decade, while the percentage of younger workers is expected to decrease. This obviously increases the need for succession planning at many organizations to ensure the continuity of leadership. Due to the aging of the U.S. workforce, and to the clearly differentiated characteristics of

Figure 2.2

The labor force in the United States is getting older. For example, as shown here, between 2006 and 2016 the number of U.S. workers between the ages of 65 and 74 grew by 83.4 percent, and the percentage of workers 75 and older grew by 84.3 percent. In contrast, the number of workers between the ages of 25 and 54 grew only by 2.4 percent.

Projected Percentage Change in the U.S. Labor Force by Age from 2006 to 2016

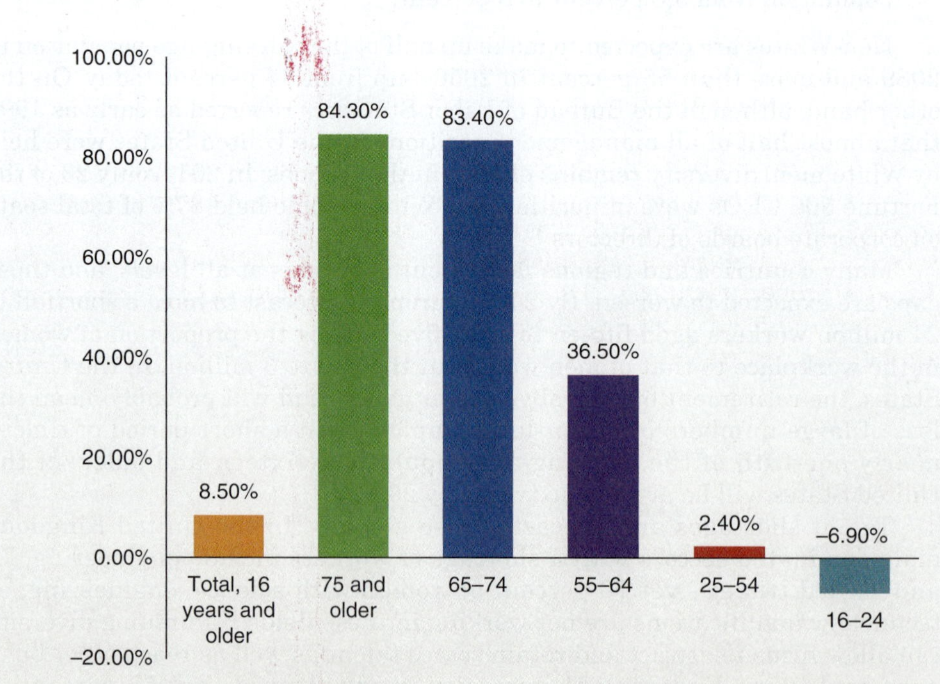

the generations that comprise it (discussed next), firms are also paying more attention to how workers of different ages work together.

For instance, work teams are often age diverse, and it is increasingly likely that an older employee will report to a younger supervisor. A survey conducted by the Society for Human Resource Management found that in organizations with 500 or more employees, 58 percent of HR professionals reported conflict between younger and older workers, largely due to their different perceptions of work ethics and work-life balance.[14] As Ed Reilly, President of the American Management Association, says, younger workers "are going to be the eventual managers. They will be as interested in keeping older workers as older workers today are interested in figuring out how to work with the younger generations."[15]

Most experts characterize today's workforce as comprising four generations. According to date of birth, they are: seniors (1922–1943); baby boomers (1943–1963); Generation X (1964–1980); and Generation Y, also referred to as the Millennial Generation (1980–2000). As each generation brings their unique experiences, values, and worldview, each also brings changes to workplace policies and procedures. For example, many seniors are staying in the workforce longer than previous generations, leading many firms to revamp their retirement policies and offer these experienced workers part-time jobs. Baby boomers' interest in wellness is changing the fitness programs and wellness benefits many employers provide. Many Generation Xers are concerned about maintaining balance in their lives, increasing many companies' interest in work-life balance programs. Generation Y members are technologically savvy, the most diverse of any generation, and are considered to be the biggest workplace influence since the baby boomers.

The U.S. workforce is aging at the same time Generation Y, the largest generation since the baby boomers, is entering the workforce. This increases the importance of understanding the role of age in organizations, and how to manage generational differences at work. Danielle Robinson, Director of Diversity, Talent, and Organizational Design for global premium drinks company Diageo, believes that Generation Y's entrance into the workplace "has added a layer of complexity to an already complex work environment."[16]

Age tends to be positively related to job performance,[17] although not all research has supported this relationship.[18] The influence of age in training environments has been extensively studied. Age was negatively associated with learning scores in an open learning program for managerial skills.[19] Older trainees demonstrated lower motivation, reduced learning, and less post-training confidence in comparison to younger trainees.[20] This suggests that age has a negative relationship with learning, and that part of its influence may be due to motivation. This could be because speed of processing slows as age increases.[21] Such speed is likely to be most important in jobs requiring high levels of intense, rapid processing of information (e.g., air-traffic controllers). It is important to note that this relationship does not hold for everyone—some older employees are likely to be good learners, and some younger employees are likely to perform poorly in training.

Increasing conscientiousness and knowledge counteract some of the negative effects of aging that result from reductions in information processing speed and motivation to learn.[22] It is likely that age is related to anxiety and other emotional variables, particularly in a complex or technologically oriented setting. Older trainees also may have concerns about their ability to rapidly process new complex information and as a result, suffer from a variation of the stereotype threat that ethnic minorities sometimes experience. Consistent with this view, older workers may not participate in learning and development activities as much as younger workers, in part due to a decline in confidence in their skills.[23] Beliefs in the adequacy of our skills influence decisions to exert and maintain effort, particularly in the face of challenges. Older adults may benefit from self-paced learning environments, which may allow additional time. Additionally, confidence-boosting interventions can help to address the negative effects of anxiety and reduced confidence.

Some organizations are using reverse mentoring to bridge generational differences and transfer the technology skills younger workers bring to the workplace to more senior employees. Reverse mentoring pairs a senior employee with a junior employee, but unlike the top-down focus of traditional mentoring, the focus is on transferring the skills of the junior employee to the senior employee.[24]

Reverse mentoring was made popular by former GE CEO Jack Welch, who realized that the web was going to transform business and knew that GE's younger, "webified" employees had better Internet skills and e-business knowledge than did GE's older and higher-ranking executives. He decided to pair an Internet savvy employee with one of GE's 600 worldwide executives to share their expertise about the new technology. In addition to building the e-business capabilities of his managers, this unique "mentoring up" program made managers at all levels more comfortable with each other, and transferred a lot of technology knowledge throughout GE.[25]

Diversity Issues for Managers

Why should we care about diversity? Because as employees, the better we are able to work with all types of people, the more effective we will be in our jobs. As managers, diversity awareness will enable us to hire, retain, and engage the best talent, which will help to maximize the organization's performance. Diversity also fosters greater creativity and innovation.[26] Indeed, a strong business case can be made for diversity.

The Business Case for Diversity

One reason that organizations should promote diversity is performance. Recent research has found that firm performance increases when employees have more positive attitudes toward diversity.[27] Diversity contributes to a firm's competitive advantage when it enables all employees to contribute their full talents and motivation to the company.

THE DIVERSITY INC TOP 20 LIST	
1. Novartis Pharmaceuticals Corporation	11. Wells Fargo
2. Kaiser Permanente	12. Deloitte
3. PricewaterhouseCoopers	13. Marriott International
4. EY	14. Abbott
5. Sodexo	15. Accenture
6. MasterCard	16. Merck & Co.
7. AT&T	17. Cox Communications
8. Prudential Financial	18. KPMG
9. Johnson & Johnson	19. General Mills
10. Procter & Gamble	20. ADP

Organizations should pursue diversity for many reasons. One very practical reason is that inclusion and diversity can often lead to improved business performance. Each of the firms on this list, for instance, has performed very well over the last several years.

ADAPTED FROM DIVERSITYINC TOP 50 LIST

The primary motivation for effectively managing diversity is the fact that doing so brings out the best in all employees, allowing each of them to contribute maximally to the firm's performance in an increasingly competitive business environment.

Some people even argue that diversity can be a source of competitive advantage for organizations.[28] For example, some studies have found that culturally diverse work teams make better decisions over time than do homogeneous teams.[29] Diverse groups can use their diverse backgrounds to develop a more comprehensive view of a problem and a broader list of possible solutions. The broader social network of diverse employees also can give workgroups and organizations access to a wider variety of information and expertise. Further, diversity can be a source of creativity and innovation that can create a competitive advantage.[30] A review of decades of research found that diversity can enhance creativity and improve a team's decision making.[31] Research by noted management expert Rosabeth Moss Kanter found that innovative companies intentionally use heterogeneous teams to solve problems and do a better job of eliminating racism, sexism, and classism.[32] Having more women in top management positively affects the performance of firms pursuing an innovation strategy.[33]

Diversity management is also important for legal reasons. Although many other antidiscrimination laws exist, one of the most important is Title VII of the Civil Rights Act of 1964, amended in 1991. It prohibits employment discrimination based on race, color, religion, sex, or national origin. Title VII prohibits not only intentional discrimination but also practices that have the effect of discriminating against individuals because of their race, color, national origin, religion, or sex. Other laws offer protections to additional groups, including employees with disabilities[34] and workers over the age of forty.[35]

The Civil Rights Act of 1991 allows monetary damages in cases of intentional employment discrimination. One of the largest employment discrimination lawsuits was settled for more than $11.7 million against Walmart and Sam's Club.[36] Thousands of female employees filed a class-action suit over alleged denial of advancement, equal pay, promotions, and raises based on the fact that they were women.[37] Obeying the law and promoting diversity is consistent with hiring the people best suited for the job and organization.

Barriers to Inclusion

Given both the performance benefits and legal imperatives of diversity, then, what prevents companies from becoming inclusive and making the most of their diversity? A report of the U.S. Equal Employment Opportunity Commission identified several common diversity barriers that exist in many organizations.[38] These barriers, summarized in Table 2.2, stem from a variety of decision-making and psychological factors as well as from employee unawareness. Understanding and proactively addressing the barriers can minimize their impact and enhance inclusion:

1. *The "Like Me" Bias:* Consciously or unconsciously, we tend to associate with others whom we perceive to be like ourselves. This bias is part of human nature. Although it can create a higher comfort level in working relationships, the "like me" bias can also lead to a tendency to employ and work with people like ourselves in terms of protected characteristics such as race, color, sex, disability, and age; and it can result in an unwillingness to employ people unlike ourselves. Perceived cultural and religious differences and ethnocentrism can feed on the "like me" bias and restrict inclusion. Because the "like me" bias can influence the assessment of

Table 2.2

Barriers to Inclusion

The "like me" bias	People prefer to associate with others they perceive to be like themselves.
Stereotypes	A belief about an individual or a group based on the idea that everyone in a particular group will behave the same way or have the same characteristics.
Prejudice	Outright bigotry or intolerance for other groups.
Perceived threat of loss	If some employees perceive a direct threat to their own career opportunities, they may feel that they need to protect their own prospects by impeding diversity efforts.
Ethnocentrism	The belief that one's own language, native country, and cultural rules and norms are superior to all others.
Unequal access to organizational networks	Women and minorities are often excluded from organizational networks, which can be important to job performance, mentoring opportunities, and being seen as a candidate for promotion.

performance norms, there may be a perception that someone "different" is less able to do a job and that someone "like me" is better able to do a job.

2. *Stereotypes:* A stereotype is a belief about an individual or a group based on the idea that everyone in that particular group will behave the same way. For example, "all men are strong," "all women are nurturing," and "people who look a certain way are dangerous" are all examples of stereotypes. A male research scientist who tends to believe that women make poor scientists is unlikely to hire, mentor, or seek the opinion of a female scientist. Stereotypes can reduce inclusion opportunities for minorities, women, persons with disabilities, and both younger and older workers. Stereotypes are harmful because they result in judgments about an individual based solely on his or her being part of a particular group, regardless of his or her unique identity. People may have stereotypes of other individuals based on their race, color, religion, national origin, sex, disability, or age, among other things. Stereotypes are often negative and erroneous, and thus adversely affect the targeted individuals.[39] Because stereotypes can breed subtle racism, sexism, prejudice, and discomfort, they must be addressed in the diversity context. Recruiters and hiring managers may have stereotypes of what makes good or poor employees that can adversely affect equal employment opportunities and undermine diversity efforts.
3. *Prejudice:* It is also possible that outright bigotry still occurs on the part of an employer or its management for or against a targeted group, despite Title VII now having been in existence for more than forty years.[40] Even if an organization has a strong commitment to inclusion, it is possible that the beliefs and actions of individual employees or managers are inconsistent with the organization's policies and values. Organizations can help to reduce the occurrence of prejudice by carefully selecting and training managers and employees, evaluating their inclusion behaviors, and tracking the promotion rates of members of different groups who work for different supervisors to identify possible discriminatory trends that warrant further attention.

4. *Perceived Threat of Loss:* As voluntary efforts are made by companies to promote inclusion, members of groups who traditionally have been the predominant employees of a particular workforce or occupation may grow anxious or angry. If they perceive a direct threat to their own career opportunities, they may feel that they need to protect their own prospects by impeding the prospects of others.[41] This can influence employees' willingness to help minority employees, recruit diverse candidates for a position, and support diversity initiatives.
5. *Ethnocentrism:* Ethnocentrism reflects the belief that one's own language, native country, and cultural rules and norms are superior to all others. Ethnocentrism often has less to do with prejudice and more to do with inexperience or ignorance about other people and environments. Because people know more about the cultural and behavioral norms of their home country, they have a better understanding of people from that country. Education and experiences that promote greater cross-cultural awareness can foster a conscious effort to value and promote cultural diversity.
6. *Unequal Access to Organizational Networks:* All organizations have formal and informal networks. These organizational networks influence knowledge sharing, resource accessibility, and work opportunities. Women and minorities are often excluded from informal organizational networks, which can be important to job performance, mentoring opportunities, and being seen as a candidate for promotion.[42] Research has associated male domination at the upper ranks of a firm with female executives' reports of barriers to advancement and exclusion from informal networks.[43]

Managing Diversity

In addition to awareness of the barriers to inclusion discussed above, there are also other proactive things managers can do to promote diversity. The most important element in effectively leveraging the positive potential of diversity is top management support for diversity and for diversity initiatives. If top managers do not promote inclusion and respect diversity, lower-level managers and employees are not likely to do so either. In addition, an inclusive environment is created when all employees' cultural awareness and empathy are enhanced through diversity training and all employees are given equal access to mentors and other influential company employees. Creating fair company policies and practices that give all employees equal access to performance feedback, training and development, and advancement opportunities is also critical.

Diversity is more likely to positively affect companies that support diverse employees in higher-level positions and help all employees effectively interact with people who are different from them. Diversity initiatives are more successful when the company is able to keep employees thinking about diversity issues, even when they do not feel a direct, negative impact.[44] This chapter's *Case Study* highlights what grocer Wegmans does to effectively manage diversity.

Training and mentoring can also help. *Reciprocal mentoring*, which matches senior employees with diverse junior employees to allow both individuals to learn more about a different group, is one technique used to promote diversity awareness and inclusion. Some organizations use career development programs, networking opportunities, and mentoring programs for all employees to promote diversity.[45] Diversity training and diversity education need to communicate that bias is a part of being human. It is not realistic to claim or to pursue an "I'm totally unbiased" stance with regard to diversity. Everyone has biases whether or not they are aware of them—diversity training should enable

LOSKUTNIKOV/SHUTTERSTOCK.COM

CASE STUDY Diversity At Wegmans

East coast grocer Wegmans views diversity as more than just a legal or moral obligation or business necessity—to them it is a business opportunity.[46] Diversity is part of Wegmans everyday culture and viewed as something that enables them to being the very best at serving the needs of all customers. The company strives to attract and retain a workforce that reflects different backgrounds, experiences, and viewpoints and mirrors the communities in which it operates.[47]

Wegmans believes that to be a great place to shop, they must first be a great place to work. Wegmans looks to hire people who love food and who have a natural propensity to serve and good skills working with the public. Wegmans emphasizes diversity in hiring to refresh stores with new ideas. The workforce includes people from a wide variety of backgrounds, from high school students to retired professionals. Corporate values including respect, caring, empowerment, and high standards have helped the company repeatedly appear on *Fortune's* list of the 100 Best Companies to Work For.[48]

Questions:

1. In what ways can diverse employees contribute to Wegmans' business performance?
2. What types of diversity do you think Wegmans should focus on? Why?
3. What are the downsides, if any, of building a diverse workforce?

PHANT/SHUTTERSTOCK.COM

employees to become aware of them and learn to control them to prevent both explicit and implicit displays of bias.

GLOBALIZATION AND BUSINESS

globalization
The internationalization of business activities and the shift toward an integrated global economy

Another, and some ways related, environmental factor that affects OB is ***globalization***. Of course, in many ways, globalization and international management are not new. Centuries ago, the Roman army was forced to develop a management system to deal with its widespread empire.[49] Moreover, many notable early explorers such as Christopher Columbus and Magellan were not actually seeking new territory but instead were looking for new trade routes to boost international trade. Likewise, the Olympic Games, the Red Cross, and other organizations have international roots. From a business standpoint, however, the widespread effects of globalization are relatively new, at least in the United States.

Trends in Globalization

In 2014, the volume of international trade in current dollars was about 50 times greater than the amount

BRENT LEWIN/BLOOMBERG/ GETTY IMAGES

Globalization is a major part of the changing environment of business. Fast food businesses like KFC and McDonald's, for example, have set up shop around the world. Their challenge is to maintain the identify and appeal that led them to become so recognizable while also adapting to customer tastes and workplace practices in different countries.

in 1960. Indeed, while international trade actually declined by 11 percent in 2009 due to the global recession, it increased by that same amount in 2010 as the economy began a slow rebound and has remained on an upward trajectory ever since. Four major factors account for much of the growth in international trade.

First, communication and transportation have improved dramatically over the past several decades. Telephone service has improved, communication networks span the globe and can interact via satellite, and once-remote areas have become routinely accessible. Telephone service in some developing countries is now almost entirely by cellular phone technology rather than land-based wired telephone service. Fax and email technologies allow managers to send documents around the world in seconds as opposed to the days it took just a few years ago. And new applications such as text messaging and digital conferencing have made global communication even easier. In short, it is simply easier to conduct international business today than was the case just a few years ago.

Second, businesses have expanded internationally to increase their markets. Companies in smaller countries, such as Nestlé in Switzerland and Heineken in the Netherlands, recognized long ago that their domestic markets were too small to sustain much growth and therefore moved into the international arena. Many U.S. firms, on the other hand, have only found it advantageous to enter foreign markets in the last half-century. Now, though, most midsize and even many small firms routinely buy and/or sell products and services in other countries.

Third, more and more firms are moving into international markets to control costs, especially to reduce labor costs. Pursuing the lowest possible labor costs has raised ethical questions, however, and strategies to cut costs in this way do not always work out as planned. This is in part because the process has sometimes drawn criticism due to media and consumer activist concern about the labor standards employed in other countries. Nonetheless, many firms are successfully using inexpensive labor in Asia and Mexico.[50] In searching for lower labor costs, some companies have discovered well-trained workers and built more efficient plants that are closer to international markets. India, for instance, has emerged as a major force in the high-tech sector. Turkey and Indonesia are also growing in importance. And many foreign automakers have built plants in the United States. Finally, many organizations have become international in response to competition. If an organization starts gaining strength in international markets, its competitors often must follow suit to avoid falling too far behind in sales and profitability. U.S. oil companies like Exxon Mobil Corporation and Chevron realized they had to increase their international market share to keep pace with foreign competitors such as BP and Royal Dutch Shell. Although labor cost control is often cited as a primary reason for offshoring, many organizations are increasingly offshoring innovation projects not for labor arbitrage but merely to access

One major reason that businesses move into international markets is to take advantage of lower labor costs. For instance, many firms moved production facilities to Mexico several years ago because of low labor costs. China then became a magnet for business with its own low labor costs. But as wages have started in climb there some businesses are looking at other manufacturing locations such as Vietnam.

the qualified talent missing at home or that they are having difficulty acquiring due to increased competition from other employers.

Cultural Competence

Italians often perceive people from the United States as people who are always working, talking about business over lunch and drinking their coffee while running in the street instead of enjoying those activities with others. Does this mean that Italians are lazy and Americans are hyperactive? No, it means that people from different cultures give different meanings to some activities. In Italy, where relationships are highly valued, lunch, dinner, and pauses for coffee have a social purpose—people get together to relax and to get to know each other better. In the United States, where time is money, business can be part of lunch, deals are discussed during dinner, and contracts are signed over coffee.[51]

One of the worst, yet easiest, mistakes people can make is to assume that other people are just like them. People from different cultures see and do things in different ways. ***Cultural competence*** is the ability to interact effectively with people of different cultures. A culturally competent person has a respectful awareness and understanding of cultural differences. There are four components of cultural competence:[52]

cultural competence
The ability to interact effectively with people of different cultures

1. *Awareness of our own cultural worldview, and of our reactions to people who are different*–A security guard who knows that she profiles teenagers as "troublemakers" is culturally aware of her reactions to this group.
2. *Our attitude toward cultural differences*–This reflects a willingness to honestly understand our beliefs and values about cultural differences.
3. *Knowledge of different worldviews and cultural practices*–Research has found that our values and beliefs about equality may be inconsistent with our behaviors. Many people whose answers on a test indicated they did not have prejudices did things in cross-cultural situations that reflected prejudice.[53]
4. *Cross-cultural skills*–This component addresses the importance of practicing cultural competence, including nonverbal communication, to become effective cross-culturally.

Although some people are naturally culturally competent, most of us have to put effort into developing this skill. This requires honestly examining our prejudices and biases, actively developing cross-cultural skills, learning from role models, and having a positive attitude about cultural issues. The key to cross-cultural success is awareness—being aware of how culture influences your interpretations of others, your own behavior, and how people from other cultures may see you. Understanding why we do things in certain ways, how we see the world, and why we react as we do is an important part of being culturally aware. Cultural awareness can improve performance in culturally diverse organizations, or when a firm's customers are diverse. This chapter's *Improve Your Skills* feature will help you understand some of the characteristics of your own culture that are likely to differ in other areas of the world.

Just for fun, take the *Cultural Etiquette Quiz* in this chapter's *Global Issues feature* and see how much you know about working and doing business in other cultures.

IMPROVE YOUR SKILLS

UNDERSTANDING YOUR CULTURE

As you have learned in this chapter, cultural competence requires an awareness of your own cultural practices and worldview. This worksheet will help you to analyse some of the features of your own societal culture. For each cultural feature, identify an example that represents most of the people in your primary culture. Then take a minute to reflect on how other cultures might differ, and how these differences might lead to misunderstanding.

Cultural Feature	Example of Feature Representing Your Primary Culture	How Feature Might Differ and Cause Misunderstanding in Other Cultures
1. Social greetings		
2. Attitudes toward privacy		
3. Appropriate decision-making speed		
4. Openness of communication		
5. Gestures that reflect that you understand what you have just been told		
6. Personal grooming		
7. Deference to authority figures		
8. Acceptable personal space		
9. Timeliness		
10. Work ethic		

Cross-Cultural Differences and Similarities

The primary concern of this book is human behavior in organizational settings, so we now turn our attention to differences and similarities in behavior across cultures. While there is relatively little research in this area, interesting findings have begun to emerge.[54]

General Observations

At one level, it is possible to make several general observations about similarities and differences across cultures. For one thing, cultural and national boundaries do not necessarily coincide. Some areas of Switzerland are very much like Italy, other parts like France, and still other parts like Germany. Similarly, within the United States there are large cultural differences across, say, Southern California, Texas, and the East Coast.[55]

Given this basic assumption, one major review of the literature on international management reached five basic conclusions.[56] First, behavior in organizational settings does indeed vary across cultures. Thus, employees in companies based in Japan, the United States, and Germany are likely to have different attitudes and patterns of behavior. The behavior patterns are also likely to be widespread and pervasive within an organization.

GLOBAL ISSUES

CULTURAL ETIQUETTE QUIZ

Successfully managing or conducting business across cultures involves knowing what to say, when to arrive for meetings, what to wear, what gifts are acceptable, and what greeting to give, among many other things. It takes a continued effort to recognize and appreciate the other party's expectations and business practices. This quiz will give you an idea of how aware you are of the business cultures of other areas of the world. Answers are at the bottom of the quiz.[57]

_____________ 1. Which culture often views professional titles as arrogant?

_____________ 2. Where should you not use red ink on your business card because the color red has a negative connotation?

_____________ 3. In this culture, it may be considered an insult to leave immediately following a meeting, as this may suggest that you are not interested in getting to know the other party.

_____________ 4. If you compliment someone in this country on one of their personal items, they may insist that you accept it as a gift.

_____________ 5. In this country, tapping your nose signals that something is to be kept secret or confidential.

_____________ 6. In this country, beckoning someone with your palm up while wagging one finger can be taken as an insult.

_____________ 7. In what country do people who have worked together for years still shake hands every morning as if they were meeting for the first time?

_____________ 8. In this country, negotiations usually take a long time and are chaotic, with numerous people often speaking simultaneously.

_____________ 9. The "thumbs up" gesture is offensive in this country.

_____________ 10. Be sensitive to the volume of your voice in this country. Loud voices are known to be offensive in meetings as well as in restaurants and on the street.

_____________ 11. Negotiations and meetings with people from this country often involve flared tempers, and tantrums and walkouts often occur. Standing with your hands in your pockets is also considered rude in this culture.

_____________ 12. Because saving face is so important in this culture, you will often hear "It's inconvenient" or "I'll look into it" instead of being told "No."

Answers: (1) Ireland; (2) Madagascar; (3) Colombia; (4) Bahrain; (5) England; (6) India (and China); (7) Germany; (8) Spain; (9) Saudi Arabia; (10) France; (11) Russia; (12) China

culture
The set of shared values, often taken for granted, that help people in a group, organization, or society understand which actions are considered acceptable and which are deemed unacceptable

Second, culture itself is one major cause of this variation. ***Culture*** is the set of shared values, often taken for granted, that help people in a group, organization, or society understand which actions are considered acceptable and which are deemed unacceptable. Thus, although the behavioral differences just noted may be caused in part by different standards of living, different geographical conditions, and so forth, culture itself is a major factor apart from other considerations.

Third, although the causes and consequences of behavior within organizational settings remain quite diverse across cultures, organizations and the ways they are structured appear to be growing increasingly similar.

Hence, managerial practices at a general level may be becoming more and more alike, but the people who work within organizations still differ markedly.

Fourth, the same individual behaves differently in different cultural settings. A manager may adopt one set of behaviors when working in one culture but change those behaviors when moved to a different culture. For example, Japanese executives who come to work in the United States may slowly begin to act more like U.S. managers and less like Japanese managers. This, in turn, may be source of concern for them when they are transferred back to Japan.

Finally, cultural diversity can be an important source of synergy in enhancing organizational effectiveness. More and more organizations are coming to appreciate the virtues of diversity, but they still know surprisingly little about how to manage it. Organizations that adopt a multinational strategy can—with effort—become more than a sum of their parts. Operations in each culture can benefit from operations in other cultures through an enhanced understanding of how the world works.[58]

Specific Cultural Issues

Geert Hofstede, a Dutch researcher, studied workers and managers in 60 countries and found that specific attitudes and behaviors differed significantly because of the values and beliefs that characterized those countries.[59] Table 2.3 shows how Hofstede's categories help us summarize differences for several countries.

individualism
Exists to the extent that people in a culture define themselves primarily as individuals rather than as part of one or more groups or organizations

The two primary dimensions that Hofstede found are the individualism/collectivism continuum and power distance. ***Individualism*** exists to the extent that people in a culture define themselves primarily as individuals rather than as part of one or more groups or organizations. At work, people from more individualistic cultures tend to be more concerned about

Table 2.3

Work-Related Differences in 10 Countries

Country	Individualism/ Collectivism	Power Distance	Uncertainty Avoidance	Masculinity	Long-Term Orientation
CANADA	H	M	M	M	L
GERMANY	M	M	M	M	M
ISRAEL	M	L	M	M	(no data)
ITALY	H	M	M	H	(no data)
JAPAN	M	M	H	H	H
MEXICO	H	H	H	M	(no data)
PAKISTAN	L	M	M	M	L
SWEDEN	H	M	L	L	M
UNITED STATES	H	M	M	M	L
VENEZUELA	L	H	M	H	(no data)

Note: H = high; M = moderate; L = low for INDIVIDUALISM/COLLECTIVISM. H means High Individualism, L means High Collectivism and M means a balance of individualism and collectivism. These are only 10 of the more than 60 countries that Hofstede and others have studied.

References: Adapted from Geert Hofstede and Michael Harris Bond, "The Confucius Connection: From Cultural Roots to Economic Growth," *Organizational Dynamics,* Spring 1988, pp. 5–21; Geert Hofstede, "Motivation, Leadership, and Organization: Do American Theories Apply Abroad?" *Organizational Dynamics,* Summer 1980, pp. 42–63.

collectivism
Characterized by tight social frameworks in which people tend to base their identities on the group or organization to which they belong

power distance (also orientation to authority)
The extent to which people accept as normal an unequal distribution of power

uncertainty avoidance (also preference for stability)
The extent to which people feel threatened by unknown situations and prefer to be in clear and unambiguous situations

masculinity (also assertiveness or materialism)
The extent to which the dominant values in a society emphasize aggressiveness and the acquisition of money and other possessions as opposed to concern for people, relationships among people, and overall quality of life

long-term values
Include focusing on the future, working on projects that have a distant payoff, persistence, and thrift

themselves as individuals than about their work group, individual tasks are more important than relationships, and hiring and promotion are usually based on skills and rules. ***Collectivism***, on the other hand, is characterized by tight social frameworks in which people tend to base their identities on the group or organization to which they belong. At work, this means that employee–employer links are more like family relationships, relationships are more important than individuals or tasks, and hiring and promotion are based on group membership. In the United States, a very individualistic culture, it is important to perform better than others and to stand out from the crowd. In Japan, a more collectivistic culture, an individual tries to fit in with the group, strives for harmony, and prefers stability.

Power distance, which might also be called ***orientation to authority***, is the extent to which people accept as normal an unequal distribution of power. In countries such as Mexico and Venezuela, for example, people prefer to be in a situation in which authority is clearly understood and lines of authority are never bypassed. On the other hand, in countries such as Israel and Denmark, authority is not as highly respected and employees are quite comfortable circumventing lines of authority to accomplish something. People in the United States tend to be mixed, accepting authority in some situations but not in others.

Hofstede also identified other dimensions of culture. ***Uncertainty avoidance***, which might also be called ***preference for stability***, is the extent to which people feel threatened by unknown situations and prefer to be in clear and unambiguous situations. People in Japan and Mexico prefer stability to uncertainty, whereas uncertainty is normal and accepted in Sweden, Hong Kong, and the United Kingdom. ***Masculinity***, which might be more accurately called ***assertiveness or materialism***, is the extent to which the dominant values in a society emphasize aggressiveness and the acquisition of money and other possessions as opposed to concern for people, relationships among people, and overall quality of life. People in the United States tend to be moderate on both the uncertainty avoidance and masculinity scales. Japan and Italy score high on the masculinity scale while Sweden scores low.

Hofstede's framework has recently been expanded to include long-term versus short-term orientation. ***Long-term values*** include focusing on the future, working on projects that have a distant payoff, persistence, and thrift. ***Short-term values*** are more oriented toward the past and the present and include respect for traditions and social obligations. Japan, Hong Kong, and China are highly long-term oriented. The Netherlands, the United States, and Germany are moderately long-term oriented. Pakistan and West Africa tend to be more short-term oriented.

Hofstede's research presents only one of several ways of categorizing differences across many different countries and cultures. His findings, however, are now widely accepted and have been used by many companies. They have also prompted

TOSHIFUMI KITAMURA/AFP/GETTY IMAGES

Collectivism tends to be a dominant cultural value in many Asian countries. As a result, workers such as these have a tight social framework and closely identify with their co-workers.

ongoing research by others. The GLOBE project, one major extension of Hofstede's work specifically related to leadership, is discussed in Chapter 12. The important issue to remember at this point is that people from diverse cultures value things differently from each other and that people need to take these differences into account as they work.

short-term values
More oriented toward the past and the present and include respect for traditions and social obligations

Global Perspective

A ***global perspective*** is distinguished by a willingness to be open to and learn from the alternative systems and meanings of other people and cultures, and a capacity to avoid assuming that people everywhere are the same.[60] A person with a global perspective scans the world from a broad view, always seeking unexpected trends and opportunities. People with global perspectives are more likely to see a broad context and accept life as a balance of conflicting forces. They are not threatened by surprises or uncertainties, and value diversity.[61] They are also able to navigate through unfamiliar cultures with an open and external focus.[62] Given globalization trends and the multicultural nature of the U.S. workforce, managers increasingly need a global perspective and a supportive set of skills and knowledge to be most effective.[63] To meet this need, business schools are increasing their efforts to develop students' global managerial skills.[64] This chapter's *Understand Yourself* feature gives you the opportunity to assess your own global perspective and better understand how to enhance it.

global perspective
A willingness to be open to and learn from the alternative systems and meanings of other people and cultures, and a capacity to avoid assuming that people from everywhere are the same

TECHNOLOGY AND BUSINESS

Technology also represents a major environmental issue that affects businesses today. ***Technology*** refers to the methods used to create products, including both physical goods and intangible services. Technological change has become a major driver for other forms of organization change. Moreover, it also has widespread effects on the behaviors of people inside an organization. Three specific areas of technology worth noting here are: (1) the shift toward a service-based economy, (2) the growing use of technology for competitive advantage, and (3) mushrooming change in information technology.[65]

technology
Refers to the methods used to create products, including both physical goods and intangible services

Manufacturing and Service Technologies

Manufacturing is a form of business that combines and transforms resources into tangible outcomes that are then sold to others. The Goodyear Tire and Rubber Company is a manufacturer because it combines rubber and chemical compounds and uses blending equipment and molding machines to create tires. Broyhill is a manufacturer because it buys wood and metal components, pads, and fabric and then combines them into furniture. And Apple is a manufacturer because it uses electronic, metal, plastic, and composite components to build smartphones, computers, and other digital products.

manufacturing
A form of business that combines and transforms resources into tangible outcomes that are then sold to others

Manufacturing was once the dominant technology in the United States. During the 1970s, manufacturing entered a long period of decline, primarily because of foreign competition. U.S. firms had grown lax and sluggish, and new foreign competitors came onto the scene with better equipment and much

UNDERSTAND YOURSELF

GLOBAL PERSPECTIVE

This self-assessment gives you the opportunity to better understand your global perspective. Place your response on the line to the left of each statement using the scale below, and then follow the scoring instructions and read the interpretation at the end.

strongly disagree	disagree	slightly disagree	neutral	slightly agree	agree	strongly agree
1	2	3	4	5	6	7

Conceptualization

___ 1. I think it is necessary today to develop strategic alliances with organizations around the globe.
___ 2. Projects that involve international dealings are long-term.
___ 3. I believe that in the next ten years the world will be the same as it is today.
___ 4. In this interlinked world of ours, national boundaries are meaningless.
___ 5. We really live in a global village.
___ 6. In discussions, I always drive for a bigger, broader picture.
___ 7. I believe life is a balance of contradictory forces that are to be appreciated, pondered, and managed.
___ 8. I find it easy to rethink boundaries and to change direction and behavior.
___ 9. I feel comfortable with change, surprise, and ambiguity.
___ 10. I believe I can live a fulfilling life in another culture.

Contextualization

___ 11. I enjoy trying food from other countries.
___ 12. I enjoy working on world community projects.
___ 13. I mostly care about the local news.
___ 14. I am at my best when I travel to worlds that I do not understand.
___ 15. I get very curious when I meet somebody from another country.
___ 16. I enjoy reading foreign books or watching foreign movies.
___ 17. I have a lot of empathy for people who struggle to speak my own language.
___ 18. When something unexpected happens, it is easier to change the process than the structure.
___ 19. In trying to accomplish my objectives, I find that diversity and multicultural teams play a valuable role.
___ 20. I have close friends from other cultural backgrounds.

Scoring: The sum of your scores for statements 1 to 10 is your Conceptualization score: _____. Plot your score on the following continuum:

10 20 30 40 50 60 70

The sum of your scores for statements 11 to 20 is your Contextualization score: _____. Plot your score on the following continuum:

10 20 30 40 50 60 70

Interpretation: The higher your Conceptualization score, the better you are able to think globally. The higher your Contextualization score, the better you are able to act locally and adapt to the local environment. Global perspective is characterized by high levels of both conceptualization and contextualization. Training in international management, living in a foreign country, and working in a foreign country are all related to having higher global perspective.[66] Although both thinking globally and acting locally are important to managers, most managers are more adept at thinking globally than at acting locally because of the uniqueness of local cultures.

If you are interested in enhancing your global perspective, reflect on the statements above that you rated lower than others and identify ways of improving in those areas. Joining international organizations and seeking out multicultural experiences can enhance your global perspective.

Source: Adapted from *Arora, A.*, Jaju, A., Kefalas, A.G., & Perenich, T. (2004). An Exploratory Analysis of Global Managerial Mindsets: A Case of U.S. Textile and Apparel Industry. *Journal of International Management, 10,* 393–411.

SEAN PAVONE/SHUTTERSTOCK.COM

Service organizations create time or place utility for customers. Restaurants and snack bars, for example, provide convenient dining options for people too busy to cook at home or who just want to eat out.

higher levels of efficiency. For example, steel companies in the Far East were able to produce high-quality steel for much lower prices than large U.S. steel companies like such as Bethlehem Steel and U.S. Steel. Faced with a battle for survival, some companies disappeared, but many others underwent a long and difficult period of change by eliminating waste and transforming themselves into leaner and more efficient and responsive entities. They reduced their workforces dramatically, closed antiquated or unnecessary plants, and modernized their remaining plants. Over the last decade or so, their efforts have started to pay dividends as U.S. manufacturing has regained a competitive position in many different industries. While low wages continue to center a great deal of global manufacturing in Asia, some manufacturers are now thriving in the United States.

During the decline of the manufacturing sector, a tremendous growth in the service sector kept the overall U.S. economy from declining at the same rate. A ***service organization*** is one that transforms resources into an intangible output and creates time or place utility for its customers. For example, Merrill Lynch makes stock transactions for its customers, Uber provides real-time transportation for passengers, and your local hairdresser cuts your hair. In 1947, the service sector was responsible for less than half of the U.S. gross national product (GNP). By 1975, however, this figure reached 65 percent, and by 2006 had surpassed 75 percent. The service sector has been responsible for almost 90 percent of all new jobs created in the United States since 1990. Moreover, employment in service occupations is expected to grow 20.9 percent between 2012 and 2022.[67]

service organization
One that transforms resources into an intangible output and creates time or place utility for its customers

Managers have come to see that many of the tools, techniques, and methods that are used in a factory are also useful to a service firm. For example, managers of automobile plants and hair salons each have to decide how to design their facility, identify the best location for it, determine optimal capacity, make decisions about inventory storage, set procedures for purchasing raw materials, and set standards for productivity and quality. At the same time, though, service-based firms must hire and train employees based on a different skill set than is required by most manufacturers. For instance, consumers seldom come into contact with the Toyota employee who installs the seats in their car, so that person can be hired based on technical skills. But Avis must recruit people who not only have the technical skills for managing car rentals but who can also effectively interface with a variety of consumers.

Technology and Competition

Technology is the basis of competition for some firms, especially those whose goals include being the technology leaders in their industries. A company, for example, might focus its efforts on being the lowest-cost producer or on always having the most technologically advanced products on the market. But because of the rapid pace of new developments, keeping a leadership position based on technology is becoming increasingly challenging. Another challenge is meeting constant demands to decrease cycle time (the time that it takes a firm to accomplish some recurring activity or function from beginning to end).

Businesses have increasingly found that they can be more competitive if they can systematically decrease cycle times. Many companies, therefore, now focus on decreasing cycle times in areas ranging from developing products to making deliveries and collecting credit payments. Twenty years ago, it took a carmaker about five years from the decision to launch a new product until it was available in dealer showrooms. Now most companies can complete the cycle in less than two years. The speedier process allows them to more quickly respond to changing economic conditions, consumer preferences, and new competitor products while recouping their product-development costs faster. Some firms compete directly on how quickly they can get things done for consumers. In the early days of personal computers, for instance, getting a made-to-order system took six to eight weeks. Today, firms such as Dell can usually ship exactly what the customer wants in a matter of days.

Information Technology

Most people are very familiar with the swift advances in information technology. Cellular telephones and electronic datebooks have been replaced by smart phones, while use of e-books and digital cameras has been enhanced by the invention of tablets. These devices, and the technologically based social networking sites like Facebook and Twitter, are just a few of the many recent innovations that have changed how people live and work.[68] Breakthroughs in information technology have resulted in leaner organizations, more flexible operations, increased collaboration among employees, more flexible work sites, and improved management processes and systems. On the other hand, they have also resulted in less personal communication, less "down time" for managers and employees, and an increased sense of urgency vis-à-vis decision making and communication—changes that have not necessarily always been beneficial. We discuss information technology and its relationship to OB more fully in Chapter 9.

ETHICS AND CORPORATE GOVERNANCE

ethics
A person's beliefs regarding what is right or wrong in a given situation

Ethics and related issues have also engendered renewed interest in recent years. While ethics have long been of relevance to businesses, what seems like an epidemic of ethical breaches in recent years has placed ethics in the mainstream of managerial thought today. One special aspect of business ethics, corporate governance, has also taken on increased importance. Ethics also increasingly relate to information technology. Before discussing these issues, however, it is useful to understand how best to frame ethical relationships in organizations.

Framing Ethical Issues

Figure 2.3 illustrates how many ethical situations can be framed. Specifically, most ethical dilemmas faced by managers relate to how the organization treats its employees, how employees treat the organization, and how employees and organizations treat other economic agents.

How an Organization Treats Its Employees

One important area of managerial ethics is the treatment of employees by the organization. This area includes policies such as hiring and firing, wages and working conditions, and employee privacy and respect. For example, both ethical and legal guidelines suggest that hiring and firing decisions should be based solely on an individual's ability to perform the job. A manager who discriminates against African Americans in hiring is exhibiting both unethical and illegal behavior. But consider the case of a manager who does not discriminate in general but who hires a family friend when other applicants might be just as—or perhaps more—qualified. Although these hiring decisions may not be illegal, they may be objectionable on ethical grounds.

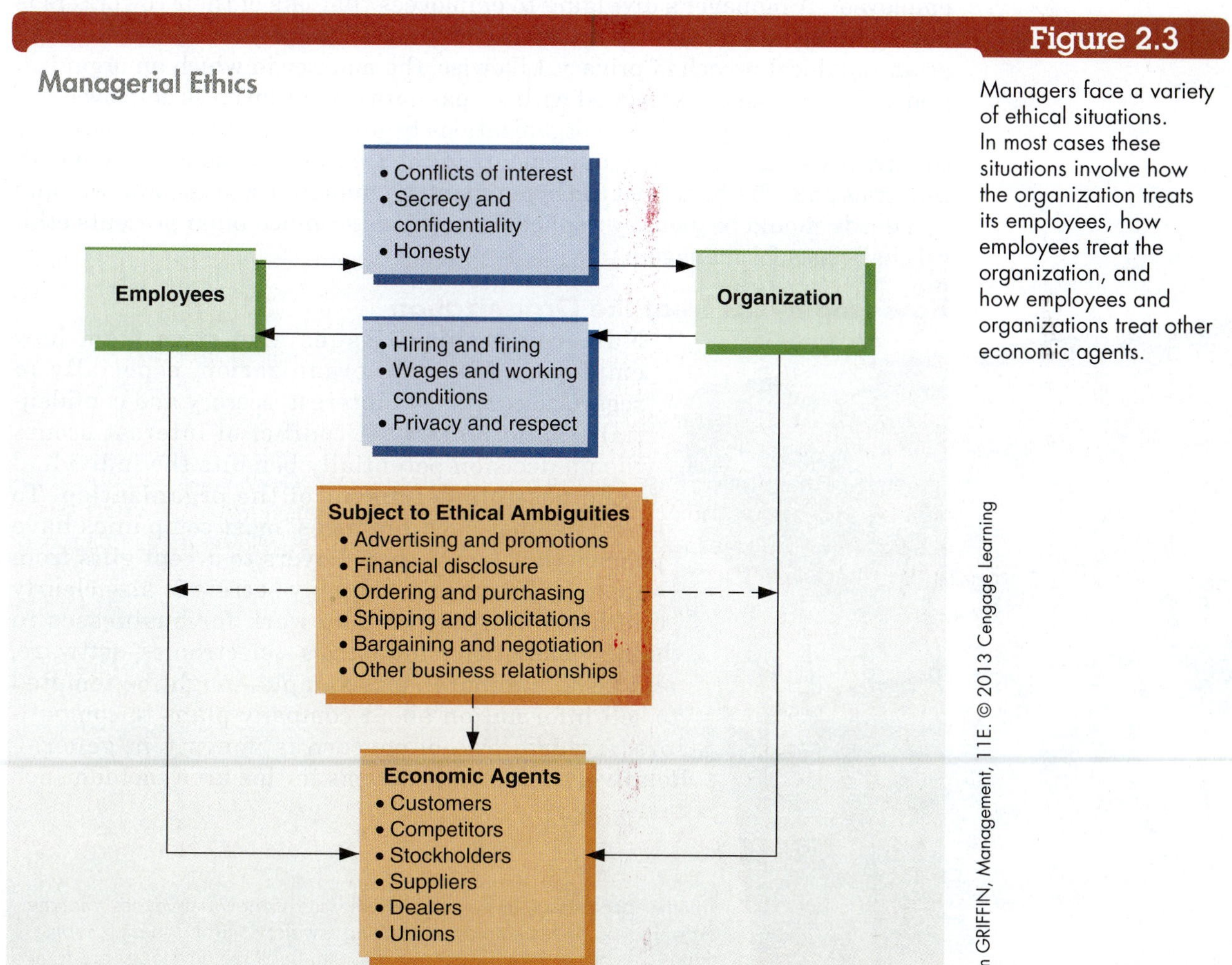

Figure 2.3

Managers face a variety of ethical situations. In most cases these situations involve how the organization treats its employees, how employees treat the organization, and how employees and organizations treat other economic agents.

STEVE BYLAND/SHUTTERSTOCK.COM

One important perspective in framing ethical issues is how the organization treats its employees. Take this closed business, for example. If its employees showed up for work one day and found this sign on the door, more people would agree that the business owners did not treat their employees ethically or responsibly by not giving them more advance notice of the impending closure.

Wages and working conditions, although tightly regulated, are also areas for potential controversy. For example, a manager paying an employee less than he deserves, simply because the manager knows the employee cannot afford to quit or risk losing his job by complaining, might be considered unethical. The same goes for employee benefits, especially if an organization takes action that affects the compensation packages—and welfare—of an entire workforce or segment of it. Finally, most observers would also agree that an organization is obligated to protect the privacy of its employees. A manager's divulging to employees that one of their coworkers is having financial problems or an affair with another employee is generally seen as an unethical breach of privacy. Likewise, the manner in which an organization addresses issues associated with sexual harassment involves employee privacy and related rights. When organizations begin to conduct business in other countries, the lack of clear requirements in the treatment of employees in both countries and whether or not the home country's human resources practices and standards should be globally applied or locally determined often presents ethical challenges for managers.

How Employees Treat the Organization

Numerous ethical issues also stem from how employees treat the organization, especially in regard to conflicts of interest, secrecy and confidentiality, and honesty. A conflict of interest occurs when a decision potentially benefits the individual to the possible detriment of the organization. To guard against such practices, most companies have policies that forbid their buyers to accept gifts from suppliers. Divulging company secrets is also clearly unethical. Employees who work for businesses in highly competitive industries—electronics, software, and fashion apparel, for example—might be tempted to sell information about company plans to competitors. A third area of concern is honesty in general. Relatively common problems in this area include such

BLEND IMAGES/SHUTTERSTOCK.COM

Another perspective in framing ethical issues is how employees treat the organization. If this employee is taking envelopes for business reasons that is, of course, ethical and appropriate. But if the envelopes are for personal use then most people would see this as unethical.

activities as using a business telephone to make personal calls, stealing supplies, and padding expense accounts.

In recent years, new issues regarding such behaviors as personal Internet use at work have also become more pervasive. Another disturbing trend is that more workers are calling in sick simply to get extra time off. One survey, for instance, found that the number of workers who reported taking more time off for personal needs was increasing substantially. A more recent CareerBuilder survey found that 29 percent of workers surveyed admitted to having called in sick when they were actually well.[69] Yet another survey found that two-thirds of U.S. workers who call in sick do so for reasons other than illness. Although most employees are basically honest, organizations must nevertheless be vigilant to avoid problems resulting from such behaviors.

How Employees and the Organization Treat Other Economic Agents

Managerial ethics also come into play in the relationship between the firm and its employees with other economic agents. As shown above in Figure 2.3, the primary agents of interest include customers, competitors, stockholders, suppliers, dealers, and unions. The interactions between the organization and these agents that may be subject to ethical ambiguity include advertising and promotions, financial disclosures, ordering and purchasing, shipping and solicitations, bargaining and negotiation, and other business relationships.

For example, state pharmacy boards are charged with overseeing prescription drug safety in the United States. All told, there are almost 300 pharmacists who serve on such boards. It was recently reported that 72 of these pharmacists were employees of major drugstore chains and supermarket pharmacies. These arrangements, while legal, could create the potential for conflicts of interest, because they might give the pharmacist's employers influence over the regulatory system designed to monitor their own business practices.[70]

Another area of concern in recent years involves financial reporting by some e-commerce firms. Because of the complexities inherent in valuing the assets and revenues of these firms, some of them have been very aggressive in presenting their financial positions in highly positive lights. In at least a few cases, some firms have substantially overstated their earnings projections to entice more investment. After Time-Warner merged with AOL, it discovered that its new online partner had overstated its value through various inappropriate accounting methods. Some of today's accounting scandals in traditional firms have stemmed from similarly questionable practices.[71] For instance, Diamond Foods, maker of Emerald snack nuts and Pop Secret popcorn, recently had to restate its earnings after an audit uncovered several accounting irregularities.[72]

Hilton Hotels hired two senior executives away from rival Starwood Hotels. It was later determined that the executives took eight boxes of electronic and paper documents with them; much of the material in the boxes related to plans and details for starting a new luxury-hotel brand. When Hilton announced plans to start such a chain itself, to be called Denizen Hotels, officials at Starwood became suspicious and investigated. When they learned about the theft of confidential materials, which Hilton subsequently returned, Starwood filed a lawsuit against Hilton.[73]

Additional complexities faced by many firms today include the variations in ethical business practices in different countries. In some countries, bribes and side payments are a normal and customary part of doing business. However, U.S. laws forbid these practices, even if a firm's rivals from other countries are paying them. For example, a U.S. power-generating company once lost a $320 million contract in the Middle East because government officials demanded a $3 million bribe. A Japanese firm paid the bribe and won the contract. Another major American company once had a big project in India cancelled because newly elected officials demanded bribes. And Walmart has been charged with paying $24 million in bribes to Mexican officials to sidestep local regulations and obtain expedited building permits for new stores.[74] Although such payments are illegal under U.S. law, other situations are more ambiguous. In China, for example, local journalists expect their cab fare to be paid if they are covering a business-sponsored news conference. In Indonesia, the normal time for a foreigner to get a driver's license is over a year, but it can be "expedited" for an extra $100. In Romania, building inspectors routinely expect a "tip" for a favorable review.[75] And the government of Bahrain charged Alcoa with involvement in a 15-year conspiracy involving overcharging, fraud, and bribery.[76] Alcoa, for instance, billed Bahraini clients for "overhead," a normal and understood charge in some countries but not in parts of the Middle East. Similarly, gifts provided to some local officials by Alcoa were seen by other officials as bribes.

Ethical Issues in Corporate Governance

corporate governance
Refers to the oversight of a public corporation by its board of directors

A related area of emerging concern relates to ethical issues in ***corporate governance***—the oversight of a public corporation by its board of directors. The board of a public corporation is expected to ensure that the business is being properly managed and that the decisions made by its senior management are in the best interests of shareholders and other stakeholders. But in far too many cases the recent ethical scandals alluded to previously have actually started with a breakdown in the corporate governance structure. For instance, in a now-classic ethical scandal involving governance issues, WorldCom's board approved a personal loan to the firm's CEO, Bernard Ebbers, for $366 million even though there was little evidence that he could repay it. Likewise, Tyco's board approved a $20 million bonus for one of its own members for helping with the acquisition of a firm owned by that individual (this bonus was in addition to the purchase price!).

Boards of directors are also increasingly being criticized even when they are not directly implicated in wrongdoing. The biggest complaint here often relates to board independence. Disney, for instance, has faced this problem in the past. Several key members of the firm's board of directors were from companies that do business with Disney, and others were long-time friends of senior Disney executives. While board members need to have some familiarity with both the firm and its industry in order to function effectively, they also need to have sufficient independence to carry out their oversight function.[77]

Ethical Issues and Information Technology

Another set of issues that have emerged in recent times involves information technology. Among the specific questions in this area are individual rights to privacy and the potential abuse of information technology by companies. Indeed, online privacy has become a hot issue as companies sort out the related ethical and management issues. DoubleClick, an online advertising network, is one of the firms at the center of the privacy debate. The company has collected data on the habits of millions of web surfers, recording which sites they visit and which ads they click on. DoubleClick insists that the profiles are anonymous and are used to better match surfers with appropriate ads. However, after the company announced a plan to add names and addresses to its database, it was forced to back down because of public concerns over invasion of online privacy.

DoubleClick isn't the only firm gathering personal data about people's Internet activities. People who register at Yahoo! are asked to list date of birth, among other details. Amazon, eBay, and other sites also ask for personal information. And GPS and other tracking technologies allow firms to potentially know where their subscribers are physically located at any point in time. Disney now uses wrist bands for guests entering its theme parks. These bands are efficient for visitors, as they are used for park admissions, purchases, access to their hotel rooms, bypassing long wait lines for rides, and so forth. At the same time, though, the bands allow Disney to track visitor locations and use facial recognition software to connect photographs with visitors. As awareness of these capabilities increases, surveys show that people are troubled by the amount of information being collected, who gets to see it, and other issues associated with privacy.

One way management can address these concerns is by posting a privacy policy on its website. The policy should explain exactly what data the company collects and who gets to see the data. It should also allow people a choice about having their information shared with others and indicate how people can opt out of data collection. Disney, IBM, and other companies support this position by refusing to advertise on websites that have no posted privacy policies.

In addition, companies can offer web surfers the opportunity to review and correct information that has been collected, especially medical and financial data. In the offline world, consumers are legally allowed to inspect credit and medical records. In the online world, this kind of access can be costly and cumbersome, because data are often spread across several computer systems. Despite the technical difficulties, government agencies are already working on Internet privacy guidelines; this means, in turn, that companies will also need internal guidelines, training, and leadership to ensure compliance.

Social Responsibility

A related business challenge relevant to OB is adopting a broader stakeholder perspective and looking beyond shareholder value or the short-term stock price. In general, this view is called social responsibility.[78] Definitions of corporate ***social responsibility*** often include businesses living and working together for the common good and valuing human dignity. An important part of this is how employers treat their employees. When the social responsibility issues involve the creation of a "green" strategy intended to protect the natural environment it is often called corporate sustainability. Organizations are increasingly interested in balancing their financial performance with their employees' quality of life, and improving the local community and broader society. One expert defined corporate social responsibility this way: "Regardless of how many people with whom you come in contact, every one of them should be better off for having known you and your company."[79]

social responsibility
Businesses living and working together for the common good and valuing human dignity

Corporate social responsibility has become increasingly important in recent years. Some firms actively engage in social responsibility by promoting fitness activities such as fun runs, bicycle races, and so forth.

Is it really the responsibility of businesses to be good citizens? Doing so can help a firm attract the best talent, and customers are increasingly favoring companies that do the right thing. Ethical behavior and socially responsible business practices have been extensively discussed and have been accepted as significant aspects of management practice. Although most agree with their importance in principle, some people still believe that managers should focus solely on stockholders' interests. Others argue that because business is an influential element of society, it has an obligation to solve problems of public concern, that it is in the enlightened self-interest of organizations to be socially responsible. In other words, social responsibility supporters believe that ethical behavior is more profitable and more rational than unethical behavior, and crucial for the effectiveness of business organizations.

To have lasting effects, social responsibility efforts should be integrated into the culture of the organization.[80] Corporate social responsibility has the biggest impact when it is integrated with business priorities, relevant to achieving business objectives, inclusive of both internal and external stakeholder needs, and consistent with the firm's cultural values and brand identity.[81] Serving stockholders as well as the larger population of stakeholders, which includes workers, customers, the community, and even the planet, are not mutually exclusive.

Corporate sustainability initiatives can be top-down, with someone in a position of authority dictating to managers and employees what to do. Corporate sustainability efforts can also be grassroots, with employees identifying projects and taking the initiative to organize their own activities. Indeed, employee participation in social responsibility initiatives not only can motivate employees, but also can generate some good ideas. When a major printing company set a goal to reduce its waste by 20 percent over five years, its executive team naturally focused on finding ways to streamline its printing operations to reduce paper waste. After a series of brainstorms, a receptionist pointed out that the number of individual lunches delivered to the office every day created a significant amount of food packaging waste. By investing in a small café and encouraging employees to eat a buffet-style lunch, the printer reduced twice as much waste as it did by streamlining its printing operations.[82] Google calculates that it takes over 2,000 cars off the road every day through its free electric car charging stations, its electric car-sharing program for employees, and its employee shuttle.[83] Nearly 50 percent of Walmart employees signed up for the company's personal sustainability project, which encourages employees to live more sustainable lives by educating them on ways to conserve resources and reduce energy consumption at home.[84]

The International Organization for Standardization (ISO) has created a variety of standards that help organizations gain international acceptance of their practices and outcomes.[85] In addition to environmentally related standards such as sustainability and carbon emissions, the ISO publishes management standards including those for leadership, customer focus, involvement of people, and continual improvement. These standards can help managers meet their environmental and social responsibility objectives.

NEW EMPLOYMENT RELATIONSHIPS

A final significant area of environmental change that is particularly relevant for businesses today involves what we call new employment relationships. While we discuss employment relationships from numerous perspectives in Part 2 of this book, two particularly important areas today involve the management of knowledge workers and the outsourcing of jobs to other businesses, especially when those businesses are in other countries. Managing temporary and contingency workers and tiered workforces is also becoming increasingly complex. The nature of psychological contracts is also changing.

The Management of Knowledge Workers

Traditionally, employees added value to organizations because of what they did or because of their experience. However, during today's "information age," many employees add value simply because of what they know.[86] These employees are often referred to as ***knowledge workers***. How well these employees are managed is seen as a major factor in determining which firms will be successful in the future.[87] Knowledge workers include computer scientists, physical scientists, engineers, product designers, and video game developers. They tend to work in high-technology firms and are usually experts in some abstract knowledge base. They often believe they have the right to work in an autonomous fashion, and they identify more strongly with their profession than with any organization—even to the extent of defining performance primarily in terms recognized by other members of their profession.[88]

knowledge workers
Those employees who add value in an organization simply because of what they know

As the importance of information-driven jobs grows, the need for knowledge workers will grow as well. However, these employees require extensive and highly specialized training, and not everyone is willing to make the human capital investments necessary to move into these jobs. In fact, even after knowledge workers are on the job, retraining and training updates are critical so that their skills do not become obsolete. It has been suggested, for example, that the "half-life" for a technical education in engineering is about three years. Further, the failure to update the required skills will not only result in the organization's losing competitive advantage but will also increase the likelihood that the knowledge worker will go to another firm that is more committed to updating those skills.[89]

Compensation and related policies for knowledge workers must also be specially tailored. For example, in many high-tech organizations, engineers and scientists have the option of entering a technical career path that parallels a management career path. This allows the knowledge worker to continue to carry out specialized work without taking on large management

DAVID PEARSON/ALAMY

Outsourcing and offshoring have become increasingly commonplace–and often controversial. These call-center workers in India, for example, are providing support services for a U.S. company. But some critics charge that such practices reduce jobs in the United States.

responsibilities, while at the same time offering that worker compensation that is equivalent to that available to management. In other high-tech firms, the emphasis is on pay for performance, with profit sharing based on projects or products developed by the knowledge workers. In addition, in most firms employing these workers there has been a tendency to reduce the number of levels of the organization to allow the knowledge workers to react more quickly to the external environment by reducing the need for bureaucratic approvals.[90]

Outsourcing and Offshoring

outsourcing
The practice of hiring other firms to do work previously performed by the organization itself; when this work is moved overseas, it is often called offshoring

Outsourcing is the practice of hiring other firms to do work previously performed by the organization itself. It is an increasingly popular strategy because it helps firms focus on their core activities and avoid getting sidetracked by secondary activities. The snack bar at a large commercial bank may be important to employees and some customers, but running it is not the bank's main line of business and expertise. Bankers need to focus on money management and financial services, not food-service operations. That's why most banks outsource snack bar operations to food-service management companies whose main line of business includes cafeterias. The result, ideally, is more attention to banking by bankers, better food service for snack bar customers, and formation of a new supplier–client relationship (food-service company/bank). Firms today often outsource numerous activities, including payroll, employee training, facility maintenance, and research and development.

Up to a point, at least, outsourcing makes good business sense in areas that are highly unrelated to a firm's core business activities. However, what has attracted considerably more attention in recent years is the growing trend toward outsourcing abroad in order to lower labor costs; this practice is often called ***offshoring***. One recent estimate suggests that 3.3 million white-collar jobs performed in the United States in 2005 have been moved abroad; this same study suggests that 1 out of 10 IT jobs once held by U.S. workers are now handled by non-U.S. workers.[91]

offshoring
Outsourcing to workers in another country

Many software firms, for example, have found that there is an abundance of talented programmers in India who are willing to work for much lower salaries than their American counterparts. Likewise, many firms that operate large call centers find that they can handle those operations for much lower costs from other parts of the world. As a result, domestic jobs are lost. Some firms have attracted additional criticism when they require their domestic workers—soon to be out of jobs—to train their newly hired foreign replacements! Clearly, there are numerous behavioral and motivational issues involved in practices such as these.

Temp and Contingency Workers

Another trend that has impacted employment relationships in business involves the use of contingent or temporary workers. Indeed, recent years have seen an explosion in the use of such workers by organizations. A ***contingent worker*** is a person who works for an organization on something other than a permanent or full-time basis. Categories of contingent workers include independent contractors, on-call workers, temporary employees (usually hired through outside agencies), and contract and leased employees. Another category is part-time workers. The financial services giant Citigroup, for example, makes extensive use of part-time sales agents to pursue new clients. About 10 percent of the U.S. workforce currently has one of these alternative forms of employment relationships. Moreover, almost 80 percent of U.S. employers use some form of nontraditional staffing arrangement. Most employers find these kinds of arrangements to be less expensive than adding permanent staff. They also provide greater flexibility. Some employees, though, take such jobs only because they can't find a traditional job. Others value the flexibility they often accompanies a nontraditional job.

contingent worker
A person who works for an organization on something other than a permanent or full-time basis

Managing contingent workers is not always straightforward, however, especially from a behavioral perspective. Expecting too much from such workers, for example, is a mistake that managers should avoid. An organization with a large contingent workforce must make some decisions about the treatment of contingent workers relative to the treatment of permanent, full-time workers. Should contingent workers be invited to the company holiday party? Should they have the same access to such employee benefits as counseling services and childcare? There are no right or wrong answers to such questions. Managers must understand that they need to develop a strategy for integrating contingent workers according to some sound logic and then follow that strategy consistently over time.[92]

Tiered Workforce

Yet another emerging issue in new employment relationships is what we call the tiered workforce. A ***tiered workforce*** exists when one group of an organization's workforce has a contractual arrangement with the organization objectively different from that of another group performing the same jobs. For example, during the 2008–2010 recession Harley-Davidson negotiated a new agreement with its labor union for wages and job security at its large motorcycle factory in York, Pennsylvania. The change was needed to help the plant remain competitive and to prevent Harley from moving York jobs to other factories. Under terms of the agreement, the wage for the lowest-paid production worker on staff at the time of the agreement was set as $24.10 an hour. All new employees hired for that same job in the future, however, would earn $19.28 an hour. Yet another group of employees, called "casual" workers, work on an "as needed" basis and would be paid $16.75 an hour.[93] Similarly, under contracts negotiated with the United Auto Workers during the recession, new hires at Ford, General Motors, and Chrysler earn a lower hourly wage and reduced benefits compared to workers already on the payroll when the agreement was signed.[94] General Motors, for example, pays its pre-contract employees a minimum of $28 an hour, but all new employees start at $14 an hour.

tiered workforce
When one group of an organization's workforce has a contractual arrangement with the organization objectively different from another group performing the same jobs

These and similar arrangements, of course, may pose new challenges in the future. For instance, recently hired workers may come to feel resentment towards their more senior colleagues who are getting paid more for the same work. Likewise, as the job market improves and workers have more options, firms may face higher turnover among their newer lower-paid employees.

The Changing Nature of Psychological Contracts

psychological contract
A person's set of expectations regarding what he or she will contribute to an organization and what the organization, in return, will provide to the individual

A final element of the business environment that both affects and is affected by employment relationships such as those discussed above is the ***psychological contract***. Whenever we buy a car or sell a house, both buyer and seller sign a contract that specifies the terms of the agreement—who pays what to whom, when it's paid, and so forth. A psychological contract resembles a standard legal contract in some ways, but it is less formal and less well defined. Specifically, a psychological contract is a person's overall set of expectations regarding what he or she will contribute to the organization and what the organization will provide in return.[95] Unlike any other kind of business contract, a psychological contract is not written on paper, nor are all of its terms explicitly negotiated.

Figure 2.4 illustrates the essential nature of a psychological contract. The individual makes a variety of *contributions* to the organization—such things as effort, skills, ability, time, and loyalty. Jill Henderson, a branch manager for Merrill Lynch, uses her knowledge of financial markets and investment opportunities to help her clients make profitable investments. Her MBA in finance, coupled with hard work and motivation, have allowed her to become one of the firm's most promising young managers. The firm believed she had these attributes when it hired her, of course, and expected that she would do well.

In return for these contributions, the organization provides *inducements* to the individual. Some inducements, such as pay and career opportunities, are tangible rewards. Others, such as job security and status, are more intangible. Jill Henderson started at Merrill Lynch at a very competitive salary and has received an attractive salary increase each of the six years she has been with the firm. She has also been promoted twice and expects another promotion—perhaps to a larger office—in the near future.

Figure 2.4

The Psychological Contract

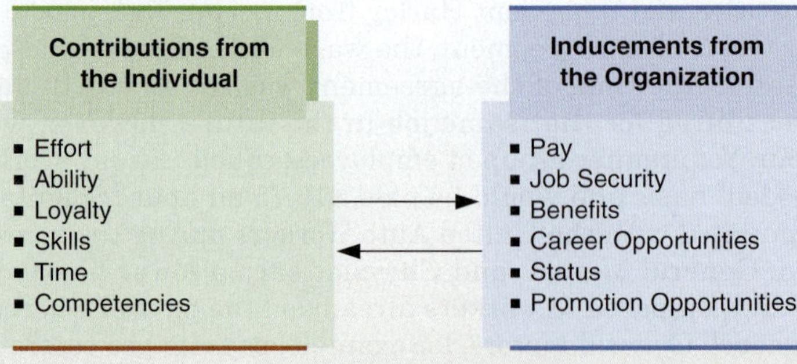

Contributions from the Individual
▪ Effort
▪ Ability
▪ Loyalty
▪ Skills
▪ Time
▪ Competencies
Inducements from the Organization
▪ Pay
▪ Job Security
▪ Benefits
▪ Career Opportunities
▪ Status
▪ Promotion Opportunities

Psychological contracts govern the basic relationship between people and organizations. Individuals contribute such things as effort and loyalty. In turn, organizations offer such inducements as pay and job security.

In this instance, both Jill Henderson and Merrill Lynch apparently perceive that the psychological contract is fair and equitable. Both will be satisfied with the relationship and will do what they can to maintain it. Henderson is likely to continue to work hard and effectively, and Merrill Lynch is likely to continue to increase her salary and give her promotions. In other situations, however, things might not work out as well. If either party sees an inequity in the contract, that party may initiate a change. The employee might ask for a pay raise or promotion, put forth less effort, or look for a better job elsewhere. The organization can also initiate change by training the worker to improve his skills, by transferring him to another job, or by firing him.

All organizations face the basic challenge of managing psychological contracts. They want value from their employees, and they need to give employees the right inducements. For instance, underpaid employees may perform poorly or leave for better jobs elsewhere. An employee may even occasionally start to steal organizational resources as a way to balance the psychological contract. Overpaying employees who contribute little to the organization, though, incurs unnecessary costs.

Recent trends in downsizing and cutbacks have complicated the process of managing psychological contracts, especially during the recession of 2008–2010. For example, many organizations used to offer at least reasonable assurances of job permanence as a fundamental inducement to employees. Now, however, job permanence is less likely, so alternative inducements may be needed.[96] Among the new forms of inducements that some companies are providing are additional training opportunities and increased flexibility in working schedules.

Increased globalization of business also complicates the management of psychological contracts. For example, the array of inducements that employees deem to be of value varies across cultures. U.S. workers tend to value individual rewards and recognition, but Japanese workers are more likely to value group-based rewards and recognition. Workers in Mexico and Germany highly value leisure time and may thus prefer more time off from work, whereas workers in China may place a lower premium on time off. The Lionel Train Company, maker of toy electric trains, once moved its operations to Mexico to capitalize on cheaper labor. The firm encountered problems, however, when it could not hire enough motivated employees to maintain quality standards and ended up making a costly move back to the United States. That is, the prevailing low wages in Mexico (which prompted the firm to move there to begin with) were not sufficient inducement to motivate the high quality performance the firm expected.

A related problem faced by international businesses is the management of psychological contracts for expatriate managers. In some ways, this process is more like a formal contract than are other employment relationships. Managers selected for a foreign assignment, for instance, are usually given some estimate of

PHOTOGRAPHEE.EU/ SHUTTERSTOCK.COM

A psychological contract is an unwritten agreement about expectations between an organization and its employees. This manager and employee, for example, are finalizing an understanding about how a new project will be managed. The agreement is not written, but both sides understand what they are supposed to do and what they can expect in return.

the duration of the assignment and receive various adjustments in their compensation package, including cost-of-living adjustments, education subsidies for children, reimbursement of personal travel expenses, and so forth. When the assignment is over, the manager must then be integrated back into the domestic organization. During the time of the assignment, however, the organization itself may have changed in many ways—new managers, new coworkers, new procedures, new business practices, and so forth. Thus, returning managers may very well come back to an organization that is quite different from the one they left and to a job quite different from what they expected.[97]

SUMMARY AND APPLICATION

Diversity is much more than demographics and can reflect combinations of characteristics in addition to a single attribute. Each individual also has a variety of characteristics that can be considered diverse. There are many types of diversity, including surface-level and deep-level diversity. Diversity can be examined as a group characteristic, as in "this group is diverse with regard to gender, race, and experience," or as an individual characteristic in terms of a person's similarity to or difference from the other group members. Having a token minority member in a group affects the majority members' perceptions of that minority group, placing greater performance pressures on minority group members, increasing stereotyping, and creating more boundaries between majority and minority group members.

Diversity affects individual and organizational outcomes through processes including social integration, differences in status and power, task conflict, relationship conflict, inclusion, and information processing. Barriers to inclusion include the "like me" bias, stereotypes, prejudice, perceptions of loss by persons who feel threatened by diversity initiatives, ethnocentrism, and unequal access to organizational networks. Organizations promote diversity through top management commitment, staffing, training, and mentoring.

Societal culture reflects language, politics, religion, and values among other things, and societal culture can vary within a single country or across nearby countries. Because societal culture influences the diverse values, customs, language, and expectations we bring with us to work, it is important to understand its effects on our own as well as on other people's behaviors. Societal cultures can differ on a variety of characteristics, including collectivism, power distance, future orientation, and gender egalitarianism as well as determine what employees consider desirable leadership characteristics. You will be a more effective performer and leader if you are culturally aware.

Globalization is playing a major role in the environment of many firms today. The volume of international trade has grown significantly and continues to grow at a very rapid pace. There are four basic reasons for this growth: (1) communication and transportation have advanced dramatically over the past several decades; (2) businesses have expanded internationally to increase their markets; (3) firms are moving into international markets to control costs, especially to reduce labor costs; and (4) many organizations have become international in response to competition. There are numerous cross-cultural differences and similarities that affect behavior within organizations.

Technology refers to the methods used to create products, including both physical goods and intangible services. Technological change has become a

LOSKUTNIKOV/SHUTTERSTOCK.COM

REAL WORLD RESPONSE
GLOBAL DIVERSITY AT COCA-COLA

Diversity is taken seriously at all levels in The Coca-Cola Company. Senior executives including the Chairman and CEO are involved with many nonprofits involving underrepresented groups, and corporate goals are linked to individuals' diversity metrics including being a cross-cultural mentor and the recruitment, promotion, engagement, and retention of diverse employees.[98] The company also offers a variety of diversity education programs that have evolved from minimizing conflict to strengthening the company's ability to amplify, respect, value, and leverage employee differences to influence sustainable business outcomes.[99]

The company has created a movement where its global business leaders see the benefits of and take responsibility for creating a diverse and inclusive working environment. Rather than just focusing on diversity numbers, The Coca-Cola Company focuses on fostering an inclusive culture using social psychology research on unconscious bias and change management techniques.[100] The Coca-Cola Company's commitment to diversity has helped it to succeed in its industry and develop a strong positive corporate reputation, becoming one of *Fortune's* top 10 Most Admired Companies six years in a row.[101]

major driver for other forms of organizational change. It also has widespread effects on the behaviors of people inside an organization. Three specific areas of technology relevant to the study of organizational behavior are (1) the shift toward a service-based economy; (2) the growing use of technology for competitive advantage; and (3) mushrooming change in information technology.

Although ethics has long been relevant to businesses and managers, what seems like an epidemic of ethical breaches in recent years have placed ethics in the mainstream of managerial thought today. One special aspect of business ethics, corporate governance, has also taken on increased importance. Ethics also increasingly relate to information technology. A central issue today revolves around the fact that rapid changes in business relationships, organizational structures, and financial systems pose unsurpassed difficulties in keeping accurate track of a company's financial position.

A final significant area of organizational change facing organizations today involves new employment relationships. Knowledge workers add value to a business because of what they know. How well these employees are managed is seen as a major factor in determining which firms will succeed. Outsourcing is the practice of hiring other firms to do the work previously performed by the organization itself. It is an increasingly popular strategy because it helps firms focus on their core activities and avoid getting sidetracked by secondary activities. However, it grows controversial when the jobs being outsourced are really being exported to foreign countries in ways that reduce domestic job opportunities. Contingent and temporary workers and the creation of a tiered workforce also pose special challenges. These challenges center around the treatment of various groups (such as contingent or lower-tier workers) compared to other groups (such as permanent or higher-tier employees).

DISCUSSION QUESTIONS

1. Which do you think is more important to team performance, surface-level or deep-level diversity? Why?
2. How can diversity create a competitive advantage for a firm?
3. If a subordinate came to you and said that they felt the company's new diversity hiring initiative was unfair and would compromise their well-deserved opportunities for advancement, how would you respond?
4. What can leaders do to be effective when team members are from different cultures and have different expectations about how the leader should behave?
5. Identify at least three ways in which the globalization of business affects businesses in your community.
6. What roles do changing technologies play in your daily activities?
7. Do you think that concerns regarding ethics will become more or less important in business? Why?
8. What are your personal opinions about international outsourcing in the garment industry? Do you think that lower prices are worth sending U.S. jobs to other countries? Explain your answer.

UNDERSTAND YOURSELF EXERCISE

Global Perspective

This Chapter's *Understand Yourself* feature gave you the opportunity to evaluate your global perspective. Global perspective is characterized by high levels of both conceptualization, or the ability to think globally, and contextualization, or the ability to act locally and adapt to the local environment. Although both thinking globally and acting locally are important to managers, most managers are more adept at thinking globally than at acting locally because of the uniqueness of local cultures.

Reflect on the nature of some of the interactions that you have had with people from other cultures. These interactions could have been in person during class, at a store, or even over the phone with a customer service agent. Next, answer the following questions:

1. Do you think that you were equally able to think and act locally as you interacted with people from other cultures?
2. What did you do well, and what could you have done better in these interactions?
3. What multicultural experiences can you seek out to enhance your global perspective?

GROUP EXERCISE

What Does Culture Mean to You?

This exercise is done as a class, and the instructor plays the role of class secretary. First working alone, think about what "societal culture" means. For five minutes, think about your own culture. Write down how you think a dictionary would define the word, then write down all of the cultural dimensions you can think of that you would use to describe it.

After five minutes, the instructor will call on students to share some of their ideas and record them on a chalkboard, flip chart, or something else. Try to identify categories into which the ideas can be placed. Then answer the following questions as a class.

Questions

1. How might multiculturalism create a competitive advantage for an organization?
2. What categories are the most important to teams working in organizations?
3. What categories are the least important to teams working in organizations?
4. What does your list suggest that managers wanting to promote a multicultural workplace might do?

VIDEO EXERCISE

Ethical Decision Making at Black Diamond Equipment

Black Diamond Equipment specializes in climbing and skiing equipment. The global company looks for employees who share the company's attitude, values, and passion toward outdoor sports and ethical values. Black Diamond also promotes fair labor practices, sustainability, and low environmental impact.

As a class, watch "Black Diamond Equipment" and then individually consider the following questions. After you have come up with your own ideas, form groups of four to five people and discuss your insights. Be sure to nominate someone to serve as a spokesperson to share your ideas with the class.

1. How does Black Diamond integrate social responsibility into its culture?
2. How does the global nature of the company and its markets influence how it thinks about employee diversity?
3. How would you describe Black Diamond's ethics in terms of how it treats its employees at the company's factory partners in Vietnam, China, and Bangladesh? Do you think that it is appropriate for firms like Black Diamond to scrutinize its partner factories like this? Why or why not?

VIDEO CASE Now What?

PERCOM/SHUTTERSTOCK.COM

Imagine trying to write a project status report for Happy Time Toys with three other team members when an older team member tries to take the project over, believing that you're too inexperienced to do a good job. *What do you say or do?* Go to this chapter's "Now What?" video, watch the challenge video, and choose a response. Be sure to also view the outcomes of the two responses you didn't choose.

Discussion Questions

1. What type(s) of barriers to inclusion exist for this group?
2. How can diversity be leveraged as a source of competitive advantage for this group?
3. If you were the CEO of Happy Time Toys, how would you create a culture of inclusion to help your company realize the benefits of not only age-related diversity but all types of diversity?

ENDNOTES

[1]The Coca-Cola Company: No. 33 in the DiversityInc Top 50. 2015. Available online: http://www.coca-colacompany.com/our-company/diversity/global-diversity-mission.

[2]Global Diversity Mission. The Coca Cola Company. 2015. Available online: http://www.coca-colacompany.com/our-company/diversity/global-diversity-mission.

[3]2020 Vision: Roadmap for Winning Together: TCCC & Our Bottling Partners. The Coca-Cola Company. Available online: http://assets.coca-colacompany.com/22/b7/ba47681f420fbe7528bc43e3a118/2020_vision.pdf.

[4]2011 U.S. Diversity Stewardship Report. The Coca-Cola Company. 2011. Available online: http://assets.coca-colacompany.com/dd/6f/f4e3125c49e4bb504d3a4df2a08e/2011-US-Diversity-Report-Final.pdf.

[5]See Fox, A. (2010, January). At Work in 2020. *HR Magazine*, 18–23.

[6]Bloom, M., & Michel, J. G. (2002). The Relationships Among Organizational Context, Pay Dispersion, and Managerial Turnover. *Academy of Management Journal*, *45*, 33–42.

[7]Linnehan, F., & Konrad, A. M. (1999). Diluting Diversity: Implications for Inter-Group Inequality in Organizations. *Journal of Management Inquiry*, *8*, 399–414.

[8]Harrison, D. A., & Klein, K. J. (2007). What's the Difference? Diversity Constructs as Separation, Variety, or Disparity in Organizations. *Academy of Management Review*, *32*, 1199–1228.

[9]Toossi, M. (2012, January). Labor Force Projections to 2020: A More Slowly Growing Workforce, *Monthly Labor Review*, 43–64.

[10]Zillman, C. (2014, February 4). Microsoft's New CEO: One Minority Exec in a Sea of White. *Fortune*. Available online: http://fortune.com/2014/02/04/microsofts-new-ceo-one-minority-exec-in-a-sea-of-white/.

[11]Desvaux, G., Devillard-Hoellinger, S., & Meany, M. C (2008, September). A Business Case for Women. *The McKinsey Quarterly*. Available online: http://www.mckinseyquarterly.com /Organization/Talent/A_business_case_for_women_2192.

[12]See Wittenberg-Cox, A., & Maitland, A. (2008). *Why Women Mean Business: Understanding the Emergence of Our Next Economic Revolution*. Chichester, UK: John Wiley & Sons.

[13]Desvaux, G., Devillard-Hoellinger, S., & Meaney, M. C. (2008, September). A Business Case for Women. *The McKinsey Quarterly*. Available online: http://www.mckinseyquarterly.com / Organization/Talent/A_business_case_for_women_2192.

[14]Schramm, J. (2006, June). *SHRM Workplace Forecast*. Alexandria, VA: Society for Human Resource Management.

[15]Frauenheim, E. (2007, March 12). Aging Boomers Require Workplace Flexibility, Says American Management Association. *Workforce Management*, *6*.

[16]Grillo, J. (2009, May/June). Gen Y: How Millennials Are Changing the Workplace. *Diversity Executive*, 20.

[17]Waldman, D. A., & Avolio, B. J. (1986). A Meta-Analysis of Age Differences in Job Performance. *Journal of Applied Psychology*, *71*, 33–38.

[18]McEvoy, G. M., & Cascio, W. F. (1989). Cumulative Evidence of the Relationship Between Employee Age and Job Performance. *Journal of Applied Psychology*, *74*, 11–17.

[19]Warr, P., & Bunce, D. (1995). Trainee Characteristics and the Outcomes of Open Learning. *Personnel Psychology*, *48*(2), 347–375.

[20]Colquitt, J. A., LePine, J. A., & Noe, R. A. (2000). Toward an Integrative Theory of Training Motivation: A Meta-Analytic Path Analysis of 20 Years of Research. *Journal of Applied Psychology*, *85*(5), 678–707.

[21]Hertzog, C. (1989). Influences of Cognitive Slowing on Age Differences in Intelligence. *Developmental Psychology*, *25*, 636–651.

[22]Gully, S. M., & Chen, G. (2010). Individual Differences, Attribute-Treatment Interactions, and Training Outcomes. In *Learning, Training, and Development in Organizations*,

eds. S. W. J. Kozlowski & E. Salas (pp. 3–64). SIOP Organizational Frontiers Series. San Francisco, CA: Jossey-Bass.

[23]Maurer, T. J. (2001). Career-Relevant Learning and Development, Worker Age, and Beliefs About Self-Efficacy for Development. *Journal of Management*, *27*(2), 123–140; Maurer, T. J., Weiss, E. M., & Barbeite, F. G. (2003). A Model of Involvement in Work-Related Learning and Development Activity: The Effects of Individual, Situational, Motivational, and Age Variables. *Journal of Applied Psychology*, *88*(4), 707–724.

[24]Chaudhuri, S. & Ghosh, R. (2012). Reverse Mentoring: A Social Exchange Tool for Keeping the Boomers Engaged and Millennials Committed. *Human Resource Development*, *11*, 55–76.

[25]Breen, B. (2001, November). Trickle-Up Leadership. *Fast Company,* 52, 70.

[26]Yang, Y. & Konrad, A.M. (2010). Diversity and Organizational Innovation: The Role of Employee Involvement, *Journal of Organizational Behavior*, *32*, 1062–1083; Harrison, D. A., & Klein, K. J. (2007). What's the Difference? Diversity Constructs as Separation, Variety, or Disparity in Organizations. *Academy of Management Review*, *32*, 1199–1228.

[27]McKay, P. F., Avery, D. R., & Morris, M. A. (2008). Mean Racial-Ethnic Differences in Employee Sales Performance: The Moderating Role of Diversity Climate. *Personnel Psychology*, *61*, 349–374.

[28]Ragins, B. R., & Gonzalez, J. A. (2003). Understanding Diversity in Organizations: Getting a Grip on a Slippery Construct. In *Organizational Behavior: The State of the Science,* ed. J. Greenberg (pp. 125–163). Mahwah, NJ: Lawrence Erlbaum Associates.

[29]Triandis, H. C., Kurowski, L. L., & Gelfand, M. J. (1993). Workplace Diversity. In *Handbook of Industrial and Organizational Psychology*, eds. H. C. Triandis, M. Dunnette, & L. Hough (4th ed., pp. 769–827). Palo Alto, CA: Consulting Psychologists Press; McLeod, P. L., Lobel, S., & Cox, T. H. (1996). Ethnic Diversity and Creativity in Small Groups. *Small Group Research*, *27*, 248–264.

[30]Bassett-Jones, N. (2005). The Paradox of Diversity Management, Creativity and Innovation. *Creativity and Innovation Management*, *14*, 169–175.

[31]Williams, K. Y. (1998). Demography and Diversity in Organizations: A Review of 100 Years of Research. In *Research in Organizational Behavior,* eds. B. M. Staw and L. L. Cummings (Vol. 20, pp. 77–140). Greenwich, CT: JAI Press.

[32]Kanter, R. M. (1983). *The Change Masters*. New York: Simon & Schuster.

[33]Deszõ, C. L., & Gaddis Ross, D. (2008, July 17). "Girl Power": Female Participation in Top Management and Firm Quality. Working paper series.

[34]For more information, see http://www.ada.gov.

[35]U.S. Equal Employment Opportunity Commission. The Age Discrimination in Employment Act of 1967. Available online: http://www.eeoc.gov/policy/adea.html.

[36]EEOC. (2010, March 1). Walmart to Pay More Than $11.7 Million to Settle EEOC Sex Discrimination Suit. U.S. Equal Employment Opportunity Commission. Available online: http://www.eeoc.gov/eeoc/newsroom/release/3-1-10.cfm.

[37]Glater, J. D. (2004, June 27). Attention Wal-Mart Plaintiffs: Hurdles Ahead. *The New York Times.* Available online: http://select.nytimes.com/gst/abstract.html?res=F00B13FD3D5C0C748EDDAF0894DC404482&n=Top%2fNews%2fBusiness%2fCompanies%2fWal%2dMart%20Stores%20Inc%2e.

[38]U.S. Equal Employment Opportunity Commission. (2012). *Best Practices of Private Sector Employers.* Available online: http://www.eeoc.gov/eeoc/task_reports/best_practices.cfm.

[39]Federal Glass Ceiling Commission. (1995, March). *Good for Business: Making Full Use of the Nation's Human Capital.* Fact-Finding Report of the Federal Glass Ceiling Commission.

[40]Federal Glass Ceiling Commission. (1995, March). *Good for Business: Making Full Use of the Nation's Human Capital* (pp. 28–29). Fact-Finding Report of the Federal Glass Ceiling Commission.

[41]Federal Glass Ceiling Commission. (1995, March). *Good for Business: Making Full Use of the Nation's Human Capital* (pp. 31–32). Fact-Finding Report of the Federal Glass Ceiling Commission.

[42]Perrewé, P. L., & Nelson, D. L. (2004, December). Gender and Career Success: The Facilitative Role of Political Skill. *Organizational Dynamics,* 366–378.

[43]Lyness, K. S., & Thompson, D. E. (2000). Climbing the Corporate Ladder: Do Female and Male Executives Follow the Same Route? *Journal of Applied Psychology*, *85*, 86–101.

[44]Spelman, D., Addison-Reid, B., Avery, E., & Crary, M. (2006). Sustaining a Long-Term Diversity Change Initiative: Lessons from a Business University. *The Diversity Factor*, *14*(4), 19–25.

[45]Diversity at PNC. (2010). Available online: https://www.pnc.com/webapp/unsec/Blank.do?siteArea=/PNC/Careers/Why+PNC /Diversity+at+PNC..

[46]What Makes Working Here Different. Wegmans, 2015. Available online: http://www.wegmans.com/webapp/wcs/stores/servlet/CategoryDisplay?storeId=10052&catalogId=10002&identifier=CATEGORY_5673.

[47]Diversity at Wegmans. Wegmans, 2015. Available online: http://www.wegmans.com/webapp/wcs/stores/servlet/ProductDisplay?productId=758917&storeId=10052&langId=-1.

[48]Owens, Donna. (2009, October 1). Treating Employees Like Customers. *HR Magazine*, *54*(10). Available online: http://www.shrm.org/publications/hrmagazine/editorialcontent/2009/1009/pages/1009owens.aspx.

[49]Gent, M. J. (1984, January-February). Theory X in Antiquity, or the Bureaucratization of the Roman Army. *Business Horizons*, 53–54.

[50]Griffin, R. & Pustay, M. (2012). *International Business* (7th ed.). Upper Saddle River, NJ: Prentice Hall.

[51]Quappe, S., & Cantatore, G. (2007, November). What Is Cultural Awareness, Anyway? How Do I Build It? Culturosity.com. Available online: http://www.culturosity.com/articles/whatisculturalawareness.htm.

[52]Adapted from Martin, M., & Vaughn, B. (2007, Spring). Cultural Competence: The Nuts and Bolts of Diversity and Inclusion. *Strategic Diversity & Inclusion Management Magazine,* 31–38.

[53]Kassof, A. (1958). The Prejudiced Personality: A Cross-Cultural Test. *Social Problems*, *6*, 59–67.

[54]Chen, Y.-R., Leung, K., & Chen, C. C. (2009). Bringing National Culture to the Table: Making a Difference with Cross-Cultural Differences and Perspectives. In *The Academy of Management Annals,* eds. J. Walsh & A. Brief (Vol. 3,

pp. 217–250). London: Routledge, Taylor & Francis Group. See also Erez, M. (2010). Cross-Cultural and Global Issues In Organizational Psychology. In *Handbook of Industrial and Organizational Psychology*. ed. S. Zedeck. Washington, DC: American Psychological Association.

[55]Ronen, S. & Shenkar, O. (1985, July). Clustering Countries on Attitudinal Dimension: A Review and Synthesis. *Academy of Management Review*, 435–454.

[56]Adler, N. J, Doktor, R. & Redding, G. (1986, Summer). From the Atlantic to the Pacific Century. *Journal of Management*, 295–318.

[57]Based on Cultural Business Etiquette. U.S. Commercial Service, United States of America Department of Commerce. Available online at: http://www.buyusa.gov/iowa/etiquette.html.; "United Kingdom," International Business Etiquette and Manners. Available online at: http://www.cyborlink.com/besite/united_kingdom.htm.; "India," International Business Etiquette and Manners. Available online at: http://www.cyborlink.com/besite/india.htm.; "Germany," International Business Etiquette and Manners. Available online at: http://www.cyborlink.com/besite/germany.htm.; "Spain," International Business Etiquette and Manners. Available online at: http://www.cyborlink.com/besite/spain.htm.; "Saudia Arabia," International Business Etiquette and Manners. Available online at: http://www.cyborlink.com/besite/saudi-arabia.htm.; "France," Interna

[58]Yamaguchi, T. (1988, February). The Challenge of Internationalization. *Academy of Management Executive*, 33–36; see also Tsui, A. (2007). From Homogenization to Pluralism in International Management. *Academy of Management Journal*, *50*(6), 1353–1364.

[59]Hofstede, G. (1980). *Culture's Consequences: International Differences in Work-Related Values*. Beverly Hills, CA: Sage Publications.

[60]Kedia, B. L., & Mukherji, A. (1999). Global Managers: Developing a Mindset for Global Competitiveness. *Journal of World Business*, *34*, 230–251.

[61]Rhinesmith, S. H. (1992). Global Mindsets for Global Managers. *Training & Development*, *46*, 63–69.

[62]Levy, O., Beechler, S., Taylor, S., & Boyacigiller, N. (2007). What We Talk About When We Talk About "Global Mindset": Managerial Cognition in Multinational Corporations. *Journal of International Business Studies*, *38*, 231–258.

[63]Wankel, C. (2007). *21st Century Management: A Reference Handbook* (Vol. 1). New York: Sage.

[64]Kedia, B. L. & Englis, P. D. (2011). Transforming Business Education to Produce Global Managers. *Business Horizons*, *54*(4), 325–331.

[65]See Fox, A. (2010, January). At Work in 2020. *HR Magazine*, 18–23.

[66]Arora, A., Jaju, A., Kefalas, A. G., & Perenich, T. (2004). An Exploratory Analysis of Global Managerial Mindsets: A Case of U.S. Textile and Apparel Industry. *Journal of International Management*,*10*, 393–411.

[67]Employment Projections: 2012–2022 Summary, U.S. Bureau of Labor Statistics, December 19, 2014.

[68]Quittner, J. (2010, March 1). The Future of Reading. *Fortune*, 62–67.

[69]CareerBuilder Releases Annual List of the Most Unusual Excuses for Calling in Sick, According to U.S. Employers. *CareerBuilder*, October 27, 2010.

[70]Chains' Ties Run Deep on Pharmacy Boards. *USA Today*, December 31, 2008, 1B, 2B.

[71]Kahn, J. (2000, March 20). Presto Chango! Sales Are Huge. *Fortune*, 90–96; More Firms Falsify Revenue to Boost Stocks. *USA Today*, March 29, 2000, 1B.

[72]Diamond Foods Restating Profits After an Audit. *Bloomberg Businessweek*, February 13–February 19, 2012, 28.

[73]U.S. Probes Hilton Over Theft Claims. *Wall Street Journal*, April 22, 2009, B1, B4.

[74]Walmart's Discounted Ethics. *Time*, May 7, 2012, p. 19.

[75]How U.S. Concerns Compete in Countries Where Bribes Flourish. *Wall Street Journal*, September 29, 1995, pp. A1, A14; Digh, P. (1997, April). Shades of Gray in the Global Marketplace. *HR Magazine*, 90–98.

[76]Alcoa Faces Allegation by Bahrain of Bribery. *Wall Street Journal*, February 28, 2009, A2.

[77]How to Fix Corporate Governance. *Business Week*, May 6, 2002, 68–78.

[78]Carroll, A. B. & Buchholtz, A. K. (2012). *Business & Society: Ethics, Sustainability, and Stakeholder Management* (8th ed.). Mason, OH: Cengage Learning.

[79]Sanders, T. (2008). *Saving the World at Work.* New York: Doubleday Business.

[80]Maon, F., Lindgreen, A., & Swaen, V. (2010). Organizational Stages and Cultural Phases: A Critical Review and a Consolidative Model of Corporate Social Responsibility Development. *International Journal of Management Reviews*, *12*, 20–38.

[81]Rupp, D. E., Williams, C. & Aguilera, R. (2011). Increasing Corporate Social Responsibility through Stakeholder Value Internalization (and the Catalyzing Effect of New Governance): An Application of Organizational Justice, Self-Determination, and Social Influence Theories. In *Managerial Ethics: Managing the Psychology of Morality*, ed. M. Schminke. New York: Routledge/Psychology Press.

[82]McClellan, J. (2008, June 27). Get Your Employees Excited About Sustainability. Society for Human Resource Management. Available online: http://www.shrm.org/hrdisciplines/ethics/-articles/pages/employeesandsustainability.aspx.

[83]Wasserman, T. (2011, June 9). Google Offers Employees 30 More Electric Cars to Share, Mashable.com. Available online: http://mashable.com/2011/06/09/google-electric-vehicles/.

[84]McClellan, J. (2008, June 27). Get Your Employees Excited About Sustainability. Society for Human Resource Management. Available online: http://www.shrm.org/hrdisciplines/ethics/-articles/pages/employeesandsustainability.aspx.

[85]For additional information, see http://www.iso.org/iso/iso_ catalogue/management_standards/iso_9000_iso_14000/qmp.htm.

[86]Boisot, M. (1998). *Knowledge Assets.* Oxford, UK: Oxford University Press.

[87]Tushman, M. L., & O'Reilly, C. A. (1996). *Winning Through Innovation.* Cambridge, MA: Harvard Business School Press.

[88]Von Glinow, M. A. (1988). *The New Professionals*. Cambridge, MA: Ballinger.

[89]Lee, T. W., & Maurer, S. D. (1997). The Retention of Knowledge Workers with the Unfolding Model of Voluntary Turnover. *Human Resource Management Review* 7, 247–276.

[90]Milkovich, G. T. (1987). Compensation Systems in High-Technology Companies. In *High Technology Management,* eds.

A. Klingartner and C. Anderson. Lexington, MA: Lexington Books.

[91]http://www.hewittassociates.com/OutsourcingStudy_2009_Results.pdf, March 21, 2010.

[92]Zeidner, R. (2010, February). Heady Debate—Rely on Temps or Hire Staff? *HR Magazine*, 28–33.

[93]Harley Union Makes Concessions. *Wall Street Journal*, December 3, 2009, B3.

[94]Ford to Begin Hiring at New Lower Wages. *Wall Street Journal*, January 26, 2010, B1.

[95]Rousseau, D. M., & Parks, J. M. (1993). The Contracts of Individuals and Organizations. In *Research in Organizational Behavior*, eds. L. L. Cummings & B. M. Staw (Vol. 15, pp. 1–43). Greenwich, CT: JAI Press. See also Rousseau, D. M. (2010). The Individual-Organization Relationship: The Psychological Contract. In *Handbook of Industrial and Organizational Psychology,* ed. S. Zedeck. Washington, DC: American Psychological Association.

[96]Rousseau, D. M. (1996, February). Changing the Deal While Keeping the People. *Academy of Management Executive*, 50–58; see also Ho, V. (2005, January). Social Influence on Evaluations of Psychological Contract Fulfillment. *Academy of Management Review*, 113–128.

[97]Guzzo, R. A., Noonan, K. A., & Elron, E. (1994). Expatriate Managers and the Psychological Contract. *Journal of Applied Psychology, 79*(4), 617–626.

[98]The Coca-Cola Company: No. 33 in the DiversityInc Top 50. 2015. Available online: http://www.diversityinc.com/the-coca-cola-company/.

[99]Diversity Education and Training. The Coca-Cola Company, 2015. Available online: http://www.coca-colacompany.com/our-company/diversity/diversity-education-training.

[100]Coca-Cola Enterprises—Thais Compoint. *Profiles in Diversity Journal*, 2015. Available online: http://www.diversityjournal.com/14365-coca-cola-enterprises-thais-compoint/.

[101]Coca-Cola No. 10 on Fortune's 2015 List of World's Most Admired Companies. Coca-Cola Journey, February 19, 2015. Available online: http://www.coca-colacompany.com/coca-cola-unbottled/coca-cola-no-10-on-fortunes-2015-list-of-worlds-most-admired-companies.

PART 2 INDIVIDUAL BEHAVIORS AND PROCESSES IN ORGANIZATIONS

As we discussed in Chapter 1, managers strive to enhance performance behaviors, enhance commitment and engagement, promote citizenship behaviors, and minimize dysfunctional behaviors by their employees. Chapter 2 identified how various environmental factors—diversity, globalization, technology, ethics, and new employment relationships—all impact organizational behavior.

We now turn to a fundamental question underlying organizational behavior: Why do individuals do what they do? Chapter 3 identifies and discusses critical individual characteristics that affect people's behaviors in organizations. The discussion of other important individual characteristics is continued in Chapter 4. Core theories and concepts that drive employee motivation are introduced and discussed in Chapter 5. Finally, in Chapter 6 we focus on how managers can implement motivation theories and concepts.

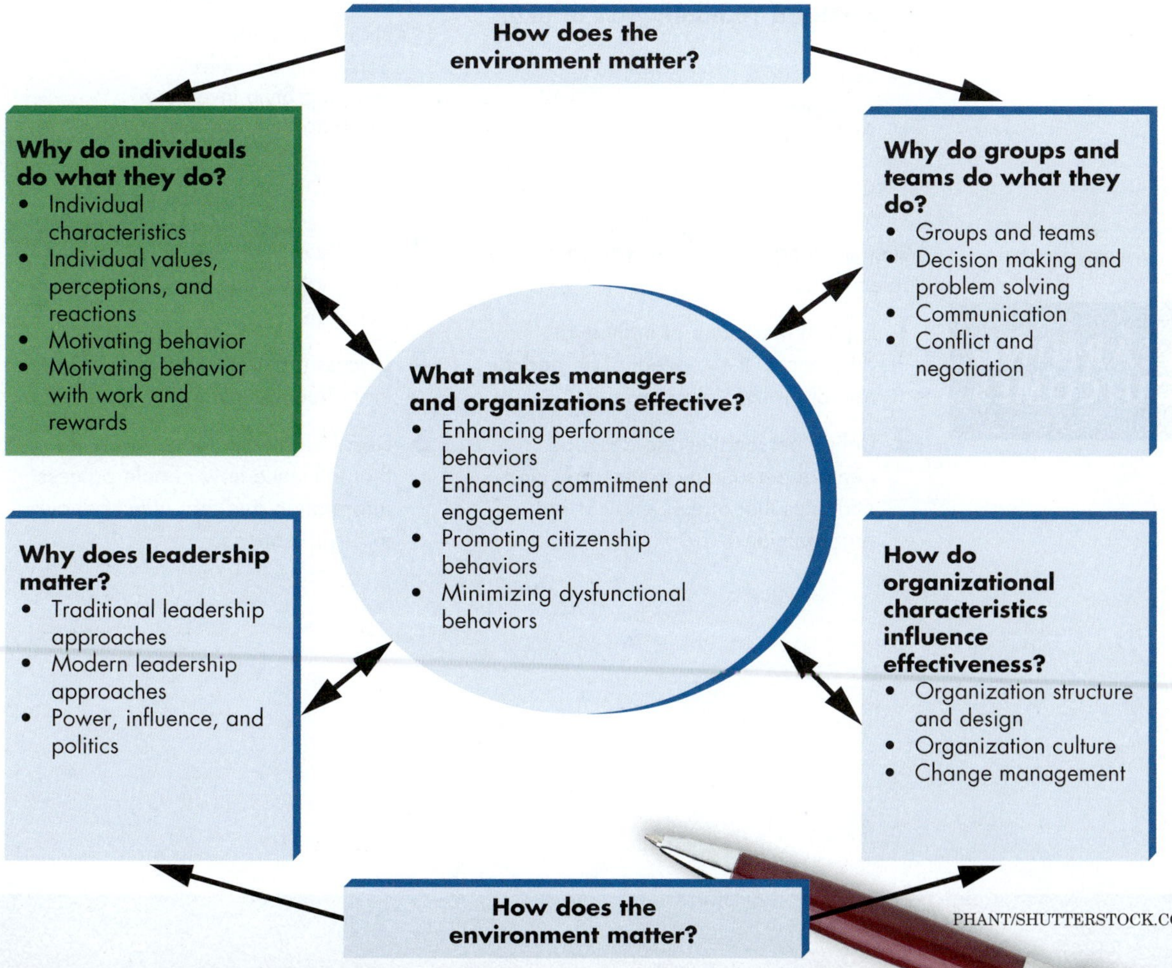

How does the environment matter?

Why do individuals do what they do?
- Individual characteristics
- Individual values, perceptions, and reactions
- Motivating behavior
- Motivating behavior with work and rewards

Why do groups and teams do what they do?
- Groups and teams
- Decision making and problem solving
- Communication
- Conflict and negotiation

What makes managers and organizations effective?
- Enhancing performance behaviors
- Enhancing commitment and engagement
- Promoting citizenship behaviors
- Minimizing dysfunctional behaviors

Why does leadership matter?
- Traditional leadership approaches
- Modern leadership approaches
- Power, influence, and politics

How do organizational characteristics influence effectiveness?
- Organization structure and design
- Organization culture
- Change management

How does the environment matter?

LOSKUTNIKOV/SHUTTERSTOCK.COM

CHAPTER

3 INDIVIDUAL CHARACTERISTICS

CHAPTER OUTLINE

LEARNING OUTCOMES

After studying this chapter, you should be able to:

1. Explain the nature of individual differences, the concept of fit, and the role of realistic job previews.
2. Define personality and describe general personality frameworks and attributes that affect behavior in organizations.
3. Identify and discuss other important personality traits that affect behavior in organizations.
4. Discuss different kinds of intelligence that affect behavior in organizations.
5. Describe different learning styles that influence how people process information and that affect behavior in organizations.

LOSKUTNIKOV/SHUTTERSTOCK.COM

REAL WORLD CHALLENGE

INDIVIDUAL DIFFERENCES THAT MAKE A DIFFERENCE AT SOUTHWEST AIRLINES

Fun and friendly customer service is essential to the success of Southwest Airlines' business strategy.[1] Southwest's Vice President of People feels that fun balances the stress of hard work. Because Southwest believes that fun is about attitude, it hires for personality and attitude. Former CEO Herb Kelleher believes that with the exception of a few technically oriented positions such as pilots, Southwest can train new hires on whatever they need to do, but it cannot change employees' inherent nature.[2]

Southwest Airlines' mission statement includes, "Creativity and innovation are encouraged for improving the effectiveness of Southwest Airlines."[3] To support its goals of hiring fun, creative, innovative employees, Southwest Airlines looks for leadership and a sense of humor in the people it hires. The company looks for empathetic people with other-oriented, outgoing personalities who work hard and have fun at the same time. Southwest's learning-oriented, fun culture gives employees the freedom to be themselves and become passionate about their jobs.[4]

Southwest asks for your advice about how to better hire empathetic employees with creativity and fun-loving characteristics who fit with the company's unique culture. After reading this chapter, you should have some good ideas.

BRIAN CAHN/CORBIS WIRE/CORBIS

Think about human behavior as a jigsaw puzzle. Puzzles consist of various pieces that fit together in precise ways. And of course, no two puzzles are exactly alike. They have different numbers of pieces, the pieces are of different sizes and shapes, and they fit together in different ways. The same can be said of human behavior and its determinants. Each of us is a whole picture, like a fully assembled jigsaw puzzle, but the puzzle pieces that define us and the way those pieces fit together are unique. Every person in an organization is fundamentally different from everyone else. To be successful, managers must recognize that these differences exist and attempt to understand them.

In this chapter we explore some of the key characteristics that differentiate people from one another in organizations. We first introduce the essential nature of individual differences and how people "fit" as individuals in organizations. We then look at personality frameworks that shed considerable light on different personality profiles. Next, we examine other specific personality traits and discuss different types of intelligence. We close this chapter with an examination of different styles for processing information and learning.

PEOPLE IN ORGANIZATIONS

As a starting point for understanding the behavior of people in organizations, let's first examine the basic nature of the individual–organization relationship. First we expand a bit further on the concept of individual differences and then introduce different forms of "fit" between people and organizations.

Individual Differences

individual differences
Personal attributes that vary from one person to another

As already noted, every individual is unique. ***Individual differences*** are personal attributes that vary from one person to another. Individual differences may be physical, psychological, and emotional. The individual differences that characterize a specific person make that person unique. As we see in both this chapter and Chapter 4, basic categories of individual differences include personality, intelligence, learning styles, attitudes, values and emotions, perception, and stress.

Are the specific differences that characterize a given person good or bad? Do they contribute to or detract from performance? The answer, of course, is that it depends on the circumstances. One person may be dissatisfied, withdrawn, and negative in one job setting but satisfied, outgoing, and positive in another. Working conditions, coworkers, and leadership are just a few of the factors that affect how a person performs and feels about a job. Thus, whenever a manager attempts to assess or account for individual differences among her employees, she must also be sure to consider the situation in which behavior occurs. In addition, as discussed in Chapter 2, managers should also be aware of psychological contracts that exist between the organization and its employees. In an ideal situation, then, understanding differences across people and creating effective psychological contracts can help facilitate a good fit between people and the organization.

The Concept of Fit

Why are some very talented people undesirable coworkers or employees despite being very talented at what they do? The answer lies in the many ways in which people need to fit with an employment opportunity to be a successful match. Being good at our job is important, but is not enough—we need to fit with our organization and workgroup as well. That is, there are actually different forms of fit.[5] These different forms of fit are summarized in Table 3.1.

Person-Job Fit

Person-job fit is the fit between a person's abilities and the demands of the job, and the fit between a person's desires and motivations and the attributes and rewards of a job.[6] An employee's talents need to meet a job's requirements, and the job needs to meet the employee's needs and motivations.[7] Because job performance is usually the most important determinant of an employee's success, person-job fit is usually the primary focus of most staffing efforts. From the employee's perspective, if the job does not meet his or her financial, career, lifestyle, and other needs, then the match is not ideal. An individual motivated by commissions and merit pay is not likely to be a good fit with a job based on teamwork and group rewards. Similarly, an individual who does not enjoy working with people is not likely to succeed in a sales position. It is important

person-job fit
The fit between a person's abilities and the demands of the job, and the fit between a person's desires and motivations and the attributes and rewards of a job

Table 3.1

Dimensions of Fit

Type of Fit	Possible Dimensions of Fit
Person-Job Fit: Does the person meet the needs of the job and does the job meet the needs of the person?	Intelligence Job-related skills Job knowledge Previous work experience Personality related to performing job tasks
Person-Group Fit: Does the employee fit the workgroup, including the supervisor?	Teamwork skills Knowledge and ability relative to other team members Conflict management style Preference for teamwork Communication skills Personality related to working well with others
Person-Organization Fit: Do the individual's values, beliefs, and personality fit the values, norms, and culture of the organization?	Alignment between personal motivations and the organization's culture, mission, and purpose Values Goals
Person-Vocation Fit: Do the person's interests, abilities, values, and personality fit his or her occupation?	Aptitudes Interests Personal values Long-term goals

IMAGE SOURCE/GETTY IMAGES

Fit is an important concept in organizations. Take this woman, for example. Her job appears to require her to deal with binders full of information. She may find this work interesting, or she may find it tedious and boring. Person-job, person-group, person organization, and person-vocation fit are all important factors in organizational behavior.

to consider not only the fit between an individual's talents and the job requirements, but also the fit between an individual's motivations and the rewards offered by the job. Research suggests that person-job fit leads to higher job performance, satisfaction, organizational commitment, and intent to stay with the company.[8] Because people differ in their personality and motivations as well as their skills, consider individual differences beyond skills when making hiring decisions.

Person-Group Fit

In addition to fit with the job, the fit between the employee and his or her workgroup and supervisor is also important. Good ***person-group fit*** (or ***person-team fit***) means that an individual fits with the workgroup's work styles, skills, and goals. Person-group fit recognizes that employees often must work effectivelywith their supervisor, workgroup, and teammates to be successful. Person-group fit leads to improved job satisfaction, organizational commitment, and intent to stay with the company.[9] Teamwork, communication, and interpersonal competencies can be as critical to team performance as team members' ability to perform core job duties. Person-group fit is thus particularly important in team-oriented work environments.[10] An executive at Men's Wearhouse once terminated one of the men's suits retail store's most successful salespeople because he focused only on maximizing his own sales as opposed to working with the other sales staff as a team. After firing the salesperson, sales at the store where he worked increased significantly.[11]

person-group fit (or person-team fit)
The extent to which an individual fits with the workgroup's and supervisor's work styles, skills, and goals

Person-Organization Fit

Person-organization fit is the fit between an individual's values, beliefs, and personality and the values, norms, and culture of the organization.[12] The strength of this fit influences important organizational outcomes including job performance, retention, job satisfaction, and organizational commitment.[13] Organizational values and norms that are important for person-organization fit include integrity, fairness, work ethic, competitiveness, cooperativeness, and compassion for fellow employees and customers. Person-organization fit has a strong positive relationship with job satisfaction, organizational commitment, and intent to stay with the company, and can influence employee attitudes and citizenship behaviors beyond the job requirements, such as helping others or talking positively about the firm.[14] It also has a modest impact on turnover and tenure, but little to no impact on meeting job requirements.[15] Despite the potential overlap between

person-organization fit
The fit between an individual's values, beliefs, and personality and the values, norms, and culture of the organization

Person-group fit is the fit between an individual and their group or team. The bored individual on the left may not be a good fit with the rest of her team members, who seem engaged and attentive.

WAVEBREAKMEDIA/SHUTTERSTOCK.COM

person-job and person-organization fit, research suggests that people may experience differing degrees of fit with the job and with the organization.[16] Essentially, it is possible to like what you do but not where you do it, or to like where you work but not what you do there.

So how can you maximize person-organization fit? A good place to start is to identify those qualifications, competencies, and traits that relate to the organization's strategy, values, and processes and hire people with those characteristics. For example, even if Maria is technically well qualified as a researcher, if she avoids risk, is indecisive, and tends to ruminate over a decision, she may be unsuccessful in an innovative, fast-paced company. Online shoe retailer Zappos.com attributes its success to its culture of great customer service, high energy, and employee autonomy. Because it does not monitor its customer service agents' call times or give them scripts, it is critical to make sure they are a good fit with the Zappos culture. One of the ways the company does that is to offer new customer service agents $2,000 to leave the company after the initial training period if they feel that they are a poor fit.[17] To find the best matches for their culture and business, The Container Store's online application includes questions asking job candidates to reveal their favorite Container Store product. Additional questions explore communications skills and other characteristics. Using the website also helps the candidate learn more about the company and be better prepared for an interview. This process helps to persuade strong candidates that The Container Store is a good fit for their interests and needs.

Employees must be able and willing to adapt to a company by learning, negotiating, enacting, and maintaining the behaviors appropriate to the company's environment.[18] To successfully adapt, employees must be open-minded and have sufficient information about organizational expectations and standards and their own performance in light of those standards. Employees also must be able and willing to learn new behaviors and habits (e.g., low anxiety, high self-esteem, good time management skills, etc.). Of course, hiring for any type of fit does not mean simply hiring those with whom we are most comfortable, which can lead to dysfunctional stereotyping and discrimination against people who may actually contribute a great deal to the company's success.

Person-Vocation Fit

person-vocation fit
The fit between a person's interests, abilities, values, and personality and a profession

Person-vocation fit is the fit between a person's interests, abilities, values, and personality and a profession.[19] Our adjustment and satisfaction are greater when our occupation meets our needs. For example, a social individual who is low in conscientiousness and dislikes working with numbers would be a poor fit with the engineering vocation. Although individuals usually choose a vocation long before applying to an organization, understanding person-vocation fit can still be useful to organizations and managers. Companies wanting to develop their own future leaders, or smaller organizations that need employees to fill multiple roles, may be able to use vocational interests in determining whether job applicants would be a good fit with the organization's future needs.

Some people pursue two or more different vocations over the course of their careers because they have diverse interests or because they become bored working a long time in the same career. Organizations may better retain valued career changers by understanding their vocational preferences and designing career tracks for them that place them in new roles in the organization over time that are consistent with their vocational interests and aptitudes. This allows valued employees who would otherwise be likely to leave the organization to pursue a different type of vocation to pursue multiple vocations within the company.

Realistic Job Previews

When communicating the nature of the work and the organization to job candidates, companies can choose how objective to be. Many firms choose to disclose as little potentially undesirable information as possible to reduce the chance that it will make the position unappealing. Essentially, some firms believe that if they tell recruits what it is really like to work there, the recruits will not want the job. However, this focus on hiring people without giving them a thorough understanding of what they are getting themselves into can backfire. Different people prefer different types of jobs and organizations. Once hired, they will obviously learn what the work and organizational culture are really like. If the fit is not good once people start work, they tend to leave. Companies are increasingly putting interactive features and questionnaires on their websites to communicate their culture and give applicants insights into what it is like to work there. This increases the accuracy of new employees' expectations, and decreases psychological contract violations.

realistic job previews (RJPs)
Involve the presentation of both positive and potentially negative information to job candidates

Realistic job previews (***RJPs***) involve the presentation of both positive and potentially negative information to job candidates. Rather than trying to sell candidates on the job and company by presenting the job opportunity in the most positive light, the company strives to present an accurate picture through an RJP. The goal is not to deter candidates, but rather to provide accurate information about the job and organization and build trust.[20] Hiring customers and using employee referrals are among the methods many companies use to give job candidates realistic information about what it would be like to work at that company.

If a common reason for employees leaving an organization is that the job is not what they expected, this is a good sign that the recruiting message can be improved. Giving applicants the opportunity to self-select out of the hiring process if they do not perceive themselves to be good fits with the position or organization increases the likelihood that the applicants ultimately hired will be good fits and will be better employees as a result. Given the relatively low cost associated with their development, RJPs may be useful for organizations trying to reduce turnover rates for jobs that departing employees say were not what they expected when they accepted job offers.

PERSONALITY AND INDIVIDUAL BEHAVIOR

Let's now begin to focus more specifically on the role and importance of an individual's personality as it relates to both work outcomes and the various forms of it. ***Personality*** is the relatively stable set of psychological attributes that distinguish one person from another. A longstanding debate among psychologists—often expressed as "nature versus nurture"—concerns the extent to which personality attributes are inherited from our parents (the "nature" argument) or shaped by our environment (the "nurture" argument). In reality, both biological and environmental factors play important roles in determining our personalities.[21] Although the details of this debate are beyond the scope of our discussion here, managers should strive to understand basic personality attributes and how they can affect people's behavior and fit in organizational situations, not to mention their perceptions of and attitudes toward the organization.

personality
The relatively stable set of psychological attributes that distinguish one person from another

The "Big Five" Framework

Psychologists have identified literally thousands of personality traits and dimensions that differentiate one person from another. But in recent years, researchers have identified five fundamental personality traits that are especially relevant to organizations.[22] These traits, illustrated in Figure 3.1, are now commonly called the ***"Big Five" personality traits***. As suggested by the figure, the personality of any given person can fall anywhere along each of these five traits.

"Big Five" personality traits
A set of five fundamental traits that are especially relevant to organizations

Agreeableness refers to a person's ability to get along with others. Agreeableness causes some people to be gentle, cooperative, forgiving, understanding, and good-natured in their dealings with others. Lack of it results in others' being irritable, short-tempered, uncooperative, and generally antagonistic toward other people. Researchers have not yet fully investigated the effects of agreeableness, but it seems likely that highly agreeable people are better at developing good working relationships with coworkers, subordinates, and higher-level managers, whereas less agreeable people are not likely to have particularly good working relationships. The same pattern might extend to relationships with customers, suppliers, and other key organizational constituents.

agreeableness
The ability to get along with others

Figure 3.1

The "big five" personality framework is currently very popular among researchers and managers. These five dimensions represent fundamental personality traits presumed to be important in determining the behaviors of individuals in organizations. In general, experts agree that personality traits closer to the left end of each dimension are more positive in organizational settings, whereas traits closer to the right are less positive.

"Big Five" personality traits

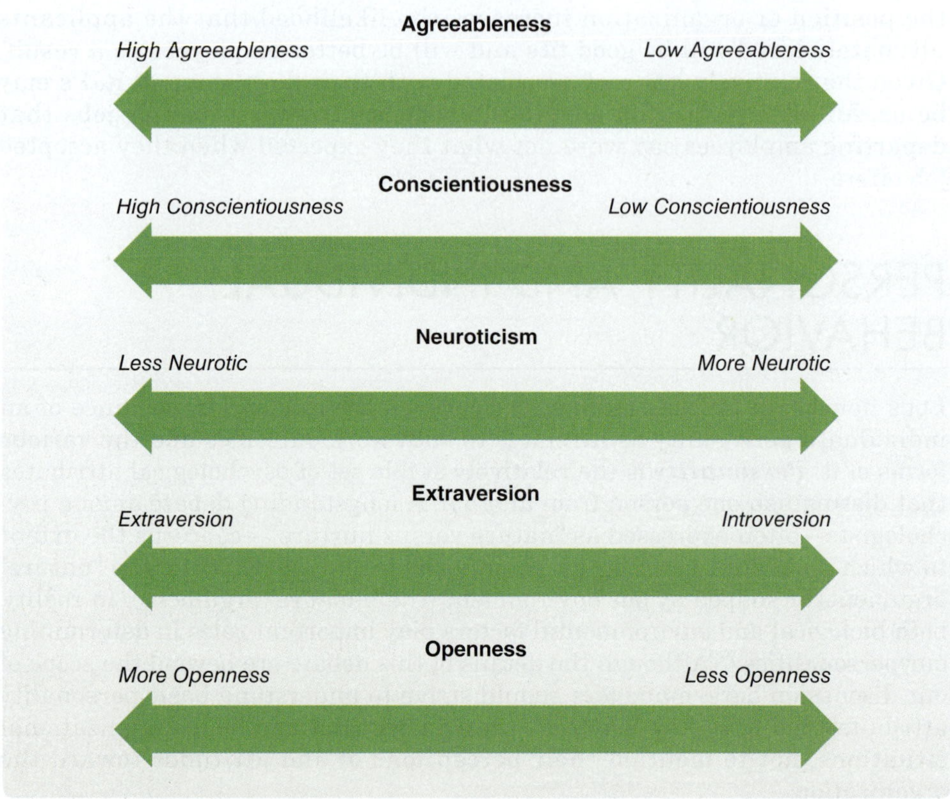

conscientiousness
Refers to an individual being dependable and organized

Conscientiousness refers to the extent to which a person can be counted on to get things done. Some people, for example, are organized, detail-oriented, responsible, dependable, and plan carefully to order to meet deadlines. These individuals can be characterized as being strong on conscientiousness. Less conscientious people may be prone to missing deadlines, overlooking various tasks, being unorganized, and being generally less dependable. In general, research suggests that being strong on conscientiousness is often a good predictor of job performance for many jobs.

neuroticism
Characterized by a person's tendency to experience unpleasant emotions such as anger, anxiety, depression, and feelings of vulnerability

The third of the Big Five personality dimensions is ***neuroticism***. People who are relatively more neurotic tend to experience unpleasant emotions such as anger, anxiety, depression, and feelings of vulnerability more often than do people who are relatively less neurotic. People who are less neurotic are relatively poised, calm, resilient, and secure; people who are more neurotic are more excitable, insecure, reactive, and subject to extreme mood swings. People with less neuroticism might be expected to better handle job stress, pressure, and tension. Their stability might also lead them to be seen as being more reliable than their less stable counterparts.

extraversion
The quality of being comfortable with relationships

Extraversion reflects a person's comfort level with relationships. Extroverts are sociable, talkative, assertive, and open to establishing new relationships. Introverts are much less sociable, talkative, and assertive, and more reluctant to begin new relationships. Research suggests that extroverts

Conscientiousness refers to the extent that a person can be counted on to get things done. This group is acknowledging the work of one of their colleagues and his efforts to help them complete a project on time. He most likely has a high level of conscientiousness. Further, given how his colleagues seem to genuinely like him he most likely also has a high degree of agreeableness.

DAVID WOOLLEY/DIGITAL VISION/GETTY IMAGES

tend to be higher overall job performers than introverts and that they are more likely to be attracted to jobs based on personal relationships, such as sales and marketing positions. For this particular trait, the opposite version is also given a name—***introversion***. An introvert tends to be less comfortable in social situations.

Finally, ***openness*** reflects a person's rigidity of beliefs and range of interests. People with high levels of openness are willing to listen to new ideas and to change their own ideas, beliefs, and attitudes in response to new information. They also tend to have broad interests and to be curious, imaginative, and creative. On the other hand, people with low levels of openness tend to be less receptive to new ideas and less willing to change their minds. Further, they tend to have fewer and narrower interests and to be less curious and creative. People with more openness might be expected to be better performers due to their flexibility and the likelihood that they will be better accepted by others in the organization. Openness may also encompass a person's willingness to accept change; people with high levels of openness may be more receptive to change, whereas people with little openness may resist change.

introversion
The tendency to be less comfortable in relationships and social situations

openness
The capacity to entertain new ideas and to change as a result of new information

The Big Five framework continues to attract the attention of both researchers and managers. The potential value of this framework is that it encompasses an integrated set of traits that appear to be valid predictors of certain behaviors in certain situations. Thus, managers who can both understand the framework and assess these traits in their employees are in a good position to understand how and why they behave as they do. On the other hand, managers must be careful to not overestimate their ability to assess the Big Five traits in others. Even assessment using the most rigorous and valid measures is likely to be somewhat imprecise. There are also times when using more specific personality traits to predict outcomes such as turnover or performance are more useful than the more general Big Five traits because the more specific trait more directly influences the intended outcome. For example, if you are trying to hire a strong team player for a diverse creative team, individual differences including a preference for teamwork and other group orientation (a preference for working with diverse others) may outperform any of the Big Five traits in predicting performance. Another limitation of the Big Five framework is that it is primarily based on research conducted in the United States. Thus, generalizing it to other cultures presents unanswered questions. Even within the United States, a variety of other factors and traits are also likely to affect behavior in organizations.

The Myers-Briggs Framework

The Myers-Briggs framework is also a popular framework that some people use to characterize personality. Many people know of this framework through a widely-used questionnaire called the Myers-Briggs Type Indicator, or MBTI.[23] More than 2 million people worldwide take the self-assessment inventory every year.[24] It is based upon Carl Jung's work on psychological types. Psychologist Carl Jung was a contemporary of Sigmund Freud and a leading exponent of Gestalt personality theory. The MBTI was first developed by Isabel Briggs Myers (1897–1979) and her mother, Katharine Cook Briggs, to help people understand themselves and each other so that they could find work that matches their personality. They put Jung's concepts into everyday language. Isabel Myers's 1980 book *Gifts Differing*, and her philosophy of celebrating individual differences, encouraged the workplace diversity movement. The MBTI uses four scales with opposite poles to assess four sets of preferences. The four scales are:[25]

1. *Extroversion (E)/Introversion (I)*: Extroverts are energized by things and people. They are interactors and "on the fly" thinkers whose motto is, "ready, fire, aim." Introverts find energy in ideas, concepts, and abstractions. They can be social, but also need quiet time to recharge their batteries. They are reflective thinkers whose motto is, "ready, aim, aim." Do you like to focus on the outer world (extroversion) or on your own inner world (introversion)?
2. *Sensing (S)/Intuition (N)*: Sensing people are detail oriented. They want and trust facts. Intuitive people seek out patterns and relationships among the facts they have learned. They trust their intuition and look for the "big picture." Do you prefer to focus on the information you take in (sensing) or do you like to interpret and add meaning (intuition)?
3. *Thinking (T)/Feeling (F)*: Thinkers value fairness, and decide things impersonally based on objective criteria and logic. Feelers value harmony, and focus on human values and needs as they make decisions or judgments. When you make decisions, do you like to first look at logic and consistency (thinking) or at the people and special circumstances involved (feeling)?
4. *Judging (J)/Perceiving (P)*: Judging people are decisive and tend to plan. They focus on completing tasks, take action quickly, and want to know the essentials. They develop plans and follow them, adhering to deadlines. Perceptive people are adaptable, spontaneous, and curious. They start many tasks, and often find it difficult to complete them. Deadlines are meant to be stretched. In dealing with the world, do you like to get things decided quickly (judging) or do you prefer to stay open to new information and options (perceiving)?

The possible combinations of these preferences result in sixteen personality types, which are identified by the four letters that represent one's tendencies on the four scales. For example, ENTJ reflects extraversion, intuition, thinking, and judging. You can complete a brief Myers-Briggs type self-assessment online at http://www.humanmetrics.com/cgi-win/JTypes2.asp.

Although the framework and Myers-Briggs instrument were not developed or intended to be used to identify personality profiles and label people, too often this is what is done with the results. This is problematic as it can lead to discrimination and poor career counseling. Employers should not hire, fire, or assign employees by personality type, because the MBTI is not even reliable at identifying a person's type. When retested, even after intervals as short as five weeks, as many as 50 percent of people are classified into a different type. There is little support for the claim that the MBTI can justify job discrimination or be a reliable aid to someone seeking career guidance.[26] Jung never intended for his work to be applied to a personality inventory. He noted, "My scheme of typology is only a scheme of orientation. There is such a factor as introversion, there is such a factor as extraversion. The classification of individuals means nothing, nothing at all. It is only the instrumentarium for the practical psychologist to explain, for instance, the husband to a wife or vice versa."[27] Nonetheless, the MBTI has become so popular that it is likely that you will encounter it during your career.[28] It can be a fun team-building tool for illustrating some of the ways that people differ, but it should not be used in making organizational decisions including hiring and promotions.

OTHER IMPORTANT PERSONALITY TRAITS

Besides these complex models of personality, several other specific personality traits are also likely to influence behavior in organizations. Among the most important are locus of control, self-efficacy, self-esteem, authoritarianism, Machiavellianism, tolerance for risk and ambiguity, Type A and Type B traits, and tendencies to bully. The role of the situation is also important.

Locus of Control

Locus of control is the extent to which people believe that their behavior has a real effect on what happens to them.[29] Some people, for example, believe that if they work hard they will succeed. They may also believe that people who fail do so because they lack ability or motivation. People who believe that individuals are in control of their lives are said to have an internal locus of control. Other people think that fate, chance, luck, or other people's behavior determines what happens to them. For example, an employee who fails to get a promotion may attribute that failure to a politically motivated boss or just bad luck, rather than to her or his own lack of skills or poor performance record. People who think that forces beyond their control dictate what happens to them are said to have an external locus of control. Table 3.2 summarizes the effects of locus of control on important organizational factors. This chapter's *Understand Yourself* feature gives you the opportunity to evaluate your locus of control when it comes to work.

locus of control
The extent to which one believes one's circumstances are a function of either one's own actions or of external factors beyond one's control

Table 3.2

Effects of Locus of Control on Organizational Outcomes

Organizational Outcome	Internal versus External Locus of Control
Job satisfaction	Internals are generally more satisfied with their job, pay, supervisor, and coworkers.
Commitment	Internals are more committed and have lower absenteeism.
Job motivation	Internals have greater task motivation, job involvement, and self-confidence than do externals.
Job performance	Internals tend to have higher job performance than externals.
Career success	Internals tend to earn a higher salary than do externals.
Conflict and stress	Internals report lower role conflict, work-family conflict, burnout, and stress than do externals.
Social integration	Internals tend to be more socially integrated at work and report more favorable relationships with their supervisors.

Source: See Ng, T.W.H., Sorensen, K.L., & Eby, L.T. (2006). Locus of Control at Work: A Meta-Analysis, *Journal of Organizational Behavior*, 27, 1057–1087.

Self-Efficacy

self-efficacy
A person's confidence in his or her ability to organize and execute the courses of action necessary to accomplish a specific task

general self-efficacy
Your generalized belief that you will be successful at whatever challenges or tasks you might face

Self-efficacy is our confidence in our ability to cope, perform, and be successful on a specific task. It is possible to have high self-esteem (I generally like myself and feel that I am a competent person) but low self-efficacy for certain tasks (I am poor at learning foreign languages). Self-efficacy is a key factor influencing motivation and engagement in an activity. It has also been found to reduce the negative effect of low job autonomy on psychological and physical stress.[30]

General self-efficacy reflects a generalized belief that we will be successful at whatever challenges or tasks we might face.[31] Because self-efficacy and general self-efficacy are related to setting higher goals, persisting in the face of obstacles, and performing better, it is important for you to maintain a positive sense of self-efficacy. Self-efficacy is even related to developing your skills, setting more challenging goals, seeking social support, and persisting longer in the face of challenges can help to build self-efficacy.

Self-Esteem

self-esteem
Our feelings of self-worth and our liking or disliking of ourselves

Self-esteem refers to our feelings of self-worth and our liking or disliking of ourselves.[32] Research suggests that self-esteem is strongly related to motivational processes such as specific self-efficacy, self-set goals, and effort as well as emotional processes, such as anxiety and regulating emotion.[33] Self-esteem is positively related to job performance[34] and learning.[35]

Authoritarianism

authoritarianism
The belief that power and status differences are appropriate within hierarchical social systems such as organizations

Another important personality characteristic is ***authoritarianism***, the extent to which a person believes that power and status differences are

UNDERSTAND YOURSELF

WORK LOCUS OF CONTROL

Using the scale below, write the number from 1 to 7 that reflects your agreement or disagreement with the statements below. When you are finished, follow the scoring instructions at the bottom to interpret your score.

strongly disagree	disagree	slightly disagree	neutral	slightly agree	agree	
1	2	3	4	5	6	7

___ 1. A job is what you make of it.

___ 2. On most jobs, people can pretty much accomplish whatever they set out to accomplish.

___ 3. If you know what you want out of a job, you can find a job that gives it to you.

___ 4. If employees are unhappy with a decision made by their boss, they should do something about it.

___ 5. Getting the job you want is mostly a matter of luck.

___ 6. Making money is primarily a matter of good fortune.

___ 7. Most people are capable of doing their jobs well if they make the effort.

___ 8. In order to get a really good job, you need to have family members or friends in high places.

___ 9. Promotions are usually a matter of good fortune.

___ 10. When it comes to landing a really good job, who you know is more important than what you know.

___ 11. Promotions are given to employees who perform well on the job.

___ 12. To make a lot of money you have to know the right people.

___ 13. It takes a lot of luck to be an outstanding employee on most jobs.

___ 14. People who perform their jobs well generally get rewarded for it.

___ 15. Most employees have more influence on their supervisors than they think they do.

___ 16. The main difference between people who make a lot of money and people who make a little money is luck.

Scoring: First recalculate your responses to items 1, 2, 3, 4, 7, 11, 14, and 15 by subtracting the number you wrote from 7. (6 = 1; 5 = 2; 4 = 3; 3 = 4; 2 = 5; 1 = 6). Cross out the number you initially wrote and replace it with the recoded value; only the new values will be used in scoring. Now add up your scores to all sixteen items to get your work locus of control score.

Interpretation: Higher scores reflect a more external locus of control. Managers tend to have a more internal locus of control.[36] If your score is not as low as you would like, review the questions and try to find ways to view yourself as being more in control of what happens to you.

Source: Copyright Paul E. Spector, All rights reserved, 1988.

appropriate within hierarchical social systems such as organizations.[37] For example, a person who is highly authoritarian may accept directives or orders from someone with more authority purely because the other person is "the boss." On the other hand, a person who is not highly authoritarian, although she or he may still carry out reasonable directives from the boss, is more likely to question things, express disagreement with the boss, and even refuse to carry out orders if they are for some reason objectionable. During the aftermath of the Enron and Arthur Anderson scandals that destroyed both firms, charges were brought against some accountants who shredded important documents before they could be seized by the authorities. The defense these individuals used was that they were simply following orders. To the extent a person engages in these kinds of behaviors knowing they are wrong but does

STUART JENNER/SHUTTERSTOCK.COM

Authoritarianism is the extent to which a person believes that power and status differences within organizations are appropriate. This individual is listening closely to instructions from his boss and seems intent on following those instructions. A person lower on authoritarianism might not be as receptive to direction.

so anyway in order to follow orders would suggest that the person is highly authoritarian.

Machiavellianism

Machiavellianism is another important personality trait. This concept is named after Niccolo Machiavelli, a sixteenth-century author. In his book *The Prince*, Machiavelli explained how the nobility could more easily gain and use power. The term "Machiavellianism" is now used to describe behavior directed at gaining power and controlling the behavior of others. Research suggests that the degree of Machiavellianism varies from person to person. More Machiavellian individuals tend to be rational and unemotional, may be willing to lie to attain their personal goals, put little emphasis on loyalty and friendship, and enjoy manipulating others' behavior. Less Machiavellian individuals are more emotional, less willing to lie to succeed, value loyalty and friendship highly, and get little personal pleasure from manipulating others. By all accounts, Dennis Kozlowski, the indicted former CEO of Tyco International, had a high degree of Machiavellianism. He apparently came to believe that his position of power in the company gave him the right to do just about anything he wanted with company resources.[38]

Machiavellianism
A trait causing a person to behave in ways to gain power and control the behavior of others

Tolerance for Risk and Ambiguity

Two other closely related traits are tolerance for risk and tolerance for ambiguity. ***Tolerance for risk*** (also called **risk propensity**) is the degree to which a person is comfortable accepting risk, willing to take chances and to make risky decisions. A manager with a high tolerance for risk, for example, might experiment with new ideas and gamble on new products. Such a manager might also lead the organization in new and different directions. This manager might be a catalyst for innovation or, if the risky decisions prove to be bad ones, might jeopardize the continued well-being of the organization. A manager with low tolerance for risk might lead an organization to stagnation and excessive conservatism, or might help the organization successfully weather turbulent and unpredictable times by maintaining stability and calm. Thus, the potential consequences of a manager's risk propensity depend heavily on the organization's environment.

tolerance for risk (or risk propensity)
The degree to which a person is comfortable with risk and is willing to take chances and make risky decisions

Tolerance for ambiguity reflects the tendency to view ambiguous situations as either threatening or desirable.[39] Intolerance for ambiguity reflects a tendency to perceive or interpret vague, incomplete, or fragmented information or information with multiple, inconsistent, or contradictory meanings as an actual or potential source of psychological discomfort or threat.[40] Being tolerant of ambiguity is related to creativity, positive attitudes toward risk, and orientation to diversity.[41] Managers with a low tolerance for ambiguity

tolerance for ambiguity
Reflects the tendency to view ambiguous situations as either threatening or desirable

A Type B personality describes someone who is relaxed easygoing, and less overtly competitive. This manager seems to be calm and relaxed as she completes a project. While we can't be certain, it would appear likely that she has a Type B personality.

MICHAELJUNG/SHUTTERSTOCK.COM

tend to be more directive with their staff and do not empower them to make their own decisions at work. The best managerial strategy is to place individuals with a low tolerance for ambiguity in well-defined and regulated tasks.

Type A and B traits

Two cardiologists identified a pair of different personality profiles they called Type A and Type B. The ***Type A personality*** is impatient, competitive, ambitious, and uptight. The ***Type B personality*** is more relaxed and easygoing and less overtly competitive than Type A. Type Bs are not without stress, but they confront challenges and external threats less frantically. Unlike Type As, Type Bs rarely experience a frustrated sense of wasting time when not actively engaged in productive activity.[42] Although Type As often have higher job performance than Type Bs,[43] Type As are also more prone to stress and coronary heart disease. Although the idea that a cause-and-effect relationship exists between Type A behavior and coronary artery disease is controversial, some effects of Type A stress are definitely known. Stress causes an increase in blood pressure; if the stress is constant, the heart and arteries begin to show signs of damage. It has been estimated that 14 to 18 percent of sudden heart attacks occur immediately after an emotional stress and are more likely to occur when a person is angry.[44] However, as shown in Figure 3.2, Type A and B profiles reflect extremes with most people simply tending toward one or the other.

Type A personality
Impatient, competitive, ambitious, and uptight

Type B personality
More relaxed and easygoing and less overtly competitive than Type A

Figure 3.2

Type A

- More competitive
- More devoted to work
- Stronger sense of time urgency

Type B

- Less competitive
- Less devoted to work
- Weaker sense of time urgency

Few people have extreme Type A or Type B personality profiles. Instead, people tend toward one type or the other. This is reflected by the overlap between the profiles shown here.

Understanding the personality type of your coworkers and boss can help you to better understand and manage this potential source of work conflicts. Recognizing your personality type can help you to identify work situations that are good fits for you. High Type As need greater stimulation than Type Bs and are more likely to overschedule themselves. In managers, having a high Type A personality and an external locus of control is associated with greater levels of perceived stress, lower job satisfaction, and poorer physical and mental health compared to those with a Type B personality and an internal locus of control. Some researchers have even suggested that negative health consequences may outweigh the superficial attractiveness of the Type A personality in a managerial position.[45]

The Bullying Personality

workplace bullying
Repeated mistreatment of another employee through verbal abuse; conduct that is threatening, humiliating, or intimidating; or sabotage that interferes with the other person's work

Workplace bullying is a repeated mistreatment of another employee through verbal abuse; conduct that is threatening, humiliating, or intimidating; or sabotage that interferes with the other person's work.[46] Popular media such as *Time, Management Today*, and *Psychology Today* have all featured stories on the pervasiveness of bullying. Bullying costs employers through higher turnover, greater absenteeism, higher workers' compensation costs, and higher disability insurance rates, not to mention a diminished reputation as a desirable place to work.[47] Fifty percent of the U.S. workforce reports either being bullied at work (35 percent) or witnessing bullying (15 percent). It is four times more common than harassment. Eighty-one percent of bullying behavior is done by supervisors.[48] Forty-five percent of targets report stress-related health problems; targeted individuals suffer debilitating anxiety, panic attacks, clinical depression, and even post-traumatic stress. Once targeted, employees have a 64 percent chance of losing their job for no reason. Despite this, 40 percent of targets never report it. Only 3 percent sue and 4 percent complain to state or federal agencies.[49]

Who tends to become a bully? Bullying is complex and comes in a variety of forms, but common to all types is the abuse of authority and power, stemming from the bully's need to control another person. Machiavellianism may lead to bullying. High Machiavellians exhibit a resistance to social influence, an orientation to cognitions (rational thoughts) rather than emotions, and a tendency toward initiating and controlling structure (components of bossiness). High Machiavellians manipulate and exploit others to advance their personal agendas, which is the foundation of bullying. If personality helps to explain why some people are bullies, can it also help us understand why some people are more likely to be targets of bullying? Although there is no clear personality profile that predicts who will be targeted, people who are more introverted, less agreeable, less conscientious, less open to experience, and more emotionally unstable seem to be more likely to be bullied.[50] This chapter's *Improve Your Skills* feature describes ways managers can be bullies (or just toxic), and describes various survival tactics (that we hope you'll never have to use!).

IMPROVE YOUR SKILLS

CHALLENGING MANAGERIAL BEHAVIORS AND HOW TO RESPOND

TYPES OF NARCISSISTIC MANAGERS

Varieties	Primary Traits	Objective	Subordinate Survival Tactics	Superior's Actions
Grandiose: Psychodynamic	Outward grandiose self-image; exploits others; devalues others; enraged if self-esteem threatened; limited conscience and capacity for empathy; desperately protects underlying fragile self-esteem	Be admired	Show admiration; avoid criticizing them; consult with mentor or executive coach	Close oversight of managers is needed to continually assess their treatment of others
Grandiose: Learned	Grandiose self-image; exploits others out of carelessness; is inconsiderate in treatment of others due to not receiving negative feedback for behavior	Be admired	Show admiration; avoid criticizing them; consult with mentor or executive coach	Do not automatically believe superiors over subordinates
Control Freak	Micromanages; seeks absolute control of everything; inflated self-image and devaluation of others' abilities; fears chaos	Control others	Avoid direct suggestions; let them think new ideas are their own; don't criticize them; show admiration and respect; don't outshine them; play down your accomplishments and ambition; document your work; build relationship with a mentor; look for other positions	360-degree feedback; place them where they cannot do serious harm; consider getting rid of them; don't ignore signs of trouble
Antisocial	Takes what he or she wants; lies to get ahead and hurts others if they are in his or her way; lacks both a conscience and capacity for empathy	Excitement of violating rules and abusing others	Avoid provoking them; transfer out before they destroy you; do not get dragged into their unethical or illegal activities; seek allies in coworkers and mentors; seek executive coach to help you cope	Consider possible presence of depression, anxiety, alcohol

Source: From Lubit, R. (2004, March/April). The Tyranny of Toxic Managers: Applying Emotional Intelligence to Deal with Difficult Personalities. *Ivey Business Journal*, p. 4.

Role of the Situation

The relationship between personality and behavior changes depending on the strength of the situation we are in. We might be extroverted in nature but, in a situation like a lecture or an important meeting, suppress our tendencies and behave in a more quiet and reserved way. When situational pressures are weak, we are better able to be ourselves and let our personalities guide our behaviors. Strong organizational cultures might decrease the influence of personality on employee behaviors by creating clear guidelines for employee behavior. Weaker organizational cultures might allow greater individual employee expression, resulting in a wider variety of employee behaviors.

You now have a good understanding of some of the ways we all differ. It is also interesting to think about how frequently there are differences in how people from other cultures perceive us. Asking foreigners to describe people from your country is a powerful way to understand how others perceive you. This chapter's *Global Issues* feature is from a *Newsweek* survey reporting the characteristics foreigners most and least often associate with Americans. It may give you some insight into how an American might be perceived differently in different parts of the world.

BALDYRGAN/SHUTTERSTOCK.COM

HOW OTHERS SEE AMERICANS

Characteristics Most Commonly Associated with Americans

France	Japan	Western Germany	Great Britain	Brazil	Mexico
Industrious	Nationalistic	Energetic	Friendly	Intelligent	Industrious
Energetic	Friendly	Inventive	Self-indulgent	Inventive	Intelligent
Inventive	Decisive	Friendly	Energetic	Energetic	Inventive
Decisive	Rude	Sophisticated	Industrious	Industrious	Decisive
Friendly	Self-indulgent	Intelligent	Nationalistic	Nationalistic	Greedy

Characteristics Least Commonly Associated with Americans

France	Japan	Western Germany	Great Britain	Brazil	Mexico
Lazy	Industrious	Lazy	Lazy	Lazy	Lazy
Rude	Lazy	Sexy	Sophisticated	Self-indulgent	Honest
Honest	Honest	Greedy	Sexy	Sexy	Rude
Sophisticated	Sexy	Rude	Decisive	Sophisticated	Sexy

Source: Adler, N. J. (2008). International Dimensions of Organizational Behavior. Mason, OH: Thompson/South-Western, p. 82, Table 3-1.

INTELLIGENCE

In addition to personality and personality traits, another important set of individual differences is intelligence. There are many types of intelligence, or mental abilities, including general mental ability, information processing capacity, verbal ability, and emotional intelligence.

General Mental Ability

General mental ability is the capacity to rapidly and fluidly acquire, process, and apply information. It involves reasoning, remembering, understanding, and problem solving. It is associated with the increased ability to acquire, process, and synthesize information and has been defined simply as the ability to learn.[51] The strong association between measures of general mental ability and performance in a wide variety of task domains is one of the most consistent findings in the field of organizational behavior.[52] Research has supported the idea that mental ability is most important in complex jobs, when individuals are new to the job, and when there are changes in the workplace that require workers to learn new ways of performing their jobs.[53] Some companies, including Google, prefer to hire for general mental ability rather than experience.[54]

general mental ability
The capacity to rapidly and fluidly acquire, process, and apply information

Information processing capacity involves the manner in which individuals process and organize information. Information processing capacity also helps explain differences between experts and novices on task learning and performance, as experts process and organize information more efficiently and accurately than novices.[55] General mental ability influences information processing capacity.[56] Age also explains differences in information processing capacity. Relative to younger adults, older adults tend to have access to a wider amount and variety of information, although they are less able to process novel information quickly.[57]

information processing capacity
Involves the manner in which individuals process and organize information

Mental ability tests typically use computerized or paper-and-pencil test formats to assess general mental abilities, including verbal or mathematical reasoning, logic, and perceptual abilities. Because scores on these tests can predict a person's ability to learn in training or on the job,[58] be adaptable and solve problems, and tolerate routine, their predictive value may increase given the trend toward jobs requiring innovation, continual training, and nonroutine problem solving. There are many different types of mental ability tests, including the Wonderlic Personnel Test, Raven's Progressive Matrices, the Kaufman Brief Intelligence Test, and the Wechsler Abbreviated Scale of Intelligence. Table 3.3 presents example items similar to those incorporated into the Wonderlic test.

Despite being easy to use and one of the most valid selection methods for all jobs, mental ability tests produce racial differences that are three to five times larger than other methods that are also valid predictors of job performance such as structured interviews.[59] Although the reasons for the different results are not fully understood, it is thought that factors including culture, differential access to test coaching and test preparation programs, and different test motivation levels could be important factors.[60] Job applicants also often dislike mental ability tests because they do not necessarily seem to be job related.[61]

Table 3.3

Mental Ability Test Items

The following questions are similar to those found on the Wonderlic Personnel Test measuring mental ability. The answers are at the bottom of the table.

1. Assume the first two statements are true. Is the final one (1) true (2) false or (3) not certain?
   - The girl plays soccer.
   - All soccer players wear cleats.
   - The girl wears cleats.
2. Paper sells for $0.36 per pad. What will three pads cost?
3. How many of the five pairs of items listed below are exact duplicates?

Pullman, K. M.	Puilman, K. M.
Jeffrey, C. K.	Jeffrey, C. K.
Schoeft, J. P.	Shoeft, J. P.
Lima, L. R.	Lima, L. R.
Woerner, K. E.	Woerner, K. C.

4. PRESENT PRESERVE—Do these words
   1. Have similar meanings?
   2. Have contradictory meanings?
   3. Mean neither the same nor the opposite?

Answers: (1) true; (2) $1.08; (3) 1; (4) 2.

Because hiring discrimination can be legally problematic when using mental ability tests,[62] it is best to evaluate the effect of mental ability tests on protected groups before using them on job candidates. Because mental ability tests can be combined with other predictors to reduce adverse impact and increase prediction accuracy, and because alternative predictors with less adverse impact can be used to predict job success comparably to mental ability tests used alone, generally mental ability tests should not be used alone.[63] Many organizations use mental ability tests, including the National Football League.[64]

Multiple Intelligences

Intelligence tests often involve a range of abstract questions designed to assess your language, spatial awareness, and numerical ability. However, to think that your score on a single test reflects your actual intelligence ignores your many other mental abilities. A lower score on a particular intelligence test result simply means you are less skilled at whatever type of intelligence that particular test measures—while reflecting nothing about your level of any other type of intelligence.

multiple intelligences
Suggests that there are a number of distinct forms of intelligence that each individual possesses in varying degrees

Increasingly, researchers and scholars are realizing that there is more than one way to be smart.[65] Gardner's theory of ***multiple intelligences*** suggests that there are a number of distinct forms of intelligence that each individual possesses in varying degrees:[66]

1. Linguistic: words and language
2. Logical-mathematical: logic and numbers
3. Musical: music, rhythm, and sound
4. Bodily-kinesthetic: body movement and control
5. Spatial-visual: images and space
6. Interpersonal: other people's feelings
7. Intrapersonal: self-awareness

The different intelligences represent not only different content domains but also learning preferences. The theory suggests that assessment of abilities should measure all forms of intelligence, not just linguistic and logical-mathematical, as is commonly done (e.g., in college admissions tests like the ACT, SAT, GMAT, and GRE).[67] According to this theory, learning and teaching should focus on the particular intelligences of each person. For example, if you have strong spatial or linguistic intelligences, you should be encouraged to develop these abilities.[68] The theory also emphasizes the cultural context of multiple intelligences. For instance, Gardner observed that the needs of different cultures lead them to emphasize different types of intelligence. For example, the high spatial abilities of the Puluwat people of the Caroline Islands enable them to navigate their ocean canoes, and a balance of personal intelligences is required in Japanese society.[69]

Knowing your strongest areas of intelligence can guide you to the most appropriate job and learning environments to enable you to achieve your potential. For example, compare your intelligence strengths to the job types in Table 3.4. As a manager, it is possible to develop the same skills in different ways for different subordinates. For example in diversity training, bodily-kinesthetic learners could engage in role-plays while spatial-visual subordinates could create posters conveying the material being taught. Using a person's preferred learning style helps to make learning easy and enjoyable.

Emotional Intelligence

Emotional intelligence (***EI***) is an interpersonal capability that includes the ability to perceive and express emotions, to understand and use them, and to manage emotions in oneself and other people.[70] Expert Daniel Goleman defines emotional intelligence as "the capacity for recognizing our own feelings and those of others, for motivating ourselves, and for managing emotions well in ourselves and in our relationships."[71] He describes five dimensions of EI that include three personal competencies (self-awareness, self-regulation, and motivation) and two social competencies (empathy and social skills). Emotional capabilities may operate at multiple levels to influence change in organizations.[72] EI may also influence employee emotional reactions to job insecurity and their coping with associated stresses.[73] Emotional intelligence involves using emotional regulatory processes to control anxiety and other negative emotional reactions and to generate positive emotional reactions.[74]

emotional intelligence (EI)
An interpersonal capability that includes the ability to perceive and express emotions, to understand and use them, and to manage emotions in oneself and other people

Table 3.4

Matching Intelligence Types with Career Choices

Type of Intelligence	Related Careers	Preferred Learning Style
*Bodily-Kinesthetic:*physical agility and balance; body control; hand-eye coordination	Athletes, firefighters, chefs, actors, gardeners	Touch and feel, physical experience
Interpersonal: ability to relate to others and perceive their feelings; interprets behaviors of others; relates to emotional intelligence	Psychologists, doctors, educators, salespeople, politicians	Human contact, teamwork
Intrapersonal: self-awareness; understands oneself and one's relationship to others and to the world; relates to emotional intelligence	Related to success in almost all careers	Self-reflection, self-discovery
*Linguistic:*verbal and written language; explaining and interpreting ideas and information	Authors, speakers, lawyers, TV and radio hosts, translators	Verbal and written words and language
Logical-Mathematical: logic and pattern detection; analytical; problem solving; excels at math	Engineers, directors, scientists, researchers, accountants, statisticians	Logic and numbers
*Musical:*recognition of rhythm and tonal patterns; musical ability; high awareness and use of sound	Musicians, DJs, music teachers, acoustic engineers, music producers, composers	Music, sounds, rhythm
Spatial-Visual: creation and interpretation of visual images; visual and special perception	Artists, engineers, photographers, inventors, beauty consultants	Pictures, shapes, visually

Source: Based on Gardner, H. (1983). *Frames of Mind.* New York: Basic Books; Gardner, H. (1993a). *Multiple Intelligences: The Theory in Practice.* NY: Basic Books; Gardner, H. (1993b). Creating Minds. NY: Basic Books; Marks-Tarlow, T. (1995). Creativity Inside Out: Learning Through Multiple *Intelligences.* Reading, MA: Addison-Wesley.

Negative emotions, such as anxiety or frustration, are distracting and result in diminished learning and performance.[75] Emotional regulation and control may also be important in managing distracting positive emotions at work. The five dimensions comprising emotional intelligence are:

1. Self-awareness: being aware of what you are feeling
2. Self-motivation: persisting in the face of obstacles, setbacks, and failures
3. Self-management: managing your own emotions and impulses
4. Empathy: sensing how others are feeling
5. Social skills: effectively handling the emotions of others

People differ in the degree to which they are able to recognize the emotional meaning of others' facial expressions, although seven universal emotions are expressed in the face in exactly the same way regardless of race, culture, ethnicity, age, gender, or religion.[76] These emotions are joy, sadness, fear, surprise, anger, contempt, and disgust. Recognizing and understanding these emotions is important in communicating, establishing relationships, building rapport, negotiating, and many other managerial tasks. More effective communicators better recognize the emotions being conveyed by peoples' facial expressions.[77]

CASE STUDY Emotional Intelligence at FedEx

Global shipping company FedEx has a "people first" philosophy and believes that for the company to deliver world class customer service its managers must also have an attitude of service in managing their associates. FedEx has received numerous awards for being one of the world's most respected and admired companies for over ten years,[78] and is one of the world's most successful businesses. Although the company is focused on speed and logistics, from the start it recognized that its employees were the key to the company's success, and that leadership would be essential to effective management.[79] Fit with a service-oriented culture is taken so seriously that one of FedEx's core managerial values is to be a servant leader.[80]

FedEx recognizes that leadership has grown more complex, and wants to develop leadership capabilities in its managers to manage its changing workforce. The company wants leaders who make fast and accurate decisions, are able to influence others and motivate them to give their full effort, and who can help build a culture where employees drive for exceptional performance in a sustainable way that creates value for all of its stakeholders.[81] Jimmy Daniel, senior leadership facilitator at the FedEx Global Leadership Institute, said, "Some leaders have an innate ability to provide what's needed to create a satisfying and rewarding work environment for employees, but many others need to develop this skill set."[82] To measure leadership performance, FedEx administers an annual survey where all employees can provide feedback about their managers. The survey's themes include fairness, respect, listening, and trust. A recognition that all of these characteristics are related to relationships and emotions created an interest in emotional intelligence as a learnable skillset that would enhance managers' ability to lead in the FedEx way.[83]

FedEx decided to increase its focus on emotional intelligence in its leadership development training to give all new managers a strong people-first foundation on which to build their managerial careers. To build teams in which employees give their full effort, FedEx believes that task-based management is insufficient and leaders need to manage their own emotions and behaviors to effectively serve as role models, mentors, and motivators at an emotional level.[84] A five-day course and six-month follow up coaching process was developed to identify new managers' strengths and give them specific emotional intelligence competencies to improve on.

The emotional intelligence training and coaching program focused on showing managers how to manage themselves first and take charge of their own emotions and behaviors so that they can be effective influencers and role models. The majority of leaders showed large improvements in relationships, influence, and decision making as a result of their improved empathy, emotional literacy, and ability to navigate emotions.[85] FedEx has been extremely pleased with the success of the emotional intelligence development program, training over 100 facilitators to run the program and coach new leaders worldwide.[86]

Questions:

1. Do you think that emotional intelligence would be important for a manager at FedEx to have? Explain your answer.
2. How does FedEx develop its new leaders' emotional intelligence?
3. What else do you think that FedEx can do to enhance its managers' emotional intelligence?

There is some evidence that components of EI are malleable skills that can be developed, including facial expression recognition.[87] The ability to understand what others think and feel, knowing how to appropriately persuade and motivate them, and knowing how to resolve conflicts and forge cooperation are some of the most important skills of successful managers. You can get a rough estimate of your EI by taking the EI self-assessment from About.com at http://psychology.about.com/library/quiz/bl_eq_quiz.htm.

There is also controversy associated with the concepts of EI.[88] Some have argued that its theoretical conceptualization is unclear because it is overly inclusive, lacks specificity, and encompasses both static trait components and malleable state components. It is not clear if it is simply a learned skill or an innate capability. Several researchers have also argued that EI is simply a surrogate for general intelligence and well-established personality traits.[89] However, a number of studies have supported the usefulness of EI.[90] EI has been found to be related to, and yet distinct from, personality dimensions; and various measures of EI provided incremental predictive power regarding life satisfaction and job performance, even after controlling for Big Five personality dimensions.[91] It appears that, although controversies still exist, EI is distinct from other ability and personality trait measures. There is some ambiguity about the degree to which EI is considered a malleable and trainable set of competencies versus a stable set of personality traits or emotional abilities; however, EI does relate to job performance, adjustments to stressful situations, and pro-social behaviors. This chapter's *Case Study* explores how FedEx incorporated emotional intelligence into its new leader training program.

LEARNING STYLES

The final individual difference we will address in this chapter is learning style. ***Learning style*** refers to individual differences and preferences in how we process information when problem solving, learning, or engaging in similar activities.[92] There are numerous typologies, measures, and models that capture these differences and preferences. Most of these approaches have focused on child learning, but there is evidence that these differences are important for adults as well.[93] Next we'll discuss several of the most popular approaches to learning styles.

learning style
Refers to individual differences and preferences in how we process information when problem solving, learning, or engaging in similar activities

Sensory Modalities

One approach addresses our preference for sensory modality. A *sensory modality* is a system that interacts with the environment through one of the basic senses.[94] The most important sensory modalities are:

- Visual: learning by seeing
- Auditory: learning by hearing
- Tactile: learning by touching
- Kinesthetic: learning by doing

According to researchers, about 20 to 30 percent of American students are auditory; about 40 percent are visual; and the remaining 30 to 40 percent are either tactile/kinesthetic, visual/tactile, or some combinations of the above major senses.[95]

Learning Style Inventory

A second approach to understanding learning styles, the Kolb Learning Style Inventory, is one of the more dominant approaches to categorizing cognitive styles.[96] According to David Kolb, the four basic learning modes are active experimentation, reflective observation, concrete experience, and abstract conceptualization. In addition, the learning process is considered from the two dimensions of active/passive and concrete/abstract.[97] Kolb suggests that there are four basic learning styles:[98]

1. Convergers: depend primarily on active experimentation and abstract conceptualization to learn. People with this style are superior in technical tasks and problems and inferior in interpersonal learning settings.
2. Divergers: depend primarily on concrete experience and reflective observation. People with this style tend to organize concrete situations from different perspectives and structure their relationships into a meaningful whole. They are superior in generating alternative hypotheses and ideas, and tend to be imaginative and people or feeling-oriented.
3. Assimilators: depend on abstract conceptualization and reflective observation. These individuals tend to be more concerned about abstract concepts and ideas than about people. They also tend to focus on the logical soundness and preciseness of ideas, rather than the ideas' practical values; they tend to work in research and planning units.
4. Accommodators: rely mainly on active experimentation and concrete experience, and focus on risk taking, opportunity seeking, and action. Accommodators tend to deal with people easily and specialize in action-oriented jobs, such as marketing and sales.

Although much has been written about cognitive styles, there are wide gaps in our current understanding. There are many differences in how styles are conceptualized,[99] and there have been numerous criticisms of Kolb's measures and the underlying theory.[100] These measures are subject to a variety of statistical and inferential problems, and many show low reliability.[101] Most of the research has also focused on children—less work has focused on how the styles influence adult learning. Despite these limitations, evidence suggests that cognitive and learning styles may be important for understanding human behavior and performance in a variety of contexts.

Learning Style Orientations

Finally, Annette Towler and Robert Dipboye[102] developed a learning style orientation measure to address some of the limitations of the Kolb inventory and identify key styles and preferences for learning. They demonstrated that learning style orientations predict preferences for instructional methods beyond the Big Five personality traits. They identified five key factors:

1. Discovery learning: an inclination for exploration during learning. Discovery learners prefer subjective assessments, interactional activities, informational methods, and active-reflective activities.
2. Experiential learning: a desire for hands-on approaches to instruction. Experiential learning is positively related to a preference for action activities.
3. Observational learning: a preference for external stimuli such as demonstrations and diagrams to help facilitate learning. Observational learning is positively related to preference for informational methods and active-reflective methods.

4. Structured learning: a preference for processing strategies such as taking notes, writing down task steps, and so forth. Structured learning is related to preferences for subjective assessments.
5. Group learning: a preference to work with others while learning. Group learning is related to preferences for action and interactional learning.

SUMMARY AND APPLICATION

Understanding individuals in organizations is important for all managers. A basic framework for facilitating this understanding is the psychological contract—people's expectations regarding what they will contribute to the organization and what they will get in return. Organizations strive to achieve an optimal person-job fit, but this process is complicated by the existence of individual differences.

Personalities are the relatively stable sets of psychological and behavioral attributes that distinguish one person from another. The Big Five personality traits are agreeableness, conscientiousness, neuroticism, extraversion, and openness. Myers-Briggs dimensions and emotional intelligence also offer insights into personalities in organizations. Other important traits are locus of control, self-efficacy, self-esteem, authoritarianism, Machiavellianism, tolerance for risk and ambiguity, Type A and Type B traits, and tendencies to bully. The role of the situation is also important. Learning styles, or individual differences and preferences in how we process information when problem solving, learning, or engaging in similar activities, are also important individual differences and preferences, and there are numerous typologies, measures, and models that capture them. (In Chapter 5 we will discuss learning from a different perspective—the role of learning in work motivation.)

Everyone is different. We each have different personalities, demographics, and intelligences. By understanding the characteristics of your coworkers, managers, and subordinates, you will be best able to choose the OB tool or management style that will be most effective. Remember, flexibility is the key to effective management. We next continue our discussion of other important individual differences that affect organizational behavior in Chapter 4. Among the major topics we will cover in that chapter are attitudes, values, emotions, perception, and stress.

DISCUSSION QUESTIONS

1. What is a psychological contract? Why is it important? What psychological contracts do you currently have?
2. What individual differences do you feel are most important to organizations? Why?
3. If you were denied a job because of your score on a personality test, what would be your reaction?
4. If your supervisor exhibited bullying behaviors, what would you do?
5. Which of Gardner's multiple intelligences do you feel are most important for managers?

LOSKUTNIKOV/SHUTTERSTOCK.COM

REAL WORLD RESPONSE

INDIVIDUAL DIFFERENCES THAT MAKE A DIFFERENCE AT SOUTHWEST AIRLINES

Southwest Airlines looks for employees with positive attitudes and leadership skills, who fit well with the company's fun and unique culture. Their investment of time and resources in finding the right talent has paid off in lower turnover, increased internal promotion rates, and higher productivity.[103]

Instead of evaluating flight attendant candidates on a fixed set of skills, Southwest looks for their attitude toward others, work ethic, and their ability to work effectively on a team.[104] Flight attendant candidates do more than interview for a job, they audition—and the audition begins the moment they request an application. Managers jot down anything memorable about the initial conversation, both good and bad. When flying candidates out for interviews, their special tickets alert gate agents, flight attendants, and others to pay special attention to them. Employees observe whether recruits are consistently friendly to the crew and to other passengers or if they are complaining and drinking cocktails at 9 A.M., and they pass these observations on to the People Department.[105]

Flight attendant recruits are evaluated even when they think that they are not being assessed. During the five-minute speeches flight attendant job candidates must give about themselves in front of as many as fifty other recruits, managers watch the audience as closely as the speaker. Unselfish people who enthusiastically support their potential coworkers are the ones who catch Southwest's eye, not the applicants who seem bored or use the time solely to improve their own presentations.[106]

Prospective employees are often asked during an interview how they recently used their sense of humor in a work environment and how they have used humor to defuse a difficult situation. Southwest also looks for humor in the interactions people have with each other during group interviews.[107] To assess leadership, Southwest Airlines uses a group assessment exercise called Fallout Shelter, in which candidates imagine they are a committee charged with rebuilding civilization after a nuclear war. Groups are given a list of fifteen people from different occupations, including nurse, teacher, all-sport athlete, biochemist, and pop singer, and have ten minutes to make a unanimous decision about which seven people can remain in the only available fallout shelter. Each candidate is graded on a scale ranging from "passive" to "active" to "leader" as they propose, discuss, and debate the decision.[108]

Southwest consistently has the highest productivity numbers in the industry.[109] Southwest's hiring methods not only ensure that it hires people whose personalities fit the company's culture, but also help the company execute its customer service strategy.

6. Do you think emotional intelligence is important to managers? How would you assess emotional intelligence in deciding who to promote to a managerial position?
7. If you were a manager, what individual differences would be important to you in hiring an assistant? Why?

UNDERSTAND YOURSELF EXERCISE

Work Locus of Control

This chapter's Understand Yourself feature gave you the chance to self-assess your work locus of control. Higher scores on the measure reflect a more external locus of control. Managers tend to have a more internal locus of control. After completing the self-assessment, answer the following questions:

1. Do you think that your score accurately reflects your locus of control at work? Why or why not?
2. How do you think that work locus of control might influence your effectiveness as a manager?
3. What do you think is the ideal locus of control in a work setting and why?
4. What might you do in the next year to make your work locus of control consistent with your answer to number 3?

GROUP EXERCISE

Strengths-Based Development

When drought threatened the survival of Ohio farming co-op Auglaize Provico, CEO Larry Hammond realized that he would have to change the business model. Grain elevators were sold, headcount was carefully reduced 25 percent, and the co-op took on work outside of its previous core business. Hammond even cut his own pay.

Hammond then implemented strengths-based development to leverage the unique strengths and talents of each employee. The strengths approach recognizes that everyone has different talents and natural patterns of thought, feeling, and behavior. Recognizing and building on those talents with pertinent skills and knowledge creates strengths. People who are applying a true strength tend to perform well. Hammond hoped that encouraging employees to leverage their innate talents would enable them to drive the business forward.

Auglaize's management had previously used a "deficit" development approach, spending a lot of time identifying employees' weaknesses and trying to correct them. This meant that a lot of Auglaize's management was relatively negative. Hammond wanted to change that approach. He says, "If you really want to [excel], you have to know yourself—you have to know what you're good at, and you have to know what you're not so good at, and a lot of people don't. Most of us know what we're not good at because people tell us. And we also tend to want to fix it." The idea that workers should "fix" their weaknesses is common, but it can be problematic because attempts to fix weaknesses take time, attention, and energy away from maximizing naturally powerful talents.

Employees also enjoy using their talents and doing something well instead of struggling against their weaknesses to produce mediocre work.

Every employee in the co-op took an assessment to measure and identify his or her top five talents, and received at least two consultations on their individual strengths. This enabled Auglaize to build on what its employees naturally do best. Employees became more engaged, productive, and energized, and the organization became more successful. As one expert says, "One issue is that the people who are really valued often don't know who they are, especially in times of change. If managers regularly give positive feedback to key performers, it increases their confidence to undertake greater challenges and reinforces their commitment."

Questions:

1. Do you think it is better to focus on assessing and developing employees' weaknesses, or to focus on their strengths? Why?
2. Why would strengths-based development increase employee engagement?
3. If you were a manager, how might you interact with employees differently if you were using strengths-based development rather than deficit-based development?

Source: Robison, J. (2007). Great Leadership Under Fire. *Gallup Management Journal*. Available online at: http://gmj.gallup.com/content/26569/Great-Leadership-Under-Fire.aspx; Local Ag Companies Merge to Form New Cooperative. *Sidney Daily News*, February 20, 2008, 8; Zelm, A. (2008). Farm Firm Poised for Expansion. *The Evening Leader*. March 10, page A1.

VIDEO EXERCISE

Barcelona Restaurant Group is always trying to attract and retain only those employees who reinforce its service-oriented culture and provide top quality customer service. The manager being interviewed in the video is constantly recruiting and hiring new employees and letting low performers and poor fits go. He also tries to provide job candidates with a realistic description of the company's expectations to ensure that they know what they would be getting into if they took a job with the company.

As a class, watch "Barcelona" (6:04) and then individually consider the following questions. After you have come up with your own ideas, form groups of 4-5 people and discuss your insights. Be sure to nominate someone to serve as a spokesperson to share your ideas with the class.

1. How does the Barcelona Restaurant Group focus on fit? What types of fit does Barcelona try to optimize when hiring?
2. How does sending managerial candidates on a $100 "Shop" serve as a realistic job preview? Explain why you think this would or would not be effective in helping job candidates assess their fit with the Barcelona Restaurant Group.
3. Besides the "Shop", how else does Barcelona try to maximize employee fit? What other suggestions do you have for the company to improve new hires' fit with the job and organization?

VIDEO CASE Now What?

PERCOM/SHUTTERSTOCK.COM

While waiting for a customer phone call with two subordinates, imagine that another subordinate walks into the room and exhibits agitated behavior after being unable to find something. The other employees in the room clearly feel uncomfortable as a result of this behavior. *What do you say or do?* Go to this chapter's "Now What?" video, watch the challenge video, and choose a response. Be sure to also view the outcomes of the two responses you didn't choose.

Discussion Questions

1. Which aspects of management and organizational behavior discussed in this chapter are illustrated in these videos? Explain your answer.
2. Which do you feel is more important at work, an employee's behavior or performance? Why?
3. As a manager, what else might you do to effectively handle this situation?

ENDNOTES

[1]Pfeffer, J. (1998). The Human Equation: Building Profits by Putting People First. Boston, MA: Harvard Business School Press.

[2]Rutherford, L. (2012). How Does Southwest Airlines Screen Candidates for Culture? *Workforce.com*, April 3. Available online: http://www.workforce.com/article/20120403/DEAR_WORKFORCE/120409976.

[3]The Mission of Southwest Airlines. Available online: http://www.southwest.com/about_swa/mission.html.

[4]Maxon, T. (2010, February 17). Southwest Airlines Ranks No. 2 on List of "Best Companies for Leadership." *Dallas News*. Available online: http://aviationblog.dallasnews.com/archives/2010/02/southwest-airlines-ranks-no-2.html.

[5]Towler, A., & Dipboye, R. L. (2003) Development of a Learning Style Orientation Measure. *Organizational Research Methods*, *6*, 216–235. © 2003 by SAGE Publications. Reprinted by permission of SAGE Publications.

[6]Mount, M. K., & Barrick, M. R. (1995). The Big Five Personality Dimensions. *Research in Personnel and Human Resource Management*, *13*, 153–200.

[7]For a more extensive discussion, see Kristof-Brown, A. L., Zimmerman, R. D., & Johnson, E. C. (2005). Consequences of Individuals' Fit at Work: A Meta-Analysis of Person-Job, Person-Organization, Person-Group, and Person-Supervisor Fit. *Personnel Psychology*, *58*, 281–342.

[8]Adapted from Edwards, J. R. (1991). Person-Job Fit: A Conceptual Integration, Literature Review, and Methodological Critique. In *International Review of Industrial and Organizational Psychology*, eds. C. L. Cooper and I. T. Robertson (Vol. 6, pp. 283–357). New York: John Wiley & Sons.

[9]Kristof-Brown, A. L., Zimmerman, R. D., & Johnson, E. C. (2005). Consequences of Individuals' Fit at Work: A Meta-Analysis of Person-Job, Person-Organization, Person-Group, and Person-Supervisor Fit. *Personnel Psychology*, *58*, 281–342.

[10]Werbel, J. D., & Gilliland, S. W. (1999). Person-Environment Fit in the Selection Process. In *Research in Personnel and Human Resource Management*, ed. G. R. Ferris (Vol. 17, pp. 209–243). Stamford, CT: JAI Press.

[11]Sinton, P. (2000, February 23). Teamwork the Name of the Game for Ideo. *San Francisco Chronicle*, B3.

[12]Kristof, A. L. (1996). Person-Organization Fit: An Integrative Review of Its Conceptualizations, Measurement, and Implications. *Personnel Psychology*, *49*, 1–50; Kristof, A. L. (2000). Perceived Applicant Fit: Distinguishing Between Recruiters' Perceptions of Person-Job and Person-Organization Fit. *Personnel Psychology*, *53*, 643–671.

[13]E.g., Chatman, J. (1989). Improving Interactional Organizational Research: A Model of Person-Organization Fit. *Academy of Management Review*, *14*, 333–349; Chatman, J. (1991). Matching People and Organizations: Selection and Socialization in Public Accounting Firms. *Administrative Science Quarterly*, *36*, 459–484; Vancouver, J. B., & Schmitt. N. W. (1991). An Exploratory Examination of Person-Organization Fit: Organizational Goal Congruence. *Personnel Psychology*, *44*, 333–352.

[14]Kristof-Brown, A. L., Zimmerman, R. D., & Johnson, E. C. (2005). Consequences of Individuals' Fit at Work: A Meta-Analysis of Person-Job, Person-Organization, Person-Group, and Person-Supervisor Fit. *Personnel Psychology*, *58*, 281–342.

[15]Kristof-Brown, A. L., Zimmerman, R. D., & Johnson, E. C. (2005). Consequences of Individuals' Fit at Work: A Meta-Analysis of Person-Job, Person-Organization, Person-Group, and Person-Supervisor Fit. *Personnel Psychology*, *58*, 281–342.

[16]Sekiguchi, T. & Huber, V. L. (2011). The Use of Person-Organization Fit and Person-Job Fit Information in Making Selection Decisions, *Organizational Behavior and Human Decision Processes, 116*(2), 203–216; O'Reilly, III, C. A., Chatman, J., & Caldwell, D. V. (1991). People and Organizational Culture: A Profile Comparison Approach to Assessing Person-Organization Fit. *Academy of Management Journal*, *34*, 487–516.

[17]McGregor, J. (2009, March 23 & 30). Zappos' Secret: It's an Open Book. *BusinessWeek,* 62.

[18]Ashford, S. J., & Taylor, M. S. (1990). Adaptations to Work Transitions: An Integrative Approach. In *Research in Personnel and Human Resources Management*, eds. G. Ferris & K. Rowland (Vol. 8, pp. 1–39). Greenwich, CT: JAI Press.

[19]Holland, J. L. (1985). *Making Vocational Choices: A Theory of Vocation Personalities and Work Environments.* Englewood Cliffs, NJ: Prentice-Hall.

[20]See Earnest, D. R., Allen, D. G. & Landis, R. S. (2011). Mechanisms Linking Realistic Job Previews with Turnover: A Meta-Analytic Path Analysis, *Personnel Psychology*, *64*(4), 865–897; Phillips, J. M. (1998). Effects of Realistic Job Previews on Multiple Organizational Outcomes: A Meta-Analysis. *Academy of Management Journal*, *41*, 673–690.

[21]See McAdams, D. & Olson, B. (2010). Personality Development: Continuity and Change Over the Life Course. In *Annual Review of Psychology*, eds. Fiske, S., Schacter, D., & Sternberg, R. (Vol. 61, pp. 517–542). Palo Alto, CA: Annual Reviews.

[22]Barrick, M. R., & Mount, M. K. (1991). The Big Five Personality Dimensions and Job Performance: A Meta-Analysis, *Personnel Psychology*, *44*, 1–26.

[23]The MBTI instrument is available from Consulting Psychological Press in Palo Alto, California.

[24]*MBTI Basics.* (2009). The Myers & Briggs Foundation. Available online: http://www.myersbriggs.org/my-mbti-personality-type/mbti-basics/.

[25]Based on Briggs Myers, I. (1995). *Gifts Differing: Understanding Personality Type.* Palo Alto, CA: Davies-Black; Brightman, H. J. (2009). *GMU Master Teacher Program: On Learning Styles.* Available online: http://www2.gsu.edu/~dschjb/wwwmbti.html; *MBTI Basics*. (2009). The Myers & Briggs Foundation. Available online: http://www.myersbriggs.org/my-mbti-personality-type/mbti-basics/.

[26]Pittenger, D. J. (1993, Fall). Measuring the MBTI and Coming Up Short. *Journal of Career Planning and Placement.* Available online: http://www.indiana.edu/~jobtalk/HRMWebsite/hrm/articles/develop/mbti.pdf.

[27]McGuire, W., & Hull, R. F. C. (eds.). (1977). *C. G. Jung Speaking* (p. 305). Princeton, NJ: Princeton University Press.

[28]Lloyd, J. B. (2012). The Myers-Briggs Type Indicator and Mainstream Psychology: Analysis and Evaluation of an Unresolved Hostility. *Journal of Beliefs & Values: Studies in Religion & Education*, *33*, 23–34, Waters, R. J. (2012). Learning Style Instruments: Reasons Why Research Evidence Might Have a Weak Influence on Practitioner Choice. *Human Resource Development International*, *15*(1), 119–129.

[29]Rotter, J. B. (1966). Generalized Expectancies for Internal vs. External Control of Reinforcement. *Psychological Monographs* (Vol. 80, pp. 1–28). Washington, DC: American Psychological Association; De Brabander, B. & Boone, C. (1990). Sex Differences in Perceived Locus of Control. *Journal of Social Psychology, 130*, 271–276.

[30]Spector, P. E. (1988). Development of the Work Locus of Control Scale. *Journal of Occupational Psychology*, *61*, 335–340.

[31]Nauta, M.M., Liu, C. & Li, C. (2010). A Cross-National Examination of Self-Efficacy as a Moderator of Autonomy/Job Strain Relationships, *Applied Psychology, 59*(1), 159–179.

[32]Chen, G., Gully, S. M., & Eden, D. (2001). Validation of a New General Self-Efficacy Scale. *Organizational Research Methods, 4,* 62–83.

[33]Brockner, J. (1988). *Self-Esteem at Work: Research, Theory, and Practice*. Lexington, MA: Lexington Books; Chen, G., Gully, S. M., & Eden, D. (2004). General Self-Efficacy and Self-Esteem: Toward Theoretical and Empirical Distinction Between Correlated Self-Evaluations. *Journal of Organizational Behavior, 25,* 375–395.

[34]Chen, G., Gully, S. M., & Eden, D. (2004). General Self-Efficacy and Self-Esteem: Toward Theoretical and Empirical Distinction Between Correlated Self-Evaluations. *Journal of Organizational Behavior, 25,* 375–395.

[35]Judge, T. A., & Bono, J. E. (2001). Relationship of Core Self-Evaluations Traits—Self-Esteem, Generalized Self-Efficacy, Locus of Control, and Emotional Stability—With Job Satisfaction and Job Performance: A Meta-Analysis. *Journal of Applied Psychology, 86*(1), 80–92.

[36]Chen, G., Gully, S. M., & Eden, D. (2004). General Self-Efficacy and Self-Esteem: Toward Theoretical and Empirical Distinction Between Correlated Self-Evaluations. *Journal of Organizational Behavior, 25,* 375–395.

[37]Adorno, T. W., Frenkel-Brunswick, E., Levinson, D. J., & Sanford, R. N. (1950). *The Authoritarian Personality.* New York: Harper & Row.

[38]The Rise and Fall of Dennis Kozlowski. *Business Week*, December 23, 2002, 64–77.

[39]Budner, S. (1962). Intolerance of Ambiguity as a Personality Variable. *Journal of Personality*, *30*, 29–50; MacDonald, A. P., Jr. (1970). Revised Scale for Ambiguity Tolerance: Reliability and Validity. *Psychological Reports*, *26*, 791–798.

[40]Furnham, A. (1995). Tolerance of Ambiguity: A Review of the Concept, Its Measurement and Applications. *Current Psychology*, *14*, 179.

[41]See Kirton, M. J. (2004). *Adaption-Innovation in the Context of Diversity and Change.* Oxford: Oxford University Press; Wilkinson, D. (2006). *The Ambiguity Advantage: What Great Leaders Are Great At.* London: Palgrave Macmillan; Lauriola, M., & Levin, I. P. (2001). Relating Individual Differences in Attitude Toward Ambiguity to Risky Choices. *Journal of Behavioral Decision Making*, *14*, 107–122.

[42]Applebaum, S. H. (1981). *Stress Management for Health Care Professionals.* Rockville, MD: Aspen Publications.

[43]Kunnanatt, J. T. (2003). Type A Behavior Pattern and Managerial Performance: A Study Among Bank Executives in India. *International Journal of Manpower*, *24*, 720–734.

[44]Ferroli, C. (1996, January/February). Anger Could Be a Fatal Fault. *The Saturday Evening Post,* 18–19.

[45]Kirkcaldy, B. D., Shephard, R. J., & Furnham, A. F. (2002). The Influence of Type A Behaviour and Locus of Control upon Job Satisfaction and Occupational Health. *Personality and Individual Differences*, *33*(8), 1361–1371.

[46]Fitzpatrick, M. E., Cotter, E. W., Bernfeld, S. J., Carter, L. M., Kies, A., & Fouad, N. A. (2011). The Importance of Workplace Bullying to Vocational Psychology: Implications for Research and Practice. *Journal of Career Development*, *38*, 479–499; Workplace Bullying Institute (2010). Results of the 2010 and 2007 WBI U.S. Workplace Bullying Survey. Workplace Bullying Institute. Available online: http://www.workplacebullying.org/wbiresearch/2010-wbi-national-survey/.; Namie, G. (2007). The Challenge of Workplace Bullying. *Employment Relations Today*, *34*(2), 43–51.

[47]Namie, G. (2008). U.S. Workplace Bullying Survey. Workplace Bullying Institute. Available online: www.workplacebullying.org/wbiresearch/wbi-2014-us-survey/

[48]Namie, G., & Namie, R. (2000, Autumn). Workplace Bullying: Silent Epidemic. *Employee Rights Quarterly*.

[49]Workplace Bullying Institute (2010). Results of the 2010 and 2007 WBI U.S. Workplace Bullying Survey. Workplace Bullying Institute. Available online: http://www.workplacebullying.org/wbiresearch/2010-wbi-national-survey/.

[50]Glaso, L., Matthiesen, S. B., Nielsen, M. B., & Einarsen, S. (2007). Do Targets of Workplace Bullying Portray a General Victim Personality Profile? *Scandinavian Journal of Psychology*, *48*(4), 313–319; Coyne, I., Seigne, E., & Randall, P. (2000). Predicting Workplace Victim Status from Personality. *European Journal of Work and Organizational Psychology*, *9*, 335–349.

[51]Hunter, J. E. (1986). Cognitive Ability, Cognitive Aptitudes, Job Knowledge, and Job Performance. *Journal of Vocational Behavior*, *29*, 340–362.

[52]Hunter, J. E., & Hunter, R. F. (1984). Validity and Utility of Alternative Predictors of Job Performance. *Psychological Bulletin*, *96*, 72–98; Ree, M. J., Carretta, T. R., & Teachout, M. S. (1995). Role of Ability and Prior Knowledge in Complex Training Performance. *Journal of Applied Psychology*, *80*(6), 721–730.

[53]Hunter, J. E. (1986). Cognitive Ability, Cognitive Aptitudes, Job Knowledge, and Job Performance. *Journal of Vocational Behavior*, *29*(3), 340–362; Murphy, K. (1989). Is the Relationship Between Cognitive Ability and Job Performance Stable Over Time? *Human Performance*, *2*, 183–200; Ree, M. J., & Earles, J. A. (1992). Intelligence Is the Best Predictor of Job Performance. *Current Directions in Psychological Science*, *1*, 86–89.

[54]Conlin, M. (2006, June). Champions of Innovation. *IN*, 18–26.

[55]Chase, W. G., & Simon, H. A. (1973). The Mind's Eye in Chess. In *Visual Information Processing,* ed. W. G. Chase (pp. 215–281). New York: Academic Press; Chi, M. T. H., Glaser, R., & Rees, E. (1982). Expertise in Problem Solving. In *Advances of the Psychology of Human Intelligence*, ed. R. J. Sternberg (Vol. 1, pp. 7–75). Hillsdale, NJ: Lawrence Erlbaum Associates.

[56]Ree, M. J., Carretta, T. R., & Teachout, M. S. (1995). Role of Ability and Prior Knowledge in Complex Training Performance. *Journal of Applied Psychology*, *80*(6), 721–730; Schmidt, F. L., & Hunter, J. E. (1981). Employment Testing: Old Theories and New Research Findings. *American Psychologist*, *36*, 1128–1137; Schmidt, F. L., & Hunter, J. E. (1998). The Validity and Utility of Selection Methods in Personnel Psychology: Practical and Theoretical Implications of 85 Years of Research Findings. *Psychological Bulletin*, *124*, 262–274.

[57]Kanfer, R., & Ackerman, P. L. (2004). Aging, Adult Development and Work Motivation. *Academy of Management Review*, *29*, 1–19.

[58]Gully, S. M., Payne, S. C., & Koles, K. L. K. (2002). The Impact of Error Training and Individual Differences on Training Outcomes: An Attribute-Treatment Interaction Perspective. *Journal of Applied Psychology*, *87*, 143–155.

[59]Outtz, J. L. (2002). The Role of Cognitive Ability Tests in Employment Selection. *Human Performance*, *15*, 161–171.

[60]Hough, L., Oswald, F. L., & Ployhart, R. E. (2001). Determinants, Detection and Amelioration of Adverse Impact in Personnel Selection Procedures: Issues, Evidence and Lessons Learnt. *International Journal of Selection and Assessment*, *9*(1/2), 152–194.

[61]Smither, J. W., Reilly, R. R., Millsap, R. E., Pearlman, K., & Stoffey, R. W. (1993). Applicant Reactions to Selection Procedures. *Personnel Psychology*, *46*, 49–76.

[62]Roth, P. L., Bevier, C. A., Bobko, P., Switzer, F. S., & Tyler, P. (2001). Ethnic Group Differences I Cognitive Ability in Employment and Educational Settings: A Meta-Analysis. *Personnel Psychology*, *54*(2), 297–330; Murphy, K. R. (2002). Can Conflicting Perspectives on the Role of g in Personnel Selection Be Resolved? *Human Performance*, *15*, 173–186; Murphy, K. R., Cronin, B. E., & Tam, A. P. (2003). Controversy and Consensus Regarding Use of Cognitive Ability Testing in Organizations. *Journal of Applied Psychology*, *88*, 660–671.

[63]Outtz, J. L. (2002). The Role of Cognitive Ability Tests in Employment Selection. *Human Performance*, *15*, 161–171.

[64]Walker, S. (2005, September 30). The NFL's Smartest Team. *Wall Street Journal Online.* Available online: http://online.wsj.com/article_email/SB112804210724556355-IRjf4NjlaZ4n56rZH2JaqWHm4.html.

[65]For more information, see Sternberg, R. J. (1997). *Thinking Styles.* New York: Cambridge University Press; Guilford, J. P. (1967). *The Nature of Human Intelligence.* New York: McGraw-Hill.

[66]Gardner, H. (1983). *Frames of Mind.* New York: Basic Books; Gardner, H. (1993a). *Multiple Intelligences: The Theory in Practice.* New York: Basic Books; Gardner, H. (1993b). *Creating Minds.* New York: Basic Books; Marks-Tarlow, T. (1995). *Creativity Inside Out: Learning Through Multiple Intelligences.* Reading, MA: Addison-Wesley.

[67]Gardner, H. (1983). *Frames of Mind.* New York: Basic Books; Gardner, H. (1993a). *Multiple Intelligences: The Theory in Practice.* New York: Basic Books; Gardner, H. (1993b). *Creating Minds.* New York: Basic Books; Marks-Tarlow, T. (1995). *Creativity Inside Out: Learning Through Multiple Intelligences.* Reading, MA: Addison-Wesley.

[68]Gardner, H. (2011). Frames of Mind: The Theory of Multiple Intelligences. Philadelphia, PA: Basic Books.

[69]Gardner, H. (1983). *Frames of Mind.* New York: Basic Books; Gardner, H. (1993a). *Multiple Intelligences: The Theory in Practice.* New York: Basic Books.

[70]Mayer, J. D., & Salovey, P. (1993). The Intelligence of Emotional Intelligence. *Intelligence*, *17*, 433–442; Mayer, J. D., & Salovey, P. (1997). What Is Emotional Intelligence? In *Emotional Development and Emotional Intelligence*, eds. P. Salovey & D. J. Sluyter. New York: Basic Books.

[71]Goleman, D. (1998). *Working with Emotional Intelligence* (p. 317). New York: Bantam Books.

[72]Huy, Q. N. (1999). Emotional Capability, Emotional Intelligence, and Radical Change. *Academy of Management Review*, *24*(2), 325–345.

[73]Jordan, P. J., Ashkanasy, N. M., & Hartel, C. E. J. (2002). Emotional Intelligence as a Moderator of Emotional and Behavioral Reactions to Job Insecurity. *Academy of Management Review*, *27*(3), 361–372.

[74]Kanfer, R., Ackerman, P. L., & Heggestad, E. D. (1996). Motivational Skills and Self-Regulation for Learning: A Trait Perspective. *Learning and Individual Differences*, *8*, 185–209; Kanfer, R., & Heggestad, E. D. (1997). Motivational Traits and Skills: A Person-Centered Approach to Work Motivation. In *Research in Organizational Behavior*, eds. L. L. Cummings and B. M. Staw (Vol. 19, pp. 1–56). Greenwich, CT: JAI Press.

[75]Chen, G., Gully, S. M., Whiteman, J. A., & Kilcullen, B. N. (2000). Examination of Relationships Among Trait-Like Individual Differences, State-Like Individual Differences, and Learning Performance. *Journal of Applied Psychology*, *85*, 835–847; Colquitt, J. A., LePine, J. A., & Noe, R. A. (2000). Toward an Integrative Theory of Training Motivation: A Meta-Analytic Path Analysis of 20 Years of Research. *Journal of Applied Psychology*, *85*(5), 678–707.

[76]Ekman, P., & Friesen, W. V (1969). The Repertoire of Nonverbal Behavior: Categories, Origins, Usage, and Coding. *Semiotica*, 1, 49–98.

[77]Law, K. S., Wong, C. S., & Song, L. J. (2004). The Construct and Criterion Validity of Emotional Intelligence and Its Potential Utility for Management Studies. *Journal of Applied Psychology*, *89*(3), 483–496.

[78]FedEx Careers. FedEx.com, 2015. Available online: http://careers.van.fedex.com/.

[79]Case Study: Emotional Intelligence for People-First Leadership at FedEx Express. 6Seconds.org, January 14, 2014. Available online: http://www.6seconds.org/2014/01/14/case-study-emotional-intelligence-people-first-leadership-fedex-express/.

[80]Fields, C. (2013). Don't Hire Without the HR Culture Interview. *Smart Recruiters Blog*, November 6. Available online: https://www.smartrecruiters.com/blog/dont-hire-without-the-hr-culture-interview/.

[81]Case Study: Emotional Intelligence for People-First Leadership at FedEx Express. 6Seconds.org, January 14, 2014. Available online: http://www.6seconds.org/2014/01/14/case-study-emotional-intelligence-people-first-leadership-fedex-express/.

[82]Emotional Intelligence Movement Comes of Age: Six Seconds Says Companies that Leverage "EQ" Training Save Money, Gain a Happier, More Productive Workforce . *BusinessWire*, April 23, 2013. Available online: http://www.businesswire.com/news/home/20130423005674/en/Emotional-Intelligence-Movement-Age-Seconds-Companies-Leverage#.VQMaYfnF9d0.

[83]Emotional Intelligence Movement Comes of Age: Six Seconds Says Companies that Leverage "EQ" Training Save Money, Gain a Happier, More Productive Workforce . *BusinessWire*, April 23, 2013. Available online: http://www.businesswire.com/news/home/20130423005674/en/Emotional-Intelligence-Movement-Age-Seconds-Companies-Leverage#.VQMaYfnF9d0.

[84]Emotional Intelligence Movement Comes of Age: Six Seconds Says Companies that Leverage "EQ" Training Save Money, Gain a Happier, More Productive Workforce . *BusinessWire*, April 23, 2013. Available online: http://www.businesswire.com/news/home/20130423005674/en/Emotional-Intelligence-Movement-Age-Seconds-Companies-Leverage#.VQMaYfnF9d0.

[85]Emotional Intelligence Movement Comes of Age: Six Seconds Says Companies that Leverage "EQ" Training Save Money, Gain a Happier, More Productive Workforce . *BusinessWire*, April 23, 2013. Available online: http://www.businesswire.com/news/home/20130423005674/en/Emotional-Intelligence-Movement-Age-Seconds-Companies-Leverage#.VQMaYfnF9d0.

[86]Goleman, D. (2006). *Social Intelligence: The New Science of Human Relationships.* New York: Bantam Books.

[87]Dulewicz, V., & Higgs, M. (2004). Can Emotional Intelligence Be Developed? *International Journal of Human Resource Management*, *15*(1), 95–111.

[88]Locke, E. A. (2005). Why Emotional Intelligence Is an Invalid Concept. *Journal of Organizational Behavior*, *26*(4), 425–431.

[89]Schulte, M. J., Ree, M. J., & Carretta, T. R. (2004). Emotional Intelligence: Not Much More than g and Personality. *Personality and Individual Differences*, *37*(5), 1059–1068.

[90]O'Boyle, E. H., Humphrey, R. H., Pollack, J. M., Hawver, T. H., & Story, P. A. (2011). The Relation Between Emotional Intelligence and Job Performance: A Meta-Analysis, *Journal of Organizational Behavior*, *32*(5), 788–818; Cote, S., & Miners, C. T. H. (2006). Emotional Intelligence, Cognitive Intelligence, and Job Performance. *Administrative Science Quarterly*, *51*(1), 1–28; Fox, S., & Spector, P. E. (2000). Relations of Emotional Intelligence, Practical Intelligence, General Intelligence, and Trait Affectivity with Interview Outcomes: It's Not All Just "G." *Journal of Organizational Behavior*, *21*, 203–220; Law, K. S., Wong, C. S., & Song, L. J. (2004). The Construct and Criterion Validity of Emotional Intelligence and Its Potential Utility for Management Studies. *Journal of Applied Psychology*, *89*(3), 483–496; Tett, R. P., & Fox, K. E. (2006). Confirmatory Factor Structure of Trait Emotional Intelligence in Student and Worker Samples. *Personality and Individual Differences*, *41*(6), 1155–1168; Van Rooy, D. L., & Viswesvaran, C. (2004). Emotional Intelligence: A Meta-Analytic Investigation of Predictive Validity and Nomological Net. *Journal of Vocational Behavior*, *65*(1), 71–95; Van Rooy, D. L., Viswesvaran, C., & Pluta, P. (2005). An Evaluation of Construct Validity: What Is This Thing Called Emotional Intelligence? *Human Performance*, *18*(4), 445–462.

[91]Emotional Intelligence Movement Comes of Age: Six Seconds Says Companies that Leverage "EQ" Training Save Money, Gain a Happier, More Productive Workforce . *BusinessWire*, April 23, 2013. Available online: http://www.businesswire.com/news/home/20130423005674/en/Emotional-Intelligence-Movement-Age-Seconds-Companies-Leverage#.VQMaYfnF9d0.

[92]Liu, Y., & Ginther, D. (1999). Cognitive Styles and Distance Education. *Online Journal of Distance Learning Administration*, *2*(3). State University of West Georgia, Distance Education. Available online: http://www.westga.edu~distance/ojdla/fall23/liu23.html/; Robertson, I. T. (1985). Human

Information-Processing Strategies and Style. *Behavior and Information Technology*, *4*(1), 19–29; Sadler-Smith, E. (1997). "Learning Style": Frameworks and Instruments. *Educational Psychology*, *17*(1–2), 51–63; Sternberg, R. J., & Zhang, L. (eds.). (2001). *Perspectives on Thinking, Learning, and Cognitive Styles.* Mahwah, NJ: LEA; Zhang, L., & Sternberg, R. J. (2006). *The Nature of Intellectual Styles*. Mahwah, NJ: LEA.

[93]Sternberg, R. J., & Zhang, L. (eds.). (2001). *Perspectives on Thinking, Learning, and Cognitive Styles.* Mahwah, NJ: LEA.

[94]Bissell, J., White, S., & Zivin, G. (1971). Sensory Modalities in Children's Learning. In *Psychology and Educational Practice*, ed. G. S. Lesser (pp. 130–155). Glenview, IL: Scott, Foresman, & Company.

[95]Dunn, R. S., & Dunn, K. J. (1979). Learning Styles/Teaching Styles: Should They & Can They & Be Matched? *Educational Leadership*, *36*, 238–244.

[96]Tennant, M. (1988). *Psychology and Adult Learning.* London: Routledge.

[97]Kolb, D. A. (1984). *Experiential Learning: Experience as the Source of Learning and Development.* Englewood Cliffs, NJ: Prentice-Hall.

[98]Kolb, D. A. (1984). *Experiential Learning: Experience as the Source of Learning and Development.* Englewood Cliffs, NJ: Prentice-Hall.

[99]Cassidy, S. (2004). Learning Styles: An Overview of Theories, Models, and Measures. *Educational Psychology*, *24*(4), 419–444.

[100]Towler, A., & Dipboye, R. L. (2003). Development of a Learning Style Orientation Measure. *Organizational Research Methods*, *6*, 216–235.

[101]Duff, A., & Duffy, T. (2002). Psychometric Properties of Honey and Mumford's Learning Styles Questionnaire. *Personality and Individual Differences*, *33*, 147–163; Newstead, S. E. (1992). A Study of Two "Quick-and-Easy" Methods of Assessing Individual Differences in Student Learning. *British Journal of Educational Psychology*, *62*(3), 299–312; Wilson, D. K. (1986). An Investigation of the Properties of Kolb's Learning Style Inventory. *Leadership & Organization Development Journal*, *7*(3), 3–15.

[102]Towler, A., & Dipboye, R. L. (2003). Development of a Learning Style Orientation Measure. *Organizational Research Methods*, *6*, 216–235.

[103]Rutherford, L. (2012). How Does Southwest Airlines Screen Candidates for Culture? Workforce.com, April 3. Available online: http://www.workforce.com/article/20120403/DEAR_WORKFORCE/120409976.

[104]Rutherford, L. (2012). How Does Southwest Airlines Screen Candidates for Culture? Workforce.com, April 3. Available online: http://www.workforce.com/article/20120403/DEAR_WORKFORCE/120409976.

[105]Kaihla, P. (2006, March 23). Best-Kept Secrets of the World's Best Companies. *Business 2.0.* Available online: http://money.cnn.com/2006/03/23/magazines/business2/business2_bestkeptsecrets/index.htm.

[106]Kaihla, P. (2006, March 23). Best-Kept Secrets of the World's Best Companies. *Business 2.0.* Available online: http://money.cnn.com/2006/03/23/magazines/business2/business2_bestkeptsecrets/index.htm; Freiberg, K., & Freiberg, J. (1996). Nuts! Southwest Airlines' Crazy Recipe for Business and Personal Success. Austin: Bard Press.

[107]Freiberg, K., & Freiberg, J. (1996). Nuts! Southwest Airlines' Crazy Recipe for Business and Personal Success. Austin: Bard Press.

[108]Carbonara, P. (1996, August). Hire for Attitude, Train for Skill. *Fast Company*, *4*, 73.

[109]Lichtenwalner, B. (2011). Southwest Airlines 2011 Results Reflect Benefits of Servant Leadership, Modern Servant Leader. Available online: http://modernservantleader.com/servant-leadership/southwest-airlines-2011-results-reflect-benefits-of-servant-leadership/.

CHAPTER 4

INDIVIDUAL VALUES, PERCEPTIONS, AND REACTIONS

CHAPTER OUTLINE

LEARNING OUTCOMES

After studying this chapter, you should be able to:

1. Discuss how attitudes are formed, describe the meaning of cognitive dissonance, and identify and describe three important work-related attitudes.
2. Describe the role and importance of values and emotions in organizational behavior.
3. Describe basic perceptual processes and how perception affects fairness, justice, and trust in organizations.
4. Discuss the nature of stress, identify the basic causes and consequences of stress, and describe how stress can be managed.

LOSKUTNIKOV/SHUTTERSTOCK.COM

REAL WORLD CHALLENGE

ATTITUDE IS A CHOICE AT PIKE PLACE FISH MARKET[1]

John Yokoyama did not plan on owning Seattle's Pike Place Fish Market. Selling fish is a tough job. The days are long—most employees at Seattle's Pike Place Fish work from 6:30 A.M. to 6:30 P.M.—and the work can be boring and tiring. But when the owner of the business decided to get out, Yokoyama decided to buy the business instead of losing his job.

As a manager, Yokoyama demanded results from his employees and came down hard on their mistakes. He never went on vacation, and insisted on managing all of his company's activities himself. He emulated the previous owner's negative attitudes, anger, and fear-based management style. No one working there was having fun, including Yokoyama.

As his business struggled, employee turnover was high and morale was low. Yokoyama knew he was not getting the best from his employees and recognized that he needed to change his managerial values and style to save his business. He realized that if he could better involve his employees and improve their attitudes, his business would be likely to improve. Yokoyama asks you for advice on improving his employees' attitudes. After reading this chapter, you should have some good ideas for him.

JOSEPH SOHM/SHUTTERSTOCK.COM

If your boss asked you to work harder, could you? Most of us could probably give at least some additional effort if we chose to do so. Because attitudes, values, and perceptions all influence our behavior and job satisfaction, effectively managing them is one way to increase employees' discretionary effort and improve performance. Employees work harder and are less likely to quit their jobs when their personal values are consistent with the organization's values, when they are satisfied with their jobs, and when they have positive attitudes about the company and the work environment.[2]

Chapter 3 introduced the concept of individual differences and explored personality, intelligence, and learning styles. This chapter continues our focus on individual behavior in organizations. We begin with a discussion of attitudes, examining how attitudes are formed and changed, cognitive dissonance, and three key work-related attitudes. Next we look at how values and emotions affect organizational behavior. The role of perception, especially as it relates to issues of fairness and trust, is then discussed. Finally, our chapter concludes with a section devoted to stress in organizations—its causes and consequences and how it can be managed.

ATTITUDES IN ORGANIZATIONS

attitudes
A person's complexes of beliefs and feelings about specific ideas, situations, or other people

People's attitudes obviously affect their behavior in organizations. ***Attitudes*** are complexes of beliefs and feelings that people have about specific ideas, situations, or other people. Attitudes are important because they are the mechanism through which most people express their feelings. An employee's statement that he feels underpaid by an organization reflects his feelings about his pay. Similarly, when a manager says that she likes a new advertising campaign, she is expressing her feelings about the organization's marketing efforts.

How Attitudes Are Formed

Attitudes are formed by a variety of forces, including our personal values, our experiences, and our personalities. For example, if we value honesty and integrity, we may form especially favorable attitudes toward a manager whom we believe to be very honest and moral. Similarly, if we have had negative and unpleasant experiences with a particular coworker, we may form an unfavorable attitude toward that person. Any of the "Big Five" or individual personality traits discussed in Chapter 3 may also

CARLO ALLEGRI/REUTERS

Attitudes are our beliefs and feelings about ideas, situations, or people. During a presidential campaign we form attitudes about various candidates–some good, others bad. But if our preferred candidate is eliminated or drops out of the race we may need to form new attitudes about those candidates who remain.

influence our attitudes. Understanding the basic structure of an attitude helps us see how attitudes are formed and can be changed.

Attitudes are usually viewed as stable dispositions to behave toward objects in a certain way. For any number of reasons, a person might decide that he or she does not like a particular political figure or a certain restaurant (a disposition). We would expect that person to express consistently negative opinions of the candidate or restaurant and to maintain the consistent, predictable intention of not voting for the political candidate or not eating at the restaurant. In this view, as illustrated in Figure 4.1, attitudes contain three components: cognition, affect, and intention.

Cognition is the knowledge a person presumes to have about something. You may believe you like a class because the textbook is excellent, the class meets at your favorite time, the instructor is outstanding, and the workload is reasonable. This "knowledge" may be true, partially true, or totally false. For example, you may intend to vote for a particular candidate because you think you know where the candidate stands on several issues. In reality, depending on the candidate's honesty and your understanding of his or her statements, the candidate's thinking on the issues may be exactly the same as yours, partly the same, or totally different. Cognitions are based on perceptions of truth and reality, and, as we note later, perceptions agree with reality to varying degrees.

cognition
The knowledge a person presumes to have about something

A person's ***affect*** is his or her feelings toward something. In many ways, affect is similar to emotion—it is something over which we have little or no conscious control. For example, most people react to words such as "love," "hate," "sex," and "war" in a manner that reflects their feelings about what those words convey. Similarly, you may like one of your classes, dislike another, and be indifferent toward a third. If the class you dislike is an elective, you may not be particularly concerned. But if it is the first course in your chosen major, your affective reaction may cause you considerable anxiety.

affect
A person's feeling toward something

Intention guides a person's behavior. If you like your instructor, you may intend to take another class from him or her next semester. Intentions are not always translated into actual behavior, however. If the instructor's course

intention
Component of an attitude that guides a person's behavior

Figure 4.1

Attitude Formation

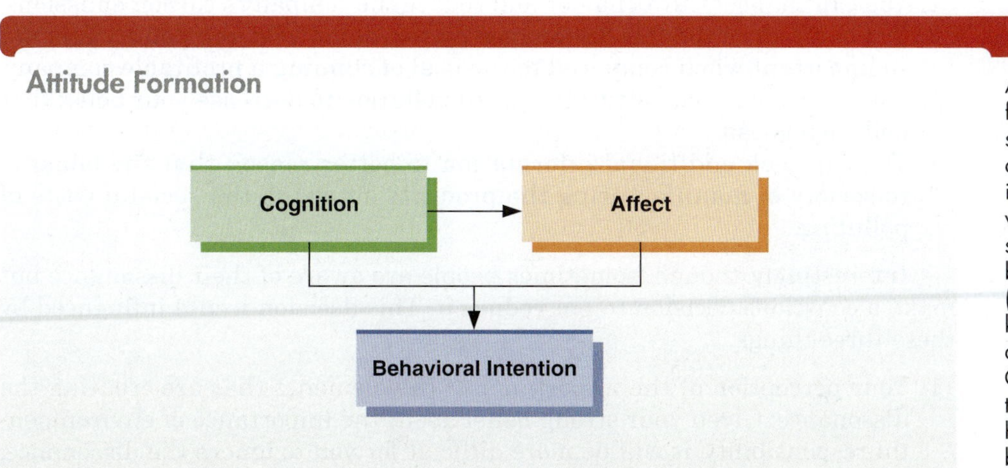

Attitudes are generally formed around a sequence of cognition, affect, and behavioral intention. That is, we come to know something that we believe to be true (cognition). This knowledge triggers a feeling (affect). Cognition and affect then together influence how we intend to behave in the future.

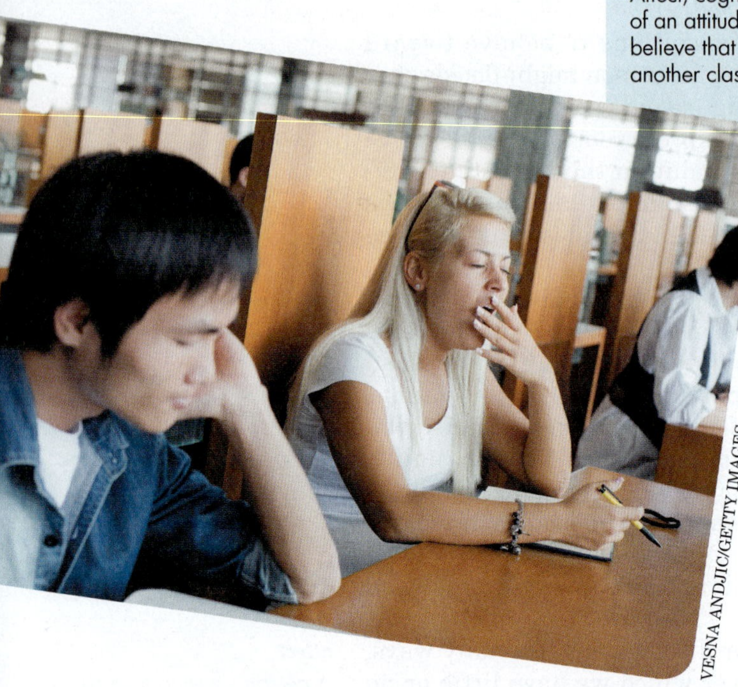

Affect, cognition, and behavioral intention are the primary components of an attitude. For instance, you may like a particular professor (affect), believe that she or he is a great instructor (cognition), and plan to take another class from the professor next semester (behavioral intention). However, if the class ends up scheduled at 8:00 am you may reconsider if you have an early morning job or just like to sleep late!

next semester is scheduled for 8 a.m., you may decide that another instructor is just as good. Some attitudes, and their corresponding intentions, are much more central and significant to an individual than others. You may intend to do one thing (take a particular class) but later alter your intentions because of a more significant and central attitude (fondness for sleeping late).

Cognitive Dissonance

Cognitive dissonance plays an important role in how attitudes affect our behavior. For instance, suppose that you strongly believe that all companies need to be both profitable and environmentally responsible, and that you are the new CEO of a company that is a terrible polluter. You learn that reducing your company's carbon emissions would be so expensive that the company would no longer be profitable. What would you do? The gap between your environmentally responsible attitude and your attitude that your responsibility is to run a profitable company creates what is called cognitive dissonance. ***Cognitive dissonance*** is an incompatibility or conflict between behavior and an attitude or between two different attitudes.[3] When people experience dissonance, they often use one of four approaches to cope with it. Using the scenario above, these would include:

cognitive dissonance
An incompatibility or conflict between behavior and an attitude or between two different attitudes

1. You can change your behavior and reduce the company's carbon emissions.
2. You can reduce the felt dissonance by reasoning that the pollution is not so important when compared to the goal of running a profitable company.
3. You can change your attitude toward pollution to decrease your belief that pollution is bad.
4. You can seek additional information to better reason that the benefits to society of manufacturing the products outweigh the societal costs of polluting.

Interestingly, though, sometimes people are aware of their dissonance but make a conscious decision to not reduce it. This decision would influenced by these three things:

1. Your perception of the importance of the elements that are creating the dissonance: Given your strong belief about the importance of environmental responsibility, it will be more difficult for you to ignore the dissonance. If the elements involved in the dissonance are less important to you, it is easier to ignore it.

2. The amount of influence you feel you have over these elements: If you are being prevented by the Board of Directors from investing in pollution-reducing technology, it would be easier to rationalize the dissonance and not take action. If you are making the decision alone, however, then you are more likely to address the dissonance in a more active way.
3. The rewards involved in the dissonance: Rewards for dissonance tend to decrease our reactions to it. If your sizeable annual bonus is based on the firm's financial performance, for example, and not its environmental record, then you would likely be less inclined to take action to address the dissonance.

Attitude Change

Attitudes are not as stable as personality attributes. For example, new information may change attitudes. A manager may have a negative attitude about a new colleague because of the colleague's lack of job-related experience. After working with the new person for a while, however, the manager may come to realize that he is actually very talented and subsequently develop a more positive attitude. Likewise, if the object of an attitude changes, a person's attitude toward that object may also change. Suppose, for example, that employees feel underpaid and as a result have negative attitudes toward the company's reward system. A big salary increase may cause these attitudes to become more positive.

Attitudes can also change when the object of the attitude becomes less important or less relevant to the person. For example, suppose an employee has a negative attitude about his company's health insurance. When his spouse gets a new job with an organization that has outstanding insurance benefits, his attitude toward his own insurance may become more moderate simply because he no longer has to worry about it. Finally, as noted earlier, individuals may change their attitudes as a way to reduce cognitive dissonance.

Deeply rooted attitudes that have a long history are, of course, resistant to change. For example, over a period of years a former airline executive named Frank Lorenzo developed a reputation in the industry of being antiunion and of cutting wages and benefits. As a result, employees throughout the industry came to dislike and distrust him. When he took over Eastern Airlines, its employees had such a strong attitude of distrust toward him that they could never agree to cooperate with any of his programs or ideas. Some of them actually cheered months later when Eastern went bankrupt, even though it was costing them their own jobs!

STEFANOLUNARDI/SHUTTERSTOCK.COM

Cognitive dissonance is sometimes experienced by people who smoke. Their cognition "tells" them that smoking is not healthy, but their behavior (smoking) contradicts this knowledge. To cope with the dissonance they may set goals for themselves to quit at some point in the future.

BLUESKYIMAGE/SHUTTERSTOCK.COM

Job satisfaction is caused by a variety of factors in the workplace, including such things as the work itself and the pay an individual receives. The attitudes expressed by coworkers, colleagues, and others in the organization can also play a role. For instance, if our coworkers are happy and excited about the work and the organization their enthusiasm may be contagious and contribute to our own job satisfaction.

Key Work-Related Attitudes

People in an organization form attitudes about many different things. Employees are likely to have attitudes about their salary, their promotion possibilities, their boss, employee benefits, the food in the company cafeteria, and the color of the company softball team uniforms. Of course, some of these attitudes are more important than others. Especially important attitudes are job satisfaction, organizational commitment, and employee engagement.

Job Satisfaction

job satisfaction *Reflects our attitudes and feelings about our job*

Job satisfaction is one of the most commonly studied organizational outcomes in the field of organizational behavior. Our ***job satisfaction*** reflects our attitudes and feelings about our job. As illustrated in Figure 4.2, the factors that have the greatest influence on job satisfaction

Figure 4.2

Job satisfaction is one of the most important job-related attitudes in organizations. It reflects both our attitudes and our feelings about our job. Job satisfaction is strongly influenced by our personality, values, other attitudes, and the work itself.

Influences on Job Satisfaction

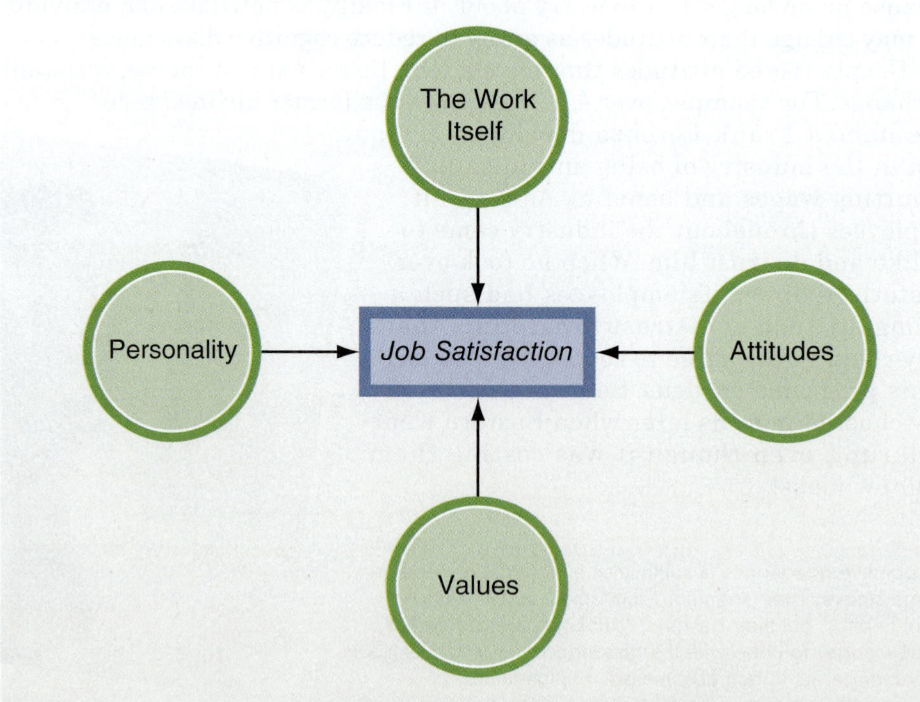

are: the work itself, attitudes, values, and personality. Satisfaction with the nature of the work itself is the largest influence on job satisfaction. If you do not like the work you are doing, it is hard to be satisfied with your job. Challenging work, autonomy, variety, and job scope also increase job satisfaction.[4] As a manager, if you want to increase your subordinates' job satisfaction, focus first on improving the nature of the work they do.[5] Coworkers, bosses, and subordinates are part of the work experience and can also influence job satisfaction. Their attitudes and perceptions can be contagious, especially for new hires forming impressions about the job and company. If coworkers are unhappy and dissatisfied with their jobs, new hires are more likely to be dissatisfied than if they regularly interact with happy and satisfied coworkers.

Our attitudes and values about work also influence our job satisfaction. Someone with a negative attitude toward work is less likely to be satisfied with any job than someone with a positive attitude toward work. Employees who find intrinsic value in their work are doing what is important to them. If someone values challenge and variety in work, that person will be more satisfied with jobs with these characteristics than with monotonous work.

Interestingly, our job satisfaction is somewhat stable over time, even when we change jobs or employers. [6] Some people are rarely satisfied with their jobs, and others tend to be satisfied no matter what job they have. Research evidence suggests that differences in job satisfaction are due in part to differences in employees' genetics and personality.[7] In particular, core self-evaluation,[8] extroversion, and conscientiousness[9] influence job satisfaction. Accordingly, selecting extroverted, conscientious people who are a good fit with the job and who have high core self-evaluations (a broad, general, positive self-regard[10]) can enhance employees' job satisfaction.

Are happy employees really more productive employees? The answer is yes. And the positive relationship between job satisfaction and job performance is even stronger for complex, professional jobs.[11] Satisfied employees also benefit organizations because job satisfaction positively influences employees' attitudes and organizational citizenship behaviors (as discussed in Chapter 1).[12] Conversely, job dissatisfaction is related to higher absenteeism and turnover, as well as to other withdrawal behaviors such as lateness, drug abuse, grievances, and retirement decisions.[13] It isn't just the level of job satisfaction that matters, however. If job satisfaction is declining, turnover intentions and actual turnover are particularly likely to increase.[14] Because of the potentially high cost of these employee behaviors, the financial impact of improving employees' job satisfaction can make it worthwhile for managers to invest in improving employee attitudes toward their jobs and the company.

Organizational Commitment

Organizational commitment reflects the degree to which an employee identifies with the organization and its goals and wants to stay with the organization. There are three ways we can feel committed to an employer:

organizational commitment
Reflects the degree to which an employee identifies with the organization and its goals and wants to stay with the organization

1. *Affective commitment*: positive emotional attachment to the organization and strong identification with its values and goals. Employees of a children's hospital may be affectively committed to the organization because of its goal of providing top-quality health care to kids. Affective commitment leads employees to stay with an organization because they want to, and is related to higher performance.

2. *Normative commitment*: feeling obliged to stay with an organization for moral or ethical reasons. An employee who has just finished an MBA paid for by a firm's tuition reimbursement program might feel a moral obligation to stay with the employer for at least a few years to repay the debt. Normative commitment is related to higher performance and leads employees to stay with an organization because they feel they should.
3. *Continuance commitment*: staying with an organization because of perceived high economic (taking another job would mean losing valuable stock options) and/or social costs (friendships with coworkers) involved with leaving. Continuance commitment leads employees to stay with an organization because they feel that they have to.

These three types of organizational commitment are not mutually exclusive. It is possible to be committed to an organization in affective, normative, and continuance ways at the same time, at varying levels of intensity. At any point in time, an employee has a "commitment profile" that reflects high or low levels of all three types of organizational commitment.[15] Different profiles have different effects on workplace behavior such as job performance, absenteeism, and the chance that the organization member will quit.[16]

Employee Engagement

If you did not like your coworkers, your boss was mean, and you did not have the resources you needed to get your job done, how would you feel about your job? Would you put 100 percent into your work? When we feel respected and see how our work matters to the company and to others, we feel more enthusiastic and engaged. ***Employee engagement*** is "a heightened emotional and intellectual connection that an employee has for his/her job, organization, manager, or coworkers that, in turn, influences him/her to apply additional discretionary effort to his/her work."[17]

employee engagement
Heightened emotional and intellectual connection that an employee has for his/her job, organization, manager, or coworkers that, in turn, influences him/her to apply additional discretionary effort to his/her work

Engaged employees give their full effort to their jobs, often going beyond what is required because they are passionate about the firm and about doing their jobs well. Disengaged workers do not perform close to their potential capability, lacking the emotional and motivational connections to their employer that drive discretionary effort. Rather than wanting to do the work and wanting to do their best, disengaged workers feel they have to do the work, and generally do only what they have to do as a result.

One study found that more than 50 percent of senior executives have "less than ideal emotional connection and alignment" to their organization.[18] This is particularly troubling given the financial consequences of low engagement. High employee engagement is related to superior business performance. Towers Perrin found that high-engagement organizations have a 28 percent earnings-per-share (EPS) growth rate compared to low-engagement organizations' 11 percent EPS decline.[19] A report from the Society for Human Resource Management found that strengthening employee engagement saved one company $1.7 million in just one year.[20] As a manager, remember that the drivers of employee engagement can differ from the drivers of employee attraction and retention—what gets employees into an organization is not the same as what keeps them engaged and keeps them from leaving.[21] Engagement is enhanced when employees:

- Have clear goals and roles
- Have the resources needed to do a good job
- Get meaningful feedback on their performance

Table 4.1

Top Three Worldwide Drivers of Employee Attraction, Retention, and Engagement for Different Age Groups

Top Drivers of Attraction for 18- to 24-Year-Olds	Top Drivers of Retention for 18- to 24-Year-Olds	Top Drivers of Engagement for 18- to 24-Year-Olds
Career advancement opportunities	Have excellent career advancement opportunities	Organization develops leaders at all levels
Competitive base pay	Work in an environment where new ideas are encouraged	Organization quickly resolves customer concerns
Learning and development opportunities	Satisfaction with the organization's business decisions	Senior management is sincerely interested in employee well-being
Top Drivers of Attraction for 45- to 54-Year-Olds	Top Drivers of Retention for 45- to 54-Year-Olds	Top Drivers of Engagement for 45- to 54-Year-Olds
Competitive base pay	Organization's reputation as a great place to work	Senior management is sincerely interested in employee well-being
Challenging work	Satisfaction with the organization's people decisions	Improved my skills and capabilities over the last year
Convenient work location	Understand potential career track within the organization	The organization's reputation for social responsibility

Source: Based on information provided in Exhibits 14, 15, and 16 of *Towers Perrin Global Workforce Study—Global Report* at http://www.towersperrin.com/tp/ getwebcachedoc?webc=HRS/USA/2008/200803/GWS_Global_Report20072008_31208.pdf.

- Are able to use their talents
- Are recognized for doing a good job
- Have positive relationships with coworkers
- Have opportunities to learn and grow
- Have supportive leadership

Table 4.1 summarizes the results of a recent global Towers Perrin survey on the different worldwide drivers of employee attraction, retention, and engagement by generation.

VALUES AND EMOTIONS IN ORGANIZATIONS

Values and emotions are also important elements of individual behavior in organizations. ***Values*** are ways of behaving or end-states that are desirable to a person or to a group. Values can be conscious or unconscious.[22] Although our values tend to be fairly well established by the time we are teenagers, they can be reshaped by major life events including the birth of a child, going to war, the death of a loved one, illness, or even business failure. Work values influence important individual and organizational outcomes including performance and retention, and are often considered to be important work outcomes in themselves.[23]

values
Ways of behaving or end-states that are desirable to a person or to a group

A company leader's personal values affect the firm's business strategy[24] and all aspects of organizational behavior including staffing, reward systems, manager–subordinate relationships, communication, conflict management styles, and negotiation approaches.[25] Personal values also influence ethical choices. When there are no clear rules for dealing with specific ethical problems, we tend to respond to each situation on an individual basis depending on our values at that time.[26] Our personal values combine with organizational influences like company culture to generate decisions that can be significantly different from those made based solely on our personal values.[27] Strong company cultures help to guide us when making these ambiguous choices. However, if personal values conflict with the organization's cultural values, it is difficult to maintain ethical norms.[28]

Types of Values

Values can be described as terminal or instrumental, and as intrinsic or extrinsic. Let's explore each of these distinctions.

Terminal and Instrumental Values

terminal values
Reflect our long-term life goals, and may include prosperity, happiness, a secure family, and a sense of accomplishment

One noted researcher has identified two types of values: terminal and instrumental.[29] ***Terminal values*** reflect our long-term life goals, and may include prosperity, happiness, a secure family, and a sense of accomplishment. People who value family more than career success will work fewer hours and spend more time with their kids than people whose values put career success first. Of course, this does not mean that having strong family values will prevent one from having a successful career. Terminal values can change over time depending on our experiences and accomplishments. When a career-oriented person sells her business for a lot of money, her prosperity goals may be reached and family may then become most important.

instrumental values
Our preferred means of achieving our terminal values or our preferred ways of behaving

Instrumental values are our preferred means of achieving our terminal values or our preferred ways of behaving. Terminal values influence what we want to accomplish; instrumental values influence how we get there. Honesty, ambition, and independence are examples of instrumental values that guide our behavior in pursuit of our terminal goals. The stronger an instrumental value is, the more we act on it. People who value honesty behave more ethically in pursuing the terminal value of prosperity and a sense of accomplishment than do people with a lower honesty instrumental value.

Intrinsic and Extrinsic Work Values

intrinsic work values
Relate to the work itself

extrinsic work values
Relate to the outcomes of doing work

Intrinsic work values relate to the work itself.[30] For example, some employees want challenging jobs with a lot of variety that require them to continually learn new things, whereas others prefer simpler jobs they can perform in the same way every day. Most people need to find some personal intrinsic value in their work to feel truly satisfied with it.[31] Valuing challenging work and learning new skills can help advance your career. ***Extrinsic work values*** are related to the outcomes of doing work.[32] Employees who work to earn money or to have health benefits are satisfying extrinsic work values. Having high status in the company, getting recognized for quality work, and having job security are extrinsic work values.

Extrinsic work values relate to the outcomes of doing work. For instance, if a person works to earn money, achieve status, or get a large corner office such as this one then that individual is largely driven by extrinsic work values.

RACORN/SHUTTERSTOCK.COM

Conflicts among Values

Intrapersonal, interpersonal, and individual-organization value conflicts all influence employee attitudes, retention, job satisfaction, and job performance. When highly ranked instrumental and terminal values conflict and both cannot be met, we experience inner conflict and stress. At some point in their career, many managers experience an ***intrapersonal value conflict*** between the instrumental value of ambition and the terminal value of happiness. If being happy pulls us to spend quality time with our family or pursuing a hobby we love, but personal ambition pulls us to work longer hours and pursue promotions, we feel conflicted. People are generally happier and less stressed when their instrumental and terminal values are aligned.

intrapersonal value conflict
Conflict between the instrumental value of ambition and the terminal value of happiness

Unlike intrapersonal value conflicts, which are internal to an individual, ***interpersonal value conflicts*** occur when two different people hold conflicting values. Interpersonal value conflicts are often the cause of personality clashes and other disagreements. If one coworker values individual rewards and the other values group recognition the two may clash over how to approach a new project. As a manager, it is important to remember that people's constellations of instrumental and terminal values differ. These differences can lead to differences in work styles, work preferences, and reactions to announcements or events.

interpersonal value conflict
Occurs when two different people hold conflicting values

Finally, just as two different employees' values can conflict, an employee's values can conflict with the values of the organization, creating ***individual-organization value conflict***. Lower individual-organization value conflict leads to greater job satisfaction, higher performance, lower stress, and greater job commitment.[33]

individual-organization value conflict
When an employee's values conflict with the values of the organization

How Values Differ around the World

Global differences in values can also lead to different managerial behaviors. For example, Latin Americans tend to highly value family loyalty, which leads them to hire competent family members whenever possible.[34] Managers in the United States tend to strongly value individual achievement, which leads them to emphasize a candidate's previous performance and skill assessments rather than family ties.

Values are influenced by culture. Research has found that a large number of basic values can be condensed into two major dimensions that vary across cultures: (1) traditional/secular-rational values and (2) survival/self-expression values.[35] Traditional/secular-rational values reflect the contrast between societies in which religion is very important and those in which it is not. More traditional societies emphasize the importance of parent-child ties and deference to authority, which is reflected in high levels of national pride and a nationalistic outlook. Societies with secular-rational values have the opposite characteristics.

Survival values emphasize economic and physical security. Self-expression values emphasize subjective well-being, self-expression, and quality of life, giving high priority to environmental protection, diversity tolerance, and participation in decision making. Societies that rank high on self-expression values also tend have higher interpersonal trust and tolerance and value individual freedom and self-expression.[36] Figure 4.3 illustrates how these two major dimensions of values differ in a variety of countries.

The Role of Emotions in Behavior

Emotions also play an important role in organizations. Do you behave the same way or perform as well when you are excited as you do when you are unhappy or afraid? Of course not—which is the reason why emotions play an important role in the workplace. It is easy to imagine the performance difference of unhappy salespeople compared to a happy sales staff. Employees who effectively manage their emotions and moods can create a competitive advantage for a company. Would Starbucks or Nordstrom be as successful with moody employees? It is not likely.

We all experience emotions at work. Our behaviors are not guided solely by conscious, rational thought. In fact, emotion often plays a larger role in our behaviors than does conscious reasoning. ***Emotions*** are intense, short-term physiological, behavioral, and psychological reactions to a specific object, person, or event that prepare us to respond to it. Let's break this definition down into its four important elements:

emotions
Intense, short-term physiological, behavioral, and psychological reactions to a specific object, person, or event that prepare us to respond to it

1. Emotions are short events or episodes. Emotions are relatively short-lived. Excitement about making a big sale or anxiety over a looming deadline subsides after a little while.
2. Emotions are directed at something or someone. This differentiates emotions from moods, which are short-term emotional states that are not directed toward anything in particular.[37] Moods are less intense than emotions and can change quickly. The cause of emotions can be readily identified—making a big sale or facing a deadline, for example.
3. Emotions are experienced. They involve involuntary changes in heart rate, blood pressure, facial expressions, animation, and vocal tone. We *feel* emotion.
4. Emotions create a state of physical readiness through physiological reactions. Increased heart rate, adrenaline, and eye movements prepare our bodies to take action. Particularly strong emotions including fear, anger, and surprise can demand our attention, interrupt our thoughts, and motivate us to respond by focusing our attention on whatever is generating the emotion.

Figure 4.3

How Values Differ Around the World

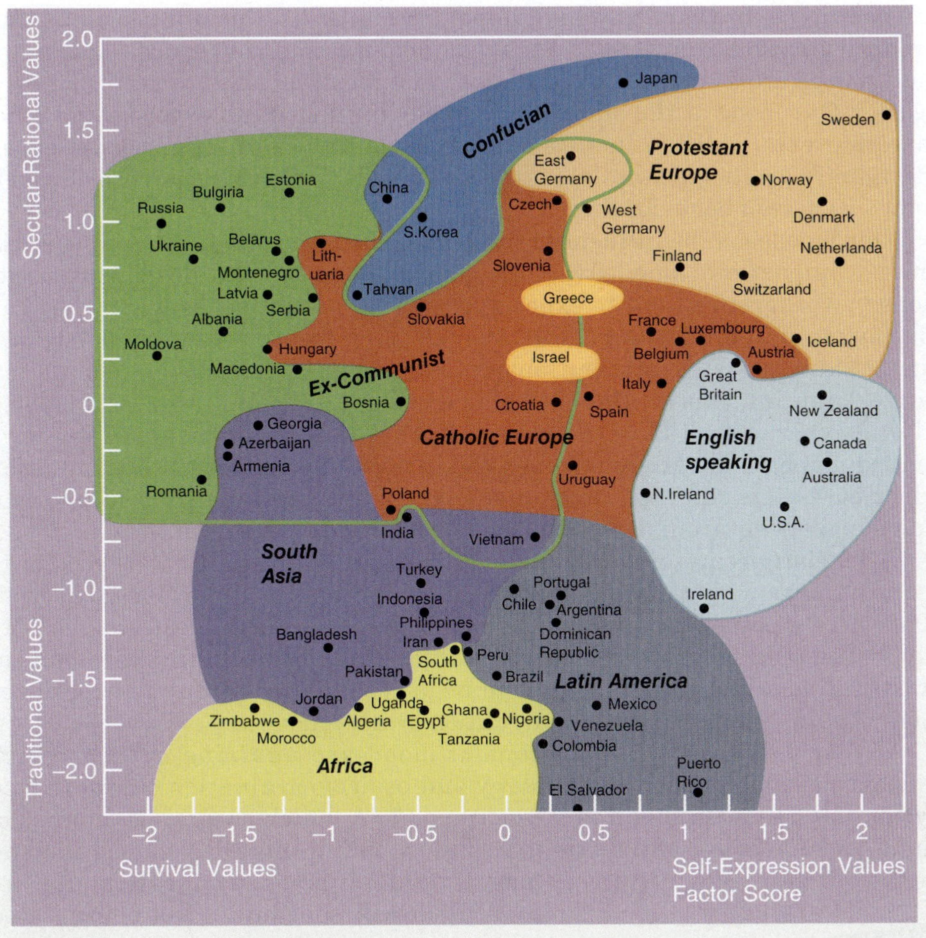

Values differ around the world. One useful way to understand differences in values is in terms of secular/rational values and survival/self-expression values. This figure illustrates how different regions of the world reflect these two sets of values.

Source: Inglehart, R., & Welzel, C. (2005). Modernization, Cultural Change and Democracy (p. 64). New York: Cambridge University Press. Based on the World Values Surveys, see http://www.worldvaluessurvey. Org. Copyright © 2005 Ronald Inglehart and Christian Welzel. Reprinted with the permission of Cambridge University Press.

Whereas an attitude can be thought of as a judgment about something, an emotion is experienced or felt. Emotions do not last as long as attitudes. Emotions influence how we perceive the world, help us interpret our experiences, and prime us to respond. Why is understanding the role of emotions important to organizations? First, because emotions are malleable, effective employees and managers know how to positively influence their own emotions and the emotions of others.[38] Second, emotions influence both the creation and maintenance of our motivation to engage or to not engage in certain behaviors. Third, research has found that emotion can influence turnover, decision making, leadership, helping behaviors, and teamwork behaviors.[39] The quality of subordinates' emotional exchanges with their leader also influences the affective tone of the workgroup.[40] Effective leaders use emotion to generate positive follower behaviors.

Affect and Mood

moods
Short-term emotional states that are not directed toward anything in particular

Although the cause of emotions tends be obvious, the cause of mood tends to be more unfocused and diffused. ***Moods*** are short-term emotional states that are not directed toward anything in particular. Unlike instant reactions that produce emotion, and that change with expectations of future pleasure or pain, moods are harder to cope with, can last for days, weeks, months, or even years.[41] Our mood at the start of a workday influences how we see and react to work events, which influences our performance.[42] Because moods reflect an individual's emotional state, researchers typically infer the existence of moods from a variety of behavioral cues.

Our moods can be influenced by others. Nasty interactions with coworkers can impact our mood five times more strongly than positive interactions.[43] Workgroups tend to experience shared group moods when they can display mood information to each other through facial, vocal, and behavioral cues. [44] Subordinates' attributions of their leader's sincere versus manipulative intentions also influence their emotional responses to the leader.[45] Altering characteristics of the group's work, changing elements of the work context, or changing group membership in a way that changes the manner in which coworkers interact can change the amount and type of mood information members get from each other and influence employees' moods.

affectivity
Represents our tendency to experience a particular mood or to react to things with certain emotions

positive affect
Reflects a combination of high energy and positive evaluation characterized by emotions like elation

negative affect
Comprises feelings of being upset, fearful, and distressed

Affectivity represents our tendency to experience a particular mood or to react to things with certain emotions.[46] Researchers have identified two types of affectivity: positive and negative. Individuals with a high positive affectivity experience tend to experience more positive emotions, including cheerfulness or enthusiasm. Individuals higher in negative affectivity tend to experience more negative emotions, such as irritation or nervousness.

The two dominant dimensions of mood are ***positive affect***, which reflects a combination of high energy and positive evaluation characterized by emotions like elation, and ***negative affect***, which comprises feelings of being upset, fearful, and distressed.[47] As shown in Figure 4.4, positive and negative affect are not opposites, but are two distinct dimensions.[48] Not being elated does not mean that you are upset, and not being sad does not mean that you are elated. Affect tends to be somewhat dispositional and fairly stable over time. Some people just tend to be more positive and optimistic than others.[49] Negative affect is related to lower organizational citizenship behaviors, greater withdrawal and counterproductive work behaviors, lower job satisfaction, and greater injuries.[50] Affectivity can also be important to training outcomes.

TERRENCE VACCARO/© 2007 NBAE/ GETTY IMAGES

Affect and mood play important roles in how we perform our jobs and how others perceive us. These two Starbucks baristas, for example, are happy and engaging. Their positive mood and affect, in turn, can make their customers feel good as well.

Figure 4.4

Positive and Negative Affect

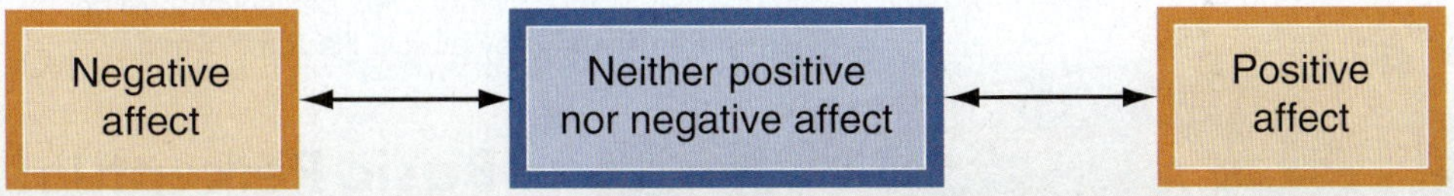

Affect can vary anywhere along a continuum ranging from positive affect to negative affect. As illustrated here, it is also possible to fall in between these extremes and reflect neither positive nor negative affect.

Source: Thompson, E. R., Development and Validation of an Internationally Reliable Short-Form of the Positive and Negative Affect Schedule (PANAS), *Journal of Cross-Cultural Psychology,* *38* (2), 227–242. © 2007 by SAGE Publications. Reprinted by Permission of SAGE Publications.

Employees with greater positive affect or lower negative affect experience a greater increase in self-efficacy after training. This suggests that affectivity may be an important thing to consider when choosing people to participate in development programs.[51]

Moods and emotions can also influence our satisfaction with our jobs and employers. Higher positive affect is related to increased creativity, openness to new information, and efficient decision making.[52] Positive affectivity also increases the likelihood of cooperation strategies in negotiations, improving the results.[53] Numerous studies show that happy individuals are successful in many areas of their lives, including marriage, health, friendship, income, and work performance.[54]

PERCEPTION IN ORGANIZATIONS

Perception—the set of processes by which an individual becomes aware of and interprets information about the environment—is another important element of workplace behavior. If everyone perceived everything the same way, things would be a lot simpler (and a lot less exciting!). Of course, just the opposite is true: People perceive the same things in very different ways.[55] Moreover, people often assume that reality is objective and that we all perceive the same things in the same way.

perception
The set of processes by which an individual becomes aware of and interprets information about the environment

To test this idea, we could ask students at the University of Michigan and Ohio State University to describe the most recent football game between their schools. We probably would hear two conflicting stories. These differences would arise primarily because of perception. The fans "saw" the same game but interpreted it in sharply contrasting ways. Since perception plays a role in a variety of workplace behaviors, managers should understand basic perceptual processes. As implied in our definition, perception actually consists of several distinct processes. Moreover, in perceiving we receive information in many guises, from spoken words to visual images of movements and forms. Through perceptual processes, the receiver assimilates the varied types of incoming information for the purpose of interpreting it.[56]

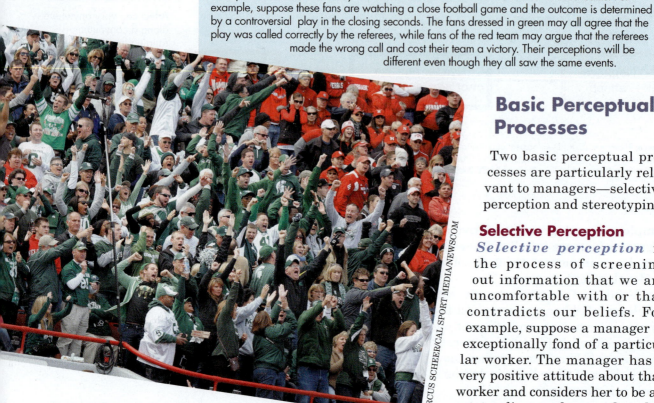

Perception is often illustrated by the different reactions of fans of two rival athletic teams. For example, suppose these fans are watching a close football game and the outcome is determined by a controversial play in the closing seconds. The fans dressed in green may all agree that the play was called correctly by the referees, while fans of the red team may argue that the referees made the wrong call and cost their team a victory. Their perceptions will be different even though they all saw the same events.

MARCUS SCHEER/CAL SPORT MEDIA/NEWSCOM

Basic Perceptual Processes

Two basic perceptual processes are particularly relevant to managers—selective perception and stereotyping.

Selective Perception

selective perception
The process of screening out information that we are uncomfortable with or that contradicts our beliefs

Selective perception is the process of screening out information that we are uncomfortable with or that contradicts our beliefs. For example, suppose a manager is exceptionally fond of a particular worker. The manager has a very positive attitude about that worker and considers her to be an outstanding performer. One day the manager observes this individual apparently sleeping at her desk. The manger may assume that the worker stayed up working late the night before and is just taking a short nap. Alternatively, suppose the manager has a very negative attitude about the worker and observes the same behavior. In this case the manager might assume that the worker was out late partying the night before, perhaps reinforcing the negative attitude.

Stereotyping

stereotyping
The process of categorizing or labeling people on the basis of a single attribute

Stereotyping is categorizing or labeling people on the basis of a single attribute. Certain forms of stereotyping can be useful and efficient. Suppose, for example, that a manager believes that communication skills are important for a particular job and that speech communication majors tend to have exceptionally good communication skills. As a result, whenever he interviews candidates for jobs he pays especially close attention to speech communication majors. To the extent that communication skills truly predict job performance and that majoring in speech communication does indeed provide those skills, this form of stereotyping can be beneficial. Common attributes from which people often stereotype are race and sex. Of course, stereotypes along these lines are inaccurate and can be harmful. For example, suppose a human resource manager forms the stereotype that women can only perform certain tasks and that men are best suited for other tasks. To the extent that this affects the manager's hiring practices, he or she is (1) costing the organization valuable talent for both sets of jobs, (2) violating federal law, and (3) behaving unethically.

Errors in Perception

As you might expect, errors may creep into how we interpret the things we perceive. Stereotyping and selection perception are often the underlying causes of these errors, but other factors may also come into play. Perception shortcuts, for example, may play a role. One perception shortcut is categorization, which reflects our tendency to put things into groups or categories (e.g., Southerner, energetic, athlete, etc.). We then exaggerate the similarities within and the differences between the groups. This explains our tendency to see members of a particular group to which we do not belong as being more alike than they actually are. Have you ever seen someone work quickly and thought to yourself how good he or she is at that job? If so, you may have put that person into a "high performer" category.

After we put people into categories, selective perception leads to selectively interpreting what we see based on our interests, expectations, experience, and attitudes. Once we categorize someone (a cashier named Sue, for our running example) as a high performer, we focus more on (and will better remember) information related to her high performance, and we tend to disregard information reflecting her low performance. If we saw Sue make an error on the cash register, we might discount it by attributing it to a fluke or to a problem with the machine, and focus only on her superior item-scanning speed. Selective perception reinforces stereotypes as the perceiver focuses on information and behaviors that confirm rather than negate the assigned stereotype. A supervisor who believes that a subordinate has high potential will interpret what is observed through that positively biased lens, while a supervisor who believes a subordinate has low ability will interpret the same information negatively to reinforce expectations of low performance. Managers need to be aware of this bias in order to evaluate subordinates more objectively and accurately.

The *halo effect* is when we form a general impression about something or someone based on a single (typically good) characteristic. For example, people tend to associate beauty with other positive characteristics. We often assume that physically attractive people possess more socially desirable personalities than less beautiful people do, and that they lead happier and more successful lives.[57] Similarly, because you perceive Sue to be a high performer, you might assume that she is also intelligent, energetic, or whatever else you associate with high performers.

The *contrast effect* occurs when we evaluate our own or another person's characteristics through comparisons with other people we have recently encountered who rank higher or lower on the same characteristics. After encountering Sue, if we see an average cashier, we might evaluate him as below average because we thought so highly of Sue's performance. The contrast effect is common among college students who—because they are used to being around people who have relatively high intelligence and ambition compared to the general public, and because they compare themselves to other smart, motivated people—conclude that they are only average when, in fact, they are above average. *Projection* occurs when we project our own characteristics onto other people. If a hiring manager is interviewing someone who reminds him of himself when he was just starting out, he may assume that the candidate also shares his values, work ethic, and abilities.

First impression bias may also be relevant. Research has found that not only do we tend to avoid people after we have had a negative reaction to

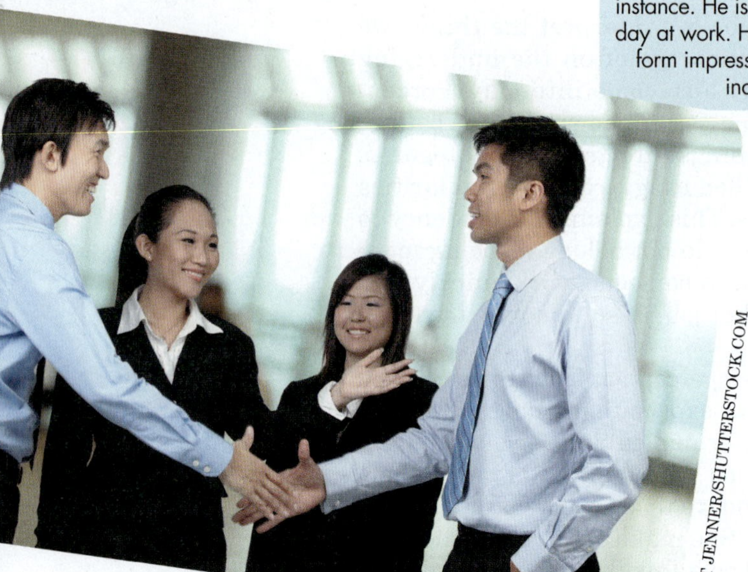

First impressions are formed quickly. Take this new employee, for instance. He is being introduced to his new colleagues during his first day at work. He will quickly form impressions of them just as they form impressions of him. First impression bias, though, may result in inaccurate impressions which may then be hard to overcome.

STUART JENNER/SHUTTERSTOCK.COM

them,[58] but also negative impressions are harder to change than positive ones.[59] First impressions are formed quickly. If you find yourself making negative assumptions about someone you have just met, it can be a good idea to quickly look for positive information that disconfirms your negative assumptions before they become too strongly held. Our social perceptions can obviously be flawed—even the most skilled observers can misperceive and misjudge others. Once we form wrong impressions, they are likely to persist. When we have the motivation and the resources to think carefully about something, we usually will, but even then the various cognitive biases can influence our perceptions.

Our impressions and expectations of others also can become *self-fulfilling prophecies*. If we categorize a person as untrustworthy, we are likely to treat that individual with suspicion and distrust. These actions then evoke appropriate guarded reactions from the other person, whose reactions serve to confirm our initial impressions. One of the first experiments on the self-fulfilling prophecy effect in work settings was conducted in a job training program for disadvantaged employees.[60] Trainees labeled "high aptitude" (though randomly selected) achieved more on objective tests, were rated higher by their supervisors and peers, and had lower dropout rates than the trainees who were not labeled in that way. Self-fulfilling prophecies are widespread in organizations. High expectations have a stronger effect on disadvantaged groups or those stereotyped as low achievers, and on people who are unsure of their abilities in a particular situation.[61] Self-fulfilling prophecies also seem to work best in newly established relationships.

Perception and Attribution

Have you ever noticed that when classmates do well on a test, they often attribute it to their own effort and ability, but when they learn that you did well, they seem to attribute it more to luck or to easy grading by the instructor? This tendency is a perfectly normal outcome of attributions. ***Attribution*** refers to the way we explain the causes of our own as well as other people's behaviors and achievements, and understand why people do what they do.[62] Our job performance and even our ultimate survival in an organization often depend on the accuracy of our attributions for our own and supervisor, coworker, and customer behaviors and outcomes.

attribution
The way we explain the causes of our own as well as other people's behaviors and achievements, and understand why people do what they do

UNDERSTAND YOURSELF

POSITIVE AND NEGATIVE AFFECTIVITY

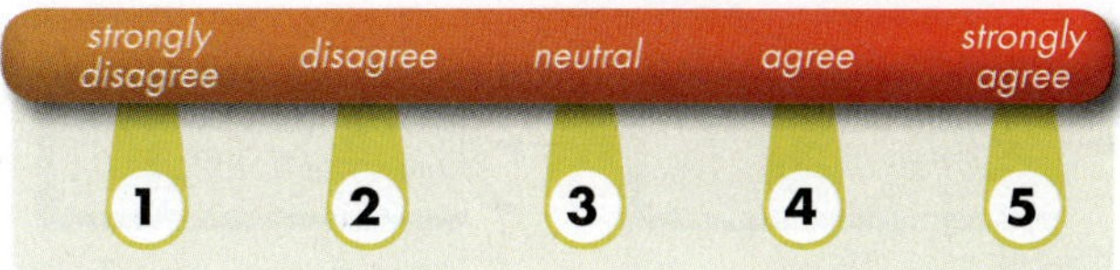

Using the scale above, and thinking about yourself and how you usually feel, indicate before each item below to what extent you generally feel:

___ 1. Upset

___ 2. Hostile

___ 3. Alert

___ 4. Ashamed

___ 5. Inspired

___ 6. Nervous

___ 7. Determined

___ 8. Attentive

___ 9. Afraid

___ 10. Active

Scoring: Add up your scores for items 3, 5, 7, 8, and 10. This is your positive affectivity score. Now add up your scores for items 1, 2, 4, 6, and 9. This is your negative affectivity score.

Interpretation: If your *positive affectivity score is greater than 19.7*, it is above average compared to a sample of 411 U.S. undergraduates. If your *negative affectivity score is greater than 11.3*, it is above average compared to the same sample of 411 U.S. undergraduates. To reduce your negative affectivity, try to think more positively and focus on those things for which you can be grateful. Keeping a gratitude journal can help you reflect positively on the things that happen in your life.

Source: Thompson, E. R., Development and validation of an internationally reliable short-form of the positive and negative affect schedule (PANAS), *Journal of Cross-Cultural Psychology, 38*(2), 227–242.

The strongest attribution people tend to make is whether their own or others' behaviors or outcomes are due to the individual (internal factors) because of things like effort or ability or to the environment (external factors) because of things like luck, a lack of resources, or other people. As shown in Figure 4.5, we rely on three rules to evaluate whether to assign an internal or an external attribution to someone's behavior or outcome:[63]

1. *Consistency*: Has the person regularly behaved this way or experienced this outcome in the past? If your roommate consistently earns good grades in a subject, you are more likely to attribute a recent high test grade to an internal cause like ability or effort. If his or her grades earlier in the semester have been lower, you are more likely to attribute the grade to an external cause like luck. Consistency leads to internal attributions.
2. *Distinctiveness*: Does the person act the same way or receive similar outcomes in different types of situations? Low distinctiveness occurs when the person frequently acts in a certain way or receives certain outcomes and leads to internal attributions. If your roommate is a straight-A student, the distinctiveness of his or her recent high grade would be low, and you would make internal attributions for it. If your roommate is a C student, the distinctiveness of the recent high grade would be high and you would attribute it to external causes.

Figure 4.5

The attribution process involves observing behavior and then attributing causes to it. Observed behaviors are interpreted in terms of their consensus, their consistency, and their distinctiveness. Based on these interpretations, behavior is attributed to either internal or external causes.

The Attribution Process

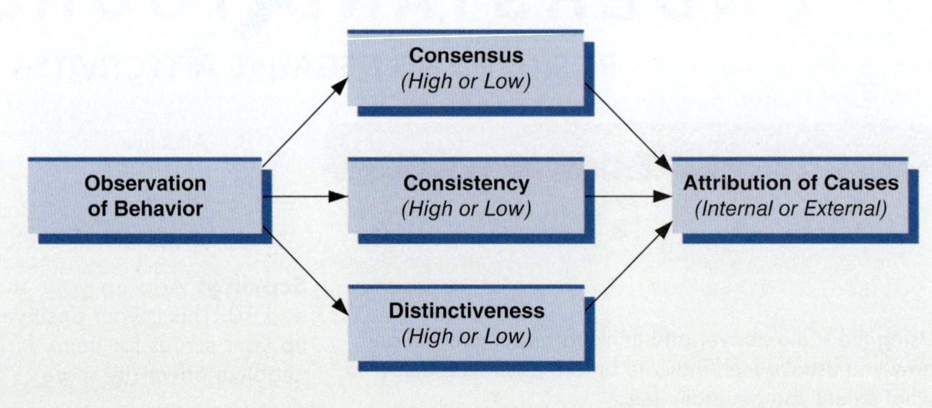

3. *Consensus*: Would others behave similarly in the same situation, or receive the same outcome? If almost everyone earns an A in the course in which your roommate just did well, consensus would be high and you would make external attributions for your roommate's grade. If consensus is low and few students do well in the class, you would make internal attributions for the grade.

A related aspect of attribution is self-handicapping. *Self-handicapping* occurs when people create obstacles for themselves that make success less likely. Examples include using drugs and alcohol, refusing to practice, and reducing effort. Creating these impediments obviously decreases motivation and performance. These behaviors may sound silly, but they are very real and serve to protect the person's sense of self-competence. If a self-handicapping person does poorly, the obstacle creates an easy explanation for the failure. If the person succeeds in spite of the obstacle, the success seems even greater.

Self-handicapping occurs when people create obstacles for themselves that make success less likely. This man, for example, is having a drink while working. Alcohol, in turn, may affect his performance and lead to bad decisions. Even if he doesn't drink too much, others who observe his behavior may start to question his judgment. In either case he may be hurting his chances for a promotion.

Students sometimes use self-handicapping attributions, perhaps by not studying for a test. They might feel that:

- If they study hard and give it their best shot but fail, they will look and feel incompetent.
- If they study hard and pass, the hard work will reduce the meaning of the success. (If they were really smart, they would not have had to work so hard.)
- If they do not study and fail, the failure can be easily explained by the lack of effort. They can still believe that they could have succeeded if they had really tried. Even if they fail the test, no one will have evidence that they are stupid.
- If they do not study but still manage to succeed, then the only explanation for the success is that they have really high ability.

This kind of reasoning is obviously counterproductive, because someone who expends less effort is obviously less likely to succeed. Self-handicapping tends to emerge during adolescence among persons with a high concern about looking competent. Focusing on effort attributions and developing feelings of self-efficacy help overcome this behavior.

As a manager, understanding that a subordinate's own perceptions or attributions for success or failure determine the amount of effort he or she will expend on that activity in the future is a powerful motivational tool. Employees' perceptions and attributions determine the amount of effort they will exert on that activity in the future, and those attributions may differ across people. An employee may believe that she expended a great deal of effort when in fact she did not, or perceive an objectively easy task to be difficult. Attributing success to internal causes builds self-efficacy and increases the motivation to try hard and persist in the face of failure.

Perception and Fairness, Justice, and Trust

Perception and perceptual processes play a major role in how people feel about fairness, justice, and trust. Think of a time when you felt unfairly treated at work or school. Why did you feel that way? What did you do about it? When we perceive

HOW CULTURE CAN INFLUENCE ATTRIBUTIONS

In intercultural interactions, the interpretations of behaviors are often more important than the actual behaviors themselves.[64] Because Western cultures emphasize individual freedom and autonomy, people in these cultures prefer dispositional explanations, while people from collectivist cultures that emphasize group membership and conformity to group norms tend to prefer situational explanations.[65]

One study showed American and Chinese participants a picture of an individual fish swimming in front of a group of fish. More American than Chinese participants attributed the individual fish's behavior as internally rather than externally caused.[66] This attributional difference may be due to the way people with different cultural orientations perceive themselves in their environment. Westerners, who tend to be more individualistic, often see themselves as independent entities and therefore tend to notice individual objects more than contextual details.[67]

Understanding a coworker's behavior requires understanding his or her subjective culture. Attributional training can help us understand the appropriate attributions for the behaviors of diverse coworkers.

unfairness, we are often motivated to do something about it. In organizations, perceptions of unfairness (also referred to as injustice) can exist in numerous situations. Layoffs and downsizings are often seen as unfair by those dismissed as well as by the employees who remain. Hiring and promotion decisions are often seen as unfair by those not chosen. In unionized settings, both managers and union representatives often perceive the other to be unfair. Even organizational change can be viewed as unfair by those asked to learn new systems or do new things.

organizational fairness *Refers to employees' perceptions of organizational events, policies, and practices as being fair or not fair*

The term ***organizational fairness*** refers to employees' perceptions of organizational events, policies, and practices as being fair or not fair.[68] Fairness is a primary concern in relationships where subordinates must rely on others in higher positions.[69] Why should you care about fairness? You should care because perceptions of fairness affect a wide variety of employee attitudes and behaviors including satisfaction, commitment, trust, and turnover. A number of negative behaviors can result from perceptions of unfairness, including theft, sabotage, and other unethical behaviors.[70] Perceived unfairness also increases the chances that employees will file lawsuits against their employers.[71] Most of these outcomes of fairness perceptions can have an obvious economic impact on organizations.

As a manager, it is critical to remember that it is insufficient to just *be* fair; you must also be *perceived* as fair by your subordinates. Perceptions are what drive responses, and subordinates' attributions and interpretations of your behaviors and decisions may not reflect your intentions or your own beliefs. The demographic diversity of the U.S. workforce requires many managers to handle differences among employees regarding characteristics ranging from ethnicity to religion to political ideology—all of which can be a source of conflict and misunderstanding.[72] Effectively managing organizational fairness perceptions and attributions can help managers prevent or effectively manage any conflict or misunderstandings that occur.

Understanding fairness is important for ethical reasons as well.[73] There has been no shortage of high-profile ethical lapses in recent years, ranging from Enron to Bernie Madoff to mortgage fraud. Training all employees, including company leaders, in organizational fairness principles helps guide them in making ethical decisions. When employees perceive general organizational fairness and an organizational desire to follow through on formal ethics programs, unethical behavior is reduced and employees are more willing to report problems to management.[74] Also, individuals' expectations for fairness produce expectations that those who violate ethical expectations will be disciplined.[75] Failure to meet employees' fairness expectations can lead them to engage in unethical behavior.[76] We think of fairness in three main ways, discussed next.

Distributive Fairness

distributive fairness *Refers to the perceived fairness of the outcome received, including resource distributions, promotions, hiring and layoff decisions, and raises*

Distributive fairness refers to the perceived fairness of the outcome received, including resource distributions, promotions, hiring and layoff decisions, and raises.[77] Imagine that you and a friend both apply for a job with a local company at the same time. Although you believe that you are more qualified, your friend is offered a job and you are not. Would this feel fair? Your belief about the fairness of you not getting the job reflects your perception of distributive fairness. Distributive fairness relates only to the outcome received, not to the fairness of the process that generated the decision.

Procedural Fairness

procedural fairness *Addresses the fairness of the procedures used to generate the outcome*

A fair process is as important as a fair outcome. ***Procedural fairness*** addresses the fairness of the procedures used to generate the outcome (e.g., what rules were followed, whether people had the opportunity to express opinions and influence the outcome, etc.).[78] For example, let's continue the example of your applying for a job at the same time as your friend but your friend getting the position. What if you learned that the hiring manager is your friend's cousin, so your friend was offered the job even though you were more qualified? Bending the rules for a relative would probably violate your standards for what constitutes a fair hiring procedure. Low procedural fairness increases negative outcomes, such as lower job performance and withdrawal behaviors like coming to work late or putting in less effort. But if procedural fairness is high, negative reactions are much less likely. Why does procedural fairness matter so much? There are two reasons.[79] First, employees use perceptions of the current decision-making procedures to predict how they will likely fare in the organization in the future. Second, fair procedures signal that employees are valued and accepted by the organization.

Interactional Fairness

Interactional fairness is whether the amount of information about the decision and the process was adequate, and the perceived fairness of the interpersonal treatment and explanations received during the decision-making process. Does an employee who did not receive a performance bonus feel that the supervisor adequately explained the reason? When we assess undesirable outcomes, how we are treated can be just as important as the outcomes we receive. It is difficult to give our best effort to someone who treats us rudely or disrespects us. Deception or abusive words or actions can be seen as having low interactional fairness.[80]

interactional fairness
Whether the amount of information about the decision and the process was adequate, and the perceived fairness of the interpersonal treatment and explanations received during the decision-making process

Interactional fairness describes two specific types of interpersonal treatment.[81] The first type is interpersonal fairness, which reflects the degree to which people are treated with politeness, dignity, and respect by authorities or third parties involved in executing procedures or determining outcomes. The second type is informational fairness, which focuses on the extent to which employees receive adequate information and explanations about decisions affecting their working lives.[82] It is important that a high degree of interactional fairness exist in the relationship between a supervisor and a subordinate. Low interactional fairness can lead to feelings of resentment toward either the supervisor or the organization.[83] A victim of interactional unfairness often has increased expressions of hostility toward the supervisor or company, which can lead to negative work behaviors and decrease the effectiveness of organizational communication.[84] Explanations increase job applicants' fairness perceptions, perceptions of the hiring organization, test-taking motivation, and performance on cognitive ability tests.[85]

Perception and Trust

One of the most important outcomes of consistently treating others fairly is trust. ***Trust*** is the expectation that another person will not act to take advantage of us regardless of our ability to monitor or control them.[86] Trust is critical to long-term relationships and is positively related to job performance.[87] Trusting work relationships enable employees to focus on their work and not waste time and energy "watching their backs." Trust is particularly important to the developmental stages of relationships,[88] and is positively related to a company's financial performance.[89] One survey of 500 business professionals found that having a trusting relationship with one's manager was the main factor in deciding to stay.[90]

trust
The expectation that another person will not act to take advantage of us regardless of our ability to monitor or control them

CASE STUDY What to Do When the Boss Releases His Inner Toddler

Put yourself in the following scenario:
You're one of 10 VPs at a small chain of regional clothing stores, where you're in charge of the women's apparel departments. One of your jobs is to review each month's performance at a meeting of all 10 department heads and the company president. Like your fellow VPs, you prepare a PowerPoint presentation showing the results for the previous month and your projections for the upcoming month, and during your presentation you take the podium and lead the discussion from the front of the room.

On the whole, the meeting is part of a pretty sound overall strategy that allows everyone to know what's going on and what to expect across the board. Typically, the only drawback to an informative and productive session is the president's apparent inability to deal with bad news. He gets irritable and likes to lambaste "underperformers," and as a result, you and your colleagues always enter the meeting with stomachs in knots and leave it with full-blown gastric distress. The president himself thinks he's fostering open and honest discussion, but everyone else in the room knows plain old-fashioned bullying when they see it.

As luck would have it, you now find yourself at the front of the room, looking up at the floor-to-ceiling screen on which are emblazoned, in what looks to you like 500-point font (red, of course), your less than stellar monthly numbers. Sweating profusely, you're attempting to explain some disappointing sales figures when you hear a noise—a sort of thudding and rattling—against the wall behind you. Startled, you spin around toward the room and are surprised to see that everyone seems to be looking for something on the floor or checking the weather through the windows on one side of the room. Finally you glance toward the wall behind you, where you discover a bent meeting-room chair lying on the floor, and as you look up again, you see that the president is standing, his arms crossed and his face scowling. "The next time you show me numbers like those," he snarls, "I won't miss!"

Believe it or not, this is a true story (although we've changed a few details—very few—in the interest of plausibility and dramatic impact). It's told by John McKee, a consultant to professionals and businesspeople who want to move up the management ladder as quickly—and, presumably, with as little violence—as possible. McKee was actually an eyewitness to the episode, and although he admits that it's "the clearest example of a boss behaving badly" that he's ever seen, he hastens to add that he won't be the least bit surprised when someone comes up with an even better one.

Consultant Lynn Taylor, who specializes in the development of work and management teams, calls bosses like the one in our scenario *Terrible Office Tyrants*, or *TOTs*—managers who can't control their power when they're placed under stress. Taylor believes that the characterization is apt in light of research showing that bosses like the one we've described actually "return to their misbehaving 'inner toddler' to handle unwieldy pressures." In other words, they revert to the kind of behavior that produced "self-serving results" when they were children. In the adult workplace, explains Taylor, they "occasionally find that their ability to master the world is limited, as it is with most mortal beings. This revelation, on top of their inability to communicate clearly in the moment, makes them furious and frustrated."

According to Taylor, there are 20 "core, parallel traits [shared by] TOTs and toddlers." The following, which are fairly aggressive, she catalogs under "Bratty Behavior":

- Bragging
- Bullying
- Demanding
- Ignoring
- Impulsiveness
- Lying
- Self-centeredness
- Stubbornness
- Tantrums
- Territorialism
- Whining

"Most tantrums," Taylor assures us, "don't involve things being thrown across the room," and TOT behavior, especially in its less aggressive forms—fickleness, mood swings, neediness—can be "proactively managed" by employees who don't care

CASE STUDY (Continued)

to be treated as emotional punching bags. She recommends "humor, common sense, rational thinking, and setting limits to bad behavior." And remember, she adds, "You are the parent with the proverbial cookie jar when it comes to managing a TOT."

Taylor's approach to understanding and dealing with bad bosses isn't entirely metaphorical, and she does suggest that beleaguered employees translate her general advice into some concrete coping techniques. When confronted by managerial neediness, for example, a good "pacifier" might be a reply such as: "It'll be the first thing on my to-do list tomorrow." If you're looking for a handy toolbox of effective techniques, you can find dozens on the Internet, most of them posted by psychologists and organizational consultants. The following was compiled by Karen Burns, *U.S. News* columnist and specialist on career advice for women:

- Put everything in writing. Write and date progress reports. When you get verbal instructions, summarize them in a reply e-mail.
- Be a star performer. Beyond just being a good employee, maintain a positive demeanor; it's hard for someone to ambush you when you're doing your job and smiling in the process.
- Pick your moments. Rather than simply avoiding your boss, study her patterns. Steer clear when she's a nutcase and schedule interactions for times when she's stabilized.
- Seek community. Anchor your sanity in ties to coworkers and other managers. Find a mentor inside the workplace and someone outside to talk (and vent) to.
- Control what you can. You can't control your boss's irrational behavior, so control what you can—namely, the way you respond to it. Ignore the cranky tone of voice and respond to the substance of what she says. Also, eat right, exercise, get enough sleep, and spend the rest of your time with sane people.
- Know your rights. If you want to take your grievance to the HR department (or further), be sure that you've documented your problem and your efforts to resolve it, and be specific about the remedy you're asking for (transfer, severance package, etc.).
- Identify the exits. Come up with a plan, and don't be bullied into taking action before you're ready.

Questions

1. According to some experts, the sort of behavior recorded here is more prevalent in the business world than in the rest of society. Assuming that this is true, why do you suppose that's the case?
2. Are you something of a perfectionist? Are you easily frustrated? How well suited are you—at this point in your life—to the task of managing other people?
3. How might attitudes, values, and perceptions affect the behaviors illustrated in this case?
4. How would stress come into play?

Sources: McKee, J. (2007, Feruary 8). Worst Boss Ever. *TechRepublic*. Available at http://www.techrepublic.com/blog/career-management/worst-boss-ever/; Taylor, L. (2009, August 27). Why Bad Bosses Act Like Toddlers. *Psychology Today*. Available at https://www.psychologytoday.com/blog/tame-your-terrible-office-tyrant/200908/why-bad-bosses-act-toddlers; Taylor, L. (2009, December 15). 10 Ways to Manage Bad Bosses. *CNN Living*. Available at http://www.cnn.com/2009/LIVING/worklife/12/14/bad.bosses.deal.with.cb/; Burns, K. (2009, November 4). How to Survive a Bad Boss. *U.S. News & World Report*. Available at http://money.usnews.com/money/blogs/outside-voices-careers/2009/11/04/how-to-survive-a-bad-boss.

STRESS IN ORGANIZATIONS

The finally element of individual behavior we will discuss in this chapter is stress. Many people think of stress as a simple problem. In reality, however, stress is complex and often misunderstood.[91] To learn how job stress truly works, we must first define it and then describe the process through which it develops.

Stress affects different people in different ways. This man, for example, seems to be very stressed about his work. However, none of his coworkers seem to be experiencing the same degree of stress. Of course, it may also be the case that his stress is unrelated to work but instead comes from other sources.

The Nature of Stress

Stress has been defined in many ways, but most definitions say that stress is caused by a stimulus, that the stimulus can be either physical or psychological, and that the individual responds to the stimulus in some way.[92] Therefore, we define ***stress*** as a person's adaptive response to a stimulus that places excessive psychological or physical demands on him or her.

stress
A person's adaptive response to a stimulus that places excessive psychological or physical demands on that person

Given the underlying complexities of this definition, we need to examine its components carefully. First is the notion of adaptation. As we discuss presently, people may adapt to stressful circumstances in any of several ways. Second is the role of the stimulus. This stimulus, generally called a stressor, is anything that induces stress. Third, stressors can be either psychological or physical. Finally, the demands the stressor places on the individual must be excessive for stress to actually result. Of course, what is excessive for one person may be perfectly tolerable for another. The point is simply that a person must perceive the demands as excessive or stress will not actually be present.

There has been a marked increase in stress reported by airline workers in the last few years. A combination of increased pressure for salary and benefit reductions, threats to pensions, demotions, layoffs, and heavier workloads have all become more pronounced since September 11. And today's rising energy prices are likely to increase these pressures. As a result, more airline workers than ever before are seeking counseling services; turnover and absenteeism are also on the rise.[93]

The Stress Process

Much of what we know about stress today can be traced to the pioneering work of Hans Selye.[94] Among Selye's most important contributions were his identification of the general adaptation syndrome and the concepts of eustress and distress. Figure 4.6 offers a graphical representation of the ***general adaptation syndrome (GAS)***. According to this model, each of us has a normal level of resistance to stressful events. Some of us can tolerate a great deal of stress and others much less, but we all have a threshold at which stress starts to affect us.

general adaptation syndrome (GAS)
Identifies three stages of response to a stressor: alarm, resistance, and exhaustion

The GAS begins when a person first encounters a stressor. The first stage is called "alarm." At this point, the person may feel some degree of panic and begin to wonder how to cope. The individual may also have to resolve a "fight-or-flight" question: "Can I deal with this, or should I run away?" For example, suppose a manager is ordered to prepare a lengthy report overnight. His first reaction might be, "How will I ever get this done by tomorrow?"

Figure 4.6

The General Adaptation System

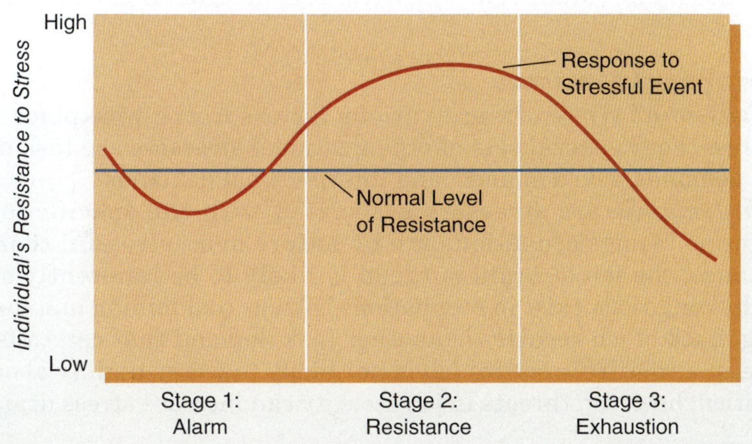

The general adaptation syndrome (GAS) perspective describes three stages of the stress process. The initial stage is called alarm. As illustrated here, a person's resistance often dips slightly below the normal level during this stage. Next comes actual resistance to the stressor, usually leading to an increase above the person's normal level of resistance. Finally, in stage 3, exhaustion may set in, and the person's resistance declines sharply below normal levels.

If the stressor is too extreme, the person may simply be unable to cope with it. In most cases, however, the individual gathers his or her strength (physical or emotional) and begins to resist the negative effects of the stressor. The manager with the long report to write may calm down, call home to tell her kids that she's working late, roll up her sleeves, order out for dinner, and get to work. Thus, at stage two of the GAS, the person is resisting the effects of the stressor.

Often, the resistance phase ends the GAS. If the manager completes the report earlier than she expected, she may drop it in her briefcase, smile to herself, and head home tired but happy. On the other hand, prolonged exposure to a stressor without resolution may bring on phase threeof the GAS: exhaustion. At this stage, the person literally gives up and can no longer fight the stressor. For example, the manager may fall asleep at her desk at 3 a.m. and fail to finish the report.

Distress and Eustress

Selye also pointed out that the sources of stress need not be bad. For example, receiving a bonus and then having to decide what to do with the money can be stressful. So can getting a promotion, making a speech as part of winning a major award, getting married, and similar "good" things. Selye called this type of stress ***eustress***. As we will see later, eustress can lead to a number of positive outcomes for the individual. Of course, there is also negative stress. Called ***distress***, this is what most people think of when they hear the word *stress*. Excessive pressure, unreasonable demands on our time, and bad news all fall into this category. As the term suggests, this form of stress generally results in negative consequences for the individual. For purposes of simplicity, we will continue to use the simple term *stress* throughout this chapter. As you read and study the chapter, remember that stress can be either good or bad. It can motivate and stimulate us, or it can lead to any number of dangerous side effects.

eustress
The pleasurable stress that accompanies positive events

distress
The unpleasant stress that accompanies negative events

Common Causes of Stress

Many things can cause stress. Figure 4.7 shows two broad categories: organizational stressors and life stressors. It also shows three categories of stress consequences: individual consequences, organizational consequences, and burnout.

Organizational Stressors

organizational stressors
factors in the workplace that can cause stress

Organizational stressors are various factors in the workplace that can cause stress. Four general sets of organizational stressors are task demands, physical demands, role demands, and interpersonal demands.

Task demands are stressors associated with the specific job a person performs. Some occupations are by nature more stressful than others. For instance, the job of brain surgeon is likely to be inherently stressful. Unhealthy conditions exist in occupations such as coal mining and toxic waste handling. Lack of job security is another task demand that can cause stress. Someone in a relatively secure job is not likely to worry unduly about losing that position; however, threats to job security can increase stress dramatically.

Figure 4.7

The causes and consequences of stress are related in complex ways. As shown here, most common causes of stress can be classified as either organizational stressors or life stressors. Similarly, common consequences include individual and organizational consequences, as well as burnout.

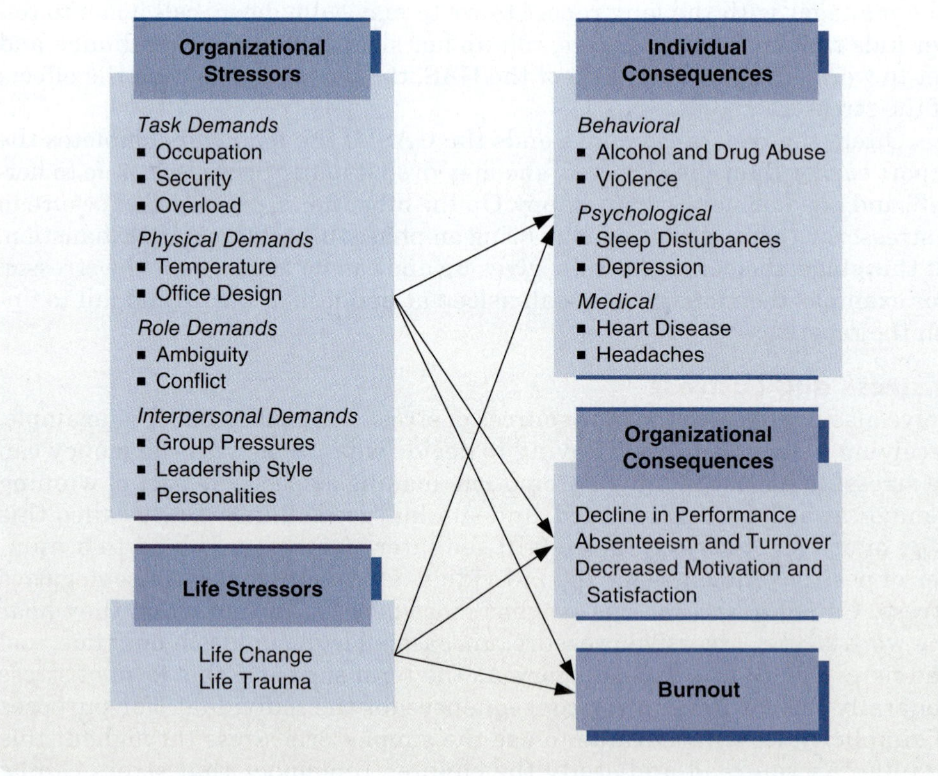

Reference: Adapted from James C. Quick and Jonathan D. Quick, Organizational Stress and Preventive Management (McGraw-Hill, 1984) pp. 19, 44, and 76. Used by permission of James C. Quick.

Organizational stressors are factors in the workplace that can cause stress. Task, physical, role, and interpersonal demands are all types of organizational stressors. This man, for example, may be stressed because he is behind on a project, just had a disagreement with his boss or coworkers, has been working too many hours, or is working in a hot office with no air conditioning.

STOCK-ASSO/SHUTTERSTOCK.COM

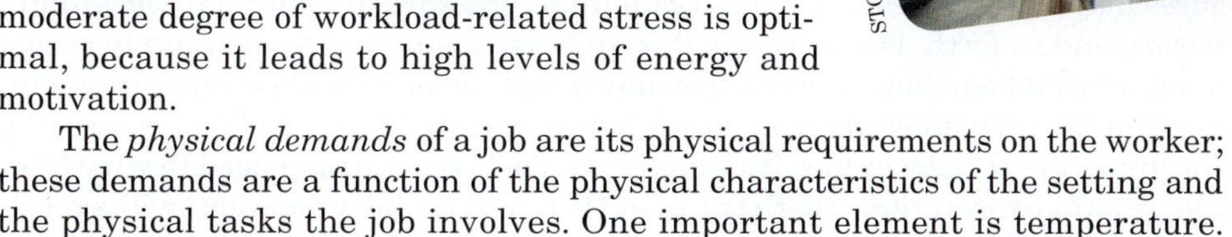

For example, stress generally increases throughout an organization during a period of layoffs or immediately after a merger with another firm. A final task demand stressor is overload. Overload occurs when a person simply has more work than he or she can handle. The overload can be either quantitative (the person has too many tasks to perform or too little time to perform them) or qualitative (the person may believe he or she lacks the ability to do the job). We should note that the opposite of overload may also be undesirable. As Figure 4.8 shows, low task demands can result in boredom and apathy just as overload can cause tension and anxiety. Thus, a moderate degree of workload-related stress is optimal, because it leads to high levels of energy and motivation.

The *physical demands* of a job are its physical requirements on the worker; these demands are a function of the physical characteristics of the setting and the physical tasks the job involves. One important element is temperature.

Figure 4.8

Workload, Stress, and Performance

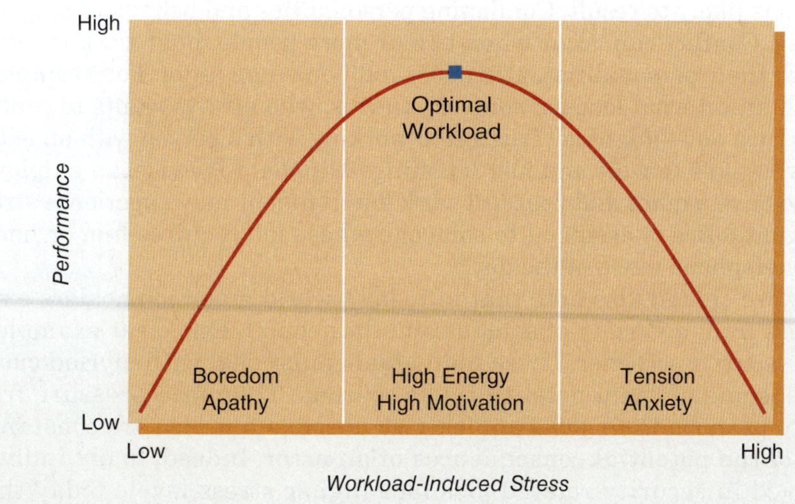

Too much stress is clearly undesirable, but too little stress can also lead to unexpected problems. For example, too little stress may result in boredom and apathy and be accompanied by low performance. And although too much stress can cause tension, anxiety, and low performance, for most people there is an optimal level of stress that results in high energy, motivation, and performance.

Working outdoors in extreme temperatures can result in stress, as can working in an improperly heated or cooled office. Strenuous labor such as loading heavy cargo or lifting packages can lead to similar results. Office design can be a problem, as well. A poorly designed office can make it difficult for people to have privacy or promote too much or too little social interaction. Too much interaction may distract a person from his or her task, whereas too little may lead to boredom or loneliness. Likewise, poor lighting, inadequate work surfaces, and similar deficiencies can create stress. Shift work can cause disruptions for people because of the way it affects their sleep and leisure-time activities.

Role demands can also be stressful to people in organizations. A role is a set of expected behaviors associated with a particular position in a group or organization. As such, it has both formal (i.e., job-related and explicit) and informal (i.e., social and implicit) requirements. People in an organization or work group expect a person in a particular role to act in certain ways. They transmit these expectations both formally and informally. Individuals perceive role expectations with varying degrees of accuracy and then attempt to enact that role. However, "errors" can creep into this process, resulting in stress-inducing problems called role ambiguity, role conflict, and role overload.

A final set of organizational stressors consists of three *interpersonal demands*: group pressures, leadership, and interpersonal conflict. Group pressures may include pressure to restrict output, pressure to conform to the group's norms, and so forth. For instance, it is quite common for a workgroup to arrive at an informal agreement about how much each member will produce. Individuals who produce much more or much less than this level may be pressured by the group to get back in line. An individual who feels a strong need to vary from the group's expectations (perhaps to get a pay raise or promotion) will experience a great deal of stress, especially if acceptance by the group is also important to him or her. Leadership style also may cause stress. Suppose an employee needs a great deal of social support from his leader. The leader, however, is quite brusque and shows no concern or compassion for him. This employee will probably feel stressed. Similarly, assume an employee feels a strong need to participate in decision making and to be active in all aspects of management. Her boss is very autocratic and refuses to consult subordinates about anything. Once again stress is likely to result. Conflicting personalities and behaviors may also cause stress. Conflict can occur when two or more people must work together even though their personalities, attitudes, and behaviors differ. For example, a person with an internal locus of control—that is, who always wants to control how things turn out—might get frustrated working with a person with an external locus who likes to wait and just let things happen. Likewise, an employee who likes to have a quiet and peaceful work environment may experience stress if the adjacent office is assigned to someone whose job requires him or her to talk on the telephone much of the day.[95]

Finally, we should also note that in today's world many job holders experience stress from a variety of sources simultaneously. One clear example is an airport security screener. These individuals must deal with myriad carry-on articles, some of them potentially dangerous. They face pressure from travelers to perform their job as quickly as possible but also are constantly reminded of the potential consequences of an error. Indeed, many individuals involved in security-related jobs face higher stress levels today than ever before. It is also the case that stress in organizational settings can be influenced by events that take place outside the organization. An individual dealing with financial problems, a sick child, or the death of a close family member will undoubtedly experience stress from those events. And understandably, an individual facing these and similar issues outside of work will still be affected by them while at work.

Consequences of Stress

Stress can have a number of consequences. As we already noted, if the stress is positive, the result may be more energy, enthusiasm, and motivation. Of more concern, of course, are the negative consequences of stress. Referring back to Figure 4.7, we see that stress can produce individual consequences, organizational consequences, and burnout. We should first note that many of the factors listed are obviously interrelated. For example, alcohol abuse is shown as an individual consequence, but it also affects the organization the person works for. An employee who drinks on the job may perform poorly and create a hazard for others. If the category for a consequence seems somewhat arbitrary, be aware that each consequence is categorized according to the area of its primary influence.

Individual Consequences

The individual consequences of stress, then, are the outcomes that mainly affect the individual. The organization also may suffer, either directly or indirectly, but it is the individual who pays the real price.[96] Stress may produce behavioral, psychological, and medical consequences.

The *behavioral consequences* of stress may harm the person under stress or others. One such behavior is smoking. Research has clearly documented that people who smoke tend to smoke more when they experience stress. There is also evidence that alcohol and drug abuse are linked to stress, although this relationship is less well documented. Other possible behavioral consequences are accident proneness, aggression and violence, and appetite disorders. The *psychological consequences* of stress relate to a person's mental health and well-being. When people experience too much stress at work, they may become depressed or find themselves sleeping too much or not enough.[97] Stress may also lead to family problems and sexual difficulties. The *medical consequences* of stress affect a person's physical well-being. Heart disease and stroke, among other illnesses, have been linked to stress. Other common medical problems resulting from too much stress include headaches, backaches, ulcers and related stomach and intestinal disorders, and skin conditions such as acne and hives.

Organizational Consequences

Clearly, any of the individual consequences just discussed can also affect the organization. Other results of stress have even more direct consequences for organizations. These include decline in performance, withdrawal, and negative changes in attitudes.

One clear organizational consequence of too much stress is a decline in performance. For operating workers, such a decline can translate into poor-quality work or a drop in productivity. For managers, it can mean faulty decision making or disruptions in working relationships as people become irritable and hard to get along with.[98] Withdrawal behaviors also can result from stress. For the organization, the two most significant forms of withdrawal behavior are absenteeism and quitting. People who are having a hard time coping with stress in their jobs are more likely to call in sick or consider leaving the organization for good. Stress can also produce other, more subtle forms of withdrawal. A manager may start missing deadlines or taking longer lunch breaks. An employee may withdraw psychologically by ceasing to care about the organization and the job. As noted above, employee violence is a potential individual consequence of stress. This also has obvious organizational implications, especially if the violence is directed at another employee or at the organization in general.[99] Another direct organizational consequence of employee stress relates to attitudes. As we just noted, job satisfaction, morale, and organizational commitment can all suffer, along with motivation to perform at high levels. As a result, people may be more prone to complain about unimportant things, do only enough work to get by, and so forth.

burnout
A general feeling of exhaustion that develops when an individual simultaneously experiences too much pressure and has too few sources of satisfaction

Burnout, another consequence of stress, has clear implications for both people and organizations. ***Burnout*** is a general feeling of exhaustion that develops when a person simultaneously experiences too much pressure and has too few sources of satisfaction.[100] People with high aspirations and strong motivation to get things done are prime candidates for burnout under certain conditions. They are especially vulnerable when the organization suppresses or limits their initiative while constantly demanding that they serve the organization's own ends.

In such a situation, the individual is likely to put too much of himself or herself into the job. In other words, the person may well keep trying to meet his or her own agenda while simultaneously trying to fulfill the organization's expectations. The most likely effects of this situation are prolonged stress, fatigue, frustration, and helplessness under the burden of overwhelming demands. The person literally exhausts his or her aspirations and motivation, much as a candle burns itself out. Loss of self-confidence and psychological withdrawal follow. Ultimately, burnout may be the result. At this point, the individual may start dreading going to work in the morning, may put in longer hours but accomplish less than before, and may generally display mental and physical exhaustion.[101]

Managing and Controlling Stress

Given that stress is widespread and so potentially disruptive in organizations, it follows that people and organizations should be concerned about how to manage it more effectively. And in fact they are. Many strategies have been developed to help manage stress in the workplace. Some are for individuals, and others are geared toward organizations.[102]

Individual Coping Strategies

Many strategies for helping individuals manage stress have been proposed. Exercise is one method of managing stress. People who exercise regularly are less likely to have heart attacks than inactive people. More directly, research has suggested that people who exercise regularly feel less tension and stress, are more self-confident, and show greater optimism. People who do not exercise regularly feel more stress, are more likely to be depressed, and experience other negative consequences.

IMPROVE YOUR SKILLS

STRESS MANAGEMENT TIPS

We all feel stress from time to time. Knowing how to manage your stress will help to keep you healthy and productive. Two main strategies for managing stress are: (1) generate calm or relaxed feelings to counteract the biological state of exhaustion or over-arousal, and (2) change your appraisal of the stress-inducing situation to reduce negative emotions. Below are some tips for using each strategy.

Generating Calm or Relaxed Feelings

1. Eat healthy and avoid too much caffeine.
2. Get enough high-quality sleep; take a nap if necessary.
3. Exercise.
4. Practice relaxation techniques including meditation. These are known to relax muscles and reduce adrenaline levels.
5. Develop affectionate relationships. Giving and getting hugs, petting a dog or cat, or having conversations with friends can all reduce feelings of stress.
6. Prioritize your to-do list. As Scarlett O'Hara says in the movie *Gone with the Wind*, "I can't think about that right now. If I do, I'll go crazy. I'll think about that tomorrow."
7. Learn to say "No," "Not now," and "I really can't"—no one can do everything!

Changing Your Appraisal of the Situation

1. Try to view crises or stressful events as opportunities. The Chinese character for crisis, *wei ji*, is made up of two component characters. One is the character for danger, and the other is the character for opportunity. Framing a crisis as an opportunity decreases negative emotions and increases positive emotions, reducing stress.
2. Reframe the stressor. Casting the situation in a less stressful or threatening way can decrease negative emotions and stress. For example, the boss is not really trying to make your job difficult; she is just very busy and has deadlines to meet.
3. Try to find the silver lining. Your boss's moving up the deadline for that big report is challenging, but it gives you a chance to show your talent, and it will soon be done!

A related method of managing stress is relaxation. We noted at the beginning of the chapter that coping with stress requires adaptation. Proper relaxation is an effective way to adapt. Relaxation can take many forms. One way to relax is to take regular vacations. One study found that people's attitudes toward a variety of workplace characteristics improved significantly following a vacation.[103] People can also relax while on the job. For example, it has been recommended that people take regular rest breaks during their normal workday.[104] A popular way of resting is to sit quietly with closed eyes for ten minutes every afternoon. (Of course, it might be necessary to have an alarm clock handy!)

Time management is often recommended for managing stress. The idea is that many daily

People can adopt a variety of techniques to help cope with stress. Exercise, relaxation, and better time management are all common methods. These coworkers are engaging in deep breathing exercises to help control their stress.

pressures can be eased or eliminated if a person does a better job of managing time. One popular approach to time management is to make a list every morning of the things to be done that day. Then you group the items on the list into three categories: critical activities that must be performed, important activities that should be performed, and optional or trivial things that can be delegated or postponed. Then, of course, you do the things on the list in their order of importance. This strategy helps people get more of the important things done every day. It also encourages delegation of less important activities to others.

Somewhat related to time management is the idea of role management, in which the individual actively works to avoid overload, ambiguity, and conflict. For example, if you do not know what is expected of you, you should not sit and worry about it. Instead, ask for clarification from your boss. Another role management strategy is to learn to say "No." As simple as saying "No" might sound, a lot of people create problems for themselves by always saying "Yes." Besides working in their regular jobs, they agree to serve on committees, volunteer for extra duties, and accept extra assignments. Sometimes, of course, we have no choice but to accept an extra obligation (if our boss tells us to complete a new project, we will probably have to do it). In many cases, however, saying "No" is an option.[105]

A final method for managing stress is to develop and maintain support groups. A support group is simply a group of family members or friends with whom a person can spend time. Going out after work with a couple of coworkers to a basketball game, for example, can help relieve the stress that builds up during the day. Supportive family and friends can help people deal with normal stress on an ongoing basis. Support groups can be particularly useful during times of crisis. For example, suppose an employee has just learned that she did not get the promotion she has been working toward for months. It may help her tremendously if she has good friends to lean on, be it to talk to or to yell at.

Organizational Coping Strategies

Organizations are also increasingly realizing that they should be involved in managing their employees' stress.[106] There are two different rationales for this view. One is that because the organization is at least partly responsible for creating the stress, it should help relieve it. The other is that workers experiencing lower levels of harmful stress will function more effectively. Two basic organizational strategies for helping employees manage stress are institutional programs and collateral programs.

Institutional programs for managing stress are undertaken through established organizational mechanisms. For example, properly designed jobs and work schedules (both discussed in Chapter 6) can help ease stress. Shift work, in particular, can cause major problems for employees, because they constantly have to adjust their sleep and relaxation patterns. Thus, the design of work and work schedules should be a focus of organizational efforts to reduce stress. The organization's culture also can be used to help manage stress. In some organizations, for example, there is a strong norm against taking time off or going on vacation. In the long run, such norms can cause major stress. Thus, the organization should strive to foster a culture that reinforces a healthy mix of work and nonwork activities. Finally, supervision can play an important institutional role in managing stress. A supervisor can be a major source of overload. If made aware of their potential for assigning stressful amounts of work, supervisors can do a better job of keeping workloads reasonable.

In addition to institutional efforts aimed at reducing stress, many organizations are turning to collateral programs. A collateral stress program is an organizational program specifically created to help employees deal with stress. Organizations have adopted stress management programs, health promotion programs, and other kinds of programs for this purpose. More and more companies are developing their own programs or adopting existing programs of this type. For example, Lockheed Martin offers screening programs for its employees to detect signs of hypertension. Many firms today also have employee fitness programs. These programs attack stress indirectly by encouraging employees to exercise, which is presumed to reduce stress. On the negative side, this kind of effort costs considerably more than stress management programs because the firm must invest in physical facilities. Still, more and more companies are exploring this option.[107] L. L. Bean, for example, has state-of-the-art fitness centers for its employees, and many technology companies such as Google and Facebook provide on-site massages and gyms for their employees.

Finally, organizations try to help employees cope with stress through other kinds of programs. For example, existing career development programs, such as the one at General Electric, are used for this purpose. Other companies use programs promoting everything from humor to massage to yoga as antidotes for stress.[108] Of course, little or no research supports some of the claims made by advocates of these programs. Thus, managers must take steps to ensure that any organizational effort to help employees cope with stress is at least reasonably effective.

The Republic of Tea, a small, privately held company that promotes healthy lifestyles centered around the consumption of tea, has measured its stress-reduction efforts' effectiveness. The firm recently added a comprehensive program called the Health Ministry to help its employees live healthier lives. A nutritionist provided free counseling to employees about their diet and weight, employees got a $500 credit for gym memberships, and a workday walking program encouraged all employees to take 10- to 15-minute walks on company time. Employees were even provided with high-quality walking shoes. The firm says that its health management efforts have boosted its order processing efficiency by 11 percent, increased order accuracy by 7 percent, and decreased employee absenteeism.[109]

Work-Life Balance

At numerous points in this chapter we have alluded to relationships between a person's work and life. In this final brief section we will make these relationships a bit more explicit.

Fundamental Work-Life Relationships

Work-life relationships can be characterized in any number of ways. Consider, for example, the basic dimensions of the part of a person's life tied specifically to work. Common dimensions would include such things as an individual's current job (including working hours, job satisfaction, and so forth), his or her career goals (the person's aspirations, career trajectory, and so forth), interpersonal relations at work (with the supervisor, subordinates, coworkers, and others), and job security.[110]

Part of each person's life is also distinctly separate from work. These dimensions might include the person's spouse or life companion, dependents (such as children or elderly parents), personal life interests (hobbies, leisure-time interests, religious affiliations, community involvement), and friendship networks. ***Work-life relationships***, then, include any relationships between dimensions of the person's work life and the person's personal life. For example, a person with numerous dependents (a nonworking spouse or domestic partner, dependent children, dependent parents, etc.) may prefer a job with a relatively high salary, few overtime demands, and little travel. On the other hand, a person with no dependents may be less interested in salary and more receptive to overtime, and may enjoy job-related travel. Stress will occur when there is a basic inconsistency or incompatibility between a person's work and life dimensions. For example, if a person is the sole care provider for a dependent elderly parent but has a job that requires considerable travel and evening work, stress is likely to result.

work-life relationships
Interrelationships between a person's work life and personal life

Balancing Work-Life Linkages

Balancing work-life linkages is, of course, no easy thing to do. Demands from both sides can be extreme, and people may need to be prepared to make trade-offs. The important thing is to recognize the potential trade-offs in advance so that they can be carefully weighed and a comfortable decision made. Some of the strategies for doing this were discussed earlier. For example, working for a company that offers flexible work schedules may be an attractive option.[111]

Individuals must also recognize the importance of long-term versus short-term perspectives in balancing their work and personal lives. For example, people may have to respond a bit more to work demands than to life demands in the early years of their careers. In mid-career, they may be able to achieve a more comfortable balance. And in later career stages, they may be able to put life dimensions first by refusing to relocate, working shorter hours, and so forth.

People also have to decide for themselves what they value and what trade-offs they are willing to make. For instance, consider the dilemma faced by a dual-career couple when one partner is being transferred to another city. One option is for one of the partners to subordinate her or his career for the other partner, at least temporarily. For example, the partner being transferred can turn the offer down, risking a potential career setback or the loss of the job. Or the other partner may resign from his or her current position and seek another one in the new location. The couple might also decide to live apart, with one moving and the other staying. The partners might also come to realize that their respective careers are more important to them than their relationship and decide to go their separate ways.[112]

SUMMARY AND APPLICATION

Attitudes, values and emotions, perception, and stress are all important factors that influence organizational behavior. Our beliefs and feelings about something influence our attitudes about it. Our attitudes then affect our behavior through our intentions. The three most important job-related attitudes are job satisfaction, organizational commitment, and employee engagement. Job satisfaction reflects our attitudes and feelings about our job. Organizational commitment is the degree to which an employee identifies with the organization and its goals and wants to stay with the organization.

Employee engagement reflects a heightened emotional and intellectual connection that an employee has for his or her job, organization, manager, or coworkers that, in turn, influences the employee to apply additional discretionary effort to his or her work.

There are many different kinds of values that can be held by people. Not surprisingly, then, it is somewhat common for an individual to have conflicting values. Values also differ across cultures in different parts of the globe. Emotions, affect, and mood are also important contributors to behavior. Emotions are intense, short-term physiological, behavioral, and psychological reactions to a specific object, person, or event that prepare us to respond to it. Mood, on the other hand, is a short-term emotional state not directed toward anything in particular. Affect represents our tendency to experience a particular mood or to react to things with certain emotions.

Perception is the set of processes by which a person becomes aware of and interprets information about the environment. Basic perceptual processes include selective perception and stereotyping. The halo effect occurs when we form an overall impression about someone on the basis of a single (typically good) characteristic. The contrast effect happens when we evaluate someone by comparing that person to other people we have recently encountered who rank higher or lower on the same characteristics. We also project our own characteristics onto others whom we perceive to be similar to us in some ways. Perception and attribution are also closely related. Internal attributions include ability and effort. External attributions include luck, not having sufficient resources, and the interference or help of other people. Distributive fairness is the perception of fairness of the outcome received. Procedural fairness is the fairness of the policies and procedures used to make the decision and determine the outcomes. Interpersonal fairness refers to the politeness, dignity, and respect with which people were treated during the decision-making process. Informational fairness focuses on the adequacy of the information and explanations received during the decision-making process. Trust is an outcome of fairness.

Stress is an individual's response to a strong stimulus. Challenging events are stressful only when also accompanied by negative emotions. Some stress is actually beneficial. Functional stress is the experience of a manageable level of stress for a reasonable period of time that generates positive emotions including satisfaction, excitement, and enjoyment. Dysfunctional stress is an overload of stress from a situation of either under- or over-arousal that continues for too long.

The General Adaptation Syndrome outlines the basic stress process. Stress can be caused by task, physical, role, and interpersonal demands. Consequences of stress include organizational and individual outcomes, as well as burnout. Several things can be done to manage stress.

DISCUSSION QUESTIONS

1. If your boss was not sure it would be worth the investment to change the company's hiring practices to include an evaluation of applicants' attitudes, what would you tell him or her?
2. Do you think that it would be easy to influence a subordinate's attitudes, values, or emotions? Why? Which would have the largest influence on the employee's behavior? Why?

REAL WORLD RESPONSE

ATTITUDE IS A CHOICE AT PIKE PLACE FISH MARKET

John Yokoyama had recently purchased Seattle's Pike Place Fish Market. Continuing the previous owner's fear-based management style led to low morale, high turnover, and bad employee attitudes. To revive his flagging business, he decided to share his vision of being world famous with his employees, and empowered them to pursue this vision. He gave his employees permission to have fun with their jobs and to perform their best by bringing their whole selves to work every day. Together, Yokoyama and his employees developed four guiding principles:

1. *Choose your attitude*: We may have no control over what job we have, but we do control how we approach our job.
2. *Make their day*: Engage and delight customers and coworkers; don't grudgingly do the bare minimum.
3. *Be present*: Don't dwell on where you aren't; instead, make the most of where you are. When talking to customers and coworkers, look them in the eye and give them your full attention.
4. *Play*: Have as much fun as you can at whatever you're doing to cultivate a spirit of innovation and creativity.

As one fishmonger explains, "My buddies and I realized that each day when we come to the fish market we bring an attitude. We can bring a moody attitude and have a depressing day. We can bring a grouchy attitude and irritate our coworkers and customers. Or we can bring a sunny, playful, cheerful attitude and have a great day. We can choose the kind of day we will have. We spent a lot of time talking about this choice, and we realized that as long as we are going to be at work, we might as well have the best day we can have."[113]

Yokoyama's goal of being world famous has also been realized. The market is known worldwide for its fun atmosphere and positive employee attitudes. The fishmongers enjoy letting customers know they are important whether they buy anything or not, and constantly entertain them. Employees sing, throw fish, and play jokes on each other and on customers.

Throwing fish and playing jokes on customers obviously would not work as well for every business as it did for Seattle's Pike Place Fish Market. By developing healthy work relationships and creating positive attitudes and emotions in employees and customers, the business is now worth 1,000 times more than Yokoyama paid for it more than thirty-five years ago. The market has been featured on numerous television shows, and was even named one of the most fun places to work in America by CNN.

Sources: Christensen, J. (2003). First Person: Gone Fishin'. *Sales and Marketing Management, 155*(4), 53; Hein, K. (2002). Hooked on Employee Morale. *Incentive, 176*(8), 56–57; Lundin, S. C., Paul, H., & Christensen, J. (2000). Fish! A remarkable Way to Boost Morale and Improve Results. New York: Hyperion; Yerkes, L. (2007). Fun Works: Creating Places Where People Love to Work. San Francisco: Berrett-Koehler.

3. What are the components of an individual's attitude? Relate each component to an attitude your currently have about something.
4. Do terminal or instrumental values have a larger influence on your behavior at work? Explain.
5. Think of a person you know who seems to have positive affectivity. Think of another who has more negative affectivity. How constant are they in their expressions of mood and attitude?
6. How does perception affect behavior? What stereotypes do you form about people? Are they good or bad?
7. Recall a situation in which you made attributions and describe them using the framework supplied in Figure 4.5.
8. Do you consider yourself a Type A or a Type B person? Why? Do you think a person who is a Type A can change to become more like a Type B? If so, how?
9. What are the major stressors for a student? What consequences are students most likely to suffer as a result of too much stress?
10. Do you agree that a certain degree of stress is necessary to induce high energy and motivation?

UNDERSTAND YOURSELF

Positive and Negative Affectivity*

Recall that affectivity represents our tendency to experience a particular mood or to react to things with certain emotions. Individuals with a high positive affectivity experience tend to experience more positive emotions including cheerfulness or enthusiasm. Individuals higher in negative affectivity tend to experience more negative emotions, such as irritation or nervousness.

Complete and score the positive and negative affectivity self-assessment on page 141 in this chapter. Your instructor will pair you with another student. The two of you should spend two minutes discussing anything you like. After the two minutes are up, each of you should try to guess the other's emotional disposition (you do not have to reveal your actual score if you do not want to).

*We thank Professor Paul Harvey at the University of New Hampshire for suggesting this exercise.

GROUP EXERCISE

The Effect of Emotion on Team Performance

In this exercise you will be asked to role-play a particular emotion as a member of a work team. After dividing into teams of four people, count off one to four to identify your role in the team by reading the description below. If your team has more than four people, restart the numbering at 1 when you get to the fifth person.

Role 1: Grouchy, negative affect

Role 2: Calm

Role 3: Happy, positive affect

Role 4: Calm

For the next five to ten minutes (until the instructor tells you to stop), your team's task is to discuss possible slogans for the field of organizational behavior and identify your team's favorite idea. When your instructor tells you, your role will change to the following:

Role 1: Calm

Role 2: Happy, positive affect

Role 3: Calm

Role 4: Grouchy, negative affect

You will spend the next five to ten minutes (until the instructor tells you to stop) discussing the best ways for the manager of a local McDonald's restaurant to improve the employees' job engagement and deciding on your group's favorite three ideas. When your instructor ends the task, address the following questions as a group and be prepared to share your answers with the class.

Questions

1. Did your emotion influence your own performance or behavior in your team?
2. Did any emotional contagion occur in your team? If so, was the positive (happy) or negative (grouchy) emotion more contagious? Why do you think this was so?
3. What could a leader do to effectively manage a team's emotion? Is it worth trying?

VIDEO EXERCISE

Recycline Preserve: Strategy and the Partnership Advantage

Recycline began in 1996 when founder Eric Hudson designed an innovative toothbrush out of all-recycled material. Today, Recycline's eco-friendly product line, Preserve, includes a range of personal care items, tableware, and kitchen goods. Recycline's materials may be recycled, but its strategy is completely new. By offering products that make consumers feel good about their purchases, Recycline not only delivers higher value products but also introduces fresh ideas in the industry.

In 2007, Whole Foods and Recycline launched a line of kitchenware products that included colanders, cutting boards, mixing bowls, and storage containers. "Together we did the competitive research, we speced out the products, and we developed the pricing strategy and designs," Webb said. "It created less risk on both sides."

Through its various partnerships, Recycline was able to take an untested product and sell it at the nation's largest and most respected natural foods store. Whole Foods in turn used its experience and resources to ensure the product sold well. "We gave Whole Foods a twelve-month exclusive on the line," Webb said, "which in turn gave them a great story to tell."

Watch the video "Recycline Preserve: Strategy and the Partnership Advantage" as a class. Next, form small groups with 3-4 of your classmates and develop responses to these questions.

Discussion Questions

1. What roles do attitudes, values, and emotions play at a firm like Recycline? What role do your existing attitudes about recycling affect how you see a company like Recycline?
2. What is your perception of CEO Eric Hudson? On what do you base your perception? What is the public's perception of green products according to Marketing Director C. A. Webb? Why do some people have that perception, and what can Recycline do to change it?
3. Would you want to work for Recycline? Why or why not?

Now What?

VIDEO CASE

PERCOM/SHUTTERSTOCK.COM

Imagine meeting with a subordinate who has been working at Happy Time Toys for a month and can't yet meet the company's goals. The subordinate tried hard to perform well during the training session to look good compared to the other new hires, but the others are doing a lot better on the job. The subordinate communicates frustration about being unable to learn the new job. *What do you say or do?* Go to this chapter's "Now What?" video, watch the challenge video, and choose a response. Be sure to also view the outcomes of the two responses you didn't choose.

Discussion Questions

1. What attitudes did the employee develop about his performance on the job? How were they formed?
2. What role do attributions play in how the employee responded to challenges of learning to do his job? What role do attributions play in how a manager might respond to a subordinate's performance?
3. In what ways does fairness influence how the subordinate responded to the situations you viewed?
4. What other solutions might you have suggested to address the situation? Explain your answer using concepts from the chapter.

ENDNOTES

[1]Powell, D. J. (2011, February 8). Learning From Fish. *Counselor*. Available online: http://www.counselormagazine.com/component/content/article/44-clinical-supervision/1160-learning-from-fish; Chittim, G. (2011, November 11). Monkfish Scares Last Tourist at Pike Place Market. *King5.com*. Available online: http://www.king5.com/news/environment/Fish-Market-Releases-Fan-Favorite-133722773.html; Christensen, J. (2003). First Person: Gone Fishin'. *Sales and Marketing Management*, *155*(4), 53; Lundin, S. C., Paul, H., & Christensen, J. (2000). *Fish! A Remarkable Way to Boost Morale and Improve Results.* New York: Hyperion.

[2]Hom, P. W., & Griffeth, R. W. (1995). *Employee Turnover.* Cincinnati, OH: Southwestern.

[3]Festinger, L. (1957). *A Theory of Cognitive Dissonance.* Stanford, CA: Stanford University Press.

[4]Gagné, M. & Bhave, D. (2011). Autonomy in the Workplace: An Essential Ingredient to Employee Engagement and Well-Being in Every Culture. In *Human Autonomy in Cross-Cultural Context: Cross-Cultural Advancements in Positive Psychology.* eds. V. I. Chirkov, R. M. Ryan, & K. M. Sheldon, (Vol. 1, pp. 163–187). New York: Springer.; Fried, Y., & Ferris, G. R. (1987). The Validity of the Job Characteristics Model: A Review and Metaanalysis. *Personnel Psychology*, *40*(2), 287–322; Parisi, A. G., & Weiner, S. P. (1999, May). Retention of Employees: Country-Specific Analyses in a Multinational Organization. Poster at the Fourteenth Annual Conference of the Society for Industrial and Organizational Psychology, Atlanta, GA.

[5]Saari, L., & Judge, T. A. (2004). Employee Attitudes and Job Satisfaction. *Human Resource Management*, *43*(4), 395–407.

[6]Staw, B. M., & Ross, J. (1985). Stability in the Midst of Change: A Dispositional Approach to Job Attitudes. *Journal of Applied Psychology*, *70*, 469–480.

[7]Judge, T.A., Ilies, R., & Zhang, Z. (2012). Genetic Influences on Core Self-Evaluations, Job Satisfaction, and Work Stress: A Behavioral Genetics Mediated Model. *Organizational Behavior and Human Decision Processes*, *117*(1), 208–220; House, R. J., Shane, S. A., & Herold, D. M. (1996). Rumors of the Death of Dispositional Research Are Vastly Exaggerated. *Academy of Management Review*, *21*, 203–224.

[8]Judge, T. A., & Bono, J. E. (2001). Relationship of Core Self-Evaluations Traits—Self-Esteem, Generalized Self-Efficacy, Locus of Control, and Emotional Stability—With Job Satisfaction and Job Performance: A Meta-Analysis. *Journal of Applied Psychology*, *86*, 80–92.

[9]Judge, T. A., Heller, D., & Mount, M. K. (2002). Five-Factor Model of Personality and Job Satisfaction: A Meta-Analysis. *Journal of Applied Psychology*, *87*, 530–541.

[10]Judge, T. A., Erez, A., Bono, J. E., & Thoresen, C. J. (2003). The Core Self-Evaluations Scale: Development of a Measure. *Personnel Psychology*, *56*, 304.

[11]Judge, T. A., Thoresen, C. J., Bono, J. E., & Patton, G. K. (2001). The Job Satisfaction–Job Performance Relationship: A Qualitative and Quantitative Review. *Psychological Bulletin*, *127*, 376–407.

[12]Organ, D. W. (1988). *Organizational Citizenship Behavior—The Good Soldier Syndrome* (1st ed.). Lexington, MA/Toronto: D.C. Heath; Smith, C. A., Organ, D. W., & Near, J. P. (1983). Organizational Citizenship Behavior: Its Nature and Antecedents. *Journal of Applied Psychology*, *68*, 653–663; Williams, L. J., & Anderson, S. E. (1991). Job Satisfaction and Organizational Commitment as Predictors of Organizational Citizenship and In-Role Behaviors. *Journal of Management*, *17*, 601–617; LePine, J. A., Erez, A., & Johnson, D. E. (2002). The Nature and Dimensionality of Organizational Citizenship Behavior: A Critical Review and Meta-Analysis. *Journal of Applied Psychology*, *87*, 52–65.

[13]Hulin, C. L., Roznowski, M., & Hachiya, D. (1985). Alternative Opportunities and Withdrawal Decisions: Empirical and Theoretical Discrepancies and an Integration. *Psychological Bulletin*, *97*, 233–250; Kohler, S. S., & Mathieu, J. E. (1993). An Examination of the Relationship Between Affective Reactions, Work Perceptions, Individual Resource Characteristics, and Multiple Absence Criteria. *Journal of Organizational Behavior*, *14*, 515–530.

[14]Chen, G., Ployhart, R. E., Thomas, H. C., Anderson, N., & Bliese, P. D. (2011). The Power of Momentum: A New Model of Dynamic Relationships between Job Satisfaction Change and Turnover Intentions. *Academy of Management Journal*, *54*(1), 159–181.

[15]Meyer, J. P., & Allen, N. J. (1997). *Commitment in the Workplace: Theory, Research, and Application.* Thousand Oaks, CA: Sage.

[16]Meyer, J. P., Stanley, L. J., & Parfyonova, N. M. (2012). Employee Commitment in Context: The Nature and Implication of Commitment Profiles. *Journal of Vocational Behavior*, *80*(1), 1–16; Taylor, S. G., Bedeian, A. G., & Kluemper, D. H. (in press). Linking Workplace Incivility to Citizenship Performance: The Combined Effects of Affective Commitment and Conscientiousness. *Journal of Organizational Behavior*; Meyer, J., Stanley, D., Herscovich, L., & Topolnytsky, L. (2002). Affective, Continuance, and Normative Commitment to the Organization: A Meta-Analysis of Antecedents, Correlates, and Consequences. *Journal of Vocational Behavior*, *61*, 20–52; Klein, H., Becker, T., & Meyer, J. (2009). *Commitment in Organizations: Accumulated Wisdom and New Directions.* New York: Taylor & Francis.

[17]Gibbons, J. (2006). *Employee Engagement: A Review of Current Research and Its Implications* (p. 5). New York: The Conference Board.

[18]In Gurchiek, K. (2008, April 23). Many Senior Executives Not Engaged with Their Organizations. Society for Human Resource Management. Available online: http://www.shrm.org/publications/hrnews/pages/seniorexecutivesnotengaged.aspx.

[19]Towers Perrin (2008). Closing the Engagement Gap: A Road Map for Driving Superior Business Performance. Towers Perrin Global Workforce Study 2007–2008. Available online: https://c.ymcdn.com/sites/www.simnet.org/resource/group/066D79D1-E2A8-4AB5-B621-60E58640FF7B/leadership_workshop_2010/towers_perrin_global_workfor.pdf.

[20]Gurchiek, K. (2008, April 23). Many Senior Executives Not Engaged with Their Organizations. Society for Human Resource Management. Available online: http://www.shrm.org/publications/hrnews/pages/seniorexecutivesnotengaged.aspx.

[21]Macey, W. H., Schneider, B. Barbera, K., & Young, S. A. (2009). *Employee Engagement: Tools for Analysis, Practice and Competitive Advantage*. Boston: Wiley-Blackwell.

[22]Kluckhohn, F., & Strodtbeck, F. L. (1961). *Variations in Value Orientations*. Evanston, IL: Row, Peterson.

[23]Schleicher, D. J., Hansen, S., Fox, D., & Kevin, E. (2011). Job Attitudes and Work Values. In *APA Handbook of Industrial and Organizational Psychology: Maintaining, Expanding, and Contracting the Organization*, ed. S. Zedeck (Vol. 3, pp. 137–189). Washington, DC: American Psychological Association.

[24]Boyacigiller, N., Kleinberg, J. M., Phillips, M. E., & Sackman, S. (1996). Conceptualizing Culture. In *Handbook for International Management Research*, eds. B. J. Punnett & O. Shenkar (pp. 157–208). Cambridge: Blackwell; Erez, M., & Earley, C. P. (1993). *Culture, Self-Identity, & Work*. New York: Oxford University Press; Hampden-Turner, C., & Trompenaars, F. (1993). *The Seven Cultures of Capitalism: Value Systems for Creating Wealth in the United States, Britain, Japan, Germany, France, Sweden, and the Netherlands*. New York: Doubleday.

[25]Bartlett, C. A., & Sumantra, G. (1998). *Managing Across Borders: The Transnational Solution* (2nd ed.). Boston: Harvard Business School Press; Porter, M. E. (1990). *The Competitive Advantage of Nations*. New York: Free Press; Posner, B. Z., & Munson, J. M. (1979). The Importance of Values in Understanding Organizational Behavior. *Human Resource Management*, *18*, 9–14.

[26]Fritzsche, D. J., & Becker, H. (1982). Business Ethics of Future Marketing Managers. *Journal of Marketing Education*, *4*, 2–7.

[27]Fritzsche, D. J. (1991). A Model of Decision-Making Incorporating Ethical Values. *Journal of Business Ethics*, *10*, 841–852.

[28]Paine, L. S. (1994). Managing for Organizational Integrity. *Harvard Business Review*, *72*(2), 106–117.

[29]Rokeach, M. (1973). *The Nature of Values*. New York: Free Press.

[30]Nord, W. R., Brief, A. P., Atieh, J. M., & Doherty, E. M. (1988). Work Values and the Conduct of Organizational Behavior. In *Research in Organizational Behavior*, eds. B. M. Staw and L. L. Cummings (pp. 1–42). Greenwich, CT: JAI Press.

[31]Malka, A., & Chatman, J. A. (2003). Intrinsic and Extrinsic Work of the Effect of Annual Income on Subjective Well-Being: A Longitudinal Study. *Society for Personality and Social Psychology, Inc.*, *29*, 737–746.

[32]Nord, W. R., Brief, A. P., Atieh, J. M., & Doherty, E. M. (1988). Work Values and the Conduct of Organizational Behavior. In *Research in Organizational Behavior*, eds. B. M. Staw and L. L. Cummings (pp. 1–42). Greenwich, CT: JAI Press.

[33]Edwards, J. R. (2004). Complementary and Supplementary Fit: A Theoretical and Empirical Integration. *Journal of Applied Psychology*, *89*, 822–834; Amos, E. A., & Weathington, B. L. (2008). An Analysis of the Relation Between Employee-Organization Value Congruence and Employee Attitudes. *Journal of Psychology: Interdisciplinary and Applied*, *142*(6), 615–632.

[34]Adler, N. J. (2008). *International Dimensions of Organizational Behavior*. Mason, OH: Thompson/South-Western.

[35]Inglehart R., & Welzel, C. (2005). *Modernization, Cultural Change and Democracy*. New York: Cambridge University Press.

[36]Inglehart R., & Welzel, C. (2005). *Modernization, Cultural Change and Democracy*. New York: Cambridge University Press.

[37]Kanfer, R., & Klimoski, R. J. (2002). Affect and Work: Looking Back to the Future. In *Emotions in the Workplace*, eds. R. G. Lord, R. J. Klimoski, & R. Kanfer (pp. 473–490). San Francisco, CA: Jossey-Bass.

[38]Elfenbein, H. A. (2007). Emotion in Organizations: A Review of Theoretical Integration. In *The Academy of Management Annals*, eds. J. P. Walsh & A. P. Brief (Vol. 1, pp. 315–386). New York: Taylor & Francis.

[39]Amabile, T., Barsade, S., Mueller, J., & Staw, B. (2005). Affect and Creativity at Work. *Administrative Science Quarterly*, *50*(3), 367–403.

[40]Tse, H. M., & Dasborough, M. T. (2008). A Study of Exchange and Emotions in Team Member Relationships. *Group & Organization Management: An International Journal*, *33*, 194–215.

[41]Schucman, H., & Thetford, C. (1975). *A Course in Miracles*. New York: Viking Penguin.

[42]Rothbard, N. P. & Wilk, S. L. (2011). Waking Up on the Right or Wrong Side of the Bed: Start-of-Workday Mood, Work Events, Employee Affect, and Performance. *Academy of Management Journal*, *54*(5), 959–980.

[43]Miner, A. G., Glomb, T. M., & Hulin, C. (2005, June). Experience Sampling Mood and Its Correlates at Work: Diary Studies in Work Psychology. *Journal of Occupational and Organizational Psychology*, *78*(2), 171–193.

[44]Bartel, C. A., & Saavedra, R. (2000). The Collective Construction of Work Group Moods. *Administrative Science Quarterly*, *45*, 197–231.

[45]Dasborough, M. T., & Ashkanasy, N. M. (2002). Emotion and Attribution of Intentionality in Leader-Member Relationships. *The Leadership Quarterly*, *13*, 615–634.

[46]Smith, C. A., & Lazarus, R. S. (1993). Appraisal Components, Core Relational Themes, and the Emotions. *Cognition and Emotion*, *7*, 233–269.

[47]Watson, D., & Tellegen, A. (1985). Toward a Consensual Structure of Mood. *Psychological Bulletin*, *98*, 219–235.

[48]Watson, D., & Tellegen, A. (1985). Toward a Consensual Structure of Mood. *Psychological Bulletin*, *98*, 219–235.

[49]Watson, D., Clark, L. A., & Tellegen, A. (1988). Development and Validation of Brief Measures of Positive and Negative Affect: The PANAS Scales. *Journal of Personality and Social Psychology*, *54*, 1063–1070.

[50]Dimotakis, N., Scott, B. A., & Koopman, J. (2011). An Experience Sampling Investigation of Workplace Interactions, Affective States, and Employee Well-Being. *Journal of Organizational Behavior*, *32*(4), 572–588; Kaplan, S., Bradley, J. C., Luchman, J. N., & Haynes, D. (2009). On the Role of Positive and Negative Affectivity in Job Performance: A Meta-Analytic Investigation. *Journal of Applied Psychology*, *94*, 162–176.

[51]Gerhardt, M. W., & Brown, K. G. (2006). Individual Differences in Self-Efficacy Development: The Effects of Goal Orientation and Affectivity. *Learning and Individual Differences*, *16*, 43–59.

[52]Isen, A. M. (2004). An Influence of Positive Affect on Decision Making in Complex Situations: Theoretical Issues with Practical Implications. *Journal of Consumer Psychology*, *11*(2), 75–85.

[53]Forgas, J. P. (1998). On Feeling Good and Getting Your Way: Mood Effects on Negotiator Cognition and Behavior. *Journal of Personality and Social Psychology*, *74*, 565–577; Van Kleef, G. A., De Dreu, C. K. W., & Manstead, A. S. R. (2004). The Interpersonal Effects of Anger and Happiness in Negotiations. *Journal of Personality and Social Psychology*, *86*, 57–76.

[54]Lyubomirsky, S., King, L., & Diener, E. (2005). The Benefits of Frequent Positive Affect: Does Happiness Lead to Success? *Psychological Bulletin*, *131*(6), 803–855.

[55]One Man's Accident Is Shedding New Light on Human Perception. *Wall Street Journal*, September 30, 1993, A1, A13.

[56]Starbuck, W. H., & Mezias, J. M. (1996). Opening Pandora's Box: Studying the Accuracy of Managers' Perceptions. *Journal of Organizational Behavior*, *17*, 99–117.

[57]Dion, K. K., Berscheid, E., & Walster, E. (1972). What Is Beautiful Is Good. *Journal of Personality and Social Psychology*, *24*, 285–290.

[58]Denrell, J. (2005). Why Most People Disapprove of Me: Experience Sampling in Impression Formation. *Psychological Review*, *112*(4), 951–978.

[59]Kammrath, L. K., Ames, D. R., & Scholer, A. A. (2007). Keeping Up Impressions: Inferential Rules for Impression Change Across the Big Five. *Journal of Experimental Social Psychology*, *43*(3), 450–457.

[60]King, A. S. (1971). Self-Fulfilling Prophecies in Training the Hard-Core: Supervisors' Expectations and the Underprivileged Workers' Performance. *Social Science Quarterly*, *52*, 369–378.

[61]Eden, D. (1990). *Pygmalion in Management.* Lexington, MA: Lexington Books/D.C. Heath.

[62]Weiner, B. (1974). *Achievement Motivation and Attribution Theory.* Morristown, NJ: General Learning Press; Weiner, B. (1980). *Human Motivation.* New York: Holt, Rinehart & Winston; Weiner, B. (1986). *An Attributional Theory of Motivation and Emotion.* New York: Springer-Verlag.

[63]Kelley, H. H. (1973, February). The Process of Causal Attribution. *American Psychologist,* 107–128.

[64]Matsumoto, D. & Juang. L. (2012). Culture and Psychology (5th ed.). Independence, KY: Wadsworth Publishing; Albert, R. A., & Triandis, H. C. (1979). Cross Cultural Training: A Theoretical Framework and Observations. In *Bilingual Multicultural Education and the Professional from Theory to Practice*, eds. H. Trueba & C. Barnett-Mizrahi. Rowley, MA: Newbury House.

[65]Miller, J. G. (1984). Culture and the Development of Everyday Social Explanation. *Journal of Personality and Social Psychology*, *46*, 961–978.

[66]Morris, M. W., & Peng, K. (1994). Culture and Cause: American and Chinese Attributions for Social and Physical Events. *Journal of Personality and Social Psychology*, *67*, 949–971.

[67]Markus, H. R., & Kitayama, S. (1991). Culture and the Self: Implications for Cognition, Emotion, and Motivation. *Psychological Review*, *98*, 224–253.

[68]Greenberg, J. (1987). A Taxonomy of Organizational Justice Theories. *Academy of Management Review*, *12*, 9–22.

[69]Lind, E. A., & Tyler, T. R. (1988). *The Social Psychology of Procedural Justice.* New York: Plenum.

[70]E.g., Greenberg, J. (1990). Employee Theft as a Response to Underemployment Inequity: The Hidden Costs of Pay Cuts. *Journal of Applied Psychology*, *75*, 561–568; Greenberg, J. (1998). The Cognitive Geometry of Employee Theft: Negotiating "The Line" Between Taking and Stealing. In *Dysfunctional Behavior in Organizations*, eds. R. W. Griffin, A. O'Leary-Kelly, & J. M. Collins (Vol. 2, pp. 147–193). Stamford, CT: JAI; Greenberg, J. (2002). Who Stole the Money and When? Individual and Situational Determinants of Employee Theft. *Organizational Behavior and Human Decision Processes*, *89*, 985–1003; Colquitt, J., & Greenberg, J. (2003). Organizational Justice: A Fair Assessment of the State of the Literature. In *Organizational Behavior: The State of the Science*, ed. J. Greenberg (2nd ed., pp. 165–210). Mahwah, NJ: Lawrence Erlbaum Associates.

[71]Wallace, J. C., Edwards, B. D., Mondore, S., & Finch, D. M. (2008). The Interactive Effects of Litigation Intentions and Procedural Justice Climate on Employee–Employer Litigation. *Journal of Managerial Issues*, *20*, 313–326.

[72]Latham, G. P., & McCauley, C. D. (2005). Leadership in the Private Sector: Yesterday Versus Tomorrow. In *The Twenty-First Century Manager*, ed. C. Cooper. Oxford, UK: Oxford University Press.

[73]Greenberg, J., & Bies, R. J. (1992). Establishing the Role of Empirical Studies of Organizational Justice in Philosophical Inquiries into Business Ethics. *Journal of Business Ethics*, *11*, 97–108.

[74]Treviño, L. K., & Weaver, G. R. (2001). Organizational Justice and Ethics Program Follow Through: Influences on Employees' Helpful and Harmful Behavior. *Business Ethics Quarterly*, *11*(4), 651–671.

[75]Treviño, L. K., & Weaver, G. R. (1998). Punishment in Organizations: Descriptive and Normative Perspectives. In *Managerial Ethics: Moral Management of People and Processes,* ed. M. Schminke (pp. 99–114). Mahwah, NJ: Lawrence Erlbaum Associates.

[76]Treviño, L. K., Weaver, G. R., Gibson, D., & Toffler, B. (1999). Managing Ethics and Legal Compliance: What Works and What Hurts. *California Management Review*, *41*(2), 131–151.

[77]Deutsch, M. (1975). Equity, Equality, and Need: What Determines Which Value Will Be Used as the Basis for Distributive Justice? *Journal of Social Issues*, *31*, 137–149.

[78]Leventhal, G. S. (1980). What Should Be Done with Equity Theory? New Approaches to the Study of Fairness in Social Relationships. In *Social Exchange: Advances in Theory and Research*, eds. K. Gergen, M. Greenberg, & R. Willis (pp. 27–55). New York: Plenum; Thibaut, J., & Walker, L. (1975). *Procedural Justice: A Psychological Analysis*. Hillsdale, NJ: Lawrence Erlbaum Associates.

[79]See Lind, E. A., & Tyler, T. R. (1988). *The Social Psychology of Procedural Justice*. New York: Plenum.

[80]Bies, R. J. (2001). Interactional (In)justice: The Sacred and the Profane. In *Advances in Organizational Justice*, eds. J. Greenberg & R. Cropanzano (pp. 89–118). Stanford, CA: Stanford University Press.

[81]Colquitt, J. A. (2001). On the Dimensionality of Organizational Justice: A Construct Validation of a Measure. *Journal of Applied Psychology*, *86*, 386–400; Colquitt, J. A., Conlon, D. E., Wesson, M. J., Porter, C. O., & Ng, K. Y. (2001). Justice at the Millennium: A Meta-Analytic Review of 25 Years of Organizational Justice Research. *Journal of Applied Psychology*, *86*(3), 425–445.

[82]Greenberg, J. (1993). The Social Side of Fairness: Interpersonal and Informational Classes of Organizational Justice. In *Justice in the Workplace,* ed. R. Cropanzano (Vol. 1, pp. 79–103). Hillsdale, NJ: Lawrence Erlbaum Associates.

[83]Aryee, S., Chen, Z., Sun, L., & Debrah, Y. (2007, January). Antecedents and Outcomes of Abusive Supervision: Test of a Trickle-Down Model. *Journal of Applied Psychology*, *92*(1), 191–201.

[84]Baron, R. A., & Neuman, J. H. (1996). Workplace Violence and Workplace Aggression: Evidence on Their Relative Frequency and Potential Causes. *Aggressive Behavior*, *22*, 161–173.

[85]Truxillo, D. M., Bodner, T. E., Bertolino, M., Bauer, T. N., & Yonce, C. A. (2009). Effects of Explanations on Applicant Reactions: A Meta-Analytic Review. *International Journal of Selection and Assessment*, *17*, 346–361.

[86]Mayer, R. C., Davis, J. H., & Schoorman, F. D. (1995). An Integrative Model of Organizational Trust. *Academy of Management Review*, *20*(3), 709–734.

[87]Colquitt, J. A., Scott, B. A., & LePine, J. A. (2007). Trust, Trustworthiness, and Trust Propensity: A Meta-Analytic Test of Their Unique Relationships with Risk Taking and Job Performance. *Journal of Applied Psychology*, *92*, 909–927.

[88]McKnight, D. H., Cummings, L. L., & Chervany, N. L. (1998). Initial Trust Formation in New Organizational Relationships. *Academy of Management Review*, *23*, 473–490.

[89]Davis, J. H., Schoorman, F. D., Mayer, R. C. & Tan, H. H. (2000). The Trusted General Manager and Business Unit Performance: Empirical Evidence of a Competitive Advantage. *Strategic Management Journal*, *21*, 563–576.

[90]Barbian, J. (2002, June). Short Shelf Life. *Training*, 52.

[91]For a recent review, see DeFrank, R. S., & Ivancevich, J. M. (1998). Stress on the Job: An Executive Update. *Academy of Management Executive*, *12*(3), 55–65.

[92]For a review, see Quick, J. C, & Quick, J. D. (1984). *Organizational Stress and Preventive Management*. New York: McGraw-Hill. See also Griffin, M. A. & Clarke, S. (2010). Stress and Well-Being at Work. In *Handbook of Industrial and Organizational Psychology*, ed. S. Zedeck (pp. 359–397). Washington, DC: American Psychological Association.

[93]Job Stress Beginning to Take Toll on Some Airline Workers. *USA Today*, November 30, 2004, 1B, 2B.

[94]Selye, H. (1976). *The Stress of Life.* New York: McGraw-Hill.

[95]Frew, D. R., & Bruning, N. S. (1987, December). Perceived Organizational Characteristics and Personality Measures as Predictors of Stress/Strain in the Work Place. *Academy of Management Journal*, 633–646.

[96]Wright, T. (2010, January–March). The Role of Psychological Well-Being in Job Performance, Employee Retention, and Cardiovascular Health. *Organizational Dynamics*, 13–23.

[97]I Can't Sleep. *Business Week*, January 26, 2004, 66–74.

[98]Hallowell, E. (2005, January). Why Smart People Underperform. *Harvard Business Review*, 54–62.

[99]Employers on Guard for Violence. *Wall Street Journal*, April 5, 1995, 3A; Neuman, J. H., & Baron, R. A. (1998). Workplace Violence and Workplace Aggression: Evidence Concerning Specific Forms, Potential Causes, and Preferred Targets. *Journal of Management*, *24*(3), 391–419.

[100]Lee, R. T., & Ashforth, B. E. (1996). A Meta-Analytic Examination of the Correlates of the Three Dimensions of Job Burnout. *Journal of Applied Psychology*, *81*(2), 123–133.

[101]For a recent update, see Densten, I. (2001). Re-thinking Burnout. *Journal of Organizational Behavior*, *22*, 833–847.

[102]Kelly, J. M. (1997, February). Get a Grip on Stress. *HR Magazine*, 51–57.

[103]Lounsbury, J. W., & Hoopes, L. L. (1986). A Vacation from Work: Changes in Work and Nonwork Outcomes. *Journal of Applied Psychology*, *71*, 392–401.

[104]Overloaded Staffers Are Starting to Take More Time Off Work. *Wall Street Journal*, September 23, 1998, B1.

[105]Eight Ways to Help You Reduce the Stress in Your Life. *Business Week Careers*, November 1986, 78. See also Weeks, H. (2001, July–August). Taking the Stress out of Stressful Conversations. *Harvard Business Review*, 112–116.

[106]For a recent review, see Macik-Frey, M., Quick, J. C., & Nelson, D. (2007). Advances in Occupational Health: From a Stressful Beginning to a Positive Future. *Journal of Management*, *33*(6), 809–840.

[107]Wolfe, R. A., Ulrich, D. O., & Parker, D. F. (1987, Winter). Employee Health Management Programs: Review, Critique, and Research Agenda. *Journal of Management*, 603–615.

[108]Workplace Hazard Gets Attention. *USA Today*, May 5, 1998, 1B, 2B.

[109]Recession Plans: More Benefits, *Time*, May 10, 2010, p. Global 8.

[110]See Premeaux, S., Adkins, C., & Mossholder, K. (2007). Balancing Work and Family: A Field Study of Multi-Dimensional, Multi-Role, and Work-Family Conflict. *Journal of Organizational Behavior*, *28*, 705–727.

[111]Work and Family. *Business Week*, September 15, 1997, 96–99. See also Hammer, L. B., & Zimmerman, K.L. (2010). Quality of Work Life. In *Handbook of Industrial and Organizational Psychology*, ed. S. Zedeck (pp. 399–431). Washington, DC: American Psychological Association.

[112]Aryee, S., Srinivas, E. S., & Tan, H. H. (2005). Rhythms of Life: Antecedents and Outcomes of Work-Family Balances in Employed Parents. *Journal of Applied Psychology*, *90*(1), 132–146.

[113]Lundin, S. C., Paul, H., Christensen, J., & Blanchard, K. (2000). *Fish! A Proven Way to Boost Morale and Improve Results* (p. 38). New York: Hyperion.

LOSKUTNIKOV/SHUTTERSTOCK.COM

CHAPTER

5

MOTIVATING BEHAVIOR

CHAPTER OUTLINE

LEARNING OUTCOMES

After studying this chapter, you should be able to:

1. Characterize the nature of motivation, including its importance and basic historical perspectives.
2. Identify and describe the need-based perspectives on motivation.
3. Identify and describe the major process-based perspectives on motivation.
4. Describe learning-based perspectives on motivation.

LOSKUTNIKOV/SHUTTERSTOCK.COM

—REAL WORLD CHALLENGE—

MOTIVATING CAST MEMBERS AT DISNEY

The Walt Disney Company started out in 1923 as a small animation studio. In the decades since then the company has grown to become the largest entertainment business in the world. Disney owns or operates eleven theme parks, operates its own cruise line, and owns several television networks, including ABC, ESPN, and, of course, the Disney channel. The company also continues to extend its reach, recently purchasing such properties as Pixar Animation Studios, Marvel Comics, and Lucasfilm.[1]

One of Disney's hallmarks is legendary customer service, especially at its theme parks and on its cruise ships. Theme park employees are called "cast members" and are taught that the ultimate goal is guest happiness and that no matter what role they play, they are expected to smile, project a positive image, and be friendly. Disney wants to motivate its cast members to provide the four service basics of projecting a positive image and energy, being courteous and respectful to all guests, staying in character and playing the part, and going above and beyond expectations, and asks you for suggestions.[2] After reading this chapter, you should have some good ideas.

RSBPHOTO1 / ALAMY

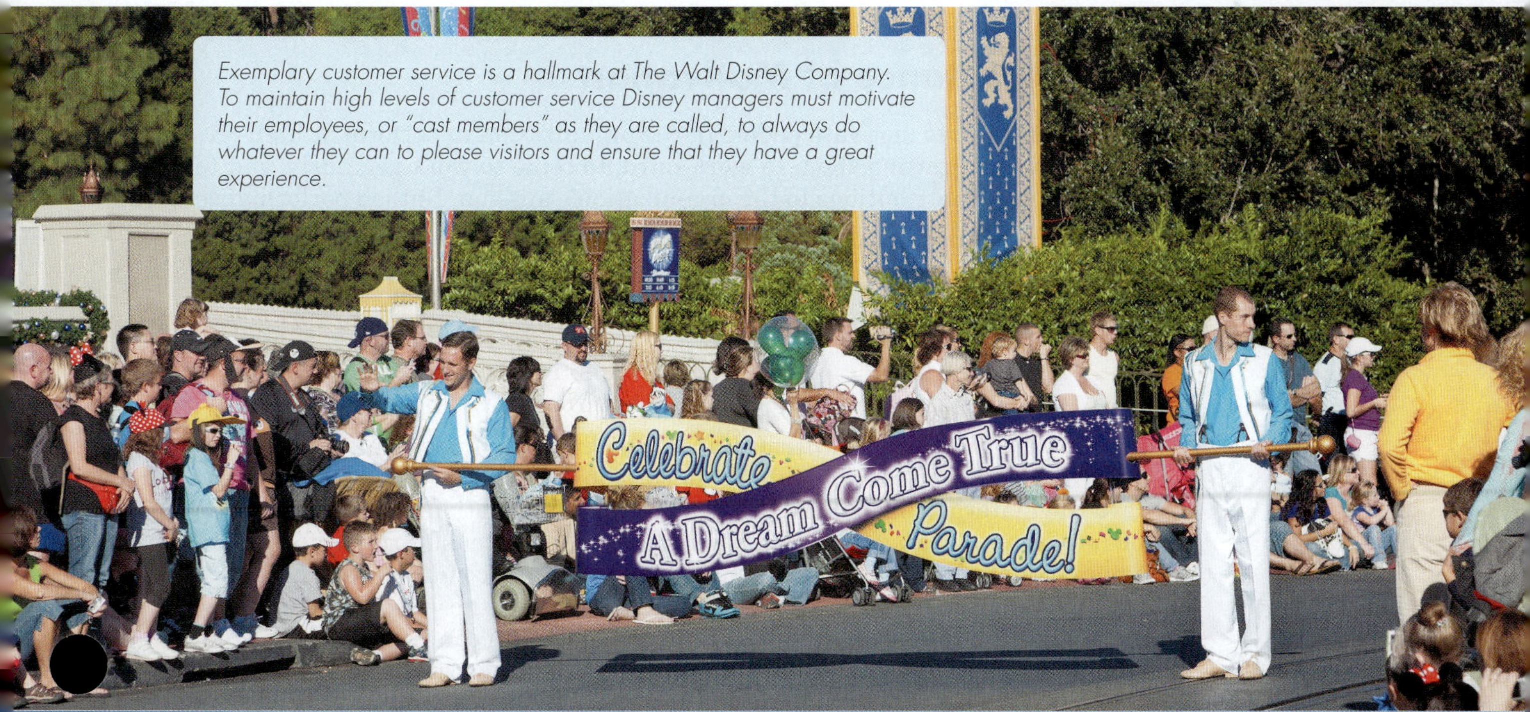

Exemplary customer service is a hallmark at The Walt Disney Company. To maintain high levels of customer service Disney managers must motivate their employees, or "cast members" as they are called, to always do whatever they can to please visitors and ensure that they have a great experience.

Celebrate A Dream Come True Parade!

Given the complex array of individual differences discussed in Chapter 3 (and extended later in this chapter), it should be obvious that people work for a wide variety of reasons. Some people want money, some want a challenge, and some want power. What people in an organization want from work and how they think they can achieve it plays an instrumental role in determining their motivation to work. As we see in this chapter, motivation is vital to all organizations. Indeed, the difference between highly effective organizations and less effective ones often lies in the motivations of their members. Thus, managers need to understand the nature of individual motivation, especially as it applies to work situations. In this chapter we first explore various need-based perspectives on motivation. We then turn our attention to the more sophisticated process-based perspectives. We conclude with a discussion of learning-based perspectives on motivation.[3]

THE NATURE OF MOTIVATION

motivation
The set of forces that leads people to behave in particular ways

Motivation is the set of forces that causes people to engage in one behavior rather than some alternative behavior.[4] Students who start assignments several weeks before they are due to ensure that their term papers are the best they can be, salespeople who work on Saturdays to get ahead, and doctors who make follow-up phone calls to patients to check on their conditions are all motivated people. Of course, students who avoid the term paper by spending the day at the beach, salespeople who go home early to escape a tedious sales call, and doctors who skip follow-up calls to have more time for golf are also motivated, but their goals are different. From the manager's viewpoint, the objective is to motivate people to behave in ways that are in the organization's best interest.[5]

The Importance of Motivation

Managers strive to motivate people in the organization to perform at high levels. This means getting them to work hard, to come to work regularly, and to make positive contributions to the organization's mission. But job performance depends on ability and environment as well as motivation. This relationship can be stated as follows:

$$P = M \times A \times E$$

where

P = performance, M = motivation,
A = ability, and E = environment

To reach high levels of performance, an employee must want to do the job well (motivation); must be able to do the job effectively (ability); and must have the materials, resources, equipment, and information required to do the job (environment). A deficiency in any one of these areas hurts performance. A manager should thus strive to ensure that all three conditions are met.[6]

In most settings, motivation is the most difficult of these factors to manage. If an employee lacks the ability to perform, she or he can be sent to training programs to learn new job skills. If the person cannot learn those skills, she or he can be transferred to a simpler job and replaced with a more skilled worker.

If an employee lacks materials, resources, equipment, and/or information, the manager can take steps to provide them. For example, if a worker cannot complete a project without sales forecast data from marketing, the manager can contact marketing and request that information. But if motivation is deficient, the manager faces the more complex situation of determining what will motivate the employee to work harder.[7] Of course, it is also important to understand what motivates us personally.

The Motivational Framework

We can start to understand motivation by looking at need deficiencies and goal-directed behaviors. Figure 5.1 shows the basic motivational framework we use to organize our discussion. A ***need***—something an individual requires or wants—is the starting point.[8] Motivated behavior usually begins when a person has one or more important needs. Although a need that is already satisfied may also motivate behavior (for example, the need to maintain a standard of living one has already achieved), unmet needs usually result in more intense feelings and behavioral changes. For example, if a person has yet to attain the standard of living she desires, this unmet need may stimulate her to action.

need
Anything an individual requires or wants

A need deficiency usually triggers a search for ways to satisfy it. Consider a person who feels her salary and position are deficient because they do not reflect the importance to the organization of the work she does and because she wants more income. She may feel she has three options: to simply ask for a raise and a promotion, to work harder in the hope of earning a raise and a promotion, or to look for a new job with a higher salary and a more prestigious title.

Next comes a choice of goal-directed behaviors. Although a person might pursue more than one option at a time (such as working harder while also looking for another job), most effort is likely to be directed at one option. In the next phase, the person actually carries out the behavior chosen to satisfy the need. She will probably begin putting in longer hours, working harder, and

Figure 5.1

Motivational Framework

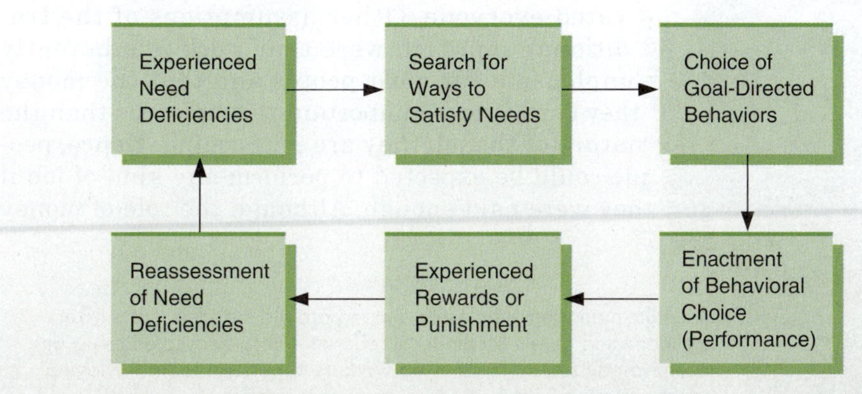

This framework provides a useful way to see how motivational processes occur. When people experience a need deficiency, they seek ways to satisfy it, which results in a choice of goal-directed behaviors. After performing the behavior, the individual experiences rewards or punishments that affect the original need deficiency.

Motivation begins with a need deficiency. Few people aspire to work as custodians or maids, but the need for money to buy basic necessities can motivate people to accept these kinds of jobs. Of course, the motivation for higher levels of income can also drive people to work harder and seek advancement.

ANDREY_POPOV/SHUTTERSTOCK.COM

so forth. She will next experience either rewards or punishment as a result of this choice. She may perceive her situation to be punishing if she ends up earning no additional recognition and not getting a promotion or pay raise. Alternatively, she may actually be rewarded by getting the raise and promotion because of her higher performance.

Finally, the person assesses the extent to which the outcome achieved fully addresses the original need deficiency. Suppose the person wanted a 10 percent raise and a promotion to vice president. If she got both, she should be satisfied. On the other hand, if she got only a 7 percent raise and a promotion to associate vice president, she will have to decide whether to keep trying, to accept what she got, or to choose one of the other options considered earlier. (Sometimes, of course, a need may go unsatisfied altogether, despite the person's best efforts.)

Early Perspectives on Motivation

Historical views on motivation, although not always accurate, are of interest for several reasons. For one thing, they provide a foundation for contemporary thinking about motivation. For another, because they generally were based on common sense and intuition, an appreciation of their strengths and weaknesses can help managers gain useful insights into employee motivation in the workplace.

scientific management
Approach to motivation that assumes that employees are motivated by money

The Traditional Approach

One of the first writers to address work motivation—over a century ago—was Frederick Taylor. Taylor developed a method for structuring jobs that he called ***scientific management***. As one basic premise of this approach, Taylor assumed that employees are economically motivated and work to earn as much money as they can.[9] Hence, he advocated incentive pay systems. He believed that managers knew more about the jobs being performed than did workers, and he assumed that economic gain was the primary thing that motivated everyone. Other assumptions of the traditional approach were that work is inherently unpleasant for most people and that the money they earn is more important to employees than the nature of the job they are performing. Hence, people could be expected to perform any kind of job if they were paid enough. Although the role of money

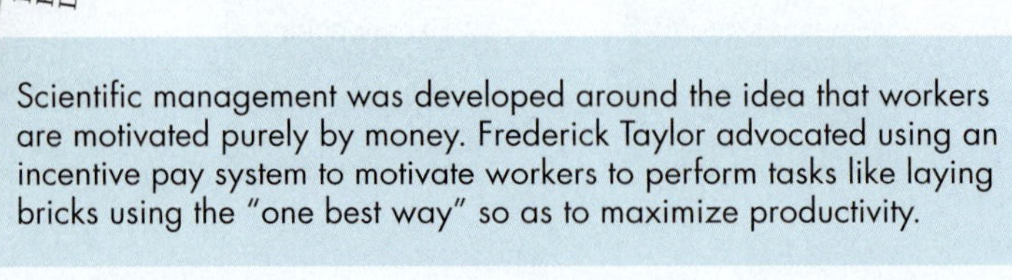

LIBRARY OF CONGRESS PRINTS AND PHOTOGRAPHS DIVISION[LC-USF33-012458-M4]

Scientific management was developed around the idea that workers are motivated purely by money. Frederick Taylor advocated using an incentive pay system to motivate workers to perform tasks like laying bricks using the "one best way" so as to maximize productivity.

as a motivating factor cannot be dismissed, proponents of the traditional approach took too narrow a view of the role of monetary compensation and also failed to consider other motivational factors.

The Human Relations Approach

The human relations approach supplanted scientific management in the 1930s.[10] The ***human relations approach*** assumed that employees want to feel useful and important, that employees have strong social needs, and that these needs are more important than money in motivating employees. Advocates of the human relations approach advised managers to make workers feel important and to allow them a modicum of self-direction and self-control in carrying out routine activities. The feelings of involvement and importance were expected to satisfy workers' basic social needs and result in higher motivation to perform. For example, a manager might allow a workgroup to participate in making a decision to enhance the quality even if he had mostly determined what the decision would be. The gesture of allowing participation was expected to enhance motivation and involvement of the workers.

human relations approach
Suggests that fostering a sense of employees' inclusion in decision making will result in positive employee attitudes and motivation to work hard

The Human Resource Approach

The ***human resource approach*** to motivation carries the concepts of needs and motivation one step farther. Whereas the human relationists believed that feelings of contribution and participation would enhance motivation, the human resource view, which began to emerge in the 1950s, assumes that the contributions themselves are valuable to both individuals and organizations. It assumes that people want to contribute and are able to make genuine contributions. Management's task, then, is to encourage participation and to create a work environment that makes full use of the human resources available. This philosophy guides most contemporary thinking about employee motivation. At Ford, Apple, Texas Instruments, and Hewlett-Packard, for example, work teams are being called upon to solve a variety of problems and to make substantive contributions to the organization.

human resource approach
Assumes that people want to contribute and are able to make genuine contributions

Individual Differences and Motivation

We noted earlier that individual differences play a key role in motivation. Simply put, different things motivate different people. As we explored in detail in our last two chapters, people have different abilities, needs, personalities, values, and self-concepts. Because of these myriad differences, there is no one best way to motivate everyone. For example, consider this conversation:

> Nancy: "I can't believe you quit your job. Your work seemed so interesting, and you always had a chance to learn new things. I like jobs that challenge me. Your new job sounds so boring that I'd go crazy."
>
> Chris: "Well, it is tedious work, but it pays better than any other job around."

What seems to be motivating to Chris? Money. But Nancy places a higher value on challenging herself and doing a variety of tasks. This simple example highlights the fact that to motivate others, it is critical that you first understand what does and what does not motivate them. Our *Global Issues* feature describes how differences between people also extend to cultural differences as well.

An easy mistake to make when trying to motivate others is assuming that the same things that motivate you also motivate them. People are diverse in the personality, values, needs, abilities, cultures, and interests they bring to their jobs. These individual characteristics motivate us to work harder at some things than at others. Individual characteristics are internal motivational factors that are a part of who we are and compel us to try harder and exert more effort toward reaching some goals as compared to others. The starting point for motivated employees is hiring people whose individual characteristics lead to high motivation on the job. A job requiring high-quality work will not be as motivating to someone who lacks attention to detail as it will to a conscientious, detail-oriented person. In your own career, finding a job that has the potential to fulfill your needs, meet your goals, and complement your attitudes can help you to maintain your motivation as well.

In addition to the various individual differences we have already discussed, one additional element is often very specifically related to the motivation to perform a specific task. If you did not think that you could sell enough products to meet your quota, would you be motivated to try very hard? Because people are motivated in part by what they expect to be able to do, you would probably not be very motivated. Alternatively, if you are very confident that you can meet your quota, and having met that quota receive a large commission, you would probably be very motivated to work hard. Recall our discussion of general self-efficacy as an individual difference back in Chapter 3. A specific form of self-efficacy is especially related to employee motivation. ***Task-specific self-efficacy*** is a person's beliefs in his or her capabilities to do what is required to accomplish a specific task.[11] Task-specific self-efficacy influences an individual's effort and persistence in the face of challenges related to performing a specific task.[12] Task-specific self-efficacy beliefs have three dimensions:

task specific self-efficacy
A person's beliefs in his or her capabilities to do what is required to accomplish a specific task

1. *Magnitude*: beliefs about how difficult a specific task can be accomplished
2. *Strength*: beliefs about how confident the person is that the specific task can be accomplished
3. *Generality*: beliefs about the degree to which similar tasks can be accomplished.

Because task-specific self-efficacy perceptions are changeable, good managers proactively enhance subordinates' perceptions of their abilities. Managers can raise task-specific self-efficacy through coaching and encouragement, assuming the employee really does have the potential to perform better. If an employee fails at a task he or she should be able to do, the manager can express confidence in the employee and guide him or her through successful experiences. When an employee is successful, the manager can discuss how the success was due to the employee's skills and effort (rather than to luck) to enhance his or her task-specific self-efficacy.

Similarly, if you find yourself lacking the confidence that you can do a task, you can take steps to eliminate the performance barriers you identify. Perhaps more practice, seeking a coach, or watching others perform the task successfully will increase your task-specific self-efficacy and motivation. One of the most important determinants of motivation, and thus success, is whether you believe you can accomplish the things you are trying to do.

GLOBAL ISSUES

MOTIVATING A GLOBAL WORKFORCE

Effectively motivating employees located across the globe is a significant challenge. Managers must be sensitive to cultural differences in values and needs and understand that what is acceptable in one culture may be taboo in another.

The American culture is more individualistic and egocentric than many other cultures. Because American culture values individual achievement, Americans often have a desire to be singled out and praised. In some cultures, people would be embarrassed or even ashamed if they received the attention Americans strive for. In Japan, for example, there is a saying, "It's the nail that sticks up that gets pounded." Motivation and reward programs in the Far East also tend to be more paternal than in the United States. In Indonesia, if a company has a good year, bonuses are not a function of individual performance but rather of each employee's organizational loyalty as measured by the number of years worked with the company, plus the size of his or her family.[13]

Some motivation principles, like treating people with respect, apply equally well around the world. For example, Colgate-Palmolive operates in more than 170 countries and receives about 70 percent of its $7 billion revenues from overseas markets. A truly global company, Colgate expects managers everywhere to show respect for their employees. Colgate-Palmolive's performance-evaluation system, for instance, evaluates how managers exemplify and reinforce respect.[14] Employees from different cultures may differentially value things like equality and individualism, but being treated with fairness and respect resonates globally.

NEED-BASED PERSPECTIVES ON MOTIVATION

Need-based perspectives represent the starting point for most contemporary thought on motivation, although these theories also attracted critics.[15] The basic premise of ***need-based theories*** and models, consistent with our motivation framework introduced earlier, is that humans are motivated primarily by deficiencies in one or more important needs or need categories. Need theorists have attempted to identify and categorize the needs that are most important to people.[16] (Some observers call these "content theories" because they deal with the content, or substance, of what motivates behavior.) The best-known need theories are the hierarchy of needs and the ERG theory.

need-based theories
Assume that need deficiencies cause behavior

The Hierarchy of Needs

The hierarchy of needs, developed by psychologist Abraham Maslow in the 1940s, is the best-known need theory.[17] Influenced by the human relations school, Maslow argued that human beings are "wanting" animals: They have innate desires to satisfy a given set of needs. Furthermore, Maslow believed that these needs are arranged in a hierarchy of importance, with the most basic needs at the foundation of the hierarchy.

Figure 5.2 shows Maslow's ***hierarchy of needs***. The three sets of needs at the bottom of the hierarchy are called deficiency needs because they must be satisfied for the individual to be fundamentally comfortable. The top two sets of needs are termed *growth needs* because they focus on personal growth and development.

hierarchy of needs
Assumes that human needs are arranged in a hierarchy of importance

Figure 5.2

Maslow's hierarchy of needs consists of five basic categories of needs. This figure illustrates both general and organizational examples of each type of need. Of course, each individual has a wide variety of specific needs within each category.

The Hierarchy of Needs

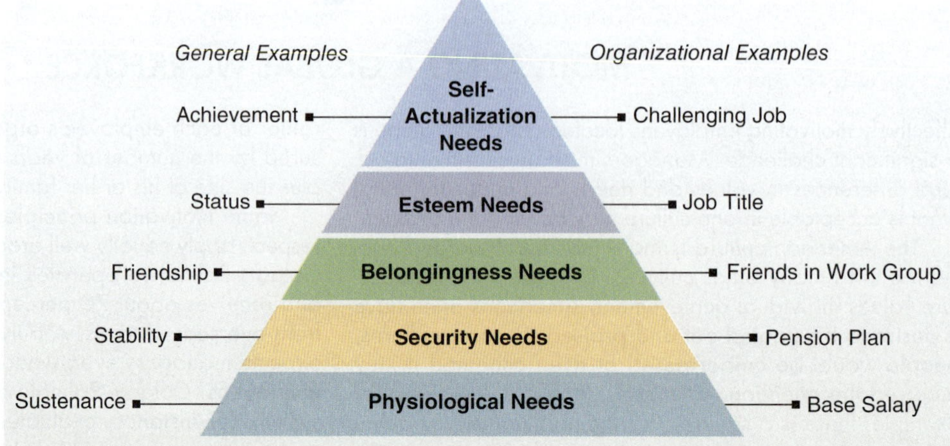

Source: Adapted from Abraham H. Maslow, "A Theory of Human Motivation," Psycho-logical Review, 1943, vol., 50, pp. 374–396.

The most basic needs in the hierarchy are *physiological needs*. These include the needs for food, sex, and air. Next in the hierarchy are *security needs*: things that offer safety and security, such as adequate housing and clothing and freedom from worry and anxiety. *Belongingness needs*, the third level in the hierarchy, are primarily social. Examples include the need for love and affection and the need to be accepted by peers. The fourth level, *esteem needs*, actually encompasses two slightly different kinds of needs: the need for a positive self-image and self-respect and the need to be respected by others. At the top of the hierarchy are *self-actualization* needs. These involve a person's realizing his or her full potential and becoming all that he or she can be.

Maslow believed that each need level must be satisfied before the level above it can become important. Thus, once physiological needs have been satisfied, their importance diminishes, and security needs emerge as the primary sources of motivation. This escalation up the hierarchy continues until the self-actualization needs become the primary motivators. Suppose, for example, that Jennifer Wallace earns all the money she needs and is very satisfied with her standard of living. Additional income may have little or no motivational impact on her behavior. Instead, Jennifer will strive to satisfy other needs, such as a desire for higher self-esteem.

However, if a previously satisfied lower-level set of needs becomes deficient again, the individual returns to that level. For example, suppose that Jennifer unexpectedly loses her job. At first, she may not be too worried because she has savings and confidence that she can find another good job. As her savings dwindle, however, she will become increasingly motivated to seek new income. Initially, she may seek a job that both pays well and satisfies her esteem needs. But as her financial situation grows worse, she may lower her expectations regarding esteem and instead focus almost exclusively on simply finding a job with a reliable paycheck.

In most businesses, physiological needs are probably the easiest to evaluate and to meet. Adequate wages, clean restrooms, ventilation, and comfortable temperatures and working conditions are measures taken to satisfy this most basic level of needs. Security needs in organizations can be satisfied by such things as job continuity (no layoffs), a grievance system (to protect against arbitrary supervisory actions), and an adequate insurance and retirement system (to guard against financial loss from illness and to ensure retirement income).

Most employees' belongingness needs are satisfied by family ties and group relationships both inside and outside the organization. In the workplace, people usually develop friendships that provide a basis for social interaction and can play a major role in satisfying social needs. Managers can help satisfy these needs by fostering interaction and a sense of group identity among employees. At the same time, managers can be sensitive to the probable effects on employees (such as low performance and absenteeism) of family problems or lack of acceptance by coworkers. Esteem needs in the workplace are met at least partially by job titles, choice offices, merit pay increases, awards, and other forms of recognition. Of course, to be sources of long-term motivation, tangible rewards such as these must be distributed equitably and be based on performance.

Self-actualization needs are perhaps the hardest to understand and the most difficult to satisfy. For example, it is difficult to assess how many people completely meet their full potential. In most cases, people who are doing well on Maslow's hierarchy will have satisfied their esteem needs and will be moving toward self-actualization. Working toward self-actualization, rather than actually achieving it, may be the ultimate motivation for most people. In recent years there has been a pronounced trend toward people leaving well-paying but less fulfilling jobs to take lower-paying but more fulfilling jobs such as nursing and teaching. This might indicate that they are actively working toward self-actualization.[18]

Research shows that the need hierarchy does not generalize very well to other countries. For example, in Greece and Japan, security needs may motivate employees more than self-actualization needs. Likewise, belongingness needs are especially important in Sweden, Norway, and Denmark. Research has also found differences in the relative importance of different needs in Mexico, India, Peru, Canada, Thailand, Turkey, and Puerto Rico.[19]

Maslow's needs hierarchy makes a certain amount of intuitive sense. And because it was the first motivation theory to become popular, it is also one of the best known among practicing managers. However, research has revealed a number of deficiencies in the theory. For example, five levels of needs are not always present; the actual hierarchy of needs does not always conform to Maslow's model; and need structures are more unstable and variable than the theory would lead us to believe.[20] And sometimes managers are overly clumsy or superficial in their attempts to use a theory such as this one. Thus, the

ANDRESR/SHUTTERSTOCK.COM

According to Abraham Maslow people may be motivated by a hierarchy of needs, including social needs to belong to groups and be part of friendships. These co-workers are apparently helping meet their belongingness needs through close working relationships at work.

theory's primary contribution seems to lie in providing a general framework for categorizing needs.

The ERG Theory

ERG theory
Describes existence, relatedness, and growth needs

The ***ERG theory***, developed by Yale psychologist Clayton Alderfer, is another historically important need theory of motivation.[21] In many respects, ERG theory extends and refines Maslow's needs hierarchy concept, although there are also several important differences between the two. The E, R, and G stand for three basic need categories: existence, relatedness, and growth. Existence needs—those necessary for basic human survival—roughly correspond to the physiological and security needs of Maslow's hierarchy. Relatedness needs—those involving the need to relate to others—are similar to Maslow's belongingness and esteem needs. Finally, *growth needs* are analogous to Maslow's needs for self-esteem and self-actualization.

In contrast to Maslow's approach, ERG theory suggests that more than one kind of need—for example, both relatedness and growth needs—may motivate a person at the same time. A more important difference from Maslow's hierarchy is that ERG theory includes a satisfaction-progression component and a frustration-regression component. The satisfaction-progression concept suggests that after satisfying one category of needs, a person progresses to the next level. On this point, the need hierarchy and ERG theory agree. The need hierarchy, however, assumes that the individual remains at the next level until the needs at that level are satisfied. In contrast, the frustration-regression component of ERG theory suggests that a person who is frustrated by trying to satisfy a higher level of needs eventually will regress to the preceding level.[22]

Suppose, for instance, that Nick Hernandez has satisfied his basic needs at the relatedness level and now is trying to satisfy his growth needs. That is, he has many friends and social relationships and is now trying to learn new skills and advance in his career. For a variety of reasons, such as organizational constraints (i.e., few challenging jobs, a glass ceiling, etc.) and the lack of opportunities to advance, he is unable to satisfy those needs. No matter how hard he tries, he seems stuck in his current position. According to ERG theory, frustration of his growth needs will cause Nick's relatedness needs to once again become dominant as motivators. As a result, he will put renewed interest into making friends and developing social relationships.

The Two-Factor Theory

two-factor theory (dual-structure theory)
Identifies motivation factors, which affect satisfaction, and hygiene factors, which determine dissatisfaction

Another important need-based theory of motivation is the ***two-factor theory***, also called the ***dual-structure theory***. This theory is in many ways similar to the need theories just discussed. The two-factor theory once played a major role in managerial thinking about motivation, and though few researchers today accept the theory, it is nevertheless still widely known and accepted among practicing managers.

Development of the Theory

Frederick Herzberg and his associates developed the two-factor theory in the late 1950s and early 1960s.[23] Herzberg began by interviewing approximately

200 accountants and engineers in Pittsburgh. He asked them to recall times when they felt especially satisfied and motivated by their jobs and times when they felt particularly dissatisfied and unmotivated. He then asked them to describe what caused the good and bad feelings. The responses to the questions were recorded by the interviewers and later subjected to content analysis. (In a content analysis, the words, phrases, and sentences used by respondents are analyzed and categorized according to their meanings.)

To his surprise, Herzberg found that entirely different sets of factors were associated with the two kinds of feelings about work. For example, a person who indicated "low pay" as a source of dissatisfaction would not necessarily identify "high pay" as a source of satisfaction and motivation. Instead, people associated entirely different causes, such as recognition or achievement, with satisfaction and motivation. The findings led Herzberg to conclude that the prevailing thinking about satisfaction and motivation was incorrect. As Figure 5.3 shows, at the time, job satisfaction was being viewed as a single construct ranging from satisfaction to dissatisfaction. If this were the case, Herzberg reasoned, one set of factors should therefore influence movement back and forth along the continuum. But because his research had identified differential influences from two different sets of factors, Herzberg argued that two different dimensions must be involved. Thus, he saw motivation as a two-factor phenomenon.

Figure 5.3 also illustrates the two-factor concept that there is one dimension ranging from satisfaction to no satisfaction and another ranging from dissatisfaction to no dissatisfaction. The two dimensions must presumably be associated with the two sets of factors identified in the initial interviews. Thus, this theory proposed, employees might be either satisfied or not satisfied and, at the same time, dissatisfied or not dissatisfied.[24]

In addition, Figure 5.3 lists the primary factors identified in Herzberg's interviews. ***Motivation factors*** such as achievement, recognition, and the opportunity to plan and control their own work were often cited by people as primary causes of satisfaction and motivation. When present in a job, these factors apparently could cause satisfaction and motivation; when they were absent, the result was feelings of no satisfaction rather than dissatisfaction. The other set of factors, ***hygiene factors***, came out in response to the questions about dissatisfaction and lack of motivation. The respondents suggested that pay, job security, supervisors, and working conditions, if seen as inadequate, could lead to feelings of dissatisfaction. When these factors were considered acceptable, however, the person still was not necessarily satisfied; rather, he or she was simply not dissatisfied.[25]

motivation factors
Are intrinsic to the work itself and include factors such as achievement and recognition

hygiene factors
Are extrinsic to the work itself and include factors such as pay and job security

To use the two-factor theory in the workplace, Herzberg recommended a two-stage process. First, the manager should try to eliminate situations that cause dissatisfaction, which Herzberg assumed to be the more basic of the two dimensions. For example, suppose that Susan Kowalski wants to use the two-factor theory to enhance motivation in the group of seven technicians she supervises. Her first goal would be to achieve a state of no dissatisfaction by addressing hygiene factors. Imagine, for example, that she discovers that their pay is a bit below market rates and that a few of them are worried about job security. Her response would be to secure a pay raise for them and to allay their concerns about job security.

According to the theory, once a state of no dissatisfaction exists, trying to improve motivation further through hygiene factors is a waste of time.[26] At

Figure 5.3

The traditional view of satisfaction suggested that satisfaction and dissatisfaction were opposite ends of a single dimension. Herzberg's Two Factor theory found evidence of a more complex view. In this theory, motivation factors affect one dimension, ranging from satisfaction to no satisfaction. Other workplace characteristics, called "hygiene factors," are assumed to affect another dimension, ranging from dissatisfaction to no dissatisfaction.

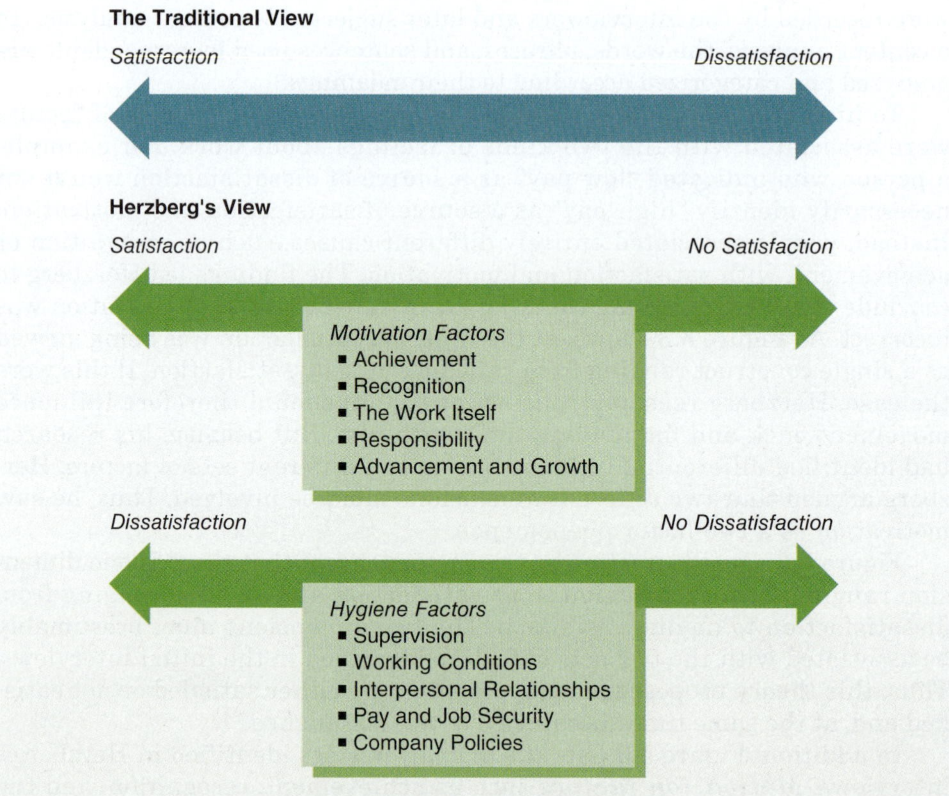

that point, the motivation factors enter the picture. Thus, when Susan is sure that she has adequately dealt with hygiene issues, she should try to increase opportunities for achievement, recognition, responsibility, advancement, and growth. As a result, she would be helping her subordinates feel satisfied and motivated.

Unlike many other theorists, Herzberg described explicitly how managers could apply his theory. In particular, he developed and described a technique called "job enrichment" for structuring employee tasks.[27] (We discuss job enrichment in Chapter 6.) Herzberg tailored this technique to his key motivation factors. This unusual attention to application may explain the widespread popularity of the two-factor theory among practicing managers.

Evaluation of the Theory

Because it gained popularity so quickly, the two-factor theory has been scientifically scrutinized more than almost any other organizational behavior theory.[28] The results have been contradictory, to say the least. The initial study by Herzberg and his associates supported the basic premises of the theory, as did a few follow-up studies.[29] In general, studies that use the same methodology as Herzberg did (content analysis of recalled incidents) tend to support the theory. However, this methodology has itself been criticized, and studies that use other methods to measure satisfaction and dissatisfaction frequently obtain results quite different from Herzberg's.[30] If the theory is "method bound," as it appears to be, its validity is therefore questionable.

Several other criticisms have been directed against the theory. Critics say the original sample of accountants and engineers may not represent the general working population. Furthermore, they maintain that the theory fails to account for individual differences. Subsequent research has found that a factor such as pay may affect satisfaction in one sample and dissatisfaction in another and that the effect of a given factor depends on the individual's age and organizational level. In addition, the theory does not define the relationship between satisfaction and motivation.

Research has also suggested that the two-factor framework varies across cultures. Only limited studies have been conducted, but findings suggest that employees in New Zealand and Panama assess the impact of motivation and hygiene factors differently from U.S. workers.[31] It is not surprising, then, that the two-factor theory is no longer held in high esteem by organizational behavior researchers. Indeed, the field has since adopted far more complex and valid conceptualizations of motivation, most of which we discuss in Chapter 6. But because of its initial popularity and its specific guidance for application, the two-factor theory merits a special place in the history of motivation research.

The Acquired Needs Framework

Next, we will discuss one final need-based motivation perspective. The ***acquired needs framework*** was advanced by David McClelland and centers on the needs for achievement, affiliation, and power (these needs are also sometimes referred to as *manifest needs*).[32] A key differentiating element of this framework is the argument that these needs are acquired, or learned, from cultural, societal, and family influences.

acquired needs framework
Centers on the needs for achievement, affiliation, and power

The Need for Achievement

The ***need for achievement*** arises from an individual's desire to accomplish a goal or task more effectively than in the past. Individuals who have a high need for achievement tend to set moderately difficult goals and to make moderately risky decisions. Suppose, for example, that Mark Cohen, a regional manager for a national retailer, sets a sales increase goal for his stores of either 1 percent or 50 percent. The first goal is probably too easy, and the second is probably impossible to reach; either would suggest a low need for achievement. But a mid-range goal of, say, 15 percent might present a reasonable challenge but also be within reach. Setting this goal might more accurately reflect a high need for achievement.

need for achievement
The desire to accomplish a task or goal more effectively than was done in the past

High need-achievers also want immediate, specific feedback on their performance. They want to know how well they did something as quickly after finishing it as possible. For this reason, high need-achievers frequently take jobs in sales, where they get almost immediate feedback from customers, and often avoid jobs in areas such as research and development, where tangible progress is slower and feedback comes at longer intervals. If Mark only asks his managers for their sales performance on a periodic basis, he might not have a high need for achievement. But if he is constantly calling each store manager in his territory to ask about their sales increases, this activity indicates a high need for achievement on his part.

Preoccupation with work is another characteristic of high need-achievers. They think about it on their way to the workplace, during lunch, and at home.

They find it difficult to put their work aside, and they become frustrated when they must stop working on a partly completed project. If Mark seldom thinks about his business in the evening, he may not be a high need-achiever. However, if work is always on his mind, he might indeed be a high need-achiever.

Finally, high need- achievers tend to assume personal responsibility for getting things done. They often volunteer for extra duties and find it difficult to delegate part of a job to someone else. Accordingly, they derive a feeling of accomplishment when they have done more work than their peers without the assistance of others. Suppose Mark visits a store one day and finds that the merchandise is poorly displayed, the floor is dirty, and the sales clerks don't seem motivated to help customers. If he has a low need for achievement, he might point the problems out to the store manager and then leave. But if his need for achievement is high, he may very well stay in the store for a while, personally supervising the changes that need to be made.

Although high need-achievers tend to be successful, they often do not achieve top management posts. The most common explanation is that although high need for achievement helps these people advance quickly through the ranks, the traits associated with the need often conflict with the requirements of high-level management positions. Because of the amount of work they are expected to do, top executives must be able to delegate tasks to others. In addition, they seldom receive immediate feedback, and they often must make decisions that are either more or less risky than those with which a high need-achiever would be comfortable.[33] High need-achievers tend to do well as individual entrepreneurs with little or no group reinforcement. Bill Gates, cofounder of Microsoft, Reed Hasting, founder and CEO of Netflix, and Marissa Mayer, CEO of Yahoo! are all recognized as being high need-achievers.

The Need for Affiliation

need for affiliation
The need for human companionship

Individuals also experience the ***need for affiliation***—the need for human companionship.[34] Researchers recognize several ways that people with a high need for affiliation differ from those with a lower need. Individuals with a high need tend to want reassurance and approval from others and usually are genuinely concerned about others' feelings. They are likely to act and think as they believe others want them to, especially those with whom they strongly identify and desire friendship. As we might expect, people with a strong need for affiliation most often work in jobs with a lot of interpersonal contact, such as sales and teaching positions.

For example, suppose that Watanka Jackson is seeking a job as a geologist or petroleum field engineer, a job that will take her into remote areas for long periods of time with little interaction with coworkers. Aside from her academic training, one reason for the nature of her job search might be that she has a low need for affiliation. In contrast, a classmate of hers, William Pfeffer, may be seeking a job in the corporate headquarters

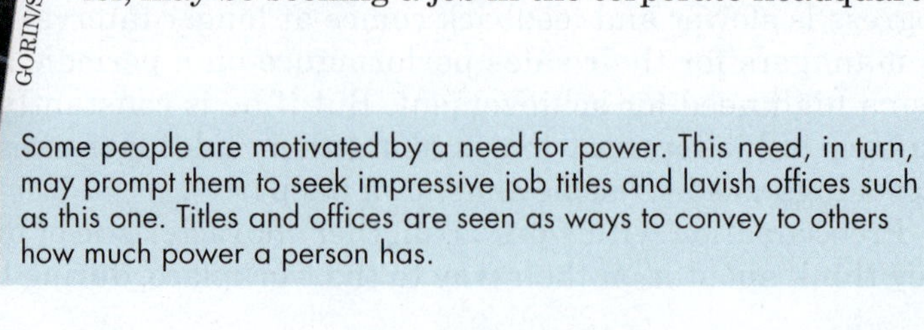

GORIN/SHUTTERSTOCK.COM

Some people are motivated by a need for power. This need, in turn, may prompt them to seek impressive job titles and lavish offices such as this one. Titles and offices are seen as ways to convey to others how much power a person has.

of a petroleum company. His preferences might be dictated, at least in part, by a desire to be around other people in the workplace; thus, he has a higher need for affiliation. A recent Gallup survey suggests that people who have at least one good friend at work are much more likely to be highly engaged with their work and to indicate higher levels of job satisfaction.[35]

The Need for Power

The third so-called acquired need is the ***need for power***—the desire to control one's environment, including financial, material, informational, and human resources.[36] People vary greatly along this dimension. Some individuals spend much time and energy seeking power; others avoid power if at all possible. People with a high need for power can be successful managers if three conditions are met. First, they must seek power for the betterment of the organization rather than for their own interests. Second, they must have a fairly low need for affiliation because fulfilling a personal need for power may well alienate others in the workplace. Third, they need plenty of self-control to curb their desire for power when it threatens to interfere with effective organizational or interpersonal relationships.[37] Our *Understand Yourself* feature will give you personal insights into how you may be motivated by these acquired needs.

need for power
The desire to control the resources in one's environment

UNDERSTAND YOURSELF

WHAT MOTIVATES YOU?

For each of the following fifteen statements, circle the number that most closely agrees with how you feel. Consider your answers in the context of your current job or past work experience.

1.	I work very hard to continually improve my work performance.	1	2	3	4	5
2.	I enjoy competition. I like to win in sports and other things I do.	1	2	3	4	5
3.	When working, I often chat with fellow employees about nonwork matters.	1	2	3	4	5
4.	I enjoy difficult challenges. At work, I like to take on the hard jobs.	1	2	3	4	5
5.	I enjoy being a manager. I like being in charge of things and people.	1	2	3	4	5
6.	It is important to me to be liked by other people.	1	2	3	4	5
7.	When I am working, I like to know how I am doing and how the work is progressing.	1	2	3	4	5
8.	If I disagree with someone, I let them know it. I am not afraid of disagreement.	1	2	3	4	5
9.	Many of my coworkers are also my friends. I enjoy spending my leisure time with them.	1	2	3	4	5
10.	I typically set realistic goals and tend to achieve them.	1	2	3	4	5
11.	It is important to me to get others to agree with my ideas.	1	2	3	4	5
12.	I enjoy belonging to clubs, groups, and other organizations.	1	2	3	4	5
13.	I enjoy the satisfaction of successfully completing a difficult job.	1	2	3	4	5
14.	One of my important objectives is to get more control over events around me.	1	2	3	4	5
15.	I would rather work with other people than work alone.	1	2	3	4	5

(Continued)

Scoring: Record your score for each of the fifteen statements on the appropriate line below, putting your response to the first statement on the top left line marked "1," your response to the second statement on the top middle line marked "2," and so on. Then add up each column to learn your achievement, power, and affiliation scores.

Achievement	Power	Affiliation
1. _____	2. _____	3. _____
4. _____	5. _____	6. _____
7. _____	8. _____	9. _____
10. _____	11. _____	12. _____
13. _____	14. _____	15. _____
TOTALS: _____	_____	_____

Use the following values to guide your interpretation of each of the totals:

5 = very low; 10 = low; 15 = moderate; 20 = high; 25 = very high

Question: How do you think your motivations influence the way that you lead or that you will lead in the future?

Source: From *Journal of Vocational Behavior*, 9(2), Steers, R., & Braunstein, D. A Behaviorally Based Measure of Manifest Needs in Work Settings, pp. 251–266.

PROCESS-BASED PERSPECTIVES ON MOTIVATION

process-based perspectives
Focus on how people behave in their efforts to satisfy their needs

Process-based perspectives are concerned with how motivation occurs. Rather than attempting to identify specific motivational stimuli, such as pay or recognition, process perspectives focus on why people choose certain behavioral options to satisfy their needs (regardless of the needs themselves) and how they evaluate their satisfaction after they have attained these goals. Two useful process perspectives on motivation are the equity and expectancy theories.

The Equity Theory of Motivation

equity theory
Focuses on people's desire to be treated with what they perceive as equity and to avoid perceived inequity

equity
The belief that we are being treated fairly in relation to others; inequity is the belief that we are being treated unfairly in relation to others

The ***equity theory*** of motivation is based on the relatively simple premise that people in organizations want to be treated fairly.[38] The theory defines ***equity*** as the belief that we are being treated fairly in relation to others and inequity as the belief that we are being treated unfairly compared with others. Equity theory is just one of several theoretical formulations derived from social comparison processes. Social comparisons involve evaluating our own situation in terms of others' situations. In this chapter, we focus mainly on equity theory because it is the most highly developed of the social comparison approaches and the one that applies most directly to the work motivation of people in organizations.

Forming Equity Perceptions

People in organizations form perceptions of the equity of their treatment through a four-step process. First, they evaluate how they are being treated by the firm. Second, they form a perception of how a "comparison-other" is being treated. The comparison-other might be a person in the same workgroup, someone in another part of the organization, or even a composite of several people scattered throughout the organization.[39] Third, they compare their own circumstances with those of the comparison-other and then use this comparison as the basis for forming an impression of either equity or inequity. Fourth, depending on the strength of this feeling, the person may choose to pursue one or more of the alternatives discussed in the next section.

Equity theory describes the equity comparison process in terms of an input-to-outcome ratio. Inputs are an individual's contributions to the organization—such factors as education, experience, effort, and loyalty. Outcomes are what the person receives in return—pay, recognition, social relationships, intrinsic rewards, and similar things. In effect, then, this part of the equity process is essentially a personal assessment of one's psychological contract. A person's assessments of inputs and outcomes for both self and others are based partly on objective data (for example, the person's own salary) and partly on perceptions (such as the comparison-other's level of recognition). The equity comparison thus takes the following form:

$$\frac{\text{Outcomes (self)}}{\text{Inputs (self)}} \text{ compared with } \frac{\text{Outcomes (other)}}{\text{Inputs (other)}}$$

If the two sides of this psychological equation are comparable, the person experiences a feeling of equity; if the two sides do not balance, a feeling of inequity results. We should stress, however, that a perception of equity does not require that the perceived outcomes and inputs be equal, but only that their ratios be the same. A person may believe that his comparison-other deserves to make more money because she works harder, thus making her outcomes (higher pay) acceptable because it is proportional to her higher input (harder work). Only if the other person's outcomes seem disproportionate to her inputs does the comparison provoke a perception of inequity.

Responses to Equity and Inequity

Figure 5.4 summarizes the results of an equity comparison. If a person feels equitably treated, she is generally motivated to maintain the status quo. For example, she will continue to provide the same level of input to the organization as long as her outcomes do not change and the ratio of inputs and outcomes of the comparison-other do not change. But a person who is experiencing inequity—real or imagined—is motivated to reduce it. Moreover, the greater the inequity, the stronger the level of motivation.

People may use one of six common methods to reduce inequity.[40] First, we may change our own inputs. Thus, we may put more or less effort into the job, depending on which way the inequity lies, as a way to alter

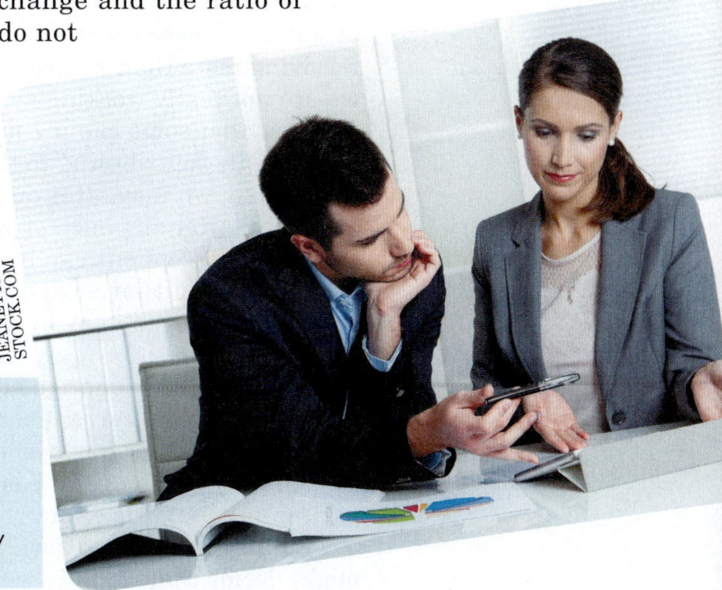

JEANETTE DIETL/SHUTTERSTOCK.COM

Perceptions of equity or inequity can play a strong role in motivating an individual. Take these two colleagues, for example. If she feels that she is equitably rewarded relative to him, then she may be motivated to maintain the status quo and be a productive and loyal employee. But if he feels that he is being inequitably rewarded relative to her, he may be motivated to ask for a raise or look for another job.

Figure 5.4

Responses to Perceptions of Equity and Inequity

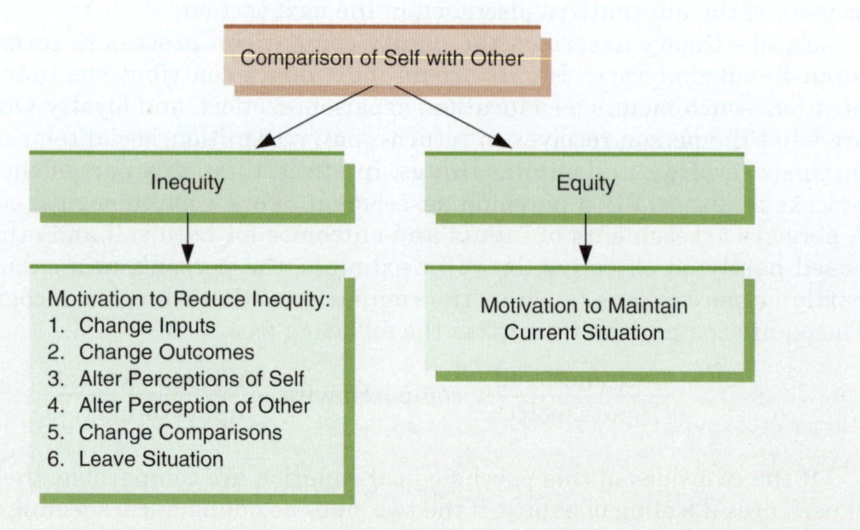

People form equity perceptions by comparing their situation with that of someone else's. If they perceive equity, they are motivated to maintain the current situation. If they perceive inequity, they are motivated to use one or more of the strategies shown here to reduce the inequity.

our ratio. If we believe we are being underpaid, for example, we may decide not to work as hard.

Second, we may change our own outcomes. We might, for example, demand a pay raise, seek additional avenues for growth and development, or even resort to stealing as a way to "get more" from the organization. Or we might alter our perceptions of the value of our current outcomes, perhaps by deciding that our present level of job security is greater and more valuable than we originally thought.

A third, more complex response is to alter our perceptions of ourselves and our behavior. After perceiving an inequity, for example, we may change our original self-assessment and decide that we are really contributing less but receiving more than we originally believed. For example, we might decide that we are not really working as many hours as we had first thought—admitting, perhaps, that some of our time spent in the office is really just socializing and not actually contributing to the organization.

Fourth, we may alter our perception of the comparison-other's inputs or outcomes. After all, much of our assessment of other people is based on perceptions, and perceptions can be changed. For example, if we feel underrewarded, we may decide that our comparison-other is working more hours than we originally believed—say by coming in on weekends and taking work home at night.

Fifth, we may change the object of comparison. We may conclude, for instance, that the current comparison-other is the boss's personal favorite, is unusually lucky, or has special skills and abilities. A different person would thus provide a more valid basis for comparison. Indeed, we might change comparison-others fairly often.

Finally, as a last resort, we may simply leave the situation. That is, we might decide that the only way to feel better about things is to be in a different situation altogether. Transferring to another department or seeking a new job may be the only way to reduce the inequity.

Evaluation and Implications

Most research on equity theory has been narrowly focused, dealing with only one ratio—between pay (hourly and piece-rate) and the quality or quantity of worker output given overpayment and underpayment.[41] Findings support the predictions of equity theory quite consistently, especially when the worker feels underpaid. When workers being paid on a piece-rate basis experience inequity, they tend to reduce their inputs by decreasing quality and tend to increase their outcomes by producing more units of work. When a person paid by the hour experiences inequity, the theory predicts an increase in quality and quantity if the person feels overpaid and a decrease in quality and quantity if the person feels underpaid. Research provides stronger support for responses to underpayment than for responses to overpayment; overall, however, most studies appear to uphold the basic premises of the theory. One interesting new twist on equity theory suggests that some people are more sensitive than others to perceptions of inequity. That is, some people pay a good deal of attention to their relative standing within the organization. Others focus more on their own situation without considering the situations of others.[42]

Social comparisons clearly are a powerful factor in the workplace. For managers, the most important implication of equity theory concerns organizational rewards and reward systems. Because "formal" organizational rewards (pay, task assignments, and so forth) are more easily observable than "informal" rewards (intrinsic satisfaction, feelings of accomplishment, and so forth), they are often central to a person's perceptions of equity.

Equity theory offers managers three messages. First, everyone in the organization needs to understand the basis for rewards. If people are to be rewarded more for the quality of work rather than for quantity of work, for instance, that fact needs to be clearly communicated to everyone. Second, people tend to take a multifaceted view of their rewards; they perceive and experience a variety of rewards, some tangible and others intangible. Finally, people base their actions on their perceptions of reality. If two people make exactly the same salary but each thinks the other makes more, each will base his or her experience of equity on the perception, not the reality. Hence, even if a manager believes two employees are being fairly rewarded, the employees themselves may not necessarily agree if their perceptions differ from the manager's. Our *Improve Your Skills* feature will help you better understand the complexities of equity and fairness in the workplace.

The Expectancy Theory of Motivation

Expectancy theory is a more encompassing model of motivation than equity theory (Expectancy theory is also known as **VIE theory**). Over the years since its original formulation, the theory's scope and complexity have continued to grow.

expectancy theory
Suggests that people are motivated by how much they want something and the likelihood they perceive of getting it

The Basic Expectancy Model

Victor Vroom is generally credited with first applying the theory to motivation in the workplace.[43] The theory attempts to determine how individuals choose among alternative behaviors. The basic premise of expectancy theory is that

IMPROVE YOUR SKILLS

FRAMING EQUITY AND FAIRNESS

This exercise will provide you with insights into how different people may frame equity and fairness and how you as a manager may need to help people address these framing issues.

Assume that you are a manager of a group of professional employees in the electronics industry. Ray Lambert, one of your employees, asks to meet with you. The company has just announced an opening for a team leader position in your group, and you know that Ray wants the job. You are unsure as to how to proceed. Ray feels that he has earned the opportunity on the basis of his consistently positive work record, but you see things a bit differently. Since you hired him about ten years ago he has been a solid but not an outstanding employee. As a result, he has consistently received average performance evaluations, pay increases, and so forth. He actually makes somewhat less money today than a couple of other people with less tenure in the group because they have had stronger performance records.

You really want to appoint another employee, Margot Sylvant, to the job. She has worked for the firm only six years, but during that time she has consistently been your top performer. You want to reward her performance, and you think she will do an excellent job as team leader. On the other hand, you don't want to lose Ray, a solid member of the group. In anticipation of both your upcoming meeting with Ray and how things will work out after you appoint Margot, perform the following activities.

1. Itemize the inputs and outcomes for both Ray and Margot. Think beyond the simple items described here and note other likely inputs and outcomes.
2. Describe how Ray and Margot are likely to see the situation.
3. Outline a conversation with Ray in which you convey your decision to hire Margot for the new position.
4. Note what advice you might offer to Margot about interacting with Ray in the future.
5. Identify other possible rewards you might offer Ray to keep him motivated.

motivation depends on how much we want something and how likely we think we are to get it.

A simple example further illustrates this premise. Suppose a recent 24-year-old college graduate is looking for her first managerial job. While scanning online job postings she sees that Apple is seeking a new executive vice president to oversee its foreign operations. The starting salary is $2,000,000. The student would love the job, but she does not bother to apply because she recognizes that she has no chance of getting it. Reading on, she sees a position that involves scraping bubble gum from underneath desks in college classrooms. The starting pay is $9.25 an hour, and no experience is necessary. Again, she is unlikely to apply—even though she assumes she could get the job, she does not want it.

Then she comes across a posting for a management training position with a successful large company known for being an excellent place to work. No experience is necessary, the primary requirement is a college degree, and the starting salary is $50,000. She will probably apply for this position because (1) she wants it and (2) she thinks she has a reasonable chance of getting it. (Of course, this simple example understates the true complexity of most choices. Job-seeking students may have strong geographic preferences, have other job opportunities, and also be considering graduate school. Most decisions of this type, in fact, are quite complex.)

Figure 5.5 summarizes the basic expectancy model. The model's general components are effort (the result of motivated behavior), performance, and outcomes. Expectancy theory emphasizes the linkages among these elements, which are described in terms of expectancies, instrumentalities, and valences.

Figure 5.5

The Expectancy Theory of Motivation

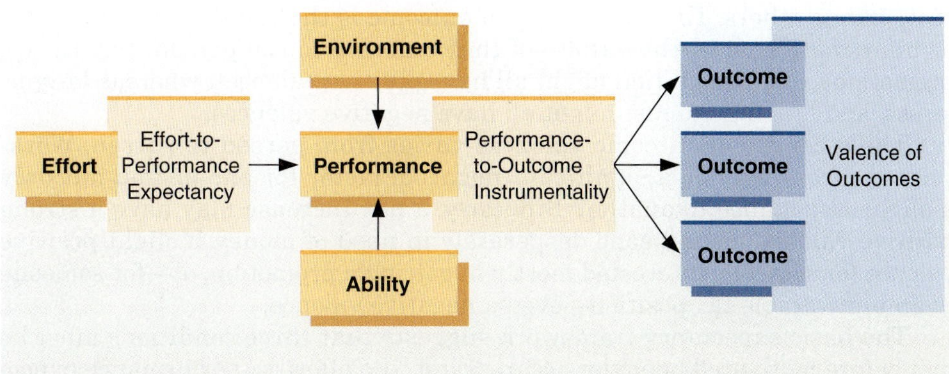

The expectancy theory is the most complex model of employee motivation in organizations. As shown here, the key components of expectancy theory are effort-to-performance expectancy, performance-to-outcome instrumentality, and outcomes, each of which has an associated valence. These components interact with effort, the environment, and the ability to determine an individual's performance.

Effort-to-Performance Expectancy

Effort-to-performance expectancy is a person's perception of the probability that effort will lead to successful performance. If we believe our effort will lead to higher performance, this expectancy is very strong, perhaps approaching a probability of 1.0, where 1.0 equals absolute certainty that the outcome will occur. If we believe our performance will be the same no matter how much effort we make, our expectancy is very low—perhaps as low as 0, meaning that there is no probability that the outcome will occur. A person who thinks there is a moderate relationship between effort and subsequent performance—the normal circumstance—has an expectancy somewhere between 1.0 and 0. Alex Morgan, a star soccer player who believes that when she puts forth maximum effort she has a great chance of scoring higher than any opponent, clearly sees a link between her effort and performance. (Some versions of this theory simply call this component *expectancy*.)

effort-to-performance expectancy
A person's perception of the probability that effort will lead to performance

Performance-to-Outcome Instrumentality

Performance-to-outcome instrumentality (also known as performance-to-outcome expectancy) is a person's perception of the probability that performance will lead to certain other outcomes. If a person thinks a high performer is certain to get a pay raise, this instrumentality is close to 1.0. At the other extreme, a person who believes raises are entirely independent of performance has an instrumentality close to 0. Finally, if a person thinks performance has some bearing on the prospects for a pay raise, his or her instrumentality is somewhere between 1.0 and 0. In a work setting, several performance-to-outcome instrumentalities are relevant because, as Figure 5.5 shows, several outcomes might logically result from performance.

performance-to-outcome instrumentality
The individual's perception of the probability that performance will lead to certain outcomes

Each outcome, then, has its own instrumentality. Green Bay Packers quarterback Aaron Rodgers may believe that if he plays aggressively all the time (performance), he has a great chance of leading his team to the playoffs. Playing aggressively may win him individual honors like the Most Valuable Player award, but he may also experience more physical trauma and throw more interceptions. (All three anticipated results are outcomes.)

Outcomes and Valences

outcome
Anything that results from performing a particular behavior

valence
The degree of attractiveness or unattractiveness a particular outcome has for a person

An ***outcome*** is anything that might potentially result from performance. High-level performance conceivably might produce such outcomes as a pay raise, a promotion, recognition from the boss, fatigue, stress, or less time to rest, among others. The ***valence*** of an outcome is the relative attractiveness or unattractiveness—the value—of that outcome to the person. Pay raises, promotions, and recognition might all have positive valences, whereas fatigue, stress, and less time to rest might all have negative valences.

The strength of outcome valences varies from person to person. Work-related stress may be a significant negative factor for one person but only a slight annoyance to another. Similarly, a pay increase may have a strong positive valence for someone desperately in need of money, a slight positive valence for someone interested mostly in getting a promotion, or—for someone in an unfavorable tax position—even a negative valence!

The basic expectancy framework suggests that three conditions must be met before motivated behavior occurs. First, the effort-to-performance expectancy must be well above zero. That is, the worker must reasonably expect that exerting effort will produce high levels of performance. Second, the performance-to-outcome instrumentalities must be well above zero. In other words, the person must believe that performance will realistically result in valued outcomes. Third, the sum of all the valences for the potential outcomes relevant to the person must be positive. One or more valences may be negative as long as the positives outweigh the negatives. For example, stress and fatigue may have moderately negative valences, but if pay, promotion, and recognition have very high positive valences, the overall valence of the set of outcomes associated with performance will still be positive.

Conceptually, the valences of all relevant outcomes and the corresponding pattern of expectancies and instrumentalities are assumed to interact in an almost mathematical fashion to determine a person's level of motivation. Most people do assess likelihoods of and preferences for various consequences of behavior, but they seldom approach them in such a calculating manner.

The Porter-Lawler Model

The original presentation of expectancy theory placed it squarely in the mainstream of contemporary motivation theory. Since then, the model has been refined and extended many times. Most modifications have focused on identifying and measuring outcomes and expectancies. An exception is the variation of expectancy theory developed by Lyman Porter and Edward Lawler. These researchers used expectancy theory to develop a novel view of the relationship between employee satisfaction and performance.[44] Although the conventional wisdom was that satisfaction leads to performance, Porter and Lawler argued the reverse: If rewards are adequate, high levels of performance may lead to satisfaction.

The Porter-Lawler model appears in Figure 5.6. Some of its features are quite different from the original version of expectancy theory. For example, the extended model includes abilities, traits, and role perceptions. At the beginning of the motivational cycle, effort is a function of the value of the potential reward for the employee (its valence) and the perceived effort-reward probability (an expectancy). Effort then combines with abilities, traits, and role perceptions to determine actual performance.

Figure 5.6

The Porter-Lawler Model

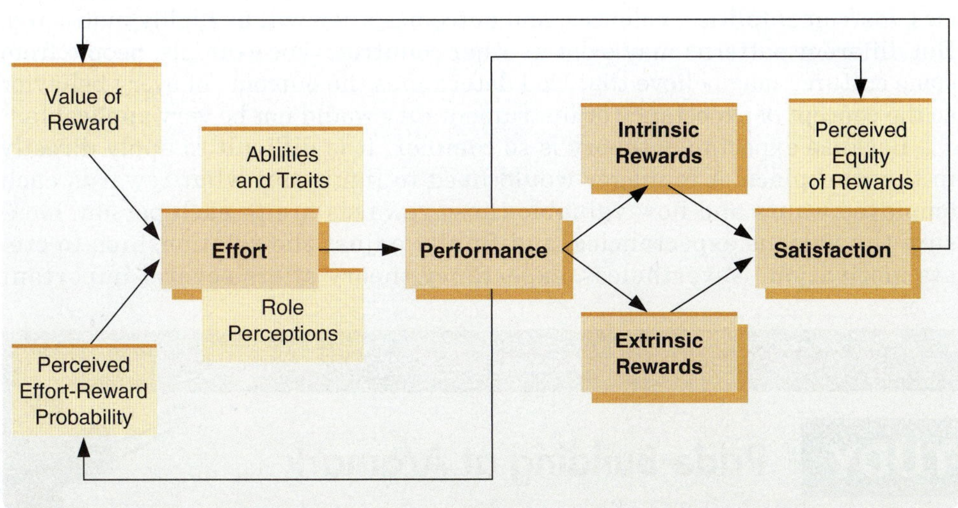

The Porter and Lawler expectancy model provides interesting insights into the relationships between satisfaction and performance. As illustrated here, this model predicts that satisfaction is determined by the perceived equity of intrinsic and extrinsic rewards for performance. That is, rather than satisfaction causing performance, which many people might predict, this model argues that it is actually performance that eventually leads to satisfaction.

Source: Figure from Lyman W. Porter and Edward E. Lawler, Managerial Attitudes and Performance. Copyright © 1968. McGraw-Hill, Inc. Used by permission of Lyman W. Porter.

Performance results in two kinds of rewards. Intrinsic rewards are intangible—a feeling of accomplishment, a sense of achievement, and so forth. Extrinsic rewards are tangible outcomes such as pay and promotion. The individual judges the value of his or her performance to the organization and uses social comparison processes (as in equity theory) to form an impression of the equity of the rewards received. If the rewards are regarded as equitable, the employee feels satisfied. In subsequent cycles, satisfaction with rewards influences the value of the rewards anticipated, and actual performance following effort influences future perceived effort-reward probabilities.

Evaluation and Implications

Expectancy theory has been tested by many different researchers in a variety of settings and using a variety of methods.[45] As noted earlier, the complexity of the theory has been both a blessing and a curse.[46] Nowhere is this double-edged quality more apparent than in the research undertaken to evaluate the theory. Several studies have supported various parts of the theory. For example, expectancies, instrumentalities, and valence have been found to be associated with effort and performance in the workplace.[47] Research has also confirmed expectancy theory's claims that people will not engage in motivated behavior unless they (1) value the expected rewards, (2) believe their efforts will lead to performance, and (3) believe their performance will result in the desired rewards.[48]

However, expectancy theory is so complicated that researchers have found it quite difficult to test. In particular, the measures of various parts of the model may lack validity, and the procedures for investigating relationships among the variables have often been less scientific than researchers would like. Moreover, people are seldom as rational and objective in choosing behaviors as expectancy theory implies. Still, the logic of the model, combined with the consistent, albeit modest, research support for it, suggests that the theory has much to offer.

Research has also suggested that expectancy theory is more likely to explain motivation in the United States than in other countries. People from the United States tend to be very goal oriented and tend to think that they can influence their own success. Thus, under the right combinations of expectancies, instrumentalities, valences, and outcomes, they will be highly motivated. But different patterns may exist in other countries. For example, people from some cultures may believe that God determines the outcome of every behavior so the concept of expectancy or instrumentality would not be very applicable.[49]

Because expectancy theory is so complex, it is difficult to apply directly in the workplace. A manager would need to figure out what rewards each employee wants and how valuable those rewards are to each person, measure the various expectancies, and finally adjust the relationships to create motivation. Nevertheless, expectancy theory offers several important

LOSKUTNIKOV/SHUTTERSTOCK.COM

CASE STUDY Pride-Building at Aramark

PHANT/SHUTTERSTOCK.COM

Aramark, a leader in professional services headquartered in Philadelphia, has approximately 270,000 employees serving clients in twenty-two countries.[50] Aramark wanted to better motivate its employees who clean airplanes for Delta and Southwest Airlines. Turnover of the low-paid staff of largely immigrant employees once exceeded 100 percent a year. Morale was low, and wallets and other valuable items that passengers left on planes had a tendency to disappear.

To turn things around, Aramark manager Roy Pelaez believed that he had to break some rules to get employees to feel motivated. "Managers are not supposed to get involved with the personal problems of their employees, but I take the opposite view," he says. "Any problem that affects the employee will eventually affect your account. If you take care of the employees, they will take care of you and your customer." Besides the typical "Employee of the Month" recognition programs, he brought in an English-language teacher to tutor employees twice a week on their own time, added Friday citizenship classes to help employees become U.S. citizens, and arranged for certified babysitters subsidized by government programs to keep single mothers showing up for work. He even created a small computer lab with three used computers so that employees could train each other in word processing and spreadsheets. "All of these things are important, because we want employees who really feel connected to the company," says Pelaez.

Employees who had perfect attendance over a six-month period or who turned in a wallet or pocketbook filled with cash and credit cards were rewarded with a day off with pay. Workers in the "Top Crew of the Month" were rewarded with movie passes, telephone calling cards, or "burger bucks." Turnover fell to 12 percent per year—amazing for jobs that pay only minimum wage to start. And crews started to recover large amounts of money from the airplanes, returning to passengers some 250 lost wallets with more than $50,000 in cash.[51]

In five years, Pelaez's efforts helped to increase Aramark's revenue in this area from $5 million to $14 million.[52] Since 1998, programs such as these have helped Aramark consistently rank as one of the top three most admired companies in its industry in *Fortune* magazine's list of "America's Most Admired Companies."[53]

Questions:

1. What motivation theories apply to the workers at Aramark?
2. If you were the manager of these employees, what would you do to motivate them? Be honest regarding your personal management style and beliefs rather than trying to be like Roy Pelaez.
3. What are some possible barriers to the effectiveness of your motivation ideas? What could you do to overcome them?

guidelines for the practicing manager. The following are some of the more fundamental guidelines:

1. Determine the primary outcomes each employee wants.
2. Decide what levels and kinds of performance are needed to meet organizational goals.
3. Make sure the desired levels of performance are possible.
4. Link desired outcomes and desired performance.
5. Analyze the situation for conflicting expectancies and instrumentalities.
6. Make sure the rewards are large enough.
7. Make sure the overall system is equitable for everyone.[54]

LEARNING-BASED PERSPECTIVES ON MOTIVATION

Learning is another key component in employee motivation. We discussed learning styles in Chapter 3, and now we examine learning from the perspective of motivation. In any organization, employees quickly learn which behaviors are rewarded and which are ignored or punished. Thus, learning plays a critical role in maintaining motivated behavior. ***Learning*** is a relatively permanent change in behavior or behavioral potential that results from direct or indirect experience. For example, we can learn to use a new software application program by practicing and experimenting with its various functions and options.

learning
A relatively permanent change in behavior or behavioral potential resulting from direct or indirect experience

How Learning Occurs

The Traditional View: Classical Conditioning

The most influential historical approach to learning is classical conditioning, developed by Ivan Pavlov in his famous experiments with dogs.[55] ***Classical conditioning*** is a simple form of learning in which a conditioned response is linked with an unconditioned stimulus. In organizations, however, only simple behaviors and responses can be learned in this manner. For example, suppose an employee receives very bad news one day from his boss. It's possible that the employee could come to associate, say, the color of the boss's suit that day with bad news. Thus, the next time the boss wears that same suit to the office, the employee may experience dread and foreboding.

classical conditioning
A simple form of learning that links a conditioned response with an unconditioned stimulus

But this form of learning is obviously simplistic and not directly relevant to motivation. Learning theorists soon recognized that although classical conditioning offered some interesting insights into the learning process, it was inadequate as an explanation of human learning. For one thing, classical conditioning relies on simple cause-and-effect relationships between one stimulus and one response; it cannot deal with the more complex forms of learned behavior that typify human beings. For another, classical conditioning ignores the concept of choice; it assumes that behavior is reflexive, or involuntary. Therefore, this perspective cannot explain situations in which people consciously and rationally choose one course of action from among many. Because of these shortcomings of classical conditioning, theorists eventually moved on to other approaches that seemed more useful in explaining the processes associated with complex learning.

The Contemporary View: Learning as a Cognitive Process

Although it is not tied to a single theory or model, contemporary learning theory generally views learning as a cognitive process; that is, it assumes that people are conscious, active participants in how they learn.[56]

First, the cognitive view suggests that people draw on their experiences and use past learning as a basis for their present behavior. These experiences represent knowledge, or cognitions. For example, an employee faced with a choice of job assignments will use previous experiences in deciding which one to accept. Second, people make choices about their behavior. The employee recognizes that she has two alternatives and chooses one. Third, people recognize the consequences of their choices. Thus, when the employee finds the job assignment rewarding and fulfilling, she will recognize that the choice was a good one and will understand why. Finally, people evaluate those consequences and add them to prior learning, which affects future choices. Faced with the same job choices next year, the employee will probably be motivated to choose the same one. As implied earlier, several perspectives on learning take a cognitive view. Perhaps foremost among them is reinforcement theory. Although reinforcement theory per se is not really new, it has only been applied to organizational settings in the last few years.

Reinforcement Theory and Learning

reinforcement theory
Based on the idea that behavior is a function of its consequences

Reinforcement theory (also called "operant conditioning") is generally associated with the work of B. F. Skinner.[57] In its simplest form, ***reinforcement theory*** suggests that behavior is a function of its consequences.[58] Behavior that results in pleasant consequences is more likely to be repeated (the employee will be motivated to repeat the current behavior), and behavior that results in unpleasant consequences is less likely to be repeated (the employee will be motivated to engage in different behaviors). Reinforcement theory also suggests that in any given situation, people explore a variety of possible behaviors. Future behavioral choices are affected by the consequences of earlier behaviors. Cognitions, as already noted, also play an important role. Therefore, rather than assuming the mechanical stimulus-response linkage suggested by the traditional classical view of learning, contemporary theorists believe that people consciously explore different behaviors and systematically choose those that result in the most desirable outcomes.

Suppose a new employee wants to learn the best way to get along with his boss. At first, the employee is very friendly and informal, but the boss responds by acting aloof and, at times, annoyed. Because the boss does not react positively, the employee is unlikely to continue this behavior. In fact, the employee next starts acting more formal and professional and finds the boss much more receptive to this posture. The employee will probably continue this new set of behaviors because they have resulted in positive consequences. We will examine how these processes work in more detail, but first let's consider one more basic aspect of learning based on the experiences of others.

Social Learning

In recent years, managers have begun to recognize the power of social learning. ***Social learning*** occurs when people observe the behaviors of others, recognize their consequences, and alter their own behavior as a result (some experts refer to social learning as *social cognitive theory*). A person can learn to do a new job by observing others or by watching videos. Or an employee may learn to avoid being late by seeing the boss chew out fellow workers. Social learning theory, then, suggests that individual behavior is determined by a person's cognitions and social environment. More specifically, people are presumed to learn behaviors and attitudes at least partly in response to what others expect of them.

social learning
When people observe the behaviors of others, recognize the consequences, and alter their own behavior as a result

Several conditions must be met to produce an appropriate environment for social learning. First, the behavior being observed and imitated must be relatively simple. Although we can learn by watching someone else how to push three or four buttons to set specifications on a machine or to turn on a computer, we probably cannot learn a complicated sequence of operations for the machine or how to run a complex software package without also practicing the various steps ourselves. Second, social learning usually involves observed and imitated behavior that is concrete, not intellectual. We can learn by watching others how to respond to the different behaviors of a particular manager or how to assemble a few component parts into a final assembled product. But we probably cannot learn through simple observation how to write computer software, how to write complicated text, how to conceptualize, or how to think abstractly. Finally, for social learning to occur, we must possess the physical ability to imitate the behavior observed. Most of us, even if we watch televised baseball games or tennis matches every weekend, cannot hit a fastball like Miguel Cabrera or execute a backhand like Serena Williams.

Social learning influences motivation in a variety of ways. Many of the behaviors we exhibit in our daily work lives are learned from others. Suppose a new employee joins an existing workgroup. She already has some basis for knowing how to behave from her education and previous

Social learning occurs when people observe the behaviors of others, recognize the consequences, and alter their won behavior as a result. This individual is getting a reward and promotion. His co-workers may now be motivated to perform their jobs in the same way as him.

experience. However, the group provides a set of very specific cues she can use to tailor her behavior to fit her new situation. The group may indicate how the organization expects its members to dress, how people are "supposed" to feel about the boss, and so forth. Hence, the employee learns how to behave in the new situation partly in response to what she already knows and partly in response to what others suggest and demonstrate.

Behavior Modification

behavior modification
The application of reinforcement theory to influence the behaviors of people in organizational settings

Learning theory alone has important implications for managers, but organizational behavior modification has even more practical applications. ***Behavior modification*** is the application of reinforcement theory to influence the behaviors of people in organizational settings.[59] One aspect of behavior modification is the use of various kinds of reinforcement when employees are observed behaving in desired or undesired ways. Figure 5.7 summarizes these kinds of reinforcement. We will now discuss these different kinds of reinforcement in more detail, and then look at different times to apply time.

Kinds of Reinforcement

There are four types of reinforcers, as shown in Figure 5.7. *Positive reinforcement* involves the use of rewards to increase the likelihood that a desired behavior—high performance, for instance—will be repeated. For example, when a manufacturing employee wears uncomfortable but important safety gear, the manager can give the employee praise to increase the likelihood that the employee will wear the safety equipment in the future. Positive reinforcement has been used at a Sears Department Store in Pennsylvania. A manager was having a difficult time getting his staff to prompt customers to apply for credit cards. He offered employees a bonus on their paycheck for every credit card application that was processed. In addition, every 90 days, the employee with the most submitted applications would be recognized at work and receive a gift card. As a result, the Sears store became the number one store for credit card applications in the state.

Figure 5.7

Individual behavior can be affected when stimulus is either presented or removed after a particular behavior. This is also dependent on whether the stimulus is positive or negative.

Types of Reinforcers[60]

		Nature of the Stimulus	
		Positive	**Negative**
Action	**Present the Stimulus**	*Positive reinforcement;* increases the behavior	*Punishment;* decreases the behavior
	Remove the Stimulus	*Extinction;* decreases the behavior	*Negative reinforcement;* increases the behavior

Sources: Based on B. Lachman, F. Camm, & S. A. Resetar, Integrated Facility Environmental Management Approaches: Lessons from Industry for Department of Defense Facilities, 2001. Santa Monica, CA: RAND Corporation. http://www.rand.org/pubs/monograph_reports/MR1343/.

Negative reinforcement is based on the removal of current or future unpleasant consequences to increase the likelihood that someone will repeat a behavior. In other words, avoidance or removal of something undesirable can be motivating. For example, suppose a piece of hazardous manufacturing equipment is set so that when it is turned on the machine operator hears a continuous loud buzzer. After the machine operator runs a series of safety checks the buzzer stops. Because the machine operator wants the buzzer to stop she or he is motivated to engage in safe work behaviors (running the safety checks). If an employee has a long or unpleasant commute, allowing her to work from home one or two days a week if her performance stays high can also be rewarding and motivate good performance.

Punishment is the application of negative outcomes to decrease the likelihood of a behavior. For example, a manager might reduce the work hours of low-performing employees. Other common forms of punishment include verbal and written reprimands, formal disciplinary activities, and reduced involvement in decision making. Because of a variety of consequences that can follow punishment, most organizations rely on rules and policies to govern the use of punishment.

Finally, *extinction* involves the removal of other reinforcement (positive or negative) following the incidence of the behavior to be extinguished to decrease the likelihood of that behavior being repeated. For example, suppose that a manager laughs at an off-color joke told by an employee. The laughter serves as positive reinforcement so the employee may continue to tell off-color jokes. The manager realizes that this could lead to trouble and wants the employee to stop. The manager can begin ignoring the jokes. Over time, the lack of a positive reaction from the manager reduces the employee's motivation and the behavior is extinguished.

For reinforcement to work, people must associate the reward with the behavior. In other words, people need to know exactly why they are receiving a reward. To best reinforce a behavior, the reward should come as quickly as possible after the behavior. The reward can be almost anything, and does not need to cost a lot of money, but it must be something desired by the recipient. Some of the most powerful rewards are symbolic—things that cost very little but mean a lot to the people who get them. Examples of symbolic rewards are things like plaques or certificates.

Rewards also impact ethical behavior choices. Although multiple studies have shown that incentives can increase unethical behavior,[61] the effects of rewards and punishments on ethical behavior are complex. Rewards do not always increase ethical behavior because the presence of the reward can undermine the intrinsic value of the ethical behavior.[62] Providing economic incentives for voluntary helping behavior undermines people's motivation for engaging in it.[63] Because the presence of sanctions makes it more likely that individuals will view a decision from a more narrow, business-driven framework rather than an ethical decision-making framework, weak sanctions can undermine ethical behavior more than no sanctions at all.[64] Instead of choosing a course of action based on what is right, the decision becomes an evaluation of whether the unethical behavior is "worth" the risk of the punishment.

The Timing of Reinforcement

As noted above, reinforcement should ideally come immediately after the behavior bring influenced. For a variety of reasons, though, this may not always be possible. Therefore, it is useful to understand the various schedules that can be used to provide reinforcement. A *continuous reinforcement* schedule is one in which the desired behavior is reinforced each time that it occurs. A *partial reinforcement* schedule is one in which the desired behavior is reinforced only part of the time. There are four types of partial reinforcement schedules:

1. *Fixed-ratio*: Desired behavior is reinforced after a specified number of correct responses—for example, receiving pay bonuses for every ten error-free pieces made per hour.
2. *Fixed-interval*: Desired behavior is reinforced after a certain amount of time has passed—for example, receiving weekly paychecks.
3. *Variable-ratio*: Desired behavior is reinforced after an unpredictable number of behaviors—for example, a supervisor praises a call center representative after the third call, then the seventh call after that, and then the fourth call after that.
4. *Variable-interval*: Desired behavior is reinforced after an unpredictable amount of time has elapsed—for example, not knowing when a regional supervisor will visit your location for an inspection.

Fixed-ratio schedules produce a high, consistent rate of responding with desired behaviors but with fast extinction when the reinforcement stops. Fixed-interval schedules produce high performance near the end of the interval, but lower performance immediately after the reinforcement occurs. Variable-ratio schedules produce a high, steady rate of responding with desired behaviors and the behaviors are difficult to extinguish. With variable-interval schedules, the behavior of the individual does not influence the availability of reinforcement so it has a minimal effect on motivation.

Research suggests that the fastest way to get someone to learn is to use continuous reinforcement and reinforce the desired behavior every time it occurs. The downside to this approach is that as soon as the reward is stopped, the desired behavior decreases in frequency (extinction). The most effective schedule for sustaining a behavior is variable reinforcement. This requires reinforcing the desired behavior every few times it occurs, around some average number of times, rather than every time it occurs. Because performing the behavior could result in a reward at any time, this approach is a strong motivator of behavior. A good example of variable reinforcement is a slot machine—players know that their machine will eventually pay out, but they do not know when, so they are motivated to continue playing for a long time even when they are losing and not being reinforced.

In terms of behavior modification, any behavior can be understood as being a result of its consequences. In other words, as a manager, you get whatever behaviors you are rewarding. If an employee continually comes to work late, it is because you are not providing the right positive consequences for coming to work on time, the negative consequences for coming in late are inappropriate, or both. To motivate the right behavior, an expert in behavior modification would identify the desired behaviors and then carefully reinforce them. This process involves five steps:[65]

1. Define the problem—what is it that could be improved?
2. Identify and define the specific behavior(s) you wish to change.
3. Record and track the occurrence of the target behavior.
4. Analyze the current negative consequences of the undesired behavior and arrange for more positive consequences to follow the desired behavior.
5. Evaluate whether the behavior has improved, and by how much.

This chapter has covered a variety of theories that can be used by managers to motivate employee performance. Table 5.1 summarizes how different motivation concepts covered in this chapter can be applied to a variety of common management challenges. Understanding *why* and *how* a motivational perspective works helps managers better match motivational techniques with motivation opportunities and enhances the likelihood of success. In Chapter 6 we will explore in more detail different ways that work and rewards can be used to motivate employee performance. These motivational methods, techniques, and programs are derived from the various theories discussed in this chapter, but also provide more operational guidance for managers.

Table 5.1

Different motivation concepts and theories can be applied to various managerial challenges to enhance employee motivation.

Managerial Challenges	**Motivation Theories**					
	Self-Efficacy	**McClelland's Needs Theory**	**Herzberg's Two-Factor Theory**	**Expectancy Theory**	**Equity Theory**	**Reinforcement**
Firm has a low-cost business strategy but needs to motivate employees	x	x	x	x	x	x
An employee feels he cannot meet his performance goals	x			x		
An employee feels underpaid relative to her coworkers			x		x	
An employee engages in inappropriate behavior (bullying, ridiculing coworkers)						x
A talented employee is not feeling challenged at work		x	x	x		
Because the work is repetitive, some employees find it boring and hard to stay motivated		x	x			

SUMMARY AND APPLICATION

Motivation is the set of forces that cause people to behave as they do. Motivation starts with a need. People search for ways to satisfy their needs and then behave accordingly. Their behavior results in rewards or punishment. To varying degrees, an outcome may satisfy the original need. Scientific management asserted that money is the primary human motivator in the workplace. The human relations view suggested that social factors are primary motivators. Individual differences can play an important role in motivation.

According to Abraham Maslow, human needs are arranged in a hierarchy of importance, from physiological to security to belongingness to esteem to, finally, self-actualization. The ERG theory is a refinement of Maslow's original hierarchy that includes a frustration-regression component. In Herzberg's two-factor theory, satisfaction and dissatisfaction are two distinct dimensions instead of opposite ends of the same dimension. Motivation factors are presumed to affect satisfaction and hygiene factors are presumed to affect dissatisfaction. Herzberg's theory is well known among managers but has several

LOSKUTNIKOV/SHUTTERSTOCK.COM

REAL WORLD RESPONSE

MOTIVATING CAST MEMBERS AT DISNEY

To motivate cast members at Disney theme parks to provide exemplary customer service, the company begins by thoroughly training new hires in topics ranging from performance expectations, to how to dress, to how to anticipate guests' needs. Cast members are then rewarded daily by managers and cast members with verbal complements, written praise, and other monetary and nonmonetary rewards. Because it is easiest to be motivated and perform well on a job we are good at, Disney also uses performance evaluations to put cast members in the best job for their unique talents.[66]

Disney believes that the key to rewards is the frequency and the immediacy with which they are administered. Disney tries to avoid time lags between when an employee does a good deed and the subsequent reward or recognition. Cast members are encouraged to give "Great Service Fanatic" cards to fellow Cast Members when they see each other going above and beyond to deliver outstanding service. After receiving a card, the Cast Member must have it signed by his/her manager to inform him or her of the praise. Disney believes that this type of praise is the key to building a highly motivated workforce and making guests happy.[67]

Whatever the reward given, Disney feels strongly that the purpose must be clear and motivational. Disney uses a variety of rewards, from a numbered bottle of green tabasco sauce to an entry in a drawing for a family Disney cruise, to motivate employees to maintain a high level of service quality and idea generation.[68]

deficiencies. Other important acquired needs include the needs for achievement, affiliation, and power.

The equity theory of motivation assumes that people want to be treated fairly. It hypothesizes that people compare their own input-to-outcome ratio in the organization with the ratio of a comparison-other. If they feel their treatment has been inequitable, they take steps to reduce the inequity. Expectancy theory, a somewhat more complicated model, follows from the assumption that people are motivated to work toward a goal if they want it and think that they have a reasonable chance of achieving it. Effort-to-performance expectancy is the belief that effort will lead to performance. Performance-to-outcome instrumentality is the belief that performance will lead to certain outcomes. Valence is the desirability to the individual of the various possible outcomes of performance. The Porter-Lawler version of expectancy theory provides useful insights into the relationship between satisfaction and performance. This model suggests that performance may lead to a variety of intrinsic and extrinsic rewards. When perceived as equitable, these rewards lead to satisfaction.

Learning also plays a role in employee motivation. Various kinds of reinforcement provided according to different schedules can increase or decrease motivated behavior. People are affected by social learning processes. Organizational behavior modification is a strategy for using learning and reinforcement principles to enhance employee motivation and performance. This strategy relies heavily on the effective measurement of performance and the provision of rewards to employees after they perform at a high level.

DISCUSSION QUESTIONS

1. When has your level of performance been directly affected by your motivation? By your ability? By the environment?
2. Identify examples from your own experience that support, and others that refute, Maslow's hierarchy of needs theory.
3. Have you ever experienced inequity in a job or a class? How did it affect you?
4. Which is likely to be a more serious problem—perceptions of being underrewarded or perceptions of being overrewarded?
5. Do you think expectancy theory is too complex for direct use in organizational settings? Why or why not?
6. Do the relationships between performance and satisfaction suggested by Porter and Lawler seem valid? Cite examples that both support and refute the model.
7. Think of occasions on which you experienced each of the four types of reinforcement.
8. Identify the five forms of reinforcement that you receive most often (i.e., wages, grades, etc.). On what schedule do you receive each of them?

UNDERSTAND YOURSELF

Managerial Motivation Skills

The goal of this exercise is to better understand and develop your managerial motivation skills. After you are assigned a partner, decide who will play the role of manager and who will play the role of the subordinate. The subordinate's task is to fold a paper airplane out of a single sheet of paper that flies farther than any other paper airplane made in the class. Your instructor will give the subordinate a confidential role assignment that is NOT to be shared with the manager. After reading the role sheet, the subordinate will act out the situation described in the role assignment. As the subordinate, DO NOT tell the manager what you will be doing—just act it out by behaving as a real employee would in the situation you have been assigned. The subordinate is responsible for folding the airplane under the supervision of the manager.

As the manager, your job is to identify the motivational problem, analyze the situation, and try different strategies to motivate the subordinate. As the subordinate, your job is to realistically portray the employee in the role description and respond realistically to the manager's attempts at increasing your motivation and changing your behavior.

When the instructor indicates, stop the role play. The subordinate should then show the manager his or her role assignment and talk about what the manager did well and less well in trying to analyze and improve the situation. Give honest, constructive feedback to help your partner improve his or her managerial skills.

Now switch roles, and the instructor will give the new subordinate a different role assignment. Repeat the process, including giving feedback to the manager when the exercise is complete.

GROUP EXERCISE

Motivating Your Sales Staff

The goal of this exercise is to give you practice aligning individual and organizational goals, and thinking like a manager in managing employee motivation. After dividing into groups of four to five students, read the scenario below:

Imagine that you are the management team of a new high-end retail clothing store named Threads. Your company's business strategy is to provide high-quality customer service and to provide high-quality products. You are not the cheapest store in town, but you expect your employees to create a service-oriented atmosphere that customers will be willing to pay a little extra for.

You recognize that your sales staff will be essential to your store's success, and you want to create a system that motivates them to help create a competitive advantage for your business. Because this is the first store you have opened, you have some latitude to decide how to best motivate your staff. Market competitive starting salaries have already established, but you have decided to allocate 10 percent of the store's profits to use to motivate your sales staff in any way you see fit.

Working as a team, discuss your answers to the following questions. Be prepared to share your answers with the class.

Questions

1. What behaviors would you want from your sales staff?
2. What goals would you set for your sales staff, given your answer to question 1?
3. What type of system would you set up to reward these behaviors?
4. What challenges would you be on the lookout for? How would you proactively address these potential challenges to prevent them from happening?

VIDEO EXERCISE

Mike Boyle Strength & Conditioning

Mike Boyle is the co-owner and manager of Mike Boyle Strength and Conditioning, a gym based in Woburn, Massachusetts. Mike's vision for his gym is that it is a place where he and his staff enjoy spending their time and do not really see their jobs as "work." Rather, he wants everyone to see the gym simply as a place they go each day to help people.

Mike Boyle Strength & Conditioning employs a number of people performing in multiple roles. For example, one of his staff members serves as both a personal trainer and a nutritionist. Another serves as both a personal training and a sports masseuse. Mike himself, along with his co-founder, also work as personal trainers in addition to managing the gym.

Mike understands that the fitness industry is characterized by high turnover. Some trainers are simply working while they pursue other career opportunities. Others move from gym to gym. Consequently, he focuses on trying to motivate his staff to both grow and develop as fitness professionals while also seeing his gym as a place they want to stay.

Watch the video "Mike Boyle Strength & Conditioning" as a class. Next, form small groups with 3-4 of your classmates and develop responses to these questions.

Questions

1. Can you relate Mike Boyle's views on employee motivation to the need theories discussed in this class? If so, how?
2. How does expectancy theory explain Ana's view of her work at Mike Boyle's Strength & Conditioning?
3. Marco speaks about the pride he takes in both his work and the gym. Describe how his pride can be explained by any of the eed perspectives on motivation.
4. How do Bob's ideas about training and learning relate to employee motivation?

Now What?

VIDEO CASE

PERCOM/SHUTTERSTOCK.COM

Imagine working in a group with two other members asked by your boss to brainstorm names for a new product. The other two members stop after quickly generating three to four weak ideas and want to quit. One group member doesn't see the point of the task. The other group member claims to not be good at this kind of creative stuff and would rather get back to work doing something else. *What do you say or do?* Go to this chapter's "Now What?" video, watch the challenge video, and choose a response. Be sure to also view the outcomes of the two responses you didn't choose.

Discussion Questions

1. Which aspects of motivation discussed in this chapter are illustrated in these videos? Explain your answer.
2. What do you feel is the biggest challenge facing this team in the challenge video?
3. As a manager, what motivational techniques would you apply in this situation?

ENDNOTES

[1]Company Overview, Disney, 2015. Available online: http://corporate.disney.go.com/corporate/overview.html.

[2]Barrett, S. (2011, April 7). Customer Service Secrets from Disney. *The Locker Room.* Available online: http://ggfablog.wordpress.com/2011/04/07/customer-service-secrets-from-disney/.

[3]See Pinder, C. (2008). *Work Motivation in Organizational Behavior* (2nd ed.). Upper Saddle River, NJ: Prentice Hall. See also Lord, R., Diefendorff, J., Schmidt, A., & Hall, R. (2010.) Self-Regulation at Work. In *Annual Review of Psychology*, eds. S. Fiske, D. Schacter, & R. Sternberg (Vol. 61, pp. 543–568). Palo Alto, CA: Consulting Psychologists Press; and Diefendorff, J. M., & Chandler M. M. (2010). Motivating Employees. In *Handbook of Industrial and Organizational Psychology,* ed. S. Zedeck. Washington, DC: American Psychological Association.

[4]Steers, R. M., Bigley, G. A., & Porter, L. W. (2002). *Motivation and Leadership at Work* (7th ed.). New York: McGraw-Hill. See also Kanfer, R. "Motivational Theory and Industrial and Organizational Psychology," In *Handbook of Industrial and Organizational Psychology,* eds. M. D. Dunnette and L. M. Hough (2nd ed., Vol. 1, pp. 75–170). Palo Alto, CA: Consulting Psychologists Press; and Ambrose, M. L. (1999). Old Friends, New Faces: Motivation Research in the 1990s. *Journal of Management*, *25*(2), 110–131.

[5]Kidwell, R. E., Jr., & Bennett, N. (1993, July). Employee Propensity to Withhold Effort: A Conceptual Model to Intersect Three Avenues of Research. *Academy of Management Review*, 429–456; see also Grant, A. (2008). Does Intrinsic Motivation Fuel the Prosocial Fire? Motivational Synergy in Predicting Persistence, Performance, and Productivity. *Journal of Applied Psychology*, *93*(1), 48–58.

[6]Pfeiffer, J. (1998). *The Human Equation.* Boston: Harvard Business School Press.

[7]See Fox, A. (2010, May). Raising Engagement. *HR Magazine*, 35–40.

[8]Deci, E. L., & Ryan, R. M. (2000). The "What" and "Why" of Goal Pursuits: Human Needs and the Self-Determination of Behavior. *Psychological Inquiry*, *11*(4), 227–269.

[9]Taylor, F. W. (1911). *Principles of Scientific Management.* New York: Harper & Row.

[10]Mayo, E. (1945). *The Social Problems of an Industrial Civilization.* Boston: Harvard University Press; Rothlisberger, F. J., & Dickson, W. J. (1939). *Management and the Worker.* Boston: Harvard University Press.

[11]Bandura, A. (1997). *Self-Efficacy: The Exercise of Control* (p. 3). New York: W.H. Freeman.

[12]Judge, T. A., Jackson, C. L., Shaw, J. C., Scott, B. A., & Rich, B. L. (2007). Self-Efficacy and Work-Related Performance: The Integral Role of Individual Differences. *Journal of Applied Psychology*, *92*, 107–127.

[13]Odell, P. (2005, November 9). Motivating Employees on a Global Scale: Author Bob Nelson. PROMO P&I. Available online: http://www.chiefmarketer.com/motivating-employees-on-a-global-scale-author-bob-nelson/.

[14]Solomon, C. M. (1994, July). Global Operations Demand That HR Rethinks Diversity. *Personnel Journal*, *73*(7), 40–50.

[15]Salancik, G. R., & Pfeiffer, J. (1977, September). An Examination of Need-Satisfaction Models of Job Attitudes. *Administrative Science Quarterly*, 427–456.

[16]Amabile, T., & Kramer, S. (2010, January–February). What Really Motivates Workers. *Harvard Business Review*, 44–45.

[17]Maslow, A. H. (1943). A Theory of Human Motivation. *Psychological Review*, *50*, 370–396; Maslow, A. H. (1954). *Motivation and Personality.* New York: Harper & Row. Maslow's most famous works include Maslow, A. H., Stephens, D. C., & Heil, G. (1998). *Maslow on Management*. New York: John Wiley and Sons; and Maslow. A. H., & Lowry, R. (1999). *Toward a Psychology of Being.* New York: John Wiley and Sons.

[18]See Professionals Sick of Old Routine Find Healthy Rewards in Nursing, *USA Today*, August 16, 2004, 1B, 2B.

[19]See Adler, N. (2007). *International Dimensions of Organizational Behavior* (5th ed.). Cincinnati, OH: Southwestern Publishing.

[20]Wahba, M. A., & Bridwell, L. G. (1976, April). Maslow Reconsidered: A Review of Research on the Need Hierarchy Theory. *Organizational Behavior and Human Performance*, 212–240.

[21]Alderfer. C. P. (1972). *Existence, Relatedness, and Growth.* New York: Free Press.

[22]Alderfer. C. P. (1972). *Existence, Relatedness, and Growth.* New York: Free Press.

[23]Herzberg, F., Mausner, B., & Synderman, B. (1959). *The Motivation to Work*. New York: John Wiley and Sons; Herzberg, F. (1968, January–February). One More Time: How Do You Motivate Employees? *Harvard Business Review*, 53–62.

[24]Herzberg, F., Mausner, B., & Synderman, B. (1959). *The Motivation to Work*. New York: John Wiley and Sons.

[25]Herzberg, F., Mausner, B., & Synderman, B. (1959). *The Motivation to Work*. New York: John Wiley and Sons.

[26]Herzberg, F., Mausner, B., & Synderman, B. (1959). *The Motivation to Work*. New York: John Wiley and Sons.

[27]Griffin, R. W. (1982). *Task Design: An Integrative Approach*. Glenview, IL: Scott, Foresman.

[28]Pinder, C. (2008).*Work Motivation in Organizational Behavior* (2nd ed.). Upper Saddle River, NJ: Prentice Hall.

[29]Herzberg, F. (1966). *Work and the Nature of Man*. Cleveland, OH: World Publishing; Bookman, V. M. (1971, Summer). The Herzberg Controversy. *Personnel Psychology*, 155–189; Grigaliunas, B., & Herzberg, F. (1971, February). Relevance in the Test of Motivation-Hygiene Theory. *Journal of Applied Psychology*, 73–79.

[30]Dunnette, M., Campbell, J., & Hakel, M. (1967, May). Factors Contributing to Job Satisfaction and Job Dissatisfaction in Six Occupational Groups. *Organizational Behavior and Human Performance*, 143–174; Hulin, C. L., & Smith, P. (1967, October). An Empirical Investigation of Two Implications of the Two-Factor Theory of Job Satisfaction. *Journal of Applied Psychology*, 396–402.

[31]Adler, N. (2007). *International Dimensions of Organizational Behavior* (5th ed.). Cincinnati, OH: Southwestern Publishing.

[32]McClelland, D. C. (1961). *The Achieving Society*. Princeton, NJ: Nostrand. See also McClelland, D. C. (1988). *Human Motivation*. Cambridge, UK: Cambridge University Press.

[33]Stahl, M. J. (1983, Winter). Achievement, Power, and Managerial Motivation: Selecting Managerial Talent with the Job Choice Exercise. *Personnel Psychology*, 775–790.

[34]Schachter, S. (1959). *The Psychology of Affiliation*. Palo Alto, CA: Stanford University Press.

[35]As reported in: Best Friends Good for Business, *USA Today*, December 1, 2004, 1B, 2B.

[36]McClelland, D. C., & Burnham, D. H. (1976, March–April). Power Is the Great Motivator. *Harvard Business Review*, 100–110.

[37]Pinder, C. (2008). *Work Motivation in Organizational Behavior* (2nd ed.). Upper Saddle River, NJ: Prentice Hall; McClelland, D. C., & Burnham, D. H. (1976, March–April). Power Is the Great Motivator. *Harvard Business Review*, 100–110.

[38]J. Stacy Adams, J. S. (1963, November). Toward an Understanding of Inequity. *Journal of Abnormal and Social Psychology*, 422–436. See also Mowday, R. T. (1987). Equity Theory Predictions of Behavior in Organizations. In *Motivation and Work Behavior,* eds. R. M. Steers & L. W. Porter *Motivation and Work Behavior* (4th ed., pp. 89–110). New York: McGraw-Hill.

[39]Shah, P. P. (1998). Who Are Employees' Social Referents? Using a Network Perspective to Determine Referent Others. *Academy of Management Journal*, *41*(3), 249–268.

[40]Adams, J. S. (1965). Inequity in Social Exchange. In *Advances in Experimental Social Psychology,* ed. L. Berkowitz (Vol. 2, pp. 267–299). New York: Academic Press.

[41]Pinder, C. (2008). *Work Motivation in Organizational Behavior* (2nd ed.). Upper Saddle River, NJ: Prentice Hall.

[42]See Sauler, K., & Bedeian, A. (2000). Equity Sensitivity: Construction of a Measure and Examination of Its Psychometric Properties. *Journal of Management*, *26*(5), 885–910; Bing, M., & Burroughs, S. (2001). The Predictive and Interactive Effects of Equity Sensitivity in Teamwork-Oriented Organizations. *Journal of Organizational Behavior*, *22*, 271–290.

[43]Vroom, V. (1964). *Work and Motivation*. New York: John Wiley and Sons.

[44]Porter, L. W., & Lawler, E. E. (1968) *Managerial Attitudes and Performance*. Homewood, IL: Dorsey Press.

[45]See Mitchell, T. R. (1974). Expectancy Models of Job Satisfaction, Occupational Preference, and Effort: A Theoretical, Methodological, and Empirical Appraisal. *Psychological Bulletin*, *81*, 1096–1112; and Campbell, J. P., & Pritchard, R. D. (1976). Motivation Theory in Industrial and Organizational Psychology. In *Handbook of Industrial and Organizational Psychology*, ed. M. D. Dunnette (pp. 63–130). Chicago, IL: Rand McNally, for reviews.

[46]Pinder, C. (2008). *Work Motivation in Organizational Behavior* (2nd ed.). Upper Saddle River, NJ: Prentice Hall.

[47]Pinder, C. (2008). *Work Motivation in Organizational Behavior* (2nd ed.). Upper Saddle River, NJ: Prentice Hall.

[48]Campbell, J. P., & Pritchard, R. D. (1976). Motivation Theory in Industrial and Organizational Psychology. In *Handbook of Industrial and Organizational Psychology,* ed. M. D. Dunnette (pp. 63–130). Chicago, IL: Rand McNally.

[49]Adler, N. (2007). *International Dimensions of Organizational Behavior* (5th ed.). Cincinnati, OH: Southwestern Publishing.

[50]Aramark 2015 Fact Sheet. (2015). Available online: http://www.aramark.com/~/media/Files/aramark-fun-facts.ashx?la=en.

[51]Byrne, J. A. (2003, August). How to Lead Now: Getting Extraordinary Performance When You Can't Pay for It. *Fast Company*, *73*, 62.

[52]Byrne, J. A. (2003, August). How to Lead Now: Getting Extraordinary Performance When You Can't Pay for It. *Fast Company*, *73*, 62.

[53]Aramark: Creating Experiences that Engage and Inspire. (2015). Available online: http://www.aramark.com/about-us.

[54]Nadler, D. A., & Lawler, E. E. (1983). Motivation: A Diagnostic Approach. In *Perspectives on Behavior in Organizations*, eds. J. R. Hackman, E. E. Lawler, & L. W. Porter (2nd ed., pp. 67–78). New York: McGraw-Hill; see also Fisher, A. (2004, March 22). Turning Clock-Watchers into Stars. *Fortune*, 60.

[55]Pavlov, I. P. (1927). *Conditional Reflexes.* New York: Oxford University Press.

[56]Bandura, A. (2001). Social Cognitive Theory: An Agentic Perspective. *Annual Review of Psychology*, *52*, 1–26.

[57]Skinner, B. F. (1953). *Science and Human Behavior.* New York: Macmillian; and Skinner, B. F. (1972). *Beyond Freedom and Dignity.* New York: Knopf.

[58]Luthans, F., & Kreitner, R. (1985). *Organizational Behavior Modification and Beyond.* Glenview, IL: Scott, Foresman.

[59]Luthans, F., & Kreitner, R. (1975). *Organizational Behavior Modification.* Glenview, IL: Scott Foresman; Luthans, F., & Kreitner, R. (1985). *Organizational Behavior Modification and Beyond.* Glenview, IL: Scott, Foresman.

[60]Lachman, B., Camm, F., & Resetar, S. A. (2001). Integrated Facility Environmental Management Approaches: Lessons from Industry for Department of Defense Facilities. Santa Monica, CA: RAND Corporation. Available online: http://www.rand.org/pubs/monograph_reports/MR1343/.

[61]Ashkanasy, N. M., Windsor, C. A., & Treviño, L. K. (2006). Bad Apples in Bad Barrels Revisited: Cognitive Moral Development, Just World Beliefs, Rewards, and Ethical Decision Making. *Business Ethics Quarterly*, *16*, 449–474; Treviño, L. K., & Youngblood, S. A. (1990). Bad Apples in Bad Barrels: A Causal Analysis of Ethical Decision Making Behavior. *Journal of Applied Psychology*, *75*(4), 447–476.

[62]Treviño, L. K., & Youngblood, S. A. (1990). Bad Apples in Bad Barrels: A Causal Analysis of Ethical Decision Making Behavior. *Journal of Applied Psychology*, *75*(4), 447–476.

[63]Frey, B. S., & Oberholzer-Gee, F. (1997). The Cost of Price Incentives: An Empirical Analysis of Motivation Crowding-Out. *American Economic Review*, *87*(4), 746–755.

[64]Tenbrunsel, A. E., & Messick, D. M. (2004). Ethical Fading: The Role of Self-Deception in Unethical Behavior. *Social Justice Research*, *17*(2), 223–235.

[65]The following is based on: Connellan, T. (1978). *How to Improve Human Performance: Behaviorism in Business.* New York: Harper & Row; Miller, L. (1978). *Behavior Management: The New Science of Managing People at Work* (p. 253). New York: John Wiley and Sons.

[66]Kalogridis, G. (2010). Chain of Excellence. *Leadership Excellence*, *27*(8), 7.

[67]James, J. (2012, April 19). Encouraging and Motivating Leaders, Talking Point: The Disney Institute Blog. Available online: http://disneyinstitute.com/blog/blog_posting.aspx?bid=52#.T7ENCOvLxNM.

[68]Ligos, M. (2009). How Mickey Makes Magic. *Successful Promotions*, *42*(5), 44–47.

LOSKUTNIKOV/SHUTTERSTOCK.COM

CHAPTER 6

MOTIVATING BEHAVIOR WITH WORK AND REWARDS

CHAPTER OUTLINE

LEARNING OUTCOMES

After studying this chapter, you should be able to:

1. Identify and describe different approaches to job design and relate each to motivation.
2. Discuss employee participation, empowerment, and flexible work arrangements and identify how they can impact motivation.
3. Describe the goal setting theory of motivation and discuss broader perspectives on goal setting.
4. Discuss performance management and its role in motivation.
5. Describe how organizations use various kinds of rewards to motivate employees.

LOSKUTNIKOV/SHUTTERSTOCK.COM

REAL WORLD CHALLENGE

ORCHESTRATING OUTCOMES

Reviewing a concert by the Orpheus Chamber Orchestra, *New York Times* music critic Vivien Schweitzer wrote that the orchestra played Robert Schumann's Symphony No. 2 "with remarkable coordination"; the "balance among strings, winds, and brass," she added, "was impressively well proportioned." Was Schweitzer, as we sometimes say, damning with faint praise? Isn't a *symphony*, which means "harmony of sounds," supposed to be played with remarkable coordination? Aren't the various sections of the orchestra supposed to be well balanced? Had the conductor, whose job is to ensure a consummate performance of the music, achieved little more than coordination and balance? Actually, New York–based Orpheus doesn't play with a conductor, and Schweitzer was remarking on the fact that the orchestra had "bravely—and successfully—attempted" such a complex work without the artistic and managerial leadership of someone who directs rehearsals and stands at a podium waving an authoritative baton.

"For us at Orpheus," explains executive director Graham Parker, "it's the *way* we make the music that's the difference." Orpheus holds to the principle that its product—the music performed for audiences—is of the highest quality when its workers—the musicians—are highly satisfied with their jobs. All professional orchestra musicians, of course, are highly trained and skilled, but make no mistake about it: A lot of them are not very happy workers. An organizational psychologist at Harvard surveyed workers in 13 different occupational categories, including orchestra players, to determine relative levels of job motivation and satisfaction. On the one hand, musicians ranked at the top in motivation, "fueled by their own pride and professionalism," according to this study. But when it came to general satisfaction with their jobs, orchestra players ranked seventh (just below federal prison guards and slightly above beer sales and delivery teams). On the question of satisfaction with growth opportunities, they ranked ninth (again, below prison guards, though a little higher than O.R. nurses and hockey players).[1] An orchestra leader has asked you how to imitate the Orpheus's success. After reading this chapter you will have some suggestions on how to do this.

HIROYUKI ITO/HULTON ARCHIVE/GETTY IMAGES

Chapter 5 described a variety of perspectives on motivation. But no single theory or model completely explains motivation—each covers only some of the factors that actually result in motivated behavior. Moreover, even if one theory were applicable in a particular situation, a manager might still need to translate that theory into operational terms. Thus, while using the actual theories as tools or frameworks, managers need to understand various operational procedures, systems, and methods for enhancing motivation and performance.

Figure 6.1 illustrates a basic framework for relating various theories of motivation to potential and actual motivation and to operational methods for translating this potential and actual motivation into performance. The left side of the figure illustrates that motivated behavior can be induced by need-based or process-based circumstances. That is, people may be motivated to satisfy various specific needs or through various processes such as perceptions of inequity, expectancy relationships, and reinforcement contingencies.

These need-, process-, and learning-based concepts result in the situation illustrated in the center of the figure—a certain potential exists for motivated behavior directed at enhanced performance. For example, suppose that an employee wants more social relationships—that is, he wants to satisfy belongingness, relatedness, or affiliation needs. This means that there is potential for the employee to want to perform at a higher level if he thinks that higher performance will satisfy those social needs. Likewise, if an employee's high performance in the past was followed by strong positive reinforcement, there is again a potential for motivation directed at enhanced performance.

Figure 6.1

Enhancing Performance in Organizations

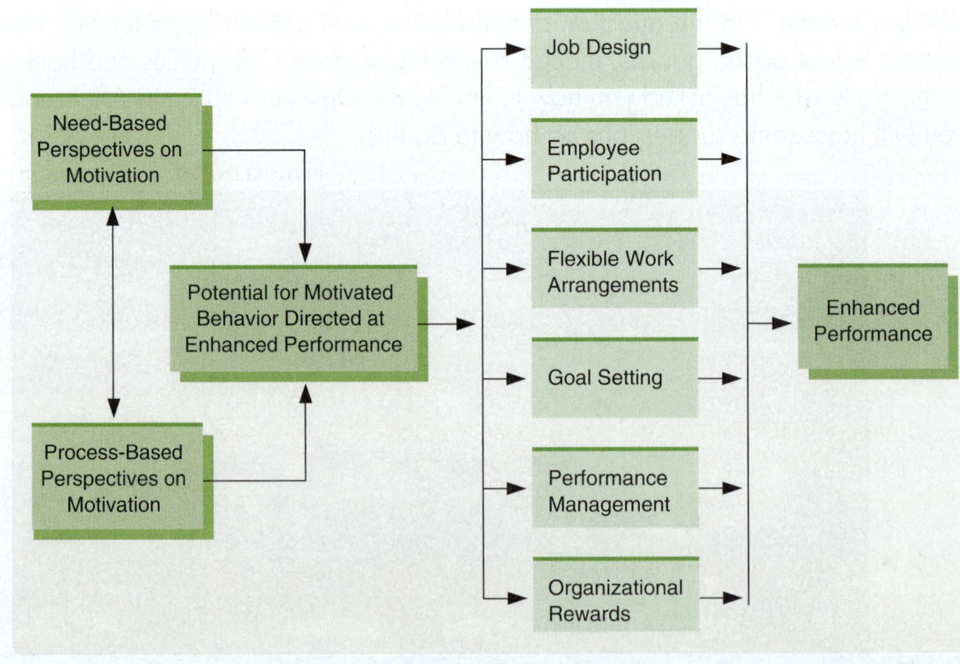

Managers can use a variety of methods to enhance performance in organizations. The need- and process-based perspectives on motivation explain some of the factors involved in increasing the potential for motivated behavior directed at enhanced performance. Managers can then use such means as goal setting, job design, flexible work arrangements, performance management, rewards, and organizational behavior motivation to help translate this potential into actual enhanced performance.

But managers may need to take certain steps to translate the potential for motivation directed at enhanced performance into real motivation and enhanced performance. In some cases, these steps may be tied to the specific need or process that has created the existing potential. For example, providing more opportunities for social interaction contingent on improved performance might capitalize on an employee's social needs. More typically, however, a manager needs to go further to help translate potential into real performance. The right side of Figure 6.1 names some of the more common methods used to enhance performance. This chapter covers these six methods: job design, employee participation and empowerment, flexible work arrangements, goal setting, performance management, and organizational rewards.

JOB DESIGN IN ORGANIZATIONS

Job design is an important method managers can use to enhance employee performance.[2] When work design is addressed at the individual level, it is most commonly referred to as ***job design***; it can be defined as how organizations define and structure jobs. As we will see, properly designed jobs can have a positive impact on the motivation, performance, and job satisfaction of those who perform them. On the other hand, poorly designed jobs can impair motivation, performance, and job satisfaction. The first widespread model of how individual work should be designed was job specialization. For example, a worker who applies safety decals to a piece of equipment as that equipment moves down an assembly line is performing a specialized job.

job design
How organizations define and structure jobs

job specialization
Breaking jobs down into small component tasks and standardizing them across all workers doing those jobs

Job Specialization

Frederick Taylor, the chief proponent of ***job specialization***, argued that jobs should be scientifically studied, broken down into small component tasks, and then standardized across all workers doing those jobs.[3] Taylor's view grew from the historical writings about division of labor advocated by Scottish economist Adam Smith. In practice, job specialization generally brought most, if not all, of the advantages its advocates claimed. Specialization paved the way for large-scale assembly lines and was at least partly responsible for the dramatic gains in output U.S. industry achieved for several decades in the early 1900s.

On the surface, job specialization appears to be a rational and efficient way to structure jobs. The jobs in many factories, for instance, are highly specialized and are often designed to maximize productivity. In practice, however, performing

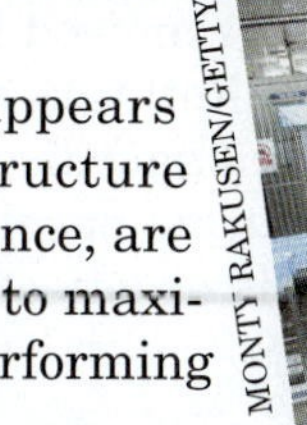

MONTY RAKUSEN/GETTY IMAGES

Job specialization involves carefully studying jobs, breaking those jobs down into small component tasks, and then standardizing how those tasks should be performed across all workers performing the jobs. These workers are following standard procedures in how they perform their specialized jobs.

those jobs can cause problems, foremost among them the extreme monotony of highly specialized tasks. Consider the job of assembling toasters. A person who does the entire assembly may find the job complex and challenging, albeit inefficient. If the job is specialized so that the worker simply inserts a heating coil into the toaster as it passes along on an assembly line, the process may be efficient, but it is unlikely to interest or challenge the worker. A worker numbed by boredom and monotony may be less motivated to work hard and more inclined to do poor-quality work or to complain about the job. For these reasons, managers began to search for job design alternatives to specialization.

Basic Alternatives to Job Specialization

In response to problems with job specialization, and a general desire to explore ways to create less monotonous jobs, managers began to seek alternative ways to design jobs. Managers initially developed two alternative approaches, job rotation and job enlargement. These approaches, along with job enrichment, remain common today.

Job Rotation

job rotation
Systematically moving workers from one job to another in an attempt to minimize monotony and boredom

Job rotation involves systematically shifting workers from one job to another to sustain their motivation and interest. Under specialization, each task is broken down into small parts. For example, assembling fine writing pens such as those made by Mont Blanc or Cross might involve four discrete steps: testing the ink cartridge, inserting the cartridge into the barrel of the pen, screwing the cap onto the barrel, and inserting the assembled pen into a box. One worker might perform step one, another step two, and so forth.

When job rotation is introduced, the tasks themselves stay the same. However, the workers who perform them are systematically rotated across the various tasks. Jones, for example, starts out with task 1 (testing ink cartridges). On a regular basis—perhaps weekly or monthly—she is systematically rotated to task 2, to task 3, to task 4, and back to task 1. Gonzalez, who starts out on task 2 (inserting cartridges into barrels), rotates ahead of Jones to tasks 3, 4, 1, and back to 2.

Unfortunately, job rotation does not entirely address issues of monotony and boredom, however.[4] That is, if a rotation cycle takes workers through the same old jobs, the workers simply experience several routine and boring jobs instead of just one. Although a worker may begin each job shift with a bit of renewed interest, the effect usually is short-lived. Rotation may also decrease efficiency. For example, it sacrifices the proficiency and expertise that grow from specialization. At the same time, job rotation is an effective training technique because a worker

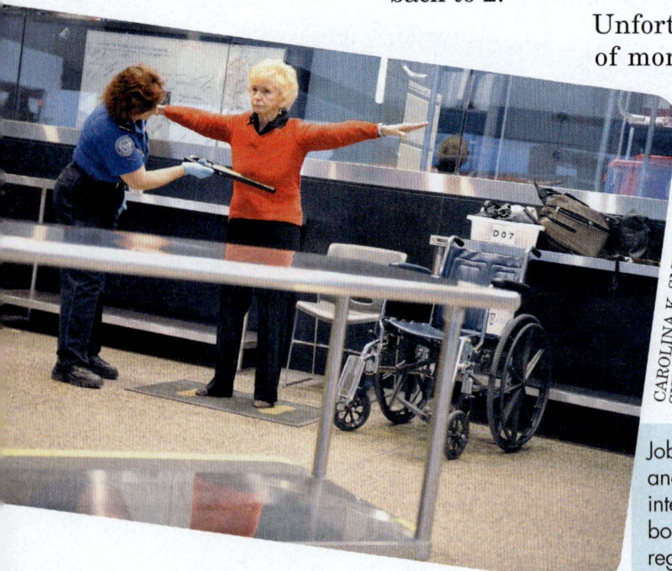

CAROLINA K. SMITH, M.D./ SHUTTERSTOCK.COM

Job rotation involves systematically shifting workers from one job to another. While job rotation was intended to sustain motivation and interest, it really does little to address the problems of monotony and boredom created by job specialization. The TSA rotates airport screeners regularly, though, in an effort to keep them focused on their jobs.

rotated through a variety of related jobs acquires a larger set of job skills. Thus, there is increased flexibility in transferring workers to new jobs. Many U.S. firms now use job rotation for training or other purposes, but few rely on it to motivate workers. Pilgrim's Pride, one of the largest chicken-processing firms in the United States, uses job rotation, but not for motivation. Workers in a chicken-processing plant are subject to cumulative trauma injuries such as carpal tunnel syndrome, and managers at Pilgrim's believe that rotating workers across different jobs can reduce these injuries. The TSA also rotates airport security screeners across different tasks every 20–30 minutes to help prevent boredom and to keep them focused on their jobs.

Job Enlargement

Job enlargement, or *horizontal job loading*, is expanding a worker's job to include tasks previously performed by other workers. For instance, if job enlargement were introduced at a Cross pen plant, the four tasks noted above might be combined into two "larger" ones. Hence, one set of workers might each test cartridges and then insert them into barrels (old steps 1 and 2); another set of workers might then attach caps to the barrels and put the pens into boxes (old steps 3 and 4). The logic behind this change is that the increased number of tasks in each job reduces monotony and boredom.

job enlargement
Involves giving workers more tasks to perform

Maytag was one of the first companies to use job enlargement.[5] In the assembly of washing machine water pumps, for example, jobs done sequentially by six workers at a conveyor belt were modified so that each worker completed an entire pump alone. Other organizations that implemented job enlargement included AT&T, the U.S. Civil Service, and Colonial Life Insurance Company. Unfortunately, job enlargement also failed to have the desired effects. Generally, if the entire production sequence consisted of simple, easy-to-master tasks, merely doing more of them did not significantly change the worker's job. If the task of putting two bolts on a piece of machinery was "enlarged" to putting on three bolts and connecting two wires, for example, the monotony of the original job essentially remained.

Job Enrichment

Job rotation and job enlargement seemed promising but eventually disappointed managers seeking to counter the ill effects of extreme specialization. They failed partly because they were intuitive, narrow approaches rather than fully developed, theory-driven methods. Consequently, a new, more complex approach to task design—job enrichment—was developed. ***Job enrichment*** is based on the two-factor theory of motivation, which is discussed in Chapter 5. That theory contends that employees can be motivated by positive job-related experiences such as feelings of achievement, responsibility, and recognition. To achieve these, job enrichment relies on *vertical job loading*—not only adding more tasks to a job, as in horizontal loading, but also giving the employee more control over those tasks.[6]

job enrichment
Entails giving workers more tasks to perform and more control over how to perform them

AT&T, Texas Instruments, IBM, and General Foods have all used job enrichment. For example, AT&T utilized job enrichment in a group of eight people who were responsible for preparing service orders. Managers believed turnover in the group was too high and performance too low. Analysis revealed several deficiencies in the work. The group worked in relative isolation, and any service representative could ask them to prepare work orders. As a result, they had little client contact or responsibility, and

WAVEBREAKMEDIA/SHUTTERSTOCK.COM

Job enrichment involves both giving workers more tasks to perform and more control over how to perform them. This clothing designer, for example, gets to select fabrics, develop new designs, and then tailor the designs into new clothing.

they received scant feedback on their job performance. The job enrichment program focused on creating a process team. Each member of the team was paired with a service representative, and the tasks were restructured: Ten discrete steps were replaced with three more complex ones. In addition, the group members began to get specific feedback on performance, and their job titles were changed to reflect their greater responsibility and status. As a result of these changes, the number of orders delivered on time increased from 27 percent to 90 percent, accuracy improved, and turnover decreased significantly.[7] Texas Instruments also used this technique to improve janitorial jobs. The company gave janitors more control over their schedules and let them sequence their own cleaning jobs and purchase their own supplies. As a direct result, turnover dropped, cleanliness improved, and the company reported estimated initial cost savings of approximately $103,000.[8]

At the same time, we should note that many job enrichment programs have failed. Some companies have found job enrichment to be cost ineffective, and others believe that it simply did not produce the expected results.[9] Several programs at Prudential Insurance, for example, were abandoned because managers believed they were benefiting neither employees nor the firm. Some of the criticism is associated with flaws in the two-factor theory of motivation on which job enrichment is based. Because of these and other problems, job enrichment is not as popular as it was a few years ago. Yet some valuable aspects of the concept can be salvaged. The efforts of managers and academic theorists ultimately have led to more complex and sophisticated viewpoints. Many of these advances are evident in the job characteristics theory, which we consider next.

The Job Characteristics Theory

job characteristics theory
Uses five motivational properties of tasks and three critical psychological to improve outcomes

The ***job characteristics theory*** focuses on the specific motivational properties of jobs. The theory, diagrammed in Figure 6.2, was developed by Hackman and Oldham.[10] At the core of the theory is the idea of critical psychological states. These states are presumed to determine the extent to which characteristics of the job enhance employee responses to the task. The three critical psychological states are:

1. *Experienced meaningfulness of the work:* the degree to which the individual experiences the job as generally meaningful, valuable, and worthwhile
2. *Experienced responsibility for work outcomes:* the degree to which individuals feel personally accountable and responsible for the results of their work
3. *Knowledge of results:* the degree to which individuals continuously understand how effectively they are performing the job

Figure 6.2

The Job Characteristics Theory

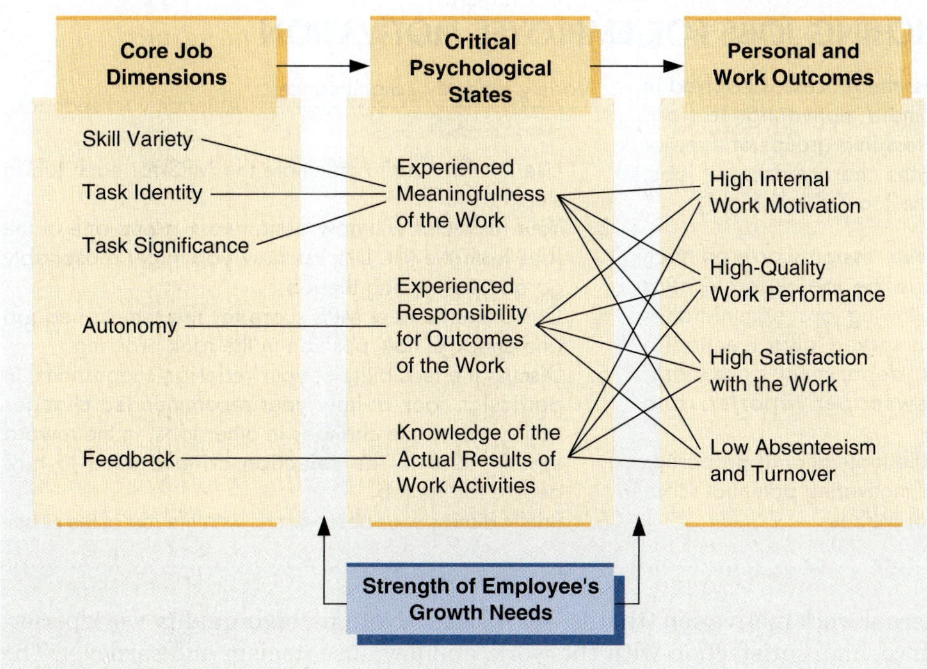

The job characteristics theory is an important contemporary model of how to design jobs. By using five core job characteristics, managers can enhance three critical psychological states. These states, in turn, can improve a variety of personal and work outcomes. Individual differences also affect how the job characteristics affect people.

If employees experience these states at a sufficiently high level, they are likely to feel good about themselves and to respond favorably to their jobs. Hackman and Oldham suggest that the three critical psychological states are triggered by the following five characteristics of the job, or core job dimensions:

1. *Skill variety:* the degree to which the job requires a variety of activities that involve different skills and talents
2. *Task identity:* the degree to which the job requires completion of a "whole" and an identifiable piece of work; that is, the extent to which a job has a beginning and an end with a tangible outcome
3. *Task significance:* the degree to which the job affects the lives or work of other people, both in the immediate organization and in the external environment
4. *Autonomy:* the degree to which the job allows the individual substantial freedom, independence, and discretion to schedule the work and determine the procedures for carrying it out
5. *Feedback:* the degree to which the job activities give the individual direct and clear information about the effectiveness of his or her performance

Figure 6.2 shows that these five job characteristics, operating through the critical psychological states, affect a variety of personal and work outcomes: high

IMPROVE YOUR SKILLS

ENRICHING JOBS FOR EMPLOYEE MOTIVATION

This exercise will help you assess the processes involved in designing jobs to make them more motivating. To start, your instructor will divide the class into groups of three or four people each. In assessing the characteristics of jobs, use a scale value of 1 ("very little") to 7 ("very high").

1. Using the scale values above, assign scores on each core job dimension used in the job characteristics theory (see below) to the following jobs: administrative assistant, professor, food server, auto mechanic, lawyer, short-order cook, department store clerk, construction worker, newspaper reporter, and telephone solicitor.
2. Researchers often assess the motivational properties of jobs by calculating their motivating potential score (MPS). The usual formula for MPS is

$$\frac{(\text{Variety} + \text{Identity} + \text{Significance})}{3} \times \text{Autonomy} \times \text{Feedback}$$

   Use this formula to calculate the MPS for each job in step 1.
3. Your instructor will now assign your group one of the jobs from the list. Discuss how you might reasonably go about enriching the job.
4. Calculate the new MPS score for the redesigned job and check its new position in the rank ordering.
5. Discuss the feasibility of your redesign suggestions. In particular, look at how your recommended changes might necessitate changes in other jobs, in the reward system, and in the selection criteria used to hire people for the job.
6. Briefly discuss your observations with the rest of the class.

internal work motivation (that is, intrinsic motivation), high-quality work performance, high satisfaction with the work, and low absenteeism and turnover. The figure also suggests that individual differences play a role in job design. People with strong needs for personal growth and development will be especially motivated by the five core job characteristics. On the other hand, people with weaker needs for personal growth and development are less likely to be motivated by the core job characteristics. Several firms, including 3M, Volvo, AT&T, Xerox, Texas Instruments, and Motorola, have successfully implemented job design changes using this theory.[11] The *Improve Your Skills* feature will help you develop stronger insights into the complexities of how jobs can be redesigned.

Much research has been devoted to this approach to job design.[12] This research has generally supported the theory, although performance has seldom been found to correlate with job characteristics.[13] Several apparent weaknesses in the theory have also come to light. First, the measures used to test the theory are not always as valid and reliable as they should be. Further, the role of individual differences frequently has not been supported by research. Finally, guidelines for implementation are not specific, so managers usually tailor them to their own particular circumstances. Still, the theory remains a popular perspective on studying and changing jobs.[14]

EMPLOYEE PARTICIPATION AND INVOLVEMENT

Employee motivation can also be enhanced in some cases through the use of participation and empowerment. In a sense, participation and empowerment are extensions of job design because each fundamentally alters how

Participation and involvement are often used to promote worker motivation. This executive, for example, is consulting with one of his employees on how best to solve a problem.

MINERVA STUDIO/SHUTTERSTOCK.COM

employees in an organization perform their jobs. ***Participation*** occurs when employees have a voice in decisions about their own work. (One important model that can help managers determine the optimal level of employee participation, Vroom's decision-tree approach, is discussed in Chapter 12.) ***Empowerment*** is the process of enabling workers to set their own work goals, make decisions, and solve problems within their spheres of responsibility and authority. Thus, empowerment is a somewhat broader concept that promotes participation in a wide variety of areas, including but not limited to work itself, work context, and work environment.[15]

The role of participation and empowerment in motivation can be expressed in terms of both the need-based perspectives and the expectancy theory discussed in Chapter 5. Employees who participate in decision making may be more committed to executing decisions properly. Furthermore, successfully making a decision, executing it, and then seeing the positive consequences can help satisfy one's need for achievement, provide recognition and responsibility, and enhance self-esteem. Simply being asked to participate in organizational decision making may also enhance an employee's self-esteem. In addition, participation should help clarify expectancies (as a component of expectancy theory, as discussed in Chapter 5). That is, by participating in decision making, employees may better understand the linkage (instrumentality) between their performance and the rewards they want most.

participation
Entails giving employees a voice in making decisions about their own work

empowerment
The process of enabling workers to set their own work goals, make decisions, and solve problems within their sphere of responsibility and authority

Areas of Employee Participation

At one level, employees can participate in addressing questions and making decisions about their own jobs. Instead of just telling them how to do their jobs, for example, managers can ask employees to make their own decisions about how to do them. Based on their own expertise and experience with their tasks, workers might be able to improve their own productivity. In many situations, they might also be well qualified to make decisions about what materials to use, which tools to use, and so forth.

Chaparral Steel, a small steel producer near Dallas, allows its workers considerable autonomy in how they perform their jobs. For example, when the firm needed a new rolling mill lathe, it budgeted $1 million for its purchase and then put the purchase decision in the hands of an operating machinist. This machinist, in turn, investigated various options, visited other mills in Japan and Europe, and then recommended an alternative piece of machinery costing less than half of the budgeted amount. The firm also helped pioneer an innovative concept called "open-book management"—any employee at Chaparral can see any company document, record, or other piece of information at any time and for any reason.

It might also help to let workers make decisions about administrative matters, such as work schedules. If jobs are relatively independent of one another, employees might decide when to change shifts, take breaks, go to lunch, and so forth. A workgroup or team might also be able to schedule vacations and days off for all of its members. Furthermore, employees are getting increasing opportunities to participate in broader issues of product quality. Involvement of this type has become a hallmark of successful Japanese and other international firms, and many U.S. companies have followed suit.

Approaches to Participation and Empowerment

In recent years many organizations have actively sought ways to extend employee participation and empowerment beyond the traditional areas. Simple techniques such as suggestion boxes and question-and-answer meetings allow a certain degree of participation, for example. The basic motive has been to better capitalize on the assets and capabilities inherent in all employees. Thus, many managers today prefer the term "empowerment" to "participation" because it implies a more comprehensive level of involvement.

One method some firms use to empower their workers is the use of work teams. This method grew out of early attempts to use what Japanese firms call "quality circles." A *quality circle* is a group of employees who voluntarily meet regularly to identify and propose solutions to problems related to quality. Quality circles quickly evolved into a broader and more comprehensive array of workgroups, now generally called "work teams." These teams are collections of employees empowered to plan, organize, direct, and control their own work. Their supervisor, rather than being a traditional "boss," plays more the role of a coach. We discuss work teams more fully in Chapter 7. The other method some organizations use to facilitate employee involvement is to change their overall method of organizing. The basic pattern is for an organization to eliminate layers from its hierarchy, thereby becoming much more decentralized. Power, responsibility, and authority are delegated as far down the organization as possible, so control of work is squarely in the hands of those who actually do it.

Netflix has high performance standards for its employees as it competes with Redbox, Amazon, and Apple in the video streaming and rental market. The firm hires talented employees, pays them generously, focuses employees on clear goals, and empowers them to do what they need to do to reach their goals.[16] It even lets employees take as much vacation time as they want as long as it does not interfere with their work.[17] Patagonia also offers every employee a lot of empowerment, which helps improve employee loyalty.[18]

Technology also helps organizations empower workers by making better and timelier information available to everyone in the organization. Although some employees are likely to feel more motivated when empowered, other employees may not react positively. Increased responsibility does not motivate everyone. Nonetheless, empowerment can be an important management tool to increase the motivation of many employees. Practical ways to empower others include:[19]

- Articulating a clear vision and goals
- Fostering personal mastery experiences to enhance self-efficacy and build skills

- Modeling successful behaviors
- Sending positive messages and arousing positive emotions in employees
- Connecting employees with the outcomes of their work and giving them feedback
- Building employee confidence by showing competence, honesty, and fairness

Regardless of the specific technique used, however, empowerment only enhances organizational effectiveness if certain conditions exist. First, the organization must be sincere in its efforts to spread power and autonomy to lower levels of the organization. Token efforts to promote participation in just a few areas are unlikely to succeed. Second, the organization must be committed to maintaining participation and empowerment. Workers will be resentful if they are given more control only to later have it reduced or taken away altogether. Third, the organization must be systematic and patient in its efforts to empower workers. Turning over too much control too quickly can spell disaster. Finally, the organization must be prepared to increase its commitment to training. Employees who are given more freedom concerning how they work are likely to need additional training to help them exercise that freedom most effectively. The *Global Issues* feature provides some insights in participation and empowerment in other countries.

BALDYRGAN/SHUTTERSTOCK.COM

PARTICIPATION AROUND THE WORLD

Some people think that it was U.S. business that pioneered the use of work teams. Not true. One of the first firms to use work teams was the Swedish (at the time) automaker Volvo. Back in the mid-1970s Volvo designed and built a totally different kind of factory in the town of Kalmar, Sweden. Rather than relying on traditional assembly lines, where workers stood along a moving conveyor built and performed simple individual assembly tasks to partially assembled cars moving along the belt, the Kalmar factory moved platforms with partially assembled cars from one team area to another. As a platform entered a team's area, the team members worked together as a team in completing a long list of tasks assigned to that team. For the most part, each team worked without direct supervision, set its own work pace, and even took breaks in its own private break area complete with shower and locker facilities. Volvo's logic for this approach was that by empowering its employees and allowing them to participate in making decisions about their work, those employees would be more motivated and produce higher-quality products.

Japanese automakers like Toyota, Nissan, and Honda also used teams long before their U.S. counterparts. The Japanese plants more closely resemble a traditional assembly line arrangement, but workers still function in teams and are not restricted to staying within a defined space and not required to perform a specialized task. Instead, the workers within each team are allowed to move from one work space to another, to help one another out, to work on tasks together, and to cover for a team member who needs a quick break. Another hallmark of the Japanese system is that any worker is empowered to stop the assembly line on his or own authority if a problem is detected. This team-oriented approach, based on participation and empowerment, is often cited as a factor in the global dominance of Japanese automobile companies, especially related to product quality.

A key reason these approaches have worked so well in Sweden and Japan is the close connection between performance and rewards. Most U.S. work systems are built around individual contributions, individual performance and individual rewards. But at Kalmar and in Japan, work is centered around teams. So, too, are rewards. That is, rewards and recognition are provided based on team performance, rather than individual performance. As a result, it is in the best interest of all team members to work together as productively as possible.

FLEXIBLE WORK ARRANGEMENTS

Beyond the actual redesigning of jobs and the use of employee involvement, many organizations today are experimenting with a variety of flexible work arrangements. These arrangements are generally intended to enhance employee motivation and performance by giving workers more flexibility about how and when they work. Among the more popular flexible work arrangements are variable work schedules, flexible work schedules, extended work schedules, job sharing, and telecommuting.[20]

Variable Work Schedules

There are many exceptions, of course, but the traditional professional work schedule in the United States has long been days that start at 8:00 or 9:00 in the morning and end at 5:00 in the evening, five days a week (and, of course, managers and other professionals often work many additional hours outside of these times). Although the exact starting and ending times vary, most companies in other countries have also used a well-defined work schedule. But such a schedule makes it difficult for workers to attend to routine personal business—going to the bank, seeing a doctor or dentist for a checkup, having a parent-teacher conference, getting an automobile serviced, and so forth. Employees locked into this work schedule may find it necessary to take a sick or vacation day to handle these activities. On a more psychological level, some people may feel so powerless and constrained by their job schedules that they grow resentful and frustrated.

compressed work schedule
Work schedule in which employees work a full forty-hour week in fewer than the traditional five days

To help counter these problems, one alternative some businesses use is a ***compressed work schedule***.[21] An employee following a compressed work week schedule works a full forty-hour week in fewer than the traditional five days. Most typically, this schedule involves working ten hours a day for four days, leaving an extra day off. Another alternative is for employees to work slightly less than ten hours a day but to complete the forty hours by lunchtime on Friday. Firms that have used these forms of compressed workweeks include Recreational Equipment (REI), USAA, Edward Jones, and Mercedes-Benz USA.[22] One problem with this schedule is that if everyone in the organization is off at the same time, the firm may have no one on duty to handle problems or deal with outsiders on the off day. On the other hand, if a company staggers days off across the workforce, people who don't get the more desirable days off (Monday and Friday, for most people) may be jealous or resentful. Another problem is that when employees put in too much time in a single day, they tend to get tired and perform at a lower level later in the day.

A popular schedule some organizations are beginning to use is called a "nine-eighty" schedule. Under this arrangement, an employee works a traditional schedule one week and a compressed schedule the next, getting every other Friday off. That is, they work eighty hours (the equivalent of two weeks of full-time work) in nine days. By alternating the regular and compressed schedules across half of its workforce, the organization is staffed at all times but still gives employees two additional full days off each month. Chevron and Marathon Oil are two businesses that currently use this schedule.

Finally, a special form of compressed work schedule is job sharing. In ***job sharing***, two part-time employees share one full-time job. Job sharing may be desirable for people who only want to work part time or when job markets are tight. For its part, the organization can accommodate the preferences of a broader range of employees and may benefit from the talents of more people. Perhaps the simplest job-sharing arrangement to visualize is that of a receptionist. To share this job, one worker would staff the receptionist's desk from, say, 8:00 A.M. to noon each day; the office might close from noon to 1:00 P.M., and a second worker would staff the desk from 1:00 p.m. in the afternoon until 5:00 P.M. To the casual observer or visitor to the office, the fact that two people serve in one job is essentially irrelevant. The responsibilities of the job in the morning and responsibilities in the afternoon are not likely to be interdependent. Thus, the position can easily be broken down into two or perhaps even more components.

job sharing
Two or more part-time employees sharing one full-time job

Extended Work Schedules

In certain cases, some organizations use another type of work scheduling called an ***extended work schedule***. An extended work schedule is one that requires relatively long periods of work followed by relatively long periods of paid time off. These schedules are most often used when the cost of transitioning from one worker to another is high and there are efficiencies associated with having a small workforce.

extended work schedule
Work schedule that requires relatively long periods of work followed by relatively long periods of paid time off

For instance, KBR is a large defense contractor that manages U.S. military installations in foreign countries, including Iraq and Afghanistan. KBR's civilian employees handle maintenance, logistics, and communications, as well as food, laundry, and mail services, among other things. The typical work schedule for a KBR employee is 12 hours a day, 7 days a week. Extended schedules such as this allow the firm to function with a smaller workforce than would be the case under a more traditional approach to work scheduling. In order to motivate employees to accept and maintain this kind of schedule, the firm pays them a compensation premium and provides them with 16 days of paid vacation and an airline ticket to any major destination in the world after every 120-day work period.

Other work settings that are conducive to this kind of extended work schedule include offshore petroleum-drilling platforms, transoceanic cargo ships, research labs in distant settings such as the South Pole, and movie crews filming in remote locations. While the specific number of hours and days and the amount of vacation time vary, most of these job settings are characterized by long periods of work followed by an extended vacation plus premium pay. Offshore drilling platform workers at ExxonMobil, for instance, generally work every day for five weeks and then have two weeks off.

INGVAR TJOSTHEIM/SHUTTERSTOCK.COM

Some organizations find it useful to use extended work hours–work schedules with relatively long periods of work followed by relatively long periods of paid time off. Firms that operate offshore drilling platforms like this one, for example, shuttle workers back-and-forth between the work site and shore by helicopter. Workers on the platform may work ten or even twelve hours a day, everyday, for several weeks straight. They then get an extended period of vacation time.

Flexible Work Schedules

***flexible work schedules* (or *flextime*)**
Give employees more personal control over the hours they work each day

Another popular alternative work arrangement is ***flexible work schedules***, sometimes called ***flextime***. The compressed work schedules previously discussed give employees time off during "normal" working hours, but they must still follow a regular and defined schedule on the days when they do work. Flextime, however, usually gives employees less say about what days they work but more personal control over the times when they work on those days.[23]

Figure 6.3 illustrates how flextime works. The workday is broken down into two categories: *flexible time* and *core time*. All employees must be at their workstations during core time, but they can choose their own schedules during flexible time. Thus, one employee may choose to start work early in the morning and finish by mid-afternoon, another to start in the late morning and work until late afternoon, and a third to start early in the morning, take a long lunch break, and work until late afternoon.

The major advantage of this approach, as already noted, is that workers get to tailor their workday to fit their personal needs. A person who needs to visit the dentist in the late afternoon can just start work early. A person who stays out late one night can start work late the next day. And the person who needs to run some errands during lunch can take a longer midday break. On the other hand, flextime is more difficult to manage because others in the organization may not be sure when a person will be available for meetings other than during the core time. Expenses such as utilities will also be higher since the organization must remain open for a longer period each day.

Some organizations use a plan in which workers set their own hours but then must follow that schedule each day. Others allow workers to modify their own schedule each day. Organizations that have used the flexible work schedule method for arranging work include Sun Microsystems, KPMG, Best Buy, Pricewaterhouse Coopers, and some offices in the U.S. government. One survey found that as many as 43 percent of U.S. workers have the option to modify their work schedules; most of those who choose to do so start earlier than normal so as to get off work earlier in the day.[24] A more recent study found

Figure 6.3

Flexible Work Schedules

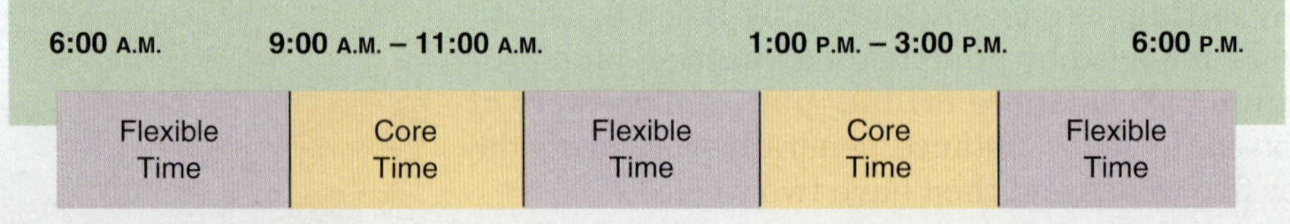

Flexible work schedules are an important new work arrangement used in some organizations today. All employees must be at work during "core time." In the hypothetical example shown here, core time is from 9 to 11 A.M. and 1 to 3 P.M. The other time, then, is flexible—employees can come and go as they please during this time, as long as the total time spent at work meets organizational expectations.

Many employers today offer flexible work schedules and the freedom for employees to work at alternative work locations. This individual, for example, is working from his home office. Of course, not all jobs are amenable to these arrangements, and even for those that are employees are still expected to meet all of the responsibilities of their jobs.

MONKEY BUSINESS IMAGES/ SHUTTERSTOCK.COM

that approximately 27 million full-time workers in the United States have some degree of flexibility in when they begin and end their work days.[25]

Alternative Workplaces

Another recent innovation in work arrangements is the use of alternative workplaces. The most common version of this approach is usually called ***telecommuting***—allowing employees to spend part of their time working off-site, usually at home. By using e-mail, web interfaces, and other technology, many employees can maintain close contact with their organization and do as much work at home as they could in their offices. The increased power and sophistication of modern communication technology—laptops and smartphones, among others—is making telecommuting easier and easier.[26] (Other terms used to describe this concept are e-commuting and working from home.)

telecommuting
Work arrangement in which employees spend part of their time working off-site

On the plus side, many employees like telecommuting because it gives them added flexibility. By spending one or two days a week at home, for instance, they have the same kind of flexibility to manage personal activities as is afforded by flextime or compressed schedules. Some employees also feel that they get more work done by staying at home because they are less likely to be interrupted. Organizations may benefit for several reasons as well: (1) they can reduce absenteeism and turnover since employees will need to take less "formal" time off, and (2) they can save on facilities such as parking spaces because fewer people will be at work on any given day. There are also environmental benefits, given that fewer cars are on the highways. On the other hand, although many employees thrive under this arrangement, others do not. Some feel isolated and miss the social interaction of the workplace. Others simply lack the self-control and discipline to walk away from the breakfast table to their desk and start working. Managers may also encounter coordination difficulties in scheduling meetings and other activities that require face-to-face contact.

GOAL SETTING AND MOTIVATION

Goal setting is another very useful method of enhancing employee performance.[27] From a motivational perspective, a ***goal*** is a meaningful objective. Goals are used for two purposes in most organizations. First, they provide a useful framework for managing motivation. Managers and employees can set goals for themselves and then work toward them. Thus, if the organization's overall goal is to increase sales by 10 percent, a manager can

goal
A meaningful objective

use individual goals to help attain that organizational goal. Second, goals are an effective control device (*control* meaning the monitoring by management of how well the organization is performing). Comparing people's short-term performances with their goals can be an effective way to monitor the organization's longer-term performance.

Social learning theory perhaps best describes the role and importance of goal setting in organizations.[28] This perspective suggests that feelings of pride or shame about performance are a function of the extent to which people achieve their goals. A person who achieves a goal will be proud of having done so, whereas a person who fails to achieve a goal will feel personal disappointment and perhaps even shame. People's degree of pride or disappointment is affected by their *self-efficacy*, the extent to which they feel that they can still meet their goals even if they failed to do so in the past.

Goal-Setting Theory

Social learning theory provides insights into why and how goals can motivate behavior. It also helps us understand how different people cope with failure to reach their goals. The research of Edwin Locke and his associates most clearly established the utility of goal-setting theory in a motivational context.[29] Locke's goal-setting theory of motivation assumes that behavior is a result of conscious goals and intentions. Therefore, by setting goals for people in the organization, a manager should be able to influence their behavior. Given this premise, the challenge is to develop a thorough understanding of the processes by which people set their goals and then work to reach them. In the original version of goal-setting theory, two specific goal characteristics—goal difficulty and goal specificity—were expected to shape performance.

Goal Difficulty

goal difficulty
The extent to which a goal is challenging and requires effort

Goal difficulty is the extent to which a goal is challenging and requires effort. If people work to achieve goals, it is reasonable to assume that they will work harder to achieve more difficult goals. But a goal must not be so difficult that it is unattainable. If a new manager asks her sales force to increase sales by 300 percent, the group may ridicule her charge as laughable because they regard it as impossible to reach. A more realistic but still difficult goal—perhaps a 20 percent increase in sales—would probably be a better objective.

A substantial body of research supports the importance of goal difficulty.[30] In one study, managers at Weyerhaeuser set difficult goals for truck drivers hauling loads of timber from cutting sites to wood yards. Over a nine-month period, the drivers increased the quantity of wood they delivered by an amount that would have required $250,000

JEANETTE DIETL/SHUTTERSTOCK.COM

Goal setting can be a very useful method for motivating employees. This is especially true if the employee gets to help set goals and is rewarded for achieving them. This manager and her subordinate are reviewing the subordinate's goals for the next quarter.

worth of new trucks at the previous per-truck average load.[31] Reinforcement also fosters motivation toward difficult goals. A person who is rewarded for achieving a difficult goal will be more inclined to strive toward the next difficult goal than will someone who received no reward for reaching the first goal.

Goal Specificity

Goal specificity is the clarity and precision of the goal. A goal of "increasing productivity" is not very specific, whereas a goal of "increasing productivity by 3 percent in the next six months" is quite specific. Some goals, such as those involving costs, output, profitability, and growth, can easily be stated in clear and precise terms. Other goals, such as improving employee job satisfaction and morale, company image and reputation, ethical behavior, and social responsibility, are much harder to state in specific or measurable terms.

goal specificity
The clarity and precision of a goal

Like difficulty, specificity has been shown to be consistently related to performance. The study of timber truck drivers previously mentioned also examined goal specificity. The initial loads the truck drivers were carrying were found to be 60 percent of the maximum weight each truck could haul. The managers set a new goal for drivers of 94 percent, which the drivers were soon able to reach. Thus, the goal was quite specific as well as difficult.

Locke's theory attracted widespread interest and research support from both researchers and managers, so Locke, together with Gary Latham, eventually proposed an expanded model of the goal-setting process. The expanded model, shown in Figure 6.4, attempts to capture more fully the complexities of goal setting in organizations. The expanded theory argues that goal-directed effort is a function of four goal attributes: difficulty and specificity (previously discussed), and acceptance and commitment. ***Goal acceptance*** is the extent to which a person accepts a goal as his or her own. ***Goal commitment*** is the extent to which he or she is personally interested in reaching the goal. The manager who vows to take whatever steps are necessary to cut costs by

goal acceptance
The extent to which a person accepts a goal as his or her own

goal commitment
The extent to which a person is personally interested in reaching a goal

Figure 6.4

The Goal-Setting Theory of Motivation

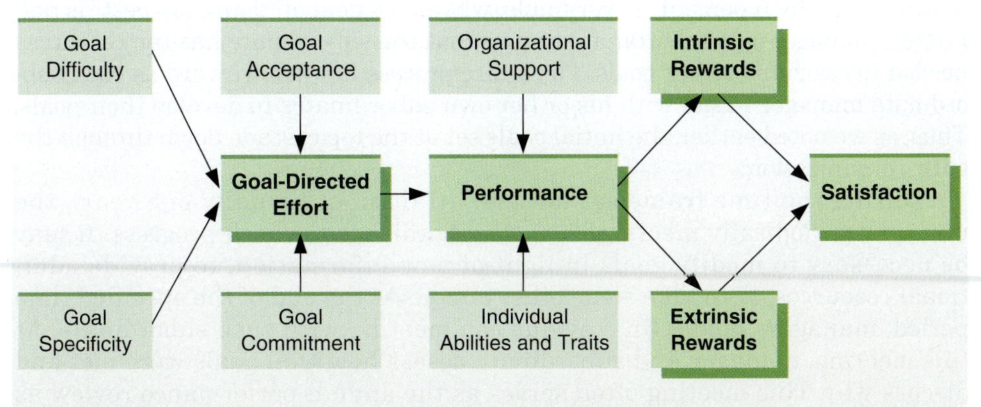

The goal-setting theory of motivation provides an important means of enhancing the motivation of employees. As illustrated here, appropriate goal difficulty, specificity, acceptance, and commitment contribute to goal-directed effort. This effort, in turn, has a direct impact on performance.

Source: Reprinted from Latham, G. P., et al. (1979, Autumn). The Goal-Setting Theory of Motivation. *Organizational Dynamics*. Copyright 1979, with permission from Elsevier.

10 percent has made a commitment to achieving the goal. Factors that can foster goal acceptance and commitment include participating in the goal-setting process, making goals challenging but realistic, and believing that goal achievement will lead to valued rewards.[32]

The interaction of goal-directed effort, organizational support, and individual abilities and traits determines actual performance. Organizational support is whatever the organization does to help or hinder performance. Positive support might mean providing whatever resources are needed to meet the goal; negative support might mean failing to provide such resources, perhaps due to cost considerations or staff reductions. Individual abilities and traits are the skills and other personal characteristics necessary to do a job. As a result of performance, a person receives various intrinsic and extrinsic rewards that in turn influence satisfaction. Note that the latter stages of this model are quite similar to those of the Porter and Lawler expectancy model discussed in Chapter 5.

Broader Perspectives on Goal Setting

management by objectives (MBO)
A collaborative goal-setting process through which organizational goals cascade down throughout the organization

Some organizations undertake goal setting from the somewhat broader perspective of ***management by objectives***, or ***MBO***. The MBO approach is essentially a collaborative goal-setting process through which organizational goals systematically cascade down through the organization. Our discussion describes a generic approach, but many organizations adapt MBO to suit their own purposes and use a variety of names for it. (Indeed, most firms today use other names. However, since no other generic label has emerged, we will continue to refer to this approach as MBO.)

A successful MBO program starts with top managers' establishing overall goals for the organization. After these goals have been set, managers and employees throughout the organization collaborate to set subsidiary goals. First, the overall goals are communicated to everyone. Then each manager meets with each subordinate. During these meetings, the manager explains the unit goals to the subordinate, and the two together determine how the subordinate can contribute to the goals most effectively. The manager acts as a counselor and helps ensure that the subordinate develops goals that are verifiable. For example, a goal of "cutting costs by 5 percent" is verifiable, whereas a goal of "doing my best" is not. Finally, manager and subordinate ensure that the subordinate has the resources needed to reach his or her goals. The entire process flows downward as each subordinate manager meets with his or her own subordinates to develop their goals. Thus, as we noted earlier, the initial goals set at the top cascade down through the entire organization.

During the time frame set for goal attainment (usually one year), the manager periodically meets with each subordinate to check progress. It may be necessary to modify goals in light of new information, to provide additional resources, or to take some other action. At the end of the specified time period, managers hold a final evaluation meeting with each subordinate. At this meeting, manager and subordinate assess how well goals were met and discuss why. This meeting often serves as the annual performance review as well, determining salary adjustments and other rewards based on reaching goals. This meeting may also serve as the initial goal-setting meeting for the next year's cycle.

Goal Setting Challenges

Goal-setting theory has been widely tested in a variety of settings. Research has demonstrated fairly consistently that goal difficulty and specificity are closely associated with performance. Other elements of the theory, such as acceptance and commitment, have been studied less frequently. A few studies have shown the importance of acceptance and commitment, but little is currently known about how people accept and become committed to goals. Goal-setting theory may also focus too much attention on the short run at the expense of long-term considerations. Despite these questions, however, goal setting is clearly an important way for managers to convert motivation into actual improved performance.

From the broader perspective, MBO remains a very popular technique. Alcoa, Tenneco, General Foods, and DuPont, for example, have used versions of MBO with widespread success. The technique's popularity stems in part from its many strengths. For one thing, MBO clearly has the potential to motivate employees because it helps implement goal-setting theory on a systematic basis throughout the organization. It also clarifies the basis for rewards, and it can stimulate communication. Performance appraisals are easier and more clear-cut under MBO. Further, managers can use the system for control purposes.

However, using MBO also presents pitfalls, especially if a firm takes too many shortcuts or inadvertently undermines how the process is supposed to work. Sometimes, for instance, top managers do not really participate; that is, the goals are actually established in the middle of the organization and may not reflect the real goals of top management. If employees believe this situation to be true, they may become cynical, interpreting the lack of participation by top management as a sign that the goals are not important and that their own involvement is therefore a waste of time. MBO also has a tendency to overemphasize quantitative goals to enhance verifiability. Another potential liability is that an MBO system requires a great deal of information processing and record keeping since every goal must be documented. Finally, some managers do not really let subordinates participate in goal setting but instead merely assign goals and order subordinates to accept them.

On balance, MBO is often an effective and useful system for managing goal setting and enhancing performance in organizations. Research suggests that it can actually do many of the things its advocates claim but that it must also be handled carefully. In particular, most organizations need to tailor it to their own unique circumstances. Properly used, MBO can also be an effective approach to managing an organization's reward system. It does require, however, individual, one-on-one interactions between each supervisor and each employee; and these one-on-one interactions can often be difficult because of the time they take and the likelihood that at least some of them will involve critical assessments of unacceptable performance.

PERFORMANCE MANAGEMENT

As described earlier, most goals are oriented toward some element of performance. Managers can do a variety of things to enhance employee motivation and performance, including designing jobs, allowing greater participation and promoting empowerment, considering alternative work arrangements, and setting goals. However, they may also fail to do things that might have improved motivation and performance, and they might even inadvertently do things that reduce motivation and performance. Thus, it is clearly important that managers understand that performance is something that can and should be managed.[33] Moreover, effective performance management is essential in order for rewards to be used effectively. The core of performance management is the actual measurement of the performance of an individual or group. ***Performance appraisal*** is the process by which someone (1) evaluates an employee's work behaviors by measurement and comparison with previously established standards, (2) documents the results, and (3) communicates the results to the employee.[34] Performance management comprises the processes and activities involved in performance appraisals.

performance appraisal
The process of assessing and evaluating an employee's work behaviors by measurement

Purposes of Performance Measurement

Performance appraisal may serve many purposes. The ability to provide valuable feedback is one critical purpose. Feedback, in turn, tells the employee where she or he stands in the eyes of the organization. Appraisal results, of course, are also used to decide and justify reward allocations. Performance evaluations may be used as a starting point for discussions of training, development, and improvement. Finally, the data produced by the performance appraisal system can be used to forecast future human resource needs, to plan management succession, and to guide other human resource activities such as recruiting, training, and development programs.

Providing job performance feedback is the primary use of appraisal information. Performance appraisal information can indicate that an employee is ready for promotion or that he or she needs additional training to gain experience in another area of company operations. It may also show that a person does not have the skills for a certain job and that another person should be recruited to fill that particular role. Other purposes of performance appraisal can be grouped into two broad categories, judgment and development, as shown in Figure 6.5.

Figure 6.5

Performance measurement plays a variety of roles in most organizations. This figure illustrates that these roles can help managers judge an employee's past performance and help managers and employees improve future performance.

Purposes of Performance Management

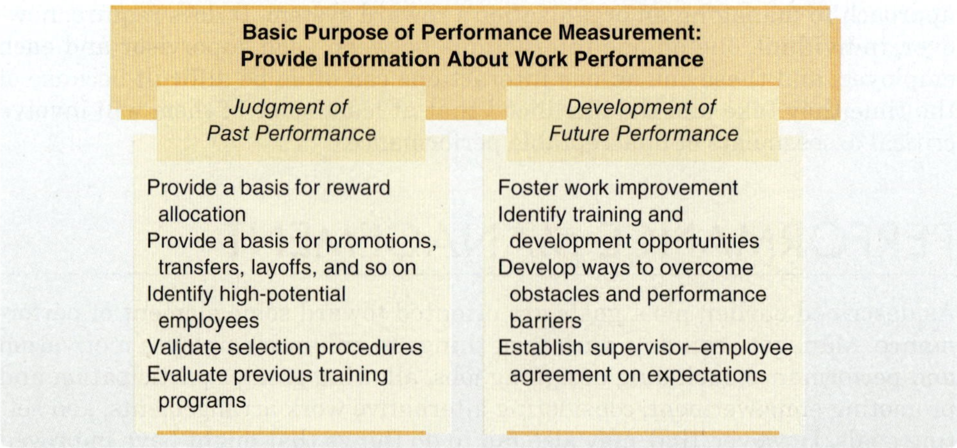

Basic Purpose of Performance Measurement: Provide Information About Work Performance

Judgment of Past Performance	*Development of Future Performance*
Provide a basis for reward allocation	Foster work improvement
Provide a basis for promotions, transfers, layoffs, and so on	Identify training and development opportunities
Identify high-potential employees	Develop ways to overcome obstacles and performance barriers
Validate selection procedures	Establish supervisor–employee agreement on expectations
Evaluate previous training programs	

Performance appraisals with a judgmental orientation focus on past performance and are concerned mainly with measuring and comparing performance and with the uses of this information. Appraisals with a developmental orientation focus on the future and use information from evaluations to improve performance. If improved future performance is the intent of the appraisal process, the manager may focus on goals or targets for the employee, on eliminating obstacles or problems that hinder performance, and on future training needs.

Elements of Performance Management

Employee appraisals are common in every type of organization, but how they are performed may vary. Many issues must be considered in determining how to conduct an appraisal. Three of the most important issues are who does the appraisals, how often they are done, and how performance is measured.

The Appraiser

In most appraisal systems, the employee's primary evaluator is the supervisor. This stems from the obvious fact that the supervisor is presumably in the best position to be aware of the employee's day-to-day performance. Further, it is the supervisor who has traditionally provided performance feedback to employees and determined performance-based rewards and sanctions. Problems often arise, however, if the supervisor has incomplete or distorted information about the employee's performance. For example, the supervisor may have little firsthand knowledge of the performance of an employee who works alone outside the company premises, such as a salesperson making solo calls on clients or a maintenance person handling equipment problems in the field. Similar problems may arise when the supervisor has a limited understanding of the technical knowledge involved in an employee's job. Our *Understand Yourself* feature will give you insight into your own style for providing feedback.

One solution to these problems is a multiple-rater system that incorporates the ratings of several people familiar with the employee's performance. One possible alternative, for example, is to use the employee as an evaluator. Although they may not actually do so, most employees are actually very capable of evaluating themselves in an unbiased manner. One of the more interesting multi-rater approaches being used in some companies today is something called ***360-degree feedback*** (it is also called multi-source feedback). This method involves employees receiving performance feedback from those on all "sides" of them in the organization—their boss, their colleagues and peers, and their own subordinates. Thus, the feedback comes from all around them, or from 360 degrees. This form of performance evaluation can be very beneficial to managers because it typically gives them a much wider range of performance-related feedback than a traditional evaluation provides. That is, rather than focusing narrowly on objective performance, such as sales increases or productivity gains, 360-degree feedback often focuses on such things as interpersonal relations and style. For example, one person may learn that she stands too close to other people when she talks, another that he has a bad temper. These are the kinds of things a supervisor might not even be aware of, much less report as part of a performance appraisal. Subordinates or peers

360-degree feedback
A performance appraisal method in which employees receive performance feedback from those on all sides of them in the organization

UNDERSTAND YOURSELF

YOUR FEEDBACK STYLE

This exercise will help you understand the dynamics of performance appraisal feedback. Diagnosing performance is critical to effective management. Performance appraisal involves both diagnosis and motivation and so is critical to the effective functioning of organizations. One of the difficulties with most performance appraisal systems is that the supervisor or manager feels uncomfortable providing feedback in a one-to-one encounter. The result often is employee vagueness about what the performance appraisal really means, what it is designed to do, and how it can improve performance. The supervisor or manager fails to address those concerns because he or she did not adequately diagnose the situation and therefore lacks an understanding of how subordinates respond to performance feedback or lacks the skill necessary to provide valuable feedback. Listed below is a set of feedback behaviors. Read the description of each behavior carefully, then select the response that best reflects the extent to which that behavior describes what you do or think you would do. Indicate your choice by circling the response. The possible responses are as follows:

Possible Responses

Y̲ = Yes, this definitely describes me.

Y = Yes I'm fairly sure this describes me.

? = I'm not sure.

N = No, I'm fairly sure this doesn't describe me.

N̲ = No, this definitely doesn't describe me.

1. When communicating, I try to seek feedback from the receiver to determine whether I'm being understood.
   1. Y̲ 2. Y 3. ? 4. N 5. N̲
2. Whenever possible, I try to ensure that my point of view is accepted and acted upon.
   1. Y̲ 2. Y 3. ? 4. N 5. N̲
3. I can easily handle and accept counterarguments to my ideas.
   1. Y̲ 2. Y 3. ? 4. N 5. N̲
4. When a communication problem occurs between another person and myself, it's usually his or her fault.
   1. Y̲ 2. Y 3. ? 4. N 5. N̲
5. I make sure the other person understands that I know what I am talking about.
   1. Y̲ 2. Y 3. ? 4. N 5. N̲
6. If someone comes to me with a personal problem, I try to listen objectively without being judgmental.
   1. Y̲ 2. Y 3. ? 4. N 5. N̲
7. When listening to someone questioning or criticizing my procedures, I often find myself engaging in mental counterarguments—thinking about my response while the person is talking.
   1. Y̲ 2. Y 3. ? 4. N 5. N̲
8. I let the other person finish an idea before intervening or finishing it for him or her.
   1. Y̲ 2. Y 3. ? 4. N 5. N̲
9. When listening to someone, I find that I can easily restate (paraphrase) that person's point of view.
   1. Y̲ 2. Y 3. ? 4. N 5. N̲
10. I try not to prejudge the speaker or the message.
    1. Y̲ 2. Y 3. ? 4. N 5. N̲
11. Whenever I provide information to someone, I prefer using facts and data.
    1. Y̲ 2. Y 3. ? 4. N 5. N̲
12. Communicating empathy for the feelings of the receiver tends to indicate weakness.
    1. Y̲ 2. Y 3. ? 4. N 5. N̲
13. I try to ensure that others know how I view their actions: good, bad, strong, weak, etc.
    1. Y̲ 2. Y 3. ? 4. N 5. N̲
14. In order to get people to do things properly, you have to tell them what to do.
    1. Y̲ 2. Y 3. ? 4. N 5. N̲
15. When talking with someone, I like saying, "What do you think?" to introduce more acceptance of the issue.
    1. Y̲ 2. Y 3. ? 4. N 5. N̲
16. If you are the boss, people expect you to tell them what to do.
    1. Y̲ 2. Y 3. ? 4. N 5. N̲
17. I try to use probing, nondirective questions in discussions with individuals.
    1. Y̲ 2. Y 3. ? 4. N 5. N̲
18. In providing negative feedback, I want to be certain the receiver knows how I view the situation.
    1. Y̲ 2. Y 3. ? 4. N 5. N̲
19. I try to listen with empathy. I listen both to what is being said and to what I think the sender is trying to say.
    1. Y̲ 2. Y 3. ? 4. N 5. N̲
20. Whenever I provide someone with feedback, I usually want to persuade him or her to act on it.
    1. Y̲ 2. Y 3. ? 4. N 5. N̲

(Continued)

Scoring:

(1) For the items listed, score your responses as follows: (2) For the items listed, the scoring system is reversed:

Item Score		Scoring	Item Score		Scoring
1.	____	Y = 2	2.	____	Y = −2
3.	____		4.	____	
6.	____	Y = 1	5.	____	Y = −1
8.	____		7.	____	
9.	____	? = 0	12.	____	? = 0
10.	____		13.	____	
11.	____	N = −1	14.	____	N = 1
15.	____		16.	____	
17.	____	N = −2	18.	____	N = 2
19.	____		20.	____	
TOTAL	____		TOTAL	____	

The items on the left assess if you are collaborative and open. The items on the right assess if you are domineering and closed in style. Stating "yes" to these items indicates a less effective feedback style so it is reverse scored (Y = −2, N = 2). A higher score on either column thus indicates a more effective style. The sum of your two scores indicates your overall feedback style. The lowest overall score is −40 and the highest overall score is +40. Most people will score in the positive range.

are much more willing to provide this sort of feedback than direct performance feedback, especially if it is used for development purposes and does not influence rewards or punishments. AT&T, Nestlé, Pitney Bowes, and JPMorgan Chase are a few of the major companies today using 360-degree feedback to help managers improve a wide variety of performance-related behaviors.[35]

Frequency of the Appraisal

Another important issue is the frequency of appraisals. Regardless of the employee's level of performance, the types of tasks being performed, or the employee's need for information on performance, the organization usually conducts performance appraisals on a regular basis, typically once a year. Annual performance appraisals are convenient for administrative purposes such as record keeping and maintaining a level of routine that helps keep everyone comfortable. Some organizations also conduct appraisals semiannually.[36] Several systems for monitoring employee performance on an "as-needed" basis have been proposed as an alternative to the traditional annual system.

Managers in international settings must ensure that they incorporate cultural phenomena into their performance-appraisal strategies. For example, in highly individualistic cultures such as that of the United States, appraising performance at the individual level is both common and accepted. But in collectivistic cultures such as Japan, performance appraisals almost always need to be focused more on group performance and feedback. And in countries where people put a lot of faith in destiny, fate, or some form of divine control, employees may not be receptive to performance feedback at all, believing that their actions are irrelevant to the results that follow them.

Measuring Performance

The foundation of good performance management is correctly identifying what should be measured and the selection of the best method(s) for measuring it. Accurately defining job performance is critical: measuring the wrong things well is not good performance management. Once the critical performance

RAGMA IMAGES/SHUTTERSTOCK.COM

Key elements of performance management are measuring and assessing performance. Performance rating scales such as this one are commonly used for assessing performance in organizations.

dimensions are known, the best way(s) of assessing them can be identified. Detailed descriptions of the many different methods for measuring performance are beyond the scope of this book; they are more appropriately covered in a course in human resource management or a specialized course in performance appraisal. However, we can present a few general comments about how to measure performance.

The measurement method provides the information managers use to make decisions about salary adjustment, promotion, transfer, training, and discipline. The courts and Equal Employment Opportunity guidelines have mandated that performance measurements be based on job-related criteria rather than on some other factor such as friendship, age, sex, religion, or national origin. In addition, to provide useful information for the decision maker, performance appraisals must be valid, reliable, and free of bias. They must not produce ratings that are consistently too lenient or too severe or that all cluster in the middle.[37] They must also be free of perceptual and timing errors.

Some of the most popular methods for evaluating individual performance are graphic rating scales, checklists, essays or diaries, behaviorally anchored rating scales, and forced choice systems. These systems are easy to use and familiar to most managers. However, two major problems are common to all individual methods: a tendency to rate most individuals at about the same level, and the inability to discriminate among variable levels of performance.

Comparative methods evaluate two or more employees by comparing them with each other on various performance dimensions. The most popular comparative methods are ranking, forced distribution, paired comparisons, and the use of multiple raters in making comparisons. Comparative methods, however, are more difficult to use than the individual methods, are unfamiliar to many managers, and may require sophisticated development procedures and a computerized analytical system to extract usable information.

balanced scorecard or ***BSC***
A relatively structured performance management technique that identifies financial and nonfinancial performance measures and organizes them into a single model

The Balanced Scorecard Approach to Performance Management

A relatively new and increasingly popular form of performance management system is the balanced scorecard approach. The ***balanced scorecard***, or ***BSC***, is a structured performance management technique that identifies financial and nonfinancial performance measures and organizes them into a single model.[38] The basic BCS is shown in Figure 6.6.

Figure 6.6

The Balanced Scorecard

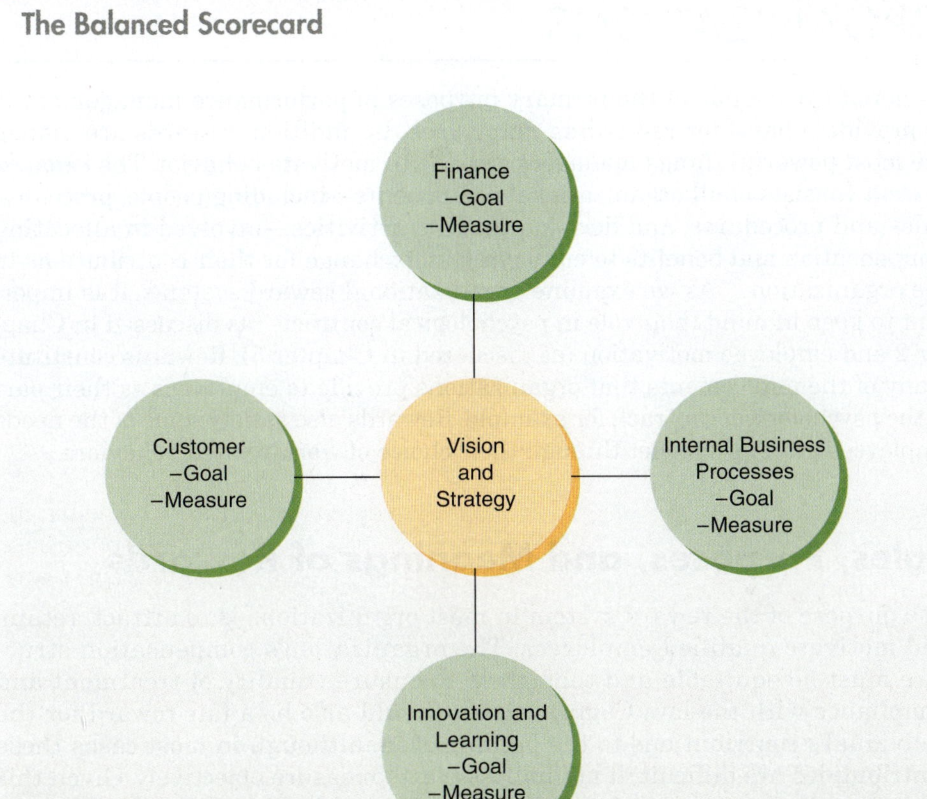

The balanced scorecard is a structured performance management technique. In its most basic form, managers establish both goals and measures for how they want to assess customer perceptions, financial performance, internal business process, and innovation and learning. Each of these sets of goals and measures need to be consistent with each other as well as with the organization's overall vision and strategy.

At the core of the BSC is organizational vision and strategy. These must be clearly established and communicated throughout the organization by the top management team. Next, managers establish a small number of objective goals and measures to support four key components of organizational success. These components are customer perceptions, financial performance, internal business processes, and innovation and learning. All subsequent performance measures are derived from this framework.

For instance, suppose that top managers have determined that they want customers to see the firm as a preferred provider of high-quality, premium-priced fashion watches (for example, Rolex). Goals and measures to support this component might be to maintain a 50 percent market share and 98 percent customer satisfaction index within the chosen market segment. One major area of individual performance evaluation, then, would focus on the extent to which a person is contributing market share, customer satisfaction, and/or a closely related area.

Not surprisingly, there are now a number of commercially available business software systems that help support the balanced scorecard approach. Moreover, a wide array of businesses report using the original BSC, a newer revised version of the BSC, or an alternative model that is patterned after the BSC. On the other hand, most of the evidence used to support the validity of the BSC is anecdotal in nature. That is, its value as a performance management system has not been demonstrated in a rigorous and empirical manner.

INDIVIDUAL REWARDS IN ORGANIZATIONS

reward system
All organizational components, including people, processes, rules and procedures, and decision-making activities, involved in allocating compensation and benefits to employees in exchange for their contributions to the organization

As noted earlier, one of the primary purposes of performance management is to provide a basis for rewarding employees. In addition, rewards are among the most powerful things managers can use to motivate behavior. The ***reward system*** consists of all organizational components—including people, processes, rules and procedures, and decision-making activities—involved in allocating compensation and benefits to employees in exchange for their contributions to the organization.[39] As we examine organizational reward systems, it is important to keep in mind their role in psychological contracts (as discussed in Chapter 2 and employee motivation (as discussed in Chapter 5). Rewards constitute many of the inducements that organizations provide to employees as their part of the psychological contract, for example. Rewards also satisfy some of the needs employees attempt to meet through their choice of work-related behaviors.

Roles, Purposes, and Meanings of Rewards

The purpose of the reward system in most organizations is to attract, retain, and motivate qualified employees. The organization's compensation structure must be equitable and consistent to ensure equality of treatment and compliance with the law. Compensation should also be a fair reward for the individual's contributions to the organization, although in most cases these contributions are difficult, if not impossible, to measure objectively. Given this limitation, managers should be as fair and as equitable as possible. Finally, the system must be competitive in the external labor market for the organization to attract and retain competent workers in appropriate fields.[40]

Beyond these broad considerations, an organization must develop its philosophy of compensation based on its own conditions and needs, and this philosophy must be defined and built into the actual reward system. For example, Walmart has a policy that none of its employees will be paid the minimum wage. Even though it may pay some people only slightly more than this minimum, the firm nevertheless wants to communicate to all workers that it places a higher value on their contributions than just having to pay them the lowest wage possible.

The organization needs to decide what types of behaviors or performance it wants to encourage with a reward system because what is rewarded tends to recur. Possible behaviors include performance, longevity, attendance, loyalty, contributions to the "bottom line," responsibility, and conformity. Performance measurement, as described earlier, assesses these behaviors, but the choice of which behaviors to reward is a function of the compensation system. A reward system must also take into account volatile economic issues such as inflation, market conditions, technology, labor union activities, and so forth.

surface value
Objective meaning or worth of a reward

It is also important for the organization to recognize that organizational rewards have many meanings for employees. Intrinsic and extrinsic rewards carry both surface and symbolic value. The ***surface value*** of a reward to an employee is its objective meaning or worth. A salary increase of 5 percent, for example, means that an individual has 5 percent more spending power than before, whereas a promotion, on the surface, means new duties and responsibilities. But managers must recognize that rewards also carry ***symbolic value***. If a person gets a 3 percent salary increase when everyone else gets 5 percent, one plausible meaning is that the organization values other employees more. But if the same person gets 3 percent and all others get only 1 percent, the meaning may be just the opposite—the individual is seen as the most valuable employee. Thus, rewards convey to people not only how much they are valued by the organization but also their importance relative to others. Managers need to tune in to the many meanings rewards can convey—not only the surface messages but the symbolic messages as well.

symbolic value
Subjective and personal meaning or worth of a reward

LOSKUTNIKOV/SHUTTERSTOCK.COM

PHANT/SHUTTERSTOCK.COM

CASE STUDY The Whole Truth

Whole Foods Market (WFM) started out in 1980 as one store with 19 employees in Austin, Texas. Today, with 370 stores and 54,000 employees in North America and Great Britain, it's the leading natural and organic foods supermarket (and ninth-largest food and drug chain in the United States). Along the way, it has also gained a considerable reputation as a socially responsible company and a good place to work. WFM's motto is "Whole Foods, Whole People, Whole Planet," and its guiding "core value," according to co-CEO Walter Robb, is "customers first, then team members, balanced with what's good for other stakeholders.... If I put our mission in simple terms," Robb continues, "it would be, No. 1, to change the way the world eats and, No. 2, to create a workplace based on love and respect."

WFM made *Fortune* magazine's very first list of the "100 Best Companies to Work For" in 1998 and has routinely appeared on the list ever since. Observers have acknowledged the company's growth (which means more jobs), salary-cap limits (the top earner gets no more than 19 times the average full-time salary), and generous health plan. The structure of the company's current health care program, which revolves around high deductibles and so-called health savings accounts (HSAs), was first proposed in 2003. Under such a plan, an employee (a "team member," in WFM parlance) pays a deductible before his or her expenses are covered.

Meanwhile, the employer funds a special account (an HSA) for each employee, who can spend the money to cover health-related expenditures. The previous WFM plan had covered 100 percent of all expenses, and when some employees complained about the proposed change, the company decided to put it to a vote. Nearly 90 percent of the workforce went to the polls, with 77 percent voting for the new plan. In 2006, employees voted to retain the plan, which now carries a deductible of around $1,300; HSAs may go as high as $1,800 (and accrue for future use). The company pays 100 percent of the premiums for eligible employees (about 89 percent of the workforce).

High-deductible plans save money for the employer (the higher the deductible, the lower the premium), and more importantly—at least according to founder and co-CEO John Mackey—they also make employees more responsible consumers. When the first $1,300 of their medical expenses comes out of their own pockets (or their own HSAs), he argues, people "start asking how much things cost. Or they get a bill and say, 'Wow, that's expensive.' They begin to ask questions. They may not want to go to the emergency room if they wake up with a hangnail in the middle of the night. They may schedule an appointment now."[41]

Questions

1. How important would benefits like those offered by Whole Foods be to you if you were working there to put yourself through school or to collect a paycheck while looking for a position in your chosen field?
2. What negative elements do you see in Whole Foods approach to pay and benefits?
3. Why don't more companies use the approach to employee health care pioneered by Whole Foods?

Types of Rewards

Most organizations use several different types of rewards. The most common are base pay (wages or salary), incentive systems, benefits, perquisites, and awards. These rewards are combined to create an individual's ***compensation package***.

compensation package
The total array of money (wages, salary, commissions), incentives, benefits, perquisites, and awards provided by the organization to an individual

Base Pay

For most people, the most important reward for work is the pay they receive. Obviously, money is important because of the things it can buy, but as we just noted, it can also symbolize an employee's worth. Pay is very important to an organization for a variety of reasons. For one thing, an effectively planned and managed pay system can improve motivation and performance. For another, employee compensation is a major cost of doing business—well over 50 percent in many organizations—so a poorly designed system can be an expensive proposition. Finally, since pay is considered a major source of employee dissatisfaction, a poorly designed system can result in problems in other areas such as turnover and low morale.

Incentive Systems

incentive systems
Plans in which employees can earn additional compensation in return for certain types of performance

Incentive systems are plans in which employees can earn additional compensation in return for certain types of performance. Examples of incentive programs include the following:

1. *Piecework programs*, which tie a worker's earnings to the number of units produced
2. *Gain-sharing programs*, which grant additional earnings to employees or workgroups for cost-reduction ideas
3. *Bonus systems*, which provide managers with lump-sum payments from a special fund based on the financial performance of the organization or a unit
4. *Long-term compensation*, which gives managers additional income based on stock price performance, earnings per share, or return on equity
5. *Merit pay plans*, which base pay raises on the employee's performance
6. *Profit-sharing plans*, which distribute a portion of the firm's profits to all employees at a predetermined rate
7. *Employee stock option plans*, which set aside stock in the company for employees to purchase at a reduced rate

Plans oriented mainly toward individual employees may cause increased competition for the rewards and some possibly disruptive behaviors, such as sabotaging a coworker's performance, sacrificing quality for quantity, or fighting over customers. A group incentive plan, on the other hand, requires that employees trust one another and work together. Of course, all incentive systems have advantages and disadvantages.

Long-term compensation for executives is particularly controversial because of the large sums of money involved and the basis for the payments. Indeed, executive compensation is one of the more controversial subjects that U.S. businesses have had to face in recent years. News reports and the popular press seem to take great joy in telling stories about how this or that executive has just received a huge windfall from his or her organization. The job of a senior executive, especially a CEO, is grueling and stressful and takes talent and decades of hard work to reach. Clearly, successful top managers deserve significant rewards. The question is whether some companies are overrewarding such managers for their contributions to the organization.[42]

When a firm is growing rapidly and its profits are also growing rapidly, relatively few objections can be raised to paying the CEO well. However, objections arise when an organization is laying off workers, its financial performance is perhaps less than might be expected, and the CEO is still earning a huge amount of money. It is these situations that dictate that a company's board of directors take a closer look at the appropriateness of its executive compensation decisions.[43]

Indirect Compensation

Another major component of the compensation package is ***indirect compensation***, also commonly referred to as the employee benefits plan. Typical ***benefits*** provided by businesses include the following:

indirect compensation
Employee benefits provided as a form of compensation

benefits
Rewards and incentives provided to employees in addition to their wages or salaries

1. *Payment for time not worked*, both on and off the job. On-the-job free time includes lunch, rest, coffee breaks, and wash-up or get-ready time. Off-the-job time not worked includes vacation, sick leave, holidays, and personal days.
2. *Social Security contributions*. The employer contributes half the money paid into the system established under the Federal Insurance Contributions Act (FICA). The employee pays the other half.
3. *Unemployment compensation*. People who have lost their jobs or are temporarily laid off get a percentage of their wages from an insurance-like program.
4. *Disability and workers' compensation benefits*. Employers contribute funds to help workers who cannot work due to occupational injury or ailment.
5. *Life and health insurance programs*. Most organizations offer insurance at a cost far below what individuals would pay to buy insurance on their own.
6. *Pension or retirement plans*. Most organizations offer plans to provide supplementary income to employees after they retire.

A company's Social Security, unemployment, and workers' unemployment compensation contributions are set by law. But deciding how much to contribute for other kinds of benefits is up to each company. Some organizations contribute more to the cost of these benefits than others. Some companies pay the entire cost; others pay a percentage of the cost of certain benefits, such as health insurance, and bear the entire cost of other benefits. Moreover, many technology companies today find it necessary to offer extravagant benefits to attract high-talent workers. For example, Google provides its employees with gourmet food, free massages, and a spa. Facebook employees also get gourmet food, plus

TDWAY/SHUTTERSTOCK.COM

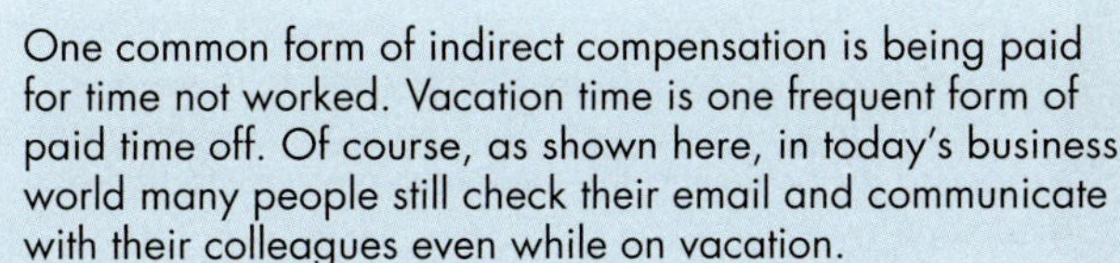

One common form of indirect compensation is being paid for time not worked. Vacation time is one frequent form of paid time off. Of course, as shown here, in today's business world many people still check their email and communicate with their colleagues even while on vacation.

wash-and-fold laundry services, free haircuts, four weeks of paid vacation, and 100 percent company-paid medical, dental, and vision insurance. Zynga provides on-site dog care, including free grooming service.[44]

Perquisites

perquisites
Special privileges awarded to selected members of an organization, usually top managers

Perquisites are special privileges awarded to selected members of an organization, usually top managers. For years, the top executives of many businesses were allowed privileges such as unlimited use of the company jet, motor home, vacation home, and executive dining room. In Japan, a popular perquisite is a paid membership in an exclusive golf club; a common perquisite in England is first-class travel. In the United States, the Internal Revenue Service has ruled that some "perks" constitute a form of income and thus can be taxed. This decision has substantially changed the nature of these benefits, but they have not entirely disappeared, nor are they likely to. Today, however, many perks tend to be more job-related. For example, popular perks currently include a car and driver (so that the executive can presumably work while being transported to and from work) and membership in airport clubs (so that the executive can more comfortably conduct business while traveling). More than anything else, though, perquisites seem to add to the status of their recipients and thus may increase job satisfaction and reduce turnover.[45]

Awards

At many companies, employees receive awards for everything from seniority to perfect attendance, from zero defects (quality work) to cost reduction suggestions. Award programs can be costly in the time required to run them and in money if cash awards are given, but award systems can improve performance under the right conditions. In one medium-size manufacturing company, careless work habits were pushing up the costs of scrap and rework (the cost of scrapping defective parts or reworking them to meet standards). Management instituted a zero-defects program to recognize employees who did perfect or near-perfect work. During the first month, two workers in shipping caused only one defect in over two thousand parts handled. Division management called a meeting in the lunchroom and recognized each worker with a plaque and a ribbon. The next month, the same two workers had two defects, so there was no award. The following month, the two workers had zero defects, and once again top management called a meeting to give out plaques and ribbons. Elsewhere in the plant, defects, scrap, and rework decreased dramatically as workers evidently sought recognition for quality work. What worked in this particular plant may or may not work in others.[46]

VOLT COLLECTION/SHUTTERSTOCK.COM

Awards and prizes are frequently used to reward outstanding performance. This manager is getting an award for achieving the most revenue growth in the company.

Related Issues in Rewarding Performance

Much of our discussion on reward systems has focused on general issues. As Table 6.1 shows, however, the organization must address other issues when developing organizational reward systems. The organization must consider its ability to pay employees at certain levels, economic and labor market conditions, and the impact of the pay system on organizational financial performance. In addition, the organization must consider the relationship between performance and rewards as well as the issues of reward system flexibility, employee participation in the reward system, pay secrecy, and expatriate compensation.

Linking Performance and Rewards

For managers to take full advantage of the symbolic value of pay, there must be a perception on the part of employees that their rewards are linked to their performance. For example, if everyone in an organization starts working for the same hourly rate and then receives a predetermined wage increase every six months or year, there is clearly no relationship between performance and rewards. Instead, the organization is indicating that all entry-level employees are worth the same amount, and pay increases are tied solely to the length of time an employee works in the organization. This holds true whether the employee is a top, average, or mediocre employee. The only requirement is that the employee works well enough to avoid being fired.

At the other extreme, an organization might attempt to tie all compensation to actual performance. Thus, each new employee might start at a different wage, as determined by his or her experience, education, skills, and other

Table 6.1

Issues to Consider in Developing Reward Systems

Issue	Important Examples
PAY SECRECY	• Open, closed, partial • Link with performance appraisal • Equity perceptions
EMPLOYEE PARTICIPATION	• By human resource department • By joint employee/management committee
FLEXIBLE SYSTEM	• Cafeteria-style benefits • Annual lump sum or monthly bonus • Salary versus benefits
ABILITY TO PAY	• Organization's financial performance • Expected future earnings
ECONOMIC AND LABOR MARKET FACTORS	• Inflation rate • Industry pay standards • Unemployment rate
IMPACT ON ORGANIZATIONAL PERFORMANCE	• Increase in costs • Impact on performance
EXPATRIATE COMPENSATION	• Cost-of-living differentials • Managing related equity issue

job-related factors. After joining the organization, the individual then receives rewards based on actual performance. One employee, for example, might start at $15 an hour because she has ten years of experience and a good performance record at her previous employer. Another might start the same job at a rate of $10.50 an hour because he has only four years' experience and an adequate but not outstanding performance record. Assuming the first employee performs up to expectations, she might also get several pay increases, bonuses, and awards throughout the year whereas the second employee might get only one or two small increases and no other rewards. Of course, organizations must ensure that pay differences are based strictly on performance (including seniority), and not on factors that do not relate to performance (such as gender, ethnicity, or other discriminatory factors).

In reality, most organizations attempt to develop a reward strategy somewhere between these two extremes. Because it is really quite difficult to differentiate among all the employees, most firms use some basic compensation level for everyone. For example, they might start everyone performing a specific job at the same rate, regardless of experience. They might also work to provide reasonable incentives and other inducements for high performers while making sure that they don't ignore the average employees. The key fact for managers to remember is simply that if they expect rewards to motivate performance, employees must see a clear, direct link between their own job-related behaviors and the attainment of those rewards.[47]

Flexible Reward Systems

flexible reward system
Allows employees to choose the combination of benefits that best suits their needs

Flexible, or cafeteria-style, reward systems are a recent and increasingly popular variation on the standard compensation system. A ***flexible reward system*** allows employees, within specified ranges, to choose the combination of benefits that best suits their needs. For example, a younger worker just starting out might prefer to have especially strong health care coverage with few deductibles. A worker with a few years of experience might prefer to have more child care benefits. A midcareer employee with more financial security might prefer more time off with pay. And older workers might prefer to have more rewards concentrated into their retirement plans.

Some organizations are starting to apply the flexible approach to pay. For example, employees sometimes have the option of taking an annual salary increase in one lump sum rather than in monthly increments. General Electric recently implemented such a system for some of its managers. UNUM Corporation, a large insurance firm, allows all of its employees the option of drawing a full third of their annual compensation in the month of January. This makes it easier for them to handle such major expenses as purchasing a new automobile, buying a home, or covering college education costs for their children. Obviously, the administrative costs of providing this level of flexibility are greater, but many employees value this flexibility and may develop strong loyalty and attachment to an employer who offers this kind of compensation package.

Participative Pay Systems

In keeping with the current trend toward worker involvement in organizational decision making, employee participation in the pay process is also increasing. A participative pay system may involve the employee in the system's design, administration, or both. A pay system can be designed by staff members of the organization's human resources department, a committee of managers in the organization, an outside consultant, the employees, or a combination of these sources. Organizations that have used a joint management employee task force to design the compensation system have generally succeeded in designing and implementing a plan that managers could use and that employees believed in. Employee participation in administering the pay system is a natural extension of having employees participate in its design. Examples of companies that have involved employees in the administration of the pay system include Romac Industries, where employees vote on the pay of other employees; Graphic Controls, where each manager's pay is determined by a group of peers; and the Friedman-Jacobs Company, where employees set their own wages based on their perceptions of their performance.[48]

Pay Secrecy

When a company has a policy of open salary information, the exact salary amounts for employees are public knowledge. State governments, for instance, make public the salaries of everyone on their payrolls. A policy of complete secrecy means that no information is available to employees regarding other employees' salaries, average or percentage raises, or salary ranges. The National Labor Relations Board recently upheld an earlier ruling that an employer's starting or enforcing a rule that forbids "employees to discuss their salaries" constitutes interference, restraint, and coercion of protected employee rights under the National Labor Relations Act. Although a few organizations have completely public or completely secret systems, most have systems somewhere in the middle.

Expatriate Compensation

Expatriate compensation is yet another important issue in managing reward systems.[49] Consider, for example, a manager living and working in Houston currently making $450,000 a year. That income allows the manager to live in a certain kind of home, drive a certain kind of car, have access to certain levels of medical care, and live a certain kind of lifestyle. Now suppose the manager is asked to accept a transfer to Tokyo, Geneva, Moscow, or London, cities where the cost of living is considerably higher than in Houston. The same salary cannot begin to support a comparable lifestyle in those cities. Consequently, the employer is almost certain to redesign the manager's compensation package so that the employee's lifestyle in the new location will be comparable to that in the old.

Now consider a different scenario. Suppose the same manager is asked to accept a transfer to an underdeveloped nation. The cost of living in this nation might be quite low by U.S. standards. But there may also be relatively few choices in housing, poorer schools and medical care, a harsh climate, greater personal danger, or similar unattractive characteristics. The firm will probably have to pay the manager some level of additional compensation to offset the decrement in quality of lifestyle. Thus, developing rewards for expatriates is a complicated process.

Figure 6.7 illustrates the approach to expatriate compensation used by one major multinational corporation. The left side of the figure shows how a U.S. employee currently uses her or his salary—part of it goes for taxes, part is saved, and the rest is consumed. When a person is asked to move abroad, a human resource manager works with the employee to develop an equitable balance sheet for the new compensation package. As shown on the right side of the figure, the individual's compensation package will potentially consist of six components. First, the individual will receive income to cover what his or her taxes and Social Security payments in the United States will be. The individual may also have to pay foreign taxes and additional U.S. taxes as a result of the move, so the company covers these as well.

Figure 6.7

The Expatriate Compensation Balance Sheet

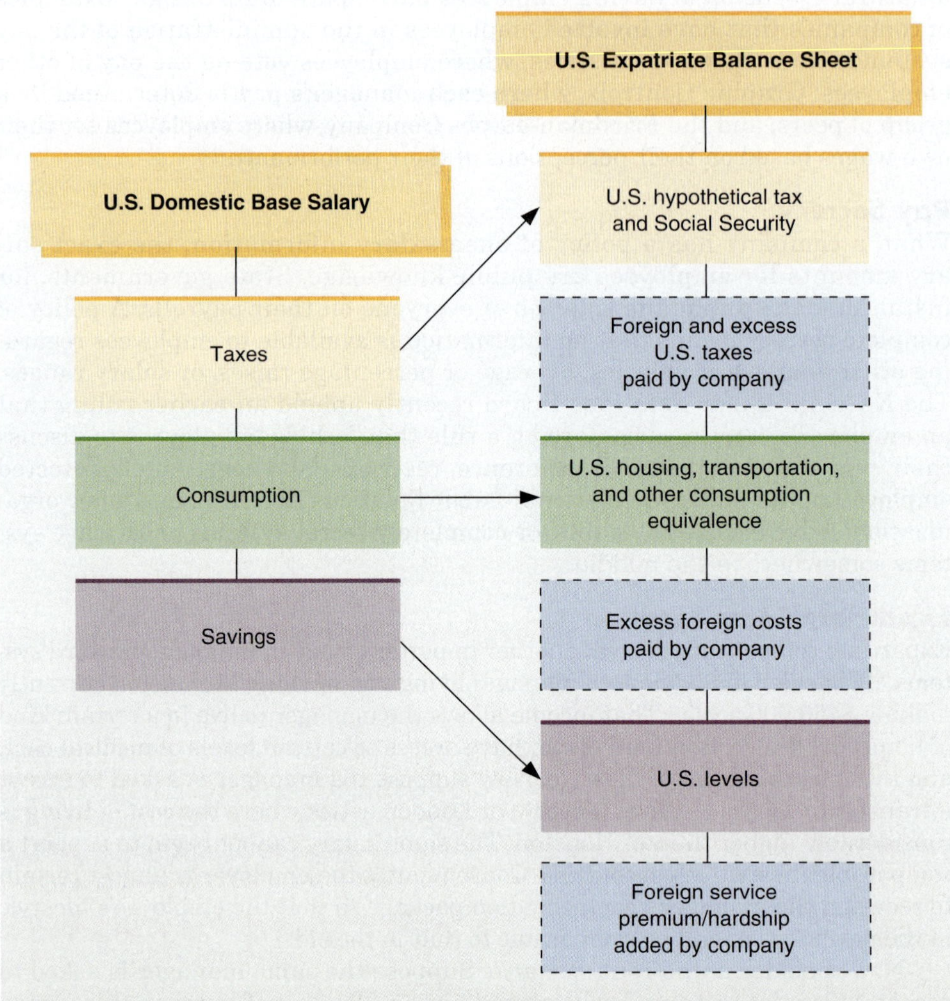

Organizations that ask employees to accept assignments in foreign locations usually must adjust their compensation levels to account for differences in cost of living and similar factors. Amoco uses the system shown here. The employee's domestic base salary is first broken down into the three categories shown on the left. Then adjustments are made by adding compensation to the categories on the right until an appropriate, equitable level of compensation is achieved.

Next, the firm also pays an amount adequate to the employee's current consumption levels in the United States. If the cost of living is greater in the foreign location than at home, the firm pays the excess foreign costs. The employee also receives income for savings comparable to what he or she is currently saving. Finally, if the employee faces a hardship because of the assignment, an additional foreign service premium or hardship allowance is added by the firm. Not surprisingly, then, expatriate compensation packages can be very expensive for an organization and must be carefully developed and managed.[50]

At the end of Chapter 5 we presented Table 5.1 to illustrate how the various theories of motivation discussed in that chapter could be used to address several representative managerial challenges. Table 6.2 shows how the various motivational tools and techniques discussed in this chapter might be used for those same challenges. Keep in mind, of course, that each situation is unique and that there are no guarantees of success. Still, though, these suggestions provide an effective starting point in helping managers know when to use different motivation methods to address various challenges the workplace.

Table 6.2

Many different management challenges related to employee motivation can be addressed through methods related to work and rewards

Managerial Challenges	Motivation Methods and Techniques					
	Job Design	Participation & Empowerment	Flexible Work	Goal Setting	Performance Management	Rewards
Firm has a low-cost business strategy but needs to motivate employees	x	x			x	x
An employee feels he cannot meet his performance goals		x		x	x	x
An employee feels underpaid relative to her coworkers			x	x	x	x
An employee engages in inappropriate behavior (bullying, ridiculing coworkers)		x		x	x	x
A talented employee is not feeling challenged at work	x	x	x		x	x
Because the work is repetitive, some employees find it boring and hard to stay motivated		x	x		x	x

SUMMARY AND APPLICATION

Managers seek to enhance employee performance by capitalizing on the potential for motivated behavior to improve performance. Methods often used to translate motivation into performance involve work design, participation and empowerment, alternative work arrangements, performance management, goal setting, and rewards.

The essence of work design is how organizations define and structure jobs. Historically, there was a general trend toward increasingly specialized jobs, but more recently the movement has consistently been away from extreme specialization. Two early alternatives to specialization were job rotation and job enlargement. Job enrichment approaches stimulated considerable interest in job design. The job characteristics theory grew from early work on job enrichment. One basic premise of this theory is that jobs can be described in terms of a specific set of motivational characteristics. Another is that managers should work to enhance the presence of those motivational characteristics in jobs but should also take individual differences into account.

Employee involvement using participative management and empowerment can help improve employee motivation in many business settings. New management practices such as the use of various kinds of work teams and of flatter, more decentralized methods of organizing are intended to empower employees throughout the organization. Organizations that want to empower their employees need to understand a variety of issues as they go about promoting participation. Flexible work arrangements are commonly used today to enhance motivated job performance. Among the more popular alternative arrangements are compressed workweeks, flexible work schedules, extended work schedules, job sharing, and telecommuting.

The goal-setting theory of motivation suggests that appropriate goal difficulty, specificity, acceptance, and commitment will result in higher levels of motivated performance. Management by objectives, or MBO, extends goal setting throughout an organization by cascading goals down from the top of the firm to the bottom.

Performance measurement is the process by which work behaviors are measured and compared with established standards and the results recorded and communicated. Its purposes are to evaluate employees' work performance and to provide information for organizational uses such as compensation, personnel planning, and employee training and development. Three primary issues in performance appraisal are who does the appraisals, how often they are done, and how performance is measured.

The purpose of the reward system is to attract, retain, and motivate qualified employees and to maintain a pay structure that is internally equitable and externally competitive. Rewards have both surface and symbolic value. Rewards take the form of money, indirect compensation or benefits, perquisites, awards, and incentives. Factors such as motivational impact, cost, and fit with the organizational system must be considered when designing or analyzing a reward system.

The effective management of a reward system requires that performance be linked with rewards. Managing rewards entails dealing with issues such as flexible reward systems, employee participation in the pay system, the secrecy of pay systems, and expatriate rewards.

LOSKUTNIKOV/SHUTTERSTOCK.COM

REAL WORLD RESPONSE

ORCHESTRATING OUTCOMES

The Orpheus Chamber Orchestra was conceived to help eliminate the disconnect between motivation and satisfaction that exists in many orchestras. Indeed, the first principle in what's now known as the "Orpheus Process" is this: "Put power in the hands of the people doing the work." In most orchestras, the conductor makes more or less autocratic decisions about what will be played and how. The input of musicians is neither sought nor welcomed, and unsolicited advice may be sharply rebuffed—and may, in fact, serve as grounds for dismissal. At Orpheus, says Parker, "we have a completely different structure to the way we approach rehearsal": A core team of players selected by the orchestra from each instrument section plans and leads rehearsals for a given piece of music.

According to Harvey Seifter, a consultant specializing in relationships between business and the arts,

(Continued)

the Orpheus Process consists of five elements designed to put this principle into practice:

1. *Choosing leaders:* For each piece of music that the orchestra decides to perform, members select a leadership team composed of five to seven musicians. This "core team" then leads rehearsals and serves as a conduit for members' input. It's also responsible for seeing that the final performance reflects "a unified vision."
2. *Developing strategies:* Prior to rehearsals, the core team decides how a piece of music will be played. Its ultimate goal is to ensure "an overall interpretive approach to the music," and it works to meet this goal by trying out various approaches to the music during rehearsals with the full orchestra.
3. *Developing the product:* Once an interpretive approach has been chosen, rehearsals are geared toward refining it. At this point, players make suggestions and critique the playing of their colleagues. It is, of course, a highly collaborative stage in the process, and its success depends on mutual respect. "We're all specialists—that's the beginning of the discussion," says violinist Martha Caplin. "When I talk to … another musician in the group, it's on an equal level. It's absolutely crucial that we have that attitude." When disagreements arise, everyone works toward a consensus, and if a consensus can't be reached, the issue is settled by a vote. Violinist Eriko Sato also emphasizes that the process of collaborative input works best when members focus their contributions on outcomes of the highest possible quality: "Fundamentally," she says, "I don't think everybody's opinion should be addressed at all times. There are certain places and times for certain things to be said. The appropriate moment. Everybody knows what's wrong, everybody can feel what's wrong. But do you have a *solution*? Do you know how to solve a problem?"
4. *Perfecting the product:* Just before each concert, a couple of members take seats in the hall to listen to the performance from the audience's perspective. Then they report to the full ensemble and may suggest some final adjustments.
5. *Delivering the product:* The final performance is the ultimate result of the Orpheus Process, but it isn't the last step. When the concert is over, members get together to share their impressions of the performance and to make suggestions for even further refinements.

"If you ask any musician in the orchestra why they love playing with Orpheus," says Parker, "it's because they feel empowered. They don't have anyone telling them what to do. They walk into the rehearsal hall and it's their opportunity to influence [and] shape music, to make music with all their experience, all their training coming together." Ask double bass player Don Palma, for instance. Palma took a sabbatical after one year with Orpheus to play with the Los Angeles Philharmonic. "I just hated it," he says. "I didn't like to be told what to do all the time, being treated like I wasn't really worth anything other than to be a good soldier and just sit there and do as I was told. I felt powerless to affect things. … I felt frustrated, and there was nothing I could … do to help make things better." By contrast, says Palma, "Orpheus keeps me involved. I have some measure of participation in the direction the music is going to take. I think that's why a lot of us have stayed involved so long."

DISCUSSION QUESTIONS

1. What are the primary similarities and differences between job enrichment and the approach proposed by job characteristics theory?
2. What are the motivational consequences of increased employee involvement from the frame of reference of expectancy and equity theories?
3. What motivational problems might result from an organization's attempt to set up work teams?
4. Which form of a flexible work schedule might you prefer? How do you think you would like telecommuting?
5. Develop a framework whereby an instructor could use goal setting in running a class such as this one.
6. Why are employees having their performance measured and evaluated all the time instead of simply being left alone to do their jobs?
7. In what ways is your performance as a student evaluated? How is the performance of your instructor measured? What are the limitations of this method?
8. Can performance on some jobs simply not be measured? Why or why not?
9. As a student in this class, what "rewards" do you receive in exchange for your time and effort?

UNDERSTAND YOURSELF EXERCISE

Making Tough Decisions

Listed below are your notes on the performance of eight managers who work for you. Working alone, recommend salary increases for eight managers who have just completed their first year with the company and are now to be considered for their first annual raise. Keep in mind that you may be setting precedents and that you need to keep salary costs down. However, there are no formal company restrictions on the kind of raises you can give. Indicate the sizes of the raises that you would like to give each manager by writing a percentage next to each name.

Variations: The instructor might alter the situation in one of several ways. One way is to assume that all of the eight managers entered the company at the same salary, say $30,000, which gives a total salary expense of $240,000. If upper management has allowed a salary raise pool of 10 percent of the current salary expenses, then you as the manager have $24,000 to give out as raises. In this variation, students can deal with actual dollar amounts rather than just percentages for the raises. Another interesting variation is to assume that all of the managers entered the company at different salaries, averaging $30,000. (The instructor can create many interesting possibilities for how these salaries might vary.) Using whatever additional information provided by your instructor, you must then suggest salaries for the different managers.

_____ % Abraham McGowan. Abe is not, as far as you can tell, a good performer. You have checked your view with others, and they do not feel that he is effective either. However, you happen to know he has one of the toughest workgroups to manage. His subordinates have low skill levels, and the work is dirty and hard. If you lose him, you are not sure whom you could find to replace him.

_____ % Benjy Berger. Benjy is single and seems to live the life of a carefree bachelor. In general, you feel that his job performance is not up to par, and some of his "goofs" are well known to his fellow employees.

_____ % Clyde Clod. You consider Clyde to be one of your best subordinates. However, it is obvious that other people do not consider him to be an effective manager. Clyde has married a rich wife, and as far as you know, he does not need additional money.

_____ % David Doodle. You happen to know from your personal relationship with "Doodles" that he badly needs more money because of certain personal problems he is having. As far as you are concerned, he also happens to be one of the best of your subordinates. For some reason, your enthusiasm is not shared by your other subordinates, and you have heard them make joking remarks about his performance.

_____ % Ellie Ellesberg. Ellie has been very successful so far in the tasks she has undertaken. You are particularly impressed by this because she has a hard job. She needs money more than many of the other people, and you are sure that they respect her because of her good performance.

_____ % Fred Foster. Fred has turned out to be a very pleasant surprise to you. He has done an excellent job, and it is generally accepted among the others that he is one of the best people at the company. This surprises you because he is constantly frivolous and does not seem to care very much about money and promotion.

_____ % Greta Goslow. Your opinion is that Greta is just not cutting the mustard. Surprisingly enough, however, when you check to see how others feel about her, you discover that her work is very highly regarded. You also know that she badly needs a raise. She was recently widowed and is finding it extremely difficult to support her household and her young family of four.

_____ % Harry Hummer. You know Harry personally, and he just seems to squander his money continually. He has a fairly easy job assignment, and your view is that he does not do it particularly well. You are, therefore, quite surprised to find that several of the other new managers think that he is the best of the new group.

After you have made the assignments for the eight people, you will have a chance to discuss them either in groups or in the larger class.

Follow-Up Questions

1. Is there a clear difference between the highest and lowest performer? Why or why not?
2. Did you notice differences in the types of information that you had available to make the raise decisions? How did you use the different sources of information?
3. In what ways did your assignment of raises reflect different views of motivation?

Source: *Lawler, E. E., III. (1975). Motivation Through Compensation, adapted by D. T. Hall. In Instructor's Manual for Experiences in Management and Organizational Behavior. New York: John Wiley & Sons.*

GROUP EXERCISE

Fad Versus Substance

Albert Q. Fixx, the founder and CEO of your company, a small manufacturer of auto parts, has long been committed to the continuous improvement of the firm's management practices through the application of modern management techniques. It seems that Mr. Fixx spent the past weekend at a seminar conducted by a nationally respected consultant on management effectiveness. The principal speaker and the group sessions focused squarely on the use of employee participation as means of improving company-wide productivity and enhancing employees' commitment to their jobs.

So inspired was Mr. Fixx by his weekend experience that he went straight back to his office on Sunday night, where he composed and sent an e-mail that all managers would find in their inboxes bright and early on Monday morning. After recapping his eye-opening weekend, he wrote the following:

> I am convinced that participative management is the key to improving productivity at this company. Because you did not have the advantage of attending the same seminar that I did, I am attaching copies of all the handouts that were given to participants. They explain everything you need to know about practicing participative management, and I expect all of you to begin putting these principles into practice, starting this week. As of now, both I myself and this company are committed to participative management. Those of you who do not undertake the application of participative-management principles in your departments will find it very difficult to remain with a forward-looking company like A.Q. Fixx.

Your instructor will divide the class into groups of four to seven people. Each member of the group will pretend to be a manager at A.Q. Fixx, and your group of "managers" will discuss each of the following issues. Be prepared to discuss the group's thinking on each issue, even if the group doesn't reach a consensus.

Questions

1. What are the chances that Mr. Fixx's e-mail will spur effective participative management at the company? Are the odds better or worse than 50/50?
2. How has each individual manager responded to the e-mail? Is your response consistent with that of most group members, or do you find yourself taking a stance that's different, even if only slightly so? If you've taken a different stance, do you think it's worthwhile trying to convince the group to come around to your way of thinking? Why or why not?
3. What is the group's opinion of Mr. Fixx's approach to implementing participative management at the company? If you don't regard his approach as the best way of implementing participative practices—or his e-mail as the best means of introducing the subject—discuss some ways in which he could he have improved his approach.

VIDEO EXERCISE

Flight 001

Until the late 1990s, Brad John and John Sencion worked in different areas of New York's fashion industry. Both traveled often between the United States, Europe, and Japan for work. No matter how many times they began a trip, they spent the days and hours racing all over town picking up last-minute essentials. By the time they got to the airport, they were sweaty, stressed, and miserable—not exactly the glamorous existence they envisioned when they got into the fashion industry.

Then, during a flight from New York to Paris in 1998, the weary travelers came up with an idea for a one-stop travel shop targeted at fashion-forward globetrotters like themselves. They called it Flight 001 and began selling guidebooks, cosmetics, laptop bags, luggage, electronic gadgets, passport covers, and other consumer products. Flight 001 is now hailed as one of the most exciting businesses in the industry. In addition to selling useful travel merchandise, the New York-based retailer offers a unique shopping experience: Flight 001 stores are shaped like airplane fuselages tricked out with retro airport décor and accessories. In the years to come, the founders expect to be in every major city in the United States, Europe, and Asia.

But as the company embarks on a new five-year plan, the stretch goal of opening as many as thirty new stores in the United States and overseas is beginning to hit turbulence. Co-founder Brad John is determined to make Flight 001 the international authority on travel, but ambitious plans will require changes to the company's staffing, merchandising, and financial planning. With all the talk about expansion and new product lines, it will be increasingly important that Flight 001 not become distracted from what makes it special in the first place: location, design, and an impeccable product line.

Questions

1. Can you describe Brad's motivation in terms of the goal-setting theory of motivation?
2. How does Emily see her job from the standpoint of motivating Flight 001 employees? What motivates her?
3. What are the roles of performance management and individual rewards in a start-up company like Flight 001?

Now What?

VIDEO CASE

PERCOM/SHUTTERSTOCK.COM

Imagine that a coworker is complaining to you about being upset after learning that another coworker is being paid more despite the complaining coworker being at the company a year longer. *What do you say or do?* Go to this chapter's "Now What?" video, watch the challenge video, and choose a response. Be sure to also view the outcomes of the two responses you didn't choose.

Discussion Questions

1. What role do rewards play in this situation? How do the surface and symbolic values of the rewards influence what happens?

2. In chapter 5 we discussed equity theory. How do the concepts from equity theory apply to this situation? Explain your answer.
3. As a manager, what could you have done to better handle the situation? Why would this be a better solution?

ENDNOTES

[1]Schweitzer, V. (2007, May 7). Players with No Conductor and, Increasingly, with No Fear. *The New York Times*; Tommasini, A. (2008, October 18). The Pluses and Minuses of Lacking a Conductor. *The New York Times*; Higgs, J. (2008, October 28). Orpheus Chamber Orchestra Embodies Democratic Principles. *Axiom News*; Gordon, A. (2009, April 25). Self-Governing Orpheus Chamber Orchestra Has Broader Lessons to Offer, Says Banking and Civic Leader John Whitehead. *New York Sun*; Seifter, H. (2001, Summer). The Conductorless Orchestra. *Leader to Leader Journal*, *21*; Hackman, J. R. (2002). *Leading Teams: Setting the Stage for Great Performances*. Cambridge, MA: Harvard Business School Press.

[2]Griffin, R. W., & McMahan, G. C. (1994). Motivation Through Job Design. In *Organizational Behavior: State of the Science,* ed. J. Greenberg (pp. 23–44). New York: Lawrence Erlbaum Associates; see also Grant, A. M., Fried, Y. & Juillerat, T. (2010). Work Matters: Job Design in Classic and Contemporary Perspectives. In *Handbook of Industrial and Organizational Psychology,* ed. S. Zedeck (pp. 417–453). Washington, DC: American Psychological Association.

[3]Taylor, F. W. (1911). *The Principles of Scientific Management*. New York: Harper & Row.

[4]Griffin, R. W. (1982) *Task Design: An Integrative Approach*. Glenview, IL: Scott, Foresman.

[5]Conant, H. & Kilbridge, M. (1965). An Interdisciplinary Analysis of Job Enlargement: Technology, Cost, Behavioral Implications. *Industrial and Labor Relations Review*, *18*(7), 377–396.

[6]Herzberg, F. (1968, January–February). One More Time: How Do You Motivate Employees? *Harvard Business Review*, 53–62; Frederick Herzberg, F. (1974, September–October). The Wise Old Turk. *Harvard Business Review*, 70–80.

[7]Ford, R. N. (1973, January–February). Job Enrichment Lessons from AT&T. *Harvard Business Review*, 96–106.

[8]Weed, E. D. (1971). Job Enrichment "Cleans Up" at Texas Instruments. In *New Perspectives in Job Enrichment,* ed. J. R. Maher. New York: Van Nostrand.

[9]Griffin, R. W. (1982) *Task Design: An Integrative Approach*. Glenview, IL: Scott, Foresman; Griffin, R. W., & McMahan, G. C. (1994). Motivation Through Job Design. In *Organizational Behavior: State of the Science,* ed. J. Greenberg (pp. 23–44). New York: Lawrence Erlbaum Associates.

[10]Hackman, J. R., & Oldham, G. (1976). Motivation Through the Design of Work: Test of a Theory. *Organizational Behavior and Human Performance*, *16*, 250–279. See also Michael A. Campion, M. A., & Thayer, P. W. (1987, Winter). Job Design: Approaches, Outcomes, and Trade-Offs. *Organizational Dynamics*, 66–78.

[11]Griffin, R. W. (1982) *Task Design: An Integrative Approach*. Glenview, IL: Scott, Foresman.

[12]Griffin, R. W. (1982) *Task Design: An Integrative Approach*. Glenview, IL: Scott, Foresman. See also Roberts, K. H., & Glick, W. (1981). The Job Characteristics Approach to Task Design: A Critical Review. *Journal of Applied Psychology*, *66*, 193–217; and Griffin, R. W. (1987). Toward an Integrated Theory of Task Design. In *Research in Organizational Behavior,* eds. L. L. Cummings & B. M. Staw (Vol. 9, pp. 79–120). Greenwich, CT: JAI Press.

[13]Ricky W. Griffin, R. W., Welsh, N. A., & Moorhead, G. (1981, October). Perceived Task Characteristics and Employee Performance: A Literature Review. *Academy of Management Review*, 655–664.

[14]See Butler, T., & Waldroop, J. (1999, September–October). Job Sculpting. *Harvard Business Review*, 144–152; see also the recent special issue of the *Journal of Organizational Behavior* (*31*, 2–3, February 2010) devoted entirely to job design.

[15]Glew, D. J., O'Leary-Kelly, A. M., Griffin, R. W., & Van Fleet, D. D. (1995). Participation in Organizations: A Preview of the Issues and Proposed Framework for Future Analysis. *Journal of Management*, *21*(3), 395–421; for a recent update, see Forrester, R. (2002). Empowerment: Rejuvenating a Potent Idea. *Academy of Management Executive*, *14*(1), 67–78.

[16]Whitney, K. (2008). Netflix Creates its Own Script for Talent Management, Talent Management, July 1. Available online: http://talentmgt.com/articles/view/netflix_creates_its _own_script_for_talent_management/1; Conlin, M. (2007, September 24). Netflix: Flex to the Max. *BusinessWeek,* 73–74.

[17]Workplacedemocracy. (2010, January 18). Netflix Takes a Vacation from Its Vacation Policy. *Workplacedemocracy.com*. http://workplacedemocracy.com/2010/01/18/netflix-takes-avacation-from-its-vacation-policy/.

[18]Henneman, T. (2011, November 7). Patagonia Fills Payroll With People Who Are Passionate, Workforce. Available online: http://www.workforce.com/article/20111104/NEWS02/111109975.

[19]Whetton, D. A., & Cameron, K. S. (2002). *Developing Management Skills* (pp. 426–427). Upper Saddle River, NJ: Prentice-Hall.

[20]George, E., & Ng, C. K. (2010). Nonstandard Workers: Work Arrangements and Outcomes. In *Handbook of Industrial and Organizational Psychology,* ed. S. Zedeck (pp. 573–596). Washington, DC: American Psychological Association.

[21]Cohen A. R., & Gadon, H. (1978). *Alternative Work Schedules: Integrating Individual and Organizational Needs*. Reading, MA: Addison-Wesley); see also Kossek, E. E., & Michel, J.

S. (2010). Flexible Work Schedules. In *Handbook of Industrial and Organizational Psychology,* ed. S. Zedeck (pp. 535–572). Washington, DC: American Psychological Association.

[22]100 Best Companies to Work For 2012. www.fortune.com.

[23]See Rau, B., & and Hyland, M. (2002). Role Conflict and Flexible Work Arrangements: The Effects on Applicant Attraction. *Personnel Psychology*, *55*(1), 111–136.

[24]Working 9-to-5 No Longer. *USA Today*, December 6, 2004, 1B, 2B.

[25]5 Flextime-Friendly Companies. *Careerbuilder.com*, December 18, 2009. Available online: www.careerbuilder.com/Article/CB-632-Job-Search-Strategies-5-Flextime-Friendly-Companies.

[26]For a recent analysis, see Raghuram, S., Garud, R., Wiesenfeld, B., & Gupta, V. (2001). Factors Contributing to Virtual Work Adjustment. *Journal of Management*, *27*, 383–406.

[27]Katzenbach, J. R., & Santamaria, J. A. (1999, May–June). Firing Up the Front Line. *Harvard Business Review*, 107–117.

[28]Bandura, A. (1977). *Social Learning Theory*. Englewood Cliffs, NJ: Prentice Hall.

[29]See Locke, E. A. (1968). Toward a Theory of Task Performance and Incentives. *Organizational Behavior and Human Performance*, *3*, 157–189.

[30]Latham, G. P., & Yukl, G. (1975). A Review of Research on the Application of Goal Setting in Organizations. *Academy of Management Journal*, *18,* 824–846.

[31]Latham, G. P., & Baldes, J. J. (1975). The Practical Significance of Locke's Theory of Goal Setting. *Journal of Applied Psychology*, *60,* 187–191.

[32]Latham, G. P. (2001). The Importance of Understanding and Changing Employee Outcome Expectancies for Gaining Commitment to an Organizational Goal. *Personnel Psychology*, *54,* 707–720.

[33]See Zacharatos, A., Barling, J., & Iverson, R. (2005, January). High-Performance Work Systems and Occupational Safety. *Journal of Applied Psychology*, *90*(1), 77–94.

[34]Bernardin, H. J., & Beatty, R. W. (1984). *Performance Appraisal: Assessing Human Behavior at Work*. Boston: Kent); see also Wildman, J. L., Bedwell, W. L., Salas, E., & Smith-Jentsch, K. A. (2010) Performance Measurement at Work: A Multilevel Perspective. In *Handbook of Industrial and Organizational Psychology,* ed. S. Zedeck (pp. 303–341). Washington, DC: American Psychological Association.

[35]Brett, J., & Atwater, L. (2001). 360° Feedback: Accuracy, Reactions, and Perceptions of Usefulness. *Journal of Applied Psychology*, *86*(5), 930–942; Beehr, T., Ivanitskaya, L., Hansen, C., Erofeev, D., & Gudanowski, D. (2001). Evaluation of 360-Degree Feedback Ratings: Relationships with Each Other and with Performance and Selection Predictors. *Journal of Organizational Behavior*, *22,* 775–788.

[36]Druskat, V. U., & Wolff, S. B. (1999). Effects and Timing of Developmental Peer Appraisals in Self-Managing Work Groups. *Journal of Applied Psychology*, *84* (1), 58–74.

[37]Sammer, J. (2008, January). Calibrating Consistency. *HR Magazine*, 73–78.

[38]See Kaplan, R., & Norton, D. (1996). *The Balanced Scorecard: Translating Strategy Into Action*. Cambridge, MA: Harvard Business Review Press; and Kaplan, R., & Norton, D. (2006). *Alignment: Using the Balanced Scorecard to Create Corporate Synergies*. Cambridge, MA: Harvard Business Review Press.

[39]See Lawler, E. E. (1981). *Pay and Organization Development*. Reading, MA: Addison-Wesley, 1981); see also Martocchio, J. J. (2010). Strategic Reward and Compensation Plans. In *Handbook of Industrial and Organizational Psychology,* ed. S. Zedeck (pp. 343–372). Washington, DC: American Psychological Association.

[40]Boyd, B, & Salamin, A. (2001). Strategic Reward Systems: A Contingency Model of Pay System Design. *Strategic Management Journal*, *22,* 777–792.

[41]References: Stossel, J., et al. (2007, September 14). Health Savings Accounts: Putting Patients in Control. *ABC News*. Available online: http://abcnews.go.com; Mackey, J. (2009, August 11). The Whole Foods Alternative to ObamaCare. *Wall Street Journal*. Available at: http://online.wsj.com; Dugan, J. (2009, August 20). Whole Foods' Crummy Insurance: What John Mackey Means by "Choice." *Consumer Watchdog*. Available online: www.consumerwatchdog.org; Emily Friedman, E. (2009, August 14). Health Care Stirs Up Whole Foods CEO John Mackey, Customers Boycott Organic Grocery Store. *ABC News*. Available online: http://abcnews.go.com; Paumgarten, N. (2010, January 4). Food Fighter. *The New Yorker*. Available online: www.newyorker.com; Whole Foods CEO John Mackey Stepping Down as Chairman. *Huffington Post*, December 25, 2009. Available online: www.huffingtonpost.com.

[42]Rappaport, A. (1999, March–April). New Thinking on How to Link Executive Pay with Performance. *Harvard Business Review*, 91–99; see also Devers, C., Cannella, A., Jr., Reilly, G., & Yoder, M. (2007). Executive Compensation: A Multidisciplinary Review of Recent Developments. *Journal of Management*, *33*(6), 1016–1072.

[43]Bates, S. (2002, May). Piecing Together Executive Compensation. *HR Magazine*, 60–69.

[44]Welcome to Silicon Valley: Perksville, USA. *USA Today*, July 5, 2012, 1A.

[45]Painless Perks. *Forbes*, September 6, 1999, 138; see also Does Rank Have Too Much Privilege? *Wall Street Journal*, February 26, 2002, B1, B4.

[46]Garvey, C. (2004, August). Meaningful Tokens of Appreciation. *HR Magazine*, 101–106.

[47]Deckop, J. R., Mangel, R., & Cirka, C. C. (1999). Getting More Than You Pay For: Organizational Citizenship Behavior and Pay-for-Performance Plans. *Academy of Management Journal*, *42*(4), 420–428.

[48]Garvey, C. (2002, May). Steering Teams with the Right Pay. *HR Magazine*, 70–80.

[49]Poe, A. (2002, April). Selection Savvy. *HR Magazine*, 77–80.

[50]Griffin, R. W., & Pustay, M. W. (2005). *International Business—A Managerial Perspective* (8th ed.). Upper Saddle River, NJ: Pearson, 2015.

PART 3

SOCIAL AND GROUP PROCESSES IN ORGANIZATIONS

As you should recall from Chapter 1, managers work to make their organizations effective by enhancing performance behaviors, enhancing commitment and engagement, promoting citizenship behaviors, and minimizing dysfunctional behaviors by their employees. Chapter 2 identified several environmental factors that must be considered. In Part 2 we asked the question "Why do individuals do what they do?' and addressed this question by discussing individual characteristics, values, perceptions, and reactions, employee motivation concepts and theories, and how work and rewards can be used to enhance motivation.

In Part 3 we ask a different question: "Why do groups and teams do what they do?" As was the case with individuals, we need to look at a number of different perspectives to better understand group and team behaviors and their role in promoting organizational effectiveness. We start in Chapter 7 by discussing groups and teams as essential parts of organizations and therefore a major determinant of the success of any organization. We then describe decision making and problem solving in Chapter 8. Although decision making may also be an individual activity, it often takes place in a group or team context and usually affects others. Communication is covered in Chapter 9. Finally, Chapter 10 addresses another important set of factors related to groups and teams, conflict and negotiation. At the conclusion of Part 3 you should have a clearer understanding of why groups and teams do what they do.

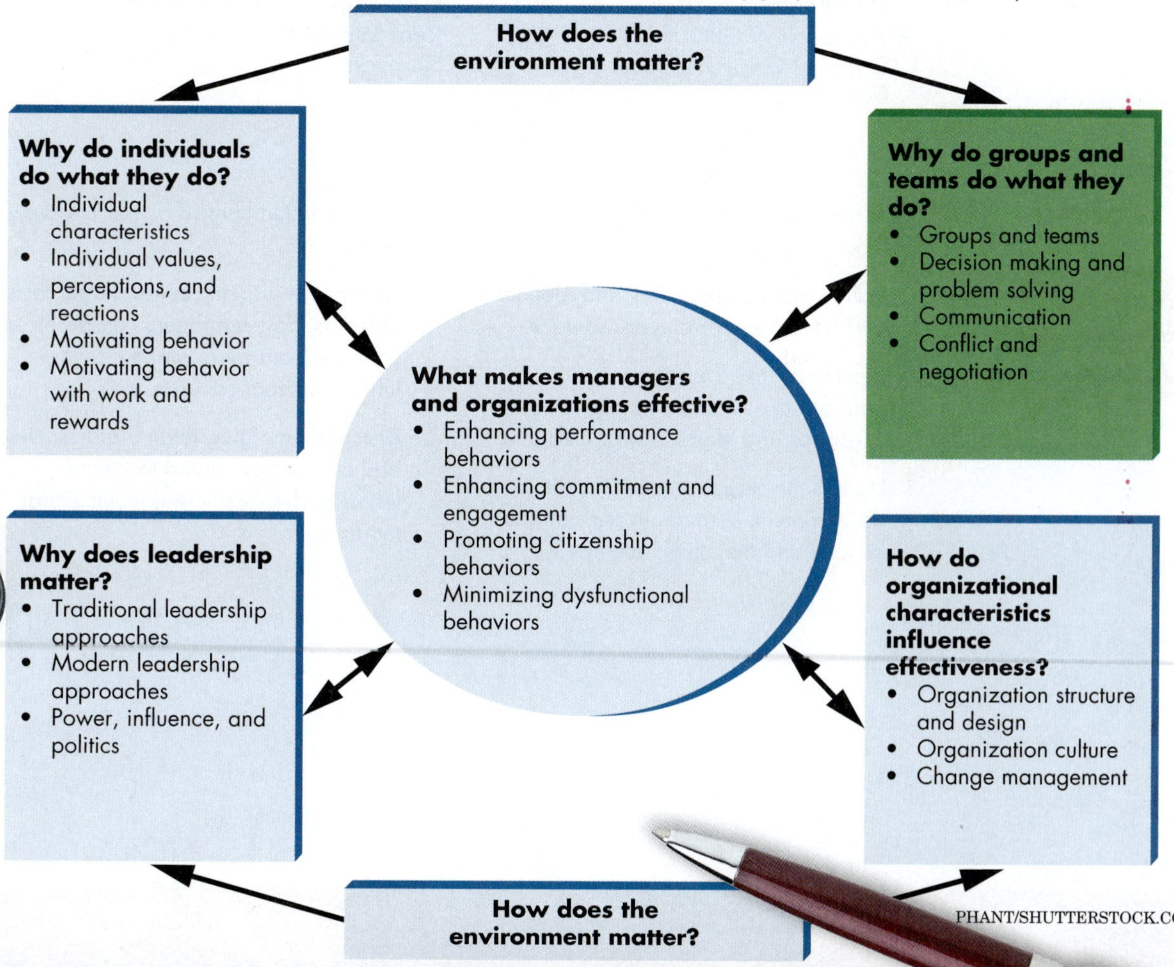

How does the environment matter?

Why do individuals do what they do?
- Individual characteristics
- Individual values, perceptions, and reactions
- Motivating behavior
- Motivating behavior with work and rewards

Why do groups and teams do what they do?
- Groups and teams
- Decision making and problem solving
- Communication
- Conflict and negotiation

What makes managers and organizations effective?
- Enhancing performance behaviors
- Enhancing commitment and engagement
- Promoting citizenship behaviors
- Minimizing dysfunctional behaviors

Why does leadership matter?
- Traditional leadership approaches
- Modern leadership approaches
- Power, influence, and politics

How do organizational characteristics influence effectiveness?
- Organization structure and design
- Organization culture
- Change management

How does the environment matter?

LOSKUTNIKOV/SHUTTERSTOCK.COM

CHAPTER 7

GROUPS AND TEAMS

CHAPTER OUTLINE

LEARNING OUTCOMES

After studying this chapter, you should be able to:

1. Define groups and teams and identify and describe several types of each.
2. Identify the five core group performance factors and relate them to groups and teams in organizations.
3. Discuss the stages of group and team development, other team performance factors, and the implementation process in the context of creating new teams.
4. Identify the primary benefits and costs of teams, how managers can promote effective team performance, and important team competencies.
5. Describe emerging team opportunities and challenges related to virtual teams and diversity and multicultural teams.

LOSKUTNIKOV/SHUTTERSTOCK.COM

REAL WORLD CHALLENGE

TEAMWORK AT STARBUCKS

Coffee giant Starbucks believes that teamwork is essential to its strategic execution and ultimate success.[1] Reinforcing this belief, Starbucks' core values include teamwork, diversity, and equal participation. Employees are called by their first names and are referred to as "partners" rather than by hierarchical titles. Teamwork is seen as so important to the company's success that new hires spend several days learning how to be part of the Starbucks team. Employees also work together on the front line, eliminating the distance between different statuses.[2]

When Starbucks started planning for its expansion into South Korea it realized that the country's culture valued hierarchical relationships and power distance, which were inconsistent with the company's equality and teamwork values. Starbucks had to decide if it wanted to change its organizational structure in South Korea to better fit the country's national culture, or stay the same to maintain its core values.[3]

Imagine that Starbucks asks for your advice on how it should handle its expansion into South Korea. After reading this chapter, you should have some good ideas.

MICHELLE GILDERS / ALAMY

In Chapter 1 we noted the pervasiveness of human behavior in organizations and the importance of interactions among people as critical to achieving important outcomes for organizations. Indeed, a great deal of all managerial work involves interacting with other people, both directly and indirectly and both inside and outside the organization. Moreover, much of the work in organizations is accomplished by people working together in groups and teams. This chapter is the first of four that deal primarily with interpersonal processes in organizations. The opening pages to this part again present the organizing framework for this book we developed back in Chapter 1. This will enable you to better understand where we are in our discussion and what lies ahead. We begin in this chapter by discussing groups and teams in organizations. In the next three chapters in this part we focus on decision making and problem solving (Chapter 8), interpersonal communication (Chapter 9), and conflict and negotiation (Chapter 10).

TYPES OF GROUPS AND TEAMS

group
Two or more people who interact with one another such that each person influences and is influenced by each other person

team
An interdependent collection of at least two individuals who share a common goal and share accountability for the team's as well as their own outcomes

There are literally hundreds of definitions of the term *group*. Groups have been defined in terms of perceptions, motivation, organization, interdependencies, interactions, and myriad other elements. We will simply define a ***group*** as two or more persons who interact with one another such that each person influences and is influenced by each other person.[4] Two people who are physically near each other are not a group unless they interact and have some influence on each other. Coworkers may work side by side on related tasks—but if they do not interact, they are not a group.

We should also note that groups and teams are not necessarily the same thing. All teams are groups, but not all groups are teams. We will define ***teams*** as an interdependent collection of at least two individuals who share a common goal and share accountability for the team's as well as their own outcomes.[5] A key part of this definition is that team members are interdependent with respect to information, resources, and skills. As tasks become more complex, they require greater coordination among team members. Team members' roles become interdependent, increasing the need for teamwork, reciprocal communication, and feedback. Communication and collaboration demands also increase dramatically.[6] So, all teams are groups, but groups are not necessarily teams. For the sake of convenience we will generally use terms 'groups' and 'teams' interchangeably in this discussion.

MONKEY BUSINESS IMAGES/SHUTTERSTOCK.COM

Groups are prevalent throughout most organizations. A variety of different kinds of workgroups and teams like this one perform many different kinds of functions and play a number of different roles.

Workgroups

Workgroups are formal groups established by the organization to do its work. Workgroups include command (or functional) groups and affinity groups (as well as teams). A ***command group*** is relatively permanent and is characterized by functional reporting relationships such as having both a group manager and those who report to the manager. Command groups are usually included in the organization chart. ***Affinity groups*** are relatively permanent collections of employees from the same level in the organization who meet on a regular basis to share information, capture emerging opportunities, and solve problems.[7]

workgroup
A formal group formed by an organization to do its work

command group
A relatively permanent, formal group with functional reporting relationships and is usually included in the organization chart

affinity groups
Collections of employees from the same level in the organization who meet on a regular basis to share information, capture emerging opportunities, and solve problems

In business organizations, most employees work in command groups, as typically specified on an official organization chart. The size, shape, and organization of a company's command groups can vary considerably. Typical command groups in organizations include the quality-assurance department, the customer service department, the cost-accounting department, and the human resource department. Other types of command groups include work teams organized as in the Japanese style of management, in which subsections of manufacturing and assembly processes are each assigned to a team of workers. The team members decide among themselves who will perform each task.

Affinity groups are a special type of formal group: They are set up by the organization, yet they are not really part of the formal organization structure. They are not really command groups because they are not part of the organizational hierarchy, yet they are not task groups because they stay in existence longer than any one task. Affinity groups are groups of employees who share roles, responsibilities, duties, and interests, and which represent horizontal slices of the normal organizational hierarchy. Because the members share important characteristics such as roles, duties, and levels, they are said to have an affinity for one another. The members of affinity groups usually have very similar job titles and similar duties but are in different divisions or departments within the organization.

Affinity groups meet regularly, and members have assigned roles such as recorder, reporter, facilitator, and meeting organizer. Members follow simple rules such as communicating openly and honestly, listening actively, respecting confidentiality, honoring time agreements, being prepared, staying focused, being individually accountable, and being supportive of each other and the group. The greatest benefits of affinity groups are that they cross existing boundaries of the organization and facilitate better communication among diverse departments and divisions throughout the organization. For instance, the Eli Lilly Company formally recognizes

MONKEY BUSINESS IMAGES/SHUTTERSTOCK.COM

Employees sometimes form groups to discuss or pursue common interests. These co-workers, for example, formed a book club. They periodically meet during their lunch break to discuss a book that they are all reading.

eight affinity groups within its organization. One focuses on Chinese Culture. Its members, including both Chinese and non-Chinese employees, meet regularly to help bridge cultural differences. Another group at Eli Lilly is called the Women's Network and focuses on gender issues. Employees in some companies form book clubs and meet regularly to discuss books of common interest.

Teams

Organizations also use a wide variety of different types of teams. The most common types of teams are summarized in Table 7.1. There are many different types of teams. Each type of team is composed of different members and responsible for different types of tasks. The members of ***functional teams*** come from the same department or functional area. A team of marketing employees and a team of finance employees are examples of functional teams.

functional team
A team whose members come from the same department or functional area

cross-functional team
A team whose members come from different departments or functional areas

Cross-functional teams have members from different departments or functional areas. This is one of the most common types of work teams. An example of a cross-functional team is a top management team with members representing different functions or units of the organization. Some organizations are organized such that the company's core work is done in cross-functional teams. For example, IDEO, a product innovation and design company, believes that interdisciplinary teamwork boosts innovation and creativity.[8] Teams share and improve ideas, building on their members' skills and providing more opportunities for problem solving. Steelcase; IDEO; Hammel, Green, and Abrahamson; and the Mayo Clinic all use cross-functional teams comprised of employees with different expertise to enhance creativity and team performance.[9]

Cross-functional teams have several strengths. In addition to getting things done faster, particularly customer service and new product development, they can increase creativity. Cross-functional teams also improve a firm's ability to solve complex problems by bringing different skill sets, perceptions, and experiences together. Because they bring diverse people from different functional areas together, they also increase employees' knowledge about other areas of the organization. The same diversity that can be a strength for

Table 7.1

Types of Teams

Functional teams	members come from the same department or functional area
Cross-functional teams	members come from different departments or functional areas
Problem-solving teams	teams created to solve problems and make improvements
Self-directed teams	set their own goals and pursue them in ways defined by the team
Venture teams	teams that operate semi-autonomously to create and develop new products, processes, or businesses
Virtual teams	teams of geographically and/or organizationally dispersed coworkers who communicate using telecommunications and information technologies
Global teams	face-to-face or virtual teams whose members are from different countries

cross-functional teams can also be a weakness if this diversity is not properly managed and conflicts are not effectively handled.

problem-solving teams
Teams established to solve problems and make improvements at work

Problem-solving teams are teams established to solve problems and make improvements at work. The core strength of problem-solving teams is that because employees are the ones actually doing the work, they usually know the job best. Putting employees on teams responsible for solving problems puts this expertise to work. For example, Colgate and JM Huber, a raw material supplier, jointly assembled a multidisciplinary team to identify ways to reduce costs. The team ultimately realized savings of hundreds of thousands of dollars.[10] Quality circles can exist for long periods whereas suggestion teams are short-lived and assembled to address specific issues. Problem-solving teams can also increase employees' commitment to decisions because they were involved in making them. Organizations are increasingly turning to outside teams to help them solve important problems. When online movie rental site Netflix sponsored a contest to improve the accuracy of its movie recommendation system, more than 40,000 teams from 186 countries formed to vie for the million dollar prize.[11]

self-directed teams
Teams that set their own goals and pursue them in ways decided by the team

Self-directed teams set their own goals and pursue them in ways decided by the team. Team members are responsible for tasks typically reserved for team leaders or managers, including scheduling work and vacations, ordering supplies, and evaluating their performance. At 3M, self-directed work teams have made improvements in products, services, and processes while increasing customer responsiveness, lowering operating costs, increasing productivity, and decreasing cycle times. Self-directed teams can improve commitment, quality, and efficiency. Cross-trained team members also help to increase the flexibility of the team during staffing shortages. Self-directed teams are difficult to implement, however, as they require specific self-management and team skills that many employees lack.

venture teams
Teams that operate semi-autonomously to create and develop new products (product development teams), processes (process design teams), or businesses (venture teams)

Venture teams are teams that operate semi-autonomously to create and develop new products (product development teams), processes (process design teams), or businesses (venture teams).[12] Separating a team from the formal structure of the rest of the organization can enhance its innovativeness and speed up cycle time.

virtual teams
Teams of geographically and/or organizationally dispersed coworkers who communicate using the Internet and other information technologies

Virtual teams are teams of geographically and/or organizationally dispersed coworkers who communicate using the Internet and other information technologies.[13] Some virtual team members may never see each other face-to-face. Many organizations use virtual teams to accomplish a variety of goals. For example, PricewaterhouseCoopers, one of the world's largest accounting firms, with more than 130,000 employees in 148 countries, uses virtual teams to bring employees from around the globe "together" for a week or two to prepare work

ANDREY_POPOV/SHUTTERSTOCK.COM

Virtual teams are becoming increasingly common in organizations. New forms of technology, coupled with pressures to reduce travel costs, make it easy for colleagues who are geographically dispersed to interact in ways that mirror face-to-face interactions. Of course, they may also have a reduced personal connection with their colleagues when meeting this way.

for a particular client. The Whirlpool Corporation used a virtual team composed of experts from the United States, Brazil, and Italy during a two-year project to develop a chlorofluorocarbon-free refrigerator.[14] You will learn more about virtual teams later in this chapter.

global teams
Teams with members from different countries

Global teams have members from different countries. Global teams can be virtual or meet face-to-face. Procter & Gamble, a multinational manufacturer of family, personal, and household care products, uses global teams to allow employees at its Cincinnati headquarters to collaborate with employees and suppliers all over the world. Bosch und Siemens Hausgeräte GmbH (BSH) is a global company that operates 31 production sites and 43 factories in 15 countries across Europe, Asia, the United States, and Latin America. The company sells household appliances under brand names including Bosch and Siemens, and uses global teams of employees from Spain, China, and Latin America to develop technologies and concepts for new products.

Informal Groups

informal group
Is established by its members

friendship group
Is relatively permanent and informal and draws its benefits from the social relationships among its members

interest group
Is relatively temporary and informal and is organized around a common activity or interest of its members

Whereas formal groups and teams are established by an organization, ***informal groups*** are formed by their members and consist of friendship groups, which are relatively permanent, and interest groups, which may be shorter-lived. ***Friendship groups*** arise out of cordial relationships among members and the enjoyment they get from being together. ***Interest groups*** are organized around a common activity or interest, although friendships may develop among members.

Good examples of interest groups are the networks of working women that have developed over the last few decades. Many of these groups began as informal social gatherings of women who wanted to meet with other women working in male-dominated organizations, but they soon developed into interest groups whose benefits went far beyond their initial social purposes. The networks became information systems for counseling, job placement, and management training. Some networks were eventually established as formal, permanent associations; some remained informal groups based more on social relationships than on any specific interest; others were dissolved. These groups may be partly responsible for the dramatic increase in the percentage of women in managerial and administrative jobs.

GROUP PERFORMANCE FACTORS

The performance of any group is affected by several factors (in addition to its reasons for forming and the stages of its development, discussed later). In a high-performing group, a group synergy often develops in which the group's performance is more than the sum of the individual contributions of its members. Several additional factors may account for this accelerated performance.[15] The five basic group performance factors are composition, size, norms, cohesiveness, and informal leadership. If you are part of a group or team that is not performing effectively, the *Improve Your Skills* feature might be a useful diagnostic tool.

ILDOGESTO/SHUTTERSTOCK.COM

IMPROVE YOUR SKILLS

DIAGNOSING TEAM PROBLEMS

Here are some questions you can ask in diagnosing team issues.

1. Clear direction
   - Can team members each articulate the purpose that the team exists to achieve?
2. A real team task
   - Is the team assigned collective responsibility for all of its customers and major outputs?
   - Does the team make collective decisions about work strategies (rather than leaving it to individuals)?
   - Are team members willing and able to help each other?
   - Does the team get team-level feedback about its performance?
3. Team rewards
   - Are more than 80 percent of all rewards available to teams only, and not to individuals?
4. Basic material resources
   - Does the team have its own meeting space?
   - Can the team easily get the basic materials it needs to do its work?
5. Authority to manage the work
   - Do team members have the authority to decide the following without first receiving special authorization?
   - How to meet client demands
   - Which actions to take, and when
   - Whether to change their work strategies when they deem necessary
6. Team goals
   - Can team members articulate specific and shared team goals?
7. Improvement norms
   - Do team members encourage each other to detect and solve problems?
   - Do members openly discuss differences in what members have to contribute to the team?
   - Do members encourage experimentation with new ways of operating?
   - Does the team actively seek to learn from other teams?

Source: Wageman, R. (1997, Summer). Critical Success Factors for Creating Superb Self-Managing Teams. *Organizational Dynamics, 26* (1), 59.

Group Composition

The composition of a group plays an important role in determining group productivity.[16] ***Group composition*** is most often described in terms of the homogeneity or heterogeneity of the members. A group is homogeneous if the members are similar in one or several ways that are critical to the work of the group, such as in age, work experience, education, technical specialty, or cultural background. In heterogeneous groups, the members differ in one or more ways that are critical to the work of the group. Homogeneous groups often are created in organizations when people are assigned to command groups based on a similar technical specialty. Although the people who work in such command groups may differ in some ways, such as in age or work experience, they are homogeneous in terms of a critical work performance variable: technical specialty.[17]

group composition
The degree of similarity or difference among group members on factors important to the group's work

A substantial amount of research has explored the relationship between a group's composition and its productivity. The group's heterogeneity in terms of age and tenure with the group has been shown to be related to turnover: Groups with members of different ages and experiences with the group tend to experience frequent changes in membership.[18] A homogeneous group is likely to be more productive when the group task is simple, cooperation is necessary, the group tasks are sequential, or quick action is required. A heterogeneous group is more likely to be productive when the task is complex, requires a collective effort (that is, each member does a different task, and the sum of these efforts constitutes the group output), demands creativity, and when speed is less important than thorough deliberations. For example, a group asked to generate ideas for marketing a new product probably needs to be heterogeneous to develop as many different ideas as possible.

The link between group composition and type of task is explained by the interactions typical of homogeneous and heterogeneous groups. A homogeneous group tends to have less conflict, fewer differences of opinion, smoother communication, and more interactions. When a task requires cooperation and speed, a homogeneous group is therefore more desirable. If, however, the task requires complex analysis of information and creativity to arrive at the best possible solution, a heterogeneous group may be more appropriate because it generates a wide range of viewpoints. More discussion and more conflict are likely, both of which can enhance the group's decision making.

Group composition becomes especially important as organizations become increasingly more culturally diverse.[19] Cultures differ in the importance they place on group membership and in how they view authority, uncertainty, and other important factors. Increasing attention is being focused on how to deal with groups made up of people from different cultures.[20] In general, a manager in charge of a culturally diverse group can expect several things. First, members will probably distrust one another. Stereotyping will present a problem, and communication problems will almost certainly arise. Thus, managers need to recognize that such groups will seldom function smoothly, at least at first. Managers may therefore need to spend more time helping a culturally diverse group through the rough spots as it matures, and they should allow a longer-than-normal time before expecting it to carry out its assigned task.

Group Size

A group can have as few as two members or as many members as can interact and influence one another. Group size—the number of people in the group—can have an important effect on performance. A group with many members has more resources available and may be able to complete a large number of relatively independent tasks. In groups established to generate ideas, those with more members tend to produce more ideas, although the rate of increase in the number of ideas diminishes rapidly as the group grows.[21] Beyond a certain point, the greater complexity of interactions and communication may make it more difficult for a large group to achieve agreement.

Interactions and communication are much more likely to be formalized in larger groups. Large groups tend to set agendas for meetings and to follow a protocol or parliamentary procedure to control discussion. As a result, time that otherwise might be available to work on tasks is taken up in administrative duties such as organizing and structuring the interactions and communications

The size of a group may impact the ability of its members to interact with one another. This group, for instance, is probably too large to function effectively as a single entity. In all likelihood the group members will form smaller sub-groups, which some of them seem to be doing.

within the group. Also, the large size may inhibit participation of some people and increase absenteeism; some people may stop trying to make a meaningful contribution and may even stop coming to group meetings if their repeated attempts to contribute or participate are thwarted by the sheer number of similar efforts by other members. Furthermore, large groups present more opportunities for interpersonal attraction, leading to more social interactions and fewer task interactions. ***Social loafing*** is the tendency of some members of groups not to put forth as much effort in a group situation as they would working alone. Social loafing often results from the assumption by some members that if they do not work hard, other members will pick up the slack. How much of a problem this becomes depends on the nature of the task, the characteristics of the people involved, and the ability of the group leadership to be aware of the potential problem and do something about it.

social loafing
The tendency of some members of groups to put forth less effort in a group than they would when working alone

The most effective size of a group, therefore, is determined by the group members' ability to interact and influence each other effectively. The need for interaction is affected by the maturity of the group, the tasks of the group, the maturity of individual members, and the ability of the group leader or manager to manage the communication, potential conflicts, and task activities. In some situations, the most effective group size is three or four; other groups can function effectively with fifteen or more members.

Group Norms

A ***norm*** is a standard against which the appropriateness of a behavior is judged. Thus, norms determine the behavior expected in a certain situation. Group norms usually are established during the second stage of group development (communication and decision making) and are carried forward into the maturity stage. By providing a basis for predicting others' behaviors, norms enable people to behave in a manner consistent with and acceptable to the group. Without norms, the activities in a group would be chaotic.

norm
A standard against which the appropriateness of a behavior is judged

Norms result from the combination of members' personality characteristics, the situation, the task, and the historical traditions of the group.[22] Norms can be positive or negative for individual and organizational outcomes because group members tend to follow them even if the consequences are negative. Lack of conformity to group norms may result in attempts to correct the deviant behavior, verbal abuse, physical threats, ostracism, or even ejection from the group. Group norms are enforced, however, only for actions that are important to group members. For example, if the office norm is for employees to wear suits to convey a professional image to clients, a staff member who wears blue jeans and a sweatshirt violates the group norm and will hear about it quickly. But if the norm is that dress is unimportant because little contact with

Groups norms reflect standards of behavior that group members establish for themselves. This group, for example, likely has norms about appropriate attire–they are each dressed very similarly to one another.

clients occurs in the office, the fact that someone wears blue jeans may not even be noticed.

Norms serve four purposes in organizations. First, they help the group survive. Groups tend to reject deviant behavior that does not help meet group goals or contribute to the survival of the group if it is threatened. Accordingly, a successful group that is not under threat may be more tolerant of deviant behavior. Second, they simplify and make more predictable the behaviors expected of group members. Because they are familiar with norms, members do not have to analyze each behavior and decide on a response. Members can anticipate the actions of others on the basis of group norms, usually resulting in increased productivity and goal attainment. Third, norms help the group avoid embarrassing situations. Group members often want to avoid damaging other members' self-images and are likely to avoid certain subjects that might hurt a member's feelings. And finally, norms express the central values of the group and identify the group to others. Certain clothes, mannerisms, or behaviors in particular situations may be a rallying point for members and may signify to others the nature of the group.[23]

Group Cohesiveness

group cohesiveness
The extent to which a group is committed to staying together

Group cohesiveness is the extent to which a group is committed to remaining together; it results from forces acting on the members to remain in the group. The forces that create cohesiveness are attraction to the group, resistance to leaving the group, and motivation to remain a member of the group.[24] As shown in Figure 7.1, group cohesiveness is related to many aspects of

Figure 7.1

The factors that increase and decrease cohesiveness and the consequences of high and low cohesiveness indicate that although it is often preferable to have a highly cohesive group, in some situations the effects of a highly cohesive group can be negative for the organization.

Factors That Affect Group Cohesiveness and Consequences of Group Cohesiveness

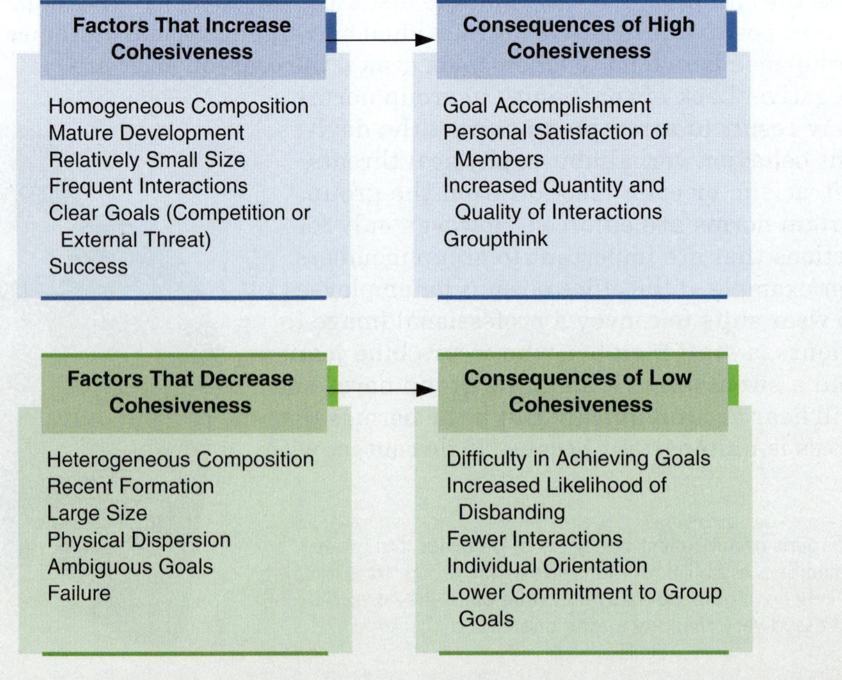

group dynamics: maturity, homogeneity, manageable size, and frequency of interactions.

The figure also shows that group cohesiveness can be increased by competition or by the presence of an external threat. Either factor can focus members' attention on a clearly defined goal and increase their willingness to work together. Finally, successfully reaching goals often increases the cohesiveness of a group because people are proud to be identified with a winner and to be thought of as competent and successful. This may be one reason behind the popular expression "Success breeds success." A group that is successful may become more cohesive and hence possibly even more successful. Of course, other factors can get in the way of continued success, such as personal differences, egos, and the lure of more individual success in other activities.

Research on group performance factors has focused on the relationship between cohesiveness and group productivity.[25] Highly cohesive groups appear to be more effective at achieving their goals than groups that are low in cohesiveness, especially in research and development groups in U.S. companies.[26] However, highly cohesive groups will not necessarily be more productive in an organizational sense than groups with low cohesiveness. As Figure 7.2 illustrates, when a group's goals are compatible with the organizational goals, a cohesive group probably will be more productive than one that is not cohesive. In other words, if a highly cohesive group has the goal of contributing to the good of the organization, it is very likely to be productive in organizational terms. If such a group decides on a goal that has little to do with the business of the organization, it will probably work to achieve its own goal even at the expense of any organizational goals that might compromised by the group's efforts.

Cohesiveness may also be a primary factor in the development of certain problems for some decision-making groups. An example is ***groupthink***, which

groupthink
when a group's overriding concern is a unanimous decision rather than critical analysis of alternatives.

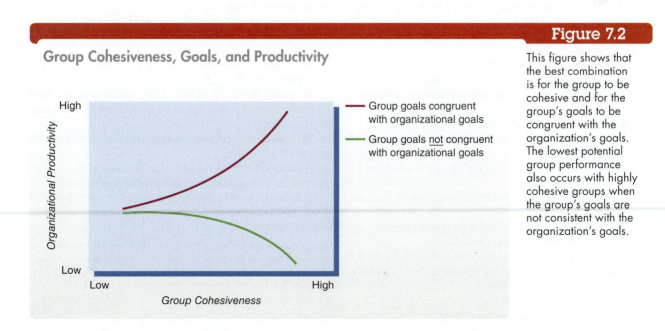

Figure 7.2

Group Cohesiveness, Goals, and Productivity

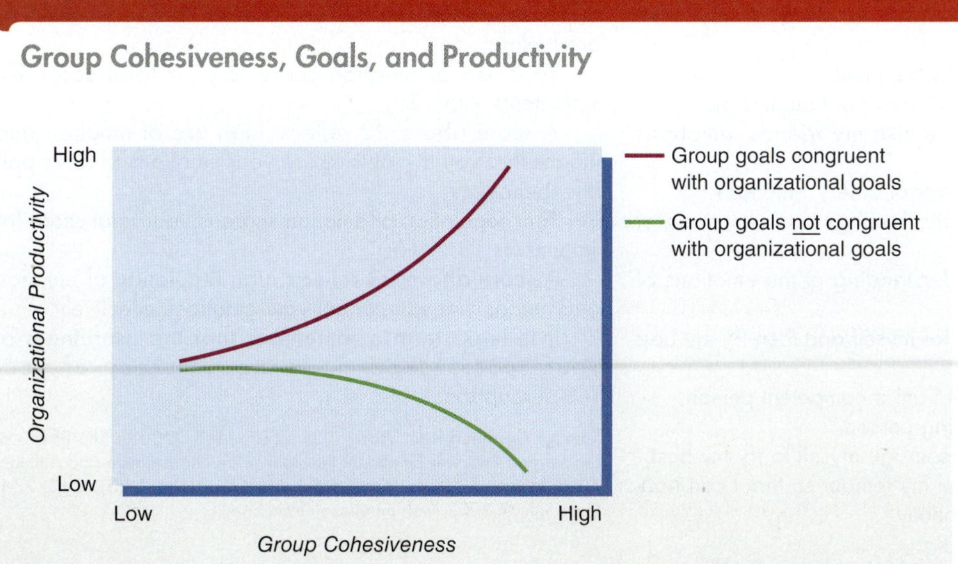

This figure shows that the best combination is for the group to be cohesive and for the group's goals to be congruent with the organization's goals. The lowest potential group performance also occurs with highly cohesive groups when the group's goals are not consistent with the organization's goals.

occurs when a group's overriding concern is a unanimous decision rather than critical analysis of alternatives.[27] (We discuss groupthink in Chapter 8.) These problems, together with the evidence regarding group cohesiveness and productivity, mean that a manager must carefully weigh the pros and cons of fostering highly cohesive groups.

Finally, there is emerging evidence that the emotional intelligence of group members can promote cohesiveness. In this context emotional intelligence refers

UNDERSTAND YOURSELF

ARE YOU EMOTIONALLY INTELLIGENT?

Emotional intelligence will help you to be a more effective group and team member, and increase your effectiveness in many other areas as well. The following sixteen questions will help you to assess yourself on four aspects of emotional intelligence. Please answer each question honestly using the following scale. Write the number from 1 to 7 that corresponds to your answer on the scale in the space to the left of each item number.

strongly disagree	disagree	slightly disagree	neutral	slightly agree	agree	strongly agree
1	2	3	4	5	6	7

___ 1. I have a good sense of why I have certain feelings most of the time.
___ 2. I have a good understanding of my own emotions.
___ 3. I really understand what I feel.
___ 4. I always know whether or not I am happy.
___ 5. I can always distinguish my friends' emotions from their behavior.
___ 6. I am a good observer of others' emotions.
___ 7. I am sensitive to the feelings and emotions of others.
___ 8. I have a good understanding of the emotions of people around me.
___ 9. I always set goals for myself and then try my best to achieve them.
___ 10. I always tell myself I am a competent person.
___ 11. I am a self-motivating person.
___ 12. I would always encourage myself to try my best.
___ 13. I am able to control my temper so that I can handle difficulties rationally.
___ 14. I am quite capable of controlling my own emotions.
___ 15. I can always calm down quickly when I am very angry.
___ 16. I have good control of my own emotions.

Scoring and Interpretation: Each score is out of a maximum score of 28. The accuracy and usefulness of your score depends on the accuracy of your self-perceptions.

Your self-emotion appraisal score is your total score for statements 1 to 4: ___

A score above 23 reflects high self-emotion appraisal and means that you have a good understanding of your own emotions.

Your others' emotion appraisal score is your total score for statements 5 to 8: ___

A score above 22 reflects high others' emotion appraisal and means that you are sensitive to what others are feeling.

Your use of emotion score is your total score for statements 9 to 12: ___

A score above 22 reflects high use of emotion and means that you are able to use your emotions to drive positive behavior.

Your regulation of emotion score is your total score for statements 13 to 16: ___

A score above 23 reflects high regulation of emotion and means that you control your emotions effectively.

It is important to remember that the usefulness of your scores depend on the accuracy of your self-perceptions.

Source: Reprinted from Wong, C.S. & Law, K.S. (2002). The Effects of Leader and Follower Emotional Intelligence on Performance and Attitude: An Exploratory Study, *The Leadership Quarterly*, *13*(3), 243–274.

to interpersonal capability that includes the ability to perceive and express emotions, to understand and use them, and to manage emotions in oneself and other people.[28] Groups with less well-defined emotional intelligence climates experience increased task and relationship conflict and increased conflict intensity.[29] The U.S. Air Force and L'Oreal use emotional intelligence training to improve team performance. This chapter's *Understand Yourself* feature will help you to evaluate and understand your emotional intelligence skills.

Informal Leadership

The final group performance factor is informal leadership. Most functional groups and teams have a formal leader—that is, one appointed by the organization or chosen or elected by the members of the group. Because friendship and interest groups are formed by the members themselves, however, any formal leader must be elected or designated by the members. Although some groups do designate such a leader (a softball team may elect a captain, for example), many do not. Moreover, even when a formal leader is designated, the group or team may also look to others for leadership. An ***informal leader*** is a person who engages in leadership activities but whose right to do so has not been formally recognized. The formal and the informal leader in any group or team may be the same person, or they may be different people. For example, most groups and teams need people to play both task and socioemotional roles. An informal leader is likely to be a person capable of carrying out both roles effectively. If the formal leader can fulfill one role but not the other, an informal leader often emerges to supplement the formal leader's functions. If the formal leader can fill neither role, one or more informal leaders may emerge to carry out both sets of functions.

informal leader
A person who engages in leadership activities but whose right to do so has not been formally recognized by the organization or group

Is informal leadership desirable? In many cases informal leaders are quite powerful because they draw from referent or expert power. When they are working in the best interests of the organization, they can be a tremendous asset. Notable athletes like Peyton Manning, LeBron James, and Abby Wambach are excellent examples of informal leaders. However, when informal leaders work counter to the goals of the organization, they can cause significant difficulties. Such leaders may lower performance norms, instigate walkouts or wildcat strikes, or otherwise disrupt the organization.

CREATING NEW GROUPS AND TEAMS

Managers frequently have the opportunity to create new groups and teams. Given the significant roles that groups and teams can play in organizational effectiveness, it its clearly important that this process

STOCKLITE/SHUTTERSTOCK.COM

When new groups are formed, or new members join an existing group, the group passes through several stages of development. For instance, this group is welcoming a new member. As they start to work together the group and its new member will need to spend some time getting to know each other, defining their expectations of each other, and so forth.

be approached logically and rationally. In general, if a new group or team is being created, managers should be aware of the stages that groups and teams go through, understand how various performance factors should be considered, and be aware of the formal process experts suggest for implementing teams.

Stages of Group and Team Development

Groups are not static, and when a new group or team is created it generally goes through some "growing pains" before it becomes fully functional. Traditional research on small groups per se (as opposed to teams) has focused on a four-stage development process: (1) mutual acceptance, (2) communication and decision making, (3) motivation and productivity, and (4) control and organization.[30] The stages and the activities that typify them are shown in Figure 7.3. We will discuss the stages as separate and distinct. It is difficult to pinpoint exactly when a group moves from one stage to another, however, because the activities in the phases tend to overlap.

Figure 7.3

Stages of Group Development

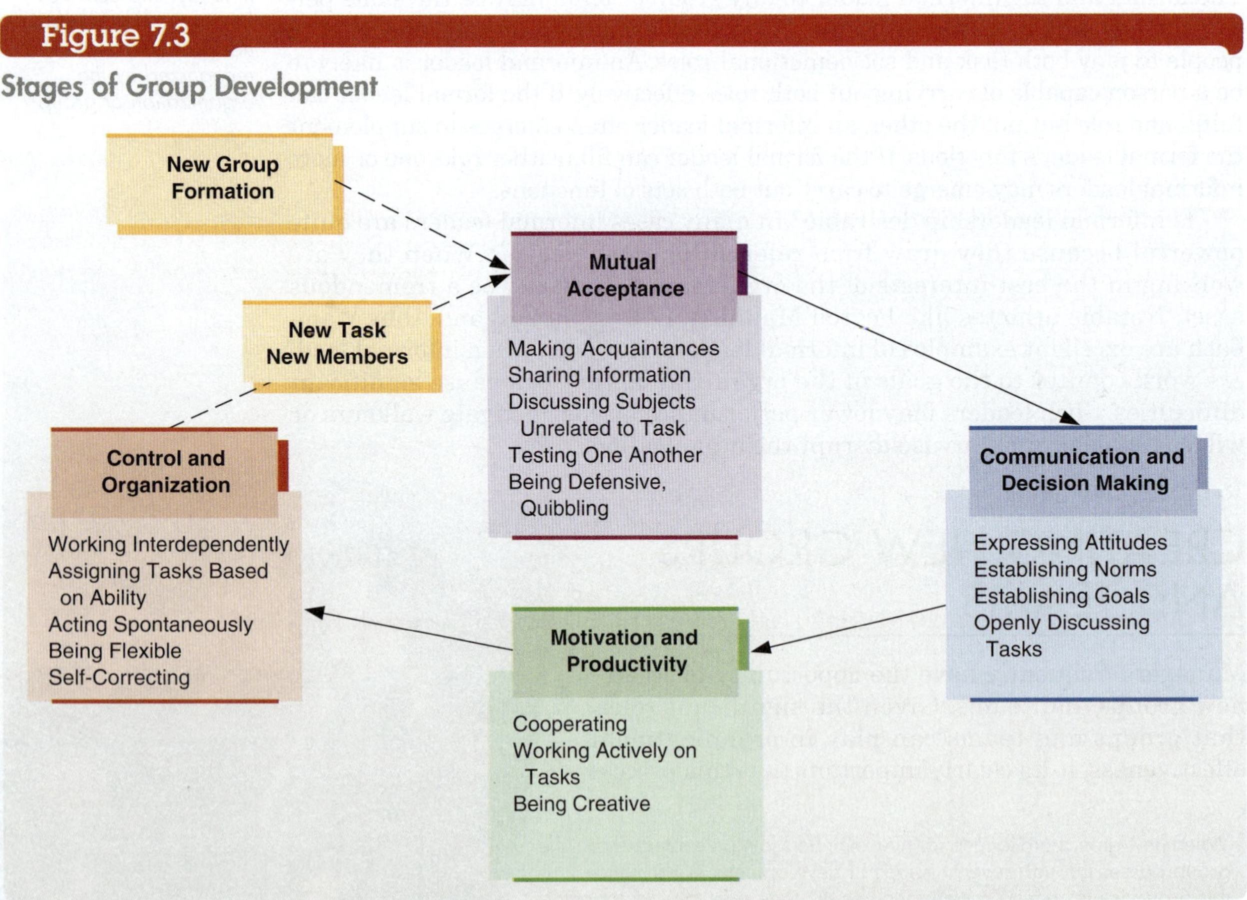

This figure shows the stages of evolution from a newly formed group to a mature group. Note that as new members are added or an existing group gets a new task, the group needs to go through the stages again.

Mutual Acceptance

In the ***mutual acceptance stage*** of group development (also called the *forming* stage), the group forms, and members get to know one another by sharing information about themselves. They often test one another's opinions by discussing subjects that have little to do with the group, such as the weather, sports, or recent events within the organization. Some aspects of the group's task, such as its formal objectives, may also be discussed at this stage. However, such discussion probably will not be very productive because the members are unfamiliar with one another and do not know how to evaluate one another's comments. If the members do happen to know one another already, this stage may be brief, but it is unlikely to be skipped altogether because this is a new group with a new purpose. Besides, there are likely to be a few members whom the others do not know well or at all.

mutual acceptance stage
Characterized by members' sharing information about themselves and getting to know each other

As the members get to know one another, discussion may turn to more sensitive issues, such as the organization's politics or recent controversial decisions. At this stage, members may have minor arguments and feud a bit as they explore one another's views on various issues and learn about each other's reactions, knowledge, and expertise. From the discussion, members come to understand how similar their beliefs and values are and the extent to which they can trust one another. Members may discuss their expectations about the group's activities in terms of their previous group and organizational experience.[31] Eventually, the conversation turns to the business of the group. When this discussion becomes serious, the group is moving to the next stage of development: communication and decision making.

Communication and Decision Making

The group progresses to the ***communication and decision-making stage*** (also called *storming* stage) once group members have begun to accept one another. In this stage, members discuss their feelings and opinions more openly, which can increase conflict; they may show more tolerance for opposing viewpoints and explore different ideas to bring about a reasonable solution or decision. The membership usually begins to develop norms of behavior during this stage. Members discuss and eventually agree on the group's goals. Then they are assigned roles and tasks to accomplish the goals.

communication and decision-making stage
Members discuss their feelings more openly and agree on group goals and individual roles in the group

Motivation and Productivity

In the next stage, ***motivation and productivity*** (also called the *norming* stage), the emphasis shifts away from personal concerns and viewpoints to activities that will benefit the group. Members perform their assigned tasks, cooperate with each other, and help others accomplish their goals. The members are highly motivated and may carry out their tasks creatively. In this stage, the group is accomplishing its work and moving toward the final stage of development.

motivation and productivity stage
Members cooperate, help each other, and work toward accomplishing tasks

Control and Organization

In the final stage, ***control and organization*** (also called the *performing* stage), the group works effectively toward accomplishing its goals. Tasks are assigned by mutual agreement and according to ability. In a mature group, the members' activities are relatively spontaneous and flexible rather than subject to rigid structural restraints. Mature groups evaluate their activities and potential outcomes and take corrective actions if necessary. The characteristics of flexibility, spontaneity, and self-correction are very important if the group is to remain productive over an extended period.

control and organization stage
The group is mature; members work together and are flexible, adaptive, and self-correcting

Not all groups, however, go through all four stages. Some groups disband before reaching the final stage. Others fail to complete a stage before moving on to the next one. Rather than spend the time necessary to get to know one another and build trust, for example, a group may cut short the first stage of development because of pressure from its leader, from deadlines, or from an outside threat (such as the boss).[32] If members are forced into activities typical of a later stage while the work of an earlier stage remains incomplete, they are likely to become frustrated: The group may not develop completely and may be less productive than it could be.[33] Group productivity depends on successful development at each stage. A group that evolves fully through the four stages of development usually becomes a mature, effective group.[34] Its members are interdependent, coordinated, cooperative, competent at their jobs, motivated to do them, self-correcting, and in active communication with one another.[35] The process does not take a long time if the group makes a good, solid effort and pays attention to the processes.

Finally, as working conditions and relationships change, either through a change in membership or when a task is completed and a new task is begun, groups may need to re-experience one or more of the stages of development to maintain the cohesiveness and productivity characteristic of a well-developed group. The San Francisco Forty-Niners, for example, once returned from an NFL strike to an uncomfortable and apprehension-filled period. Their coach conducted rigorous practices but also allowed time for players to get together to air their feelings. Slowly, team unity returned, and players began joking and socializing again as they prepared for the rest of the season.[36] Their redevelopment as a mature group resulted in two subsequent Super Bowl victories.

Although these stages are not separate and distinct in all groups, many groups make fairly predictable transitions in activities at about the midpoint of the period available to complete a task.[37] A group may begin with its own distinctive approach to the problem and maintain it until about halfway through the allotted time. The midpoint transition is often accompanied by a burst of concentrated activity, reexamination of assumptions, dropping old patterns of activity, adopting new perspectives on the work, and making dramatic progress. Following these midpoint activities, the new patterns of activity may be maintained until close to the end of the period allotted for the activity. Another transition may occur just before the deadline. At this transition, groups often go into the completion stage, launching a final burst of activity to finish the job.

Understanding Team Performance Factors

process gain
Performance improvements that occur because people work together rather than independently

process loss
Performance decrements that occur when a team performs worse than the individual members would have if they had worked alone

People working together in teams have the potential to produce more or higher-quality outputs than would have resulted if the individual efforts of team members were later combined. ***Process gain*** refers to the performance improvements that occur because people work together rather than independently. Process gain is the goal of working in teams—people working together doing more and doing it better than would be possible working alone.

Unfortunately, many teams do not realize process gain and instead experience ***process loss***. Process loss occurs when a team of people working in a group or team together performs worse than the individual members would have if they had worked alone. Process loss can be reduced by making clear role and task assignments and not tolerating free riders. Free riders do not contribute because they rely on the work of others. Paying attention to how a team does its work can help you to identify and remedy many of the factors contributing to process loss. The likelihood of process gain can be improved by awareness of several team performance factors. Some of these relate closely to the group performance factors noted earlier, while others are extend beyond those factors.

One useful technique for promoting process gain is to develop and promote team efficacy. ***Team efficacy*** is a team's shared belief that it can organize and execute the behaviors necessary to reach its goals.[38] Team efficacy is strongly related to team performance, particularly when team interdependence is high.[39] Team efficacy can be enhanced by ensuring that at least some members of a team have strong self-efficacy themselves, that team members are given appropriate support and training, and by expressing confidence in and providing encouragement to the team.

team efficacy
A team's shared belief that it can organize and execute the behaviors necessary to reach its goals

As we noted earlier, members of a highly cohesive team are motivated to stay in the team, contribute as much as they can, and conform to team norms. Because members of teams that lack cohesiveness are not strongly committed to the team or its goals and do not contribute to their full potential, team performance is compromised.[40] Therefore, managers of new groups and teams should strive to promote cohesiveness.

Managers should also try to build trust among team members. ***Trust*** is our confidence that other people will honor their commitments, especially when it is difficult to monitor or observe the other people's behavior.[41] Teams build trust through repeated positive experiences, commitment to shared goals, and an understanding of team members' needs, motives, and ideas. Because the lack of trust in a team can undermine any team activity, building trust is an important managerial task. Giving frequent task feedback and interpersonal contact can help diverse teams utilize their diversity to their advantage and create process gain.[42]

trust
Confidence that other people will honor their commitments, especially when it is difficult to monitor or observe the other people's behavior

Managers should also try to prevent social loafing. Indeed, social loafing is a primary cause of process loss. Research has documented the common practice of social loafing,[43] particularly for trivial to moderately important tasks. Social loafing is less common with very important tasks,[44] and with smaller teams.[45] Social loafing often occurs because team members feel that their individual contributions will not be evaluated or because they expect others in the team to do tasks so they choose not to do them.[46]

An opposite behavior occurs when people actually work harder and are more motivated when others are present than when they are working alone. ***Social facilitation*** happens when people are motivated to look good to others and want to maintain a positive self-image. It happens when people are working alone, but in the presence of an audience. People sometimes increase their effort when working in a group simply because others are present[47] or because of evaluation apprehension.[48]

social facilitation
Happens when people are motivated to look good to others and want to maintain a positive self-image

Keeping team size small, clarifying what the team expects each member to do, and making individual contributions to the team identifiable can help reduce social loafing and encourage social facilitation.[49] For example, giving a team member the responsibility for ensuring that meeting notes are shared with the team within two days of a meeting makes it more likely that notes will be taken and distributed. Letting team members choose which tasks they will be responsible for can also increase their motivation for getting them done.

roles
Define the behaviors and tasks each team member is expected to perform because of the position they hold

In addition, managers should establish clear roles. ***Roles*** define the behaviors and tasks each team member is expected to perform because of the position they hold. One of the primary outcomes of the process of group and team development is the establishment of clear roles in the team. Understanding what your teammates expect you to do and what you can expect your teammates to do reduces conflict and enables smooth team performance. Making team roles and expectations clear helps to reduce process loss.

It is also important to establish positive norms. By helping team members know what to expect from each other, norms help to ensure high performance. An example of a positive team norm is arriving to meetings prepared and on time, and participating fully. Team members comply with team norms (1) to avoid punishments and receive rewards; (2) to imitate team members whom they like and admire; and (3) because they have internalized the norm and believe it is the appropriate way to behave.[50]

When possible, managers should create shared team goals and provide feedback. High-performing teams have clear and challenging goals that all team members are committed to, and create sub-goals and milestones against which they measure themselves. If performance is lagging, feedback helps the team quickly adjust its behavior and processes to reach its goals.[51] As featured in this chapter's real world response, in South Korea, Starbucks created shared team goals around tasks typically performed by females to encourage its male employees to perform these tasks as well.[52]

Team rewards also motivate effective teamwork behaviors. Tying team rewards to team performance motivates team members to pursue team goals rather than individual goals.[53] Teams require firms to shift the emphasis of their compensation and rewards programs from individual to team rewards. Any remaining individual rewards should acknowledge people who are effective team players—people who freely share their expertise, help when needed, and challenge their teams to improve. A "star" system that rewards only individual performance undermines team effectiveness.

Some individual rewards may be appropriate for those who make particularly critical individual contributions to the team, but the bulk of rewards need to be made at the team level. Managers should remember the importance of integrating new team members. Team member turnover compromises team effectiveness as new members must be proactively integrated and socialized.[54] Leaders are critical to this newcomer integration and socialization process. New team member integration involves motivating all team members by promoting shared goal commitment, positive affect, and shaping team processes. Team socialization creates affective bonds that connect members to the team and its mission, and helps build trust and a sense of community. If current team members do not take the time to incorporate new members into the fabric of the team, the team will be less cohesive, new members will not be able to contribute to their full potential, and new members are likely to be less committed to the team.

The Implementation Process

Implementing teams across an organization is not easy; it takes a lot of hard work, time, training, and patience. Indeed, changing from a traditional organizational structure to a team-based structure is a major organizational change and calls for a complete cultural change for the organization. Typically, the organization is hierarchically designed to provide clear direction and control. However, many organizations need to be able to react quickly to a dynamic environment. Team procedures artificially imposed on existing processes are a recipe for disaster. In this section we present several essential elements peculiar to an organizational change to a team-based situation. This process is shown in Figure 7.4.

Phase 1: Start-Up

In phase 1, team members are selected and prepared to work in teams so that the teams have the best possible chance of success. Much of the initial training is informational or "awareness" training that sends the message that top management is firmly committed to teams and that teams are not experimental. The steering committee usually starts the training at the top, and the training and information are passed down the chain to the team members.

Figure 7.4

Phases of Team Implementations

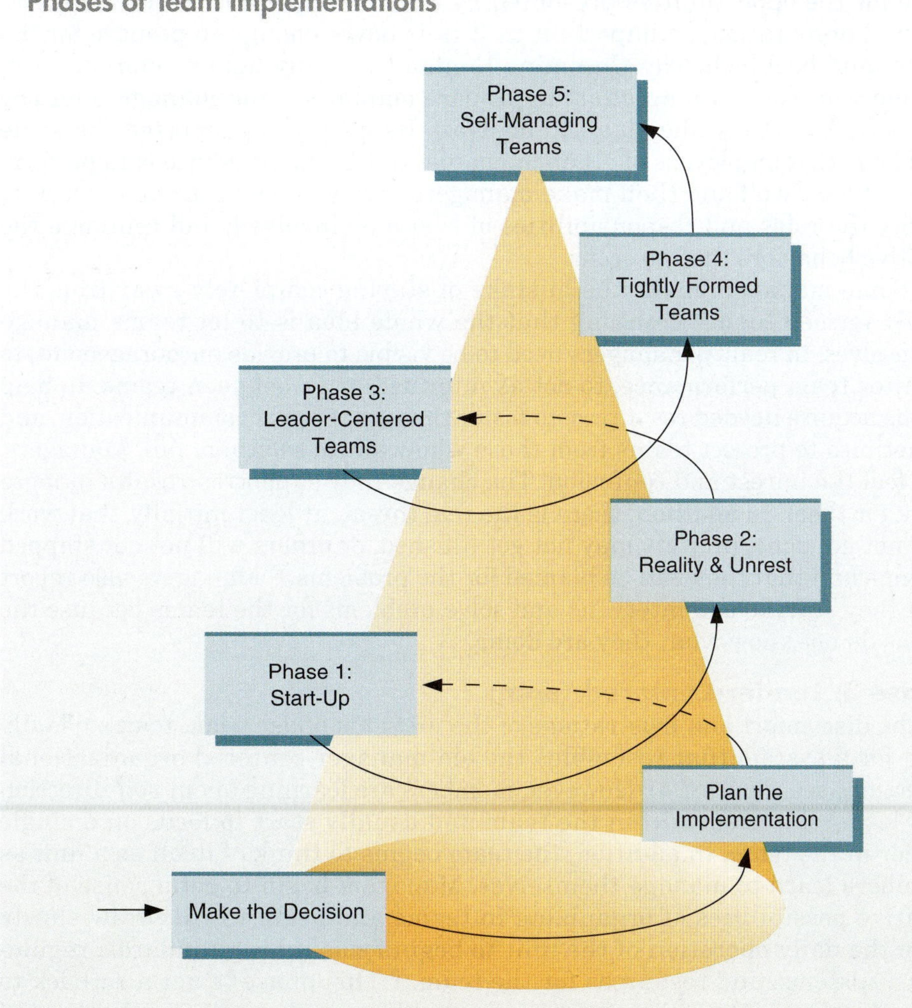

Implementation of teams in organizations is a long and arduous process. After the decision is made to initiate teams, the steering committee develops the plans for the design team, which plans the entire process. The goal is for teams to become self-managing. The time it takes for each stage varies with the organization.

Training covers the rationale for moving to a team-based organization, how teams were selected, how they work, the roles and responsibilities of teams, compensation, and job security. In general, training covers the technical skills necessary to do the work of the team, the administrative skills necessary for the team to function within the organization, and the interpersonal skills necessary to work with people in the team and throughout the organization. Sometimes the interpersonal skills are important. Perhaps most important is establishing the idea that teams are not "unmanaged" but are "differently managed." The difference is that the new teams manage themselves. Team boundaries are also identified, and the preliminary plan is adjusted to fit the particular team situations. Employees typically feel that much is changing during the first few months; enthusiasm runs high, and the anticipation of employees is quite positive. Performance by teams increases at start-up because of this initial enthusiasm for the change.

Phase 2: Reality and Unrest

After perhaps six to nine months, team members and managers report frustration and confusion about the ambiguities of the new situation. For employees, unfamiliar tasks, more responsibility, and worry about job security replace hope for the opportunities presented by the new approach. All of the training and preparation, as important as it is, is never enough to prepare for the storm and backlash. The Cummins Engine Company held numerous "prediction workshops" in an effort to prepare employees and managers for the difficulties that lay ahead, all to no avail. Its employees reported the same problems that employees of other companies did. The best advice is to perform phase 1 very well and then make managers very visible, continue to work to clarify the roles and responsibilities of everyone involved, and reinforce the positive behaviors that do occur.

Some managers make the mistake of staying completely away from the newly formed teams, thinking that the whole idea is to let teams manage themselves. In reality, managers need to be visible to provide encouragement, to monitor team performance, to act as intermediaries between teams, to help teams acquire needed resources, to foster the right type of communication, and sometimes to protect teams from those who want to see them fail. Managers, too, feel the unrest and confusion. The change they supported results in more work for them. In addition, there is the real threat, at least initially, that work will not get done, projects may not get finished, or orders will not get shipped on time and that they will be blamed for the problems.[55] Managers also report that they still have to intervene and solve problems for the teams because the teams do not know what they are doing.

Phase 3: Leader-Centered Teams

As the discomfort and frustrations of the previous phase peak, teams usually long for a system that resembles the old manager-centered organizational structure (see Figure 7.4). However, members are learning about self-direction and leadership from within the team and usually start to focus on a single leader in the team. In addition, the team begins to think of itself as a unit as members learn to manage themselves. Managers begin to get a sense of the positive possibilities of organizing in teams and begin to withdraw slowly from the daily operation of the unit to begin focusing on standards, regulations, systems, and resources for the team.[56] This phase is not a setback to team development—although it may seem like one—because development of and reliance on one internal leader is a move away from focusing on the old hierarchy and traditional lines of authority.

The design and steering committees need to be sure that two things happen during this phase. First, they need to encourage the rise of strong internal team leaders. The new leaders can either be company appointed or team appointed. Top management sometimes prefers the additional control they get from appointing the team leaders, assuming that production will continue through the team transition. On the other hand, if the company-appointed leaders are the former managers, team members have trouble believing that anything has really changed. Team-appointed leaders can be a problem if the leaders are not trained properly and oriented toward team goals.

If the team-appointed leader is ineffective, the team usually recognizes the problem and makes the adjustments necessary to get the team back on track. Another possibility for team leadership is a rotating system in which the position changes every quarter, month, week, or even day. A rotating system fosters professional growth of all members of the team and reinforces the strength of the team's self-management.

The second important issue for this phase is to help each team develop its own sense of identity. Visits to observe mature teams in action can be a good step for newly formed teams. Recognizing teams and individuals for good performance is always powerful, especially when the teams choose the recipients. Continued training in problem-solving steps, tools, and techniques is imperative. Managers need to push as many problem-solving opportunities as possible down to the team level. Finally, as team identity develops, teams develop social activities and display T-shirts, team names, logos, and other items that show off their identity. All of these are a sure sign that the team is moving into phase 4.

Phase 4: Tightly Formed Teams

In the fourth phase of team implementation, teams become tightly formed to the point that their internal focus can become detrimental to other teams and to the organization as a whole. Such teams are usually extremely confident of their ability to do everything. They are solving problems, managing their schedule and resources, and resolving internal conflicts. However, communication with external teams begins to diminish, the team covers up for underperforming members, and interteam rivalries can turn sour, leading to unhealthy competition.

To avoid the dangers of the intense team loyalty and isolation inherent in phase 4, managers need to make sure that teams continue to do the things that have enabled them to prosper thus far. First, teams need to keep the communication channels with other teams open through councils of rotating team representatives who meet regularly to discuss what works and what does not; teams who communicate and cooperate with other teams should be rewarded. At the Digital Equipment plant in Connecticut, team representatives meet weekly to share successes and failures so that all can avoid problems and improve the ways their teams operate.[57] Second, management needs to provide performance feedback through computer terminals in the work area that give up-to-date information on performance, or via regular feedback meetings. At TRW plants, management introduced peer performance appraisal at this stage of the team implementation process. It found that in phase 4, teams were ready to take on this administrative task but needed significant training in how to perform and communicate appraisals. Third, teams need to follow the previously developed plan to transfer authority and responsibility to the teams and to be sure that all team members have followed the plan to get training in all of the skills necessary to do the work of the team. By the end of phase 4, the team should be ready to take responsibility for managing itself.

Phase 5: Self-Managing Teams

Phase 5 is the end result of the months or years of planning and implementation. Mature teams are meeting or exceeding their performance goals. Team members are taking responsibility for team-related leadership functions. Managers and supervisors have withdrawn from the daily operations and are planning and providing counseling for teams. Probably most important, mature teams are flexible—taking on new ideas for improvement; making changes as needed to membership, roles, and tasks; and doing whatever it takes to meet the strategic objectives of the organization. Although the teams are mature and functioning quite well, several things need to be done to keep them on track. First and foremost, individuals and teams need to continue their training in job skills and team and interpersonal skills. Second, support systems need to be constantly improved to facilitate team development and productivity. Third, teams always need to improve their internal customer and supplier relationships within the organization. Partnerships among teams throughout the organization can help the internal teams continue to meet the needs of external customers.

MANAGING TEAMS

The ongoing management of teams requires additional insights. These include understanding the benefits and costs of teams, promoting effective performance in teams, and identifying and developing teamwork competencies.

Understanding Benefits and Costs of Teams

With the popularity of teams increasing so rapidly around the world, it is possible that some organizations are starting to use teams simply because everyone else is doing it—which is obviously the wrong reason. The reason for a company to create teams should be that teams make sense for that particular organization. The best reason to start teams in any organization is to achieve the positive benefits that can result from a team-based environment: enhanced performance, employee benefits, reduced costs, and organizational enhancements. Four categories of benefits and some examples are shown in Table 7.2. Our *Case Study* profiles another example.

Enhanced Performance

Enhanced performance can come in many forms, including improved productivity, quality, and customer service. Working in teams enables workers to avoid wasted effort, reduce errors, and react better to customers, resulting in more output for each unit of employee input. Such enhancements result from pooling of individual efforts in new ways and from continuously striving to improve for the benefit of the team.[58] For example, a General Electric plant in

Table 7.2

Benefits of Teams in Organizations

Type of Benefit	Specific Benefit	Organizational Examples
ENHANCED PERFORMANCE	Increased productivity	Ampex: On-time customer delivery rose 98%.
	Improved quality	K Shoes: Rejects per million dropped from 5,000 to 250.
	Improved customer service	Eastman: Productivity rose 70%.
EMPLOYEE BENEFITS	Quality of work life Lower stress	Milwaukee Mutual: Employee assistance program usage dropped to 40% below industry average.
REDUCED COSTS	Lower turnover, absenteeism	Kodak: Reduced turnover by 50 percent.
	Fewer injuries	Texas Instruments: Reduced costs more than 50%.
		Westinghouse: Costs down 60%.
ORGANIZATIONAL ENHANCEMENTS	Increased innovation, flexibility	IDS Mutual Fund Operations: Improved flexibility to handle fluctuations in market activity. Hewlett-Packard: Innovative order processing system.

Source: Examples derived from from Katzenbach, J., & Eisenhardt, K. (2013). *HBR's 10 Must Reads on Teams.* Boston: Harvard Business School Press; Gustasfon, P., & Liff, S. (2014). *A Team of Leaders: Empowering Every Member to Take Ownership. Develop Initiative, and Take Ownership.* New York: AMACOM; McChrysal, S., & Collins, T. (2015). New York: John Wiley and Sons.

North Carolina experienced a 20 percent increase in productivity after team implementation.[59] K Shoes reported a 19 percent increase in productivity and significant reductions in rejects in the manufacturing process after it started using teams.

Reduced Costs

As empowered teams reduce scrap, make fewer errors, file fewer worker compensation claims, and reduce absenteeism and turnover, organizations based on teams are showing significant cost reductions. Team members feel that they have a stake in the outcomes, want to make contributions because they are valued, and are committed to their team and do not want to let it down. Wilson Sporting Goods reported saving $10 million per year for five years thanks to its teams. Colgate-Palmolive reported that technician turnover was extremely low—more than 90 percent of technicians were retained after five years—once it changed to a team-based approach.

Other Organizational Benefits

Other improvements in organizations that result from moving from a hierarchically based, directive culture to a team-based culture include increased innovation, creativity, and flexibility.[60] Use of teams can eliminate redundant layers of bureaucracy and flatten the hierarchy in large organizations. Employees feel closer and more in touch with top management. Employees who think their efforts are important are more likely to make significant contributions. In addition, the team environment constantly challenges teams to innovate and solve problems creatively. If the "same old way" does not work, empowered teams are free to throw it out and develop a new way. With increasing

CASE STUDY Teamwork at IDEO

IDEO is a global award-winning design firm.[61] Every year teams of people including psychologists, mechanical engineers, biologists, and industrial designers work on projects ranging from Apple's first computer mouse to heart defibrillators to the Neat Squeeze toothpaste tube.

IDEO's corporate philosophy is that teamwork improves innovation and creativity. Group brainstorming is used to spark a lot of new ideas at once. Project teams share and improve ideas by leveraging members' skills and solving problems together. The company believes that the diversity of interdisciplinary teams allows higher quality, faster innovation.[62]

Regardless of the project, IDEO teams use the same process. First they identify similar products and experiences, then they observe people using them. The teams then visualize, evaluate, refine, and implement innovative solutions to their clients' problems drawing from their research and observations. IDEO team members lack status or formal titles, and every team member is given equal respect.[63]

Questions:

1. How does teamwork influence innovation at IDEO?
2. How does diversity influence the effectiveness of teamwork at IDEO?
3. What characteristics would you look for in staffing a project team at IDEO?

global competition, organizations must constantly adapt to keep abreast of changes. Teams provide the flexibility to react quickly. One of Motorola's earliest teams challenged a long-standing top-management policy regarding supplier inspections in an effort to reduce the cycle times and improve delivery of crucial parts.[64] After several attempts, management finally allowed the team to change the system and consequently reaped the expected benefits.

Employee Benefits

Employees tend to benefit as much as organizations in a team environment. Much attention has been focused on the differences between the baby-boom generation and the "postboomers" in their attitudes toward work, its importance to their lives, and what they want from it. In general, younger workers tend to be less satisfied with their work and the organization, tend to have lower respect for authority and supervision, and tend to want more than a paycheck every week. Teams can provide the sense of self-control, human dignity, identification with work, and sense of self-worth and self-fulfillment for which current workers seem to strive. Rather than relying on the traditional, hierarchical, manager-based system, teams give employees the freedom to grow and to gain respect and dignity by managing themselves, making decisions about their work, and really making a difference in the world around them.[65] As a result, employees have a better work life, face less stress at work, and make less use of employee assistance programs.

Costs of Teams

The costs of teams are usually expressed in terms of the difficulty of changing to a team-based organization. Managers have expressed frustration and confusion about their new roles as coaches and facilitators, especially if they developed their managerial skills under the traditional hierarchical management philosophy. Some managers have felt as if they were working themselves out of a job as they turned over more and more of their directing duties to a team.[66]

Employees may also feel like losers during the change to a team culture. Some traditional staff groups, such as technical advisory staffs, may feel that their jobs are in jeopardy as teams do more and more of the technical work formerly done by technicians. New roles and pay scales may need to be developed for the technical staff in these situations. Often, technical people have been assigned to a team or a small group of teams and become members who fully participate in team activities.

Another cost associated with teams is the slowness of the process of full team development. As discussed elsewhere in this chapter, it takes a long time for teams to go through the full development cycle and become mature, efficient, and effective. Productivity may fall before the positive effects of the new team system kick in. If top management is impatient with the slow progress, teams may be disbanded, returning the organization to its original hierarchical form with significant losses for employees, managers, and the organization.

Probably the most dangerous cost is premature abandonment of the change to a team-based organization. If top management gets impatient with the team change process and cuts it short, never allowing teams to develop fully and realize benefits, all the hard work of employees, middle managers, and supervisors is lost. As a result, employee confidence in management in general and in the decision makers in particular may suffer for a long time.[67] The losses in productivity and efficiency will be very difficult to recoup. Management must therefore be fully committed before initiating a change to a team-based organization.

Promoting Effective Performance

This chapter has described the many benefits of teams and the process of changing to a team-based organization. Teams can be utilized in small and large organizations, on the shop floor and in offices, and in countries around the world. Teams must be initiated for performance-based business reasons, and proper planning and implementation strategies must be used. In this section we discuss three essential issues that cannot be overlooked when moving to a team-based organization.

Top-Management Support

The question of where to start in team implementation is really no issue at all. Change starts at the top in every successful team implementation. Top management has three important roles to play. First, top management must decide to go to a team-based organization for sound business performance–related reasons. A major cultural change cannot be made because it is the fad, because the boss went to a seminar on teams, or because a quick fix is needed. Second, top management is instrumental in communicating the reasons for the change to the rest of the organization. Third, top management has to support the change effort during the difficult periods. As discussed previously, performance usually goes down in the early phases of team implementation. Top-management support may involve verbal encouragement of team members, but organizational support systems for the teams are also needed. Examples of support systems for teams include more efficient inventory and scheduling systems, better hiring and selection systems, improved information systems, and appropriate compensation systems.

Understanding Time Frames

Organizations often expect too much too soon when they implement teams. In fact, things often get worse before they get better.[68] Figure 7.5 shows how, shortly after implementation, team performance often declines and then rebounds to rise to the original levels and above. Management at Investors Diversified Services, a financial services firm in Minneapolis, Minnesota (and now a part of American Express), expected planning for team start-up to take three or four months. The actual planning took eight and a half months.[69] It often takes a year or more before performance levels return to at least their before-team levels. If teams are implemented without proper planning, their performance may never return to prior levels. The long lead time for improving performance can be discouraging to managers who reacted to the fad for teams and expected immediate returns.

The phases of implementation discussed in the previous sections correspond to key points on the team performance curve. At the start-up, performance is at its normal levels, although sometimes the anticipation of, and enthusiasm for, teams cause a slight increase in performance. In phase 2, reality and unrest, teams are often confused and frustrated with the training and lack of direction from top management, to the point that actual performance may decline. In phase 3, leader-centered teams become more comfortable with the team idea and refocus on the work of the team. They once again have established leadership, although it is with an internal leader rather than an

Figure 7.5

The team performance curve shows that performance initially drops as reality sets in, and team members experience frustration and unrest. However, performance soon increases and rises to record levels as the teams mature and become self-managing.

Performance and Implementation of Teams

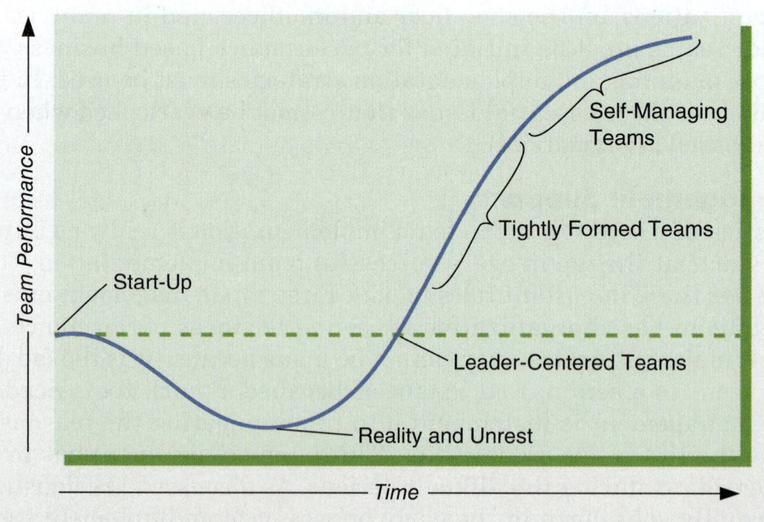

Source: From Katzenbach, J. R., & Smith, D. K. (1993). *The Wisdom of Teams: Creating the High Performance Organization* (p. 84). Boston, MA: Harvard Business School Press.

ALEX BRYLOV/SHUTTERSTOCK.COM

Organizations that increase their use of teams will likely need to change their reward systems. This organization, for example, is recognizing and rewarding high performance by work teams. In the past, the organization focused more on individual performance.

external manager or supervisor. Thus, their performance usually returns to at least their former levels. In phase 4, teams are beginning to experience the real potential of teamwork and are producing above their prior levels. Finally, in phase 5, self-managing teams are mature, flexible, and usually setting new records for performance.

Organizations changing to a team-based arrangement need to recognize the time and effort involved in making such a change. Hopes for immediate, positive results can lead to disappointment. The most rapid increases in performance occur between the leader-centered phase and the team-centered phase because teams have managed to get past the difficult, low-performance stages, have had a lot of training, and are ready to utilize their independence and freedom to make decisions about their own work. Team members are deeply committed to each other and to the success of the team. In phase 5, management needs to make sure that teams are focused on the strategic goals of the organization.

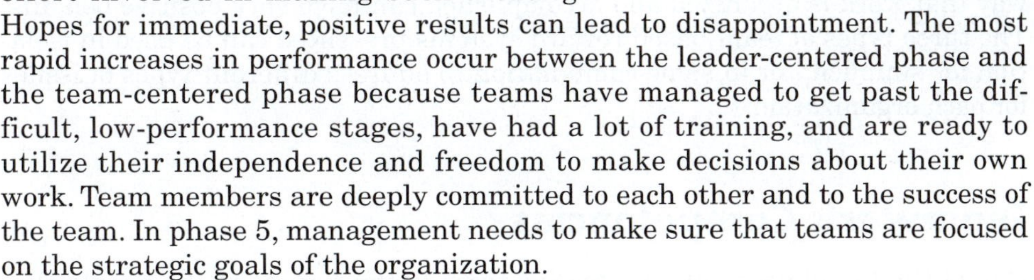

Changing Organizational Rewards

How employees are rewarded is vital to the long-term success of an organization. The traditional reward and compensation systems suitable for individual motivation are simply not appropriate in a team-based organization. In conventional settings, employees are usually rewarded on the basis of their individual performance, their seniority, or their job classification. In a team-based situation, however, team members are generally rewarded for mastering a range of skills needed to meet team performance goals, and rewards are sometimes based on team performance. Such a pay system tends to promote the flexibility that teams need to be responsive to changing environmental factors. Three types of reward systems are common in a team environment: skill-based pay, gain-sharing systems, and team bonus plans.

1. *Skill-Based Pay:* Skill-based pay systems require team members to acquire a set of the core skills needed for their particular team plus additional special skills, depending on career tracks or team needs. Some programs require all members to acquire the core skills before any member receives additional pay. Usually employees can increase their base compensation by some fixed amount, say $0.50 per hour for each additional skill acquired, up to some fixed maximum. Companies using skill-based pay systems include Eastman Chemical Company, Colgate-Palmolive, and Pfizer.
2. *Gain-Sharing Systems:* Gain-sharing systems usually reward all team members from all teams based on the performance of the organization, division, or plant. Such a system requires a baseline performance that must be exceeded for team members to receive some share of the gain

over the baseline measure. Westinghouse gives equal one-time, lump-sum bonuses to everyone in the plant based on improvements in productivity, cost, and quality. Employee reaction is usually positive because when employees work harder to help the company, they share in the profits they helped generate. On the other hand, when business conditions or other factors beyond their control make it impossible to generate improvements over the preset baseline, employees may feel disappointed and even disillusioned with the process.

3. *Team Bonus Plans:* Team bonus plans are similar to gain-sharing plans except that the unit of performance and pay is the team rather than a plant, a division, or the entire organization. Each team must have specific performance targets or baseline measures that the team considers realistic for the plan to be effective. Companies using team bonus plans include Milwaukee Insurance Company, Colgate-Palmolive, and Harris Corporation.

Changes in an organizational compensation system can be traumatic and threatening to most employees. However, matching the reward system to the way that work is organized and accomplished can have very positive benefits. The three types of team-based reward systems presented can be used in isolation for simplicity or in some combination to address different types of issues for each organization.

Teamwork Competencies

One of the foundations of an effective team is the nature of the people chosen to be in the team. Staffing teams with people who have the interpersonal skills and competencies to contribute to task performance but who are also able to work well in team settings is critical. Some of the teamwork abilities you should look for are:[70]

1. Conflict resolution abilities
   - The ability to recognize and encourage desirable and discourage undesirable team conflict
   - The ability to recognize the type and source of conflict confronting the team and implement an appropriate resolution strategy
   - The ability to employ an integrative (win-win) negotiation strategy, rather than the traditional distributive (win-lose) strategy
2. Collaborative problem-solving abilities
   - The ability to identify situations requiring participative group problem solving and to utilize the proper degree and type of participation
   - The ability to recognize the obstacles to collaborative group problem solving and implement appropriate corrective actions
3. Communication abilities
   - The ability to communicate openly and supportively
   - The ability to listen objectively and to appropriately use active listening techniques
   - The ability to maximize the congruence between nonverbal and verbal messages and to recognize and interpret the nonverbal messages of others
   - The ability to engage in small talk and ritual greetings and a recognition of their importance

4. Goal-setting and self-management abilities
   - The ability to help establish specific, challenging, and accepted team goals
   - The ability to provide constructive feedback
5. Planning and task coordination abilities
   - The ability to coordinate and synchronize activities, information, and tasks among team members
   - The ability to help establish task and role assignments for individual team members and ensure proper balancing of workload

Teamwork competencies also include an understanding of ethical behavior in teams. The more frequently and intensely we interact with peers, the stronger their influence on our own behavior.[71] Other people's ethical behavior influences our own ethical behavior.[72] This is particularly true for managers, highlighting the importance of consistently setting a good example as a manager.[73] Four ethical issues are especially important in teams:

1. How do teams fairly distribute work?
2. How do teams assign blame and award credit?
3. How do teams ensure participation, resolve conflict, and make decisions?
4. How do teams avoid deception and corruption?

A ***team contract*** is a written agreement among team members establishing ground rules about the team's processes, roles, and accountabilities. Team members must communicate and negotiate in order to identify the quality of work they all wish to achieve, how decisions will be made, and the level of participation and individual accountability they all feel comfortable with. Team contracts help to reduce the potential for team conflict stemming from an unequal division of resources and deter free riding. By enhancing personal accountability and creating clear rules and expectations, team contracts can promote ethical team behavior and improve team performance and team member satisfaction.

team contract
A written agreement among team members establishing ground rules about the team's processes, roles, and accountabilities

EMERGING TEAM OPPORTUNITIES AND CHALLENGES

As teams become increasingly common in organizations, two additional sets of opportunities and challenges must be addressed. These involve virtual teams and diversity & multicultural teams.

Virtual Teams

Managing virtual teams can be difficult.[74] Virtual team members are frequently separated by both geographic space and time, increasing the challenges of working together effectively. In such environments, team members are often isolated from one another and find it difficult to feel connected to their team.[75] It is hard enough to lead teams who see each other, and whose members share common language and culture, but these challenges multiply when teams "go virtual" and communication is via technology and involves team members with far different cultures and life experiences.[76]

Virtual teams allow organizations to access the most qualified individuals for a particular job regardless of their location, enable organizations to respond faster to increased competition, and provide greater flexibility to individuals working from home or on the road. In some cases, some members of the team may be free agents or alliance partners and not be employees of the organization. In some teams, members may never even meet face-to-face. Many virtual teams operate within a particular organization, but increasingly they cross organizational boundaries as well.[77] Hewlett-Packard, Motorola, and Bank of Boston rely on virtual teams to execute their strategies.[78]

Virtual Team Leadership Skills

The effective leadership of teams whose members are linked by technology and whose members often do not see each other requires unique skills and behaviors compared to managing and leading teams located in the same place.[79] Working from different locations introduces challenges with communication, collaboration, and the integration of the team members with the rest of the team and the broader organization. When team members rarely see each other or other employees, it can be difficult for them to feel part of the team and organizational community.

One of the most important things a virtual team leader can do is to establish a communication climate that is characterized by openness, trust, support, mutual respect, and risk taking. This helps the team establish positive working relationships, share information openly, reduce the formation of in-groups and out-groups, and avoid misinterpreting communications.[80]

One expert identified five categories of important leadership skills in virtual project team or distance management situations:[81]

1. *Communicating effectively and matching technology to the situation:* Collaborative online tools help virtual teams manage files, meetings, and task assignments.
2. *Building community among team members based on mutual trust, respect, affiliation, and fairness:* Effective leaders solicit and value the contributions of all team members, and consistently treat all team members with respect and fairness.
3. *Establishing a clear and motivating shared vision, team purpose, goals, and expectations:* Subtle messages, such as quietly reminding someone not to attack ideas during a brainstorming session, are powerful tools in shaping virtual team norms.
4. *Leading by example and focusing on measurable results:* Effective virtual leaders set clear goals and make clear task assignments. The leaders then hold team members accountable for them.
5. *Coordinating and collaborating across organizational boundaries:* Virtual team leaders need to work effectively with people in multiple organizations and with free agents and alliance partners who are not employees of the leader's organization.

Leader Behaviors

The lack of face-to-face contact with virtual team members makes it difficult for leaders to monitor team member performance and to implement solutions to work problems. It is also difficult for virtual team leaders to perform typical mentoring, coaching, and development functions. The challenge for virtual team leaders is that these tasks must be accomplished by empowering the team to perform these functions itself without the leader being physically present.[82]

For example, members of virtual teams are usually chosen for their expertise and competence, and for their prior virtual team experience. They are expected to have the technical knowledge, skills, abilities, and other attributes to be able to contribute to team effectiveness and to operate effectively in a virtual environment. Thus, the need for virtual team leaders to monitor or develop team members may not be as crucial. In addition, virtual team leaders can distribute aspects of these functions to the team itself, making it more of a self-managing team.[83]

Virtual team leaders need to provide a clear, engaging direction for the team[84] along with specific individual goals. Clear direction and goals allow team members to monitor and evaluate their own performance.[85] Although this is relevant in all teams, virtual team leaders need to be more proactive and structuring. Virtual team leaders need to develop team processes that become the way the team naturally behaves.

One way virtual team leaders can do this is by developing appropriate routines and procedures early on in the team's lifecycle.[86] Routines create consistent patterns of behavior that occur even in the leader's absence. Leaders can define desired routines (e.g., standard operating procedures), train members in them, and provide motivational incentives sufficient to ensure compliance with them. Leaders can also establish rules and guidelines that specify appropriate team member behavior. For example, computer-mediated communication tends to lead to more uninhibited individual behavior, such as strong and inflammatory expressions.[87] Therefore, virtual team leaders may need to develop standard operating procedures that specify appropriate and inappropriate computer-mediated communication. Because virtual team members are more detached from the overall team environment, it is also important for leaders to monitor the environment and inform team members of any important changes.[88]

Groupware and Group Decision Support Systems

Synchronous and asynchronous information technologies support members of virtual teams.[89] Synchronous technologies such as videoconferencing, instant messaging, electronic meetings, and even conference calls allow real-time communication and interaction. Asynchronous technologies such as e-mail, wikis, and some electronic meetings delay the communication of the message. Many virtual teams rely on both types of information technology and use the one best suited to the message being communicated and task being performed. Bausch & Lomb found that a web-based collaboration tool increased synergy by decreasing the number of meetings, giving people more free work time to get things done.[90]

Many team meetings are poorly run, take too long, and accomplish too little. Meeting management software, electronic whiteboards, and collaborative document editors facilitate meetings by allowing team members to contribute ideas, to view other people's ideas anonymously, and to comment and vote on them. Computer-mediated communication enhances team performance by helping team members communicate more effectively with each other.

The right technology is critical to making virtual teams work. Office furniture maker Steelcase relies on its cross-functional, cross-office, and even cross-company virtual teams to do business every day.[91] To reduce travel costs and to increase team productivity and efficiency, the company uses software to support its virtual teams and enable them to work together as if they were in the same location. The collaboration software connects virtual teams with members in locations around the world and helps structure the meeting process. Teams can share files, manage projects, and coordinate business processes by marking up documents and showing PowerPoint presentations within secure workspaces synchronized across all team members' PCs. Team members communicate via instant messaging, chat, or voiceover-IP using the virtual meeting tool. A meeting wizard facilitates the process of creating a meeting and inviting team members. Once a meeting is created, any participant can easily add agenda topics, create action items, attach files, and record minutes.[92]

Diversity and Multicultural Teams

Diversity can both help and hinder team effectiveness. Diversity can be a source of creativity and innovation that can create a competitive advantage[93] and improve a team's decision making.[94] Innovative companies intentionally use heterogeneous teams to solve problems.[95] Our *Global Issues* feature focuses on how to increase the effectiveness of multicultural teams.

Despite its potential for improving team performance, diversity can be a two-edged sword.[96] Diversity can create misunderstandings and conflict that can lead to absenteeism, poor quality, low morale, and loss of competitiveness[97] as well as lowered workgroup cohesiveness.[98] Diverse groups are less able to provide for all of their members' needs and tend to have less integration and communication and more conflict than do homogeneous groups.[99]

Informational diversity, or diversity in knowledge and experience, has a positive impact on team performance. Because team members' unique knowledge enlarges the team's knowledge resources and can enhance the options it is able to consider, it can enhance creativity and problem solving. *Demographic diversity*, on the other hand, often has a negative impact on performance. Team conflict tends to increase and teams tend to perform lower as they become more demographically diverse.[100] Increasing demographic diversity can result in work teams having more difficulty utilizing their informational diversity because team members are not able to work effectively with different others. When this happens, the potential for demographically diverse work teams to perform more effectively is lost.[101]

To leverage the potential benefits of diversity, many companies take steps to proactively staff their teams with informational diversity and with people who are comfortable with diversity and with teamwork. Effectively managing diversity in teams has as much to do with the attitudes of team members toward diversity as it does with the diversity of the team itself.

Just as diversity is becoming more common in organizations, so too are groups and teams also becoming more diverse. This group, for instance, reflects several different forms of diversity. Group and team diversity can promote creativity and innovation. Unfortunately it can also be a source of conflict.

INCREASING THE EFFECTIVENESS OF MULTICULTURAL TEAMS

What should you do to increase the effectiveness of multicultural teams? The best solution seems to be to make minor concessions on process—learn to adjust to and even respect another approach to decision making. For example, global managers from the U.S. have learned to keep impatient bosses away from team meetings and give them frequent updates. A comparable lesson for managers from other cultures is to be explicit about what they need—saying, for example, "We have to see the big picture before we will be ready to talk about details."[102]

Four strategies for dealing with the challenges of multicultural teams are:

1. *Adaptation*: seeing a problem as a cultural difference, and not a personality issue. This works when team members are willing and able to identify and acknowledge their cultural differences and to assume responsibility for figuring out how to live with them.
2. *Structural intervention*: changing the shape of the team. Social interaction and working can be structured to engage everyone on the team.
3. *Managerial intervention*: setting norms early or bringing in a higher-level manager. This usually works best early in a team's life. In one case, a manager set norms of respect by telling his new team that no one had been chosen for English skills; each member was chosen because he or she was technically the best person for the job, so get over the accents.[103]
4. *Exit*: removing a team member when other options have failed. If emotions get too high and too much face has been lost, it can be almost impossible to get a team to work together effectively again.[104]

As one expert says:

> The most fundamental thing is to be a role model for respect. It rubs off on the other members of the team. Helping team members see that problems are due to cultural differences and not personality helps a lot. And if you're able to help the team see that the behavior that's so frustrating and annoying is due to culture, then people get curious: How do they get anything done in that culture? And when you unleash curiosity, that inspires learning. The last thing is, don't intervene too swiftly. If they can always bring a problem to your door and you solve it, they don't learn to solve it themselves.[105]

Managers and multicultural team members must find ways to utilize each member's strengths while minimizing coordination losses resulting from communication problems, language differences, varying work styles, and misunderstandings.[106]

Multicultural teams can create frustrating dilemmas for managers. Cultural differences can create substantial obstacles to effective teamwork, but they may be difficult to recognize until significant damage has been done.[107] It is easy to assume that challenges in multicultural teams are just due to differing communication styles, but differing attitudes toward hierarchy and authority and conflicting norms for decision making can also create barriers to a multicultural team's ultimate success.[108] We next elaborate on all three of these factors.

Direct versus Indirect Communication

Communication in Western cultures is typically direct and explicit, and a listener does not have to know much about the context or the speaker to interpret it. In many other cultures, meaning is embedded in the way the message is presented. For example, people in the West obtain information about other people's preferences and priorities by asking direct questions, such as "Do you prefer option A or option B?" In cultures using indirect communication, people often have to infer preferences and priorities from changes, or the lack of them, in the other person's counterproposal. In cross-cultural settings, the non-Westerner can easily understand the direct communications of the Westerner, but the Westerner often has difficulty understanding the indirect communications of the non-Westerner.[109] Communication challenges create barriers to effective teamwork by reducing information sharing, creating interpersonal conflict, or both. Because accepted communication patterns differ across cultures, it is a good idea to familiarize yourself with the communication patterns and norms of any other cultures with which you will be interacting.

Differing Attitudes toward Hierarchy and Authority

By design, teams have a rather flat structure. But team members from cultures in which people are treated differently according to their status in an organization are often uncomfortable on flat teams. If they defer to higher status team members, their behavior will be seen as appropriate by team members from hierarchical cultures, but they may damage their credibility if most of the team comes from egalitarian cultures. For example, in multicultural teams, engineers from the culture in India are typically not culturally comfortable arguing with the team leader or with older people.[110] This decreases the ability of the team to secure everyone's input.

Conflicting Decision-Making Norms

Cultures differ substantially when it comes to how quickly decisions should be made and how much analysis is required. Compared with managers from other countries, U.S. managers like to make decisions very quickly and with relatively little analysis. A Brazilian manager at an American company made these comments about a negotiation, "On the first day, we agreed on three points, and on the second day, the company wanted to start with point four. But the Koreans wanted to go back and rediscuss points one through three. My boss almost had an attack."[111]

SUMMARY AND APPLICATION

A group is two or more persons who interact with one another such that each person influences and is influenced by each other person. Teams are an interdependent collection of at least two individuals who share a common goal and share accountability for the team's as well as their own outcomes. Groups and teams are not necessarily the same thing. All teams are groups, but not all groups are teams. Common kinds of groups in organizations include workgroups, teams, and informal groups.

The performance of any group is affected by several factors other than its reasons for forming and the stages of its development. The five basic group performance factors are composition, size, norms, cohesiveness, and informal leadership. Group composition is most often described in terms of the homogeneity or heterogeneity of the members. Group size can also have an important effect on performance. A norm is a standard against which the appropriateness of a behavior is judged and determines the behavior expected in a certain situation. Group cohesiveness is the extent to which a group is committed to remaining together; it results from forces acting on the members to remain in the group. The final group performance factor is informal leadership: the emergence of an individual who engages in leadership activities but whose right to do so has not been formally recognized.

When a new group or team is formed it typically goes through several stages of development. Traditional research on small groups per se (as opposed to teams) has focused on a four-stage development process: (1) mutual acceptance, (2) communication and decision making, (3) motivation and productivity, and (4) control and organization. In terms of teamwork, other factors that contribute to performance include process gain or loss, team efficacy, trust, social facilitation, and roles. The process of implementation of teams should be approached carefully as would be the case for any major organizational change.

Managers need to have a clear understanding of the potential benefits and costs of using teams. They should also know what they need to do to promote effective team performance, including providing top management support, understanding time frames, and planning for the likely need to change rewards. Working to develop teamwork competencies is also important.

Virtual teams and multicultural teams are important emerging areas of teamwork that are relevant to most organizations today. Managers should strive to understand how to most effectively use these two kinds of teams.

LOSKUTNIKOV/SHUTTERSTOCK.COM

REAL WORLD RESPONSE

TEAMWORK AT STARBUCKS

Starbucks' expansion into South Korea posed a challenge. Should the company change its teamwork and equality culture to better fit South Korea's hierarchical natural culture that valued hierarchical distance between employees or should it stay the same and reinforce its own values in South Korea?

Starbucks decided to stay true to its culture and values, but to be sensitive to the cultural needs and expectations of its South Korean employees. Because South Korean employees were uncomfortable calling each other by their first names rather than by traditional hierarchical titles, Starbucks' managers gave every South Korean employee an English name to use at work. This made employees more comfortable using first names while preserving Starbucks' equality values.[112]

Another teamwork issue emerged because South Korean men typically do not do "housework" chores including washing dishes and cleaning toilets. However, this type of work is expected of everyone in Starbucks' stores. To help its male employees overcome the psychological barrier to cleaning, Starbucks leveraged the South Korean cultural affinity for imitating leaders' behaviors. The international director for Starbucks' headquarters personally did all of the cleaning activities and even hung a picture of him cleaning the toilet. Because lower-level employees imitate the behavior of top leaders this helped them overcome this cultural obstacle to teamwork.[113]

DISCUSSION QUESTIONS

1. Identify several different groups that you belong to and classify them as one of the group types discuss in this chapter.
2. Think about an effective team you have been on. What made it effective? Think about an underperforming team you have been on. Why was it underperforming?
3. Are any of the groups to which you belong too large or too small to get their work done? If so, what can the leader or the members do to alleviate the problem?
4. List two norms each for two of the groups to which you belong. How are these norms enforced?
5. Discuss the following statement: "Group cohesiveness is the good, warm feeling we get from working in groups and is something that all group leaders should strive to develop in the groups they lead."
6. Some say that changing to a team-based arrangement "just makes sense" for organizations. What are the four primary reasons why this might be so?
7. Do you think a team contract would improve the effectiveness of teams? Why or why not?
8. Which do you feel is more important to team performance, informational diversity or demographic diversity? Why? Do multicultural teams increase this type of diversity? If so, how?

UNDERSTAND YOURSELF EXERCISE

How Well Do You Add Up as a Team Member?

Think about a group or team that you've been a part of. Answer the following questions about the nature of your participation by selecting the option that's most accurate. There are no right or wrong answers. You may have to be "hypothetical" in responding to a few items, and in some cases you might have to rely on "composite" answers reflecting your experience in more than one group or teamwork setting.

1. I offer information and opinions
   a. Very frequently
   b. Frequently
   c. Sometimes
   d. Rarely
   e. Never
2. I summarize what's happening in the group
   a. Very frequently
   b. Frequently
   c. Sometimes
   d. Rarely
   e. Never
3. When there's a problem, I try to identify what's happening
   a. Very frequently
   b. Frequently
   c. Sometimes
   d. Rarely
   e. Never

4. I start the group working
   a. Very frequently
   b. Frequently
   c. Sometimes
   d. Rarely
   e. Never
5. I suggest directions that the group can take
   a. Very frequently
   b. Frequently
   c. Sometimes
   d. Rarely
   e. Never
6. I listen actively
   a. Very frequently
   b. Frequently
   c. Sometimes
   d. Rarely
   e. Never
7. I give positive feedback to other members of the group
   a. Very frequently
   b. Frequently
   c. Sometimes
   d. Rarely
   e. Never
8. I compromise
   a. Very frequently
   b. Frequently
   c. Sometimes
   d. Rarely
   e. Never
9. I help relieve tension
   a. Very frequently
   b. Frequently
   c. Sometimes
   d. Rarely
   e. Never
10. I talk
    a. Very frequently
    b. Frequently
    c. Sometimes
    d. Rarely
    e. Never
11. I help to ensure that meeting times and places are arranged
    a. Very frequently
    b. Frequently
    c. Sometimes
    d. Rarely
    e. Never

12. I try to observe what's happening in the group
    a. Very frequently
    b. Frequently
    c. Sometimes
    d. Rarely
    e. Never
13. I try to help solve problems
    a. Very frequently
    b. Frequently
    c. Sometimes
    d. Rarely
    e. Never
14. I take responsibility for ensuring that tasks are completed
    a. Very frequently
    b. Frequently
    c. Sometimes
    d. Rarely
    e. Never
15. I like the group to be having a good time
    a. Very frequently
    b. Frequently
    c. Sometimes
    d. Rarely
    e. Never

How to score: Award yourself points according to the values shown in the following table. An answer of "b" on Question 5, for example, is worth 1 point, while a "b" on Question 6 is worth 3 points. To get your total score, add up all the numbers in your "Score" column.

Question	a	b	c	d	e	Score
1	1	2	3	2	1	
2	1	2	3	2	1	
3	1	2	3	2	1	
4	2	2	3	1	0	
5	0	1	3	1	0	
6	3	3	2	1	0	
7	3	3	2	1	0	
8	2	3	3	1	0	
9	1	2	3	1	0	
10	0	0	3	2	1	
11	2	3	3	1	0	
12	3	3	2	1	0	
13	2	3	3	1	0	
14	2	2	3	1	0	
15	1	1	2	1	1	
			TOTAL			

41–45 = Very effective team person

35–40 = Effective team person

Under 35 = Person who probably needs to work on his or her teamwork skills

Source: Adapted from University of South Australia, "Test Your Effectiveness as a Team Member." *'Working in Teams' Online Workshop*. Handout: "Teamwork Skills Questionnaire."

GROUP EXERCISE

1. Working alone, write the letters of the alphabet in a vertical column down the left side of a sheet of paper: A–Z.
2. Your instructor will randomly select a sentence from any written document and read out loud the first twenty-six letters in that sentence. Write these letters in a vertical column immediately to the right of the alphabet column. Everyone should have an identical set of twenty-six two-letter combinations.
3. Working alone, think of a famous person whose initials correspond to each pair of letters, and write the name next to the letters—for example, "MT Mark Twain." You will have ten minutes. Only one name per set is allowed. One point is awarded for each legitimate name, so the maximum score is twenty-six points.
4. After time expires, exchange your paper with another member of the class and score each other's work. Disputes about the legitimacy of names will be settled by the instructor. Keep your score for use later in the exercise.

Your instructor will divide the class into groups of five to ten people. All groups should have approximately the same number of members. Each group now follows the procedure given in Part 1. Again write the letters of the alphabet down the left side of the sheet of paper, this time in reverse order: Z–A. Your instructor will dictate a new set of letters for the second column. The time limit and scoring procedure are the same. The only difference is that the groups will generate the names.

Each team identifies the group member who came up with the most names. The instructor places these "best" students into one group. Then all groups repeat Part 2, but this time the letters from the reading will be in the first column and the alphabet letters will be in the second column.

Each team calculates the average individual score of its members on Part 1 and compares it with the team score from Parts 2 and 3, kept separately. Your instructor will put the average individual score and team scores from each part of each group on the board.

Follow-Up Questions

1. Are there differences in the average individual scores and the team scores? What are the reasons for the differences, if any?
2. Although the team scores in this exercise usually are higher than the average individual scores, under what conditions might individual averages exceed group scores?

Source: Adapted from Jones, J. J., & Pfeiffer, J. W. (eds.). The Handbook for Group Facilitators (pp. 19–20). Copyright © 1979 Pfeiffer.

VIDEO EXERCISE

Evo Teamwork

For years Evo has supported athletic teams, but only recently did the Seattle-based e-commerce company launch a formal work team. Like many organizations, the online retailer of snowboard, ski, skate, and wake gear used team metaphors loosely to describe anything involving random groups of employees. But Evo got an education on real work teams when the company formed a team for its creative services employees.

The new group, which is comprised of a photographer, designer, and copywriter, is responsible for producing Evo's magazine ads, promotions, and website content. Although the individuals' roles are not generally interchangeable, photographer Tre Dauenhauer might dabble in design, graphic designer Pubs One may write a few lines of copy, and copywriter Sunny Fenton might snap photos on occasion. Most team projects require a combination of eye-grabbing photos, clever words, and a compelling design, and the teammates are committed to a common purpose.

When the creative services team launched, group members moved into their own space, away from Evo's chaotic, open-plan work areas. Being together every day enabled the team members to become better acquainted and move through the "forming" stage more quickly. But even with close quarters, Dauenhauer, One, and Fenton needed help navigating the conflict-ridden, storming stage of their team's development. Before joining the team, they functioned individually and weren't used to sharing power or making decisions as a group. To help the members learn to work together, Nathan Decker, director of e-commerce, became the team leader. As a skilled negotiator, Decker makes sure his talented trio steers clear of dysfunction and delivers the goods. Any time the team finishes a project, Decker brings members together for a postmortem discussion—a method of reviewing what was learned, and how things could be executed differently. It's here that the team members identify new routines and rituals to incorporate into their process for future improvement.

Due to Decker's leadership and skillful negotiation of conflicts, members of the creative services team are learning how to communicate in ways never before possible. Having a skilled leader to facilitate work processes has helped build team cohesiveness and deliver a collective output that is greater than the sum of its parts.

Questions

1. What organizational dilemma was hurting Evo's creative output, and how did management resolve the problem using teams?
2. How might Nathan Decker lead effectively as the team starts "norming"?
3. Can you relate the group performance factors of composition, size, norms, cohesiveness, and informal leadership to Evo?

VIDEO CASE

Now What?

PERCOM/SHUTTERSTOCK.COM

Imagine being part of a group meeting with two coworkers and the boss to discuss a situation with a customer who wants a 30 percent discount on an order because it will be a week late. The team can't agree on whether to give the discount to keep the good customer happy or not give the discount to make more money on the sale, and is having trouble making a decision. *What do you say or do?* Go to this chapter's "Now What?" video, watch the challenge video, and choose a response. Be sure to also view the outcomes of the two responses you didn't choose.

Discussion Questions

1. Which team performance factors have the most influence on the decision-making process?
2. What teamwork competencies were most important for achieving a resolution and why?
3. As a manager, what might you have done to handle the situation better? Please use group or team concepts from the chapter.

ENDNOTES

[1]Strauss, S. (2002, May 20). How to Be a Great Place to Work. *USA Today*.

[2]Jargon, J. (2009, August 5). Latest Starbucks Buzzword: "Lean" Japanese Techniques. *The Wall Street Journal*. Available online: http://online.wsj.com/article/SB124933474023402611.html.

[3]Chen, X. & Tsui, A. S. (2006). An Organizational Perspective on Multi-Level Cultural Integration: Human Resource Management Practices in Cross-Cultural Contexts. In *Multi-Level Issues in Social Systems: Research in Multi-Level Issues,* eds. F. J. Yammarino & F. Dansereau (Vol. 5, pp. 81–96.). Bingley, UK: Emerald Group Publishing.

[4]Shaw, M. E. (1991). *Group Dynamics: The Psychology of Small Group Behavior* (3rd ed., p. 11). New York: McGraw-Hill. See also Cannon-Bowers, J. A., & Bowers, C. (2010). Team Development and Functioning. In *Handbook of Industrial and Organizational Psychology,* ed. S. Zedeck (pp. 597–650). Washington, DC: American Psychological Association.

[5]Sundstrom, E., DeMeuse, K. P., & Futrell, D. (1990). Work Teams: Applications and Effectiveness. *American Psychologist, 45*(2), 120–133; Thompson, L. L. (2004). *Making the Team: A Guide for Managers* (2nd ed.). Upper Saddle River, NJ: Pearson Education.

[6]Hollingshead, A. B., McGrath, J. E., & O'Connor, K. M. (1993). Group Task Performance and Communication Technology: A Longitudinal Study of Computer-Mediated Versus Face-to-Face Work Groups. *Small Group Research, 24*(3), 307–333; Hollingshead, A. B.,& McGrath, J. E. (1995). Computer-Assisted Groups: A Critical Review of the Empirical Research. In *Team Effectiveness and Decision Making in Organizations,* eds. R. Guzzo and E. Salas (pp. 46–78). San Francisco, CA: Jossey-Bass; Thompson, L. L. (2004). *Making the Team: A Guide for Managers* (2nd ed.). Upper Saddle River, NJ: Pearson Education.

[7]Sparks, W. L., Monetta, D. J., & Simmons, L. M., Jr. (1999). Affinity Groups: Developing Complex Adaptive Organizations. Washington, DC:. The PAM Institute, working paper.

[8]Piorsall, B. (2013). How Does IDEO Organize its Teams? What Creative Process do they Follow? Quora. Available online: http://www.quora.com/How-does-IDEO-organize-its-teams-What-creative-process-do-they-follow.

[9]Salter, C. (2006). A Prescription for Innovation, *Fast Company*, April. Available online: http://www.fastcompany.com/56032/prescription-innovation.

[10]Global Procurement Mission and Goals. *Colgate*. Available online: http://www.colgate.com/app/Colgate/US/Corp/ContactUs/GMLS/MissionAndGoals.cvsp.

[11]Lohr, S. (2009, July 27). Netflix Competitors Learn the Power of Teamwork. *The New York Times*. Available online: http://www.nytimes.com/2009/07/28/technology/internet/28netflix.html?_r=2; Dybwad, B. (2009). Netflix Million Dollar Prize Ends in Photo Finish. *Mashable*. Available online: http://mashable.com/2009/09/21/netflix-prize-winners/.

[12]Olson, P. (1990, January–February). Choices for Innovation Minded Corporations. *Journal of Business Strategy,* 86–90.

[13]Townsend, A. M., DeMarie, S. M., & Hendrickson, A. R. (1998). Virtual Teams: Technology and the Workplace of the Future. *Academy of Management Executive, 12*(3), 17–29, 17.

[14]Geber, B. (1995). Virtual Teams. *Training, 32*(4), 36–42.

[15]Davis, J. H. (1964). *Group Performance* (pp. 92–96). Reading, MA: Addison-Wesley.

[16]Shaw, M. E. (1991). *Group Dynamics: The Psychology of Small Group Behavior* (3rd ed.). New York: McGraw-Hill; see also Horwitz, S. K., & Horwitz, I. B. (2007). The Effects of Team Diversity on Team Outcomes: A Meta-Analytic Review of Team Demography. *Journal of Management, 33*(6), 987–1015.

[17]Jackson, S. E., & Joshi, A. (2010). Work Team Diversity. In *Handbook of Industrial and Organizational Psychology,* ed. S. Zedeck (pp. 651–686). Washington, DC: American Psychological Association.

[18]O'Reilly, C. A., III, Caldwell, D. F., & Barnett, W. P. (1999, March). Work Group Demography, Social Integration, and Turnover. *Administrative Science Quarterly, 34*, 21–37.

[19]See Webber, S. S., & Donahue, L. (2001). Impact of Highly and Less Job-Related Diversity on Work Group Cohesion and Performance: A Meta-Analysis. *Journal of Management, 27*, 141–162.

[20]Adler, N. (2002). *International Dimensions of Organizational Behavior* (4th ed., Chapter 5). Cincinnati, OH: Thomson Learning.

[21]Shaw, M. E. (1991). *Group Dynamics: The Psychology of Small Group Behavior* (3rd ed., pp. 173–177). New York: McGraw-Hill.

[22]See Chatman, J., & Flynn, F. (2001). The Influence of Demographic Heterogeneity on the Emergence and Consequences of Cooperative Norms in Work Teams. *Academy of Management Journa, 44*(5), 956–974.

[23]Feldman, D. C. (1994, January). The Development and Enforcement of Group Norms. *Academy of Management Review*, 47–53.

[24]Piper, W. E., Marrache, M., Lacroix, R., Richardson, A. M., & Jones, B. D. (1993, February). Cohesion as a Basic Bond in Groups. *Human Relations*, 93–109.

[25]Beal, D., Cohen, R., Burke, M., & McLendon, C. (2003). Cohesion and Performance in Groups: A Meta-Analytic Clarification of Construct Relations. *Journal of Applied Psychology, 88*(6), 989–1004.

[26]Keller, R. T., (1996, December). Predictors of the Performance of Project Groups in R & D Organizations. *Academy of Management Journal*, 715–726.

[27]Janis, I. L. (1992). *Groupthink* (2nd ed., p. 9). Boston: Houghton Mifflin.

[28]Mayer, J. D., & Salovey, P. (1993). The Intelligence of Emotional Intelligence. *Intelligence, 17,* 433–442; Mayer, J. D., & Salovey, P. (1997). What Is Emotional Intelligence? In *Emotional Development and Emotional Intelligence,* eds. P. Salovey & D. J. Sluyter. New York: Basic Books.

[29]Ayoki, O. B., Callan, V. J., & Hartel, C. E. J. (2008). The Influence of Team Emotional Intelligence Climate on Conflict and Team Members' Reactions to Conflict. *Small Group Research, 39*(2), 121–149.

[30]Bass, B. M., & Ryterband, E. C. (1979). *Organizational Psychology* (2nd ed., pp. 252–254). Boston: Allyn & Bacon. See also Lester, S., Meglino, B., & Korsgaard, M. A. (2002, January). The Antecedents and Consequences of Group Potency: A Longitudinal Investigation of Newly Formed Work Groups. *Academy of Management Journal, 45*(2), 352–369.

[31]Long, S. (1994, April). Early Integration in Groups: A Group to Join and a Group to Create. *Human Relations*, 311–332.

[32]For example, see Waller, M., Conte, J., Gibson, C., & Carpenter, M. (2001). The Effect of Individual Perceptions of Deadlines on Team Performance. *Academy of Management Review, 26*(4), 596–600.

[33]Obert, S. L. (1993, January). Developmental Patterns of Organizational Task Groups: A Preliminary Study. *Human Relations*, 37–52.

[34]Bass, B. M., & Ryterband, E. C. (1979). *Organizational Psychology* (2nd ed., pp. 252–254). Boston: Allyn & Bacon.

[35]Bass, B. M. (1954, September). The Leaderless Group Discussion. *Psychological Bulletin*, 465–492.

[36]Lieber, J. (1997, November 2). Time to Heal the Wounds., *Sports Illustrated*, 96–91.

[37]Gersick, C. J. G. (1999). Marking Time: Predictable Transitions in Task Groups. *Academy of Management Journal, 32*, 274–309.

[38]Bandura, A. (1997). Collective Efficacy. In *Self-Efficacy: The Exercise of Control,* ed. A. Bandura (pp. 477–525). New York: W. H. Freeman.

[39]Gully, S. M., Joshi, A., Incalcaterra, K. A., & Beaubien, J. M. (2002). A Meta-Analysis of Team-Efficacy, Potency, and Performance: Interdependence and Level of Analysis as Moderators of Observed Relationships. *Journal of Applied Psychology, 87*(5), 819–832; Jung, D. I., & Sosik, J. (2003). Group Potency and Collective Efficacy: Examining Their Predictive Validity, Level of Analysis, and Effects of Performance Feedback on Future Group Performance. *Group and Organization Management, 28*(3), 366–391.

[40]Gully, S. M., Devine, D. J., & Whitney, D. J. (2012). A Meta-Analysis of Cohesion and Performance: Effects of Levels of Analysis and Task Interdependence. *Small Group Research, 43(6)*, 702-725

[41]Thompson, L. L. (2004). *Making the Team: A Guide for Managers* (2nd ed., p. 93). Upper Saddle River, NJ: Pearson Education.

[42]Watson, W. E., Johnson, L., Kumar, K., & Critelli, J. (1998). Process Gain and Process Loss: Comparing Interpersonal Processes and Performance of Culturally Diverse and Non-Diverse Teams Across Time. *International Journal of Intercultural Relations, 22,* 409–430.

[43]Horowitz, I. A., & Bordens, K. S. (1995). *Social Psychology*. Mountain View, CA: Mayfield.

[44]Karau, S. J., & Williams, K. D. (1993). Social Loafing: A Meta-Analytic Review and Theoretical Integration. *Journal of Personality and Social Psychology, 65,* 681–706.

[45]Kerr, N. L. (1989). Illusions of Efficacy: The Effects of Group Size on Perceived Efficacy in Social Dilemmas. *Journal of Experimental Social Psychology, 25,* 287–313.

[46]Williams, K. D., Harkins, S. G., & Latané, B. (1981). Identifiability as a Deterrent to Social Loafing: Two Cheering Experiments. *Journal of Personality and Social Psychology, 40,* 303–311.

[47]Zajonc, R. (1965). Social Facilitation. *Science, 149,* 269–274.

[48]Cottrell, N. B. (1972). Social Facilitation. In *Experimental Social Psychology,* ed. C. G. McClintock. New York: Holt, Rinehart & Winston.

[49]Williams, K., Harkins, S., & Latané, B. (1981). Identifiability as a Deterrent to Social Loafing: Two Cheering Experiments. *Journal of Personality and Social Psychology, 40,* 303–311; Latané, B. (1986). Responsibility and Effort in Organizations. In *Designing Effective Work Groups,* ed. P. S. Goodman. San Francisco, CA: Jossey-Bass.

[50]Hackman, J. R. (1992). Group Influences on Individuals in Organizations. In *Handbook of Industrial and Organizational Psychology,* eds. M. D. Dunnette & L. M. Hough (2nd ed., Vol. 3). Palo Alto, CA: Consulting Psychologists Press.

[51]Katzenbach, J. R., & Smith, D. K. (1994). *The Wisdom of Teams: Creating the High-Performance Organization*. New York: HarperBusiness.

[52]Chen, X. & Tsui, A. S. (2006). An Organizational Perspective on Multi-Level Cultural Integration: Human Resource Management Practices in Cross-Cultural Contexts. In *Multi-Level Issues in Social Systems: Research in Multi-Level Issues,* eds. F. J. Yammarino & F. Dansereau (Vol. 5, pp. 81–96.). Bingley, UK: Emerald Group Publishing.

[53]Parker, G., McAdams, J., & Zielinski, D. (2000). *Rewarding Teams: Lessons from the Trenches*. San Francisco, CA: Jossey-Bass.

[54]Levine, J. M., & Moreland, R. L. (1989). Newcomers and Oldtimers in Small Groups. In *Psychology of Group Influence,* ed. P. Paulus (2nd ed., pp. 143–186). Hillsdale, NJ: Lawrence Erlbaum Associates; Levine, J. M., & Moreland, R. L. (Eds.). (2006). *Small Groups*. Philadelphia: Psychology Press.

[55]Manz, C. C., & Sims, H. P. (1995). *Business Without Bosses: How Self-Managing Teams Are Building High- Performing Companies* (pp. 27–28). New York: John Wiley and Sons.

[56]Manz, C. C., & Sims, H. P. (1995). *Business Without Bosses: How Self-Managing Teams Are Building High- Performing Companies* (pp. pp. 29–31). New York: John Wiley and Sons.

[57]Manz, C. C., & Sims, H. P. (1995). *Business Without Bosses: How Self-Managing Teams Are Building High- Performing Companies* (p. 130). New York: John Wiley and Sons.

[58]Rico, R., Sanchez-Manzanares, M., Gil, F. & Gibson, C. (2008). Team Implicit Knowledge Coordination Processes: A Team Knowledge-Based Approach. *Academy of Management Review*, *33*(1), 63–184.

[59]Orsburn, J. D., Moran, L., Musselwhite, E., & Zenger, J. H. (1990). *Self Directed Work Teams: The New American Challenge* (p. 15). New York: McGraw-Hill.

[60]Ancona, D., Bresman, H., & Kaeufer, K. (2002, Spring). The Competitive Advantage of X-Teams. *Sloan Management Review*, 33–42.

[61]About IDEO, 2012. Available online: http://www.ideo.com/about/.

[62]Innovative Product Design Team, *Invention at Play*, 2012. Available online: http://inventionatplay.org/inventors_ide.html.

[63]Dawson, I. (2012, May 28). Teamwork and Innovation the IDEO Way, *Dare Dreamer Magazine*. Available online: http://daredreamermag.com/2012/05/28/teamwork-and-innovation-the-ideo-way/.

[64]Katzenbach, J. R., & Smith, D. K. (1994). *The Wisdom of Teams: Creating the High-Performance Organization* (pp. 184–189). New York: HarperBusiness.

[65]Manz, C. C., & Sims, H. P. (1995). *Business Without Bosses: How Self-Managing Teams Are Building High- Performing Companies* (pp. 10–11). New York: John Wiley and Sons.

[66]Manz, C. C., & Sims, H. P. (1995). *Business Without Bosses: How Self-Managing Teams Are Building High- Performing Companies* (pp. 74–76). New York: John Wiley and Sons.

[67]Colquitt, J., Noe, R., & Jackson, C. (2002). Justice in Teams: Antecedents and Consequences of Procedural Justice Climate. *Personnel Psychology*, *55*, 83–95.

[68]Manz, C. C., & Sims, H. P. (1995). *Business Without Bosses: How Self-Managing Teams Are Building High- Performing Companies* (p. 200). New York: John Wiley and Sons; see also Horwitz, S. K., & Horwitz, I. B. (2007). The Effects of Team Diversity on Team Outcomes: A Meta-Analytic Review of Team Demography. *Journal of Management*, *33*(6), 987–1015.

[69]Manz, C. C., & Sims, H. P. (1995) Business Without Bosses: How Self-Managing Teams Are Building High-Performing Companies (p. 200). New York: John Wiley and Sons.

[70]From Stevens, M. J., & Campion, M. A. (1994). The Knowledge, Skill, and Ability Requirements for Teamwork: Implications for Human Resource Management. *Journal of Management, 20,* 505.

[71]Zey-Ferrell, M., & Ferrell, O. C. (1982). Role-Set Configuration and Opportunity as Predictors of Unethical Behavior in Organizations. *Human Relations, 35*(7), 587–604.

[72]Treviño, L. K., Weaver, G. R., & Reynolds, S. J. (2006). Behavioral Ethics in Organizations: A Review. *Journal of Management, 32,* 951–990.

[73]Treviño, L. K., Weaver, G. R., & Reynolds, S. J. (2006). Behavioral Ethics in Organizations: A Review. *Journal of Management, 32,* 951–990.

[74]Berry, G.R. (2011). Enhancing Effectiveness on Virtual Teams: Understanding Why Traditional Team Skills are Insufficient, *Journal of Business Communication, 48*(2), 186–206.

[75]Bhappu, A. D., Griffith, T. L., & Northcraft, G. B. (1997). Media Effects and Communication Bias in Diverse Groups. *Organizational Behavior and Human Decision Processes, 70,* 199–205.

[76]Gibson, C., & Cohen, S. (2003). *Virtual Teams That Work: Creating Conditions for Virtual Team Effectiveness*. San Francisco, CA: Jossey-Bass.

[77]Cascio, W. F. (2000). Managing a Virtual Workplace. *Academy of Management Executives, 14*(3), 81–90.

[78]Lipnack, J., & Stamps, J. (1997). *Virtual Teams: Reaching Across Space, Time, and Organizations with Technology*. New York: John Wiley and Sons.

[79]Bell, B. S., & Kozlowski, S. W. J. (2002). A Typology of Virtual Teams: Implications for Effective Leadership. *Group and Organization Management, 27*(1), 14–49.

[80]Gibson, C. B., & Gibbs, J. L. (2006). Unpacking the Concept of Virtuality: The Effects of Geographic Dispersion, Electronic Dependence, Dynamic Structure, and National Diversity on Team Innovation. *Administrative Science Quarterly, 51,* 451–495.

[81]Thompsen, J. A. (2000, September). Leading Virtual Teams. *Quality Digest*. Available online at http://www.qualitydigest.com/sept00/html/teams.html.

[82]Bell, B. S., & Kozlowski, S. W. J. (2002). A Typology of Virtual Teams: Implications for Effective Leadership. *Group and Organization Management, 27*(1), 14–49.

[83]Manz, C., & Sims, H. P. (1987). Leading Workers to Lead Themselves: The External Leadership of Self-Managing Work Teams. *Administrative Science Quarterly, 32,* 106–128.

[84]Hackman, J. R., & Walton, R. E. (1986). Leading Groups in Organizations. In *Designing Effective Work Groups,* eds. Paul S. Goodman & Associates. San Francisco, CA: Jossey-Bass.

[85]Kozlowski, S. W. J. (1998). Training and Developing Adaptive Teams: Theory, Principles, and Research. In *Decision Making Under Stress: Implications for Training and Simulation,* eds. J. A. Cannon-Bowers & E. Salas (pp. 115–153). Washington, DC: American Psychological Association; Smith, E. M., Ford, J. K., & Kozlowski, S. W. J. (1997). Building Adaptive Expertise: Implications for Training Design. In *Training for a Rapidly Changing Workplace: Applications of Psychological Research,* ed. M. A. Quinones & A. Ehrenstein (pp. 89–118). Washington, DC: American Psychological Association.

[86]Gersick, C. J. G., & Hackman, J. R. (1990). Habitual Routines in Task-Performing Teams. *Organizational Behavior and Human Decision Processes, 47,* 65–97.

[87]Siegel, J., Dubrovsky, V., Kiesler, S., & McGuire, T. W. (1986). Group Processes in Computer-Mediated Communication. *Organizational Behavior and Human Decision Processes, 37,* 157–187; Strauss, S. G., & McGrath, J. E. (1994). Does the Medium Matter? The Interaction of Task Type and Technology on Group Performance and Member Reactions. *Journal of Applied Psychology, 79,* 87–97; Thompson, L. L. (2004). *Making the Team: A Guide for Managers* (2nd ed.). Upper Saddle River, NJ: Pearson Education.

[88]Bell, B. S., & Kozlowski, S. W. J. (2002). A Typology of Virtual Teams: Implications for Effective Leadership. *Group and Organization Management, 27*(1), 14–49.

[89]Duarte, D. L., & Snyder, N. T. (1999). *Mastering Virtual Teams*. San Francisco, CA: Jossey-Bass.

[90]Rosencrance, L. (2005, January). Meet Me in Cyberspace. *Computerworld*. Available online: http://www.computerworld.com.au/article/1636/meet_me_cyberspace/?relcomp=1.

[91]Purdum, T. (2005, May 4). Teaming, Take 2. *IndustryWeek*. Available online: http://www.industryweek.com/articles/teaming_take_2_10179.aspx.

[92]Rosencrance, L. (2005, January 3). Meet Me in Cyberspace. *Computerworld*. Available online: http://www.computerworld.com.au/article/1636/meet_me_cyberspace/?relcomp=1.

[93]Bassett-Jones, N., & Lloyd, G. (2005). The Paradox of Diversity Management. *Journal of Creativity and Innovation Management, 14,* 169–175.

[94]Williams, K. Y. (1998). Demography and Diversity in Organizations: A Review of 100 Years of Research. In *Research in Organizational Behavior,* eds. B. M. Staw & L. L. Cummings (Vol. 20, pp. 77–140). Greenwich, CT: JAI Press.

[95]Kanter, R. M. (1983). *The Change Masters*. New York: Simon and Schuster.

[96]Millikin, F. J., & Martins, L. L. (1996). Searching for Common Threads: Understanding the Multiple Effects of Diversity in Organizational Groups. *Academy of Management Review, 21,* 402–433.

[97]Bassett-Jones, N., & Lloyd, G. (2005). The Paradox of Diversity Management. *Journal of Creativity and Innovation Management, 14,* 169–175.

[98]Jackson, S. E., Stone, V. K., & Alvarez, E. B. (1992). Socialization Amidst Diversity: The Impact of Demographics on Work Team Old-Timers and Newcomers. In *Research in Organizational Behavior,* L. L. Cummings & B. M. Staw (Vol. 15, pp. 45–109). Greenwich, CT: JAI.

[99]Williams, K. Y., & O'Reilly III, C. A. (1998). Demography and Diversity in Organizations: A Review of 40 Years of Research. *Research in Organizational Behavior, 20,* 77–140.

[100]Jehn, K., Northcraft, G., & Neale, M. (1999). Why Differences Make a Difference: A Field Study of Diversity, Conflict, and Performance in Workgroups. *Administrative Science Quarterly, 44*(4), 741–763.

[101]Bhappu, A. D., Zellmer-Bruhn, M., & Anand, V. (2001). The Effects of Demographic Diversity and Virtual Work Environments on Knowledge Processing in Teams. *Advances in Interdisciplinary Studies of Work Teams, 8,* 149–165.

[102]Melymuka, K. (2006, November 20). Managing Multicultural Teams. *Computerworld*. Available online: http://www.computerworld.com/s/article/271169/Managing_Multicultural_Teams.

[103]Brett, J., Behfar, K., & Kern, M. C. (2006, November). Managing Multicultural Teams. *Harvard Business Review,* 84–91.

[104]Brett, J., Behfar, K., & Kern, M. C. (2006, November). Managing Multicultural Teams. *Harvard Business Review,* 84–91.

[105]Melymuka, K. (2006, November 20). Managing Multicultural Teams. *Computerworld*. Available online: http://www.computerworld.com/s/article/271169/Managing_Multicultural_Teams.

[106]Melymuka, K. (2006, November 20). Managing Multicultural Teams. *Computerworld*. Available online: http://www.computerworld.com/s/article/271169/Managing_Multicultural_Teams.

[107]Brett, J., Behfar, K., & Kern, M. C. (2006, November). Managing Multicultural Teams. *Harvard Business Review,* 84–91.

[108]Behfar, K., Kern, M., & Brett, J. (2006). *Managing Challenges in Multicultural Teams: Research on Managing Groups and Teams* (Vol. 9, pp. 233–262). New York: Elsevier.

[109]Brett, J., Behfar, K., & Kern, M. C. (2006, November). Managing Multicultural Teams. *Harvard Business Review,* 84–91.

[110]Melymuka, K. (2006, November 20). Managing Multicultural Teams. *Computerworld*. Available online: http://www.computerworld.com/s/article/271169/Managing_Multicultural_Teams.

[111]Behfar, K., Kern, M., & Brett, J. (2006). *Managing Challenges in Multicultural Teams: Research on Managing Groups and Teams* (Vol. 9, pp. 233–262). New York: Elsevier.

[112]Chen, X. & Tsui, A. S. (2006). An Organizational Perspective on Multi-Level Cultural Integration: Human Resource Management Practices in Cross-Cultural Contexts. In *Multi-Level Issues in Social Systems: Research in Multi-Level Issues,* eds. F. J. Yammarino & F. Dansereau (Vol. 5, pp. 81–96.). Bingley, UK: Emerald Group Publishing.

[113]Chen, X. & Tsui, A. S. (2006). An Organizational Perspective on Multi-Level Cultural Integration: Human Resource Management Practices in Cross-Cultural Contexts. In *Multi-Level Issues in Social Systems: Research in Multi-Level Issues,* eds. F. J. Yammarino & F. Dansereau (Vol. 5, pp. 81–96.). Bingley, UK: Emerald Group Publishing.

LOSKUTNIKOV/SHUTTERSTOCK.COM

CHAPTER 8

DECISION MAKING AND PROBLEM SOLVING

CHAPTER OUTLINE

LEARNING OUTCOMES

After studying this chapter, you should be able to:

1 Describe the nature of decision making and distinguish it from problem solving.

2 Discuss the rational approach to decision making.

3 Identify and discuss the primary behavioral aspects of decision making.

4 Discuss group decision making in organizations.

5 Discuss the nature of creativity and relate it to decision making and problem solving.

LOSKUTNIKOV/SHUTTERSTOCK.COM

REAL WORLD CHALLENGE

AN ETHICAL CHALLENGE

The CEO of a $20 million aircraft engine repair company just received a troubling fax. An airline is reporting that eight jets repaired by his company were just grounded because the turbines no longer worked. The airline claims that the CEO's company's parts are the cause of the problem. Within two hours, more calls come in and a total of eleven planes are grounded because of what the airline claims are problems with his company's parts. Although word has not yet reached the press, the FAA has been notified of the problem. The CEO fears that if his lenders learn of the accusation, the company's loans might be pulled. Not only would this be bad for the company, but it would jeopardize his own financial stake in the firm. Because the FAA has begun an investigation, he reasons, the only thing to do is sit tight until more details are revealed.

Unfortunately, the company is also in the middle of its annual audit. As part of the process, the CEO has to sign a letter stating that the auditors have been informed of any outstanding circumstances that more than likely could have a negative financial impact on the company. Disclosing the FAA investigation could mean the financial demise of his company. The CEO states, "In my industry, there's a very tight code of ethics about the use of drugs or alcohol by a manufacturer's employees. But there's nothing that tells you how you're supposed to deal with reporting information like this."[1]

Imagine that the CEO asks you how to decide what to do. Should he disclose the information and risk the jobs of hundreds of employees and his own financial stake in the company? Or should he stay quiet until he has more information? After reading this chapter, you should have some good advice for him.

ECHO/GETTY IMAGES

Managers routinely make both tough and easy decisions. Regardless of which decisions are made, though, it is almost certain that some observers will criticize and others will applaud. Indeed, in the rough-and-tumble world of business, there are few simple or easy decisions to make. Some managers claim to be focused on the goal of what is good for the company in the long term and make decisions accordingly. Others clearly focus on the here and now. Some decisions deal with employees, some with investors, and others with dollars and cents. But all require careful thought and consideration.

This chapter describes many different perspectives of decision making. We start by examining the nature of decision making and distinguishing it from problem solving. Next, we describe several different approaches to understanding the decision-making process. We then identify and discuss related behavioral aspects of decision making. Next we discuss the major elements of group decision making. Finally, we discuss creativity, a key ingredient in many effective decisions.

THE NATURE OF DECISION MAKING

decision making
The process of choosing from among several alternatives

Decision making is choosing one alternative from among several. Consider a manager seeking a location for a new factory. The manager identifies a set of potential locations, assesses each in terms of a number of relevant criteria (such as cost of the land, access to transportation, the local labor force, property tax rates, and so forth). This assessment will allow the manager to eliminate some sites from further consideration but most likely there will still be multiple sites that best fit the firm's requirements. At this point the manager must make a decision and select one.

problem solving
Finding the answer to a question

Problem solving, on the other hand, involves finding the answer to a question. Suppose a manager identifies an ideal site for the factory and initiates the process of buying the land. However, the manager discovers that there is some ambiguity about which of two entities actually owns the site. The most likely solution would be to engage the services of a real estate attorney to sort things out. Most likely the attorney can get to the bottom of things and then the purchase can continue. In this case there is not a decision to be made, since there is one correct answer as to who owns the land.

Note that in some situations decision making and problem solving start out alike but may lead down different paths. To illustrate, let's revisit the site selection example again. If after evaluating each of the primary locations only one viable choice remains, then there is really no decision left to make—what appeared to call for a decision instead turned into a problem. Similarly, when the issue of land ownership comes up the real estate attorney might advise the manager than it may take years and a great deal of money to identify the legal owner. Now the manager has to make a decision—continue efforts to buy the land or pull out and look for another option. Most of our interest relates to decision making. However, we will identify implications for problem solving as relevant.

Figure 8.1 shows the basic elements of decision making. A decision maker's actions are guided by a goal. Each of several alternative courses of action is linked with various outcomes. Information is available on the alternatives, on the likelihood that each outcome will occur, and on the value of each outcome relative to the goal. The decision maker chooses one alternative on the basis of his or her evaluation of the information.

Figure 8.1

Elements of Decision Making

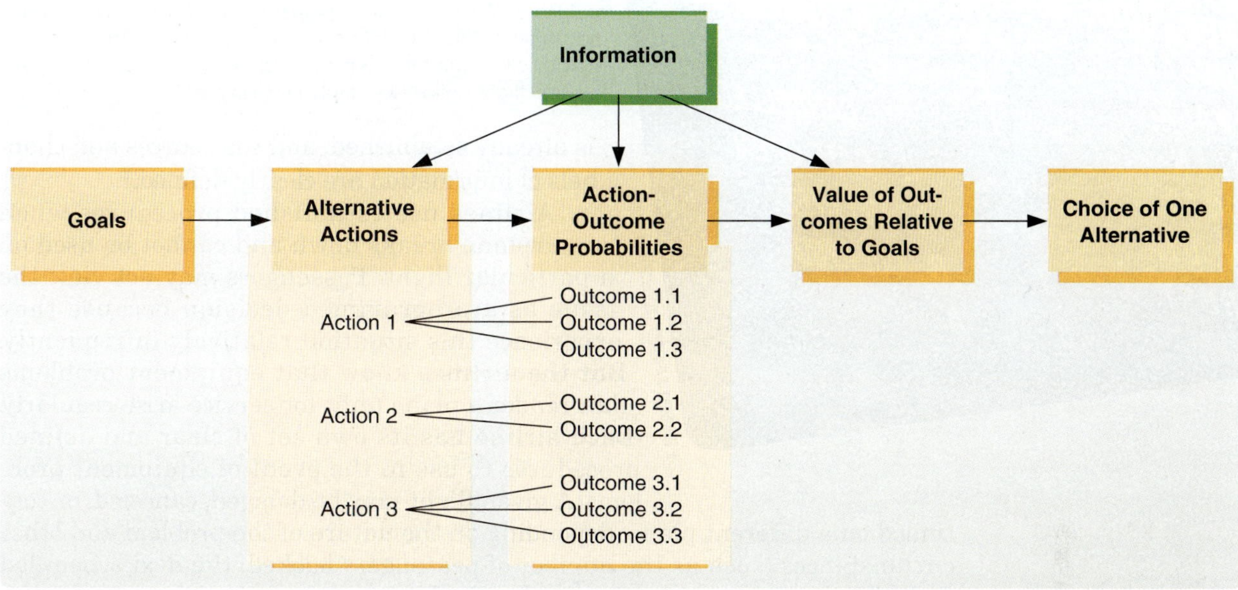

A decision maker has a goal, evaluates the outcomes of alternative courses of action in terms of the goal, and selects one alternative to be implemented

Decisions made in organizations can be classified according to frequency and to information conditions. In a decision-making context, frequency is how often a particular decision situation recurs, and information conditions describe how much information is available about the likelihood of various outcomes.

programmed decision
A decision that recurs often enough for a decision rule to be developed

decision rule
A statement that tells a decision maker which alternative to choose based on the characteristics of the decision situation

Types of Decisions

The frequency of recurrence determines whether a decision is programmed or nonprogrammed. A ***programmed decision*** recurs often enough for decision rules to be developed. A ***decision rule*** tells decision makers which alternative to choose once they have predetermined information about the decision situation. The appropriate decision rule is used whenever the same situation is encountered. Programmed decisions usually are highly structured; that is, the goals are clear and well known, the decision-making procedure

MR DOOMITS/SHUTTERSTOCK.COM

Developers targeted this tract of land as a future site of a shopping plaza. After much analysis, demographic and geographic research, and surveying, the developer selected this site.

CAAMALF/SHUTTERSTOCK.COM

Airlines often use programmed decision rules to help make decisions about such things as flight cancellations and delays. For instance, if a plane dedicated to a particular flight has a mechanical problem that will take several days to repair and the airline has no other planes available, its decision rule may indicate that the flight needs to be canceled. However, if protocols suggest the plane can be repaired in a few hours then the flight is likely to simply be delayed.

is already established, and the sources and channels of information are clearly defined.[2]

Airlines use established procedures when an airplane breaks down and cannot be used on a particular flight. Passengers may not view the issue as a programmed decision because they experience this situation relatively infrequently. But the airlines know that equipment problems that render a plane unfit for service arise regularly. Each airline has its own set of clear and defined procedures to use in the event of equipment problems. A given flight may be delayed, canceled, or continued on a different plane, depending on the nature of the problem and other circumstances (such as the number of passengers booked, the next scheduled flight for the same destination, and so forth).

nonprogrammed decision
A decision that recurs infrequently and for which there is no previously established decision rule

When a problem or decision situation has not been encountered before, however, a decision maker cannot rely on previously established decision rules. Such a decision is called a ***nonprogrammed decision***, and it requires problem solving. Problem solving is a special form of decision making in which the issue is unique—it often requires developing and evaluating alternatives without the aid of a decision rule.[3] Nonprogrammed decisions are poorly structured because information is ambiguous, there is no clear procedure for making the decision, and the goals are often vague. For instance, in 2015 a popular ice cream maker, Blue Bell Creameries, learned that its production facilities were infected with listeria, a potentially dangerous bacteria. This was the first serious health problem the firm had ever encountered and managers faced considerable ambiguity in deciding how to respond. One key element of nonprogrammed decisions is that they require good judgment on the part of leaders and decision makers.[4]

Table 8.1 summarizes the characteristics of programmed and nonprogrammed decisions. Note that programmed decisions are more common at the lower levels of the organization, whereas a primary responsibility of top management is to make the difficult, nonprogrammed decisions that determine the organization's long-term effectiveness. By definition, the strategic decisions for which

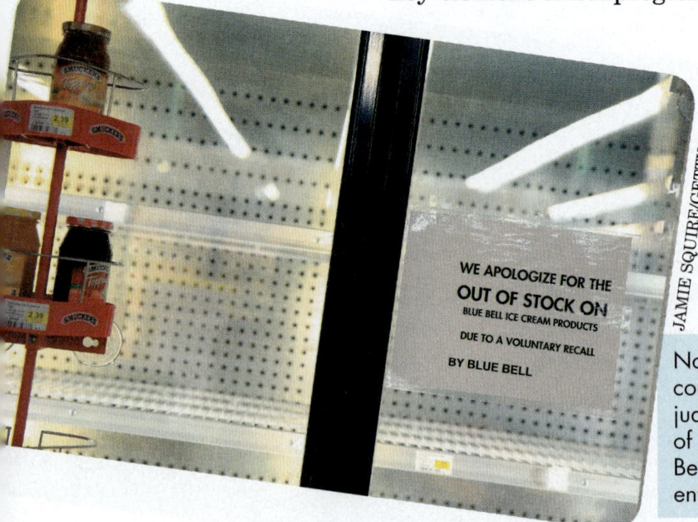

JAMIE SQUIRE/GETTY IMAGES

Nonprogrammed decisions are required when an unusual or complex situation arises that requires problem solving and judgment. When Blue Bell creameries discovered bacteria in one of its production facilities in 2015 its managers shut down all Blue Bell facilities while they worked to eradicate the bacteria. The entire process took months and cost the firm millions of dollars.

Table 8.1

Characteristics of Programmed and Nonprogrammed Decisions

Characteristics	Programmed Decisions	Nonprogrammed Decisions
Type of Decision	Well structured	Poorly structured
Frequency	Repetitive and routine	New and unusual
Goals	Clear, specific	Vague
Information	Readily available	Not available, unclear channels
Consequences	Minor	Major
Organizational Level	Lower levels	Upper levels
Time for Solution	Short	Relatively long
Basis for Solution	Decision rules, set procedures	Judgment and creativity

top management is responsible are poorly structured, nonroutine, and have far-reaching consequences.[5] Programmed decisions, then, can be made according to previously tested rules and procedures. Nonprogrammed decisions generally require that the decision maker exercise judgment and creativity. In other words, all problems require a decision, but not all decisions require problem solving.

Decision-Making Conditions

Decisions are made to bring about desired outcomes, but the information available about those outcomes varies. The range of available information can be considered as a continuum whose endpoints represent complete certainty—when all alternative outcomes are known—and complete uncertainty, when all alternative outcomes are unknown. Points between the two extremes create risk—the decision maker has some information about the possible outcomes and may be able to estimate the probability of their occurrence.

condition of certainty *Manager knows what the outcomes of each alternative of a given action will be and has enough information to estimate the probabilities of various outcomes*

Different information conditions present different challenges to the decision maker.[6] For example, suppose the marketing manager of PlayStation is trying to determine whether to launch an expensive promotional effort for a new video game (see Figure 8.2). For simplicity, assume there are only two alternatives: to promote the game or not to promote it. Under a ***condition of certainty***, the manager knows the outcomes of each alternative. If the new game is promoted heavily, the company will realize a

CHARNSITR/SHUTTERSTOCK.COM

Decision-making conditions range from certainty to risk to uncertainty. For instance, if a firm is planning to launch a new video game for PlayStation, managers will need to assess factors associated with risk and uncertainty when developing their marketing budget.

Figure 8.2

Alternative Outcomes Under Different Decision-Making Conditions

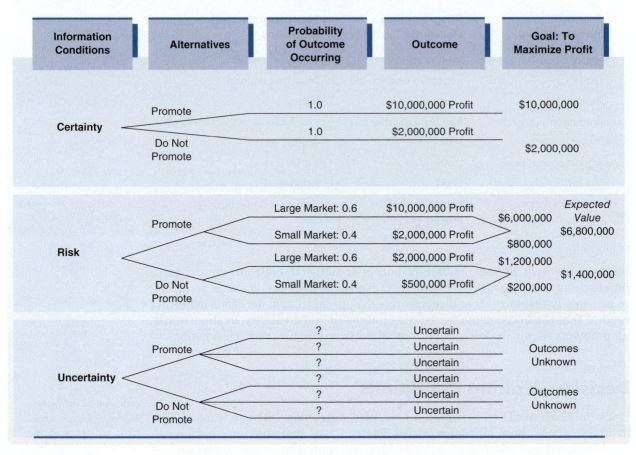

Information Conditions	Alternatives	Probability of Outcome Occurring	Outcome	Goal: To Maximize Profit	
Certainty	Promote	1.0	$10,000,000 Profit	$10,000,000	
	Do Not Promote	1.0	$2,000,000 Profit	$2,000,000	
					Expected Value
Risk	Promote	Large Market: 0.6	$10,000,000 Profit	$6,000,000	$6,800,000
		Small Market: 0.4	$2,000,000 Profit	$800,000	
	Do Not Promote	Large Market: 0.6	$2,000,000 Profit	$1,200,000	$1,400,000
		Small Market: 0.4	$500,000 Profit	$200,000	
Uncertainty	Promote	?	Uncertain	Outcomes Unknown	
		?	Uncertain		
		?	Uncertain		
	Do Not Promote	?	Uncertain	Outcomes Unknown	
		?	Uncertain		
		?	Uncertain		

The three decision-making conditions of certainty, risk, and uncertainty for the decision about whether to promote a new video game to the market.

$10 million profit. Without promotion, the company will realize only a $2 million profit. Here the decision is simple: Promote the game. (Note: These figures are created for the purposes of this example and are not actual profit figures for any company.)

condition of risk
The decision maker cannot know with certainty what the outcome of a given action will be but has enough information to estimate the probabilities of various outcomes

Under a ***condition of risk***, the decision maker cannot know with certainty what the outcome of a given action will be but has enough information to estimate the probabilities of various outcomes. Thus, working from information gathered by the market research department, the marketing manager in our example can estimate the likelihood of each outcome in a risk situation. In this case, the alternatives are defined by the size of the market. The probability for a large video game market is 0.6, and the probability for a small market is 0.4. The manager can calculate the expected value of the promotional effort based on these probabilities and the expected profits associated with each. To find the expected value of an alternative, the manager multiplies each outcome's value by the probability of its occurrence. The sum of these calculations for all possible outcomes represents that alternative's expected value.

In this case, the expected value of alternative 1—to promote the new game—is as follows:

$$0.6 \times \$10,000,000 = \$6,000,000$$
$$\pm 0.4 \times \$2,000,000 = \$800,000$$
$$\text{Expected value of alternative 1} = \$6,800,000$$

The expected value of alternative 2—not to promote the new game—is $1,400,000 (see Figure 8.2). The marketing manager should choose the first alternative, because its expected value is higher. The manager should recognize, however, that although the numbers look convincing, they are based on incomplete information and are only estimates of probability.

The decision maker who lacks enough information to estimate the probability of outcomes (or perhaps even to identify the outcomes at all) faces a ***condition of uncertainty***. In the PlayStation example, this might be the case if sales of video games had recently collapsed and it was not clear whether the precipitous drop was temporary or permanent, nor when information to clarify the situation would be available. Under such circumstances, the decision maker may wait for more information to reduce uncertainty or rely on judgment, experience, and intuition to make the decision. Of course, it is also important to remember that decision making is not always so easy to classify in terms of certainty, risk, and uncertainty.

condition of uncertainty
The decision maker lacks enough information to estimate the probability of possible outcomes

Several approaches to decision making offer insights into the process by which managers arrive at their decisions. The rational approach is appealing because of its logic and economy. Yet these very qualities raise questions about this approach because decision making often is not a wholly rational process. The behavioral approach, meanwhile, attempts to account for the limits on rationality in decision making. Of course, as we will see, many managers combine rationality with behavioral processes when making decisions. The sections that follow explore these approaches in more detail.

THE RATIONAL APPROACH TO DECISION MAKING

The ***rational decision-making approach*** assumes that managers follow a systematic, step-by-step process. It further assumes that the organization is dedicated to making logical choices and doing what makes the most sense economically and that it is managed by decision makers who are entirely objective and have complete information.[7]

rational decision-making approach
A systematic, step-by-step process for making decisions

Steps in Rational Decision Making

Figure 8.3 identifies the steps of the process, starting with stating a goal and running logically through the process until the best decision is made, implemented, and controlled.

State the Situational Goal

The rational decision-making process begins with the statement of a situational goal—that is, a goal for a particular situation. The goal of a marketing department, for example, may be to obtain a certain market share by the

Figure 8.3

The Rational Decision-Making Approach

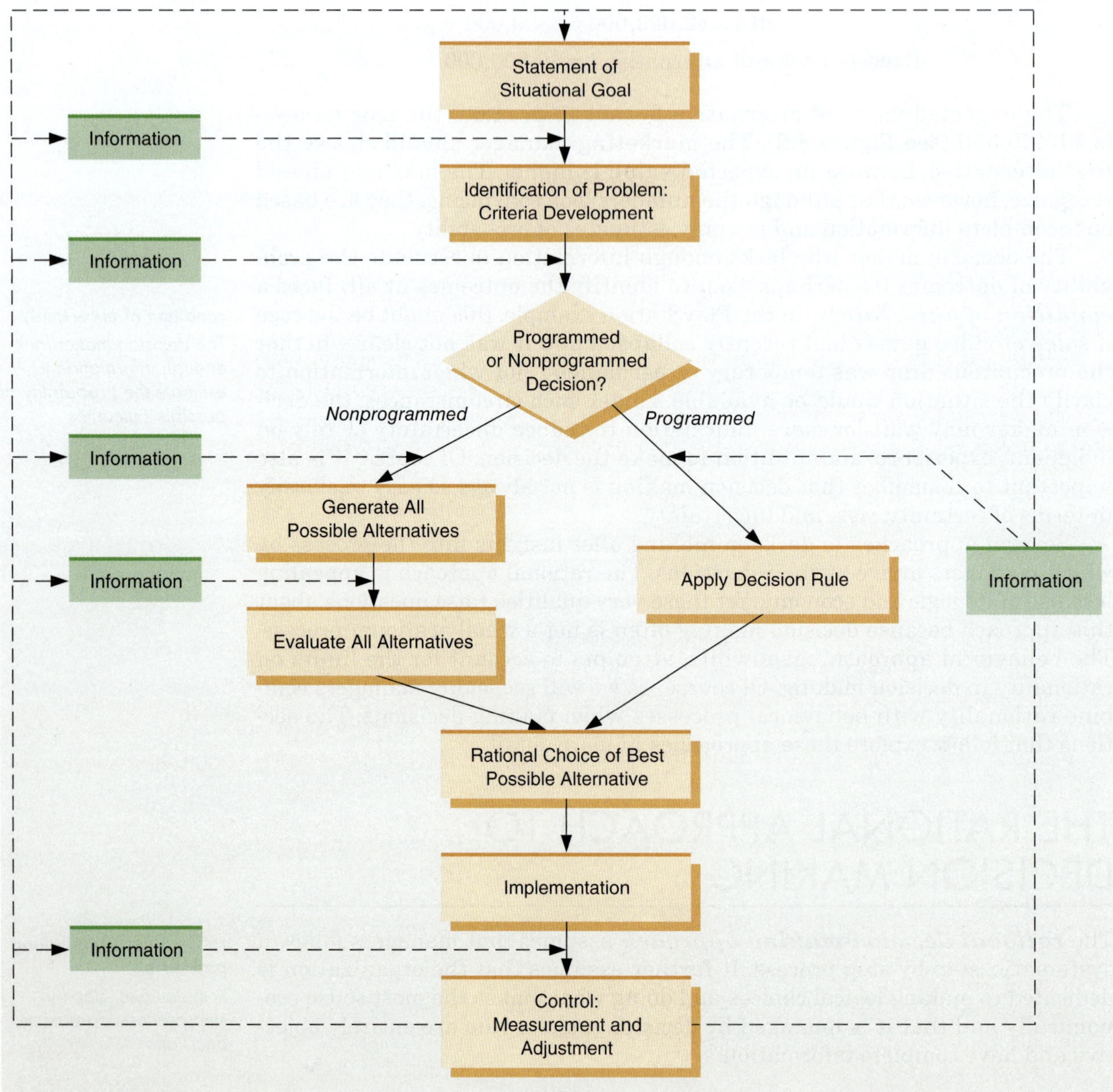

The rational model follows a systematic, step-by-step approach from goals to implementation, measurement, and control.

end of the year. (Some models of decision making do not start with a goal. We include it, however, because it is the standard used to determine whether there is a decision to be made.)

Identify the Problem

The purpose of problem identification is to gather information that bears on the goal. If there is a discrepancy between the goal and the actual state, action may be needed. In the marketing example, the group may gather information about the company's actual market share and then compare it with the desired market share. A difference between the two represents a problem that necessitates a decision. Reliable information is very important in this step. Inaccurate information can lead to an unnecessary decision or to no decision when one is required.

Determine the Decision Type

Next, the decision makers must determine whether the problem represents a programmed or a nonprogrammed decision. If a programmed decision is needed, the appropriate decision rule is invoked, and the process moves on to the choice among alternatives. A programmed marketing decision may be called for if analysis reveals that competitors are outspending the company on print advertising. Because creating print advertising and buying space for it are well-established functions of the marketing group, the problem requires only a programmed decision.

Although it may seem simple to diagnose a situation as programmed, apply a decision rule, and arrive at a solution, mistakes can still occur. Choosing the wrong decision rule or assuming the problem calls for a programmed decision when a nonprogrammed decision actually is required can result in poor decisions. The same caution applies to the determination that a nonprogrammed decision is called for. If the situation is wrongly diagnosed, the decision maker wastes time and resources seeking a new solution to an old problem, or "reinventing the wheel."

Generate Alternatives

The next step in making a nonprogrammed decision is to generate alternatives. The rational process assumes that decision makers will generate all the possible alternative solutions to the problem. However, this assumption is unrealistic because even simple business problems can have scores of possible solutions. Decision makers may rely on education and experience as well as knowledge of the situation to generate alternatives. In addition, they may seek information from other people such as peers, subordinates, and supervisors. Decision makers may analyze the symptoms of the problem for clues or fall back on intuition or judgment to develop alternative solutions.[8] If the marketing department in our example determines that a nonprogrammed decision is required, it will need to generate alternatives for increasing market share.

Evaluate Alternatives

Evaluation involves assessing all possible alternatives in terms of predetermined decision criteria. The ultimate decision criterion is "Will this alternative bring us nearer to the goal?" In each case, the decision maker must examine each alternative for evidence that it will reduce the discrepancy between the desired state and the actual state. The evaluation process usually includes (1) describing the anticipated outcomes (benefits) of each alternative, (2) evaluating the anticipated costs of each alternative, and (3) estimating the uncertainties and risks associated with each alternative.[9] In most decision situations, the decision maker does not have perfect information regarding the outcomes of all alternatives. At one extreme, as shown earlier in Figure 8.2, outcomes may be known with certainty; at the other, the decision maker has no information whatsoever, so the outcomes are entirely uncertain. But risk is the most common situation.

Choose an Alternative

Choosing an alternative is usually the most crucial step in the decision-making process. Choosing consists of selecting the alternative with the highest possible payoff, based on the benefits, costs, risks, and uncertainties of all alternatives. In the PlayStation promotion example, the decision maker evaluated the two alternatives by calculating their expected values. Following the rational approach, the manager would choose the alternative with the largest expected value.

Even with the rational approach, however, difficulties can arise in choosing an alternative. First, when two or more alternatives have equal payoffs, the decision maker must obtain more information or use some other criterion to make the choice. Second, when no single alternative will accomplish the objective, some combination of two or three alternatives may have to be implemented. Finally, if no alternative or combination of alternatives will solve the problem, the decision maker must obtain more information, generate more alternatives, or change the goals.[10]

contingency plans
Alternative actions to take if the primary course of action is unexpectedly disrupted or rendered inappropriate

An important part of the choice phase is the consideration of ***contingency plans***— alternative actions that can be taken if the primary course of action is unexpectedly disrupted or rendered inappropriate.[11] Planning for contingencies is part of the transition between choosing the preferred alternative and implementing it. In developing contingency plans, the decision maker usually asks such questions as “What if something unexpected happens during the implementation of this alternative?” or “If the economy goes into a recession, will the choice of this alternative ruin the company?” or “How can we alter this plan if the economy suddenly rebounds and begins to grow?”

Implement the Plan

post-decision dissonance
Doubt about a choice that has already been made

Implementation puts the decision into action. It builds on the commitment and motivation of those who participated in the decision-making process (and may actually bolster individual commitment and motivation). To succeed, implementation requires the proper use of resources and good management skills. Following the decision to promote the new PlayStation game heavily, for example, the marketing manager must implement the decision by assigning the project to a work group or task force. The success of this team depends on the leadership, the reward structure, the communications system, and group dynamics. Sometimes the decision maker begins to doubt a choice already made. This doubt is called ***post-decision dissonance***, a form of cognitive dissonance (as discussed in Chapter 4).[12] To reduce the tension created by the dissonance, the decision maker may seek to rationalize the decision further with new information.

Control: Measure and Adjust

In the final stage of the rational decision-making process, the outcomes of the decision are measured and compared with the desired goal. If a discrepancy remains, the decision maker may restart the decision-making process by setting a new goal (or reiterating the existing one). The decision maker, unsatisfied with the previous decision, may modify the subsequent decision-making process to avoid another mistake. Changes can be made in any part of the process, as Figure 8.3 illustrates by the arrows leading from the control step to each of the other steps. Decision making therefore is a dynamic, self-correcting, and ongoing process in organizations.

Suppose a marketing department implements a new print advertising campaign. After implementation, it constantly monitors market research data and compares its new market share with the desired market share. If the advertising has the desired effect, no changes will be made in the promotion campaign. If, however, the data indicate no change in the market share, additional decisions and implementation of a contingency plan may be necessary.

Strengths and Weaknesses of the Rational Approach

The rational approach has several strengths. It forces the decision maker to consider a decision in a logical, sequential manner, and the in-depth analysis of alternatives enables the decision maker to choose on the basis of information rather than emotion or social pressure. But the rigid assumptions of this approach often are unrealistic.[13] The amount of information available to managers usually is limited by either time or cost constraints, and most decision makers have limited ability to process information about the alternatives. In addition, not all alternatives lend themselves to quantification in terms that will allow for easy comparison. Finally, because they cannot predict the future, it is unlikely that decision makers will know all possible outcomes of each alternative.

Evidence-Based Decision Making

While rational decision making perspectives have been around for decades, some experts (most notably Jeffrey Pfeffer and Robert Sutton) have recently called for a renewed focus on rationality.[14] This new focus has been called evidence-based management. ***Evidence-based management (EBM)*** is defined as the commitment to identify and utilize the best theory and data available to make decisions. Advocates of this approach encourage the use of five basic "principles":

evidence-based management (EBM) *The commitment to identify and utilize the best theory and data available to make decisions*

1. Face the hard facts and build a culture in which people are encouraged to tell the truth, even if it's unpleasant.
2. Be committed to "fact-based" decision making—which means being committed to getting the best evidence and using it to guide actions.
3. Treat your organization as an unfinished prototype—encourage experimentation and learning by doing.
4. Look for the risks and drawbacks in what people recommend (even the best medicine has side effects).
5. Avoid basing decisions on untested but strongly held beliefs, what you have done in the past, or uncritical "benchmarking" of what winners do.

EBM advocates are particularly persuasive when they use EBM to question the outcomes of decisions based on "untested but strongly held beliefs" or on "uncritical 'benchmarking.'" Take, for instance, the popular decision to pay high performers significantly more than low performers. Pfeffer and Sutton's research shows that pay-for-performance policies get good results when employees work solo or independently. But it's another matter altogether when it comes to collaborative teams—the kind of teams that make so many organizational decisions today. Under these circumstances, the greater the gap between highest- and lowest-paid executives, the weaker the firm's financial performance. Why? According to Pfeffer and Sutton, wide disparities in pay often weaken both trust among team members and the social connectivity that contributes to strong team-based decision making.

Or consider another increasingly prevalent decision for evaluating and rewarding talent. Pioneered at General Electric by the legendary Jack Welch, the practice of "forced ranking" divides employees into three groups based on performance—the top 20 percent, middle 70 percent, and bottom 10 percent—and terminates those at the bottom. Pfeffer and Sutton found that, according to many HR managers, forced ranking impaired morale and collaboration and ultimately reduced productivity. They also concluded that automatically firing the bottom 10 percent resulted too often in the unnecessary disruption of otherwise effective teamwork. That's how they found out that 73 percent of the errors committed by commercial airline pilots occur on the first day that reconfigured crews work together.[15]

THE BEHAVIORAL APPROACH TO DECISION MAKING

Whereas the rational approach assumes that managers operate logically and rationally, the behavioral approach acknowledges the role and importance of human behavior in the decision-making process. Herbert A. Simon was one of the first experts to recognize that decisions are not always made with rationality and logic.[16] Simon was subsequently awarded the Nobel Prize in economics. Rather than prescribing how decisions should be made, his view of decision making, now called the ***administrative model***, describes how decisions often actually are made. (Note that Simon was not advocating that managers use the administrative model but was instead describing how managers actually make decisions.) Our *Understand Yourself* feature will give you some quick insights into how emotion can affect how we make decisions.

administrative model of decision making
Argues that managers use bounded rationality, rules of thumb, suboptimizing, and satisficing in making decisions

The Administrative Model

One crucial assumption of the administrative model is that decision makers operate with bounded rationality rather than with the perfect rationality assumed by the rational approach. ***Bounded rationality*** is the idea that although individuals may seek the best solution to a problem, the demands of processing all the information bearing on the problem, generating all possible solutions, and choosing the single best solution are beyond the capabilities of most decision makers. Thus, they accept less-than-ideal solutions based on a process that is neither exhaustive nor entirely rational.

bounded rationality
Idea that decision makers cannot deal with information about all the aspects and alternatives pertaining to a problem and therefore choose to tackle some meaningful subset of it

For example, one study found that under time pressure, groups usually eliminate all but the two most favorable alternatives and then process the remaining two in great detail.[17] Thus, decision makers operating with bounded rationality limit the inputs to the decision-making process and base decisions on judgment and personal biases as well as on logic.[18]

The administrative model is characterized by (1) the use of procedures and rules of thumb, (2) suboptimizing, and (3) satisficing. Uncertainty in decision making can initially be reduced by relying on procedures and rules of thumb. If, for example, increasing print advertising has increased a company's market share in the past, that linkage may be used by company employees as a rule of thumb in decision making. When the previous month's market share drops

UNDERSTAND YOURSELF

EMOTION-BASED DECISION MAKING

Using the scale below, write the number from 1 to 6 that reflects your agreement or disagreement with the statements below. When you are finished, follow the scoring instructions at the bottom to interpret your score.

strongly disagree	moderately disagree	slightly disagree	slightly agree	moderately agree	strongly agree
1	2	3	4	5	6

___ 1. I listen to my feelings when making important decisions.
___ 2. I base my goals in life on inspiration, rather than logic.
___ 3. I plan my life based on how I feel.
___ 4. I plan my life logically.
___ 5. I believe emotions give direction to life.
___ 6. I believe important decisions should be based on logical reasoning.
___ 7. I listen to my brain rather than my heart.
___ 8. I make decisions based on facts, not feelings.

Scoring: For questions 4, 6, 7, and 8, change your score as follows: 1 = 6; 2 = 5; 3 = 4; 4 = 3; 5 = 2; 6 = 1. Cross out your old response so that you can clearly see the replacement number. Now add up your responses to the eight items.

Interpretation: If you scored 36 or above, you tend to rely heavily on your feelings when making decisions. This could mean that you try to make decisions too quickly. You might try to recognize the role that emotions tend to play in your decisions, and consciously take more time to identify and consider the facts before deciding.

If you scored between 24 and 35, you tend to use a balance of logic and emotion when making decisions. Although intuition can be helpful when making complex decisions, try to remain fact- rather than emotion-focused.

If you scored 23 or less, you tend to use logic over emotions when making decisions. This can lead to effective decisions, although it also can lead to slower decision making.

Source: International Personality Item Pool: A Scientific Collaboratory for the Development of Advanced Measures of Personality Traits and Other Individual Differences. http://ipip.ori.org

below a certain level, the company might increase its print advertising expenditures by 25 percent during the following month.

Suboptimizing is knowingly accepting less than the best possible outcome. Frequently, given organizational constraints, it is not feasible to make the ideal decision in a real-world situation. The decision maker often must suboptimize to avoid unintended negative effects on other departments, product lines, or decisions.[19] An automobile manufacturer, for example, can cut costs dramatically and increase efficiency if it schedules the production of one model at a time. Thus, the production group's optimal decision is single-model scheduling. But the marketing group, seeking to optimize its sales goals by offering a wide variety of models, may demand the opposite production schedule: short runs of entirely different models. The groups in the middle—design and scheduling— may suboptimize the benefits the production and marketing groups seek by planning long runs of slightly different models. This is the practice of the large auto manufacturers such as General Motors and Ford, which make multiple body styles in different models on the same production line.

suboptimizing
Knowingly accepting less than the best possible outcome to avoid unintended negative effects on other aspects of the organization

The final feature of the behavioral approach is ***satisficing***: examining alternatives only until a solution that meets minimal requirements is found

satisficing
Examining alternatives only until a solution that meets minimal requirements is found

and then ceasing to look for a better one.[20] The search for alternatives usually is a sequential process guided by procedures and rules of thumb based on previous experiences with similar problems. The search often ends when the first minimally acceptable choice is encountered. The resulting choice may narrow the discrepancy between the desired and the actual states, but it is not likely to be the optimal solution. As the process is repeated, incremental improvements slowly reduce the discrepancy between the actual and desired states.

Other Behavioral Forces in Decision Making

In addition to those behavioral elements identified in the administrative model, the manager should also be aware of other behavioral forces that can affect decision making as well. These include political forces, intuition, escalation of commitment, risk propensity, and ethics. Prospect theory is also relevant.

Political Forces in Decision Making

coalition
An informal alliance of individuals or groups formed to achieve a common goal

Political forces can play a major role in how decisions are made. We cover political behavior in Chapter 13, but one major element of politics, coalitions, is especially relevant to decision making. A ***coalition*** is an informal alliance of individuals or groups formed to achieve a common goal. This common goal is often a preferred decision alternative. For example, coalitions of stockholders frequently band together to force a board of directors to make a certain decision. Indeed, many of the recent power struggles between management and dissident shareholders at Dell Computer have relied on coalitions as each side tried to gain the upper hand against the other.[21] The impact of coalitions can be either positive or negative. They can help astute managers get the organization on a path toward effectiveness and profitability, or they can strangle well-conceived strategies and decisions. Managers must recognize when to use coalitions, how to assess whether coalitions are acting in the best interests of the organization, and how to constrain their dysfunctional effects.[22]

Intuition

intuition
An innate belief about something without conscious consideration

Intuition is an innate belief about something without conscious consideration. Managers sometimes decide to do something because it "feels right" or they have a hunch. This feeling is usually not arbitrary, however. Rather, it is based on years of experience and practice in making decisions in similar situations. An inner sense may help managers make an occasional decision without going through a full-blown rational sequence of steps. The best-selling book by Malcolm Gladwell entitled *Blink: The Power of Thinking Without Thinking* made strong arguments that intuition is both used more commonly and results in better decisions than had previously been believed. On the other hand, some experts challenge this view and suggest that underlying understanding and experience make intuition mask the true processes used to make quick decisions.[23]

The New York Yankees once contacted three major sneaker manufacturers, Nike, Reebok, and Adidas, and informed them that they were looking to make a sponsorship deal. While Nike and Reebok were carefully and rationally assessing the possibilities, managers at Adidas quickly realized that a partnership with the Yankees made a lot of sense for them. They responded very quickly to the idea, and ended up hammering out a contract while the competitors were still analyzing details.[24] Of course, all managers, but most especially inexperienced ones, should be careful not to rely on intuition too heavily. If rationality and logic are continually flouted for what "feels right," the odds are that disaster will strike one day.

Escalation of Commitment

Another important behavioral process that influences decision making is ***escalation of commitment*** to a chosen course of action (sometimes called the *sunk cost fallacy*). In particular, decision makers sometimes make decisions and then become so committed to the course of action suggested by that decision that they stay with it or even increase their investment in it, even when it appears to have been wrong.[25] People sometimes justify continued or increased investments of time, money, or in the case of the military, even human lives, because of their prior investment in a decision, even if new evidence suggests that the decision should be changed or even reversed. For example, when people buy stock in a company, they sometimes refuse to sell it or even buy more after repeated drops in price. They chose a course of action—buying the stock in anticipation of making a profit—and then stay with it even in the face of increasing losses.

escalation of commitment
Occurs when a decision maker stays with a decision even when it appears to be wrong

For years Pan American World Airways ruled the skies and used its profits to diversify into real estate and other businesses. But with the advent of deregulation, Pan Am began to struggle and lose market share to other carriers. When Pan Am managers finally realized how ineffective the airline operations had become, the "rational" decision would have been, as experts today point out, to sell off the remaining airline operations and concentrate on the firm's more profitable businesses. But because they still saw the company as being first and foremost an airline, they instead began to slowly sell off the firm's profitable holdings to keep the airline flying. Eventually, the company was left with nothing but an ineffective and inefficient airline, and then had to sell off its more profitable routes before eventually being taken over by Delta. Had Pan Am managers made the more rational decision years earlier, chances are the firm could still be a profitable enterprise today, albeit one with no involvement in the airline industry.[26]

Thus, decision makers must walk a fine line. On the one hand, they must guard against sticking with an incorrect decision too long. To do so can bring about financial decline. On the other hand, managers should not bail out of a seemingly incorrect decision too soon, as Adidas did several years ago. Adidas once dominated the market for professional athletic shoes. It subsequently entered the market for amateur sports shoes and did well there also. But managers incorrectly interpreted a sales slowdown as a sign that the boom in athletic shoes was over. They thought that they had made the wrong decision and ordered drastic cutbacks. The market took off again with Nike at the head of the pack, and Adidas could not recover. Fortunately, a new management team has changed the way Adidas makes decisions and, as illustrated earlier, the firm is again on its way to becoming a force in the athletic shoe and apparel markets.

Risk Propensity and Decision Making

The behavioral element of ***risk propensity*** is the extent to which a decision maker is willing to gamble when making a decision. Some managers are cautious about every decision they make. They try to adhere to the rational model and are extremely conservative in what they do. Such managers are more

risk propensity
The extent to which a decision maker is willing to gamble in making a decision

likely to avoid mistakes, and they infrequently make decisions that lead to big losses. Other managers are extremely aggressive in making decisions and are willing to take risks.[27] They rely heavily on intuition, reach decisions quickly, and often risk big investments on their decisions. As in gambling, these managers are more likely than their conservative counterparts to achieve big successes with their decisions; they are also more likely to incur greater losses.[28] The organization's culture is a prime ingredient in fostering different levels of risk propensity.

Ethics and Decision Making

ethics
A person's beliefs about what constitutes right and wrong behavior

Ethics are a person's beliefs about what constitutes right and wrong behavior. Ethical behavior is that which conforms to generally accepted social norms; unethical behavior does not conform to generally accepted social norms. Some decisions made by managers may have little or nothing to do with their own personal ethics, but many other decisions are influenced by the manager's ethics. For example, decisions involving such disparate issues as hiring and firing employees, dealing with customers and suppliers, setting wages and assigning tasks, and maintaining one's expense account are all subject to ethical influences. And, of course, managers can make fatal personal decisions simply because they choose to ignore the difference between right and wrong.

In general, ethical dilemmas for managers may center on direct personal gain, indirect personal gain, or simple personal preferences. Consider, for example, a top executive contemplating a decision about a potential takeover. His or her stock option package may result in enormous personal gain if the decision goes one way, even though stockholders may benefit more if the decision goes the other way. An indirect personal gain may result when a decision does not directly add value to a manager's personal worth but does enhance her or his career. Or the manager may face a choice about relocating a company facility in which one of the options is closest to his or her residence.

Managers should carefully and deliberately consider the ethical context of every one of their decisions. The goal, of course, is for the manager to make the decision that is in the best interest of the firm, as opposed to the best interest of the manager. Doing this requires personal honesty and integrity. Managers also find it helpful to discuss potential ethical dilemmas with colleagues. Others can often provide an objective view of a situation that may help a manager avoid unintentionally making an unethical decision. The *Global Issues* feature focuses on cultural and national influences on ethical awareness.

Prospect Theory and Decision Making

prospect theory
Argues that when people make decisions under a condition of risk they are more motivated to avoid losses than they are to seek gains

Finally, prospect theory also offers useful insights into how people make decisions.[29] Essentially, ***prospect theory*** focuses on decisions under a condition of risk. The theory argues that such decisions are influenced more by the potential value of gains or losses than the final outcome itself. The theory further argues that, all else being equal, people are more motivated to avoid losses than they are to seek gains. Stated another way, people may be more motivated by the threat of losing something they have than they are by the prospect of gaining something they do not have.

For instance, one study investigated this hypothesis in a sample of public school teachers in Chicago. One group of teachers was told that they could receive a bonus of up to $8,000 at the end of the school year if their students met certain test score targets. The other group was given an upfront bonus of $4,000 at the beginning of the school year. These teachers were told that

BALDYRGAN/SHUTTERSTOCK.COM

CULTURE AND NATIONALITY INFLUENCES ON ETHICAL AWARENESS

If we do not recognize ethical issues in a situation, we are unlikely to attend to them in making subsequent decisions. Research has found that both culture and nationality influence the recognition of ethical issues. One study found that Taiwanese sales agents were more likely to perceive ethical issues associated with their companies' or competitors' agents while U.S. sales agents were more likely to perceive ethical issues with their colleagues' behavior.[30]

A second study compared the ethical awareness of Australians and Americans, argued to be "cultural cousins" because of their similar cultures. Despite having similar cultures, Americans were more likely than the Australians to identify an ethical problem in scenarios involving the withholding of information and the misleading of an appraiser.[31]

A third study asked managers from around the world to decide what they would do next in the following situation:[32]

You are riding in a car driven by a close friend. He hits a pedestrian. You know he was going at least thirty-five miles-per-hour in an area of the city where the maximum allowed speed is twenty miles-per-hour. There are no witnesses. His lawyer says that if you testify under oath that he was only driving twenty miles-per-hour, it might save him from serious consequences.

1. What right has your friend to expect you to protect him?
   a. My friend has a definite right as a friend to expect me to testify to the lower figure.
   b. He has some right as a friend to expect me to testify to the lower figure.
   c. He has no right as a friend to expect me to testify to the lower figure.
2. What do you think you would do in view of the obligations of a sworn witness and the obligations to your friend?
   a. Testify that he was going twenty miles an hour.
   b. Not testify that he was going twenty miles an hour.

Managers' responses to this situation differed widely. More than 90 percent of managers in Canada (96 percent), the United States (95 percent), Switzerland (94 percent), and Sweden (93 percent) said that because society's rules were made for everyone, their friend had no right to expect them to testify falsely. Consequently, they would not testify that their friend was driving at twenty miles-per-hour. In contrast, fewer than half of the managers from South Korea (26 percent), Venezuela (34 percent), Russia (42 percent), and China (48 percent) would refuse to support their friend.

if their students did not meet test score targets they would have to pay back some or all of the bonus; however, if their students met targets they could keep the bonus plus earn up to another $4,000 in a year-end bonus. Students of the second group of teachers had higher test scores at the end of the year. The researchers inferred that the teachers who had something to lose (some or all of the $4,000 up-front bonus) were more motivated to improve their students' test scores than were the teachers who could not lose anything.[33]

An Integrated Approach to Decision Making

Because of the unrealistic demands of the rational approach and the limited, short-term orientation of the behavioral approach, neither is entirely satisfactory. However, the worthwhile features of each can be combined into a practical approach to decision making, shown in Figure 8.4. The steps in this process are the same as in the rational approach; however, the conditions recognized by the behavioral approach are added to provide a more realistic process. For example, the integrated approach suggests that rather than generating all alternatives, the decision maker should try to go beyond rules of

Figure 8.4

Practical Approach to Decision Making with Behavioral Guidelines

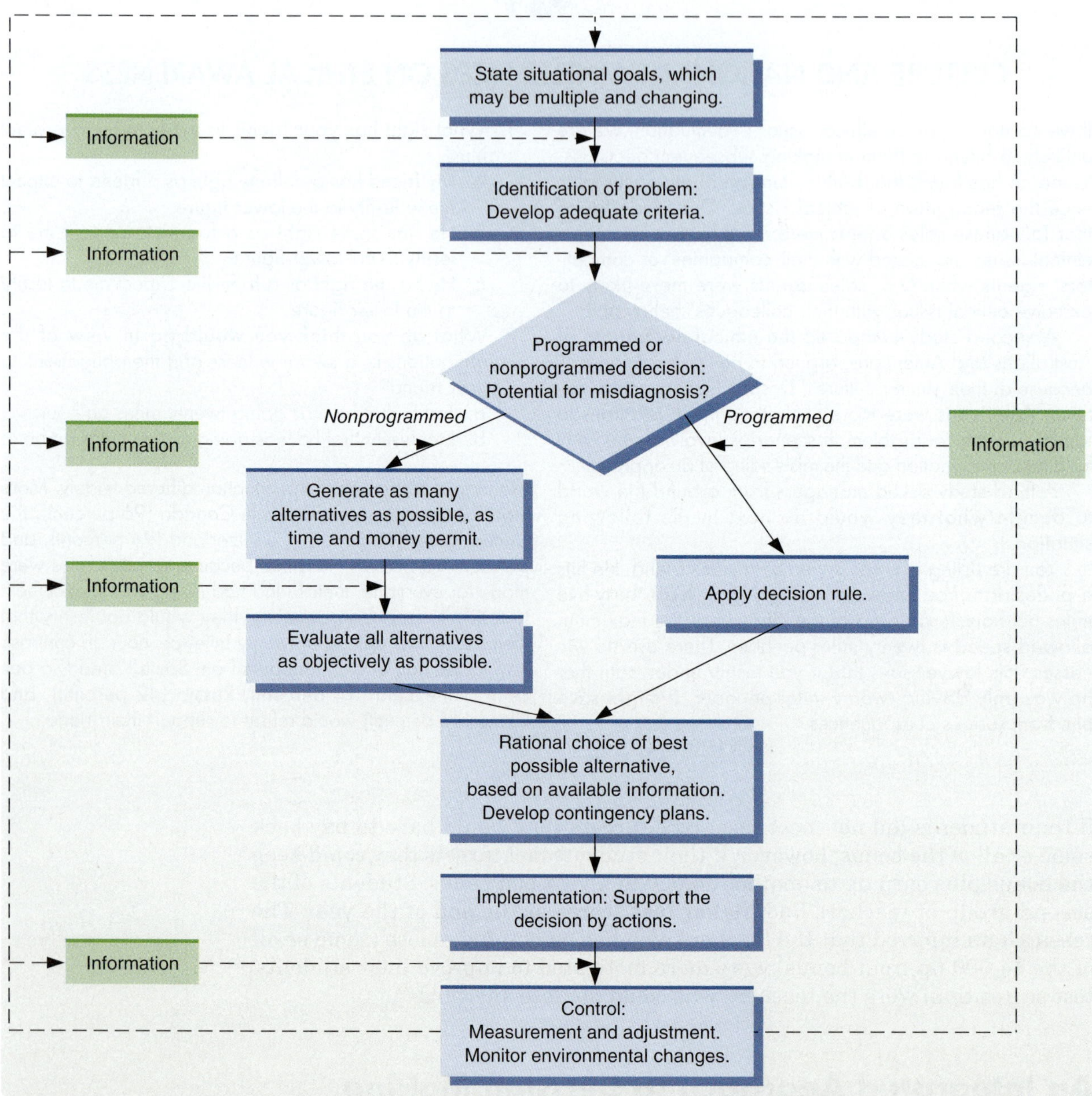

The practical model applies some of the conditions recognized by the behavioral approach to the rational approach to decision making. Although similar to the rational model, the practical approach recognizes personal limitations at each point (or step) in the process.

thumb and satisficing limitations and generate as many alternatives as time, money, and other practicalities of the situation allow. In this synthesis of the two other approaches, the rational approach provides an analytical framework for making decisions, whereas the behavioral approach provides a moderating influence.

In practice, decision makers use some hybrid of the rational, behavioral, and integrated approaches to make the tough day-to-day decisions in running organizations. Some decision makers use a methodical process of gathering as much information as possible, developing and evaluating alternatives, and seeking advice from knowledgeable people before making a decision. Others fly from one decision to another, making seemingly hasty decisions and barking out orders to subordinates. The second group would seem not to use much information or a rational approach to making decisions. Recent research, however, has shown that managers who make decisions very quickly probably are using just as much, or more, information and generating and evaluating as many alternatives as slower, more methodical decision makers.[34]

GROUP DECISION MAKING IN ORGANIZATIONS

As we discussed in Chapter 7, people in organizations work in a variety of groups—formal and informal, permanent and temporary, and various kinds of teams. Most of these groups make decisions that affect the welfare of the organization and the people in it. Therefore, we need to consider group decision making. The primary elements we will discuss are group polarization, groupthink, and group problem solving methods.

Group Polarization

Members' attitudes and opinions with respect to an issue or a solution may change during group discussion. Some studies of this tendency have showed the change to be a fairly consistent movement toward a more risky solution, called "risky shift."[35] Other studies and analyses have revealed that the group-induced shift is not always toward more risk; the group is just as likely to move toward a more conservative view.[36] Generally, ***group polarization*** occurs when the average of the group members' post-discussion attitudes tends to be more extreme than average pre-discussion attitudes.[37]

group polarization
The tendency for a group's average post-discussion attitudes to be more extreme than its average pre-discussion attitudes

Several features of group discussion contribute to polarization. When individuals discover during group discussion that others share their opinions, they may become more confident about their opinions, resulting in a more extreme view. Persuasive arguments also can encourage polarization. If members who strongly support a particular position are able to express themselves cogently in the discussion, less avid supporters of the position may become

LAUREMAR/SHUTTERSTOCK.COM

Many decisions in organizations are made by groups. While group decision making has several advantages, it also has certain risks, including group polarization. These colleagues, for instance, are involved in making a decision. They should strive to make sure that their decision is not too risky or too conservative as a result of excessive polarization.

convinced that it is correct. In addition, members may believe that because the group is deciding, they are not individually responsible for the decision or its outcomes. This diffusion of responsibility may enable them to accept and support a decision more radical than those they would make as individuals.

Polarization can profoundly affect group decision making. If group members are known to lean toward a particular decision before a discussion, it may be expected that their post-decision position will be even more extreme. Understanding this phenomenon may be useful for one who seeks to affect their decision.

Groupthink

As discussed in Chapter 7, highly cohesive groups and teams often are very successful at meeting their goals, although they sometimes have serious difficulties as well. One problem that can occur is groupthink. According to Irving L. Janis, ***groupthink*** is "a mode of thinking that people engage in when they are deeply involved in a cohesive in-group, and when the members' strivings for unanimity override their motivation to realistically appraise alternative courses of action."[38] When groupthink occurs, then, the group unknowingly makes unanimity rather than the best decision its goal. Individual members may perceive that raising objections is not appropriate. Groupthink can occur in many decision-making situations in organizations. The current trend toward increasing use of teams in organizations may increase instances of groupthink because of the susceptibility of self-managing teams to this type of thought.[39]

groupthink
A mode of thinking that occurs when members of a group are deeply involved in a cohesive in-group, and the desire for unanimity offsets their motivation to appraise alternative courses of action

Symptoms of Groupthink

The three primary conditions that foster the development of groupthink are cohesiveness, the leader's promotion of his or her preferred solution, and insulation of the group from experts' opinions. Based on analysis of the disaster associated with the explosion of the space shuttle *Challenger* in 1986, the original idea of groupthink symptoms was enhanced to include the effects of increased time pressure and the role of the leader in not stimulating critical thinking in developing the symptoms of groupthink.[40] Figure 8.5 outlines the revised groupthink process.

A group in which groupthink has taken hold exhibits eight well-defined symptoms:

1. An illusion of invulnerability, shared by most or all members, that creates excessive optimism and encourages extreme risk taking
2. Collective efforts to rationalize or discount warnings that might lead members to reconsider assumptions before recommitting themselves to past policy decisions
3. An unquestioned belief in the group's inherent morality, inclining members to ignore the ethical and moral consequences of their decisions
4. Stereotyped views of "enemy" leaders as too evil to warrant genuine attempts to negotiate or as too weak or stupid to counter whatever risky attempts are made to defeat their purposes
5. Direct pressure on a member who expresses strong arguments against any of the group's stereotypes, illusions, or commitments, making clear that such dissent is contrary to what is expected of loyal members

Figure 8.5

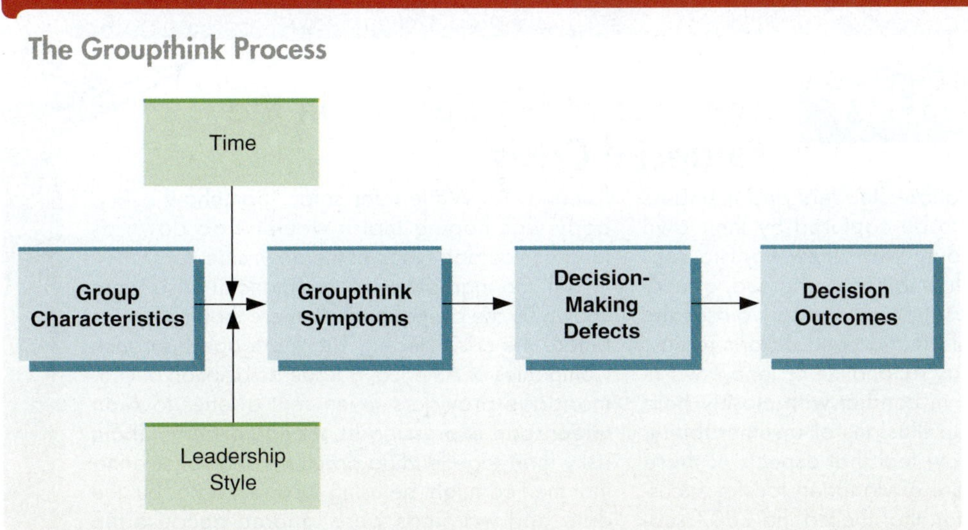

Groupthink can occur when a highly cohesive group with a directive leader is under time pressure; it can result in a defective decision-making process and low probability of successful outcomes.

Source: Moorhead, G., Ference, R., & Neck, C. P. (1991). Group Decision Fiascoes Continue: Space Shuttle *Challenger* and a Revised Groupthink Framework. *Human Relations*, *44*, 539–550.

6. Self-censorship of deviations from the apparent group consensus, reflecting each member's inclination to minimize the importance of his or her doubts and counterarguments
7. A shared illusion of unanimity, resulting partly from self-censorship of deviations, augmented by the false assumption that silence means consent[41]
8. The emergence of self-appointed "mindguards," members who protect the group from adverse information that might shatter their shared complacency about the effectiveness and morality of their decisions.[42]

Janis contends that the members of the group involved in the Watergate cover-up during President Richard Nixon's administration and reelection campaign—Nixon himself, H. R. Haldeman, John Ehrlichman, and John Dean—may have been victims of groupthink. Evidence of most of the groupthink symptoms can be found in the unedited transcripts of the group's deliberations.[43] Groupthink often helps to explain why companies and governments sometimes continue to pursue strategies and policies that are clearly failing. Our *Case Study* provides another contemporary example of groupthink.

Decision-Making Defects and Decision Quality

When groupthink dominates group deliberations, the likelihood increases that decision-making defects will occur. The group is less likely to survey a full range of alternatives and may focus on only a few (often one or two). In discussing a preferred alternative, the group may fail to examine it for nonobvious risks and drawbacks. The group may not reexamine previously rejected alternatives for nonobvious gains or some means of reducing apparent costs, even when they receive new information. The group may reject expert opinions that run counter to its own views and may choose to consider only information that supports its preferred solution. The decision to launch the space shuttle *Challenger* in January 1986 may have been a product of groupthink because, due to the increased time pressure to make a decision and the leaders' style, negative information was ignored by the group that made the decision. (Unfortunately, this same pattern apparently occurred again prior to the ill-fated

CASE STUDY The Role of Groupthink in the Financial Crisis

When an organization's leaders and members allow themselves to be captured by their own beliefs, they see only what they want to see. When coupled with ambition and greed, a feedback loop develops that increasingly biases the interpretation of information and distorts reality. Group members may rationalize or ignore warning signs that are in conflict with closely held beliefs and develop illusions of invulnerability. Many historians now feel that aspects of these processes are a core explanation for the excessive credit expansion that fuelled the 2007 subprime mortgage meltdown and subsequent financial crisis.

In the years leading up to the financial crisis, clear warnings of impending problems were ignored. The revered chairman of the U.S. Federal Reserve Bank, Alan Greenspan, was a strong advocate of the free market and supported minimal market intervention. He was also known to be unwelcoming to challenges to his ideas. As William White, the chief economist for the central bank of all central bankers, the Bank for International Settlements, recalls, "Greenspan always demanded respect."[44] And who could question Greenspan? He was an economic superstar and everything was going well. As White further states, "When you are inside the bubble, everybody feels fine. Nobody wants to believe that it can burst."[45]

White was the only central banker in the world willing to challenge or criticize Greenspan and his ideas. White predicted the approaching financial crisis years before it happened and presented a paper to the central bankers that contradicted everything Greenspan believed. Despite White's and his team's persistent criticism of the mortgage securitization business, explanations of the perils of risky loans, and provision of evidence about the rating agencies' lack of credibility, few in the highly secretive world of central banking listened. As White later said, "Somehow everybody was hoping that it wouldn't go down as long as you don't look at the downside."[46]

All the ingredients of the financial crisis were known by the central bankers more than two years before the crisis began. The Mortgage Insurance Companies of America, a trade association of U.S. mortgage providers, even sent a letter to Alan Greenspan expressing its strong concerns about risky mortgage lending practices and speculating that the Fed might be using incorrect data. But the data and warnings were ignored because the economy was doing well and billions in bonuses were being awarded on Wall Street. No one was anxious to break up the party. When Ben Bernanke succeeded Greenspan in early 2006, he also ignored the warnings. Even as the financial crisis began, Bernanke downplayed the risk of the troubles spreading further. We now know that the troubles and concerns highlighted by White and others rocked the foundations of the global economy.

To decrease the chances of groupthink undermining the financial industry again, some experts have suggested increasing the diversity of senior management and among those developing products that affect the risks in the financial system. Because similar people (age, race, education, gender, etc.) tend to think in the same way, perhaps people from different backgrounds would be more willing to question ideas and counter the effects of groupthink.

Questions:

1. How were the elements of groupthink illustrated in the financial crisis?
2. What could be done to reduce the effects of groupthink in the future?
3. Do you think that increasing the diversity of the financial companies' leadership would reduce groupthink? Why or why not?

launch of the shuttle *Columbia* in 2003.) Finally, the group may not consider any potential setbacks or countermoves by competing groups and therefore may fail to develop contingency plans. It should be noted that Janis contends that these defects may arise from other common problems as well: fatigue, prejudice, inaccurate information, information overload, and ignorance.[47]

Explosions destroyed the space shuttles *Challenger* (in 1986) and the *Columbia* (in 2003), killing everyone on board. Detailed study of decisions about each shuttle mission suggest that groupthink likely played a role in each disaster.

EVERETT HISTORICAL/SHUTTERSTOCK.COM

Defects in decision making do not always lead to bad outcomes or defeats. Even if its own decision-making processes are flawed, one side can win a battle because of the poor decisions made by the other side's leaders. Nevertheless, decisions produced by defective processes are less likely to succeed. Although the arguments for the existence of groupthink are convincing, the hypothesis has not been subjected to rigorous empirical examination. Research supports parts of the model but leaves some questions unanswered.[48]

Prevention of Groupthink

Several suggestions have been offered to help managers reduce the probability of groupthink in group decision making. Summarized in Table 8.2, these prescriptions fall into four categories, depending on whether they apply to the leader, the organization, the individual, or the process. All are designed to facilitate the critical evaluation of alternatives and discourage the single-minded pursuit of unanimity.

Table 8.2

Prescriptions for Preventing Groupthink

A. Leader prescriptions
   1. Assign everyone the role of critical evaluator.
   2. Be impartial; do not state preferences.
   3. Assign the devil's advocate role to at least one group member.
   4. Use outside experts to challenge the group.
   5. Be open to dissenting points of view.

B. Organizational prescriptions
   1. Set up several independent groups to study the same issue.
   2. Train managers and group leaders in groupthink prevention techniques.

C. Individual prescriptions
   1. Be a critical thinker.
   2. Discuss group deliberations with a trusted outsider; report back to the group.

D. Process prescriptions
   1. Periodically break the group into subgroups to discuss the issues.
   2. Take time to study external factors.
   3. Hold second-chance meetings to rethink issues before making a commitment.

Participation

A major issue in group decision making is the degree to which employees should participate in the process. Early management theories, such as those of the scientific management school, advocated a clear separation between the duties of managers and workers.

Management was to make the decisions, and employees were to implement them.[49] Other approaches have urged that employees be allowed to participate in decisions to increase their ego involvement, motivation, and satisfaction.[50] Numerous research studies have shown that whereas employees who seek responsibility and challenge on the job may find participation in the decision-making process to be both motivating and enriching, other employees may regard such participation as a waste of time and a management imposition.[51]

Whether employee participation in decision making is appropriate depends on the situation. In tasks that require an estimation, a prediction, or a judgment of accuracy— usually referred to as "judgmental tasks"—groups typically are superior to individuals simply because more people contribute to the decision-making process. However, one especially capable individual may make a better judgment than a group.

In problem-solving tasks, groups generally produce more and better solutions than do individuals. But groups take far longer than individuals to develop solutions and make decisions. An individual or very small group may be able to accomplish some things much faster than a large, unwieldy group or organization. In addition, individual decision making avoids the special problems of group decision making such as groupthink or group polarization. If the problem to be solved is fairly straightforward, it may be more appropriate to have a single capable individual concentrate on solving it. On the other hand, complex problems are more appropriate for groups. Such problems can often be divided into parts and the parts assigned to individuals or small groups who bring their results back to the group for discussion and decision making.

An additional advantage of group decision making is that it often creates greater interest in the task. Heightened interest may increase the time and effort given to the task, resulting in more ideas, a more thorough search for solutions, better evaluation of alternatives, and improved decision quality.

The Vroom decision tree approach to leadership (discussed in Chapter 12) is one popular way of determining the appropriate degree of subordinate participation.[52] The model includes decision styles that vary from "decide" (the leader alone makes the decision) to "delegate" (the group makes the decision, with each member having an equal say). The choice of style rests on seven considerations that concern the characteristics of the situation and the subordinates.

Participation in decision making is also related to organizational structure. For example, decentralization involves delegating some decision-making authority throughout the organizational hierarchy. The more decentralized the organization, the more its employees tend to participate in decision making. Whether one views participation in decision making as pertaining to leadership, organization structure, or motivation, it remains an important aspect of organizations that continues to occupy managers and organizational scholars.[53]

Group Problem Solving

A typical interacting group may have difficulty with any of several steps in the decision-making process. One common problem arises in the generation-of-alternatives phase: The search may be arbitrarily ended before all plausible alternatives have been identified. Several types of group interactions can have this effect. If members immediately express their reactions to the alternatives as they are first proposed, potential contributors may begin to censor their ideas to avoid embarrassing criticism from the group. Less confident group members, intimidated by members who have more experience, higher status, or more power, also may censor their ideas for fear of embarrassment or punishment. In addition, the group leader may limit idea generation by enforcing requirements concerning time, appropriateness, cost, feasibility, and the like. To improve the generation of alternatives, managers may employ any of three techniques to stimulate the group's problem-solving capabilities: brainstorming, the nominal group technique, or the Delphi technique.

Brainstorming

Brainstorming is most often used in the idea-generation phase of decision making and is intended to solve problems that are new to the organization and have major consequences. In brainstorming, the group convenes specifically to generate alternatives. The members present ideas and clarify them with brief explanations. Each idea is recorded in full view of all members, usually on a flip chart. To avoid self-censoring, no attempts to evaluate the ideas are allowed. Group members are encouraged to offer any ideas that occur to them, even those that seem too risky or impossible to implement. (The absence of such ideas, in fact, is evidence that group members are engaging in self-censorship.) In a subsequent session, after the ideas have been recorded and distributed to members for review, the alternatives are evaluated.

brainstorming
A technique used in the idea-generation phase of decision making that assists in development of numerous alternative courses of action

The intent of brainstorming is to produce totally new ideas and solutions by stimulating the creativity of group members and encouraging them to build on the contributions of others. Brainstorming does not provide the resolution to the problem, an evaluation scheme, or the decision itself. Instead, it should produce a list of alternatives that is more innovative and comprehensive than one developed by the typical interacting group.

nominal group technique
Group members follow a generate-discuss-vote cycle until they reach a decision

The Nominal Group Technique

The ***nominal group technique*** is another means of improving group decision making. Whereas brainstorming is used primarily to generate alternatives, this technique may be used in other phases of decision making, such as identification of the problem and of appropriate criteria for evaluating alternatives. To use this technique, a group of individuals convenes to address an issue. The issue is described to the group, and each individual writes a

Brainstorming is used to generate ideas and alternatives. These individuals are brainstorming color palettes and designs for a new advertising campaign. At this point in the process their focus is on identifying multiple alternatives. Later in the decision making process they will narrow the set down until they have made a final selection.

list of ideas; no discussion among the members is permitted. Following the five- to ten-minute idea-generation period, individual members take turns reporting their ideas, one at a time, to the group. The ideas are recorded on a flip chart, and members are encouraged to add to the list by building on the ideas of others. After all ideas have been presented, the members may discuss them and continue to build on them or proceed to the next phase. This part of the process can also be carried out without a face-to-face meeting or by mail, telephone, or computer. A meeting, however, helps members develop a group feeling and puts interpersonal pressure on the members to do their best in developing their lists.

After the discussion, members privately vote on or rank the ideas or report their preferences in some other agreed-upon way. Reporting is private to reduce any feelings of intimidation. After voting, the group may discuss the results and continue to generate and discuss ideas. The generation-discussion-vote cycle can continue until an appropriate decision is reached. The nominal group technique has two principal advantages. It helps overcome the negative effects of power and status differences among group members, and it can be used to explore problems to generate alternatives, or to evaluate them. Its primary disadvantage lies in its structured nature, which may limit creativity.

The Delphi Technique

Delphi technique
A method of systematically gathering judgments of experts for use in developing forecasts

The ***Delphi technique*** was originally developed by Rand Corporation as a method for systematically gathering the judgments of experts for use in developing forecasts. It is designed for groups that do not meet face to face. For instance, the product development manager of a major toy manufacturer might use the Delphi technique to probe the views of industry experts to forecast developments in the dynamic toy market.

The manager who wants the input of a group is the central figure in the process. After recruiting participants, the manager develops a questionnaire for them to complete. The questionnaire is relatively simple in that it contains straightforward questions that deal with the issue, trends in the area, new technological developments, and other factors the manager is interested in. The manager summarizes the responses and reports back to the experts with another questionnaire. This cycle may be repeated as many times as necessary to generate the information the manager needs. The Delphi technique is useful when experts are physically dispersed, anonymity is desired, or the participants are known to have trouble communicating with one another because of extreme differences of opinion. This method also avoids the intimidation problems that may exist in decision-making groups. On the other hand, the technique eliminates the often fruitful results of direct interaction among group members.

CREATIVITY, PROBLEM SOLVING, AND DECISION MAKING

creativity
A person's ability to generate new ideas or to conceive of new perspectives on existing ideas

Creativity is an important individual difference variable that exists in everyone. However, rather than discuss it with other individual-level concepts in Chapters 3 and 4, we describe it here because it plays such a central role in both decision making and problem solving. ***Creativity*** is the ability of an

ILDOGESTO/SHUTTERSTOCK.COM

IMPROVE YOUR SKILLS

CREATIVE DECISIONS THROUGH BORROWING IDEAS

Creative decisions are novel and useful, and borrowing ideas from other areas is often a foundation of the creative decision-making process.[54] Johannes Gutenberg's idea for a movable type printing press was inspired by the technology of the screw-type wine presses of France's Rhine Valley. It was there in 1440 that Gutenberg created his printing press, in which ink was rolled over the raised surfaces of moveable hand-set block letters held within a wooden form which was then pressed against a sheet of paper.[55] He creatively combined his knowledge of goldsmithing, linen, and presses used for other things to arrive at an innovative solution. More recently, Steve Jobs of Apple recognized Amazon's Kindle as an inspiration for the iPad.

Rather than being out of touch for most people, creative decision making can follow a deliberate process in pursuit of an existing idea that solves a related problem in some other area. It is still difficult—the borrowed ideas only provide the raw material. Noted author David Kord Murray provides six simple steps that you can practice to improve your own creativity:[56]

1. Defining: Define the problem you are trying to solve. How you define the problem will determine how you solve it. Mistakes often result from defining problems too narrowly or too broadly.
2. Borrowing: Borrow ideas from places that have faced a similar problem. One tactic is to start with your competitors, then other industries, and then outside business and to nature, the sciences, or entertainment to see how they solve similar problems.
3. Combining: Combine the borrowed ideas. This is the essence of creativity, as in Gutenberg's printing press.
4. Incubating: Give your subconscious mind time to work and listen to the ideas it generates. This can involve sleeping on it or putting it away for a little while. Sometimes not thinking at all is the most effective thinking.
5. Judging: Identify the strengths and weaknesses of the decision.
6. Enhancing: Tweak your decision to contain more positives and fewer negatives. Evolve your decisions through trial and error and make appropriate adjustments.

Sources: Murray, D. K. (2009). Borrowing Brilliance: The Six Steps to Business Innovation by Building on the Ideas of Others. New York: Gotham; Murray, D.K. (2009). What are the Six Steps? Available online: http://www.borrowingbrilliance.com/sixsteps.html; Harry Ransom Center (2009). Adapting Technology. Harry Ransom Center at the University of Texas at Austin. Available online: http://www.hrc.utexas.edu/educator/modules/gutenberg/invention/adapting/; Lienhard, J.H. (1988). No. 753: Johann Gutenberg. Available online: http://www.uh.edu/engines/epi753.htm.

individual to generate new ideas or to conceive of new perspectives on existing ideas. Hence, creativity can play a role in how a problem or decision situation is defined, what alternatives are identified, and how each is evaluated. Creativity can also enable a manager to identify a new way of looking at things.[57] Our *Improve Your Skills* feature will help you better see the connections between creativity and decision making.

What makes a person creative? How does the creative process work? Although psychologists have not yet discovered complete answers to these questions, examining a few general patterns can help us understand the sources of individual creativity within organizations and the processes through which creativity emerges.[58]

The Creative Individual

Numerous researchers have focused their efforts on attempting to describe the common attributes of creative individuals. These attributes generally fall into three categories: background experiences, personal traits, and cognitive abilities.

EVERETT HISTORICAL/SHUTTERSTOCK.COM

Creativity is sometimes associated with being raised in an environment that nurtures creativity and fosters curiosity. Thomas Edison's creativity was nurtured by his mother. Edison went on to become one of the greatest inventors in history.

Background Experiences and Creativity

Researchers have observed that many creative individuals were raised in an environment in which creativity was nurtured. Mozart was raised in a family of musicians and began composing and performing music at age 6. Pierre and Marie Curie, great scientists in their own right, also raised a daughter, Irene, who won the Nobel Prize in Chemistry. Thomas Edison's creativity was nurtured by his mother. However, people with background experiences very different from theirs have also been creative. The African American abolitionist and writer Frederick Douglass was born into slavery in Tuckahoe, Maryland, and had very limited opportunities for education. Nonetheless, his powerful oratory and creative thinking helped lead to the Emancipation Proclamation, which outlawed slavery in the United States.

Personal Traits and Creativity

Certain personal traits have also been linked to creativity in individuals. The traits shared by most creative people are openness, an attraction to complexity, high levels of energy, independence and autonomy, strong self-confidence, and a strong belief that one is, in fact, creative. Individuals who possess these traits are more likely to be creative than are those who do not have them.

Cognitive Abilities and Creativity

Cognitive abilities are an individual's power to think intelligently and to analyze situations and data effectively. Intelligence may be a precondition for individual creativity—but, although most creative people are highly intelligent, not all intelligent people necessarily are creative. Creativity is also linked with the ability to think divergently and convergently. Divergent thinking is a skill that allows people to see differences between situations, phenomena, or events. Convergent thinking is a skill that allows people to see similarities between situations, phenomena, or events. Creative people are generally very skilled at both divergent and convergent thinking.

The Creative Process

Although creative people often report that ideas seem to come to them "in a flash," individual creative activity actually tends to progress through a series of stages. Figure 8.6 summarizes the major stages of the creative process. Not all creative activity has to follow these four stages, but much of it does.

Preparation

preparation
Usually the first stage in the creative process, includes education and formal training

The creative process normally begins with a period of ***preparation***. Formal education and training are usually the most efficient ways of becoming familiar with a vast amount of research and knowledge. To make a creative contribution to business management or business services, individuals must usually receive formal training and education in business. This is one reason for the strong demand for undergraduate and master's level business education. Formal business education can be an effective way for an individual to get "up to speed" and begin making creative contributions quickly.

Experiences that managers have on the job after their formal training has finished can also contribute to the creative process. In an important sense, the education and training of creative people never really ends. It continues as long as they remain interested in the world and curious about the way things work. One such individual is Bruce Roth, who earned a Ph.D. in chemistry and then spent years working in the pharmaceutical industry learning more and more about chemical compounds and how they work in human beings.

Figure 8.6

The Creative Process

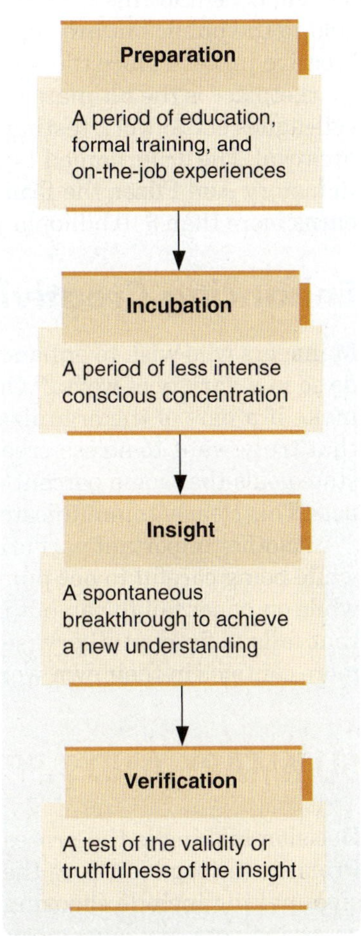

Preparation	A period of education, formal training, and on-the-job experiences
Incubation	A period of less intense conscious concentration
Insight	A spontaneous breakthrough to achieve a new understanding
Verification	A test of the validity or truthfulness of the insight

The creative process generally follows the four steps illustrated here. Of course, there are exceptions, and the process is occasionally different. In most cases, however, these steps capture the essence of the creative process.

Incubation

The second phase of the creative process is ***incubation***—a period of less intense conscious concentration during which the knowledge and ideas acquired during preparation mature and develop. A curious aspect of incubation is that it is often helped along by pauses in concentrated rational thought. Some creative people rely on physical activity such as jogging or swimming to provide a "break" from thinking. Others may read or listen to music. Sometimes sleep may even supply the needed pause. Bruce Roth eventually joined Warner-Lambert, an up-and-coming drug company, to help develop medication to lower cholesterol. In his spare time, Roth read mystery novels and hiked in the mountains. He later acknowledged that this was when he did his best thinking.

incubation
The stage of less intense conscious concentration during which a creative person lets the knowledge and ideas acquired during preparation mature and develop

Insight

Usually occurring after preparation and incubation, insight is a spontaneous breakthrough in which the creative person achieves a new understanding of some problem or situation. ***Insight*** represents a coming together of all the scattered thoughts and ideas that were maturing during incubation. It may occur suddenly or develop slowly over time. Insight can be triggered by some external event—such as a new experience or an encounter with new data that forces the individual to think about old issues and problems in new ways—or it can be a completely internal event in which patterns of thought finally coalesce in ways that generate new understanding. One day Bruce Roth was reviewing some data from some earlier studies that had found the new drug under development to be no more effective than other drugs already available. But this time he saw some statistical relationships that had not been identified previously. He knew then that he had a major breakthrough on his hands.

insight
The stage in the creative process in which all the scattered thoughts and ideas that were maturing during incubation come together to produce a breakthrough

Verification

Once an insight has occurred, ***verification*** determines the validity or truthfulness of the insight. For many creative ideas, verification includes scientific experiments

verification
The final stage of the creative process in which the validity or truthfulness of the insight is determined

to determine whether or not the insight actually leads to the results expected. Verification may also include the development of a product or service prototype. A prototype is one (or a very small number) of products built just to see whether the ideas behind this new product actually work. Product prototypes are rarely sold to the public but are very valuable in verifying the insights developed in the creative process. Once the new product or service is developed, verification in the marketplace is the ultimate test of the creative idea behind it. Bruce Roth and his colleagues set to work testing the new drug compound and eventually won FDA approval. The drug, named Lipitor, has become the largest-selling pharmaceutical in history. And Pfizer, the firm that bought Warner-Lambert in a hostile takeover, earns more than $10 billion a year on the drug.[59]

Enhancing Creativity in Organizations

Managers who wish to enhance and promote creativity in their organizations can do so in a variety of ways.[60] One important method for enhancing creativity is to make it a part of the organization's culture, often through explicit goals. Firms that truly want to stress creativity, such as 3M and Rubbermaid, for example, state goals that some percent of future revenues are to be gained from new products. This clearly communicates that creativity and innovation are valued.

Another important part of enhancing creativity is to reward creative successes, while being careful to not punish creative failures. Many ideas that seem worthwhile on paper fail to pan out in reality. If the first person to come up with an idea that fails is fired or otherwise punished, others in the organization will become more cautious in their own work. And as a result, fewer creative ideas will emerge.

SUMMARY AND APPLICATIONS

Decision making is the process of choosing one alternative from among several. Problem solving is finding the answer to a question. The basic elements of decision making include choosing a goal; considering alternative courses of action; assessing potential outcomes of the alternatives, each with its own value relative to the goal; and choosing one alternative based on an evaluation of the outcomes. Information is available regarding the alternatives, outcomes, and values.

Programmed decisions are well-structured, recurring decisions made according to set decision rules. Nonprogrammed decisions involve nonroutine, poorly structured situations with unclear sources of information; these decisions cannot be made according to existing decision rules. Decision making may also be classified based on salient conditions that exist. The classifications—certainty, risk, and uncertainty—reflect the amount of information available regarding the outcomes of alternatives.

The rational approach views decision making as a completely rational process in which goals are established, a problem is identified, alternatives are generated and evaluated, a choice is made and implemented, and control is exercised. Evidence-based decision making is a recent restatement of the need for rationality when making decisions.

The use of procedures and rules of thumb, suboptimizing, and satisficing characterize the behavioral model. A variety of other behavioral processes also influence decision making in organizations. Political activities by coalitions, managerial intuition, and the tendency to become increasingly committed to a chosen course of action are all important. Risk propensity is also an important

LOSKUTNIKOV/SHUTTERSTOCK.COM

REAL WORLD CHALLENGE

AN ETHICAL CHALLENGE

Did the CEO of the aircraft engine repair company disclose the pending claim that his company's parts were the possible cause of the grounding of eleven airplanes and risk the jobs of hundreds of employees and his own stake in the company? Or did he stay quiet until he had more information? The right choice is not always clear—this type of decision is typical of many of the tough decisions managers have to make.

In this case, the CEO considered that the bankers might call the company's loans and company investors might lose their money if word of the FAA investigation got out. He also worried about the effect on his employees if the banks started pulling loans and the company had to lay off workers. But he did not consider whether he had any responsibility to passengers regarding the situation to enable them to make their own decisions about their safety. Years later, he acknowledged that passengers' safety never crossed his mind when making the decision.

The CEO ultimately decided not to disclose the information and signed the audit papers. Eventually the FAA concluded that it was impossible to identify who was at fault for the engine failures. The company's name was never publicly disclosed as being a possible factor in the grounding of the airplanes.

behavioral perspective on decision making. Ethics also affect how managers make decisions. Prospect theory suggests that people are more motivated to avoid losses than to make gains. The rational and behavioral views can be combined into an integrated model.

Creativity is the capacity to generate new ideas. Numerous individual and background factors are likely to influence any given individual's level of creativity. The creative process itself generally involves four phases: preparation, incubation, insight, and verification. Managers can enhance or reduce creativity in their organizations through various means.

DISCUSSION QUESTIONS

1. Some have argued that people, not organizations, make decisions and that the study of "organizational" decision making is therefore pointless. Do you agree with this argument? Why or why not?
2. What information did you use in deciding to enter the school you now attend?
3. When your alarm goes off each morning, you have a decision to make: whether to get up and go to school or work, or to stay in bed and sleep longer. Is this a programmed or nonprogrammed decision? Why?
4. Describe at least three points in the decision-making process at which information plays an important role.

5. How does the role of information in the rational model of decision making differ from the role of information in the behavioral model?
6. Why does it make sense to discuss several different models of decision making?
7. Can you think of a time when you satisficed when making a decision? Have you ever suboptimized?
8. Describe a situation in which you experienced escalation of commitment to an ineffective course of action. What did you do about it? Do you wish you had handled it differently? Why or why not?
9. How comfortable or uncomfortable are you in making risky decisions?
10. Do you consider yourself to be relatively more or less creative? Recall an instance in which you made a discovery using the four phases of the creative process.

UNDERSTAND YOURSELF EXERCISE

Making a Rational Decision*

Select a personal decision that you are currently making or that you will need to make soon. It might be picking a major, buying a car, renting an apartment, choosing a job, or something else. Now apply the rational decision-making process to it by identifying criteria and goals, assigning weights to the criteria, generating and evaluating alternatives, ranking the alternatives, and making a decision.

Next, compare the outcome of this decision with the outcome you would have reached by following a more intuitive or emotional process. Are the outcomes different? Which process do you feel led you to the best decision? Why?

*We would like to thank Professor Carolyn M. Youssef of Bellevue University for providing this exercise.

GROUP EXERCISE

Superheroes*

Each student should pick his or her favorite superhero. Now assume that a large earthquake just hit a populated island. How could your superhero assist the island? Take five minutes to write down your ideas.

Now form groups of five to six students. Share which superhero you chose and the ideas you generated based on your superhero's special abilities (e.g., Batman could use his gadgets and tools to help free people trapped in rubble). The group should then work together to identify true possible solutions based on the ideas generated for the superheroes (e.g., Batman's grappling hook might be adapted for use in moving large obstacles during rescues).

*We would like to thank Professor Jim Gort of Davenport University for suggesting this exercise.

VIDEO EXERCISE

City of Greensburg Kansas

It's almost impossible to assign credit or blame to any one person for Greensburg's decision to rebuild the small Kansas town as a model green community after a tornado decimated 95 percent of its buildings. Many folks in

Greensburg would assert that whoever made the decision, made a good one. Other residents make a different case.

Former mayor Lonnie McCollum expressed interest in exploring the possibilities of running Greensburg's municipal buildings on solar and wind power well before the EF5 tornado hit in May 2004. After the storm, he saw the tragedy as an opportunity to reinvent the dying town and put it back on the map. But McCollum was not the sole decision maker; instead, he was the leader of a small community facing endless uncertainties. Ultimately, the Greensburg City Council would have to vote on this matter.

After multiple rounds of community meetings in which residents engaged in rigorous debate, Greensburg's City Council voted in favor of rebuilding the town using green methods and materials. And when the council members voted on the specifics of implementation, they decided to build all municipal buildings to the Leadership in Energy and Environmental Design (LEED) Platinum standard, which is the highest nationally accepted benchmark for the design, construction, and operation of high-performance green buildings.

But residents were divided over the decision, and the town meetings generated rancor and politicking. Mayor McCollum eventually resigned, city administrators dug in, and many residents checked out. But the rebuilding plan went forward, and today a collaborative effort among business and nonprofit groups is putting Greensburg back on the map.

There is no way to convince every Greensburg resident that going green was a good decision. Perhaps all the City Council can hope for is support from a majority of residents. In their minds, what were the alternatives? The town was dying. But Greensburg is rebuilding thanks to generous corporate sponsorships and government grants. The town also stars in a TV show on Planet Green. The TV show is aptly named, *Greensburg*.

Discussion Questions

1. Cite reasons for and against rebuilding Greensburg as a "green town." Which reasons do you find most convincing and why?
2. Do you think Greensburg's decision-making process was effective? Explain.
3. What prevented the City of Greensburg from making purely rational decisions?

Now What?

VIDEO CASE

PERCOM/SHUTTERSTOCK.COM

Imagine being part of a group with three other coworkers trying to make a decision about whether to discontinue funding an underperforming product. The group has been working together on the product line for three years, but the product is clearly a failure. When you start to question where the decision is headed you are called disloyal and told to go with the team and give the product more time. One of the team members calls for a final vote on the group's decision, which appears to be to continue funding a clearly awful and doomed-to-fail product. *What do you say or do?* Go to this chapter's "Now What?" video, watch the challenge video, and choose a response. Be sure to also view the outcomes of the two responses you didn't choose.

Discussion Questions

1. Is this decision a programmed or non-programmed decision and what is the basis for your answer?

2. How is groupthink and stereotyping illustrated in these videos? Explain your answer.
3. Would a rational decision-making approach work? Why or why not?
4. As a manager, how else might you handle this situation?

ENDNOTES

[1]Seglin, J. L. (2005, April). How to Make Tough Ethical Calls. *Harvard Management Update,* 3.

[2]Simon, H. (1960). *The New Science of Management Decision* (p. 1). New York: Harper & Row.

[3]See Bromiley, P., & Rau, D. (2010). Strategic Decision Making. In *Handbook of Industrial and Organizational Psychology,* ed. S. Zedeck (pp. 161–182). Washington, DC: American Psychological Association.

[4]Tichy, N., & Bennis, W. (2007). *Judgment—How Winning Leaders Make Great Calls*. New York: Penguin Group.

[5]Rajagopalan, N., Rasheed, A. M. A., & Datta, D. K. (1993, Summer). Strategic Decision Processes: Critical Review and Future Directions. *Journal of Management, 19*(2), 349–384.

[6]See Huber, G. P. (1980). *Managerial Decision Making* (pp. 90–115). Glenview, IL: Scott, Foresman, for a discussion of decision making under conditions of certainty, risk, and uncertainty.

[7]See Garvin, D., & Roberto, M. (2001, September). What You Don't Know About Making Decisions. *Harvard Business Review*, 108–115.

[8]'90s Style Brainstorming. *Forbes ASAP*, October 25, 1993, 44–61.

[9]Mintzberg, H., Raisinghani, D., & Thoret, A. (1976, June). The Structure of "Unstructured" Decision Processes. *Administrative Science Quarterly*, 246–275; Zeleny, M. (1991). Descriptive Decision Making and Its Application. *Applications of Management Science, 1,* 327–388.

[10]For more on choice processes, see Harrison, E. F. (1999). *The Managerial Decision-Making Process* (5th ed., pp. 55–60). Boston: Houghton Mifflin.

[11]Ginsberg, A., & Ventrakaman, N. (1985, July). Contingency Perspectives of Organizational Strategy: A Critical Review of the Empirical Research. *Academy of Management Review*, 412–434; Hambrick, D. C., & Lei, D. (1985, December). Toward an Empirical Prioritization of Contingency Variables for Business Strategy. *Academy of Management Journal*, 763–788.

[12]Festinger, L. (1957). *A Theory of Cognitive Dissonance*. Palo Alto, CA: Stanford University Press.

[13]For more on the rational approach to decision making, see Harrison, E. F. (1999). *The Managerial Decision-Making Process* (5th ed., pp. pp. 74–100). Boston: Houghton Mifflin.

[14]Pfeffer, J., & Sutton, R. I. (2006). *Hard Facts, Dangerous Half-Truths, and Total Nonsense: Profiting from Evidence-Based Management*. Cambridge, MA: Harvard Business School Press.

[15]Pfeffer, J., & Sutton, R. I. (2006). *Hard Facts, Dangerous Half-Truths, and Total Nonsense: Profiting from Evidence-Based Management*. Cambridge, MA: Harvard Business School Press.

[16]Simon, H. A. (1945). *Administrative Behavior: A Study of Decision-Making Processes in Administrative Organizations*. New York: Free Press. Simon's ideas have been refined and updated in Simon, H. A. (1976). *Administrative Behavior: A Study of Decision-Making Processes in Administrative Organizations* (3rd ed.). New York: Free Press; and Simon, H. A. (1987, February). Making Management Decisions: The Role of Intuition and Emotion. *Academy of Management Executive*, 57–63.

[17]Parks, C. D., & Cowlin, R. (1995). Group Discussion as Affected by Number of Alternatives and by a Time Limit. *Organizational Behavior and Human Decision Processes*, *62*(3), 267–275.

[18]For more on the concept of bounded rationality, see March, J. G., & Simon, H. A. (1958). *Organizations*. New York: John Wiley and Sons.

[19]Simon, H. A. (1976). *Administrative Behavior: A Study of Decision-Making Processes in Administrative Organizations* (3rd ed.). New York: Free Press.

[20]Cyert, R. M., & March, J. G. (1963). *A Behavioral Theory of the Firm* (p. 113). Englewood Cliffs, NJ: Prentice Hall; Simon, H. A. (1976). *Administrative Behavior: A Study of Decision-Making Processes in Administrative Organizations* (3rd ed.). New York: Free Press.

[21]Hoover's *Handbook of American Business 2012* (pp. 845–847). Austin, TX: Hoover's Business Press.

[22]Elsbach, K. D., & Elofson, G. (2000). How the Packaging of Decision Explanations Affects Perceptions of Trustworthiness. *Academy of Management Journal, 43*(1), 80–89.

[23]Tichy, N., & Bennis, W. (2007). *Judgment—How Winning Leaders Make Great Calls*. New York: Penguin Group.

[24]Wallace, C. P. (1997, August 18). Adidas—Back in the Game," *Fortune*, 176–182.

[25]Staw, B. M., & Ross, J. (1988, February). Good Money after Bad," *Psychology Today*, 30–33; and Bobocel, D. R., & Meyer, J. (1994). Escalating Commitment to a Failing Course of Action: Separating the Roles of Choice and Justification. *Journal of Applied Psychology*, *79*, 360–363.

[26]Keil, M., & Montealegre, R. (2000, Spring). Cutting Your Losses: Extricating Your Organization When a Big Project Goes Awry. *Sloan Management Review*, 55–64.

[27]McNamara, G., & Bromiley, P. Risk and Return in Organizational Decision Making. *Academy of Management Journal*, *42*(3), 330–339.

[28]For and example, see O'Reilly, B. (1999, June 7). What it Takes to Start a Startup. *Fortune*, 135–140.

[29]Kahneman, D., & Tversky, A. (1979). Prospect Theory: An Analysis of Decision under Risk. *Econometrica*, *47*, 263–291.

[30]Blodgett, J. G., Lu, L. C., Rose, G. M., & Vitell, S. J. (2001). Ethical Sensitivity to Stakeholder Interests: A Cross-Cultural Comparison. *Academy of Marketing Science Journal, 29*(2), 190–202.

[31]Singhapakdi, A., Karande, K., Rao, C. P., & Vitell, S. J. (2001). How Important Are Ethics and Social Responsibility? A Multinational Study of Marketing Professionals. *European Journal of Marketing, 35*(1–2), 133–152.

[32]Trompenaars, F., & Hampden-Turner, C. (1998). *Riding the Waves of Culture: Understanding Cultural Diversity in Business* (2nd ed.). New York: McGraw-Hill.

[33]As described by Weissmann, J. (2012, July 24). A Very Mean (but Maybe Brilliant) Way to Pay Teachers. *The Atlantic Monthly*, 44–46.

[34]Eisenhardt, K. M. (1989, September). Making Fast Strategic Decisions in High-Velocity Environments. *Academy of Management Journal*, 543–576.

[35]Wallach, M. A., Kogan, N., & Bem, D. J. (1962, August). Group Influence on Individual Risk Taking. *Journal of Abnormal and Social Psychology*, 75–86; Stoner, J. A. F. (1968, October). Risky and Cautious Shifts in Group Decisions: The Influence of Widely Held Values. *Journal of Experimental Social Psychology*, 442–459.

[36]Cartwright, D. (1971, December). Risk Taking by Individuals and Groups: An Assessment of Research Employing Choice Dilemmas. *Journal of Personality and Social Psychology*, 361–378.

[37]Moscovici, S., & Zavalloni, M. (1969, June). The Group as a Polarizer of Attitudes. *Journal of Personality and Social Psychology*, 125–135.

[38]Janis, I. L. (1982). *Groupthink* (2nd ed., p. 9). Boston: Houghton Mifflin.

[39]Moorhead, G., Neck, C. P., & West, M. (1998, February–March). The Tendency Toward Defective Decision Making Within Self-Managing Teams: Relevance of Groupthink for the 21st Century. *Organizational Behavior and Human Decision Processes*, 327–351.

[40]Moorhead, G., Ference, R., & Neck, C. P. (1991). Group Decision Fiascoes Continue: Space Shuttle Challenger and a Revised Groupthink Framework. *Human Relations*, *44,* 539–550.

[41]Cross, R. & Brodt, S. (2001, Winter. How Assumptions of Consensus Undermine Decision Making. *Sloan Management Review*, 86–95.

[42]Janis, I. L. (1972). *Victims of Groupthink* (pp. 197–198). Boston: Houghton Mifflin.

[43]Janis, I. L. (1982). *Groupthink* (2nd ed., p. 9). Boston: Houghton Mifflin.

[44]Balzli, B., & Schiessl, M. (2009, July 8). Global Banking Economist Warned of Coming Crisis. *Spiegel Online*. Available online: http://www.spiegel.de/international/business/0,1518,druck-635051,00.html.

[45]Balzli, B., & Schiessl, M. (2009, July 8). Global Banking Economist Warned of Coming Crisis. *Spiegel Online*. Available online: http://www.spiegel.de/international/business/0,1518,druck 635051,00.html.

[46]Balzli, B., & Schiessl, M. (2009, July 8). Global Banking Economist Warned of Coming Crisis. *Spiegel Online*. Available online: http://www.spiegel.de/international/business/0,1518,druck-635051,00.html.

[47]Janis, I. L. (1982). *Groupthink* (2nd ed., pp. 193–197). Boston: Houghton Mifflin; Moorhead, G. (1982, December). Groupthink: Hypothesis in Need of Testing. *Group & Organization Studies*, 429–444.

[48]Moorhead, G., & Montanari, J. R. (1986, May). Empirical Analysis of the Groupthink Phenomenon. *Human Relations*, 399–410; Montanari, J. R., & Moorhead, G. (1989, Spring). Development of the Groupthink Assessment Inventory. *Educational and Psychological Measurement*, 209–219.

[49]Taylor, F. W. (1911). *The Principles of Scientific Management*. New York: Harper & Row.

[50]Argyris, C. (1957). *Personality and Organization*. New York: Harper & Row; Likert, R. (1961). *New Patterns of Management*. New York: McGraw-Hill, 1961.

[51]Coch, L., & French, J. R. P. (1948). Overcoming Resistance to Change. *Human Relations*, *1,* 512–532; Morse, N. C., & Reimer, E. (1956, January). The Experimental Change of a Major Organizational Variable. *Journal of Abnormal and Social Psychology*, 120–129.

[52]Vroom, V. (2000, Spring). Leadership and the Decision-Making Process. *Organizational Dynamics*, 82–94.

[53]For a recent example, see De Dreu, C. K. W., & West, M. (2001). Minority Dissent and Team Innovation: The Importance of Participation in Decision Making. *Journal of Applied Psychology*, *86*(6), 1191–1201.

[54]Akande, A. (1991). How Managers Express Their Creativity. *International Journal of Manpower, 12,* 17–19.

[55]Bellis, M. (2009). Johannes Gutenberg and the Printing Press. About.com. Available online: http://inventors.about.com/od/gstartinventors/a/Gutenberg.htm

[56]Muray, D. K. (2009). *Borrowing Brilliance: The Six Steps to Business Innovation by Building on the Ideas of Others*. New York: Gotham.

[57]Jing Zhou, J., & Shalley, C. E. (2010). Deepening our Understanding of Creativity in the Workplace: A Review of Different Approaches to Creativity Research. In *Handbook of Industrial and Organizational Psychology,* ed. S. Zedeck (pp. 275–302). Washington, DC: American Psychological Association.

[58]Woodman, R. W., Sawyer, J. E., & Griffin, R. W. (1993, April). Toward a Theory of Organizational Creativity. *Academy of Management Review*, 293–321; see also Henessey, B., & Amabile, T. (2010). Creativity. In *Annual Review of Psychology,* eds. S. Fiske, D. Schacter, & R. Sternberg (Vol. 61, pp. 569–598). Palo Alto, CA: Annual Reviews.

[59]Simons, J. (2003, January 20). The $10 Billion Pill. *Fortune*, 58–68.

[60]Shalley, C. E., Gilson, L. L., & Blum, T. C. (2000). Matching Creativity Requirements and the Work Environment: Effects on Satisfaction and Intentions to Leave. *Academy of Management Journal*, *43*(2), 215–223; see also Tabak, F. (1997). Employee Creative Performance: What Makes it Happen? *The Academy of Management Executive*, *11*(1), 119–122.

LOSKUTNIKOV/SHUTTERSTOCK.COM

CHAPTER 9

COMMUNICATION

CHAPTER OUTLINE

LEARNING OUTCOMES

After studying this chapter you should be able to:

1 Describe the communication process, explain the difference between one-way and two-way communication, and identify barriers to effective communication.

2 Identify and discuss the major communications skills used by managers.

3 Discuss communication media and describe the richness of each.

4 Describe different forms of organizational communication.

LOSKUTNIKOV/SHUTTERSTOCK.COM

—REAL WORLD CHALLENGE—

COMMUNICATING VALUES AT NOKIA[1]

Nokia Corporation, based in Espoo, Finland, is a leader in the world of large-scale telecommunications infrastructures, mobile phone technology development and licensing, and online mapping services. Named after the Nokia River in southern Finland and employing more than 60,000 people worldwide, Nokia sold over a billion mobile phones before selling is phone business to Microsoft in order to concentrate on technology development and licensing.[2] Nokia's strong culture is based on innovation and collaboration, and the company relies on its values to keep its employees focused and energized.

Nokia has long held strong, clear values that it regularly refreshes in various communications and initiatives. Recently, though, the company has realized that its values are no longer in the forefront of employees' minds. It seems like everything that could be said about Nokia's values has been said. Now employees are not talking about them as much, and the values seem old fashioned and less engaging.

Nokia knows that it needs to do something to modernize and reenergize its values among its employees. The company asks you for advice about how to effectively establish and communicate its core values to employees. After reading this chapter, you should have some good ideas about how Nokia can renew and refresh its values among its employees.

SARI GUSTAFSSON/AFP/GETTY IMAGES

Imagine what an organization would be like without communication. Managers could not manage, employees could not collaborate, and decisions would never get made. Communication, a form of social interaction, is the glue that holds organizations together—it is not an understatement to say that if communication within an organization is consistently ineffective that organization is not likely to survive. Organizations achieve their strategies, goals, and outcomes through communication. Organizational decision makers must communicate to plan and develop strategies. Making decisions requires the communication of information. Managers then communicate these strategies and decisions to employees, who communicate among themselves to execute them. Managers also communicate with customers and suppliers and use communication to acquire information about the marketplace and competitors. In addition, communication is related to higher levels of employee engagement, which are related to higher shareholder return and increased market value.[3]

To be effective leaders, managers must have good communication skills, particularly during tough economic times. As former GE CEO Jack Welch said, in tough times, "you have to communicate like you've never communicated before. People must feel the excitement of tomorrow instead of the pain of today. You can only accomplish this by talking honestly about both."[4] When U.S. steelmaker Nucor was hit by the global recession, managers used communication to keep up morale. The CEO doubled the time he spent in the plants, and one plant's general manager sent weekly notes updating his 750-person staff on order volumes.[5] Communication is also critical to employee motivation.[6]

In this chapter, we will discuss the communication process, some of the basic issues in interpersonal communication, methods of communicating, and how information technology (IT) and the Internet have influenced organizational communications. We also discuss some specific communication skills, present some barriers to effective communication, and provide ways to overcome those barriers. This chapter should give you a good understanding of the communication process and help you to become a more effective communicator.

communication
The transmission of information from one person to another to create a shared understanding and feeling

encoding
Converting a thought, idea, or fact into a message composed of symbols, pictures, or words

THE COMMUNICATION PROCESS

Communication is the process of transmitting information from one person to another to create a shared understanding and feeling. The word communication actually comes from the Latin word *communicare*, meaning to share or make common.[7] Communication does not mean agreeing, only that information is transmitted and received as it was intended. Figure 9.1 illustrates the communications process. The six parts of the model of the communication process are:

1. ***Encoding*** occurs when the message sender converts a thought, idea, or fact into a message composed of symbols, pictures, or words.

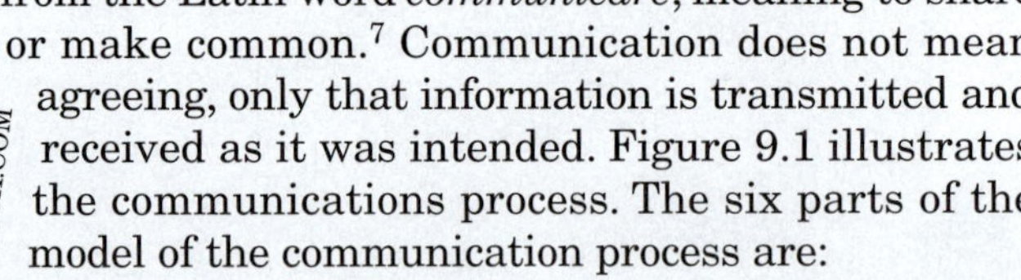

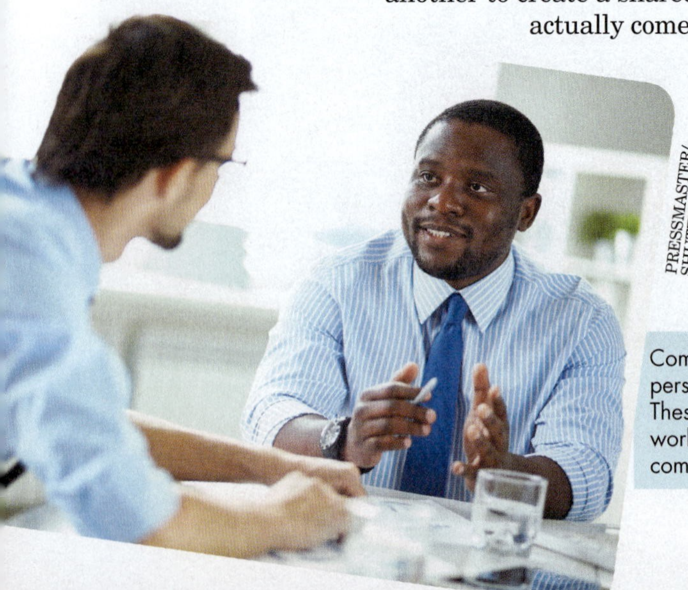

PRESSMASTER/ SHUTTERSTOCK.COM

Communication is the process of transmitting information from one person to another to create shared understanding and feeling. These two colleagues are having a conversation about a significant work issue. Both are engaged in the process and seem to be communicating effectively.

Figure 9.1

The Communication Process

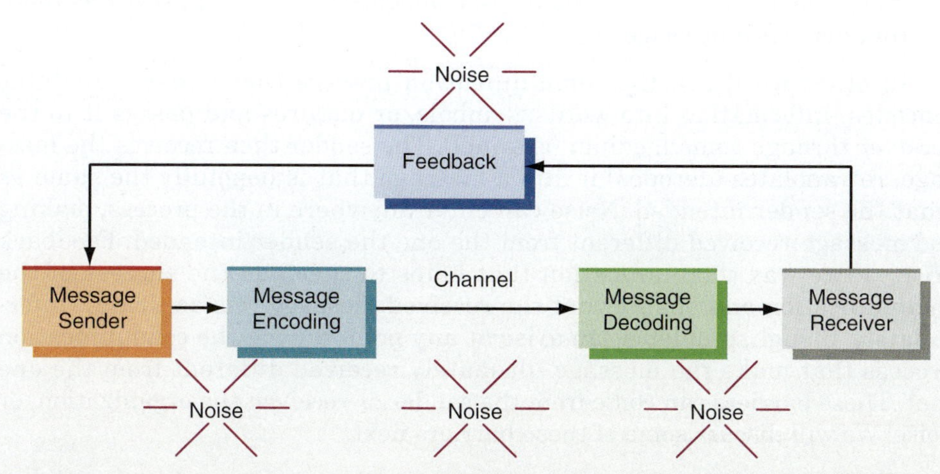

The communication process involves a number of steps. The process begins with encoding a message, then transmitting that message through a channel, and it then being decoded by the receiver. Feedback helps improve communication effectiveness, but, on the other hand, noise can block or distort it.

2. The ***message*** is the encoded information being sent. For example, a manager wants to communicate to her new employee, Zack, that he is doing well. The manager encodes that thought into words expressing that Zack's performance has been steadily increasing and that he is performing at 90 percent of his target level. These words are the message. The manager could also create a graph showing Zack's performance pattern and a line representing his target performance level.
3. The ***channel*** is the medium used to send the message to the receiver, including voice, writing, graphs, videos, intranets, the Internet, television, and body language.
4. When the message receiver sees, reads, or hears the message, it gets decoded. ***Decoding*** is the interpretation and translation of the message back into something understood by the receiver. The decoded information is hopefully the same as the information the sender intended to communicate, but this is not always the case.
5. ***Feedback*** is a check on the success of the communication. The message receiver sends a new message back to the original sender, and the original sender assesses if the receiver understood the original message as intended. Repeating or paraphrasing the original message, asking for clarification, and asking if your conclusion is correct are forms of feedback.
6. ***Noise*** is anything that blocks, distorts, or changes in any way the message the sender intended to communicate. For example, noise

message
The encoded information

channel
The medium used to send the message

decoding
Translating the message back into something that can be understood by the receiver

feedback
A check on the success of the communication

noise
Anything that blocks, distorts, or changes in any way the message the sender intended to communicate

MONKEY BUSINESS IMAGES/ SHUTTERSTOCK.COM

Noise can block or distort messages. This individual, for example, is texting during a business meeting. There is a good chance that he will not fully understand what others are saying because he is paying more attention to his texts than to the meeting itself.

can be something physical in the environment, like a ringing bell or people talking, or it can occur because the sender or receiver are distracted and are unable to concentrate on the message being sent or received. Stereotypes, biases, and one's mood or psychological state can all serve as noise that distorts a message.

In other words, in the communication process the sender translates (encodes) information into words, symbols, or pictures and passes it to the receiver through some medium (channel). The sender then receives the message, retranslates (decodes) it into a message that is hopefully the same as what the sender intended. Noise can enter anywhere in the process, making the message received different from the one the sender intended. Feedback creates two-way communication that helps to check on the success of the communication and ensure that the received message was accurate. Unfortunately, though, problems can arise at any point during the communication process that make the message ultimately received different from the one sent. These barriers can come from the sender or receiver, the organization, or noise. We will discuss some of these barriers next.

Nonverbal Communication

nonverbal communications
Communications that are not spoken or written but that have meaning to others

body language
A body movement such as a gesture or expression that conveys information to others

The way we communicate—our nonverbal behaviors and vocal tone—is more important to a message's meaning than the words we actually say. ***Nonverbal communications*** are not spoken or written. Some of the strongest and most meaningful communications are nonverbal—a fire alarm, a smile, an emoticon, a red traffic light, or a look of anger on someone's face.

Body Language

Body language is a body movement such as a gesture or expression that conveys information to others. For example, during a performance appraisal interview, an employee drumming his or her fingers on the table and fidgeting in the chair is communicating anxiety without saying a word. Research suggests that in a typical face-to-face communication exchange 7 percent of the total message is conveyed by the words, 38 percent of the total message is conveyed by vocal intonation, and 55 percent of the total message is conveyed by facial and body expressions.[8] For communication to be effective and meaningful, then, all three parts of the message need to be congruent. If any of the three parts are incongruent, conflicting messages are being sent.[9]

Consciously controlling your body language is as important a managerial skill as knowing how to interpret others' body language. Controlling your nonverbal signals and vocal tone ensures that you reinforce your intended message. For example, in the United States (although not in all cultures), shifting your eyes

STEFANOLUNARDI/SHUTTERSTOCK.COM

Nonverbal communication plays an important role in our understanding of a message. This individual, for instance, appears to be surprised or upset about something. He may be telling his colleagues that is is okay, but his nonverbal communication suggests otherwise.

and looking away while speaking tends to make people not trust your message. If you want people to see you as a leader, stand up straight, make eye contact, and smile—those signals project confidence and energy. Walking with slumped shoulders and with your head down, speaking in a flat tone, and fidgeting often communicate that you are indecisive, negative, or inexperienced.[10]

Verbal Intonation

Verbal intonation is the emphasis given to spoken words and phrases. For example, the simple words, "May I speak with you?" can be interpreted very differently if said in a cheery, upbeat tone versus a strong or angry tone.

verbal intonation *The emphasis given to spoken words and phrases*

Consider the statement, "Aiden earned a promotion" in Table 9.1. Emphasizing different words completely changes the meaning of the statement. Remember the saying, "it's not what you say that matters but how you say it," every time you communicate. When body language is inconsistent with the spoken message, receivers are more likely to interpret your body language as the "true meaning."[11]

One-Way and Two-Way Communication

In *one-way communication*, information flows in only one direction. The sender communicates a message without expecting or getting any feedback from the receiver. For example, if a manager tells an employee to help a customer and the employee does so without saying a word or if a manager tells an employee that he is doing a good job and then leaves before hearing a response, one-way communication has occurred.

Once a receiver provides feedback to a sender, the sender and receiver have engaged in *two-way communication*. If a manager tells an employee to join a telephone conference and the employee says, "I'll be right there," this is two-way communication. Feedback enhances the effectiveness of the communication process by helping to ensure that the intended message is the one received. Have you ever sent an important email and then waited and wondered if the receiver received and understood it? If so, you appreciate the value of two-way communication and feedback.

Task Interdependence

When one person or unit is dependent on another person for resources or information to get work done, communication needs increase. There are three

Table 9.1

Changes in Meaning Depending on Emphasis

Aiden earned a promotion.	Aiden, not Jenna, earned the promotion.
Aiden **earned** a promotion.	Aiden earned the promotion; it was not political.
Aiden earned **a** promotion.	Aiden earned one promotion, not two, and it may not have been the only available promotion.
Aiden earned a **promotion**.	Aiden earned a promotion, not necessarily a raise or more vacation days.

Putting emphasis on different words can alter the meaning of a message.

Figure 9.2

Task interdependence leads to an increase in communications requirements. The three major forms of interdependence, as shown here, are pooled, sequential, and reciprocal. The higher the level of interdependence the greater the requirement for effective communication.

Types of Task Interdependence

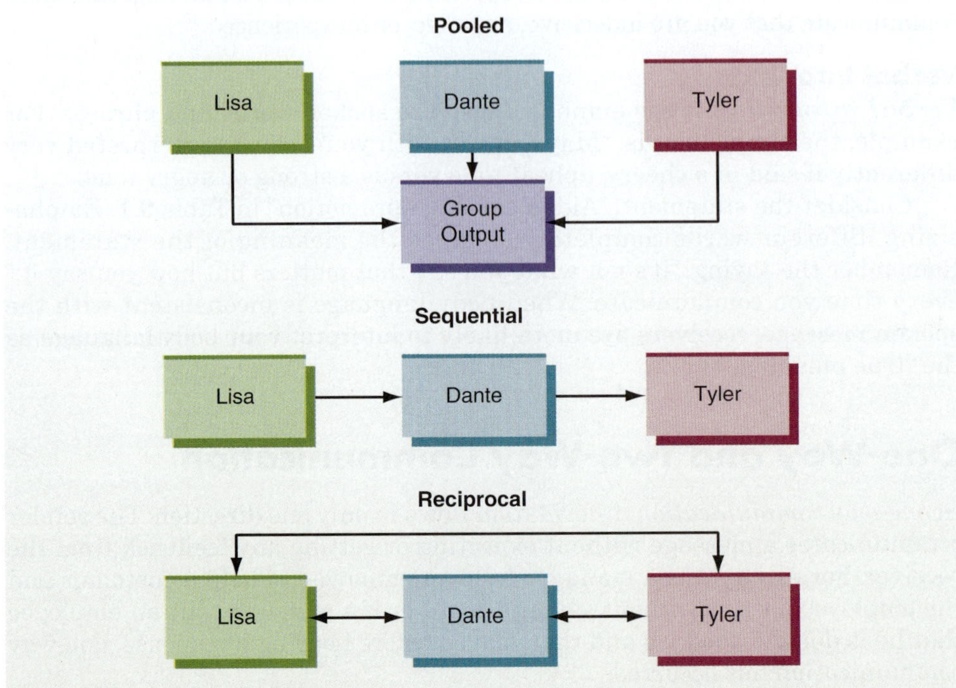

types of interdependence, illustrated in Figure 9.2. *Pooled interdependence* is when employees work independently and their output is combined into group output. An example of pooled interdependence is a call center in which customer service agents act relatively independently in handling calls. Because employees work independently, pooled interdependence has low communication requirements.

Sequential interdependence, like in an assembly line, requires tasks to be performed in a certain order. This increases the need for communication as individuals or groups are dependent on other individuals or groups for the resources they need to complete their own tasks. For example, in Figure 9.2, Lisa, Dante, and Tyler need to communicate in order to coordinate their work.

Reciprocal interdependence requires constant communication and mutual adjustment for task completion, such as a cross-functional research and development team, or an event-planning team, and creates the highest potential for conflict. As shown in Figure 9.2, this is the most interdependent way of doing work and has the highest communication needs.

Barriers to Effective Communication

A number of potential barriers to effective communication exist. Table 9.2 summarizes some of the most common barriers that can interfere with the accurate communication of a message.

Table 9.2

A number of different barriers can inhibit effective communication in organizations.

Communication Barriers

Barrier	Description
Selective perception	We selectively see and hear based on our expectations and beliefs.
Misperception	Messages are not always decoded by the receiver in the way the sender intended.
Filtering	Information is intentionally withheld, ignored, or distorted to influence the message that is ultimately received.
Information overload	It is possible to have so much information that it is impossible to process all of it.
Organizational barriers	A firm's hierarchical structure and culture can influence who is allowed to communicate what to whom, and may limit how messages can be sent.
Cultural barriers	Different national cultures have different ways of expressing things.
Noise	Anything that blocks, distorts, or changes the message the sender intended to communicate can create a barrier.

Selective Perception

People tend not to hear things that they do not want to hear, and to hear things that are consistent with what they already believe. Selective perception occurs when we selectively interpret what we see based on our interests, expectations, experience, and attitudes rather than on how things really are. Sometimes people ignore conflicting information and focus only on the information that confirms what they already believe. Selective perception leads us to receive only the part of a message that is consistent with our expectations, needs, motivations, interests, and other personal characteristics.

For example, managers' functional expertise can influence how they perceive and solve complex problems.[12] Two managers given the same information about a problem may see the problem differently—a manager with a finance background may be more likely to see the problem as finance-based, while a manager with a production background may be more likely to see it as production-based. Each manager selectively perceives information that is consistent with his or her expertise and expectations, and does not pay as much attention to other types of information.

MARCIN BALCERZAK/ SHUTTERSTOCK.COM

Selective perception may occur when people interpret messages differently because of their roles or areas of responsibility. Take these two men, for example. The manager on the left may base his understanding on information he is getting from his digital device. But the warehouse supervisor on the right may base his understanding on his practical background and understanding of how the warehouse operates.

Misperception

misperception
When a message is not decoded by the receiver in the way the sender intended

Misperception occurs when a message is not decoded by the receiver in the way the sender intended. A misperception can occur because the sender's body language is inconsistent with the sender's words, and the receiver incorrectly interprets the body language to be the true message. A misperception can also be due to the receiver selectively perceiving favorable parts of the sender's message, distorting the message's meaning. Poor listening skills can also result in misperception.

Filtering

filtering
Less than the full amount of information is received due to withholding, ignoring, or distorting information

Filtering occurs when people receive less than the full amount of information due to the withholding, ignoring, or distorting of information. Filtering can happen when a sender manipulates information so that the receiver is more likely to perceive it in a favorable way. For example, to try to look good before a performance evaluation a manager might tell his or her boss about the things that are going well in the manager's unit and fail to mention the challenges she or he is facing.

Information Overload

information overload
The amount of information available exceeds a person's ability to process it

Filtering can also occur when a receiver has too much information. When the amount of information available exceeds our ability to process it, we experience ***information overload***. When faced with too much information, we have to use some sort of filtering strategy to reduce it to a manageable amount. For example, an executive who starts the day with 500 emails in her inbox will likely apply some sort of filter, such as the email sender or the urgency conveyed by the sender, to decide which to read and which to delete or save to read later. Filtering is essential to managers because it helps to reduce the amount of noise in the communication process. Effective filtering amplifies relevant and accurate information and minimizes the rest.

Some companies use technology to reduce the filtering of messages as they move around the company. For example, to better manage its internal communications and encourage the free flow of information to better serve its clients, Medco Health Solutions built an internal broadcast facility to broadcast video with sound to all employee desktop computers in the country. The facility posts taped presentations to the company intranet, and hosts real-time interviews and panel discussions with company leaders. Employees can email questions to the people in the studio, who can answer them in real time. This prevents lower-level employees from having to go through the company's hierarchy to get information about company issues. Medco also uses polling tools on its intranet and in the broadcast studio to quickly survey employees on important issues.

The broadcast facility enables Medco managers to go right to the source to get information that has not been filtered as it

GIL C/SHUTTERSTOCK.COM

Information overload is becoming increasingly common today, in part because of the growth of digital communication. This manager's inbox, for instance, shows 110 unread emails plus another 95 emails that went directly to spam.

gets passed around and up the hierarchy. In addition, lower levels of the organization get faster resolution to their issues because the inefficient filtering and "managing up" that used to take place when the company relied on traditional linear communication channels are eliminated. An additional benefit of adopting the technology has been greater mutual visibility between the lower and higher levels of the organization, which helps to ensure that everyone shares the same goals and priorities.[13]

Organizational Barriers

Organizational barriers to communication come from the hierarchical structure and culture of the organization. Numerous hierarchical levels or department specializations can make communication across levels and departments difficult. Different hierarchical levels typically focus on different types of information, which can interfere with communication. Higher-level executives, for example, typically focus on information related to bigger picture issues and business strategy, while lower-level employees focus on customer issues, production, and deadlines.

Some organizational cultures encourage open communication while other cultures promote a limited sharing of information. Company spaces can reinforce an organization's communication culture. For example, when the music company Muzak moved from Seattle to Fort Mill, South Carolina, company leaders wanted to create more open communication paths. To do this, they designed the new workspace to be completely open with no cubicle walls. The open environment makes it easy for people to ask questions and offer ideas. This facilitates communication and allows the CEO to get ideas from people he never would previously have asked for input.[14]

Everything in the offices of animation company Pixar encourages collaboration. When designing the space, Steve Jobs, who founded the company, even included only one set of bathrooms in the entire building to force interaction among the employees. Games, couches, and a variety of gathering areas help employees move around, communicate, and collaborate.[15]

Cultural Barriers

Words and gestures can mean different things in different cultures. For example, in many parts of the world the thumb-up sign means "okay." But in Nigeria, Afghanistan, Iran, and parts of Italy and Greece, it is an obscene insult and carries the same meaning as the middle finger does in the United States.

In some cultures, people tend to say what they mean and to mean what they say, leaving little to subjective interpretation. These ***low-context cultures*** rely on the words themselves to convey meaning.[16] People in ***high-context cultures*** rely on nonverbal or situational cues or things other than words to convey meaning. For example, the Japanese tendency to say "I'll ask my boss" or "that could be difficult" when they mean "the answer is no" reflects their high-context culture. Sometimes it is what is *not* said that has the most meaning—like silence after you ask someone what she thinks of your idea.

low-context cultures *Cultures that rely on words to convey meaning*

high-context culture *Situational and nonverbal cues are used to convey meaning*

Communicating in high-context cultures like Asian or Arab cultures requires more trust and a greater understanding of the culture. In high-context cultures, managers tend to make suggestions rather than give direct instructions. In low-context cultures like Germany, Switzerland, or North American cultures, communication tends to be more direct and explicit.

One informal survey of managers from fifteen countries identified lack of cultural understanding as the biggest challenge in communicating with people around the world. Other challenges (in order) were: "being thorough and very careful with interpretations," "careful audience research," "keeping communication simple," "respecting everyone," "using technology as an asset," and "knowing similarities as well as differences."[17] This chapter's *Global Issues* feature describes additional cultural issues in communication.

Noise

As discussed earlier, noise is anything that blocks, distorts, or changes in any way the information the sender intended to communicate. It can enter anywhere in the communication process and interfere with the successful transmission and reception of a message. We will next discuss some of the most common sources of noise.

Interruptions, the sound of engines or machinery, dim computer screens, small font, or a receiver's headache are all physical barriers that create noise.

BALDYRGAN/SHUTTERSTOCK.COM

CULTURAL DIFFERENCES IN COMMUNICATION

Because they are a part of culture, verbal and written communications vary around the world.[18] The international business communication process is filtered through a range of variables including language, environment, technology, social organization, social history, authority beliefs, and different nonverbal communication.[19] Problems in cross-cultural business communication often arise when participants from one culture are unable to understand the other person's communication practices, traditions, and thinking.

People generally perceive their own behavior as logical, and tend to generalize the values and practices of their culture to apply to everyone. For example, if your culture values promptness, then you probably assume that everyone you meet does too. But in many Hispanic cultures, not being on time is culturally acceptable. Because each culture has its own set of values, some of which are quite different from the values held in other cultures, the concepts of correct and incorrect, and even right and wrong, are often blurred. In international business, questions regularly arise regarding what is proper by each culture's values, what is wise by each culture's view of the world, and what is right by each culture's standards.[20]

Managing cultural differences is particularly important in cross-cultural teams because of the potential of these differences to reduce information sharing, create interpersonal conflict, or both. For example, Western norms for direct communication often clash with Asian norms of indirect communication. In describing the problems facing her team, one American manager leading a joint U.S. and Japanese project said, "In Japan, they want to talk and discuss. Then we take a break and they talk within the organization. They want to make sure that there's harmony in the rest of the organization. One of the hardest lessons for me was when I thought they were saying yes but they just meant 'I'm listening to you.'"[21]

When the manager discovered flaws in the system that would significantly disrupt company operations, she emailed her American boss and the Japanese team members. Her Japanese colleagues were embarrassed because the manager had violated their norms. They probably would have responded better if she had pointed out the problems more indirectly—maybe by asking them what would happen if a certain part of the system was not functioning properly, even though she knew what was wrong. Because the typical Japanese response to direct confrontation is to isolate the norm violator, the American manager was isolated socially and physically. She explains, "They literally put my office in a storage room, where I had desks stacked from floor to ceiling and I was the only person there. So they totally isolated me, which was a pretty loud signal to me that I was not a part of the inside circle and that they would communicate with me only as needed."[22]

Effective managers understand how the perception of a given message changes depending on the viewpoint of those communicating. Because business is not conducted the same from culture to culture, business relations are enhanced when employees are trained to be aware of areas likely to create communication difficulties and conflict across cultures.[23]

Jargon, or technical language, may create ambiguity if the receiver is not trained to understand it. Contracts and other legal documents, tax codes and regulations, and technology instructions may be daunting to many people.

LANE V. ERICKSON/SHUTTERSTOCK.COM

Loss of transmission occurs when an Internet connection goes down, phone lines are full of static, or a videoconference link is dropped. Competition from other communication sources, such as employees checking their smartphones or whispering to each other during a meeting, can also create noise.

Ambiguity is another source of noise in communication. *Ambiguity of meaning* occurs when the receiver is not sure what the sender meant. (Does "we need to do this" mean now or next year?) *Ambiguity of intent* means the receiver is uncertain about the message's consequences. (What am I supposed to be doing to "do this"?) The clearer a message, the less chance ambiguity will cloud its meaning.

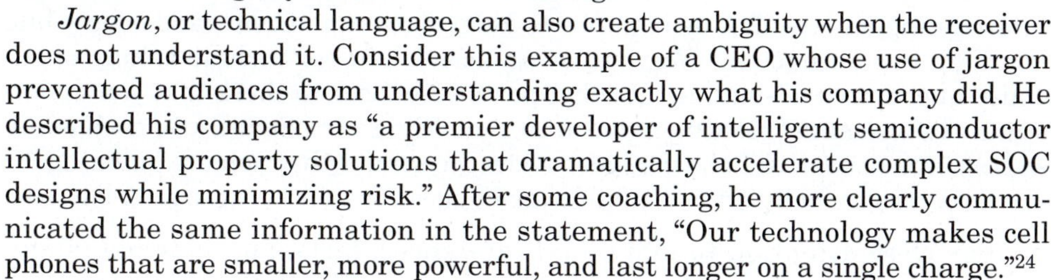

Jargon, or technical language, can also create ambiguity when the receiver does not understand it. Consider this example of a CEO whose use of jargon prevented audiences from understanding exactly what his company did. He described his company as "a premier developer of intelligent semiconductor intellectual property solutions that dramatically accelerate complex SOC designs while minimizing risk." After some coaching, he more clearly communicated the same information in the statement, "Our technology makes cell phones that are smaller, more powerful, and last longer on a single charge."[24]

Semantics are another barrier that introduces noise into communications. Words mean different things to different people. *Soon* might mean immediately to one person and in a few days or weeks to another. Asking for feedback helps the sender ensure that his or her intended meaning is the same as the one ultimately received.

Some companies rely on technology to minimize the effects of these barriers to effective communication. For example, three locations of DreamWorks Animation often need to communicate, but traditional communication media is ineffective for communicating about animation, and adds noise that distorts messages.[25] To help deal with this, the firm created a videoconferencing room that resembles a typical boardroom. Physically present meeting participants sit on one side of the table, opposite their remote colleagues shown on three giant flat-screen monitors. A fourth screen allows participants to share documents, drawings, and animated sequences. The audio system even lets people talk over one another, just as they would in a "real" meeting, rather than waiting for a speaker to finish.

COMMUNICATION SKILLS

Communicating effectively is an important managerial skill, and a skill critical for effective leadership. Many barriers exist to good communications that are beyond your control, but improving your communication skills can help to overcome these barriers.

Listening Skills

active listening
Becoming actively involved in the process of listening to what others are saying and clarifying messages' meaning

Listening is not the same as hearing. Hearing is passive; listening is an active search for meaning. ***Active listening*** plays an important role in communication and is especially important for effective leadership. It requires becoming actively involved in the process of listening to what others are saying and clarifying the meaning of messages if they are unclear. Both parties should engage in active listening until it is clear that each understands the final message.

Being an active listener requires concentration. When someone speaks to you, try to identify any ambiguous words, and any discrepancy between the words and nonverbal cues. Quickly compare the verbal and nonverbal messages to see if the messages are contradictory and to make sure you really understand the message being sent. Then reflect the message back to the sender, repeating the message in your own words. The person with whom you are speaking should either confirm your understanding or, if there is a misunderstanding, restate the message. This allows both parties to continue to work toward mutual understanding until you are both sure you understand each other.

Active listening requires the receiver to tune out noise and concentrate on the message. This is harder than it sounds—it can be as difficult to refrain from interrupting one speaker as it can be to keep your mind from wandering while listening to someone else. Ways to be an active listener include asking open-ended questions and sending the other person feedback to check that you understand the message. Making eye contact, nodding occasionally, and showing appropriate nonverbal behaviors also show the sender that you are listening.[26]

Experts generally offer the following suggestions for being a good listener:

- Pay close attention to individual inferences, facts, and judgments and make useful and logical connections between what you have heard on multiple occasions.
- Give speakers clear nonverbal evidence that you are listening attentively, including leaning toward the speaker, maintaining eye contact, and not fidgeting.
- Give speakers clear verbal evidence that you are listening attentively, including giving constructive feedback, paraphrasing, and questioning for clarification and refinement.
- Show the speaker respect by not interrupting and using an inclusive, friendly, and sharing tone rather than an exclusionary, hostile, and condescending tone.
- Follow up on unusual or inconsistent communication cues from the speaker, such as changes in tone, vocabulary, and body language to determine the real message the speaker is trying to send.
- Use what the speaker says or infers to determine the speaker's motives, self-interest, and expectation(s) of listeners.
- Offer speakers honest, clear, timely, respectful, and relevant acknowledgment of what they have said.

Listening skills play a vital role in effective communication. These individuals all seem to be concentrating and paying close attention as they listen to a business presentation. As a result, they are likely to come away with a good understanding of the presentation.

This chapter's *Understand Yourself* feature will help you to better understand your own listening skills.

Writing Skills

From memos and business letters to emails, managers frequently need to communicate in writing.[27] Effective business writing is not just about grammar and punctuation—the style and tone also have to be appropriate for the audience.[28] Business writing needs to be professional and direct, and often needs to be persuasive. Always proofread your business communications, even if they are fairly short, and ensure that spelling and grammar are correct. Experts suggest these guidelines for effective business writing:[29]

- Write to express, not to impress. Get to the point and use common language rather than jargon or difficult verbiage. For example, Mark Twain vowed never to write metropolis when paid the same for writing *city*.[30] Provide transitions between ideas.
- Back up your assertions. Support your points with statistics, examples, citation of authorities, and anecdotes. Footnote any ideas, phrases, sentences, and terms that are not your own.
- Write for your audience. Ensure that your language, length, and evidence suit your audience.
- Edit and revise. Correct grammar and spelling errors and stay focused.
- Format for readability. Make documents attractive and easy to read.
- Use graphic aids and pictures where appropriate to highlight and express ideas.
- Write with energy and conviction. Avoid passive voice.[31]

Composing effective electronic communications can be challenging. Because email is not an interactive conversation, the rules for phone conversations are not appropriate. Neither are the rules for written correspondence, which is more formal and not instantaneous. Because email falls in between a phone call and a letter, email etiquette can be difficult. Table 9.3 provides some suggestions for effectively using email at work.

Training in using all forms of electronic communication, including email, instant messaging, blogs, and wikis, can help managers and employees reduce misunderstandings and enhance communication efficiency. For example, the New Jersey Hospital Association in Princeton, New Jersey, gives all new hires email etiquette training that covers the basics including how to communicate quickly but with courtesy, what not to put in writing, and the importance of proofreading emails before sending them.

Presentation Skills

Do you ever get nervous when you are about to make a presentation? It is perfectly normal to feel this way before speaking in front of a group, even if you have a lot of experience. Fortunately, being a little nervous tends to improve with practice; taking courses on public speaking is one way to get practice. Managers need effective presentation skills to present proposals to supervisors and to communicate with other managers and groups

UNDERSTAND YOURSELF

LISTENING SELF-ASSESSMENT

Complete this fifteen-item questionnaire twice. The first time through, think about your behavior in recent meetings or social gatherings. Mark "yes" or "no" next to each question—and be honest! The second time through, mark a "+" next to your answer if you are satisfied with your response, or a "–" if you wish you had answered the question differently.

		Yes	No	+ or –
1.	I frequently attempt to listen to several conversations at the same time.			
2.	I like people to give me only the facts and then let me make my own interpretations.			
3.	I sometimes pretend to pay attention to people.			
4.	I consider myself a good judge of nonverbal communications.			
5.	I usually know what another person is going to say before he or she says it.			
6.	I usually end conversations that do not interest me by diverting my attention from the speaker.			
7.	I frequently nod, frown, or whatever to let the speaker know how I feel about what he or she is saying.			
8.	I usually respond immediately when someone has finished talking.			
9.	I evaluate what is being said while it is being said.			
10.	I usually formulate a response while the other person is still talking.			
11.	The speaker's delivery style frequently keeps me from listening to content.			
12.	I usually ask people to clarify what they have said rather than guess at the meaning.			
13.	I make a concerted effort to understand other people's point of view.			
14.	I frequently hear what I expect to hear rather than what is being said.			
15.	Most people feel that I have understood their point of view when we disagree.			

Scoring: To determine your score based on listening theory, score your answers using the upside-down answer key at the bottom of this exercise, add up the number of incorrect answers, multiply that by 7, and subtract that total from 105.

Interpretation: If you often marked "–" after a wrong answer, this suggests that you have some good insights about how you could improve your listening skills.

If you scored between 91 and 105, you have good listening habits! This skill will serve you well as a manager.

If you scored between 77 and 90, you have room for improving your listening skills. Refer to the behaviors in the questionnaire and practice some of these behaviors every day.

If you scored below 76, you are a poor listener and should work hard on improving this skill. Refer to the behaviors in the questionnaire and practice some of these behaviors every day.

Source: Reprinted by permission of the publisher from Supervisory Management © 1989 American Management Association, New York, NY. www.amanet.org

Answers: (1) No (2) No (3) No (4) Yes (5) No (6) No (7) No (8) No (9) No (10) No (11) No (12) Yes (13) Yes (14) No (15) Yes.

Table 9.3

Tips for Effective Email

Using email effectively requires practice. These suggestions are useful ways to improve the quality and professionalism of email.

1. Deliver personal information in person or by telephone.
2. Avoid unprofessional email addresses for business emails—have two email accounts if necessary. This will avoid the embarrassment of having to tell a new boss that your email address is partyon@isp.com.
3. Ensure that you are responding to every part of the email that warrants a response.
4. Respond to emails quickly, preferably by the end of the same day. If you cannot do this, email the person to let them know that you received their email and cannot address their question right now, but you will get back to them soon with an answer.
5. Read your emails once or twice before sending them to check for clarity and readability.
6. Write concise and informative subject lines. For example, "We're meeting Wednesday at 9" sends a message without the recipient even opening the email.
7. Do not criticize others via email. This can make them feel belittled and disrespected, and if others forward your email you could quickly regret ever sending it.
8. Do not use your inbox as a catchall folder. After reading an incoming item, answer immediately, delete it, or move it to a project-specific folder.
9. Agree on company acronyms for subject lines, such as "AR" for action required or "MFR" for monthly financial report. This both saves time and prevents confusion.
10. Send group mail only when useful to all recipients. Use "reply all" and "cc" sparingly.
11. Use the "out of office" feature and voice mail messages to let people know when you may not be able to respond quickly.
12. Before sending an attachment in a particular format, make sure the recipient can open it.
13. Because they are slow to download, avoid sending large attachments and graphics (especially to people who are traveling) unless it is necessary. Post large attachments on a wiki or portal instead.
14. Consolidate your messages in one organized email rather than sending one message per thought.

Sources: Hyatt, M. (2007). Email Etiquette 101, MichaelHyatt.com. Available online: http://michaelhyatt.com/e-mailetiquette-101.html. Stanley, B. (2008). 5 Rules of Email Etiquette, February 10. Smartphonemag.com. http://www.smartphonemag.com/cms/blogs/27/5_rules_of_email_etiquette Andrea C. Poe, "Don't Touch that 'Send' Button! – e-mail messaging skills," HR Magazine, July, 2001, 46 (7) pp. 74–80.

of subordinates at once. Here are some suggestions for making effective presentations:[32]

- Speak up and speak clearly.
- Quickly achieve rapport. In the first few moments, show audience members that you feel comfortable with them.
- Channel nervous energy into an enthusiastic delivery; use gestures to express your ideas.

Presentations are common methods for sharing information in organizations. Skilled presenters like this woman can inform and educate others while also keeping them interested in what she is presented. Other presenters, however, may be much less effective. Fortunately, there are techniques that people can use to improve their presentation skills.

- Move freely and naturally without pacing; look at your audience.
- Minimize notes and use them unobtrusively. Notes work best as "thought triggers."
- Highlight key ideas. Use voice volume, graphic aids, pauses, and "headlining" (telling the audience that a point is particularly important).
- Watch the audience for signs of comprehension or misunderstanding. Tilted heads and furrowed brows can signal a need for clarification and review.
- End with a bang. Your concluding words should be memorable.

Meeting Skills

Because they lead groups and teams, another way that managers often communicate is through meetings. In addition to wasting time and money, poorly led meetings are often a source of frustration. One international survey found that employee well-being was related to whether meeting time was well spent, not to the amount of meeting time or number of meetings attended. Meeting effectiveness may be improved when people come prepared to meetings, an agenda is used, meetings are punctual (start and end on time), purposes are clear, and there is widespread participation.[33]

ILDOGESTO/SHUTTERSTOCK.COM

IMPROVE YOUR INTERVIEW SKILLS

When conducting job interviews, good communication skills help you to best evaluate the job candidates and enable the candidates to do their best job in the interviews. Here are some tips to help you run an effective job interview meeting.

Do:

- Make any necessary accommodations if the candidate has a disability.
- Take the first two minutes to establish rapport and take control of the interview.
- Use open body language and present a straight, relaxed, confident posture; maintain good eye contact so that you look pleasant and engaged.
- Try to make the candidate feel relaxed; give the candidate the opportunity to ask you questions.
- Show sincerity in your vocal tone; speak at a suitable pace.
- Remember that in addition to evaluating the candidates, you also are selling them on the opportunity and trying to increase their interest in the position.
- Express interest in the candidates and their experiences; listen attentively and nod occasionally.
- Ask specific, job-relevant questions.

Avoid:

- Giving a weak or a bone-crushing handshake.
- Sitting across a table unless necessary—the formality can make some candidates nervous.
- Standing too close—respect the candidate's personal space.
- Saying, "Tell me about yourself."
- Multitasking—focus on the candidate.

Sources: Adapted from Burges-Lumsden, A. (2005, April 5). Body language for successful HR, *PersonnelToday.com*. Available online: http://www.personneltoday.com/hr/body-language-for-successful-hr/; New York State Department of Civil Service (2012). How to Conduct a Job Interview, March. http://www.cs.ny.gov/pio/interviewguide/conductinterview.cfm. Office of Disability Employment Policy (2010). Accommodating Persons with Disabilities. United States Department of Labor. http://www.zurichna.com/zna/services/searchresults.htm?k=workers%20compensation%20interviewing

Leading meetings requires skills in organizing, eliciting input from meeting participants, and conflict management. Here are some suggestions for running effective meetings:[34]

- Have a good reason to meet in the first place, or do not meet.
- Have an agenda that clearly states the purpose of the meeting and key steps to satisfying that purpose by the end of the meeting.
- Ensure that participants receive the agenda in advance, know what you expect of them, and know how they should prepare.
- Be fully prepared for the meeting and bring any relevant outside information that might be needed.
- State a time frame at the beginning of the meeting and stick to it.
- Require that participants come prepared to discuss the topics on the agenda.
- Keep participants focused on the agenda items and quickly manage any interpersonal issues so that the meeting stays productive.
- Follow up on any outside assignments made to meeting participants.

This chapter's *Improve Your Skills* feature will help you to use the right body language when conducting the important managerial task of a job interview meeting.

COMMUNICATION MEDIA

Managers can choose from a variety of communication media. Some of the most popular are the internet, collaboration software, intranets, and oral communication. Media richness is an important factor for each form.

The Internet

The Internet has fundamentally changed how many managers communicate.[35] Instead of filtering the information coming into an organization, they are now responsible for aligning information with business goals and acting as facilitators by bringing the right people together to solve business problems as a collaborative community. Individuals using the Internet are able to select only the information they want using information pull.[36] Information pull occurs when someone receives requested information.

This contrasts with the broadcast technique of information push where people receive information without requesting it, just in case they need it. International retailer Target's career site provides information and videos about the company, its brand, and its careers and benefits. By making the site self-directed and providing only small amounts of information in each area, employees are empowered and engaged as they learn about the company's culture, procedures, and policies.[37]

Although technology should never replace all face to face interaction between leaders and subordinates, it can help the communication process by giving leaders more communication choices. For example, email helps managers prioritize incoming communications and stay caught up while away from work. In many organizations, email has evolved from an informal communication channel to become a primary and formal means of business correspondence.[38]

Some companies have misused email in communicating important or sensitive information. For example, RadioShack once announced plans to cut about 400 jobs by notifying affected employees via email rather than in person. This can be seen as dehumanizing by employees.

Voice mail is similar to email but instead of writing, a spoken message is digitized and sent to someone to be retrieved and listened to later. Like emails, voice mails can be saved or sent to others to hear. In most systems today voice mail can also be converted to email.

Instant messaging enables users to see who is logged on and to chat with them in real time rather than emailing and waiting for a response. This allows employees to get in touch with each other immediately to get input or ask questions. At Medco Health Solutions, instant messaging is available companywide and is used constantly to provide high-quality customer service. Most managers are rarely without their wirelessly connected laptops. Because meeting customer needs is Medco's priority, managers are even expected to respond to customer-oriented instant messages during meetings. Although this can create some distractions, managers have become skilled at multitasking and handling the multiple communication channels simultaneously open to them.[39]

Managers can also use various software tools to meet without being face-to-face. Videoconferencing can enable leaders to communicate effectively with employees and customers. By allowing the parties to see as well as hear each other, teleconferencing can be a very effective form of communication.

Telework is work conducted in a location other than a central office or production facility with communications between coworkers and supervisors occurring via electronic communication systems.[40] There are four major types of telework:[41]

1. Home-based telecommuting includes people who work at home for some period on a regular basis, but not necessarily every day.
2. Satellite offices are offices situated to be more convenient for employees and/or customers. These offices are located away from what would normally be the main office location.
3. Neighborhood work centers provide office space for the employees of more than one company in order to save commutes to central locations.
4. Mobile work refers to work completed by traveling employees who use technology to communicate with the office as necessary from places such as client offices, airports, cars, and hotels.

Telecommuting allows organizations to reduce the amount of office space they own or rent, and decreases employees' need to commute to work. IBM saves more than $100 million a year in real estate costs because its telecommuting employees do not need offices.[42] If telecommuting employees sometimes need to work at the company's location, the company can set up a *hoteling* space for them. This gives visiting telecommuting employees who do not have dedicated office space at the company's location a cubicle or office in which to set up their laptop computer, log in, and be immediately connected to the company's intranet. They can then work effectively at the company's location when they need to.

Collaboration software allows team members to easily share information and work together on projects. People can easily interface with their team members in real time using various digital devices.

RAWPIXEL/SHUTTERSTOCK.COM

Collaboration Software

Computer software such as Microsoft's SharePoint allows members of workgroups and teams to share information to improve their communication, efficiency, and performance. Collaborative software, also called groupware, enhances the collaborative abilities of group or team members by providing an electronic meeting site. It essentially integrates work being done on a single project simultaneously by several users at different computers located anywhere in the world.

Collaborative writing systems allow group members to work simultaneously on written documents through a network of interconnected computers. As team members work on different sections of the document, each member has access to the entire document and can modify his or her section to be compatible with the rest of it. A group scheduling system lets group members input their daily schedules into a common scheduling database. This makes it faster and easier to identify the best times for meetings and to schedule them quickly.

Workflow automation systems use technology to facilitate and speed up work processes. These systems send documents, information, or tasks to the right people or places based on the established procedure. For example, imagine a nurse ordering medication for a hospital patient. A workflow automation system sends the prescription request to a doctor, and then forwards the prescription to the pharmacy. If the pharmacy does not have the medicine in stock, the system can notify the nurse that the prescription cannot be filled. If the medicine is dispensed, the system records it in the medicine dispense record and updates the pharmacy's inventory. The system can also immediately update the patient's medical record.

Decision support systems are interactive, computer-based systems that help decision-making teams find solutions to unstructured problems that require judgment, evaluation, and insights.[43] Team members can meet in the same room or in separate locations and interact via their computers. Software tools including electronic questionnaires, brainstorming tools, idea organizers, and voting tools to weight and prioritize recommended solutions help the group make decisions and complete projects. A decision support system can reduce the likelihood that one member will dominate the discussion, and helps groups avoid many of the barriers that face-to-face groups encounter.

Intranets

An intranet is a type of centralized information clearinghouse. At its simplest, an intranet is a website stored on a computer that is connected to other company computers by an internal network. Employees reach the intranet site with standard web-browser software such as Netscape or Microsoft Explorer. An intranet can be connected to the Internet at large so that suppliers and customers can visit using company-issued passwords. In such cases, firewall software can be installed to act as a barrier between the internal systems and unauthorized outsiders.

Because they centralize data in an easy-to-access way, intranets are a good idea when a company's employees need to reach the same company information. Intranets give employees controlled access to the information stored on a company's network, which can reduce the need for paper versions of documents such as manuals and company forms. Intranets are not useful if many employees do not use or have access to computers, or if no one has the expertise to set up and manage the intranet.

Portals are similar to intranets but tend to be more project-focused. Portals strongly resemble Internet sites like Yahoo.com and AOL.com. Users interact with them with a standard computer browser like Internet Explorer or Netscape, but instead of containing links to news and weather, the links lead you to sites on the company's private intranet.

Portals can make project status continually visible to managers through real-time reports and visual cues such as red-yellow-green traffic signals or digital dashboards. Portals allow managers to use their browser to get a high-level summary of project status at any time. Some portals also provide visual comparisons and metrics between projects within a program.[44]

Project managers use portals to manage schedules and any issues that arise. By centralizing a variety of information, portals allow managers to track progress and identify any problems early on. Managers can also use portals to quickly disseminate information (documents, processes, notices, etc.) to all of their team members, wherever they are located, and solicit input and feedback in a controlled manner.[45]

Portals allow team members to easily share news and ideas, enhancing collaboration and project implementation efficiency. Project managers can delegate responsibilities down to individual team members, yet still retain control of the project.[46] Portals are often customizable, allowing employees to subscribe only to the information they need.

Portals can be integrated with other applications. For example, one button on a portal might call up yesterday's production charts, another lets employees check their 401(k) balance, and a third lets employees tell colleagues about how they solved important customer problems. Portals also let everyone in a company share databases, documents, calendars, and contact lists. They make it possible to collaborate easily with coworkers in remote locations and even conduct instant employee opinion polls. By consolidating information and connecting employees with each other, they help companies function as a single unit, rather than as individual entities.[47]

Sperry Marine, a business unit of the global aerospace and defense giant Northrop Grumman, implemented a project management portal to create virtual "war rooms" for collaborating on requests for proposals and resulting projects. The portal also provides a centralized, visible location for coordinated document storage, information, schedule tracking, and status information. One manager says, "Before using the portal, people had to e-mail back and forth or call to stay informed. The wrong version of a document could be passed to somebody and team members might miss information if they missed meetings. Now everyone gets general information from the portal's home pages, reviews an up-to-date notice board, checks documents in and out, accesses process and risk information, and views live schedule and milestone reports."[48] This facilitates communication and ensures that everyone is on the same page.

Until recently, portals were strictly for big businesses due to their prohibitive cost. Their complexity also required a team of computer specialists to set up and administer them. But intranets have become more common as software vendors like IBM, Microsoft and Oracle, Plumtree, and SAP have developed packaged portal solutions to suit almost every size business and meet almost every business need.[49] In addition to portals for their customers to use in interacting with the company and employee portals to facilitate work, companies are using specialized portals to meet specific goals. For example, to help control health care premiums, insurance brokerage Keenan & Associates of Torrance, California, created a web-based portal to encourage employees to eat right and exercise more. The service, KeenanFit, offers customized fitness, nutrition, and self-improvement plans for employees and their families. The portal also allows employees to complete self-assessments to monitor specific health risks.[50]

Webcasts are live or prerecorded video segments that are broadcast over a company's intranet and archived for employees to view later. They can help higher levels of management communicate with more employees and communicate messages more effectively because the executive is able to use voice and even video to express the message through intonation and body language.

Wikis are searchable, archivable websites that allow people to comment on and edit one another's work in real time. The user-edited *Wikipedia* encyclopedia (Wikipedia.org) is one of the most popular online wikis. Wikis are well suited for collaborative writing because they allow users to quickly and easily add and edit content. Wikis are essentially a simplified system of creating webpages combined with a system that records and catalogs all revisions. This allows entries to be changed to a previous state at any time. A wiki system may also include tools designed to provide users with an easy way to monitor the constantly changing state of the wiki. A place to discuss and resolve any issues or disagreements over wiki content is also common. Wikis are easy to use and inexpensive. Because real-time project information is located in one easy-to-access place, project completion times can be greatly reduced. Unlike a portal or intranet, wikis have no inherent structure. Some popular wiki features are an automatically generated list of pages recently changed and an index of all the wiki's pages.[51] Access can be restricted to a limited group of people and even require passwords. Disney, Kodak, and Motorola have all found ways to use wikis.[52]

Information technology and the Internet have made it easier for organizations to communicate with people outside the organization. When Intuit wanted to connect with more tax professionals, it created a free wiki called TaxAlmanac.org, where thousands of professors, authors, and tax attorneys contributed thousands of articles as a tax law resource.[53]

Blogs are individuals' chronicles of personal thoughts and interests. Some blogs function as online diaries. A typical blog combines text, images, and links to other blogs, webpages, and other media related to its topic. In some cases, a CEO will create a blog to communicate more directly with employees and stakeholders.

When the investment bank Dresdner Kleinwort Wasserstein wanted to make it easier for its employees to collaborate, it used blogs and wikis.

Now that its 1,500 employees create, comment, and revise projects in real time, meeting times have been cut in half, and productivity has increased.[54] When online shoe retailer Zappos had to cut staff by 8 percent, CEO Tony Hsieh used his popular blog to reassure employees and outline the steps the company would take to avoid further cutbacks.[55] Hotelier Marriott International's CEO Bill Marriott sometimes uses video clips to supplement his blog, "Marriott on the Move."[56]

Better software and greater network bandwidth have made video presentations much easier and more effective at communicating with employees. Even smaller firms can use free or low-cost online tools, such as setting up a private area in YouTube for corporate videos.[57] Southwest Airlines' blog, Nuts About Southwest, gives new employees the opportunity to communicate with each other and also to receive important information from the company. The links to social and interactive media encourage employees to interact, form their own interest groups, and form relationships that enable them to become more personally invested in the company. The RSS feed allows employees to know instantly when new information is posted to the site. This can help keep communication flowing during emergencies, or when important meetings are posted or changed.[58]

Oral Communication

Despite the speed and convenience of technology-based message channels, many of them promote one-way communication and decrease feedback opportunities. If used improperly, this can increase the chances of miscommunication because the receiver has less opportunity to ask questions or get clarification. It can also decrease the quality of decisions if it is harder for employees to make suggestions or share concerns.

Technology has certainly changed the ways many managers communicate, but there will always be a need for managers to communicate verbally. One expert advises people to use electronic communication only for transmitting and confirming simple information, and to have actual conversations for anything that could possibly be sensitive.[59]

During its restructuring, Avon Products engaged in a large communication effort to facilitate the changes. The CEO, president, and others addressed Avon's top 150 managers to explain the rationale for the restructuring. Company leaders then went region to region to tell the same story to the top 1,000 leaders around the world. Reflecting Avon's values, they wanted employees to hear the good and bad news directly from them and from their own managers rather than through emails or communications bulletins. This honesty, respect, and transparency created a lot of trust among employees, who responded positively to the leaders' appeal for support.[60]

Communicating in person is important to building credibility and trust. One DreamWorks representative says that despite the technology, face-time is still critical, especially early in a project. "When you meet someone, there's that instinctive, involuntary chemical reaction, where you decide what you think and whether you trust them."[61] To be perceived as competent communicators, managers must share and respond to information in a timely manner, actively listen to other points of view, communicate clearly and succinctly, and utilize a variety of communication channels.[62]

Media Richness

Communication media can be classified in terms of their *richness*, or the media's ability to carry nonverbal cues, provide rapid feedback, convey personality traits, and support the use of natural language.[63] The richness of a medium depends on four things:

1. Interactivity, or the availability of feedback. Immediate feedback allows senders to adjust their messages. Richer media provide faster feedback.
2. The ability to transmit multiple cues, such as physical presence, voice inflection, nonverbal cues, and pictures. Richer media allow the communication of multiple cues.
3. Language variety for conveying a broad set of concepts and ideas. For example, ideas about a new advertising campaign cannot be expressed in as many ways in a letter as they can in a face-to-face conversation. Richer media allow for greater language variety.
4. The personal focus of the medium, or the degree to which it allows the expression of emotions and other social cues. Richer media allow for more personal focus.

The more a medium displays these attributes, the richer it is; the less it displays these attributes, the leaner it is. Face-to-face is the richest medium because it has the capacity for immediate feedback, carries multiple cues, and uses natural language.

When communicating, managers must choose the media that best matches the information richness required of the task or communication. The more ambiguous and uncertain a task is, the richer the media should be that supports it. For example, text-based computer messaging is a good fit for generating ideas, but not for negotiating conflicts. Videoconferencing is a good fit for decision-making tasks but is not rich enough for negotiating. Table 9.4 describes how different media compare in terms of their richness.

Sometimes the extra expense of face-to-face communication is worth the cost because of the richness of the communication it enables as well as the respect and sincerity it conveys. After Luxottica Group acquired rival Cole

Table 9.4

Media Richness of Various Managerial Communications

Media	Richness	Feedback Availability	Number of Cues	Language Variety	Personal Focus
Face-to-face	High	High	High	High	High
Videoconferences	High	High	High	High	High
Telephone	Moderate	Moderate	Moderate	Moderate	High
Instant messaging[64]	Moderate	High	Low	Low	Moderate
Email	Moderate	Moderate	Low	Low	Moderate
Personal written correspondence	Low	Low	Low	Low	Low
Formal written correspondence	Low	Low	Low	Low	Low

Media vary in terms of their richness. Managers should try to match media richness with their message in order to improve communication effectiveness.

National, Luxottica human resource officials made constant weeklong trips from their North American headquarters in Mason, Ohio, to the central Cole office in Twinsburg, Ohio. The visits were part of a broad effort to prevent a culture clash from undermining the merger from the start. Robin Wilson, senior director of human resources technology and analytics at Luxottica, and about a dozen HR officials made the journey to make sure that approximately

CASE STUDY Communicating Ethics at Cisco

Technology provider Cisco Systems puts a high value on ethics and corporate social responsibility. Cisco is one of only three companies to appear on the business ethics publication *Corporate Responsibility Officer*'s "100 Best Corporate Citizens" list every year in the list's first ten years. So it was no surprise that company leaders were concerned when an employee survey revealed that ethics and compliance issues training was seen as boring and dry. Cisco realized that it had been cramming ethics and compliance information down employees' throats. Because many of Cisco's employees are tech-savvy engineers who are more comfortable figuring things out for themselves, the old model of in-person PowerPoint-based training clearly was not working.

Accordingly, Cisco decided to revamp the ethics and compliance program for its 65,000 worldwide employees to make the training interesting, engaging, and fun. The company developed "Ethics Idol," a cartoon-based parody of the television reality show *American Idol*, to engage employees in ethical decision making. Featured on Cisco's intranet, employees view four cartoon "contestants," each of whom sings the tale of a different, complicated ethical situation. The three judges then give their decisions as in *American Idol*.

The themes of the song parodies include international trade regulations and chain-of-command issues when reporting malfeasance or harassment. The parodies are purposely vague to make employees really think about the ethical issues. After viewing the judges' decisions, employees vote on which of the three judges gave the most appropriate response to each situation, and instantly see how their vote matches up companywide. Cisco's ethics office then weighs in at the end of each episode to give the correct answer based on the company's official ethics and compliance standards.

Thanks to its ability to easily change the language in which it is broadcast, Ethics Idol is being rolled out to Cisco employees globally. The Ethics Idol program not only got Cisco employees to learn more about ethics and compliance, but it also gave the company momentum when it decided to rewrite its Code of Business Conduct in more simple and clear language. Cisco's new code was introduced shortly after Ethics Idol was rolled out, and within ten weeks, 99.6 percent of Cisco employees certified that they had received and read the new document. A survey of employees found that 94 percent agreed that the new code was easy to read, and 95 percent agreed that it was easy to comprehend.

Ethics Idol has been a hit among the technology-loving employees at Cisco. As one expert says, "You cannot teach people morality, but you can teach them how to deal with the ethical problems they encounter in the hopes they will make a good decision."[65] Ethics Idol has done just that by matching the communication medium to the audience and making learning fun.

Questions:

1. What are the advantages of Ethics Idol as an ethics training communication medium over in-person PowerPoint training?
2. Would you enjoy this type of training program? Why or why not?
3. Can you think of other ways ethics and corporate social responsibility information could be communicated in an engaging way?

Sources: Based on O'Brien, M. (2009, May 16). 'Idol'-izing Ethics. http://www.hreonline.com/HRE/view/story.jhtml?id=209480118; Singer, A. (2008, November /December). Cisco Transmits Ethics to a 'Wired' Workforce, *Ethikos*. http://www.singerpubs.com/ethikos/html/cisco.html.

600 former Cole employees in Twinsburg understood that they mattered and could get their questions answered. Luxottica also set up a call center exclusively to field questions from former Cole employees. "It was all designed to ensure that we demonstrated a culture of inclusiveness," Wilson says.[66]

This chapter's *Case Study* feature describes how Cisco effectively matched the communication media it used with the need for information richness in training its employees on ethics and social responsibility.

ORGANIZATIONAL COMMUNICATION

Organizational communication is the exchange of information among two or more individuals or groups in an organization that creates a common basis of understanding and feeling. Organizational communication can move in a variety of directions, and be formal or informal in nature. Figure 9.3 illustrates downward, upward, horizontal, and diagonal communication paths in organizations.

organizational communication *The exchange of information among two or more individuals or groups in an organization that creates a common basis of understanding and feeling*

Downward Communication

Downward communication occurs when higher-level employees communicate to those at lower levels the organization—for example, from a manager to a subordinate. Downward communication typically consists of messages about how to do a job, performance goals, the firm's policies, and how the company is performing.

Technology now gives many executives real-time feedback on employees' and the company's performance, but getting those executives' decisions communicated to employees often takes longer. Setting up procedures and creating a culture that enables the uninhibited flow of information is the foundation of effective communication.[67] As a senior leader of Tata Consultancy Services

Figure 9.3

Communication Paths in Organizations

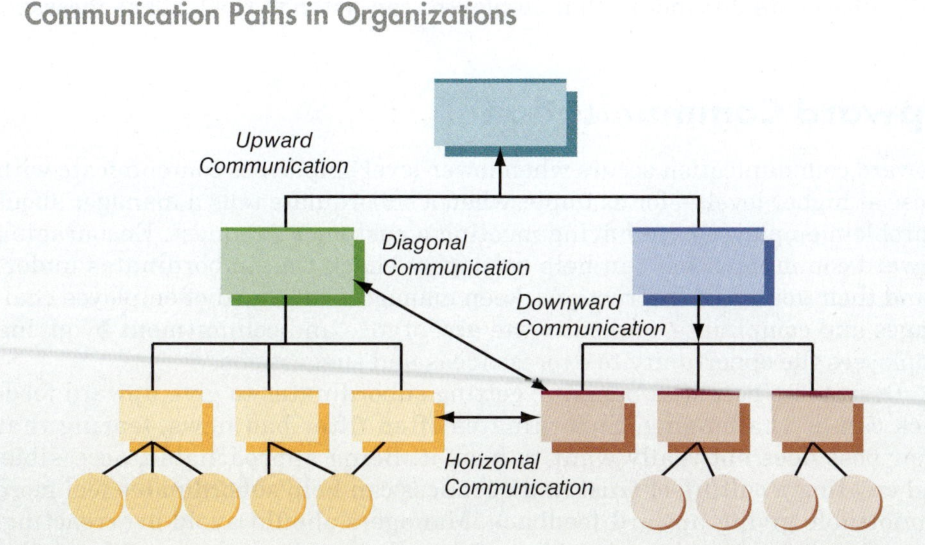

Organizational communication can follow a variety of paths. As illustrated here, these paths can be downward, upward, horizontal, or diagonal.

MICHAL KOWALSKI/SHUTTERSTOCK.COM

Senior managers can learn a lot about what is going on in their company by visiting facilities and talking to employees. This executive, for instance, is visiting one of his firm's distribution centers to better educate himself on what goes on there.

in Mumbai, India, says, "From communicating key organizational policies and initiatives to establishing a direct connection between the CEO, senior management and the employees, technology can help dissolve geographic and hierarchical barriers."[68]

Management by wandering around is a face-to-face management technique in which managers get out of their offices and spend time talking informally to employees throughout the organization.[69] Being actively engaged in the day-to-day operations of the business gives managers a feel for what is really going on in the company. For example, in the first six months after Gary Kusin became CEO of Kinko's, he went into each of Kinko's twenty-four markets in the United States, visited more than 200 stores, and met with more than 2,500 team members to learn what the company needed to do to continue evolving.[70]

Information technology and the Internet have given managers more choices in how to communicate downward, including email, instant messaging, intranets, portals, wikis, blogs, and webcasts in addition to traditional verbal and written communication. Lucent uses a variety of technologies to communicate with employees around the world and gathers employee feedback to identify what is and is not working. Through this feedback Lucent has learned how to use satellite broadcasts, email messages, and Internet publications to share information with employees. A Lucent executive says, "Global communication becomes almost instantaneous when posted to the website. We can send out an internal press release and ensure that employees are getting accurate information as quickly as possible."[71] When big news hits, Lucent quickly posts audio files on its intranet so that employees can listen to the leader's message.

Upward Communication

Upward communication occurs when lower-level employees communicate with those at higher levels—for example, when a subordinate tells a manager about a problem employees are having meeting a customer's request. Encouraging upward communication can help managers check that subordinates understand their goals and instructions, keep managers informed of employee challenges and complaints, and cultivate acceptance and commitment by giving employees the opportunity to express ideas and suggestions.[72]

Despite its potential benefits, getting subordinates to give upward feedback can be challenging. Subordinates often filter bad news, fearing that their boss does not really want to hear it. Being approachable, accessible, and creating a culture of trust and openness can help subordinates feel more comfortable giving upward feedback. Managers should avoid overreacting, becoming defensive, or acting blameful, and should respect confidentiality when a subordinate shares potentially controversial or negative information. Attitude surveys, an open-door policy, and regular face-to-face meetings with subordinates can also foster upward communication. One of the best ways to make subordinates comfortable sharing information may be sympathetically listening to them during your daily informal contacts with them in and outside of the workplace.[73] This can build the trust required for subordinates to share their ideas and honestly communicate negative information.

Technology tools such as wikis can enhance bottom-up communication in organizations. By creating an open-source workspace, all employees can be part of the brainstorming and problem-solving process. For example, when a manager at an investment bank wanted an analysis of how to double profits on a particular trade, he put the problem on a wiki page where other employees could comment, brainstorm, and edit in real time. In two days, the manager had analytics that otherwise would have taken two weeks to acquire.[74]

Horizontal Communication

Horizontal communication occurs when someone in an organization communicates with others at the same organizational level. Managers often depend on each other to help get the job done, and communication is necessary for them to coordinate resources and workflow. Although horizontal communication occurs between peers, as in all organizational communications, it is best to stay professional and avoid confrontational words and negative body language.

Managers can facilitate horizontal or interdepartmental communication by appointing liaison personnel or creating interdepartmental committees or task forces to facilitate communication and coordination and solve common problems. Technology also can help. Kraft Foods gives employees many communication tools to use in communicating with each other. KraftCast is a quarterly podcast featuring an interview with a company executive or newsmaker. On Ask the KET (short for Kraft executive team), employees ask questions about anything from recipe changes to how the financial crisis is affecting Kraft. Online videos, blogs, wikis, and discussion boards can be made available to all employees or to a particular workgroup. An online notice board even lets employees congratulate each other or thank coworkers for their help.[75]

Diagonal Communication

When employees communicate across departments *and* levels, they are engaging in diagonal communication. For example, if Ryan's subordinate Owen contacts Ryan's peer in a different department, diagonal communication has occurred. Diagonal communication is common in cross-functional project teams composed of people from different levels drawn from different departments.

Diagonal communication allows employees in different parts of an organization to contribute to creating a new product or solving a problem. Diagonal communication also helps to link groups and spread information around the firm. Almost all successful managers use these informal communication networks to monitor employee communication and to communicate quickly with employees.[76] A long-standing practice at General Motors is its "diagonal slice meetings" in which top executives seek feedback from white-collar people at all levels of the company.[77]

Diagonal communication can also be inappropriate depending on the situation and the people involved. Subordinates who engage in diagonal communication may alienate their direct supervisor who might feel "out of the loop" and punish the subordinate for disrespecting the chain of command.

Information technology and the Internet can facilitate horizontal and diagonal communication through the company's intranet, portals, and wikis. By creating a central location where employees can post questions and help solve problems other employees are dealing with, communication can occur among employees who would be unable to communicate without the use of technology. For organizations with multiple locations, IT and the Internet can create employee networks that allow employees located around the world to work together and share knowledge.[78]

Formal and Informal Communication

Formal communications are official, organization-sanctioned communications. They can be upward, downward, horizontal, or diagonal. Formal communication channels typically involve some sort of written communication that provides a permanent record of the exchange. Formal communication is usually interpreted accurately.

Informal communication is anything that is not official. Informal communications include gossip and answering another employee's question about how to do something. The grapevine is an example of an informal communication channel. The grapevine can promote the spread of gossip or rumors, which can be destructive and interfere with the functioning of the company, particularly if they are untrue.[79] You should not avoid the grapevine, but be sure to evaluate the credibility of the source before you believe what you hear.[80] If a rumor does not make sense or is inconsistent with other things you know or have heard, seek more information before reacting.

social network
The set of relationships among people connected through friendship, family, work, or other ties

As a manager, being aware of current office gossip can help to keep you informed of what is on employees' minds and prevent rumors from growing out of control. It is best to prevent rumors from starting by establishing clear communication channels, building trust with your employees, and providing employees adequate facts and information. If a rumor does start to spread, *neutralize* it by consistently and honestly communicating with employees about the issue. Not making a comment is usually seen as confirmation of a rumor.[81]

ARENA CREATIVE/
SHUTTERSTOCK.COM

Informal communication plays a powerful role in most organizations. These two co-workers, for example, have gone out to lunch and are now returning to work. They may be discussing their boss, another colleague, or a major business decision. Alternatively, they may be talking about the weather or social activities. The power of informal communication, whether inside or outside the organization, should not be overlooked.

Social Networking

A ***social network*** is the set of relationships among people connected through friendship, family, work, or other ties. People form social networks in organizations that allow for an exchange of information from one employee to another, or even to people outside the company. These informal networks can be helpful—they give employees access to people who can help solve problems and get work done. It is often recommended that new employees try to tap into existing social networks to learn how to successfully do their work.[82]

Our social networks consist of both formal and informal ties. Formal ties refer to relationships with coworkers, bosses, and others we know because of the roles we hold. Employees have formal ties with their bosses and subordinates. Informal ties are relationships based on friendship and choice. If an accounting employee and a production employee create a tie between them because they want to discuss work issues or develop a friendship, and not because they have to, this tie is an informal one.

Some people's social networks have many ties, making them central in an organization's social network. The employee who everyone goes to with a question, or who seems to know everything about everyone else, is central to that company's social network.

The pattern of relationships in a company influences its communication patterns and information flow. If employees tend to be connected to many other employees communication is more open and information flows more freely. If employees tend to be connected to very few other employees, or if employees tend to be connected only to their managers, the network is more closed and information tends to flow only to the central person.

Personal contacts are essential to the success of salespeople and managers alike. Social networking Internet sites take these personal relationships online. Hundreds of companies worldwide, including Saturn and Smart Car, use internal social networks to boost productivity and encourage collaboration. LinkedIn's service, Company Groups, digitally gathers all of a company's employees into a single, private web forum where they can talk, share ideas, and ask company-related questions. More than 1,000 companies have signed up for the service.[83] Facebook also has a service that lets people sharing company email addresses join the same group.

Social networking also has a potential downside. If employees and customers are satisfied, these networks can help build loyalty. If not, employees and customers will communicate and amplify every complaint through these networks. Both employees and managers need to be careful about what they post on Internet social networking sites like Facebook, LinkedIn, and Instagram. This information will be available for others to view for many years, and many hiring managers look at Facebook and other sites to learn more about job candidates.[84] You can use this to your advantage by posting information that reinforces and further explains your qualifications and accomplishments, rather than photos and other information that might frame you in a negative light.[85]

SUMMARY AND APPLICATION

The communication process starts when a sender translates (encodes) information into words, symbols, or pictures and passes it to the receiver through some medium (channel). The sender then receives the message, and retranslates (decodes) it into a message that is hopefully the same as what the sender intended. Noise can enter anywhere in the process, making the message received different from the one the sender intended. Feedback creates two-way communication that helps to check on the success of the communication and ensure that the received message is accurate. Nonverbal communication and task interdependence also affect the communication process, as do potential barriers to effective communication.

Successful managers usually have strong communication skills. There are actually several different forms of communication skills that are important. Effective listening skills are especially important. Writing, speaking, and meeting management skills are also all important to effective communication.

Managers and employees use a variety of communication media. These include the internet, collaboration software, and intranets, as well as various forms of oral communication. Managers need to fit the media to the message, use appropriate body language and nonverbal cues, and ensure that subordinates understand the meaning of the messages sent. It is also a good idea to understand how employees like to be communicated with and seek their feedback about how different communication channels are working.

Organizational communication can move in a variety of directions, and be formal or informal in nature. Communication paths can be downward, upward, horizontal, or diagonal. Social networks help to establish communication patterns in organizations.

REAL WORLD RESPONSE

COMMUNICATING VALUES AT NOKIA

Employees had stopped referring to Nokia's values as energizing. Because of the importance of its values to its strong culture of innovation and teamwork, Nokia wanted to reenergize employees around its core values. Nokia understood that the core of communication is getting your message into the heads of the receivers, and that the best way to do this is to engage them.

To engage employees in identifying and living the company's values, Nokia began by conducting a worldwide series of two-day workshops called Value Cafés. Over six months, 2,500 employees from all organizational levels and around the world discussed what values Nokia should have to achieve its strategic goals and how to best communicate them. Nokia then sent representatives from the Value Cafés to Helsinki to hold a Global Value Café to synthesize the input and identify what Nokia's values should look like. They then presented their ideas to Nokia's Group Executive Board, which loved them. The new values were:

1. *Engaging you:* "You" refers to the whole ecosystem of all key stakeholders—customers, suppliers, partners, communities, employees, and so on, rather than just the customer.
2. *Achieving together:* This value emphasizes the fact that teamwork and collaboration are essential to Nokia's success.

(*Continued*)

3. *Passion for innovation:* Nokia's success depends on innovation, which is encouraged and expected throughout the company.
4. *Very human:* Nokia is focused on creating very human technology with a customer-friendly human interface; this value also reflects its values when dealing with people internally.

One of the Value Café representatives then presented the new values during a gathering of about 250 of Nokia's top managers, and received standing ovations. Nokia next held a 48-hour online jam session to put the new values and strategies on the Internet and to get employees to discuss, chat, and debate them. More than 15,000 employees participated, including all of Nokia's top executives, who showed their interest and answered questions.

To further engage all of its employees, Nokia held a photo contest encouraging employees to use their mobile phones to take pictures about things at Nokia that reflected the company's values. Employees then voted on the best pictures, which were given prizes. A third-party expert who was unaware of the values was given a subset of the pictures to analyze and identify what the pictures reflected. The expert identified the four values from the pictures. The contest was very popular among employees, and Nokia received many outstanding pictures they could later use in company communications to further reinforce the company's values. The photo contest was so well received that Nokia held a similar video contest, which also was energizing and fun for employees.

Nokia understands that the ownership of values lies with its employees. By involving them in defining and capturing the company's values, employees became actively involved and engaged. In the process of taking photos and shooting videos, Nokia employees were implementing Nokia's values. The popularity of the contests ensured that almost all employees developed an idea of what the values mean to them. This made the communication of the new values thorough and personal by engaging employees, rather than simply telling them what the new values would be.

After the values initiative, Nokia saw positive trends on its next employee survey regarding values. Employees' excitement about Nokia's values and their expectations that Nokia live by them went up substantially. Whenever Nokia makes companywide decisions, the leaders always get feedback from employees about how the decisions fit with the company's values. Nokia's employees are again actively talking excitedly about the company's values.

Source: This real world response is based on a telephone interview with Hallstein Moerk, Senior Vice President and Director of Human Resources, Nokia Corporation, June 26, 2009.

DISCUSSION QUESTIONS

1. What are your preferred methods of receiving information? Does your answer differ depending on the type of information being sent?
2. What are the implications of organizational diversity on the communication media the company should use?

3. What are some of the most common sources of noise when others try to talk to you? What can you do to reduce their effects?
4. Think of a time when you have been persuaded by someone to do something. Why was the other person able to change your attitude or behavior?
5. If you had to tell your boss bad news, what communication media would you use?
6. If you were about to be fired, how would you want to hear the news? Why? How would you least want to hear the news? Why?
7. Which do you think is more important for organizations: downward communication or upward communication?
8. Which do you think is more important for organizations: formal or informal communication?
9. What role, if any, do you feel the grapevine plays in organizations?

DEVELOP YOUR SKILLS EXERCISE

Writing Conciseness

Read the following customer complaint. Write a paragraph describing the business representative's goals in responding to the complaint. Then play the role of the company representative and compose a business letter in response. Provide a solution, a reason for not complying with the complainer's request, or whatever you deem appropriate. You should use a clear, concise, business style and format your letter professionally.

Emil Tarique
101 Main Street
Chicago, IL 60610

October 17, 2016

Computer Kingdom
Consumer Complaint Division
2594 Business Drive
Tallahassee, FL 32301

Dear Sir or Madam:
Re: Account #29375403

On April 15, I bought a store-brand laptop computer at your Michigan Avenue store. Unfortunately, the computer has not performed well because of hardware issues. I am disappointed because I need the machine to do my work, and have had to take it in for repairs twice in the short time I have owned it. This has cost me time as well as decreased my productivity. I don't trust the machine, and am constantly worried about losing more data even though it has supposedly been repaired.

To resolve the problem, I would appreciate your exchanging this computer for a new one in good working order. Enclosed is a copy of my purchase receipt as well as the receipts for the two repairs.

I look forward to your reply and a resolution to my problem and will wait until August 30 before seeking help from a consumer protection agency or the Better Business Bureau. Please contact me at the above address or by email at: myfakemail.gmail.com.

Sincerely,

Emil
ENCLOSURE(S)

GROUP EXERCISE

Active Listening*

Form groups of at least four people. Each group then selects one of the following workplace scenarios:

___ 1. An employee asking for a raise
___ 2. A supervisor explaining a new vacation policy to an employee
___ 3. A new employee asking a coworker about the company's culture
___ 4. Two new employees generating potential solutions to a problem

After selecting a scenario, each group has twenty minutes to prepare two three-minute skits. The first skit, performed by team members one and two, should show the interaction without active listening techniques. The second skit, performed by team members three and four, should duplicate the conversation while clearly using active listening techniques.

*We thank Professor Jim Gort at Davenport University for suggesting this exercise.

VIDEO EXERCISE

Intermountain Healthcare

The healthcare industry today is changing rapidly. There actually seem to be two different—and conflicting—sets of pressure affecting healthcare that relate to communication. On the one hand, patient privacy and confidentiality are of great concern. At the same time, though, more comprehensive access to patient information could very well improve the quality of healthcare in many cases.

Intermountain Healthcare is a non-profit healthcare system that provides hospital and other medical services in Utah and Idaho. Intermountain uses clinical data to improve patient outcomes. With 22 hospitals in Utah, one in Idaho, and over 300 clinics, a lot of information needs to be stored, so communication is very important. The importance of communication is highlighted in the way Intermountain works, especially in a field where information can be a matter of life and death.

Watch the video Intermountain Healthcare as a class. Next, using whatever format indicated by your instructor respond t the following questions.

Discussion Questions

1. What characteristics of information are most important in Intermountain Healthcare?
2. How is the horizontal form of communication more prominent in Intermountain Healthcare?
3. In what way is digital communication an important form of communication in Intermountain?

VIDEO CASE

Now What?

PERCOM/SHUTTERSTOCK.COM

Imagine having a tight deadline requiring you to focus on writing a report for the rest of the day in order to get it done on time. A worried looking subordinate enters your office and ineffectively tries to communicate a hurried message. *What do you say or do?* Go to this chapter's "Now What?" video, watch the challenge video, and choose a response. Be sure to also view the outcomes of the two responses you didn't choose.

Discussion Questions

1. What communication barriers are illustrated in these videos?
2. How do these situations illustrate the importance of verbal and nonverbal communication as well as active listening?
3. Which other aspects of communication discussed in this chapter are illustrated in these videos? Explain your answer.

ENDNOTES

[1]This real world response is based on a telephone interview with Hallstein Moerk, Senior Vice President and Director of Human Resources, Nokia Corporation, June 26, 2009.

[2]The Nokia Story, 2012. Available online: http://company.nokia.com/en/about-us]

[3]Wyatt, W. (2010). 2009/2010 Communication ROI Study Report: Capitalizing on Effective Communication. Watson Wyatt. Available online: http://www.towerswatson.com/en-US/Insights/IC-Types/Survey-Research-Results/2009/12/20092010-Communication-ROI-Study-Report-Capitalizing-on-Effective-Communication

[4]Welch, J. (2009, June 28). Keynote address at the 2009 SHRM 61st Annual Conference and Exposition, Seattle, WA.

[5]Byrnes, N. (2009, April 6). A Steely Resolve. *BusinessWeek*, 54.

[6]Welch, M. (2011). The Evolution of the Employee Engagement Concept: Communication Implications, *Corporate Communications: An International Journal*, *16*(4), 328–346; Mayfield, J. R., Mayfield, M. R., & Kopf, J. (1998). The Effects of Leader Motivating Language on Subordinate Performance and Satisfaction. *Human Resource Management*, *37*, 235–249.

[7]Bell, A., & Smith, D. (1999). *Management Communication* (p. 19). New York: John Wiley and Sons.

[8]Mehrabian, A. (1968). Communication Without Words. *Psychology Today*, *2*(9), 52–55.

[9]Mehrabian, A. (1971). *Silent Messages*. Belmont, CA: Wadsworth; see also Mehrabian, A. (1981). *Silent Messages: Implicit Communication of Emotions and Attitudes* (2nd ed.). Belmont, CA: Wadsworth; Mehrabian, A. (1972). *Nonverbal Communication*. Chicago, IL: Aldine-Atherton.

[10]Warfield, A. (2001, April). Do You Speak Body Language? *Training and Development*, 60.

[11]Warfield, A. (2001, April). Do You Speak Body Language? *Training and Development*, 60.

[12]Dearborn, D. C., & Simon, H. A. (1958). Selective Perception: A Note on the Departmental. Identification of Executives. *Sociometry*, *21*, 140–144; Beyer, J. M., Chattopadhyay, P., George, E., Glick, W. H., Ogilvie, D. T., & Pugliese, D. (1997).

The Selective Perception of Managers Revisited. *Academy of Management Journal*, *40*(3), 716–737.

[13]Dessler, G., & Phillips, J. M. (2008). *Managing Now!* New York: Houghton-Mifflin.

[14]Lawrence, P. (2005). Designing Where We Work. *Fast Company*. Available online: http://www.fastcompany.com/918951/designing-where-we-work

[15]Herrington, A. (2011). PIXAR is Inspiration for Modea's New Headquarters, Modea, September 19. Available online: http://www.modea.com/blog/pixar-is-inspiration-for-modeas-new headquarters.

[16]Hall, E. T. (1976). *Beyond Culture*. New York: Doubleday.

[17]Geddie, T. (1998, April–May). Moving Communication Across Cultures. *Communication World*, *16*(5), 37–41.

[18]Martin, J. S., & Chaney, L. H. (2006). *Global Business Etiquette: A Guide to International Communication and Customs*. New York: Praeger.

[19]Cross-Cultural/International Communication. (2009). Small Business Encyclopedia. Available online: http://www.answers.com/topic/cross-cultural-international-communication.

[20]Cross-Cultural/International Communication. (2009). Small Business Encyclopedia. Available online: http://www.answers.com/topic/cross-cultural-international-communication.

[21]Brett, J., Behfar, K., & Kern, M. C. (2006, November). Managing Multicultural Teams. *Harvard Business Review*, 86.

[22]Brett, J., Behfar, K., & Kern, M. C. (2006, November). Managing Multicultural Teams. *Harvard Business Review*, 87.

[23]Brett, J., Behfar, K., & Kern, M. C. (2006, November). Managing Multicultural Teams. *Harvard Business Review*, 84–91.

[24]Gallo, C. (2005, December 1). Lose the Jargon or Lose the Audience. *BusinessWeek Online*. Available online: http://www.businessweek.com/stories/2005-11-30/lose-the-jargon-or-lose-the-audience.

[25]Kirsner, S. (2006, January). DreamWorks Animation Couldn't Find a Videoconferencing System That Made CEO Jeffrey Katzenberg Happy—So It Built Its Own. *Fast Company*, 90.

[26]Petress, K. C. (1999). Listening: A Vital Skill. *Journal of Instructional Psychology*, *26*(4), 261–262.

[27]Dwyer, J. (2011). The Business Communication Handbook (8th ed.), New York: Pearson.

[28]Tyler, K. (2003, March). Toning Up Communications: Business Writing Courses Can Help Employees and Managers Learn to Clearly Express Organizational Messages. *HR Magazine*, 87–89.

[29]Adapted from Bell, A. H., & Smith, D. M. (1999). *Management Communication* (p. 14). New York: John Wiley and Sons.

[30]Twainquotes.com. Available online: http://www.twainquotes.com/Word.html.

[31]Stockard, O. (2011). *The Write Approach: Techniques for Effective Business Writing*. Bingley, UK: Emerald Group.

[32]Adapted from Bell, A. H., & Smith, D. M. (1999). *Management Communication* (p. 14). New York: John Wiley and Sons.

[33]Rogelberg, S. G., Leach, D. L., Warr, P. B., & Burnfield, J. L. (2006). "Not Another Meeting!" Are Meeting Time Demands Related to Employee Well-Being? *Journal of Applied Psychology*, *91*, 86–96.

[34]Walters, J. (2003, January). Was That a Good Meeting, or a Bad One? *Inc*. Available online: http://www.inc.com/articles/2003/01/25007.html.

[35]Bloom, N., Garicano, L., Sadun, R. & Van Reenen, J. (2009, May). *The Distinct Effects of Information Technology and Communication Technology on Firm Organization*. NBER Working Paper No. 14975.

[36]Gonzalez, J. S. (1998). *The 21st-Century INTRANET*. Upper Saddle River, NJ: Prentice-Hall.

[37]Impastato, J. (2009, January). Integrate Web 2.0 into the On-Boarding Experience. *Talent Management*, 18–20.

[38]*USA Today*. (2007, March 2). RadioShack Lays Off Employees Via E-Mail. Available online: http://usatoday30.usatoday.com/tech/news/2006-08-30-radioshack-email-layoffs_x.htm

[39]Dessler, G., & Phillips, J. M. (2008). *Managing Now!* New York: Houghton-Mifflin.

[40]Martin, B. H. & MacDonnell, R. (2012). Is Telework Effective for Organizations? A Meta-Analysis of Empirical Research on Perceptions of Telework and Organizational Outcomes, *Management Research Review*, *35*(7).

[41]Kurland, N. B., & Bailey, D. E. (1999). Telework: The Advantages and Challenges of Working Here, There, Anywhere, and Anytime. *Organizational Dynamics*, *28*(2), 53–67.

[42]Stark, B. (2007, August 27). The Future of the Workplace: No Office, Headquarters in Cyberspace. ABC World News with Dianne Sawyer. Available online: http://abcnews.go.com/WN/story?id=3521725&page=1.

[43]Laudon, K.. & Laudon, J. (2006). Management Information Systems: Managing the Digital Firm (9th ed., p. 436). Upper Saddle River, NJ: Prentice-Hall.

[44]Nielsen Norman Group (2011). Usability of Intranet Portals, Fremont, CA: Nielsen Norman Group.

[45]Nielsen Norman Group (2011). Usability of Intranet Portals, Fremont, CA: Nielsen Norman Group.

[46]Nielsen Norman Group (2011). Usability of Intranet Portals, Fremont, CA: Nielsen Norman Group.

[47]Howard, N. (2009). Information Please! *Inc.com*. Available online: http://www.inc.com/partners/businessinsights/content/-Intranet.html.

[48]Nielsen Norman Group (2011). Usability of Intranet Portals, Fremont, CA: Nielsen Norman Group.

[49]Howard, N. (2009). Information Please! *Inc.com*. Available online: http://www.inc.com/partners/businessinsights/content/Intranet.html. An example of a portal can be found at http://en.wikipedia.org/wiki/Wikipedia:Community_Portal.

[50]Workforce Management. (2006, March 19–25). Get Fit. *Workforce Week: Management*, *7*(12). Available online: www.workforce.com.

[51]Wiki. (2012). Wikipedia. Available online: http://en.wikipedia.org/wiki/Wiki.

[52]Goodnoe, E. (2005, August 8). How to Use Wikis for Business. *InternetWeek*. Available online: http://www.informationweek.com/news/global-cio/showArticle.jhtml?articleID=167600331& pgno=1.

[53]Pacesetters: Collaboration. (2005, November 21). *Business Week*, 92.

[54]Pacesetters: Collaboration. (2005, November 21). *BusinessWeek*, 92.

[55]Robb, D. (2009, February). From the Top. *HR Magazine*, 61–63.

[56]Robb, D. (2009, February). From the Top. *HR Magazine*, 61–63.

[57]Robb, D. (2009, February). From the Top. *HR Magazine*, 61–63.

[58]Impastato, J. (2009, January). Integrate Web 2.0 into the On-Boarding Experience. *Talent Management*, 18–20.

[59]Wellner, A. S. (2005, September). Lost in Translation, *Inc.*, 37.

[60]Phone interview with Lucien Alziari, Senior Vice President of Human Resources at Avon, Jean Phillips, June 8, 2009.

[61]Kirsner, S. (2006, January). DreamWorks Animation Couldn't Find a Videoconferencing System That Made CEO Jeffrey Katzenberg Happy—So It Built Its Own. *Fast Company*, 90.

[62]Madlock, P. E. (2008). The Link Between Leadership Style, Communicator Competence, and Employee Satisfaction. *Journal of Business Communication*, *45*, 61–79.

[63]Daft, R. L., & Lengel, R. H. (1986). Organizational Information Requirements, Media Richness and Structural Design. *Management Science*, *32*(5), 554–571; Daft, R. L., & Lengel, R. H. (1984). Information Richness: A New Approach to Managerial Behavior and Organization Design. In *Research in Organizational Behavior*, eds. B. M. Staw and L. L. Cummings (Vol. 6, pp. 191–233). Greenwich, CT: JAI Press.

[64]Treviño, L, K., Lengel, R. H., Bodensteiner, W., Gerloff, E., & Muir, N. (1990). The Richness Imperative and Cognitive Style: The Role of Individual Differences in Media Choice Behavior. *Management Communication Quarterly*, *4*, 176–197.

[65]Kincaid, C. (2009, April 6). Corporate Ethics Training: The Right Stuff. *Training*, 46, 34–36.

[66]Frauenheim, E. (2007, March 26). Luxottica Group: Optimas Award Winner for Managing Change. *Workforce Management*, 29.

[67]Nazari, J. A., Herremans, I. M., Isaac, R. G., Manassian, A., & Kline, J. B. (2011). Organizational Culture, Climate, and IC: An Interaction Analysis, *Journal of Intellectual Capital*, *12*(2), 224–249.

[68]Robb, D. (2009, February). From the Top. *HR Magazine*, 61.

[69]Peters, T. J., & Waterman, R. H., Jr. (1982). *In Search of Excellence*. New York: Harper & Row; Bell, C. R. (2000). Managing by Wandering Around. *Journal for Quality and Participation*, *23*, 42–44.

[70]Overholt, A. (2002, May). New Leaders, New Agenda. *Fast Company*, 52.

[71]Dessler, G., & Phillips, J. M. (2008). *Managing Now!* (p. 447). New York: Houghton-Mifflin.

[72]Dessler, G. (1993). *Winning Commitment: How to Build and Keep a Competitive Workforce*. New York: McGraw-Hill.

[73]Plenty, E., & Machaner, W. (1977). Stimulating Upward Communication. In *Readings in Organizational Behavior*, eds. J. Gray and F. Starke (pp. 229–240). Columbus, OH: Charles Merrill.

[74]Conlin, M. (2005, November 28). E-Mail Is So Five Minutes Ago. *BusinessWeek*, 111.

[75]Robb, D. (2009, February). From the Top. *HR Magazine*, 61–63.

[76]Wilson, D. O. (1992). Diagonal Communication Links Within Organizations. *Journal of Business Communication*, *29*(2), 129–143.

[77]Welch, D. (2009, October 5). GM: His Way or the Highway. *BusinessWeek*, 62–63.

[78]O'Brien, M. (2009, May 16). "Idol"-izing Ethics. Available online: http://www.hreonline.com/HRE/view/story.jhtml?id=209480118

[79]Michelson, G., & Mouly, S. (2000). Rumour and Gossip in Organizations: A Conceptual Study. *Management Decision*, *38*(5), 339–346.

[80]Burke, L., & Wise, J. (2003). The Effective Care, Handling, and Pruning of the Office Grapevine. *Business Horizons*, *46*(3), 71–76.

[81]Difonzo, N., Bordia, P., & Rosnow, R. (1994). Reigning in Rumors. *Organizational Dynamics*, *23*(1), 47–62.

[82]Abrams, L. C., Cross, R., Lesser, E., & Levin, D. Z. (2003, November 17). Nurturing Interpersonal Trust in Knowledge-Sharing Networks. *Academy of Management Executive*, *17*(4), 64–77.

[83]Swartz, J. (2008, October 8). Social Networking Sites Help Companies Boost Productivity. Available online: http://usatoday30.usatoday.com/tech/products/2008-10-07-social-network-work_N.htm

[84]Roberts, C. (2009, July 14). Hey Kids, Facebook Is Forever. *NYDailyNews.com*. Available online: http://www.nydailynews.com/news/money/hey-kids-facebook-article-1.404500

[85]Schepp, D. (2012). 1 in 3 Employers Reject Applicants Based on Facebook Posts, AOL Jobs, April 19. Available online: http://jobs.aol.com/articles/2012/04/18/one-in-three-employers-reject applicants-based-on-facebook-posts/.

LOSKUTNIKOV/SHUTTERSTOCK.COM

CHAPTER 10

MANAGING CONFLICT AND NEGOTIATING

CHAPTER OUTLINE

LEARNING OUTCOMES

After studying this chapter, you should be able to:

1 Describe the nature of conflict, discuss the conflict escalation process, and describe how conflict can be de-escalated.

2 Identify and discuss the five interpersonal conflict management strategies.

3 Describe some of the best and worst conflict resolution behaviors and discuss how to create constructive conflict.

4 Describe the difference between distributive and integrative negotiation and identify the three types of alternative dispute resolution.

LOSKUTNIKOV/SHUTTERSTOCK.COM

—REAL WORLD CHALLENGE—

RESOLVING DISPUTES AT MARKS & SPENCER[1]

Global clothing, home products, and food retailer Marks & Spencer employs about 82,000 people around the world and has over 700 stores in the United Kingdom alone. Marks & Spencer understands that workplace conflicts and disputes are inevitable, and wants to handle them responsibly and ethically. The company also knows that the managerial time spent on disputes as well as damaged coworker relationships can distract employees from focusing on their jobs and performing their best.

Marks & Spencer wants to give its employees the opportunity to find fair, mutually agreed upon, constructive solutions in a safe environment and enable them to move forward after a conflict positively and confidently. Imagine that the company's management team approaches you for suggestions. What advice would you give them? After reading this chapter you should have some good ideas.

SIMON DAWSON/BLOOMBERG/GETTY IMAGES

Conflict is an inevitable result of interdependencies among people, workgroups, and organizations.[2] Given that all organizations are interdependent systems, organizations without conflict do not exist.[3] Indeed, mid-level managers spend approximately 25 percent of their time managing conflict.[4] Your ability to effectively manage conflict will influence both your individual success and organizational performance.

Although many people feel that conflict is inherently destructive, in fact some conflict is beneficial and desirable. Conflict can certainly have negative consequences in the short run, such as when a manager and staff have a conflict over customer needs or when two employees disagree about how to do something. Conflict can undermine decision quality when either or both parties withdraw and refuse to cooperate.[5] It can also lead to the departure of valued employees, as happened in the fashion company Gianni Versace when CEO Giancarlo Di Risio resigned after a conflict with Donatella Versace over creative control.[6]

In the long run, however, conflict can also lead to positive outcomes including better decisions, more motivated employees, and happier customers. When it is well managed, conflict can improve problem solving and innovation, increase employee involvement and commitment, and clarify work processes and goals. How conflict is managed is the biggest determinant of whether a conflict has positive or negative outcomes. For example, compared with a no-conflict situation, conflict can improve decision quality when it is managed through cooperative problem solving. Constructive change is typically the result of well-managed conflict.

Negotiation is an important skill in managing and resolving conflicts, as well as many other management activities, and is a part of all managers' jobs. After reading this chapter, you should have a good understanding of what conflict is, its role in organizations, and how to manage it. You will also understand how to be a more effective negotiator.

THE NATURE OF CONFLICT

conflict
A disagreement through which two or more parties perceive a threat to their interests, needs, or concerns

Conflict is a disagreement that arises when two or more parties perceive a threat to their interests, needs, or concerns. Conflict can be both constructive and destructive.[7] One major conflict resolution expert argues that whether conflict is positive or negative is determined by the parties' response to the conflict rather than by the conflict itself.[8] Focusing on the conflict management process, not just the outcomes desired by the parties, is thus a key to realizing the potential benefits of a conflict. Mismanaged conflict helps to explain why so few family businesses make it to the third generation. A survey of 1,002 family-business owners revealed that the potential for conflict increases significantly as family businesses age.[9]

dysfunctional conflict
Destructive conflict focused on emotions and differences between the two parties

Behaviors that escalate a conflict until the conflict seems to take on a life of its own generate ***dysfunctional conflict***. Dysfunctional conflicts focus on emotions and differences between the two parties and can degenerate to the extent that the parties forget the substantive issues and focus on getting even, retaliating, or even hurting the other party.

Not only can dysfunctional conflict negatively influence employee, workgroup, and company performance, but it also can lead to employee depression, absenteeism, turnover, burnout, and negative emotional states.[10] It is

Conflict is a disagreement that arises when two or more parties perceive a threat to their interests, needs, or concerns. These two colleagues are engaged in a heated argument and, therefore, are experiencing conflict. This conflict, in turn, may be dysfunctional or constructive.

characterized by feelings of contempt and at least one of the parties withdrawing from communicating.[11] No one is satisfied with the outcome of dysfunctional conflict, potential gains from the conflict are not realized, and the negative feelings at the end of one conflict are carried over to the next conflict, creating a negative spiral. As a result, dysfunctional conflict often becomes separated from the initial issue and continues even after the original conflict becomes irrelevant or is forgotten.

At the same time, though, conflict can also be positive. For example, have you ever ended a disagreement feeling better about something? When it is effectively managed, conflict can be healthy. Interpersonal conflict can lead to greater learning, flexibility, and creativity.[12] Behaviors that are adaptive and responsive to the situation, person, and issues create ***constructive conflict***. Constructive conflicts, also called *functional conflicts*, balance the interests of both parties to maximize mutual gains and the attainment of mutual goals. Constructive conflicts contain elements of creativity, adaptation, and a desire to discover a mutually acceptable outcome. Constructive conflict can lead to the identification of new alternatives and ideas.[13] Constructive conflict is a natural, inevitable, and creative force, and can be beneficial to employees and their organizations.[14]

constructive conflict
Adaptive, positive conflict (also called functional conflict)

Common Causes of Conflict

What creates conflict? The short answer is that conflict can be caused by anything that leads to a disagreement. We next discuss nine of the most common sources of conflict in organizations. These are also summarized in Table 10.1.

Differing Task Goals

Task conflict is a disagreement about the task or goals. A moderate amount of task conflict is beneficial in the early stages of a project because it increases innovation and generates more alternatives from which to choose. However, task conflict is more likely to be detrimental over time when tasks are complex.[15] Task conflict can be very productive if handled correctly. For example, marketing employees want to provide product variety to maximize sales whereas production employees focus on efficiencies and cost and prefer long, economical production runs of a limited number of products. Resolving this task conflict balances the organization's need for cost efficiencies with its goal of maximizing sales. Task conflict also occurs when employees disagree about which packaging design is best or whether quality or quantity is more important.

task conflict
A disagreement about the task or goals

Compensation systems often create differing task goals within an organization. For example, if marketing employees are compensated based on the

Table 10.1

There are many different sources of conflict in organizations.

Sources of Conflict

Differing task goals	disagreements over what is to be accomplished
Differing process goals	disagreements over how to accomplish tasks or goals
Interpersonal differences	differences in motivation, aspirations, or personality
Resource constraints	incompatible needs or competition over perceived or actual resource constraints
Change	the uncertainty of change often creates conflict and changes the relative importance of different organizational groups
Differing values	perceived or actual incompatibilities in beliefs about what is good or bad, right or wrong, or fair or unfair
Poor communication	when people lack necessary information, are misinformed, interpret information differently, or disagree about which data is relevant
Task interdependence	when one person or unit is dependent on another for resources or information, the potential for conflict increases
Organizational structure	conflict (either horizontal or vertical) can result from structural or process features of the organization

number of units the company sells but production employees are compensated based on the average cost per unit, conflict between them is understandable. Holding marketing and production employees jointly accountable for both sales and cost gives them common goals and reduces their conflict. Focusing employees, workgroups, and departments on a common enemy such as a competitor or even a challenging economy can also unite employees in their pursuit of a common goal and reduce the negative effects of conflict.

process conflict
Conflict about how to accomplish a task, who is responsible for what, and how things should be delegated

Differing Process Goals

Have you ever wanted to do a task one way but someone else preferred a different strategy? Even when we agree about what we are trying to accomplish, we can still disagree about how we should accomplish it. ***Process conflict*** reflects conflict about how to accomplish a task, who is responsible for what, or how things should be delegated.[16] Role ambiguity increases process conflict. If a manager does not clearly assign work tasks to employees, employees may experience process conflict as they jockey with each other to do the most desirable assignments and avoid the least desirable tasks.

NILOO/SHUTTERSTOCK.COM

Task conflict is a disagreement about the task or goals to be accomplished. Take this display of orange juice, for example. The marketing department prefers a wide variety of formulas, sizes, and packaging in order to give customers more choice. Production, on the other hand, may prefer fewer formulas, sizes, and packaging in order to hold down production costs.

Interpersonal Differences

Have you ever had trouble working with someone because you just did not like the person? Conflicts can arise from interpersonal differences in motivation, aspirations, or personality. Interpersonal differences are a common trigger of ***relationship conflict***, which is the result of incompatibility or differences between individuals or groups. Relationship conflict can also be triggered by personality, particularly the personality traits of dogmatism and power motivation. Relationship problems often fuel disputes and lead to an unnecessary escalating spiral of dysfunctional conflict.

relationship conflict
Conflict due to incompatibility or differences between individuals or groups

Relationship conflict is rarely a good thing. In fact, it is consistently recognized as a primary source of stress for employees of all ages, cultures, and occupations. Twenty-five percent of employees from a wide range of occupations identified interpersonal issues as the most vexing stressor at work.[17] In another study, negative social interactions at work accounted for 75 percent of all work situations that employees described as detrimental.[18]

Relationship conflict is fueled primarily by emotions (usually anger and frustration) and by perceptions about the other party's personality, character, or motives. Some conflicts occur because people ignore their own or others' feelings and emotions. Other conflicts occur when feelings and emotions differ over a particular issue. Because relationship conflict is personalized, it tends to become more extreme. In one privately held $12 million company, the relationship between the CEO and COO deteriorated to the point that they avoided each other in the hallway, seldom talked, and communicated primarily through other people.[19]

Because relationship conflict is not about concrete issues, neither party is really interested in solving the problem and may even try to create new problems. If relationship conflict cannot be converted to task conflict, it almost always gets worse because each person acts as if the other is untrustworthy, looks for and finds more problems, and gets angrier. Sometimes moving one or more team members to another team to separate the employees experiencing relationship conflict is necessary.

Effective project teams tend to have low but increasing levels of process conflict, moderate levels of task conflict in the middle of the project, and low levels of relationship conflict that increase toward the end of the project.[20] Creating a culture of respect and supporting the safe and balanced expression of perspectives and emotions can help to suppress relationship conflict. Intel trains all new employees in how to constructively manage conflict. Employees learn how to deal with others in a positive manner, use facts rather than opinion when persuading others, and focus on the problem rather than the people involved.[21]

Resource Constraints

The availability and allocation of scarce resources is a major source of conflict in organizations. Incompatible needs and competition over perceived or actual resource constraints can create conflicts of interest.[22] ***Conflicts of interest*** occur when someone believes that to satisfy his or her own needs, the needs and interests of someone else must be sacrificed. This is particularly problematic when dividing resources (like money or time) is a zero-sum game in which one party's gain is the other party's loss. Conflicts of interest can occur over:

conflicts of interest
Conflict due to incompatible needs or competition over perceived or actual resource constraints

- *Substantive issues* including time, money, and physical resources
- *Procedural issues* involving the way the conflict will be handled
- *Psychological issues* including perceptions of fairness, trust, or interest in participating

Conflicts of interest are best resolved by jointly addressing both parties' interests. If a scarce resource can be expanded, for example, say through a bigger budget or by adding more office space, a conflict can be resolved to both parties' satisfaction. Resolving conflicts of interest often increases creativity and innovation and stimulates performance.[23]

Change

Change also causes conflict. Indeed, it has been said that change is not possible without conflict.[24] One of the primary drivers of conflict is uncertainty. Organizational changes, including reorganization, downsizing, and changing business strategies, increase uncertainty and opportunities for resource conflicts. External changes can also trigger conflict if regulations or changing market conditions change the relative importance of different organizational groups. For example, if a strong new competitor enters a company's market, the firm's marketing and advertising departments may get resources previously available to the research and development or human resources departments. A big lawsuit filed against the company is likely to elevate the relative status and resources given to the legal department.

Apple Computer's shift in focus from the Apple II computer to the Macintosh PC illustrates the conflict that can accompany change. When Apple's cofounder Steve Jobs presented the new computer in the company's auditorium, Mac Division employees watched from front-row seats. Meanwhile, Apple II employees watched Jobs's presentation on closed-circuit TV in another room. This differential treatment clearly communicated Jobs's view that the Mac was the future of the company and the Apple II was much less important. Considerable internal conflict followed as the differential treatment prompted Apple cofounder and Apple II inventor Steve Wozniak to resign and the morale of the Apple II employees to plummet.[25]

Differing Values

values conflict

Conflict arising from perceived or actual incompatibilities in belief systems

People differ in their values and worldviews. These differences are the source of ***values conflict***, or conflict arising from perceived or actual incompatibilities in beliefs about what is good or bad, right or wrong, and fair or unfair. Values conflicts can arise when people or groups have different values or a different understanding of the world. For example, if some employees feel that the organization should be focused on maximizing the firm's profits while other employees feel that the firm should be focused on doing the maximum good for the maximum number of people, the two groups of employees are experiencing values conflict.

What violates someone's values differs across national cultures. Different events can trigger conflict in various cultural contexts due to different core concerns. For example, rights violations trigger greater anger in the United States, whereas violations over duties and face cause greater anger among Koreans.[26] In the United States, Americans perceive conflicts to be more about winning and violations to individual rights, whereas Japanese view the same conflicts to be about compromise and violations to duties and obligations.[27]

NORGAL/SHUTTERSTOCK.COM

When Apple cofounder Steve Jobs told the firm's employees about the firm's new directions in computer development those employees working on the Apple II (shown here) watched remotely while those working on the new Mac had front-row seats. This disparate treatment led to conflict and was instrumental in causing Apple's other cofounder, Steve Wozniak, to resign.

Poor Communication

Remember, uncertainty is one of the primary drivers of conflict. Poor communication increases uncertainty, and can thus increase the potential for conflict. ***Information conflict*** occurs when people lack important information, are misinformed, interpret information differently, or disagree about which information is relevant.

information conflict
Conflict that occurs when people lack necessary information, are misinformed, interpret information differently, or disagree about which information is relevant

If a manager tells only some subordinates (but not others) about strategy changes or upcoming scheduling changes, this increases the opportunity for conflict between the employees who have this important information and those who lack the information. Because email restricts the richness of communication and increases the chances for misunderstanding, conflicts are more likely to escalate when people communicate via email compared to face-to-face or over the telephone.[28]

Task Interdependence

When one person or unit is dependent on another for resources or information, the potential for conflict increases. Imagine writing a class paper with a partner. If you divide the assignment in half and each of you completes your section independently, there is less potential for conflict than if your ability to do a good job writing your section of a paper depends on the quality of the other student's section.

Organizational Structure

Structural conflict is the result of structural or process features of the organization. Structural conflict can be horizontal or vertical. Horizontal conflict occurs between groups at the same organizational level, such as between line and staff employees or between departments such as production and marketing. A classic example is the marketing-production conflict between marketing's long-term view of sales and production's short-term goal of cost efficiency. Because the realities of employees in each department are aligned with their identification with these dimensions, conflict is a perfectly justified response to "those people in that other department."[29]

structural conflict
Conflict resulting from structural or process features of the organization

Vertical conflict occurs across different hierarchical levels in the organization, including conflicts over wage issues or control. Union–management relationships are a classic example of vertical conflict.

Because structural conflict is due to organizational design, adjusting the design often reduces or eliminates the structural conflict. Matching a department's structural design with its needs given its environment improves its effectiveness. Structural interventions should focus on creating a moderate amount of constructive task conflict and minimal relationship conflict by addressing the sources of these conflicts for that particular unit.

Conflict Escalation

Unfortunately, as noted already, conflict has a tendency to escalate. Conflict escalation happens when one party involved in a conflict (an individual, small group, department, or entire organizations) first uses an aggressive tactic or begins using more aggressive tactics than the other party.[30] When constructive approaches to conflict resolution are unsuccessful and break down, the conflict escalates. The farther the conflict escalates, the more difficult it is to reverse and the more likely it is to become dysfunctional. Friedrich Glasl's nine-stage model of conflict escalation is summarized in Table 10.2.[31]

Table 10.2

Glasl's Nine-Stage Model of Conflict Escalation

Friedrich Glasl developed a nine-stage model that illustrates how conflict escalates.

Stage	Main Conflict Issues	Behaviors	Trigger to Move to the Next Level
1. Hardening	Objective issues	Discussion	Argumentation tactics
2. Debate	Objective issues Superiority/inferiority	Verbal confrontation Argumentation Emotional pressure Debates	Action without consultation
3. Action over Words	Objective issues Self-image Proving one's mastery	One side gets frustrated and takes action without consulting the opponent Blocking opponent's goals and forcing opponent to yield Decreased verbal and increased nonverbal communication	Covert attacks aimed directly at opponent's identity
4. Images and Coalitions	Shift from focus on issues to personalization of the conflict "Win or lose" mentality Save own reputation	Coalition formation Attacks on opponent's core identity Exploitation of gaps in norms	Loss of face
5. Loss of Face	Fundamental values Restore own dignity Expose opponent Distrust of opponent	Attacking opponent's public face Restoring own prestige	Strategic threats Ultimatums
6. Threat as a Strategy	Control opponent	Extending conflict Presenting threats and ultimatums that restrict future alternatives	Execute ultimatums or threats
7. Limited Attempts to Overthrow	Hurt opponent more than self Survival	Limited attempts to overthrow opponent Opponent not seen as a person	Effort to shatter opponent by attacking core
8. Fragmentation of the Enemy	Winning is no longer possible Survival, outlasting opponent Malice	Acts intended to shatter opponent Annihilate opponent by destroying power base No real communication	Abandon self-preservation Total war
9. Together into the Abyss	Annihilation at any cost, including personal destruction	Unlimited war with limitless violence Accept own destruction if opponent is also destroyed	

Sources: Glasl, F. (1982) The Process of Conflict Escalation and Roles of Third Parties (1982). In *Conflict management and industrial relations*, eds. G. B. J. Bomers & R. B. Peterson (pp. 119–140) The Hague: Kluwer Nijhoff Publishing; Glasl, F. (1992). Konfliktmanagement. *Ein Handbuch für Führungskräfte und Berater* (2nd ed.). Stuttgart: Bern; Glasl, F. & Kopp, P. (1999). *Confronting Conflict: A First-Aid Kit for Handling Conflict.* Binghamton, NY: Hawthorn Press.

In the first stage of conflict escalation, *hardening*, each side's opinion hardens and the two opponents adopt a collision course. The disagreement is recognized but each side believes that the issue can be resolved through discussion. In the second stage, *debate*, each side's opinion becomes polarized and emotions rise. Each side begins thinking in terms of black and white and adopts a viewpoint of self-superiority and opponent-inferiority. Constructive conflicts are generally resolved by the second stage. The third stage, *action over words*, sees a decrease in empathy for the opponent, and the idea that "talking no longer helps" emerges. The conflict becomes increasingly destructive in this stage. In the fourth stage, *images/coalitions*, negative rumors are spread and stereotypes are formed as each side prepares for a fight and conducts a search for supporters. The fifth stage, *loss of face*, marks the beginning of open and direct aggression intended to cause the opponent's loss of public face. In the sixth stage, *threat as a strategy*, threats and counter-threats increase. As ultimatums are made, conflict escalation accelerates. In the seventh stage, *limited attempts to overthrow*, the opponent is no longer viewed as a person. Slight personal damage is considered acceptable as a consequence of limited attempts to overthrow the opponent. In the eighth stage, *fragmentation of the enemy*, the goal becomes the destruction and dissolution of the system. This goal is pursued aggressively. The ninth and final stage, *together into the abyss*, sees the descent into total confrontation with no way back. Extermination of the opponent at the price of self-extermination is seen and accepted.[32]

The later stages of this conflict escalation model might sound extreme, but unfortunately workplace aggression and violence do happen. Table 10.3 summarizes some of the factors associated with an increased risk of workplace violence resulting from conflict. It is obviously a good idea to be especially vigilant for potential conflicts in these situations, and to manage them quickly when they do occur. Generating feelings of empathy and sympathy and keeping both parties focused on common goals also helps to de-escalate conflict. Fairness and the appearance of fairness often decrease the risk of workplace violence when conflicts do occur.[33]

De-Escalating Conflict

Even if it does not escalate quickly, unresolved conflict drains employees' energy and reduces their performance. It is obviously easier to manage conflict escalation in the early stages of a conflict. Unfortunately, conflicts are often hard to detect in their early stages. Because the conflict is still minimal, the parties also have little motivation to invest their time and energy in preventing further escalation.

Table 10.3

Several factors serve to increase the risk of coworker violence in organizations.

Coworker Violence Risk Factors

- Supervising others
- Working in a high-stress environment
- Personality conflicts
- Understaffed workplaces
- Economic downturns

OPOLJA/SHUTTERSTOCK.COM

Conflict can often be de-escalated by open communication and discussion. These two colleagues, for example, have resolved a dispute and are shaking hands to symbolize that they are now in agreement.

If you are involved in a conflict, one of the best ways to prevent further escalation is to react equivalently to the other party and not overreact. Sometimes underreacting can trigger de-escalation of the conflict. By being aware of the dynamic and setting personal behavior limits at the beginning of the conflict, you can often avoid being caught up in the conflict escalation process.

As a manager, you can reduce conflict escalation by modeling de-escalation processes, and by setting and enforcing limits on conflict escalation (prohibiting threats or violence, for example). Managers can serve as a conflict resolution facilitator as well. Referring to Glasl's nine-stage model of conflict escalation discussed above can help you to assess how far a conflict has progressed and how best to respond. It is also important to continue to monitor conflicts to ensure that they do not reemerge. After Ina Drew, chief investment officer at JPMorgan Chase, contracted Lyme disease and had to miss periods of work, her absences allowed tensions and relationship conflicts among her subordinates to flare up again. These issues are credited in part with JPMorgan Chase's trading loss of over $3 billion in 2012.[34] Table 10.4 summarizes what to do and some things to avoid in de–escalating conflict.

After a conflict is resolved, it is important to reestablish a sense of justice and trust among the parties. Strengthening shared goals and shared identities can help to reduce the potential for future conflict. It is also important to remember that you do not always have to intervene in a conflict, particularly if it is not affecting job performance. Letting employees learn to work out

Table 10.4

Certain actions can be used to de-escalate conflict. There are other actions that should be avoided.

De-Escalating Conflict

Do	Avoid
Be an empathetic listener	Communicating hostility verbally or through body language
Focus your attention on the other person	Rejecting all requests from the start
Use delay tactics to create time to diffuse emotions	Challenging, threatening, or daring
Control your body language—relax, uncross legs and arms, and make eye contact	Raising your voice
Remind both parties that a win-win solution can be found	Blaming either party or saying anything that would cause the parties to lose face
Stay focused on issues, not emotions	Minimizing the situation or the conflict

Emotions can play a big role in conflict. For instance, some emotions can increase our tendencies to be combative and argumentative. Similarly, once conflict arises there can also be lingering emotions that may make it hard to resolve the conflict.

ALLIANCE/SHUTTERSTOCK.COM

their differences and resolve conflicts on their own through training and experience will decrease their dependence on you to resolve their conflicts.

Role of Emotion in Conflict

When we are in conflict we often feel emotionally charged.[35]In fact, we are often unaware that we are in conflict until we recognize that we are emotional about something.[36] There is an important distinction between perceiving conflict and feeling conflict—conflict is often not recognized until it is felt.[37] One expert observes that "emotions are an important element of conflict. They define individuals' subjective interpretations of reality and reactions to current situations."[38] Even though the emotional component is most evident in relationship conflict, task and process conflict also can contain high levels of emotion.[39]

Many people let their feelings and emotions influence how they deal with conflict. Controlling your emotions and staying focused on the issues can help to prevent a conflict from escalating. Assessing and acknowledging the emotions of the other party can also help you to more effectively manage the conflict.

INTERPERSONAL CONFLICT MANAGEMENT STRATEGIES

Once you understand the source of a conflict you are engaged in, you need to identify the best strategy for addressing it. There are five conflict management strategies that differ in their concern for others and concern for your own interests.[40] Figure 10.1 illustrates how these five styles of managing interpersonal conflict compare in their focus on others and on pursuing one's self-interests.

collaborating
A conflict management style reflecting a desire to give both parties what they want

Collaborating reflects a high concern for your own interests and a high concern for the interests of the other party. This conflict management style emphasizes problem solving and pursues an outcome that gives both parties what they want. Saying, "Let's see if we can find a solution that meets both of our needs" reflects a collaborating conflict management style. Collaborating helps to build commitment to the outcome, although the communication required to reach a solution can take substantial time and energy. Even though there is a risk that one party may take advantage of the other party's trust and openness, collaboration is generally regarded as the best approach for managing most conflicts. The objective of collaboration is to fulfill both parties' needs with a goal of "I win / you win."

Figure 10.1

There are five general interpersonal conflict management styles. These differ in terms of your concerns for others versus your concerns for yourself.

Interpersonal Conflict Management Styles[41]

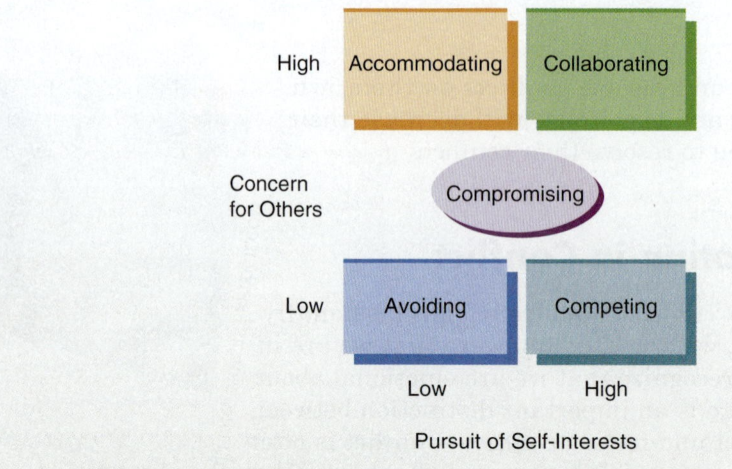

compromising
A conflict management style in which each side sacrifices something in order to end the conflict

Compromising is a conflict management style in which each side sacrifices something in order to end the conflict. This middle-ground style reflects a moderate concern for your own interests and a moderate concern for the interests of the other party. Saying, "Maybe we can meet in the middle" or "I'm willing to reconsider my initial position" reflects a compromising style. A compromising style is often used to achieve temporary solutions, to avoid destructive power struggles, or when a conflict must be resolved quickly. The goal of compromising is "I win some and lose some / you win some and lose some."

competing
Pursuing one's own interest at the expense of the other party

accommodating
A cooperative conflict management style

Competing is a conflict management style resulting from a high concern for your own interests and low concern for the other party. This approach is generally used when the conflict issue is important or to set a precedent. However, because one party is trying to dominate the other, this conflict management style can escalate the conflict and the loser may try to retaliate. A person who uses threats or ultimatums is using a competing conflict management style. Saying, "If you don't accept this offer the deal is off" reflects a competing style. The goal of competing is "I win / you lose."

Accommodating is a cooperative conflict management style. Accommodating reflects a low concern for your own interests and a high concern for the interests of the other party. This conflict management style is generally used when the issue is more important to the other party than it is to you.

PRESSMASTER/SHUTTERSTOCK.COM

There are several different strategies for managing interpersonal conflict. Compromising is often used when the parties can agree on some things but not others. In certain cases, such as conflicts between management and labor unions, compromises are then legally spelled out in the form of a contract.

This style is also appropriate when you recognize that you are wrong. Saying, "I'll go along with whatever is best for you" reflects an accommodating style. The goal of accommodating is "I lose / you win."

Avoiding is a passive conflict management style involving ignoring the conflict or denying that it exists. This style reflects a low concern for your own interests and a low concern for the interests of the other party. When this strategy is used to manage trivial conflicts no damage may be done, but it can result in maximum damage when important issues are involved. Avoidance is also used when more information is needed or when addressing the conflict has the potential to create more problems (perhaps the other party is known to be aggressive). The primary drawback to an avoidance style is that the decision may not be optimal to you and your interests. The goal of avoiding is "no winners / no losers." Because conflict is often uncomfortable, members of workgroups often resort to passive forms of conflict management such as avoidance.[42] This chapter's *Understand Yourself* feature gives you a chance to assess your preferred conflict management style.

avoiding
Ignoring the conflict or denying that it exists

In general, each style of handling interpersonal conflict is appropriate and ethical in some situations as long as it is used to attain the organization's proper goals.[43] Remember, because people differ in their preferred conflict management styles, it is important to adapt your own style accordingly. What is most important is that you proactively manage workplace conflict. Research has found that conflict leads to stress and emotional exhaustion.[44] Cultural values can also influence preferred conflict management styles, as you will learn in this chapter's *Global Issues* feature.

UNDERSTAND YOURSELF

YOUR PREFERRED CONFLICT MANAGEMENT STYLE

People tend to use a subset of the possible conflict management styles based on their personal comfort with conflict and personal management style. Understanding your preferred conflict management style can help you to reflect on how you might better use other styles when they are more appropriate.

To help you understand your conflict management style, rank order the five conflict management styles based on how often you tend to use each one:

____ Competing
____ Collaborating
____ Compromising
____ Avoiding
____ Accommodating

The styles with the lowest numbers reflect your preferred conflict management styles. Do you think this accurately reflects you? When might this style be most appropriate? When might it be least appropriate? What can you do to improve your comfort and skill with some of the other styles?

If you would like to complete a self-assessment to help analyze your conflict management style, go to: http://academic.engr.arizona.edu/vjohnson/ConflictManagementQuestionnaire/ConflictManagementQuestionnaire.asp.

Source: Adapted from Tang, T. L. P. (1992). The Meaning of Money Revisited. *Journal of Organizational Behavior, 13*, 197–202; Roberts, J. A., & Sepulveda, C. J. (1999, July). Demographics and Money Attitudes: A Test of Yamauchi and Templer's (1982) Money Attitude Scale in Mexico. *Personality and Individual Differences, 27*, 19–35; Yamauchi, K. & Templer, D. (1982). The Development of a Money Attitudes Scale. *Journal of Personality Assessment, 46*, 522–528.

BALDYRGAN/SHUTTERSTOCK.COM

CONFLICT MANAGEMENT DIFFERENCES ACROSS CULTURES

Reflecting variations in cultural values, individuals from different cultures adopt different conflict resolution strategies.[45] For example, compared to U.S. managers, Asian managers avoid explicitly discussing a conflict. Managers in the United States tend to prefer a style of dominance and assertively competing to see who can convince the other of their preferred resolution of the conflict.[46] Chinese managers favor compromise and avoidance, whereas British executives favor collaboration and competition.[47] Arab Middle Eastern executives use more of an integrating and avoiding style in handling interpersonal conflict.[48]

As another example, an employee from a culture in India who considers you a superior may be hesitant to give you direct feedback to save face for both of you. Instead, the person may tell you what he or she thinks you want to hear, especially when others are around. Because Indians may communicate only the positives when asked to give constructive feedback, you should listen carefully for what they do *not* say.[49] A desire to maintain one's own public face is related to a greater use of a dominating conflict style, and a desire to maintain the face of the other party is related to a greater use of the avoiding, integrating, and compromising styles of conflict management.[50]

Members of collective cultures also perceive and manage conflict differently from those in individualistic cultures.[51] Collectivism emphasizes group harmony and interdependence. Individualism emphasizes individual rights and independence. The Chinese culture is collective and the U.S. culture is individualistic. Collective societies tend to avoid open conflict—any conflict that emerges must be resolved in inner circles before it becomes serious enough to justify public involvement.[52]

THE CONFLICT PROCESS

Putting it all together, the conflict process is summarized in Figure 10.2. After a potential conflict is triggered, it is perceived by both parties. The true disagreement may differ from the perceived disagreement—conflict is often accompanied by misunderstandings that exaggerate the perceived disagreement. If neither party experiences emotion in reaction to the potential conflict, it does not escalate. For example, if Ryan disagrees with his boss about how to do something but Ryan does not mind doing it the boss's way, neither party experiences emotion over the disagreement and the conflict ends. On the other hand, if Ryan feels strongly that his way is better or that the boss's way will not work, emotion may be felt. In this case, the conflict will begin to escalate. Both sides will then implement one or more conflict management strategies that either will end the conflict constructively or allow the conflict to continue to escalate, perhaps to the point of becoming destructive.

Conflict Management Skills

Fortunately, most managers can learn the necessary skills for effective conflict management. Professionals in conflict resolution training suggest four areas of skill development:[53]

1. Listening (including eye contact, rephrasing, and summarizing what each side tells you to show them that you understand each side's position)
2. Questioning
3. Communicating nonverbally
4. Mediating

Figure 10.2

The Conflict Process

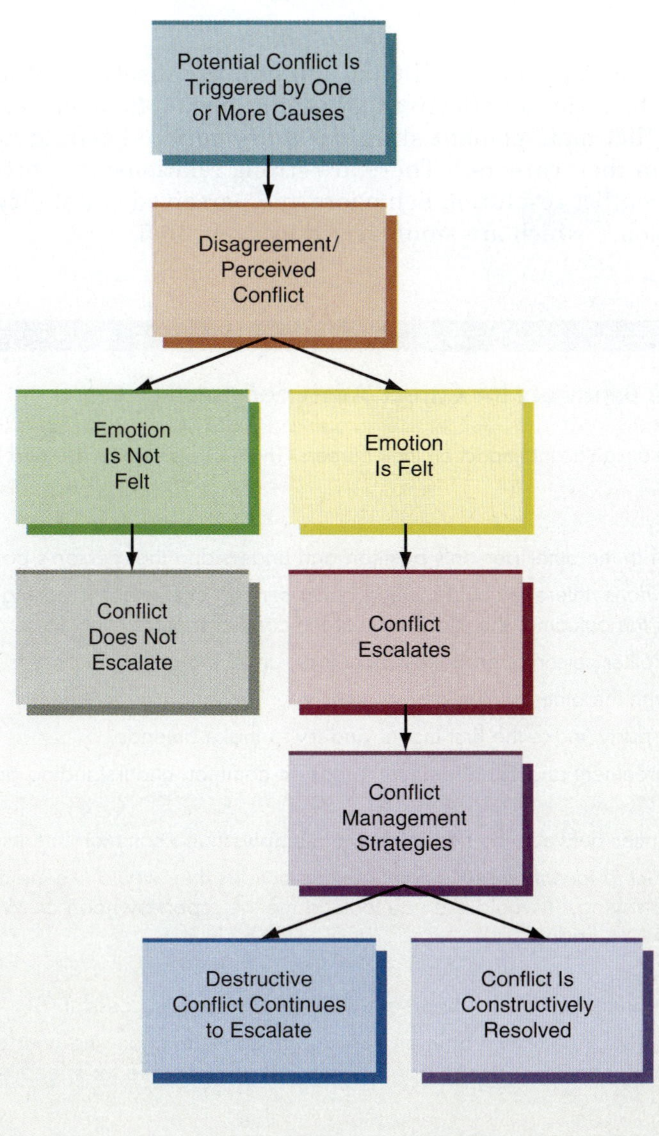

The conflict process includes several elements that define the direction and magnitude of the conflict. Disagreements, emotions, and escalation all play important roles and suggest optimal conflict management strategies.

If you are mediating a conflict, ask open rather than leading questions, and use nonverbal cues to show that you are sincerely trying to help. Read nonverbal cues to learn additional information. Mediation skills include open-mindedness, staying nonjudgmental and calm, demonstrating empathy and sensitivity, remaining neutral, respecting confidentiality, and showing flexibility and resiliency.[54] Try to identify and communicate a superordinate goal shared by both parties that cannot be reached without their mutual cooperation.

MONKEY BUSINESS IMAGES/ SHUTTERSTOCK.COM

The ability to listen is an important conflict management skill. This man is explaining why he is unhappy to a colleague. The colleague, meanwhile, is paying careful attention to what he is saying. Her listening skills will help her avoid getting too angry and will facilitate them developing a better working relationship.

A person's ability to successfully resolve conflict is related to his or her effectiveness as a leader.[55] Managers with poor conflict management skills hit a promotional ceiling much earlier in their careers.[56] There are strong relationships between certain conflict resolution behaviors and perceived suitability for promotion,[57] which are summarized in Table 10.5.

Table 10.5

Best and Worst Conflict Resolution Behaviors for Career Advancement

How managers deal with conflict can have a significant impact on their careers. There are both effective and less effective approaches.

Best Conflict Resolution Behaviors:

- *Perspective taking*: Try to put yourself in the other person's position and understand that person's point of view.
- *Focusing on interests rather than positions*: Interests could include better serving clients or increasing the clarity of work expectations. By focusing on the outcome, the root cause of the conflict is more likely to be addressed.
- *Creating solutions*: Brainstorm with the other person or group, ask questions, and try to create solutions to the problem.
- *Expressing emotions*: Talk honestly with the other person and express your thoughts and feelings.
- *Reaching out*: Reach out to the other party, make the first move, and try to make amends.
- *Documenting*: Document areas of agreement and disagreement to ensure common understanding and clear communication.
- *Smoothing*: Playing down the differences between the two sides while emphasizing common interests.
- *Asking the parties involved in a conflict to identify three or four specific actions they would like the other party to take*: An example of this would be saying, "I would like you to send me the report by noon on Wednesday so that I can meet my deadline of 10 A.M. Friday."

Worst Conflict Resolution Behaviors:

- *Avoiding the conflict*: Avoiding or ignoring the conflict, hoping it will pass, is rarely successful.
- *Winning at all costs*: Arguing vigorously for your own opinion, refusing to consider changing your position, and trying to win regardless of the interpersonal costs are approaches that do not make for speedy or satisfying conflict resolution.
- *Displaying anger*: Expressing anger, raising your voice, and using harsh, angry words will make the other person defensive and will slow down or prevent any resolution of the conflict.
- *Demeaning the other party*: Laughing at the other person, ridiculing the other's ideas, and using sarcasm are both disrespectful and not conducive to resolving conflict.
- *Retaliating*: Obstructing the other person, retaliating against the other person, and trying to get revenge are unprofessional and disrespectful behaviors and will not promote conflict resolution.
- *Meeting separately with the people in conflict*: Because the sole goal of each employee involved in a conflict is to convince you of the merits of their own case, the parties are likely to become more committed to their positions rather than committed to resolving the conflict if you talk to each party in private.

Sources: Delahoussaye, M. (2002, June). Don't Get Mad, Get Promoted. *Training, 39,* 20; Heathfield, S. M. (2009). Workplace Conflict Resolution: People Management Tips. About.com. Available online: http://humanresources.about.com/od/managementtips/a/conflict_solue.htm; Susskind, L. & Cruikshank, J. (1987). *Breaking the Impasse: Consensual Approaches to Resolving Public Disputes.* New York, NY: Basic Books.

Managers sometimes need to create constructive conflict in order to stimulate thinking and develop new ideas. In this brainstorming session, for example, team members have identified a number of alternatives and are now putting them into categories for further discussion.

CANDYBOX IMAGES/SHUTTERSTOCK.COM

Creating Constructive Conflict

As management pioneer Warren Bennis observed, "Leaders do not avoid, repress, or deny conflict, but rather see it as an opportunity."[58] You have learned that conflict can lead to better decisions, better relationships, and other positive outcomes. However, most people dislike conflict. It is seen as easier, less stressful, and less risky to one's career to avoid conflict and suppress dissenting opinions, despite their effectiveness in stimulating more creative and effective ideas and solutions. Often we are unsure of whether or not we are correct, and we also may fear ridicule or rejection.[59] Yet organizations that avoid conflict will have an increasingly difficult time competing successfully in a global environment. So what can managers do to increase the positive outcomes of conflict?

The successful design company IDEO printed the three rules of brainstorming on the wall. These rules are: (1) concentrate on the quantity of ideas; (2) don't criticize others' ideas; and (3) elaborate and build on others' ideas.[60] Emerson Electric makes conflict a fundamental element of its strategic planning process, creating an atmosphere of vigorous debate.[61] Hewlett Packard awards a medal of defiance for continuing work on an idea contrary to management's views.[62] General Electric uses workout groups to allow employees to voice their dissenting opinions.[63] The hotelier Marriott even has a policy that if managers cannot explain why they are asking an employee to do something, the employee does not have to do it.[64]

To successfully create constructive conflict, organizations often punish conflict avoiders. Rewarding employees who engage in constructive conflict can help to reduce employees' fears of ridicule or rejection. A simple "thank you" for voicing a dissenting opinion can signal to employees that it is okay to speak up. Hiring employees who are comfortable with constructive conflict and who tend to use effective conflict management strategies can also enhance constructive conflict and improve organizational performance.

Assigning one or more employees to play the role of devil's advocate can help to generate constructive conflict by providing a safer environment for the introduction of different perspectives. The dialectical method in which multiple groups discuss issues separately and then together to better synthesize different viewpoints into a common framework can help to reduce conflict by ensuring that multiple perspectives are incorporated into decisions.

THE NEGOTIATION PROCESS

At some time or another everyone has to negotiate. For instance, discussing where to meet a friend for dinner, haggling over the price of a new car, and trying to convince your boss that you deserve a pay increase are all negotiations.[65]

We often experience conflicts with other people in which we must negotiate to reach a solution. Negotiation skills thus are not only critical for managers, but also improve the effectiveness of all employees.

Negotiating Skills

negotiation
A process in which two or more parties make offers, counteroffers, and concessions in order to reach an agreement

Negotiation is a process in which two or more parties make offers, counteroffers, and concessions in order to reach an agreement. Most managers do a lot of negotiating as part of their jobs. Job offers and contracts with customers and suppliers have to be negotiated, resources have to be secured and shared with other departments, and agreements have to be made with bosses and subordinates.

distributive negotiation
Any gain to one party is offset by an equivalent loss to the other party

There are two types of negotiation, distributive and integrative. ***Distributive negotiation*** occurs under zero-sum conditions, where any gain to one party is offset by an equivalent loss to the other party.[66] Distributive negotiation essentially distributes resources among the parties involved. Because distributive negotiation structures the conflict in a win-lose way, it tends to be competitive and adversarial. For example, every dollar one manager gets from the company's total budget is a dollar another manager does not get.

Former Yahoo! CEO Jerry Yang is widely faulted for his failed negotiations with Microsoft in 2008. Yang's behavior during negotiations indicated that he misinterpreted his bargaining position in pursuing a distributive negotiation strategy. High-tech analyst Rob Enderle explains that Yang "kept saying we should get more money, we should get more money, and not realizing how precarious their position was."[67] Yang's employment was ultimately terminated by Yahoo!'s board of directors.

integrative negotiation
A win-win negotiation in which the agreement involves no loss to either party

Integrative negotiation is a win-win negotiation in which the agreement involves no loss to either party.[68] In general, integrative bargaining is better than distributive bargaining because when it is over neither party feels that they have lost. Integrative bargaining helps to build good long-term relationships, and minimizes grudges between the parties. This is particularly beneficial when the parties have to work together on an ongoing basis once the negotiations are finished.

A classic example of integrative bargaining exercise involves a dispute over an orange. Two people take the position that they want the whole orange, so the moderator of the dispute gives each person one half of the orange. However, if the parties' interests were considered, there could have been a different, win-win outcome. One person wanted to eat the meat of the orange, but the other just wanted the peel to use in baking cookies. If the mediator had understood their interests, they could have both gotten all of what they wanted, rather than just half.[69]

The four fundamental principles of integrative negotiation are:[70]

1. *Separate the people from the problem*. Separate relationship issues (or "people problems" such as emotions, misperceptions, and communication issues) from substantive issues, and deal with them independently.
2. *Focus on interests, not positions*. Negotiate about things that people really want and need, and not what they say they want or need.
3. *Invent options for mutual gain*. Look for new solutions to the problem that will allow both sides to win, rather than just fighting over the original positions that assume that for one side to win, the other side must lose.

4. *Insist on objective fairness criteria*. Outside, objective fairness criteria for the negotiated agreement are ideal if they exist (like the terms of another company's union-management contract).

ITT Senior Vice President and Director of Human Resources Scott Crum focuses on integrative bargaining in which both parties satisfy their interests without compromising. To do this, Crum focuses on establishing trust through his negotiating style and tactics. He first asks the parties to state their interests, not their demands. Identifying desired outcomes not only improves his understanding of each side's needs, but builds trust as well. Crum feels that respect builds trust, which leads to openness, which is critical to achieving lasting, final, win-win solutions.[71]

It is also helpful to research and understand the individual with whom you will be negotiating. The better you understand the person's background, interests, and negotiating style, the more effective you will be. Try to begin with a positive exchange, create an open and trusting environment, and emphasize win-win situations. Be sure to prepare well, listen actively, and think through your alternatives. The more options you feel you have, the better a negotiating position you will be in.[72]

Here are some suggestions for being an effective negotiator:[73]

- Do not look at a deal as an either/or proposition. Negotiating is about compromise.
- Make sure each side knows the other's perception of the issues and each other's interests.
- Identify what you can and cannot part with. If you are negotiating an employment contract, identify the things most important to you (e.g., more vacation, a signing bonus) and those things that are less important (e.g., a prestigious job title). Act like everything is important, and grudgingly concede ground on the things that matter less to you. The other party will count these concessions as a victory and might yield on things you value more.
- Try to identify and use sources of leverage. Leverage consists of anything that can help or hinder a party in a bargaining situation. For example, a seller who must sell is at a disadvantage, and if the other party needs to move quickly you might be able to make a tougher offer. Competing offers can also increase one party's leverage over the other.
- Show the other side that you understand their position. Help the other person to see you as an ally by mirroring their emotions. If the other person appears frustrated, let him or her know that you recognize he or she is frustrated. The other person may respond with, "I sure am frustrated!" and now you're agreeing on something. Empathizing with the other party helps to preserve a cordial and productive atmosphere.
- Suppress your emotions. Negotiations can become tense and stir emotions. Constantly reminding yourself of your goal can help you to maintain an appropriate level of detachment and continue to see the deal clearly. Stay rationally focused on the issue being negotiated, and take a break if emotions start to flare up. Also, be careful not to show too much desire for something, or your bargaining power will be reduced. If the other side can tell that you emotionally want something, this weakens your bargaining power.
- Know your "BATNA." The acronym BATNA stands for "best alternative to a negotiated agreement." It is what you could have done had no negotiation taken place, or what you will do if you cannot reach an agreement

with the other party. The purpose of negotiations is to see if you can get your interests better met by negotiating an agreement with the other party, compared to this best alternative. If the BATNA is not compared to the agreement being negotiated, negotiators can make agreements that are worse than not making an agreement at all.[74] If negotiations stall, letting the other side know that you are prepared to proceed with your backup plan can also help to get the process started up again. This chapter's *Improve Your Skills* feature gives you some tips for improving your negotiation skills.

Cultural Issues in Negotiations

Different national cultures have different preferred negotiation styles. For example, Russians tend to ignore deadlines and view concessions as a sign of weakness.[75] Some cultures, like the French, are more comfortable with conflict than other cultures. Although they also value tact or diplomacy, the French can be very direct and frequently question and probe into the other side's arguments.[76] In Saudi Arabia, saving face is essential. Causing embarrassment to the other party may be disastrous to a negotiation. Maintaining cordial relationships is also crucial to Saudi Arabians.[77] In India's group-oriented culture, asserting individual preferences may be less effective than having a sense of belonging to a group, conforming to its norms, and maintaining harmony among group members.[78] Iraqis attend more to how something is said than to what is actually said. Messages spoken in a calm and unemotional manner are given less weight and credibility than those communicated with emotion.[79] Because Americans' desire to be liked is known in other cultures, skilled negotiators from other cultures use this to their advantage by making friendship conditional on the final outcome of the negotiation.[80]

When people believe they have been treated disrespectfully as a result of differing cultural norms, the whole project can blow up. In one Korean-U.S. negotiation, the American team was having difficulty getting information from their Korean counterparts. They nearly destroyed the deal by complaining directly to higher-level Korean management. The higher-level managers were offended because the Korean culture strictly adheres to hierarchy. Their own lower-level people, not the U.S. team members, should have been the ones to come to them with a problem. The Korean team members were also mortified that the Americans involved their bosses before they themselves could brief them. The crisis was resolved only when high-level U.S. managers made a trip to Korea, conveying appropriate respect for their Korean counterparts.[81]

ZELJKODAN/SHUTTERSTOCK.COM

Cultural differences can play a major role in negotiation. For instance, people from the United States, Europe, Asia, and the Middle East all have different negotiating styles. An awareness of cultural differences can help avoid problems and misunderstandings.

IMPROVE YOUR SKILLS

IMPROVING YOUR NEGOTIATION SKILLS

Do:

Prepare well
Use silence to your advantage
Offer a warm greeting and build rapport
Understand your position and what you can and cannot part with
Maintain a confident posture, lean forward, and smile
Maintain good eye contact
Ask good-quality, open questions
Speak in a clear, measured manner
Show empathy
Display controlled energy

Avoid:

Constantly making eye contact
Ignoring members of the group
Celebrating a victory in the presence of the other party
Coldness or harshness in your voice
Closed body language (arms folded, head down, avoiding eye contact)

Clearly, intercultural negotiation requires paying attention to issues beyond what is being negotiated. The appropriateness of different negotiation tactics, the emphasis to put on developing relationships, how to respond to deadlines, and even where the negotiation should be held are all influenced by national culture. Preparation is particularly important when engaging in cross-cultural negotiations.

Alternative Dispute Resolution

Sometimes two parties are unable to reach an acceptable settlement through direct negotiations with each other. In such cases, the parties may involve a third party to overcome the stalemate and avoid a trial. This process is sometimes called ***alternative dispute resolution***. There are three types of alternative dispute resolution:

1. ***Conciliation***: A third party builds a positive relationship between the parties, improves their communication, and facilitates their discussion. Conciliation facilitates a discussion and directs the parties toward a satisfactory settlement and may issue a binding opinion if both parties agreed to that ahead of time.
2. ***Mediation***: An impartial third party (the mediator) facilitates a discussion using persuasion and logic, suggesting alternatives, and establishing each side's priorities. The mediator suggests a settlement that does not have to be accepted.
3. ***Arbitration***: A third party is involved and usually has the authority to impose a settlement on the parties.

alternative dispute resolution
Involving a third party in a negotiation to overcome a stalemate between the parties

conciliation
A third party builds a positive relationship between the parties and directs them toward a satisfactory settlement

mediation
An impartial third party (the mediator) facilitates a discussion using persuasion and logic, suggesting alternatives, and establishing each side's priorities

arbitration
A third party is involved and usually has the authority to impose a settlement on the parties

MARCIN BALCERZAK/SHUTTERSTOCK.COM

Mediation is a common form of alternative dispute resolution. This mediator (in the center) is helping two people resolve their differences. Effective mediators require training and skill in order to be able to successfully fulfill their role.

Conciliation is often the first step in the alternative dispute resolution process. Its goal is to get the parties to better communicate and resolve the problem on their own, although the conciliator may suggest a resolution that the parties can accept or reject. Arbitration and mediation also pursue the ideal of a fair outcome.

Mediation is a voluntary and nonbinding process, whereas the results of arbitration are legally binding. If the conflict has not escalated too much and both sides are motivated to resolve their conflict through bargaining, mediation can be very effective. If the mediator is not perceived as neutral, he or she is not likely to be effective.

Arbitration may be required by a contract or by law, or may be voluntary if the parties agree to it. The negotiating parties can establish rules for the arbitrator, such as restricting the arbitrator to one of the negotiators' final offers or freeing the arbitrator to make any judgment he or she wishes. Although arbitration, unlike mediation, always results in a settlement, it has greater potential to leave at least one party dissatisfied, which could cause the conflict to resurface later.

ombudsman
Someone who investigates complaints and mediates fair settlements between aggrieved parties

An ***ombudsman*** is someone who investigates complaints and mediates fair settlements between aggrieved parties. Universities often have ombudsmen to resolve conflicts between students and the institution, and large companies often have them to mediate conflicts with consumers. Ombudsmen help to resolve disputes while they are relatively small. This chapter's *Case Study* feature illustrates how ombudsmen can help companies resolve various types of internal conflicts.

CASE STUDY Ombudsman to the Rescue

A growing number of small and midsize businesses are enlisting ombudsmen to handle internal conflicts. Alan Siggia, cofounder of Sigmet, a Massachusetts data processor design company that is now a part of Vaisala Group,[82] and his cofounder Richard Passarelli did their best to manage employee squabbles, but became overwhelmed. Even small coworker disagreements could lead to a grudge match. Siggia says, "The struggles people were having were beyond what a well-intentioned but untrained person like me could handle."[83]

To better deal with the internal conflicts, the partners hired an ombudsman to spend a few hours a week at Sigmet. The ombudsman asks how things are going and counsels upset employees. She listens to employees' problems, asks questions, and helps devise solutions. An employee fed up with a colleague's unsolicited opinions, for example, might be walked through a hypothetical conversation asking the colleague to stop the behavior. The sessions are confidential, encouraging honesty, unless there is an imminent risk of harm to the company or a person. Employees wanting even more privacy can arrange an outside meeting. The ombudsman also helps the company to identify company policies that create conflicts. For instance, vague job descriptions were fueling a turf war, so the owners are crafting clear job descriptions and reviving performance reviews.

Sigmet is now enjoying better communication, less stress, and less conflict. Having a neutral person to help resolve conflicts has made a real difference—senior management has gained 30 percent more time, and colleagues are working together more efficiently. Office morale also has improved dramatically.[84]

Questions:

1. How has the ombudsman decreased conflicts at Sigmet?
2. Would you feel comfortable using an ombudsman to resolve a conflict with a coworker? Why or why not?
3. What could companies do to maximize the effectiveness of an ombudsman?

SUMMARY AND APPLICATION

Conflict is a natural part of organizational life. It can lead to positive outcomes, including better quality decisions, but it also has the potential to lead to negative outcomes if it is not properly handled. Emotion helps to convert a disagreement into a conflict. A variety of conflict management strategies can be used to help keep a conflict from escalating.

Organizational effectiveness is enhanced through an appropriate diagnosis and management of conflict.[85] To do this effectively managers need to be aware of and understand the advantages and disadvantages of five interpersonal conflict management strategies. These strategies are collaborating, compromising, competing, accommodating, and avoiding.

Some of the best conflict resolution behaviors are perspective taking, creating solutions, expressing emotions, reaching out, and documenting areas of agreement and disagreement. Some of the worst conflict management behaviors are avoiding the conflict, winning at all costs, displaying anger, demeaning the other party, and retaliating. Managers should also understand when and how to create constructive conflict.

Negotiation is one of the best ways to dissipate potential conflict. Integrative negotiation practices seeking to meet the needs of both parties are generally best for establishing long-term solutions that maintain a healthy relationship between the two parties. Alternative dispute resolution can be used when the negotiating parties are unable to negotiate a solution by themselves. The three types of alternative dispute resolution are conciliation, mediation, and arbitration.

LOSKUTNIKOV/SHUTTERSTOCK.COM

REAL WORLD RESPONSE

RESOLVING DISPUTES AT MARKS & SPENCER[86]

UK-based retailer Marks & Spencer wanted a process for its employees to use in identifying fair, mutually agreed upon, constructive conflict solutions in a safe environment. It also wanted to enable employees to move forward after a conflict positively and confidently. To accomplish these goals Marks & Spencer decided to train a team of accredited mediators to provide dispute resolution support to employees and to embed mediation and informal dispute resolution in the company's culture. The commitment of the company's CEO, Sir Stuart Rose, to mediation process was essential to the adoption of mediation as the primary dispute resolution process throughout the company.

The mediation process involves each party first separately talking with the mediator about the dispute. They then meet with the mediator a second time to discuss what they will say to each other and how they will respond during the meeting. The mediator focuses on coaching each party to help them reach a successful outcome and de-escalating strong emotions. After a lunch break the parties meet to discuss and resolve the dispute.

Mediation allows workplace problems to be addressed as early as possible to prevent escalation, and helps to make dispute resolution less adversarial. By bringing the people involved in a dispute together to explore what went wrong and what impact it had, employees' relationships with each other can even be strengthened as a result of the mediation process. By training a number of skilled mediators able to promote and offer mediation as an alternative to traditional formal grievance processes, a more healthy conflict resolution culture developed at Marks & Spencer.

DISCUSSION QUESTIONS

1. Have you ever experienced a constructive conflict? What happened? How was the disagreement resolved?
2. Have you ever experienced a dysfunctional conflict? What happened? Why was the conflict not resolved earlier?

3. How can managers promote constructive conflict?
4. Which of the conflict causes do you feel is most challenging to a manager? Why?
5. Think about a current conflict you are experiencing with a coworker, friend, or family member. Which of Glasl's conflict stages are you in? What can you do to keep the conflict from escalating to the next level?
6. If two of your subordinates were experiencing relationship conflict, what would you do to manage it? Why?
7. If two of your subordinates were experiencing task conflict, what would you do to manage it? Why?
8. What could you do to minimize the potential for negative outcomes in cross-cultural negotiations?
9. What would have to happen for you to fully accept and cooperate with a mediator's recommended settlement?

DEVELOP YOUR SKILLS EXERCISE

Union Conflict

Point your favorite browser to http://www.lasvegassun.com/news/2008/jun/28/toxic-feud-seius-top-ends-resignations/ to learn what happened when the conflict between the top two leaders of a union got out of hand. Then answer the following questions.

Questions

1. What type of conflict(s) existed between the two leaders? Explain your answer.
2. What did the two union leaders do to resolve their conflict?
3. In hindsight, what might have been done to resolve the conflict before it escalated so far?

GROUP EXERCISE

Win as Much as You Can!

Directions: For ten successive rounds, each team will select either an "X" or a "Y" and submit their choice to the instructor on a small piece of paper with their team name on it. The "payoff" for each round is determined by the patterns of choices made by the other teams as described below:

Choice Pattern	*Payout*
4 Xs	Lose $1 each
3 Xs	Win $1 each
1 Y	Lose $3
2 Xs	Win $2 each

2 Ys	Lose $2 each
1 X	Win $3
3 Ys	Lose $1 each
4 Ys	Win $1 each

Task: In each round, teammates confer and make a joint decision. Before rounds 5, 8, and 10, the teams will have a chance to confer with each other for three minutes before conferring with teammates for one minute and making a decision. Note the three bonus rounds, where the payoff is multiplied.

Round	Time Allowed	Confer with Other Teams	Your Choice	$ Won	$ Lost	Balance	Bonus?
1	2 min	No					No
2	1	No					No
3	1	No					No
4	1	No					No
5	3 + 1	Yes					**Bonus 3X**
6	1	No					No
7	1	No					No
8	3 + 1	Yes					**Bonus 5X**
9	1	No					No
10	3 + 1	Yes					**Bonus 10X**

VIDEO EXERCISE

Maine Media Workshops—Building a Contingent Workforce

Maine Media Workshops has seen some of the most talented filmmakers, photographers, and writers pass through its doors. The program began as a summer camp for artists wanting to hone their skills. Over the years, the workshops have allowed students to work with some of Hollywood's heavy-hitters, including Vilmos Zsigmond (*The Black Dahlia*), Alan Myerson (*Boston Public*), and Gene Wilder (*Willy Wonka & the Chocolate Factory*).

Staff selection is difficult for Maine Media Workshops. From January through November, the organization hires instructors to teach weeklong classes for approximately 500 courses. With the exception of a few full-timers, the organization is staffed with temporary week-to-week instructors. In the time it takes new hires to get their employee handbook and complete W2 forms, most instructors at the Maine Media Workshops have finished their course and are moving on. Job requirements workshops instructors are unique. Instructors act as mentors and coaches who dine with students, participate in social events, teach, and discuss assignments and careers. "What makes a good teacher is someone who is generous enough and open enough to share her life, her experience, her career and her knowledge 24/7 with students," said Elizabeth Greenburg, director of education.

Keeping courses staffed requires constant recruitment, and there is no time for training. As a result, the HR department seeks people who, like Elizabeth Greenburg, were once students. That way a new hire already understands what it takes to perform according to the Maine Media Workshops standard. Surprisingly, compensation is not an issue. Although the Maine Media Workshops pays a fair wage, the real compensation doesn't come in a check. "No one comes here for the money," said Mimi Edmunds, film program manager. "They come here because they love it."

Discussion Questions

1. What is the primary problem that education directors face when recruiting instructors to teach at Maine Media Workshops?
2. What sources of conflict are hampering recruitment at Maine Media Workshops?
3. What might Maine Media Workshops do to help resolve its ongoing staffing conflicts?

Now What?

VIDEO CASE

PERCOM/SHUTTERSTOCK.COM

Imagine being part of a team of two other coworkers experiencing negative task conflict as they try to finalize the design of a new toy before an imminent deadline. One team member is focused on making the toy of maximum quality and the other is focused on the conflicting goal of making the toy at the lowest cost. One of the team members is getting frustrated and feels that the team should be making better progress. The coworker asks you if there is anything the team can do to be more effective. *What do you say or do?* Go to this chapter's "Now What?" video, watch the challenge video, and choose a response. Be sure to also view the outcomes of the two responses you didn't choose.

Discussion Questions

1. What types of conflict is the team experiencing in the challenge video?
2. What aspects of the negotiation process would best resolve the conflict and why would this work?
3. What conflict resolution behaviors would you use as a manager to address this situation? Explain your answer.

ENDNOTES

[1]Papakostis, P. (2012, January 24). Marks & Spencer Case Study, The TCM Group. http://thetcmgroup.com/marks-spencer/; Sir Stuart Rose Supports the Benefits of Mediation in the Workplace (2009, October 9). Globis Mediation Group. http://www.globis.co.uk /news/2009/10/09/sir-stuart-rose-supports-the-benefits-of-mediation-in-the-workplace/; Company Overview, Marks & Spencer, 2012. Available online: http://corporate.marksandspencer.com/aboutus/company_overview.

[2]Rahim, A. (2000). *Managing Conflict in Organizations* (3rd ed.). Westport, CT: Quorum Books.

[3]Pfeffer, J. (1997). *Managing with Power: Politics and Influence in Organizations*. Boston: Harvard Business Press.

[4]Thomas, K. W., & Schmidt, W. H. (1976). A Survey of Managerial Interests with Respect to Conflict. *Academy of Management Journal*, *19*, 315–318.

[5]De Dreu, C. K. W., & Gelfand, M. J. (2008). Conflict in the Workplace: Sources, Dynamics, and Functions Across Multiple Levels of Analysis. In *The Psychology of Conflict and Conflict Management in Organizations*, eds. C. K. W. De Dreu & M. J. Gelfand (pp. 3–54). New York: Lawrence Erlbaum Associates.

[6]Forden, S. G. (2009). Versace Said Likely to Fire CEO Today After Conflict. Bloomberg. Available online: http://www.bloomberg.com/apps/news?pid=newsarchive&sid=awNvtXtoyJ9w.

[7]Pruitt, D. G., & Kim, S. H. (2004). *Social Conflict: Escalation, Stalemate, and Settlement* (3rd ed.). New York: McGraw-Hill.

[8]Deutsch, M. (1973). Conflicts: Productive and Destructive. In *Conflict Resolution Through Communication*, ed. F. E. Jandt. New York: Harper & Row.

[9]Fenn, D. (1995, July). Benchmark: Sources of Conflict in Family Businesses. *Inc*. Available online: http://www.inc.com/magazine/19950701/2343.html; Massachusetts Mutual Life Insurance Co. (1994). Telephone Survey, Springfield, MA.

[10]Dormann, C., & Zapf, D. (1999). Social Support, Social Stressors at Work, and Depressive Symptoms: Testing for Main and Moderating Effects with Structural Equations in a Three-Wave Longitudinal Study. *Journal of Applied Psychology*, *84*, 874–884; Spector, P. E., Dwyer, D. J., & Jex, S. M. (1988). Relation of Job Stressors to Affective, Health, and Performance Outcomes: A Comparison of Multiple Data Sources. *Journal of Applied Psychology*, *73*, 11–19.

[11]Wilmot, W. W., & Hocker, J. L. (1998). *Interpersonal Conflict* (5th ed.). Boston: McGraw-Hill.

[12]Schulz-Hardt, S., Mojzisch, A., & Vogelgesang, F. (2007). Dissent as a Facilitator: Individual-and Group-Level Effects on Creativity and Performance. In *The Psychology of Conflict and Conflict Management in Organizations*, eds. C. K. W. De Dreu & M. Gelfand (pp. 149–177). Hillsdale, NJ: Lawrence Erlbaum Associates.

[13]Pondy, L. R. (1992). Reflections on Organizational Conflict. *Journal of Organizational Behavior 13*, 257–262.

[14]Pondy, L. R. (1992). Reflections on Organizational Conflict. *Journal of Organizational Behavior 13*, 257–262.

[15]De Dreu, C. K. W., & Weingart, L. R. (2003). Task Versus Relationship Conflict: Team Performance, and Team Member Satisfaction: A Meta-Analysis. *Journal of Applied Psychology*, *88*, 741–749.

[16]Jehn, K. A. (1997). A Qualitative Analysis of Conflict Types and Dimensions in Organizational Groups. *Administrative Science Quarterly*, *42*, 530–557.

[17]Smith, C. S., & Sulsky, L. (1995). An Investigation of Job-Related Coping Strategies Across Multiple Stressors and Samples. In *Job Stress Interventions*, eds. L. R. Murphy, J. J. Hurrell, S. L. Aauter, & G. P. Keita (pp. 109–123). Washington, DC: American Psychological Association.

[18]Schwartz, J. E., & Stone, A. A. (1993). Coping with Daily Work Problems: Contributions of Problem Content, Appraisals, and Person Factors. *Work and Stress*, *7*, 47–62.

[19]Frank, W. S. (2005, June 24). How to Resolve Conflict Between Two Warring Executives. *Denver Business Journal*. Available online: http://denver.bizjournals.com/denver/stories/2005/06/27 /smallb3.html.

[20]Jehn, K. A., & Mannix, E. A. (2001). The Dynamic Nature of Conflict: A Longitudinal Study of Intergroup Conflict and Group Performance. *Academy of Management Journal*, *44*, 238–251.

[21]Sutton, R. I. (2007). *The No Asshole Rule: Building a Civilized Workplace and Surviving One That Isn't*. New York: Grand Central Publishing.

[22]De Dreu, C. K. W., & Gelfand, M .J. (2008). Conflict in the Workplace: Sources, Dynamics, and Functions Across Multiple Levels of Analysis. In *The Psychology of Conflict and Conflict Management in Organizations*, eds. C. K. W. De Dreu & M. J. Gelfand (pp. 3–54). New York: Lawrence Erlbaum Associates.

[23]Van de Vliert, E., & De Dreu, C. (1994). Optimizing Performance by Conflict Stimulation, *International Journal of Conflict Management*, *5*, 211–222.

[24]Coser, L. (1956). *The Functions of Social Conflict*. Glencoe, IL: Free Press.

[25]Wise, D. C., & Lewis, G. C. (1985, March 11). A Split That's Sapping Morale at Apple. *Business Week*, 106–107; Nee, S. (1985, July 29). Sculley Confirms Rift with Jobs. *Electronic News*, 22.

[26]Shteynberg, G., Gelfand, M. J., & Kim, H. G. (2005, April). The Cultural Psychology of Revenge. Paper presented at the annual conference of the Society for Industrial and Organizational Psychology, Los Angeles, CA.

[27]Gelfand, M. J., Nishii, L. H., Holcombe, K., Dyer, N., Ohbuchi, K.,& Fukumo, M. (2001). Cultural Influences on Cognitive Representations of Conflict: Interpretations of Conflict Episodes in the U.S. and Japan. *Journal of Applied Psychology*, *86*, 1059–1074.

[28]Friedman, R. A., & Curall, S. C. (2003). Conflict Escalation: Dispute Exacerbating Elements of E-Mail Communication. *Human Relations*, *56*, 1325–1347.

[29]Banner, D. K., & Gagné, E. T. (1994). Designing Effective Organizations: Traditional & Transformational Views (p. 402). New York: Sage.

[30]Pruitt, D. G. (2007). Conflict Escalation in Organizations. In *The Psychology of Conflict and Conflict Management in Organizations*, eds. C. K. W. De Dreu & M. J. Gelfand (pp. 245–265). Hillsdale, NJ: Lawrence Erlbaum Associates.

[31]Glasl, F. (1982). The Process of Conflict Escalation and Roles of Third Parties (1982). In *Conflict Management and*

Industrial Relations, eds. G. B. J. Bomers & R. B. Peterson (pp. 119–140). The Hague: Kluwer Nijhoff; Glasl, F. (1992). *Konfliktmanagement. Ein Handbuch für Führungskräfte und Berater* (2nd ed.). Stuttgart: Bern; Glasl, F., & Kopp, P. (1999). *Confronting Conflict: A First-Aid Kit for Handling Conflict*. Binghampton, NY: Hawthorn Press.

[32]Glasl, F. & Kopp, P. (1999). Confronting Conflict: A First-Aid Kit for Handling Conflict. Binghampton, NY: Hawthorn Press.

[33]Neuman, J. H., & Baron, R. A. (1998). Workplace Violence and Workplace Aggression: Evidence Concerning Specific Forms, Potential Causes, and Preferred Targets. *Journal of Management*, *24*, 391–419; Jawahar, I. M. (2002). A Model of Organizational Justice and Workplace Aggression. *Journal of Management*, *6*, 811–834; Kriesberg, L. (1998). De-Escalating Conflicts. In *Constructive Conflicts* (pp. 181–222). Lanham, MD: Rowman & Littlefield.

[34]Silver-Greenberg, J. & Schwartz, N. D. (2012, May 19). Discord at Key JPMorgan Unit is Faulted in Loss, The New York Times. Available online: http://www.cnbc.com/id/47489227.

[35]Bodtker, A. M., & Jameson, J. K. (2001). Emotion in Conflict Formation and Its Transformation: Application to Organizational Conflict Management. International *Journal of Conflict Management*, *12*(3), 259–275.

[36]Nair, N. (2008). Towards Understanding the Role of Emotions in Conflict: A Review and Future Directions. *International Journal of Conflict Management*, *19*, 359–381.

[37]Pondy, L. R. (1967). Organizational Conflict: Concepts and Models. *Administrative Science Quarterly*, *12*, 296–320.

[38]Jehn, K. A. (1997). A Qualitative Analysis of Conflict Types and Dimensions in Organizational Groups. *Administrative Science Quarterly*, *42*, 532.

[39]Jehn, K. A. (1997). A Qualitative Analysis of Conflict Types and Dimensions in Organizational Groups. *Administrative Science Quarterly*, *42*, 530–557.

[40]Rahim, M., & Bonoma, T. (1979). Managing Organizational Conflict: A Model for Diagnosis and Intervention. Psychological Reports, 44, 1323–1344; Blake, R. R., & Mouton, J. S. (1964). *The Managerial Grid*. Houston, TX: Gulf Publishing.

[41]Based on Rahim, M. A. & Blum, A. A. (Eds.) (1994). *Global Perspectives on Organizational Conflict* (p. 5). Westport, CT: Praeger.

[42]Ayoko, O. B., Hartel, C. E. J., & Cullen,V. J. (2002). Resolving the Puzzle of Productive and Destructive Conflict in Culturally Heterogeneous Work Groups: A Communication-Accommodation Approach. *International Journal of Conflict Management*, 13, 165–195.

[43]Rahim, M. A., Garrett, J. E., & Buntzman, G. F. (1992). Ethics of Managing Interpersonal Conflict in Organizations. *Journal of Business Ethics*, 11, 423–432.

[44]Jaramillo, F., Mulki, J. P., & Boles, J. S. (2011). Workplace Stressors, Job Attitude, and Job Behaviors: Is Interpersonal Conflict the Missing Link? *Journal of Personal Selling* and *Sales Management*, 31(3), 339–356; Ilies, R., Johnson, M. D., Judge, T. A., & Keeney, J. (2011). A Within-Individual Study of Interpersonal Conflict as a Work Stressor: Dispositional and Situational Moderators. *Journal of Organizational Behavior*, *21*(1), 44–64.

[45]Kirkbride, P. S., Tang, F. Y., & Westwood, R. I. (1991). Chinese Conflict Preferences and Negotiating Behaviour: Cultural and Psychological Influences. *Organization Studies*, 12, 365–386.

[46]Morris, M. W., Williams, K. Y., Leung, K., Larrick, R., Mendoza, M. T., Bhatnagar, D., Li, J., Kondo, M., Luo, J., & Hu, J. (1998). Conflict Management Style: Accounting for Cross-National Differences. *Journal of International Business Studies*, 29, 729–747; Tse, D. K., Francis, J., & Walls, J. (1994). Cultural Differences in Conducting Intra- and Intercultural Negotiation: A Sino-Canadian Comparison. *Journal of International Business Studies*, *3*, 537–555.

[47]Tang, S. F. Y., & Kirkbride, P. S. (1986). Developing Conflict Management Skills in Hong Kong: An Analysis of Some Cross-Cultural Implications. *Management Learning*, *17*, 287–301.

[48]Elsayed-Ekhouly, S., & Buda, R. (1996). Organizational Conflict: A Comparative Analysis of Conflict Styles Across Cultures. *International Journal of Conflict Management*, *1*, 71–81.

[49]Katz, L. (2007). *Negotiating International Business—The Negotiator's Reference Guide to 50 Countries Around the World*. Dallas, TX: Booksurge.

[50]Ting-Toomey, S., Gao, G., Trubisky, P., Yang, Z., Kim, H. S., Lin, S. L., & Nishida, T. (1991). Culture, Face Maintenance, and Styles of Handling Interpersonal Conflict: A Study in Five Cultures. *International Journal of Conflict Management*, *2*, 275–296.

[51]Ting-Toomey, S. (1988). Intercultural Conflicts: A Face-Negotiation Theory. In *Theories in Intercultural Communication*, eds. Y. Kim & W. Gudykunst (pp. 213–235). Newbury Park, CA: Sage.

[52]Ting-Toomey, S. (1988). Intercultural Conflicts: A Face-Negotiation Theory. In *Theories in Intercultural Communication*, eds. Y. Kim & W. Gudykunst (pp. 213–235). Newbury Park, CA: Sage; Tse, D. K., Francis, J., & Walls, J. (1994). Cultural Differences in Conducting Intra- and Intercultural Negotiation: A Sino-Canadian Comparison. *Journal of International Business Studies*, *3*, 537–555.

[53]Ramsey, R. D. (1996, August). Conflict Resolution Skills for Supervisors. *Supervision*, *57*(8), 9–12.

[54]Ramsey, R. D. (1996, August). Conflict Resolution Skills for Supervisors. *Supervision*, *57*(8), 9–12.

[55]In Delahoussaye, M. (2002, June). Don't Get Mad, Get Promoted. *Training*, *39*(6), 20.

[56]Delahoussaye, M. (2002, June). Don't Get Mad, Get Promoted. *Training*, *39*, 20; Heathfield, S. M. (2009). Workplace Conflict Resolution: People Management Tips. About.com. Available online at: http://humanresources.about.com/od/managementtips /a/conflict_solue.htm.

[57]Delahoussaye, M. (2002, June). Don't Get Mad, Get Promoted, *Training*, *39*(6), 20; Heathfield, S. M. (2009). Workplace Conflict Resolution: People Management Tips. About.com. Available online: http://humanresources.about.com/od/managementtips /a/conflict_solue.htm; Susskind, L., & Cruikshank, J. (1987). *Breaking the Impasse: Consensual Approaches to Resolving Public Disputes*. New York: Basic Books.

[58]Bennis, W. (1989). *Why Leaders Can't Lead: The Unconscious Conspiracy Continues* (p. 153). San Francisco: Jossey-Bass.

[59]Nemeth, C. J., Endicott, J., & Wachtler, J. (1977). Increasing the Size of the Minority: Some Gains and Some Losses. *European Journal of Social Psychology*, *1*, 11–23.

[60]Paulus, P. B., & Nijstad, B. A. (2003). *Group Creativity: Innovation Through Collaboration*. New York: Oxford University Press.

[61]Lagace, M. (2005, June 6). Don't Listen to "Yes." *Harvard Business School Working Knowledge*. Available online: http://hbswk.hbs.edu/item/4833.html.

[62]Sommerfield, F. (1990, May). Paying the Troops to Buck the System. *Business Month*, 77–79.

[63]Cabana, S., & Fiero, J. (1995). Motorola, Strategic Planning and the Search Conference. *Journal for Quality and Participation*, *18*, 22–31.

[64]Cabana, S., & Fiero, J. (1995). Motorola, Strategic Planning and the Search Conference. *Journal for Quality and Participation*, *18*, 22–31.

[65]Fisher, R., & Ury, W. L. (1991). Getting to Yes: Negotiating Agreement Without *Giving In*. New York: Penguin.

[66]Korda, P. (2011). In *The Five Golden Rules of Negotiation*, eds. J. M. Phillips & S. M. Gully. New York: Business Expert Press.

[67]Arnoldy, B. (2008, November 19). Why Yahoo!'s Jerry Yang Stepped Down. Available online: http://www.csmonitor.com/Money/2008/1119/p02s01-usec.html.

[68]Fisher, R., Ury, W., & Patton, B. (1991). *Getting to Yes: Negotiating Agreement Without Giving In* (2nd ed.). New York: Houghton Mifflin.

[69]De Dreu, C. K. W. (2005, June). A PACT Against Conflict Escalation in Negotiation and Dispute Resolution. *Current Directions in Psychological Science*, *14*, 149.

[70]Based on Fisher, R., Ury, W. & Patton, B. (1991). *Getting to Yes: Negotiating Agreement Without Giving In* (2nd ed.). New York: Houghton Mifflin.

[71]This vignette is based on a telephone interview with Scott Crum, Senior Vice President and Director of Human Resources at ITT, June 8, 2009.

[72]Walker, R. (2003, August). Take It or Leave It: The *Only* Guide to Negotiating You Will Ever Need. *Inc.*, *75*.

[73]Watkins, M. (2002). *Breakthrough Business Negotiation: A Toolbox for Managers*. New York: Jossey-Bass; Kaplan, M. (2005, May). How to Negotiate Anything. *Money*, *34*(5), 116–119; Stansell, K. (2000, October 1). Practice the Art of Effective Negotiation. *Inc.* Available online: http://www.inc.com/articles/2000/10/20856.html.

[74]Fisher, R., Ury, W., & Patton, B. (1991). *Getting to Yes: Negotiating Agreement Without Giving In* (2nd ed.). New York: Houghton Mifflin.

[75]Glenn, E. S., Witmeyer, D., & Stevenson, K. A. (1977). Cultural Styles of Persuasion. *Journal of Intercultural Relations*, 52–66.

[76]Katz, L. (2007). *Negotiating International Business—The Negotiator's Reference Guide to 50 Countries Around the World*. Dallas, TX: Booksurge.

[77]Katz, L. (2007). *Negotiating International Business—The Negotiator's Reference Guide to 50 Countries Around the World*. Dallas, TX: Booksurge.

[78]Katz, L. (2007). *Negotiating International Business—The Negotiator's Reference Guide to 50 Countries Around the World*. Dallas, TX: Booksurge.

[79]Triandis, H. C. (1994). *Culture and Social Behavior*. New York: McGraw-Hill.

[80]Harris, P. R., & Moran, R. T. (1999). *Managing Cultural Differences* (5th ed.). Houston: Gulf Publishing.

[81]Brett, J., Behfar, K., & Kern, M. C. (2006, November). Managing Multicultural Teams. *Harvard Business Review*, 84–91.

[82]Sigmet. (2009). Sigmet Product Line. Available online: http://www.vaisala.com/weather/products/sigmet.html.

[83]Gill, J. (2005, November 1). Squelching Office Conflicts. *Inc.* Available online: http://www.inc.com/magazine/20051101/handson-managing.html.

[84]Lynch, D. B. (2005, December 2). Say No to Office Conflict. *PR Web*. Available online: http://www.prweb.com/releases/2005/12/prweb317075.htm.

[85]Rahim, M. A. (2002). Toward a Theory of Managing Organizational Conflict. *International Journal of Conflict Management*, *13*, 206–235.

[86]Papakostis, P. (2012, January 24). Marks & Spencer Case Study, *The TCM Group*. http://www.thetcmgroup.com/news/327-http-www-thetcmgroup-com-news/?p_view=all; Sir Stuart Rose Supports the Benefits of Mediation in the Workplace (2009, October 9). *Globis Mediation Group*. http://www.globis.co.uk /news/2009/10/09/sir-stuart-rose-supports-the-benefits-of–mediation-in-the-workplace/; Company Overview, Marks & Spencer, 2012. Available online: http://corporate.marksandspencer.com/aboutus/company_overview.

PART 4

LEADERSHIP AND INFLUENCE PROCESSES IN ORGANIZATIONS

Recall that our underlying question in this book is what makes managers and organizations effective and how effectiveness is influenced by performance behaviors, commitment and engagement, citizenship behaviors, and dysfunctional behaviors. In Part 3 we examined the impact of various forms of social behaviors on these questions. We discussed groups and teams in Chapter 7. Chapter 8 focused on decision making and problem solving. We looked at communication in Chapter 9. And in Chapter 10 we discussed conflict and negotiation in organizations.

In Part 4 we ask a different but related question: why does leadership matter? Chapter 11 looks at traditional leadership approaches, while modern leadership approaches are covered in detail in Chapter 12. Chapter 13 concludes Part 4 by examining power, influence, and politics in organizations. At the end of the part you should have a strong understanding of how leadership affects employee performance behaviors, employee commitment and engagement, citizenship behaviors, and dysfunctional behaviors.

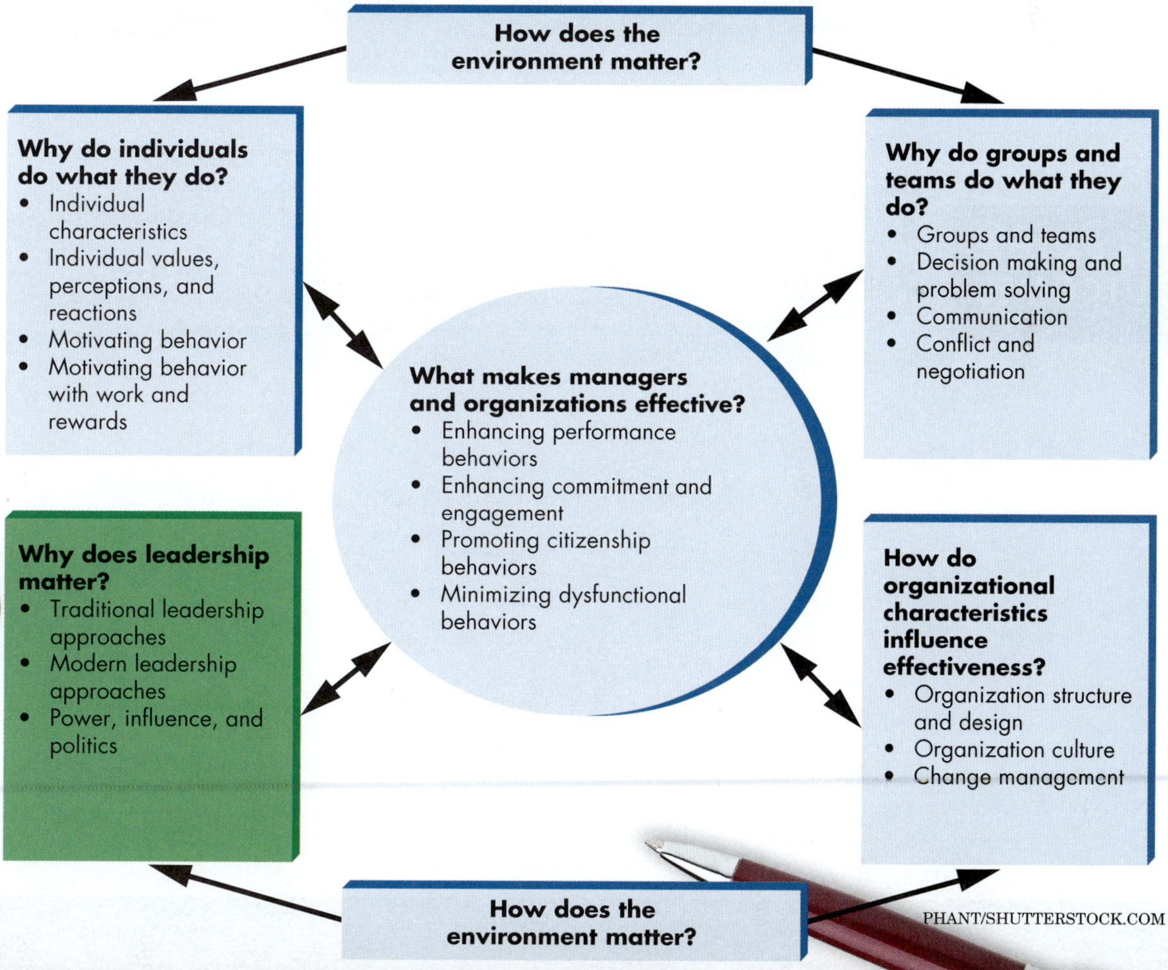

How does the environment matter?

Why do individuals do what they do?
- Individual characteristics
- Individual values, perceptions, and reactions
- Motivating behavior
- Motivating behavior with work and rewards

Why do groups and teams do what they do?
- Groups and teams
- Decision making and problem solving
- Communication
- Conflict and negotiation

What makes managers and organizations effective?
- Enhancing performance behaviors
- Enhancing commitment and engagement
- Promoting citizenship behaviors
- Minimizing dysfunctional behaviors

Why does leadership matter?
- Traditional leadership approaches
- Modern leadership approaches
- Power, influence, and politics

How do organizational characteristics influence effectiveness?
- Organization structure and design
- Organization culture
- Change management

How does the environment matter?

LOSKUTNIKOV/SHUTTERSTOCK.COM

CHAPTER 11 TRADITIONAL LEADERSHIP APPROACHES

CHAPTER OUTLINE

LEARNING OUTCOMES

After studying this chapter, you should be able to:

1. Characterize the nature of leadership.
2. Trace the early approaches to leadership.
3. Discuss the emergence of situational theories and models of leadership including the LPC and path-goal theories.
4. Describe Vroom's decision tree approach to leadership.

REAL WORLD CHALLENGE

LEADERSHIP PINBALL[1]

LOSKUTNIKOV/SHUTTERSTOCK.COM

As U.S. Senator and former presidential candidate John McCain puts it, "[Leadership is] a game of pinball, and you're the ball." Fortunately, a few of corporate America's veteran leaders have some tips for those who still want to follow in their increasingly treacherous footsteps. First of all, if you think you're being overworked—that your hours are too long and your schedule too demanding—odds are you're right: Most people—including executives—*are* overworked. And in some industries, they're particularly overworked. U.S. airlines, for example, now service 100 million more passengers annually than they did just five years ago—with 70,000 fewer workers. "I used to manage my time," quips one airline executive. "Now I manage my energy." In fact, many high-ranking managers have realized that energy is a key factor in their ability to complete tasks on tough schedules. Most top corporate leaders work 80 to 100 hours a week, and a lot of them have found that regimens that allow them to refuel and refresh make it possible for them to keep up the pace.

Carlos Ghosn, who's currently CEO and chairman of both Renault and Nissan, believes in regular respites from his workweek routine. "I don't bring my work home. I play with my four children and spend time with my family on weekends," says Ghosn. "I come up with good ideas as a result of becoming stronger after being recharged." Yahoo! CEO/president Marissa Mayer admits that "I can get by on four to six hours of sleep," but she also takes a weeklong vacation three times a year. Global HR consultant Robert Freedman devotes two minutes every morning to doodling on napkins. Not only does it give him a chance to meditate, but he's thinking about publishing both his doodles and his meditations in a coffee-table book.

Suppose someone you know is taking a leadership role in a large organization and asks your advice on how to deal with the increase in workload. After reading this chapter you should have some useful information to share.

JOE RAEDLE/GETTY IMAGES

The mystique of leadership makes it one of the most widely debated, studied, and sought-after properties of organizational life. Managers talk about the characteristics that make an effective leader and the importance of leadership to organizational success, while organizational scientists have extensively studied leadership and myriad related phenomena for decades. Paradoxically, however, while leadership is among the most widely studied concepts in the entire field of management, many unanswered questions remain. Why, then, should we continue to study leadership? First, leadership is of great practical importance to organizations. Second, in spite of many remaining mysteries, researchers have isolated and verified some key variables that influence leadership effectiveness.[2]

This chapter, the first of two devoted to leadership, introduces the fundamental traditional models that are commonly used as a basis for understanding leadership. We start with a discussion of the meaning of leadership, including its definition and the distinctions between leadership and management. Then we turn to historical views of leadership, focusing on the trait and behavioral approaches. Next, we examine three contemporary leadership theories that have formed the basis for most leadership research: the LPC theory developed by Fiedler, the path-goal theory, and Vroom's decision tree approach to leadership. In our next chapter, we explore several contemporary and emerging views of leadership.

THE NATURE OF LEADERSHIP

leadership (as process)
Involves the use of noncoercive influence

leadership (as property)
The set of characteristics attributed to someone who is perceived to use influence successfully

influence
The ability to affect the perceptions, beliefs, attitudes, motivation, and/or behaviors of others

Because "leadership" is a term that is often used in everyday conversation, you might assume that it has a common and accepted meaning. In fact, just the opposite is true. Like several other key organizational behavior terms such as "personality" and "motivation," "leadership" is used in a variety of ways. Thus, we first clarify its meaning as we use it in this book.

The Meaning of Leadership

We will define leadership in terms of both process and property.[3] As a process, ***leadership*** is the use of noncoercive influence to direct and coordinate the activities of group members to meet a goal. As a property, ***leadership*** is the set of characteristics attributed to those who are perceived to use such influence successfully.[4] ***Influence***, a common element of both perspectives, is the ability to affect the perceptions, beliefs, attitudes, motivation, and/or behaviors of others. From an organizational viewpoint, leadership is vital because it has such a powerful influence on individual and group behavior.[5] Moreover, because the goal toward which the group directs

RAWPIXEL/SHUTTERSTOCK.COM

Leadership is both a process and a property. This executive is working to affect how his audience feels about a new business strategy for their organization. Therefore, he is attempting to use leadership as a process. Further, if he is successful in engaging the support of his colleagues then they may attribute leadership characteristics to him.

its efforts is often the desired goal of the leader, it may or may not mesh with organizational goals.

Leadership involves neither force nor coercion. A manager who relies solely on force and formal authority to direct the behavior of subordinates is not exercising leadership. Thus, as discussed more fully in the next section, a manager or supervisor may or may not also be a leader. It is also important to note that on one hand, a leader may actually possess the characteristics attributed to him or her; on the other, the leader may merely be perceived as possessing them.

Leadership versus Management

From these definitions, it should be clear that leadership and management are related, but they are not the same. A person can be a manager, a leader, both, or neither.[6] Some of the basic distinctions between the two are summarized in Table 11.1. On the left side of the table are four elements that differentiate leadership from management. The two columns show how each element differs

Table 11.1

Kotter's Distinctions Between Management and Leadership

Activity	Management	Leadership
CREATING AN AGENDA	Planning and budgeting. Establishing detailed steps and timetables for achieving needed results; allocating the resources necessary to make those needed results happen	Establishing direction. Developing a vision of the future, often the distant future, and strategies for producing the changes needed to achieve that vision
DEVELOPING A HUMAN NETWORK FOR ACHIEVING THE AGENDA	Organizing and staffing. Establishing some structure for accomplishing plan requirements, staffing that structure with individuals, delegating responsibility and authority for carrying out the plan, providing policies and procedures to help guide people, and creating methods or systems to monitor implementation	Aligning people. Communicating the direction by words and deeds to all those whose cooperation may be needed to influence the creation of teams and coalitions that understand the vision and strategies and accept their validity
EXECUTING PLANS	Controlling and problem solving. Monitoring results versus plan in some detail, identifying deviations, and then planning and organizing to solve these problems	Motivating and inspiring. Energizing people to overcome major political, bureaucratic, and resource barriers to change by satisfying very basic, but often unfulfilled, human needs
OUTCOMES	Produces a degree of predictability and order and has the potential to consistently produce major results expected by various stakeholders (e.g., for customers, always being on time; for stockholders, being on budget)	Produces change, often to a dramatic degree, and has the potential to produce extremely useful change (e.g., new products that customers want, new approaches to labor relations that help make a firm more competitive)

Source: From *A Force for Change: How Leadership Differs from Management*, by John P. Kotter.

when considered from a management and a leadership point of view. For example, when executing plans, managers focus on monitoring results, comparing them with goals, and correcting deviations. In contrast, the leader focuses on energizing people to overcome bureaucratic hurdles to help reach goals.

To further underscore the differences, consider the various roles that might typify managers and leaders in a hospital setting. The chief of staff of a large hospital is clearly a manager by virtue of the position itself. At the same time, this individual may not be respected or trusted by others and may have to rely solely on the authority vested in the position to get people to do things. But an emergency room nurse with no formal authority may be quite effective at taking charge of a chaotic situation and directing others in how to deal with specific patient problems. Others in the emergency room may respond because they trust the nurse's judgment and have confidence in the nurse's decision-making skills. The head of pediatrics, supervising a staff of twenty other doctors, nurses, and attendants, may also enjoy the staff's complete respect, confidence, and trust. They readily take her advice and follow directives without question, and often go far beyond what is necessary to help carry out the unit's mission.

Thus, being a manager does not ensure that a person is also a leader—any given manager may or may not also be a leader. Similarly, a leadership position can also be formal, as when someone appointed to head a group has leadership qualities, or informal, as when a leader emerges from the ranks of the group according to a consensus of the members. The chief of staff described earlier is a manager but not really a leader. The emergency room nurse is a leader but not a manager. And the head of pediatrics is likely both.

Organizations need both management and leadership if they are to be effective. For example, leadership is necessary to create and direct change and to help the organization get through tough times.[7] Management is necessary to achieve coordination and systematic results and to handle administrative activities during times of stability and predictability. Management in conjunction with leadership can help achieve planned orderly change, and leadership in conjunction with management can keep the organization properly aligned with its environment. The *Improve Your Skills* feature will give you some insights into your readiness to assume a leadership role.

In addition, managers and leaders also play a major role in establishing the moral climate of the organization and in determining the role of ethics in its culture.[8] Maintaining one's ethical balance while discharging other leadership duties can sometimes require an executive to walk a fairly fine line. For instance, consider a CEO who knows that her firm will need to lay off several thousand workers in a few months. On the one hand, divulging this information too early may result in devaluing the firm's stock and causing top employees to look for other jobs. On the other, delaying the news until the last minute might result in longer periods of unemployment for the workers who lose their jobs.

EARLY APPROACHES TO LEADERSHIP

Although leaders and leadership have profoundly influenced the course of human events, careful scientific study of them began only about a century ago. Early studies focused on the traits, or personal characteristics, of leaders.[9] Later research shifted to examine actual leader behaviors.

IMPROVE YOUR SKILLS

ARE YOU READY TO LEAD?

This exercise is designed to help you assess both your current readiness for leadership and your current preference in leadership style. The 10 statements in the table below reflect certain preferences in the nature of work performance. Indicate the extent to which you agree or disagree with each statement by circling the number in the appropriate column.

Statement of preference	**Strongly agree**				**Strongly disagree**
1. I like to stand out from the crowd.	1	2	3	4	5
2. I feel proud and satisfied when I influence others to do things my way.	1	2	3	4	5
3. I enjoy doing things as part of a group rather than achieving results on my own.	1	2	3	4	5
4. I have a history of becoming an officer or captain in clubs or organized sports.	1	2	3	4	5
5. I try to be the one who is most influential in task groups at school or work.	1	2	3	4	5
6. In groups, I care most about good relationships.	1	2	3	4	5
7. In groups, I most want to achieve task goals.	1	2	3	4	5
8. In groups, I always show consideration for the feelings and needs of others.	1	2	3	4	5
9. In groups, I always structure activities and assignments to help get the job done.	1	2	3	4	5
10. In groups, I shift between being supportive of others' needs and pushing task accomplishment.	1	2	3	4	5

How to score: Follow the instructions in the following table to enter the numbers that you've circled:

Leadership Readiness Score	Add the numbers that you circled on items 1–5: ___
Leadership Style Score	
Task Preference Score	Add the numbers that you circled on items 7 and 9: ___
Relationship Preference Score	Add the numbers that you circled on items 6 and 8: ___ Difference between Task and Relationship scores: ___ Check the higher score: Task ___ Relationship ___
Adaptability Score	Your score on item 10 ___

How to interpret your scores:

Leadership Readiness: If your total score on items 1–5 is 20 or more, you'll probably enjoy a leadership role. If your score is 10 or less, you're probably more interested in personal achievement—at least at this point in your life. If you've scored somewhere in the middle range, your leadership potential is still flexible. You could go either way, depending on circumstances.

Leadership Style: Your responses to items 6–10 reflect your leadership style, which may be task-oriented, relationship-oriented, or flexible. Your current leadership style preference is determined by the higher of your two scores on the dimensions of task and relationship. The strength of your preference is indicated by the difference between your scores on the two dimensions.

Leadership Style Adaptability: A score of 4 or 5 on item 10 suggests that you're likely to adapt to circumstances as they arise.

Source: Adapted from Hunsaker, P. L. (2005). *Management: A Skills Approach* (2nd ed., pp. 419–20). Upper Saddle River, NJ: Pearson Education.

Trait Approaches to Leadership

trait approach (to leadership)
Attempted to identify stable and enduring character traits that differentiated effective leaders from nonleaders

Lincoln, Napoleon, Joan of Arc, Hitler, and Gandhi are names that most of us know quite well. Early researchers believed that leaders such as these had some unique set of qualities or traits that distinguished them from their peers. Moreover, these traits were presumed to be relatively stable and enduring. Following this ***trait approach***, these researchers focused on identifying leadership traits, developing methods for measuring them, and using the methods to select leaders.

Hundreds of studies guided by this research agenda were conducted during the first several decades of the twentieth century. The earliest writers believed that important leadership traits included intelligence, dominance, self-confidence, energy, activity, and task-relevant knowledge. The results of subsequent studies gave rise to a long list of additional traits. Unfortunately, the list quickly became so long that it lost any semblance of practical value. In addition, the results of many studies were inconsistent.

For example, one early argument was that effective leaders such as Lincoln tended to be taller than ineffective leaders. But critics were quick to point out that Hitler and Napoleon, both effective leaders in their own way, were not tall. Some writers have even tried to relate leadership to such traits as body shape, astrological sign, or handwriting patterns. The trait approach also had a significant theoretical problem in that it could neither specify nor prove how presumed leadership traits are connected to leadership per se. For these and other reasons, the trait approach was all but abandoned several decades ago.

In recent years, however, the trait approach has received renewed interest. For example, some researchers have sought to reintroduce a limited set of traits into the leadership literature. These traits include emotional intelligence, drive, motivation, honesty and integrity, self-confidence, cognitive ability, knowledge of the business, and charisma (which is discussed in Chapter 12).[10] Some people even believe that biological factors may play a role in leadership. Although it is too early to know whether these traits have validity from a leadership perspective, it does appear that a serious and scientific assessment of appropriate traits may further our understanding of the leadership phenomenon. And unfortunately, traits may even play a role in people not having opportunities to engage in leadership activities. Regardless of the reasons (including prejudice, stereotypes, or other factors), women, African Americans, and Hispanics are still significantly underrepresented among top management teams and boards of directors in the largest American businesses. Our *Case Study* examines these issues in more detail.

Behavioral Approaches to Leadership

In the late 1940s, most researchers began to shift away from the trait approach and started to look at leadership as an observable process or activity.

SALIM OCTOBER/SHUTTERSTOCK.COM

The trait approach to leadership focuses on stable and identifiable traits that differentiate effective leaders from nonleaders. Gandhi was seen as an outstanding leader, in part because of his integrity and humility.

CASE STUDY Getting on Board with Diversity

"It's been proven again and again," says Carl Brooks, CEO of the Executive Leadership Council, a network of senior African American executives, "that companies with board members who reflect gender and ethnic diversity also tend to have better returns on equity and sales." According to Marc H. Morial, CEO of the National Urban League, which promotes economic empowerment for African Americans, a minority presence on corporate boards is also necessary to protect the interests of minority consumers and other stakeholders: "African American voices and perspectives," he argues, "are needed on corporate boards to ensure that business decisions affecting Black America are both responsible and sensitive to the needs of our communities."

Unfortunately, says Morial, "African Americans still represent a miniscule fraction of board-level corporate leadership in America." Citing a recent study by the Executive Leadership Council, Morial points out that the number of blacks on *Fortune 500* boards has actually declined in recent years: Even though blacks comprise 13 percent of the U.S. population, representation on corporate boards stands at "a meager 7 percent."

The same trend was confirmed with the recent release of the U.S. Senate Democratic Hispanic Task Force report on minority and women representation on *Fortune 500* boards and executive teams (CEOs plus their direct reports). Here are some of the survey's findings:

- Women comprise 18 percent of all board members and just under 20 percent of executive team members (roughly 1 in 5). Those figures, of course, are far below the 50-percent proportion of women in the population.
- Minorities comprise 14.5 percent of all directors—about 1 out of every 7—and an even smaller percentage of executive-team members. That's less than half of their 35-percent proportion of the population.
- Although African Americans boast the highest minority representation on boards—8.8 percent—that's equivalent to only 69 percent of their total proportion of the population. Representation on executive teams is only 4.2 percent.
- Hispanics fared worse than any other minority. Although they represent 15 percent of the U.S. population, they comprise only 3.3 percent of board members and 3 percent of executive-team members.

The report, says task force chair Robert Menendez (one of only three Hispanic members of the U.S. Senate),

> clearly confirms what we had suspected all along—that American corporations need to do better when it comes to having the board rooms on Wall Street reflect the reality on Main Street. We need to change the dynamic and make it commonplace for minorities to be part of the American corporate structure. It is not just about doing what's right, but it's a good business decision that will benefit both corporations and the communities they're tapping into and making investments in.

Sources: African Americans Lost Ground on *Fortune 500* Boards. *UrbanMecca*, July 21, 2009. Available at: http://urbanmecca.net/news/2009/07/21/african-americans-lost-ground-on-fortune-500-boards/; Morial, M. H. (2011, April 14). National Urban League Trains African Americans for Corporate Boards. *BlackVoiceNews*. Available at: http://www.blackvoicenews.com/commentary/more-commentary/46010-national-urban-league-trains-african-americans-for-corporate-boards.html; Results of Menendez's Major *Fortune 500* Diversity Survey: Representation of Women and Minorities on Corporate Boards Still Lags Far Behind National Population. Senator Robert Menendez's website (press release), August 4, 2010. Available at: http://www.menendez.senate.gov/news-and-events/press/results-of-menendezs-major-fortune-500-diversity-survey-representation-of-women-and-minorities-on-corporate-boards-still-lags-far-behind-national-population.

behavioral approach (to leadership)
Tried to identify behaviors that differentiated effective leaders from nonleaders

The goal of the so-called ***behavioral approach*** was to determine what behaviors are associated with effective leadership.[11] The researchers assumed that the behaviors of effective leaders differed somehow from the behaviors of less effective leaders and that the behaviors of effective leaders would be the same

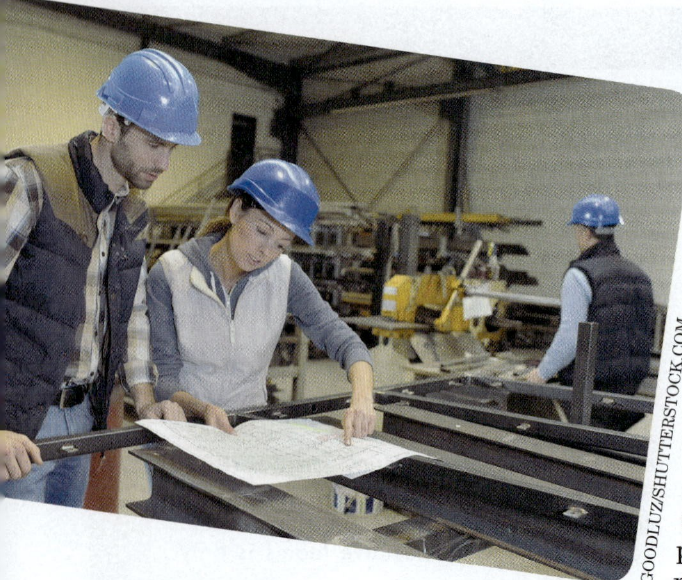

Job-centered leader behavior is associated with directing and monitoring the performance of subordinates. This manager is exhibiting job-centered leader behavior by explaining a work procedure to one of her subordinates.

across all situations. The behavioral approach to the study of leadership included the Michigan studies, the Ohio State studies, and the leadership grid.

The Michigan Studies

The ***Michigan leadership studies*** were a program of research conducted at the University of Michigan.[12] The goal of this work was to determine the pattern of leadership behaviors that result in effective group performance. From interviews with supervisors and subordinates of high- and low-productivity groups in several organizations, the researchers collected and analyzed descriptions of supervisory behavior to determine how effective supervisors differed from ineffective ones. Two basic forms of leader behavior were identified—job-centered and employee-centered—as shown in the top portion of Figure 11.1.

Michigan leadership studies
Defined job-centered and employee-centered leadership as opposite ends of a single leadership dimension

The leader who exhibits ***job-centered leader behavior*** pays close attention to the work of subordinates, explains work procedures, and is mainly interested in performance. The leader's primary concern is efficient completion of

Figure 11.1

Early Behavioral Approaches to Leadership

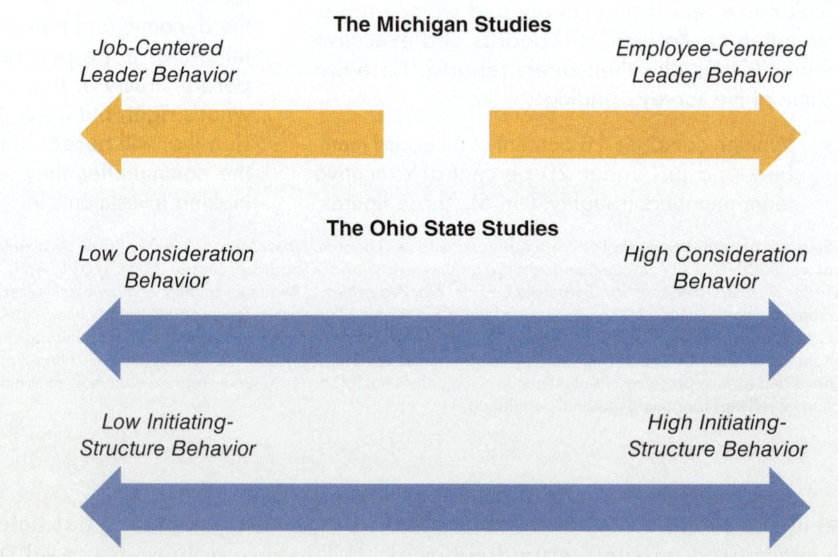

Two of the first behavioral approaches to leadership were the Michigan and Ohio State studies. The results of the Michigan studies suggested that there are two fundamental types of leader behavior, job-centered and employee-centered, which were presumed to be at opposite ends of a single continuum. The Ohio State studies also found two kinds of leadership behavior, "consideration" and "initiating-structure." These behaviors are somewhat parallel to those found in the Michigan studies but this research suggested that these two types of behavior were actually independent dimensions.

the task. The leader who engages in ***employee-centered leader behavior*** attempts to build effective work groups with high performance goals. The leader's main concern is with high performance, but that is to be achieved by paying attention to the human aspects of the group. These two styles of leader behavior were presumed to be at opposite ends of a single dimension. Thus, the Michigan researchers suggested that any given leader could exhibit either job-centered or employee-centered leader behavior, but not both at the same time. Moreover, they suggested that employee-centered leader behavior was more likely to result in effective group performance than was job-centered leader behavior.

job-centered leader behavior
Involves paying close attention to the work of subordinates, explaining work procedures, and demonstrating a strong interest in performance

employee-centered leader behavior
Involves attempting to build effective work groups with high performance goals

Ohio State leadership studies
Defined leader consideration and initiating-structure behaviors as independent dimensions of leadership

consideration behavior
Involves being concerned with subordinates' feelings and respecting subordinates' ideas

initiating-structure behavior
Involves clearly defining the leader-subordinate roles so that subordinates know what is expected of them

The Ohio State Studies

The ***Ohio State leadership studies*** were conducted at about the same time as the Michigan studies, in the late 1940s and early 1950s.[13] During this program of research, behavioral scientists at Ohio State University developed a questionnaire, which they administered in both military and industrial settings, to assess subordinates' perceptions of their leaders' behavior. The Ohio State studies identified several forms of leader behavior but tended to focus on the two most common ones: consideration and initiating-structure.

When engaging in ***consideration behavior***, the leader is concerned with the subordinates' feelings and respects subordinates' ideas. The leader-subordinate relationship is characterized by mutual trust, respect, and two-way communication. When using ***initiating-structure behavior***, on the other hand, the leader clearly defines the leader-subordinate roles so that subordinates know what is expected of them. The leader also establishes channels of communication and determines the methods for accomplishing the group's task.

Unlike the employee-centered and job-centered leader behaviors, consideration and initiating structure were not thought to be on the same continuum. Instead, as shown in the bottom portion of Figure 11.1, they were seen as independent dimensions of the leader's behavioral repertoire. As a result, a leader could exhibit high initiating-structure behavior and low consideration or low initiating-structure behavior and high consideration. A leader could also exhibit high or low levels of each behavior simultaneously. For example, a leader may clearly define subordinates' roles and expectations but exhibit little concern for their feelings. Alternatively, she or he may be concerned about subordinates' feelings but fail to define roles and expectations clearly. But the leader might also demonstrate concern for performance expectations and employee welfare simultaneously.

The Ohio State researchers also investigated the stability of leader behaviors over time. They found that a given individual's leadership pattern appeared to change little as long as the situation remained fairly constant.[14] Another topic they looked at was the combinations of leader behaviors that were related to effectiveness. At first, they believed that leaders who exhibit high levels of both behaviors would be most effective.

LDPROD/ SHUTTERSTOCK.COM

Leaders exhibit consideration behavior by showing genuine concern for the feelings and well-being of subordinates. This leader is showing consideration behavior by checking on a colleague who has just received bad news.

An early study at International Harvester (now Navistar Corporation), however, found that employees of supervisors who ranked high on initiating-structure behavior were higher performers but also expressed lower levels of satisfaction. Conversely, employees of supervisors who ranked high on consideration had lower performance ratings but also had fewer absences from work.[15] Later research showed that these conclusions were misleading because the studies did not consider all the important variables. Nonetheless, the Ohio State studies represented another important milestone in leadership research.[16]

Leadership Grid

Yet another behavioral approach to leadership is the Leadership Grid (originally called the Managerial Grid).[17] The Leadership Grid provides a means for evaluating leadership styles and then training managers to move toward an ideal style of behavior. The most current version of the Leadership Grid is shown in Figure 11.2. The horizontal axis represents concern for production

Figure 11.2

The Leadership Grid is a method of evaluating leadership styles. The overall objective of an organization using the Grid is to train its managers using organizational development techniques so that they are simultaneously more concerned for both people and production (9,9 style on the Grid).

The Leadership Grid

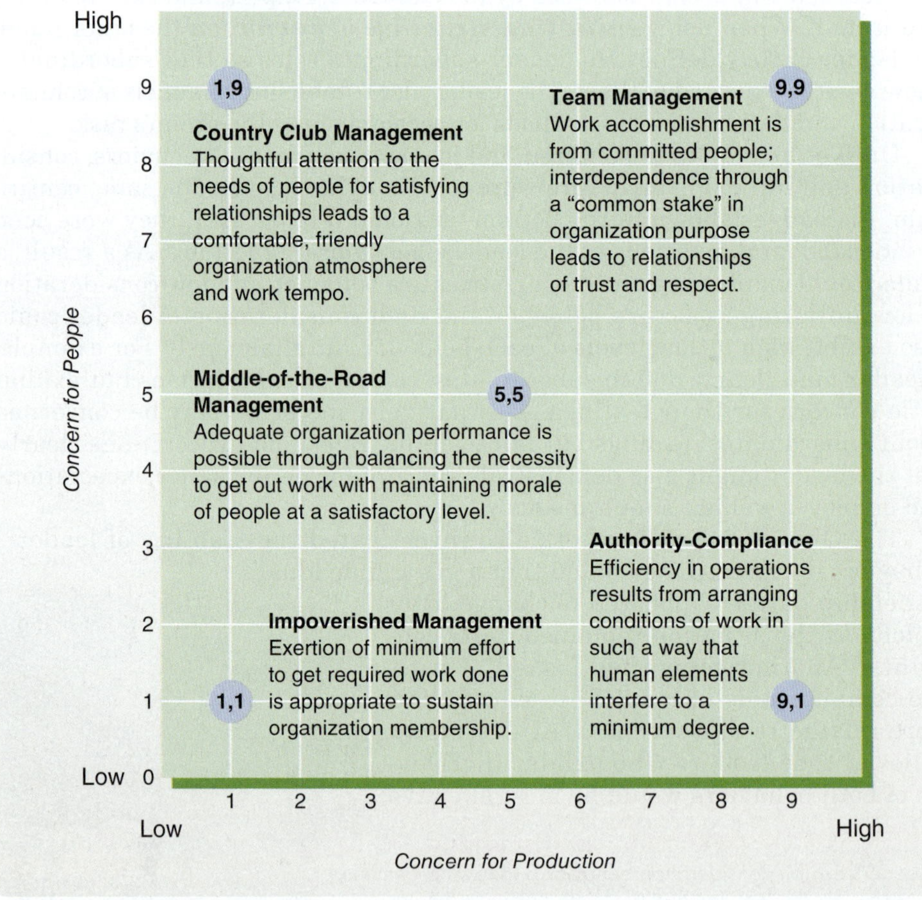

Source: Blake, R. R., & McCanse, A. A. The Leadership Grid Figure from *Leadership Dilemmas—Grid Solutions* (p. 29). Houston: Gulf Publishing Company. (Formerly *The Managerial Grid* by Robert R. Blake and Jane S. Mouton.) Copyright © 1997 by Grid International, Inc. Reproduced by permission of Grid International, Inc.

(similar to job-centered and initiating-structure behaviors), and the vertical axis represents concern for people (similar to employee-centered and consideration behavior). Note the five extremes of leadership behavior: the 1,1 manager (impoverished management), who exhibits minimal concern for both production and people; the 9,1 manager (authority-compliance), who is highly concerned about production but exhibits little concern for people; the 1,9 manager (country club management), who has the exact opposite concerns from the 9,1 manager; the 5,5 manager (middle of the road management), who maintains adequate concern for both people and production; and the 9,9 manager (team management), who exhibits maximum concern for both people and production.

According to this approach, the ideal style of leadership is 9,9. The developers of this model thus created a multiphase training and development program to assist managers in achieving this style of behavior. A.G. Edwards, Westinghouse, the FAA, Equicor, and other companies have used the Leadership Grid, and anecdotal evidence seems to confirm its effectiveness in some settings. However, there is little published scientific evidence regarding its true effectiveness and the extent to which it applies to all managers or to all settings. Indeed, as we discuss next, such evidence is not likely to actually exist.

THE EMERGENCE OF SITUATIONAL LEADERSHIP MODELS

The leader-behavior theories have played an important role in the development of more realistic, albeit more complex, approaches to leadership. In particular, they urge us not to be so preoccupied with what properties may be possessed by leaders (the trait approach), but to instead concentrate on what leaders actually do (their behaviors). Unfortunately, these theories also make universal generic prescriptions about what constitutes effective leadership. When we are dealing with complex social systems composed of complex individuals, however, few if any relationships are consistently predictable, and certainly no formulas for success are infallible.

The behavior theorists tried to identify consistent relationships between leader behaviors and employee responses in the hope of finding a dependable prescription for effective leadership. As we might expect, they often failed. Other approaches to understanding leadership were therefore needed. The catalyst for these new approaches was the realization that although interpersonal and task-oriented dimensions might be useful to describe the behavior of leaders, they were not useful for predicting or prescribing it. The next step in the evolution of leadership theory was the creation of situational models.

Situational models assume that appropriate leader behavior varies from one situation to another. The goal of a situational theory, then, is to identify key situational factors and to specify how they interact to determine appropriate leader behavior. Before discussing the major situational theories, we first discuss an important early model that in many ways laid the foundation for these theories. In a seminal article about the decision-making process, Robert Tannenbaum and Warren H. Schmidt proposed a continuum of leadership behavior. Their model is much like the original Michigan framework.[18]

Besides purely job-centered behavior (or "boss-centered" behavior, as they termed it) and employee-centered ("subordinate-centered") behavior, however, they identified several intermediate behaviors that a manager might consider. These are shown on the leadership continuum in Figure 11.3.

This continuum of behavior ranges from the one extreme of having the manager make the decision alone to the other extreme of having the employees make the decision with minimal guidance from the leader. Each point on the continuum is influenced by characteristics of the manager, subordinates, and the situation. Managerial characteristics include the manager's value system, confidence in subordinates, personal inclinations, and feelings of security. Subordinate characteristics include the subordinates' need for independence, readiness to assume responsibility, tolerance for ambiguity, interest in the problem, understanding of goals, knowledge, experience, and expectations. Situational characteristics that affect decision making include the type of organization, group effectiveness, the problem itself, and time pressures.

Hence, the leadership continuum acknowledged for the first time that leader behaviors represent a continuum rather than discrete extremes, and that various characteristics and elements of any given situation would affect the success of any given leadership style. Although this framework pointed out the importance of situational factors, it was, however, only speculative. It remained for others to develop more comprehensive and integrated theories. In the following sections, we describe three of the most important and widely

Figure 11.3

Tannenbaum and Schmidt's Leadership Continuum

The Tannenbaum and Schmidt leadership continuum was an important precursor to modern situational approaches to leadership. The continuum identifies seven levels of leadership, which range between the extremes of boss-centered and subordinate-centered leadership.

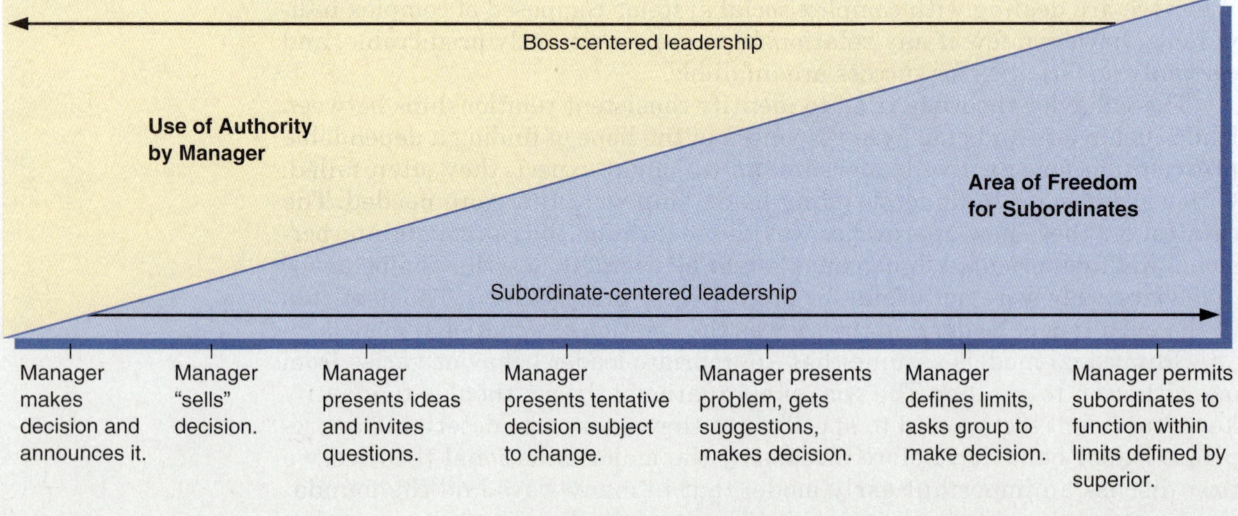

Source: Based on an exhibit from "How to Choose a Leadership Pattern" by Robert Tannenbaum and Warren Schmidt (May–June 1973).

accepted situational theories of leadership: the LPC theory, the path-goal theory, and Vroom's decision tree approach.

THE LPC THEORY OF LEADERSHIP

Fred Fiedler developed the ***LPC theory of leadership***. The LPC theory attempts to explain and reconcile both the leader's personality and the complexities of the situation. (This theory was originally called the "contingency theory of leadership." However, because this label has come to have generic connotations, new labels are being used to avoid confusion. "LPC" stands for "least-preferred coworker," a concept we explain later in this section.) The LPC theory contends that a leader's effectiveness depends on the situation and, as a result, some leaders may be effective in one situation or organization but not in another. The theory also explains why this discrepancy may occur and identifies leader-situation matches that should result in effective performance.

LPC theory of leadership
Suggests that a leader's effectiveness depends on the situation

Task versus Relationship Motivation

Fiedler and his associates maintain that leadership effectiveness depends on the match between the leader's personality and the situation. Fiedler devised special terms to describe a leader's basic personality traits in relation to leadership: "task motivation" versus "relationship motivation." He also conceptualized the situational context in terms of its favorableness for the leader, ranging from highly favorable to highly unfavorable.

In some respects, the ideas of task and relationship motivation resemble the basic concepts identified in the behavioral approaches. Task motivation closely parallels job-centered and initiating-structure leader behavior, and relationship motivation is similar to employee-centered and consideration leader behavior. A major difference, however, is that Fiedler viewed task versus relationship motivation as being grounded in personality in a way that is basically constant for any given leader.

The degree of task or relationship motivation in a given leader is measured by the ***least-preferred coworker (LPC)*** scale. The LPC instructions ask respondents (i.e., leaders) to think of all the persons with whom they have worked and to then select their least-preferred coworker. Respondents then describe this coworker by marking a series of sixteen scales anchored at each end by a positive or negative quality or attribute.[19] You can assess your own LPC score by completing this chapter's *Understand Yourself* feature.

least-preferred coworker (LPC)
Scale presumed to measure a leader's motivation

Fiedler assumed that the descriptions in the LPC scale actually say more about the leader than about the least-preferred coworker. He believed, for example, that everyone's least-preferred coworker is likely to be equally "unpleasant," and that differences in descriptions actually reflect differences in personality traits among the leaders responding to the LPC scale. Fiedler contended that high-LPC leaders are basically more concerned with interpersonal relations whereas low-LPC leaders are more concerned with task-relevant problems. Not surprisingly, controversy has always surrounded the LPC scale. Researchers have offered several interpretations of the LPC score, arguing that it may be an index of behavior, personality, or some other unknown factor. Indeed, the LPC measure and its interpretation have long been among the most debated aspects of this theory.

UNDERSTAND YOURSELF

LEAST-PREFERRED COWORKER SCALE

Think of the person with whom you can work least well. This may be a person you currently work with or someone you knew in the past. This person is not necessarily the person you like least well, but he or she should be the person with whom you had the most difficulty in getting a job done.

The following questionnaire asks you to describe this person as she or he appears to you. Look at the words at both ends of the line before you mark one box with an "x." Please remember that there are no right or wrong answers. Work quickly; your first answer is usually the most accurate. Do not omit any items, and mark only one answer for each item. When you are finished, add the numbers appearing under each line you marked with an "x." Scoring instructions are at the bottom of the table.

Pleasant	8	7	6	5	4	3	2	1	Unpleasant
Friendly	8	7	6	5	4	3	2	1	Unfriendly
Rejecting	1	2	3	4	5	6	7	8	Accepting
Helpful	8	7	6	5	4	3	2	1	Frustrating
Unenthusiastic	1	2	3	4	5	6	7	8	Enthusiastic
Tense	1	2	3	4	5	6	7	8	Relaxed
Distant	1	2	3	4	5	6	7	8	Close
Cold	1	2	3	4	5	6	7	8	Warm
Cooperative	8	7	6	5	4	3	2	1	Uncooperative
Supportive	8	7	6	5	4	3	2	1	Hostile
Boring	1	2	3	4	5	6	7	8	Interesting
Quarrelsome	1	2	3	4	5	6	7	8	Harmonious
Self-assured	8	7	6	5	4	3	2	1	Hesitant
Efficient	8	7	6	5	4	3	2	1	Inefficient
Gloomy	1	2	3	4	5	6	7	8	Cheerful
Open	8	7	6	5	4	3	2	1	Guarded

Scoring and Interpretation: Those with scores above 78 are considered high LPCs and are more people-oriented, while those with scores below 29 are considered low LPCs and are more task-oriented.

Source: Fiedler, F. E. (1967). *A Theory of Leadership Effectiveness* (p. 41). New York: McGraw-Hill.

The LPC theory of leadership suggests that what constitutes effective leader behavior depends on elements of the situation. Task structure, in turn, is one situational element that can affect what workers might need from their leader. In highly structured jobs such as these workers may not need much task-oriented leadership.

06PHOTO/SHUTTERSTOCK.COM

Situational Favorableness

Fiedler also identified three factors that determine the favorableness of the situation. In order of importance (from most to least important), these factors are leader-member relations, task structure, and leader position power.

Leader-member relations refers to the personal relationship that exists between subordinates and their leader. It is based on the extent to which subordinates trust, respect, and have confidence in their leader, and vice versa. A high degree of mutual trust, respect, and confidence obviously indicates good leader-member relations, and a low degree indicates poor leader-member relations.

Task structure is the second most important determinant of situational favorableness. A structured task is routine, simple, easily understood, and unambiguous. The LPC theory presumes that structured tasks are more favorable because the leader need not be closely involved in defining activities and can devote time to other matters. On the other hand, an unstructured task is one that is nonroutine, ambiguous, and complex. Fiedler argues that this task is more unfavorable because the leader must play a major role in guiding and directing the activities of subordinates.

Finally, *leader position power* is the power inherent in the leader's role itself. If the leader has considerable power to assign work, reward and punish employees, and recommend them for promotion, position power is high and favorable. If, however, the leader must have job assignments approved by someone else, does not control rewards and punishment, and has no voice in promotions, position power is low and unfavorable; that is, many decisions are beyond the leader's control.

Leader Motivation and Situational Favorableness

Fiedler and his associates conducted numerous studies examining the relationships among leader motivation, situational favorableness, and group performance. Table 11.2 summarizes the results of these studies.

To begin interpreting the results, let's first examine the situational favorableness dimensions shown in the table. The various combinations of these three dimensions result in eight different situations, as arrayed across the first three lines of the table. These situations in turn define a continuum ranging from very favorable to very unfavorable situations from the leader's perspective. Favorableness is noted in the fourth line of the table. For example, good relations, a structured task, and either high or low position power result in a very favorable situation for the leader. But poor relations, an unstructured

Table 11.2

The LPC Theory of Leadership

Leader-Member Relations	Good				Poor			
Task Structure	Structured		Unstructured		Structured		Unstructured	
Position Power	High	Low	High	Low	High	Low	High	Low
SITUATIONAL FAVORABLENESS	Very favorable ↓			Moderately favorable ↓			Very unfavorable ↓	
RECOMMENDED LEADER BEHAVIOR	Task-oriented behavior			Person-oriented behavior			Task-oriented behavior	

task, and either high or low position power create very unfavorable conditions for the leader.

The table also identifies the leadership approach that is supposed to achieve high group performance in each of the eight situations. These linkages are shown in the bottom line of the table. A task-oriented leader is appropriate for very favorable as well as very unfavorable situations. For example, the LPC theory predicts that if leader-member relations are poor, the task is unstructured, and leader position power is low, a task-oriented leader will be effective. It also predicts that a task-oriented leader will be effective if leader-member relations are good, the task is structured, and leader position power is high. Finally, for situations of intermediate favorableness, the theory suggests that a person-oriented leader will be most likely to achieve high group performance.

Leader-Situation Match

What happens if a person-oriented leader faces a very favorable or very unfavorable situation, or if a task-oriented leader faces a situation of intermediate favorableness? Fiedler considers these leader-situation combinations to be "mismatches." Recall that a basic premise of his theory is that leadership behavior is a personality trait. Thus, the mismatched leader cannot readily adapt to the situation and achieve effectiveness. Fiedler contends that when a leader's style and the situation do not match, the only available course of action is to change the situation through "job engineering."[20]

For example, Fiedler suggests that if a person-oriented leader ends up in a situation that is very unfavorable, the manager should attempt to improve matters by spending more time with subordinates to improve leader-member relations and by laying down rules and procedures to provide more task structure. Fiedler and his associates have also developed a widely used training program for supervisors on how to assess situational favorableness and to change the situation, if necessary, to achieve a better match.[21] Weyerhaeuser and Boeing are among the firms that have experimented with Fiedler's training program.

Evaluation and Implications

The validity of Fiedler's LPC theory has been heatedly debated because of the inconsistency of the research results. Apparent shortcomings of the theory are that the LPC measure lacks validity, the theory is not always supported by research, and Fiedler's assumptions about the inflexibility of leader behavior are unrealistic.[22] The theory itself, however, does represent an important contribution because it returned the field to a study of the situation and explicitly considered the organizational context and its role in effective leadership.

THE PATH-GOAL THEORY OF LEADERSHIP

Another important contingency approach to leadership is the path-goal theory. Developed jointly by Martin Evans and Robert House, the path-goal theory focuses on the situation and leader behaviors rather than on fixed traits of the leader.[23] In contrast to the LPC theory, the path-goal theory suggests that leaders can readily adapt to different situations.

Basic Premises

The path-goal theory has its roots in the expectancy theory of motivation discussed in Chapter 5. Recall that expectancy theory says that a person's attitudes and behaviors can be predicted from the degree to which the person believes job performance will lead to various outcomes (expectancy) and the value of those outcomes (valences) to the individual. The ***path-goal theory of leadership*** argues that subordinates are motivated by their leader to the extent that the behaviors of that leader influence their expectancies. In other words, the leader affects subordinates' performance by clarifying the behaviors (paths) that will lead to desired rewards (goals). Ideally, of course, getting a reward in an organization depends on effective performance. Path-goal theory also suggests that a leader may behave in different ways in different situations. Finally, although not directly tied to path-goal theory, this chapter's GLOBAL ISSUES feature illustrates how subordinates expect different things from their leader in different cultures.

path-goal theory of leadership
Suggests that effective leaders clarify the paths (behaviors) that will lead to desired rewards (goals)

Leader Behaviors

As Figure 11.4 shows, path-goal theory identifies four kinds of leader behavior: directive, supportive, participative, and achievement-oriented. With directive leadership, the leader lets subordinates know what is expected of them, gives specific

MONKEY BUSINESS IMAGES/SHUTTERSTOCK.COM

The path-goal theory of leadership suggests that effective leader behavior clarifies the paths, or behaviors, that will lead subordinates to desired rewards (goals). This manager is explaining to his subordinate what needs to be done in order to earn a promotion and pay raise.

THE ROLE OF LEADERS ACROSS CULTURES

An important research study* asked workers in different countries if they agreed with this simple statement:

"It is important for a manager to have at hand precise answers to most of the questions that subordinates may raise about their work."

The percentage of workers from six different countries that strongly agreed with this statement are shown below. Clearly, leaders in Italy and Japan are expected to know all of the answers their subordinates may ask, while leaders in Sweden and the United States may more comfortably indicate that they don't know the answer to a question or that they need to check before answering.

*International Studies of Management and Organization, 13, 1–2 (Spring–Summer 1983).

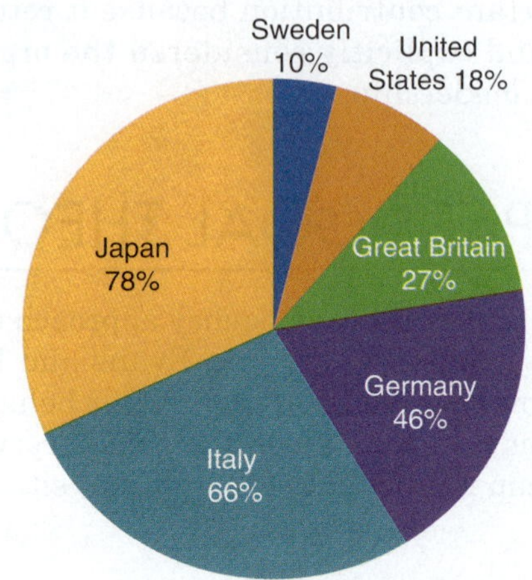

guidance as to how to accomplish tasks, schedules work to be done, and maintains definitive standards of performance for subordinates. A leader exhibiting supportive leadership is friendly and shows concern for subordinates' status, well-being, and needs. With participative leadership, the leader consults with subordinates about issues and takes their suggestions into account before making a decision. Finally, achievement-oriented leadership involves setting

Figure 11.4

The path-goal theory of leadership specifies four kinds of leader behavior: directive, supportive, participative, and achievement-oriented. Leaders are advised to vary their behaviors in response to such situational factors as personal characteristics of subordinates and environmental characteristics.

The Path-Goal Theory of Leadership

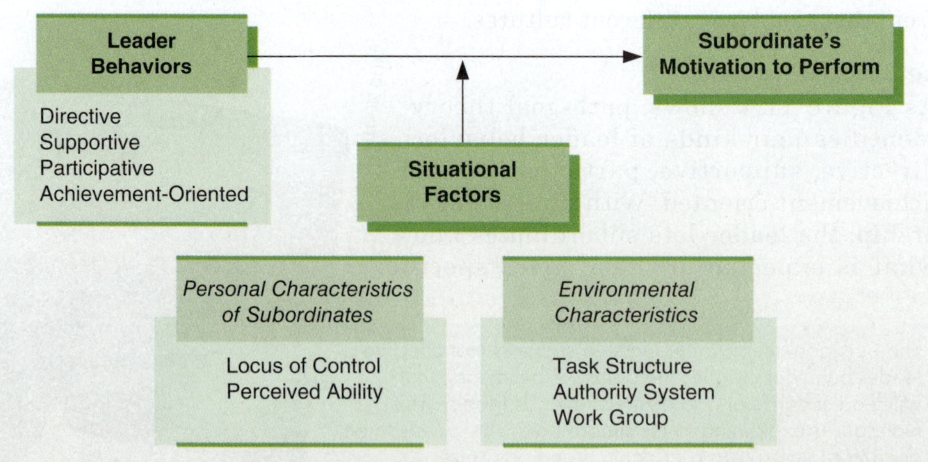

challenging goals, expecting subordinates to perform at their highest level, and showing strong confidence that subordinates will put forth effort and accomplish the goals. Unlike the LPC theory, path-goal theory assumes that leaders can change their behavior and exhibit any or all of these leadership styles. The theory also predicts that the appropriate combination of leadership styles depends on situational factors.

Situational Factors

The path-goal theory proposes two types of situational factors that influence how leader behavior relates to subordinate satisfaction: the personal characteristics of the subordinates and the characteristics of the environment (see Figure 11.4).

Two important personal characteristics of subordinates are locus of control and perceived ability. Locus of control, discussed in Chapter 3, refers to the extent to which individuals believe that what happens to them results from their own behavior or from external causes. Research indicates that individuals who attribute outcomes to their own behavior may be more satisfied with a participative leader (since they feel their own efforts can make a difference) whereas individuals who attribute outcomes to external causes may respond more favorably to a directive leader (since they think their own actions are of little consequence). Perceived ability pertains to how people view their own ability with respect to the task. Employees who rate their own ability relatively highly are less likely to feel a need for directive leadership (since they think they know how to do the job), whereas those who perceive their own ability to be relatively low may prefer directive leadership (since they think they need someone to show them how to do the job).

Important environmental characteristics are task structure, the formal authority system, and the primary work group. The path-goal theory proposes that leader behavior will motivate subordinates if it helps them cope with environmental uncertainty created by those characteristics. In some cases, however, certain forms of leadership will be redundant, decreasing subordinate satisfaction. For example, when task structure is high, directive leadership is less necessary and therefore less effective; similarly, if the work group gives the individual plenty of social support, a supportive leader will not be especially attractive. Thus, the extent to which leader behavior matches the people and environment in the situation is presumed to influence subordinates' motivation to perform.

Evaluation and Implications

The path-goal theory was designed to provide a general framework for understanding how leader behavior and situational factors influence subordinate attitudes and behaviors. The intention of the path-goal theorists was to stimulate research on the theory's major propositions, not to offer definitive answers. Researchers hoped that a more fully developed, formal theory of leadership would emerge from continued study. Further work actually has supported the theory's major predictions, but it has not validated the entire model. Moreover, many of the theory's predictions remain overly general and have not been fully refined and tested.

VROOM'S DECISION TREE APPROACH TO LEADERSHIP

Vroom's decision tree approach (to leadership)
Attempts to prescribe how much participation subordinates should be allowed in making decisions

The third major contemporary approach to leadership is ***Vroom's decision tree approach***. The earliest version of this model was proposed by Victor Vroom and Philip Yetton and later revised and expanded by Vroom and Arthur Jago.[24] Most recently, Vroom has developed yet another refinement of the original model.[25] Like the path-goal theory, this approach attempts to prescribe a leadership style appropriate to a given situation. It also assumes that the same leader may display different leadership styles. But Vroom's approach concerns itself with only a single aspect of leader behavior: subordinate participation in decision making.

Basic Premises

Vroom's decision tree approach assumes that the degree to which subordinates should be encouraged to participate in decision making depends on the characteristics of the situation. In other words, no one decision-making process is best for all situations. After evaluating a variety of problem attributes (characteristics of the problem or decision), the leader determines an appropriate decision style that specifies the amount of subordinate participation.

Vroom's current formulation suggests that managers should use one of two different decision trees.[26] To do so, the manager first assesses the situation in terms of several factors. This assessment involves determining whether the given factor is "high" or "low" for the decision that is to be made. For instance, the first factor is decision significance. If the decision is extremely important and may have a major impact on the organization (i.e., choosing a location for a new plant), its significance is high. But if the decision is routine and its consequences not terribly important (i.e., selecting a logo for the firm's softball team uniforms), its significance is low. This assessment guides the manager through the paths of the decision tree to a recommended course of action. One decision tree is to be used when the manager is primarily interested in making the fastest possible decision; the other is to be used when time is less critical and the manager wishes to help subordinates improve and develop their own decision-making skills.

The two decision trees are shown in Figures 11.5 and 11.6. The problem attributes (situational factors) are arranged along the top of the decision tree. To use the model, the decision maker starts at the left side of the diagram and assesses the first problem attribute (decision significance). The answer determines the path to the second node on the decision tree, where the next attribute (importance of commitment) is assessed. This process continues until a terminal node is reached. In this way, the manager identifies an effective decision-making style for the situation.

RIDO/SHUTTERSTOCK.COM

Vroom's decision tree approach to leadership helps leaders determine the optimal degree of participation they should allow their subordinates to have in making a decision. This leader is explaining a decision to her subordinates in order to solicit their suggestions.

Figure 11.5

Vroom's Time-Driven Decision Tree

This matrix is recommended for situations in which time is of the highest importance in making a decision. The matrix operates like a funnel. You start at the left with a specific decision problem in mind. The column headings denote situational factors that may or may not be present in that problem. You progress by selecting High or Low (H or L) for each relevant situational factor. Proceed down from the funnel, judging only those situational factors for which a judgment is called for, until you reach the recommended process.

	Decision Significance	Importance of Commitment	Leader Expertise	Likelihood of Commitment	Group Support	Group Expertise	Team Competence	
PROBLEM STATEMENT	H	H	H	H	–	–	–	Decide
				L	H	H	H	Delegate
							L	Consult (Group)
						L	–	
					L	–	–	
			L	H	H	H	H	Facilitate
							L	Consult (Individually)
						L	–	
					L	–	–	
				L	H	H	H	Facilitate
							L	Consult (Group)
						L	–	
					L	–	–	
		L	H	–	–	–	–	Decide
			L	–	H	H	H	Facilitate
							L	Consult (Individually)
						L	–	
					L	–	–	
	L	H	–	H	–	–	–	Decide
				L	–	–	H	Delegate
							L	Facilitate
		L	–	–	–	–	–	Decide

Source: Victor H. Vroom's Time-Driven Model from *A Model of Leadership Style*, copyright 1998.

Figure 11.6

This matrix is to be used when the leader is more interested in developing employees than in making the decision as quickly as possible. Just as with the time-driven tree shown in Figure 11.5, the leader assesses up to seven situational factors. These factors, in turn, funnel the leader to a recommended process for making the decision.

Vroom's Development-Driven Decision Tree

	Decision Significance	Importance of Commitment	Leader Expertise	Likelihood of Commitment	Group Support	Group Expertise	Team Competence	
PROBLEM STATEMENT	H	H	–	H	H	H	H	Decide
							L	Facilitate
						L	–	Consult (Group)
					L	–	–	
				L	H	H	H	Delegate
							L	Facilitate
						L	–	
					L	–	–	Consult (Group)
		L	–	–	H	H	H	Delegate
							L	Facilitate
						L	–	
					L	–	–	Consult (Group)
	L	H	–	H	–	–	–	Decide
				L	–	–	–	Delegate
		L	–	–	–	–	–	Decide

Source: Victor H. Vroom's Time-Driven Model from *A Model of Leadership Style*, copyright 1998.

The various decision styles reflected at the ends of the tree branches represent different levels of subordinate participation that the manager should attempt to adopt in a given situation. The five styles are defined as follows:

- *Decide:* The manager makes the decision alone and then announces or "sells" it to the group.
- *Delegate:* The manager allows the group to define for itself the exact nature and parameters of the problem and then develop a solution.
- *Consult (Individually):* The manager presents the program to group members individually, obtains their suggestions, and then makes the decision.
- *Consult (Group):* The manager presents the problem to group members at a meeting, gets their suggestions, and then makes the decision.
- *Facilitate:* The manager presents the problem to the group at a meeting, defines the problem and its boundaries, and then facilitates group member discussion as members make the decision.

Vroom's decision tree approach represents a very focused but quite complex perspective on leadership. To compensate for this difficulty, Vroom has developed elaborate expert system software to help managers assess a situation accurately and quickly and then make an appropriate decision regarding employee participation. Many firms, including Halliburton, Litton Industries, and Borland International, have provided their managers with training in how to use the various versions of this model.

Evaluation and Implications

Because Vroom's current approach is relatively new, it has not been fully scientifically tested. The original model and its subsequent refinement, however, attracted a great deal of attention and were generally supported by research.[27] For example, there is some support for the idea that individuals who make decisions consistent with the predictions of the model are more effective than those who make decisions inconsistent with it. The model therefore appears to be a tool that managers can apply with some confidence in deciding how much subordinates should participate in the decision-making process.

SUMMARY AND APPLICATIONS

Leadership is both a process and a property. Leadership as a process is the use of noncoercive influence to direct and coordinate the activities of group members to meet goals. As a property, leadership is the set of characteristics attributed to those who are perceived to use such influence successfully. Leadership and management are related but distinct phenomena.

Early leadership research primarily attempted to identify important traits and behaviors of leaders. The Michigan and Ohio State studies each identified two kinds of leader behavior, one focusing on job factors and the other on people factors. The Michigan studies viewed these behaviors as poi nts on a single continuum, whereas the Ohio State studies suggested that they were separate dimensions. The Leadership Grid further refined these concepts.

Newer situational theories of leadership attempt to identify appropriate leadership styles on the basis of the situation. The leadership continuum first proposed by Tannenbaum and Schmidt was the catalyst for these theories.

Fiedler's LPC theory states that leadership effectiveness depends on a match between the leader's style (viewed as a trait of the leader) and the favorableness of the situation. Situation favorableness, in turn, is determined by task structure, leader-member relations, and leader position power. Leader behavior is presumed to reflect a constant personality trait and therefore cannot easily be changed.

The path-goal theory focuses on appropriate leader behavior for various situations. The path-goal theory suggests that directive, supportive, participative, or achievement-oriented leader behavior may be appropriate, depending on the personal characteristics of subordinates and the characteristics of the environment. Unlike the LPC theory, this view presumes that leaders can alter their behavior to best fit the situation.

Vroom's decision tree approach suggests appropriate decision-making styles based on situation characteristics. This approach focuses on deciding how much subordinates should participate in the decision-making process. Managers assess situational attributes and follow a series of paths through a decision tree that subsequently prescribes for them how they should make a particular decision.

REAL WORLD RESPONSE

LEADERSHIP PINBALL

Many leaders report that playing racquetball, running marathons, practicing yoga, or just getting regular exercise helps them to recover from overwork. Hank Greenberg, Chairman and CEO of the financial services firm C.V. Starr, plays tennis for most of the year and skis in the winter months. "I'm addicted to exercise," he says, because it "unwinds me." PayPal cofounder Max Levchin prefers "80 or 90 hard miles on a road bike … starting early on Saturday mornings." Ninety–two-year-old Sumner Redstone, chairman of the parent company of CBS, Viacom, MTV, and Paramount Pictures, rises at 5 A.M. and hits both the exercise bike and the treadmill before the markets open. (Redstone also recommends "lots of fish and plenty of antioxidants.") Finally, Strauss Zelnick, CEO and chairman of Take-Two Interactive Software, is *really* serious about exercise:

> I try to book my exercise like a meeting and try hard never to cancel it.… Generally I try to do an exercise class at the gym once a week; I train for an hour with a trainer once or twice a week; I cycle with a group of friends for an hour once to three times a week, and I lift weights with a friend or colleague twice or three times a week.

Effective leaders also take control of information flow—which means managing it, not reducing the flow until it's as close to a trickle as they can get it. Like most executives, for example, Mayer can't get by without multiple sources of information: "I always have my laptop with me," she reports, and "I adore my cell phone." Starbucks chairman/CEO Howard Schultz receives a morning voicemail summarizing the previous day's sales results and reads three newspapers a day. Mayer watches the news all day, and Bill Gross, a securities portfolio manager, keeps an eye on six monitors displaying real-time investment data.

On the other hand, Gross stands on his head to force himself to take a break from communicating. When he's upright again, he tries to find time to concentrate. "Eliminating the noise," he says, "is critical.… I only pick up the phone three or four times a day.… I don't want to be connected—I want to be disconnected." Ghosn, whose schedule requires weekly intercontinental travel, uses bilingual assistants to screen and translate information—one assistant for information from Europe (where Renault is), one for information from Japan (where Nissan is), and one for information from the United States (where Ghosn often has to be when he doesn't have to be in Europe or Japan). Clothing designer Vera Wang also uses an assistant to filter information. "The barrage of calls is so enormous," she says, "that if I just answered calls I'd do nothing else.… If I were to go near email, there'd be even more obligations, and I'd be in [a mental hospital] with a white jacket on."

(*Continued*)

Not surprisingly, Microsoft founder Bill Gates integrates the role of his assistant into a high-tech information-organizing system:

> On my desk I have three screens, synchronized to form a single desktop. I can drag items from one screen to the next. Once you have that large display area, you'll never go back, because it has a direct impact on productivity.
>
> The screen on the left has my list of emails. On the center screen is usually the specific email I'm reading and responding to. And my browser is on the right-hand screen. This setup gives me the ability to glance and see what new has come in while I'm working on something and to bring up a link that's related to an email and look at it while the email is still in front of me.
>
> At Microsoft, email is the medium of choice.... I get about 100 emails a day. We apply filtering to keep it to that level. Email comes straight to me from anyone I've ever corresponded with, anyone from Microsoft, Intel, HP, and all the other partner companies, and anyone I know. And I always see a write-up from my assistant of any other email, from companies that aren't on my permission list or individuals I don't know....
>
> We're at the point now where the challenge isn't how to communicate effectively with email—it's ensuring that you spend your time on the email that matters most. I use tools like "in-box rules" and search folders to mark and group messages based on their content and importance.

DISCUSSION QUESTIONS

1. How would you define "leadership"? Compare and contrast your definition with the one given in this chapter.
2. Cite examples of managers who are not leaders and of leaders who are not managers. What makes them one and not the other? Also, cite examples of both formal and informal leaders.
3. What traits do you think characterize successful leaders? Do you think the trait approach has validity?
4. Recent evidence suggests that successful managers (defined by organizational rank and salary) may indeed have some of the same traits originally ascribed to effective leaders (such as an attractive appearance and relative height). How might this finding be explained?
5. What other forms of leader behavior besides those cited in the chapter can you identify?
6. Critique Fiedler's LPC theory. Are other elements of the situation important? Do you think Fiedler's assertion about the inflexibility of leader behavior makes sense? Why or why not?
7. Do you agree or disagree with Fiedler's assertion that leadership motivation is basically a personality trait? Why?
8. Compare and contrast the LPC and path-goal theories of leadership. What are the strengths and weaknesses of each?
9. Of the three major leadership theories—the LPC theory, the path-goal theory, and Vroom's decision tree approach—which is the most comprehensive? Which is the narrowest? Which has the most practical value?
10. How realistic do you think it is for managers to attempt to use Vroom's decision tree approach as prescribed? Explain.

DEVELOP YOUR SKILLS EXERCISE

What Is Your Leadership Potential?

For each pair of statements below, distribute 5 points based on how characteristic each statement is of you. If the first statement is totally like you and the second is not like you at all, give 5 points to the first and 0 to the second. If it is the opposite, use 0 and 5. If the statement is usually like you, then the distribution can be 4 and 1, or 1 and 4 if it is not usually like you. If both statements tend to be like you, the distribution should be 3 and 2, or 2 and 3. Remember, the combined score for each pair of statements must equal 5. There are no right or wrong answers. Be honest in answering the questions, so that you can better understand yourself and your behavior as it relates to leadership.

Here are the possible scoring distributions for each pair of statements:

0–5 or 5–0	One of the statements is totally like you; the other is not like you at all.
1–4 or 4–1	One statement is usually like you; the other is not.
3–2 or 2–3	Both statements are like you, although one is slightly more like you.

1. ____ I'm interested in and willing to take charge of a group.
   ____ I want someone else to be in charge of the group.
2. ____ When I'm not in charge, I'm willing to give input to the leader to improve performance.
   ____ When I'm not in charge, I do things the leader's way, rather than offer my suggestions.
3. ____ I'm interested in and willing to get people to listen to my suggestions and to implement them.
   ____ I'm not interested in influencing other people.
4. ____ When I'm in charge, I want to share management responsibilities with group members.
   ____ When I'm in charge, I want to perform the management functions for the group.
5. ____ I want to have clear goals and to develop and implement plans to achieve them.
   ____ I like to have very general goals and take things as they come.
6. ____ I like to change the way my job is done, and to learn and do new things.
   ____ I like stability, or to do my job in the same way; I don't like learning and doing new things.
7. ____ I enjoy working with people and helping them succeed.
   ____ I don't really like working with people and helping them succeed.

Scoring: To calculate your leadership potential score, add up your scores (0 to 5) for the first statements in each pair; ignore the numbers for the second statements. Your total should be between 0 and 35. Place your score on this continuum:

0———5———10———15———20———25———30———35

Low leadership potential — High leadership potential

Interpretation: Generally, the higher your score, the greater your potential to be an effective leader. Because the key to leadership success is not simply potential, but also persistence and hard work, you can develop your leadership ability by applying the principles and theories you learn from studying this book to your personal and professional lives. One good place to start is to look at the effective leadership statements to which you gave a low score and practice engaging in those behaviors.

Source: Adapted from Lussier, R. N., & Achua, C. F. (2001). *Leadership: Theory, Application and Skill Development.* Cincinnati, OH: South-Western College Publishing. © 2001 Cengage Learning.

GROUP EXERCISE

Managers and Leaders

This exercise offers you an opportunity to compare your assumptions and perspectives on managers and leaders with the assumptions and perspectives of others in your class.

Your Assignment:

1. Make a list of 10 characteristics of successful managers and a list of 10 different characteristics of successful leaders.
2. Share your lists with other students in small groups and discuss the following:
   (A). Which manager characteristics, if any, appear on different students' lists?
   (B). Which leader characteristics, if any, appear on different students' lists?
   (C). Which characteristics, if any, do students put on both their manager list and their leader list?
3. Have your group compile one list of 10 characteristics of managers and one list of 10 characteristics of leaders.
4. Share all group lists with the entire class, and see if the class can agree on a final list for managers and a final list for leaders. What, if anything, do the final two lists have in common? Do any characteristics appear on both the manager list and the leader list?

VIDEO EXERCISE

City of Greensburg, Kansas: Leadership

After working in Oklahoma City as a parks director, Steve Hewitt wanted to run an entire town. A smaller community seemed the perfect place to get hands-on leadership experience before tackling a bigger city, so Hewitt took the city administrator position in his hometown, Kansas (population: 1,500). But on May 4, 2007, while staring into a dark sky from the tattered remains of his kitchen, Hewitt realized that he got more than he'd bargained for—a tornado had struck the town.

The morning after the powerful EF-5 tornado whipped through the area, everyone knew Greensburg was gone—perhaps forever. But in a subsequent press conference, Mayor Lonnie McCollum announced that the town would rebuild as a model green community, and he convinced the city it needed a full-time administrator to make big changes. Hewitt was the man for the job.

Intense and fast-talking, Steve Hewitt provided the perfect complement to McCollum's humble, measured demeanor. Daniel Wallach, executive director of Greensburg GreenTown, describes the young leader as "the kind of guy you want taking the last shot in a basketball game." Indeed, Hewitt had the ambition and confidence necessary to get the community back on its feet. While Mayor McCollum offered a vision for rebuilding Greensburg, it is Hewitt who stepped up to ensure that the vision became a reality.

Hewitt quickly went to work on a plan for rebuilding. He took a crash course on interpersonal influence tactics, increased his staff from twenty to thirty-five people, and established full-time fire, planning, and community development departments. To keep Greensburg on everyone's radar, Hewitt spent hours each week conducting interviews with news media. The press attention kept Greensburg on the map even though it lay in ruins.

City workers give Hewitt high marks for his handling of the crisis. "He has been very open as far as information," said recovery coordinator Kim Alderfer. "He's very good about delegating authority. He gives you the authority to do your job. He doesn't have time to micromanage."

Like most good leaders, Hewitt hasn't been afraid to ruffle feathers as needed. When certain residents opposed the strict environmental building codes, Hewitt found the courage and moral leadership, to say, "No. You're going to build it right and you're going to do it to code." Asked about his management of conflict in the middle of a crisis, Hewitt answered, "I'm dumb enough not to care what people say, and young enough to have the energy to get through it."

Discussion Questions

1. Where does Hewitt's leadership fall on the Managerial Grid discussed in the chapter? Explain.
2. Would deficiencies or shortcomings would you identify in Hewitt's leadership?
3. Is Hewitt's leadership style appropriate for Greensburg's situation? Explain your answer using insights drawn from Fiedler's LPC theory.

VIDEO CASE

Now What?

PERCOM/SHUTTERSTOCK.COM

Imagine receiving a performance review from your boss about your leadership capabilities that is less favorable than you expected. *What do you say or do?* Go to this chapter's "Now What?" video, watch the challenge video, and choose a response. Be sure to also view the outcomes of the two responses you didn't choose.

Discussion Questions

1. Is Alex an effective manager? Is he an effective leader? Justify your answers for each question.
2. Does Amy demonstrate effective leadership in the challenge video? In what way is she an effective or ineffective leader?
3. In addition to the solution you think is best, what would you do as either Amy or Alex to demonstrate more effective leadership when handling this situation?

ENDNOTES

[1]Colvin, G. (2006, February 6). Catch a Rising Star. *Fortune*. 10, 2015 Available at: http://archive.fortune.com/magazines/fortune/fortune_archive/2006/02/06/toc.html; Kneale, K. (2009, April 17). Stress Management for the CEO. Available at: http://www.forbes.com/2009/04/16/ceo-network-management-leadership-stress.html; Berfield, S. (2009, July 24). The Real Effects of Workplace Anxiety. Business Week. Available at: http://www.bloomberg.com/bw/stories/2009-07-24/the-real-effects-of-workplace-anxietybusinessweek-business-news-stock-market-and-financial-advice. ess Week; Useem, J. (2006, March 15). Making Your Work Work for You. Available at: http://archive.fortune.com/magazines/fortune/fortune_archive/2006/03/20/8371789/index.htm.

[2]Stogdill, R. M. (1974). *Handbook of Leadership*. New York: Free Press. See also Bass, B., & Bass, R. (2008). *Handbook of Leadership: Theory, Research, and Application* (4th ed.). Riverside, NJ: Free Press; Tichy, N., & Bennis, W. (2007). *Judgment: How Winning Leaders Make Great Calls*. New York: Portfolio Press; see also Vinchur, A. J., & Koppes, L. L. (2010) A Historical Survey of Research and Practice in Industrial and Organizational Psychology. In *Handbook of Industrial and Organizational Psychology*, ed. S. Zedeck (pp. 3–36). Washington, DC: American Psychological Association.

[3]Yukl, G., & Van Fleet, D. D. (1992). Theory and Research on Leadership in Organizations. In *Handbook of Industrial and Organizational Psychology*, eds. M. D. Dunnette & L. M. Hough (Vol. 3, pp. 148–197). Palo Alto, CA: Consulting Psychologists Press. See also Avolio, B. J., Walumbwa, F. O., & Weber, T. J. (2009). Leadership: Current Theories, Research, and Future Decisions. In *Annual Review of Psychology 2009*, eds. S. T. Fiske, D. L. Schacter, & R. J. Sternberg (pp. 421–450). Palo Alto, CA: Annual Reviews.

[4]Jago, A. G. (1982, March). Leadership: Perspectives in Theory and Research, *Management Science*, 315–336. See also Barling, J., Christie, A., & Hoption, C. Leadership. In *Handbook of Industrial and Organizational Psychology*, ed. S. Zedeck (pp. 183–240). Washington, DC: American Psychological Association.

[5]Sorcher, M., & Brant, J. (2002, February). Are You Picking the Right Leaders? *Harvard Business Review*, 78–85.

[6]Kotter, J. P. (1990, May–June). What Leaders Really Do. *Harvard Business Review*, 103–111. See also Zaleznik, A. (1992, March–April). Managers and Leaders: Are They Different? *Harvard Business Review*, 126–135; and Kotter, J. (2001, December). What Leaders Really Do. *Harvard Business Review*, 85–94.

[7]Heifetz, R., & Linsky, M. (2002, June). A Survival Guide for Leaders. *Harvard Business Review*, 65–74.

[8]Reichheld, F. (2001, July–August). Lead for Loyalty. *Harvard Business Review*, 76–83.

[9]Van Fleet, D. D., & Yukl, G. A. (1986). A Century of Leadership Research. In *Papers Dedicated to the Development of Modern Management*, eds. D. A. Wren & J. A. Pearce II (pp. 12–23). Chicago: Academy of Management.

[10]Kirkpatrick, S. A., & Locke, E. A. (1991, May). Leadership: Do Traits Matter? *Academy of Management Executive*, 48–60; see also Sternberg, R. J. (1997). Managerial Intelligence: Why IQ Isn't Enough. *Journal of Management*, *23*(3), 475–493.

[11]Podsakoff, P. M., MacKenzie, S. B., Ahearne, M., & Bommer, W. H. (1995). Searching for a Needle in a Haystack: Trying to Identify the Illusive Moderators of Leadership Behaviors, *Journal of Management*, *21*(3), 422–470.

[12]Likert, R. (1961). *New Patterns of Management*. New York: McGraw-Hill.

[13]Fleishman, E. A., Harris, E. F., & Burtt, H. E. (1955). *Leadership and Supervision in Industry*. Columbus: Bureau of Educational Research, Ohio State University.

[14]Fleishman, E. A. (1973). Twenty Years of Consideration and Structure. In *Current Developments in the Study of Leadership*, eds. E. A. Fleishman & J. G. Hunt (pp. 1–40). Carbondale, IL: Southern Illinois University Press.

[15]Fleishman, E. A., Harris, E. F., & Burtt, H. E. (1955). *Leadership and Supervision in Industry*. Columbus: Bureau of Educational Research, Ohio State University.

[16]For a recent update, see Judge, T., Piccolo, R., & Ilies, R. (2004). The Forgotten Ones? The Validity of Consideration and Initiating Structure in Leadership Research. *Journal of Applied Psychology*, *89*(1), 36–51.

[17]Blake, R. R., & Mouton, J. S. (1964). *The Managerial Grid*. Houston, TX: Gulf Publishing; Blake, R. R., & Mouton, J. S. (1981). *The Versatile Manager: A Grid Profile* Homewood, IL: Dow Jones-Irwin.

[18]Tannenbaum, R., & Schmidt, W. H. (1958, March–April). How to Choose a Leadership Pattern. *Harvard Business Review*, 95–101.

[19]Fiedler, F. F. (1967). *A Theory of Leadership Effectiveness*. New York: McGraw-Hill. Reprinted by permission of the author.

[20]Fiedler, F. F. (1965, September–October). Engineering the Job to Fit the Manager. *Harvard Business Review*, 115–122.

[21]Fiedler, F. F., Chemers, M. M., & Mahar, L. (1976). *Improving Leadership Effectiveness: The Leader Match Concept*. New York: John Wiley and Sons.

[22]Schriesheim, C. A., Tepper, B. J., & Tetrault, L. A. (1994). Least Preferred Co-Worker Score, Situational Control, and Leadership Effectiveness: A Meta-Analysis of Contingency Model Performance Predictions. *Journal of Applied Psychology*, *79*(4), 561–573.

[23]Evans, M. G. (1970, May). The Effects of Supervisory Behavior on the Path-Goal Relationship, *Organizational Behavior and Human Performance*, 277–298; House, R. J. (1971, September). A Path-Goal Theory of Leadership Effectiveness. *Administrative Science Quarterly*, 321–339; House, R. J., & Mitchell, T. R. (1974, Autumn). Path-Goal Theory of Leadership. *Journal of Contemporary Business*, 81–98.

[24]Vroom, V. H., & Yetton, P. H. (1973). *Leadership and Decision Making*. Pittsburgh, PA: University of Pittsburgh Press; Vroom, V. H., & Jago, A. G. (1988). *The New Leadership*. Englewood Cliffs, NJ: Prentice Hall.

[25]Vroom, V. H. (2000, Spring). Leadership and the Decision-Making Process. *Organizational Dynamics*, *28*(4), 82–94.

[26]Vroom, V. H., & Jago, A. G. (1988). *The New Leadership*. Englewood Cliffs, NJ: Prentice Hall.

[27]Heilman, M. E., Hornstein, H. A., Cage, J. H., & Herschlag, J. K. (1984, February). Reaction to Prescribed Leader Behavior as a Function of Role Perspective: The Case of the Vroom-Yetton Model. *Journal of Applied Psychology*, 50–60; Field, R. H. G. (1982, February). A Test of the Vroom-Yetton Normative Model of Leadership. *Journal of Applied Psychology*, *67*(5), 523–532.

LOSKUTNIKOV/SHUTTERSTOCK.COM

CHAPTER

12 CONTEMPORARY VIEWS OF LEADERSHIP IN ORGANIZATIONS

CHAPTER OUTLINE

LEARNING OUTCOMES

After studying this chapter, you should be able to:

1. Identify and describe contemporary situational theories of leadership.
2. Discuss leadership through the eyes of followers.
3. Identify and describe alternatives to leadership.
4. Describe the changing nature of leadership and emerging leadership issues.

LOSKUTNIKOV/SHUTTERSTOCK.COM

REAL WORLD CHALLENGE

ETHICAL LEADERSHIP AT COSTCO[1]

Warehouse retailer Costco has over $50 billion in sales from its more than 500 outlets in several countries, and employs more than 120,000 workers. Costco competes by giving customers the best value at the best price. The maximum mark-up at Costco is 15 percent, which means that customers never pay more than 15 percent over what Costco paid for the item. Costco's cofounder and former CEO, Jim Sinegal, believed in treating employees with respect. He also knew that acting ethically and never losing sight of the purpose of the business was critical to his leading Costco into the future.

At the core of Sinegal's leadership philosophy was the idea that great businesses can be made and sustained on the back of a set of core values. As Costco continues to grow and become even more multinational, Sinegal still plays a role at Costco and wants to maintain the central role of ethics in the company. However, Wall Street analysts have long criticized Sinegal for paying high wages and keeping employees around too long, which increases salary and benefits costs.

Sinegal knows that good, happy employees are more productive and believes that they are the backbone of Costco's success. Sinegal attributes Costco's success to a team effort, not the work of any individual. Assume that Sinegal asks you for advice on how to effectively lead Costco into the future. After reading this chapter, you should have some good ideas.

A KATZ/SHUTTERSTOCK.COM

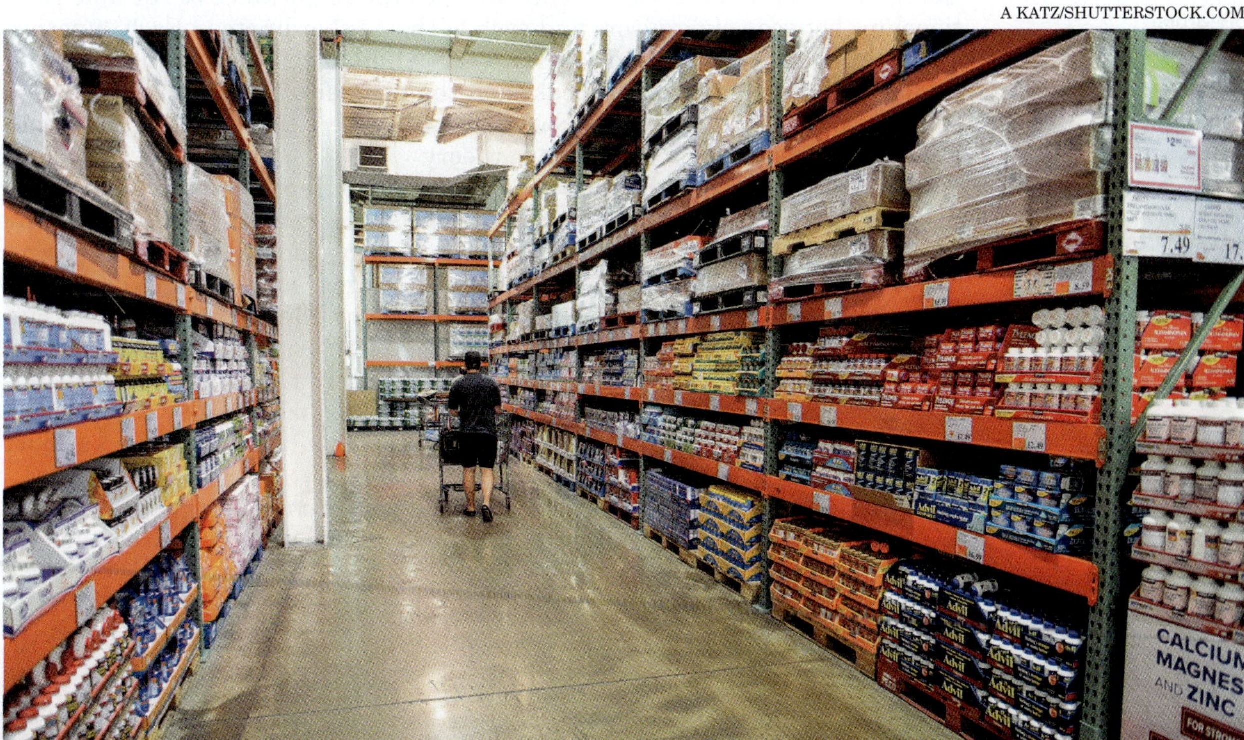

The three major situational theories of leadership discussed in Chapter 11 altered everyone's thinking about leadership. No longer did people feel compelled to search for the one best way to lead. Nor did they continue to seek universal leadership prescriptions or relationships. Instead, both researchers and practicing managers turned their attention to a variety of new approaches to leadership. These new approaches, as well as other current emerging leadership issues, are the subject of this chapter. We first describe two relatively new situational theories, as well as recent refinements to the earlier theories. We then examine leadership through the eyes of followers. Recent thinking regarding potential alternatives to traditional leadership are then explored. Next we describe the changing nature of leadership. We conclude this chapter with a discussion of several emerging issues in leadership.

leader-member exchange model (LMX) (of leadership)
Stresses the importance of variable relationships between supervisors and each of their subordinates

in-group
Often receives special duties requiring more responsibility and autonomy; they may also receive special privileges, such as more discretion about work schedules

out-group
Receive less of the supervisor's time and attention and are likely to be assigned the more mundane tasks the group must perform and not be "in the loop" when information is being shared

CONTEMPORARY SITUATIONAL THEORIES

The LPC theory, the path-goal theory, and Vroom's decision tree approach together redirected the study of leadership. Not surprisingly, then, other situational theories have also been developed. Moreover, there continue to be changes and refinements to the original situational models.

The Leader-Member Exchange Model

The ***leader-member exchange model (LMX)*** of leadership, conceived by George Graen and Fred Dansereau, stresses the importance of variable relationships between supervisors and each of their subordinates.[2] Each superior-subordinate pair is referred to as a "vertical dyad." The model differs from earlier approaches in that it focuses on the differential relationship leaders often establish with different subordinates. Figure 12.1 shows the basic concepts of the leader-member exchange theory.

The model suggests that supervisors establish a special relationship with a small number of trusted subordinates referred to as the "in-group." The ***in-group*** often receives special duties requiring more responsibility and autonomy; they may also receive special privileges, such as more discretion about work schedules. Members of the in-group are also likely to be privy to sensitive information and are likely to know about upcoming events before others. They may also receive more rewards and generally stronger support from the leader.

Subordinates who are not a part of this group are called the ***out-group***, and they receive less of

OCSKAY MARK/SHUTTERSTOCK.COM

One of the basic premises of the leader-member exchange model (LMX) of leadership is that supervisors tend to develop individual relationships with each of their subordinates. This supervisor is making a point of explaining things in a bit more detail to one of her subordinates while the rest of the group watches on. He may be a member of the in-group that gets special attention from the leader.

Figure 12.1

The Leader-Member Exchange (LMX) Model

The LMX model suggests that leaders form unique independent relationships with each of their subordinates. As illustrated here, a key factor in the nature of this relationship is whether the individual subordinate is in the leader's out-group or in-group.

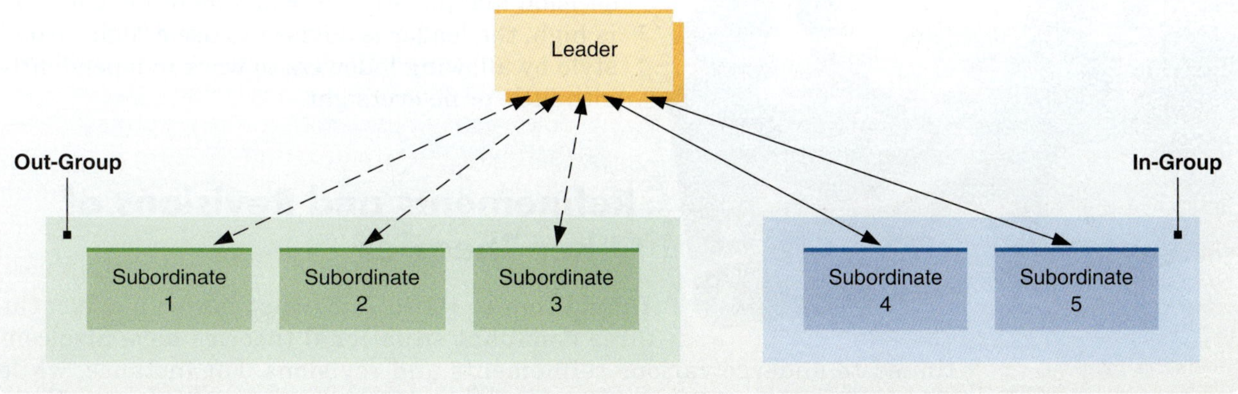

the supervisor's time and attention. Members of the out-group are likely to be assigned the more mundane tasks the group must perform and not be "in the loop" insofar as information is being shared. They may also receive fewer rewards and overall weaker support from the leader.

Note in the figure that the leader has a dyadic, or one-to-one, relationship with each of the five subordinates. Early in his or her interaction with a given subordinate, the supervisor initiates either an in-group or out-group relationship. It is not clear how a leader selects members of the in-group, but the decision may be based on personal compatibility and subordinates' competence. Research has confirmed the existence of ingroups and out-groups. In addition, studies generally have found that in-group members tend to have a higher level of performance and satisfaction than out-group members.[3]

The Hersey and Blanchard Model

Another recent situational perspective, especially popular among practicing managers, is the Hersey and Blanchard model. Like the leadership grid discussed in the previous chapter, this model was also developed as a consulting tool. The ***Hersey and Blanchard model*** is based on the notion that appropriate leader behavior depends on the "readiness" of the leader's followers.[4] In this instance, readiness refers to the subordinate's degree of motivation, competence, experience, and interest in accepting responsibility. Figure 12.2 shows the basic model.

Hersey and Blanchard model
Based on the premise that appropriate leader behavior depends on the "readiness" of the leader's followers (i.e., the subordinate's degree of motivation, competence, experience, and interest in accepting responsibility)

The figure suggests that as the readiness of followers improves, the leader's basic style should also change. When subordinate readiness is low, for example, the leader should rely on a "telling" style by providing direction and defining roles. When low to moderate readiness exists, the leader should use a "selling" style by offering direction and role definition accompanied by explanation and information. In a case of moderate to high follower readiness, the leader should use a "participating" style, allowing followers to share in

GPOINTSTUDIO/SHUTTERSTOCK.COM

The Hersey and Blanchard model of leadership suggests that appropriate leader behavior depends on the "readiness" of the leader's followers. This leader is explaining some things in a very casual and informal manner, perhaps indicating that the group "readiness" is high.

decision making. Finally, when follower readiness is high, the leader is advised to use a "delegating" style by allowing followers to work independently with little or no oversight.

Refinements and Revisions of Other Theories

In addition to these somewhat newer models, the three dominant situational theories have also continued to undergo various refinements and revisions. For instance, while the version of the LPC theory presented in Chapter 11 is still the dominant model, researchers have made several attempts to improve its validity. Fiedler added the concept of stress as a major element of situational favorableness. He also argued that the leader's intelligence and experience play a major role in enabling her or him to cope with various levels of stress that characterize any particular situation.[5]

Figure 12.2

The Hersey and Blanchard theory suggests that leader behaviors should vary in response to the readiness of followers. This figure shows the nature of this variation. The curved line suggests that a leader's relationship behavior should start low, gradually increase, but then decrease again as follower readiness increases. But the leader's task behavior, shown by the straight line, should start high when followers lack readiness and then continuously diminish as they gain readiness.

The Hersey and Blanchard Theory of Leadership

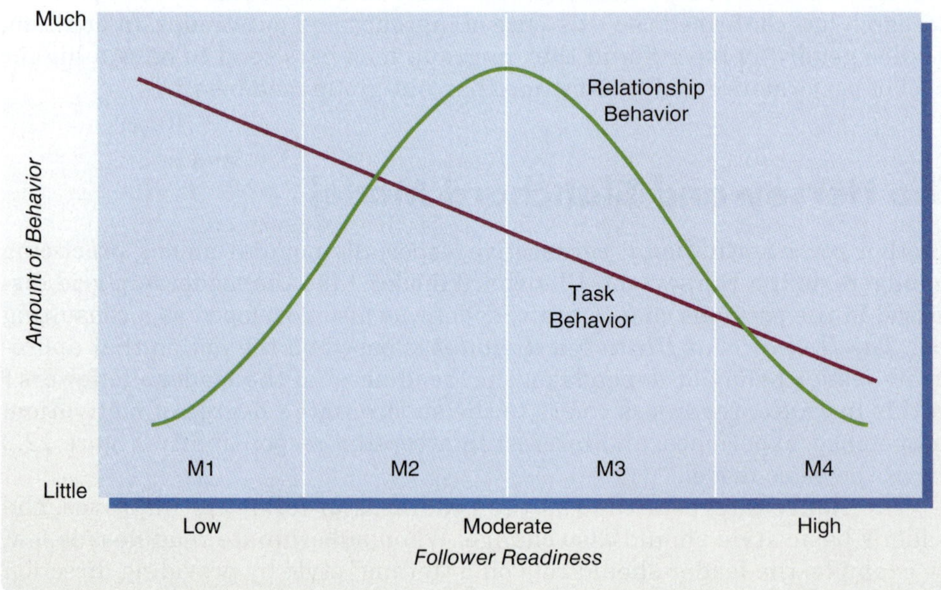

Sources: The Situational Leadership® Model is the registered trademark of the Center for Leadership Studies, Escondido, CA. Excerpt from Hersey, P., & Blanshard, K. H. (1977). *Management of Organizational Behavior: Utilizing Human Resources* (3rd ed., p. 165). Englewood Cliffs, NJ: Prentice-Hall.

The path-goal theory has also undergone major refinements over the years. Its original formulation included only two forms of leader behavior. A third was later added and then, most recently, the theory evolved to include the four forms of leader behavior discussed in Chapter 11. While there has been relatively little research on this theory in recent years, its intuitive logic and general research support make it highly likely that it will again one day emerge as a popular topic for research.

Finally, Vroom's decision tree approach also continues to evolve. The version presented in Chapter 11 was the third published version. Moreover, Vroom and his associates have continued to develop training and assessment materials to better enable managers to understand their own "natural" decision-making styles. In addition, there are software versions of the various models that now can quickly help managers determine the optimal level of participation in any given situation.

LEADERSHIP THROUGH THE EYES OF FOLLOWERS

Another perspective that has been adopted by some leadership experts focuses on how leaders are seen through the eyes of followers. That is, in what ways and to what extent is it important that followers and other observers attribute leadership to others? The three primary approaches to leadership through the eyes of followers are transformational leadership, charismatic leadership, and attributions of leadership.

Transformational Leadership

Transformational leadership focuses on the basic distinction between leading for change and leading for stability.[6] According to this viewpoint, much of what a leader does occurs in the course of normal, routine, work-related transactions—assigning work, evaluating performance, making decisions, and so forth. Occasionally, however, the leader has to initiate and manage major change, such as managing a merger, creating a workgroup, or defining the organization's culture. The first set of issues involves transactional leadership, whereas the second entails transformational leadership.[7]

Recall from Chapter 11 the distinction between management and leadership. ***Transactional leadership*** is essentially the same as management in that it involves routine, regimented activities. Closer to the general notion of leadership, however, is ***transformational leadership***, the set of abilities that allows the leader to recognize the need for change, to create a vision to guide that change, and to execute the change effectively. Only a leader with tremendous influence can hope to perform these functions successfully. Some experts believe that change is such a vital organizational function that even successful firms need to change regularly to avoid complacency and stagnation; accordingly, leadership for change is also important.[8]

transactional leadership
Leadership focused on routine, regimented activities

transformational leadership
The set of abilities that allows the leader to recognize the need for change, to create a vision to guide that change, and to execute the change effectively

Another hallmark of effective leadership is the ability to see which approach is needed. Following the death of legendary Apple co-founder and CEO Steve Jobs, Apple executive Tim Cook was elevated to the position of CEO.

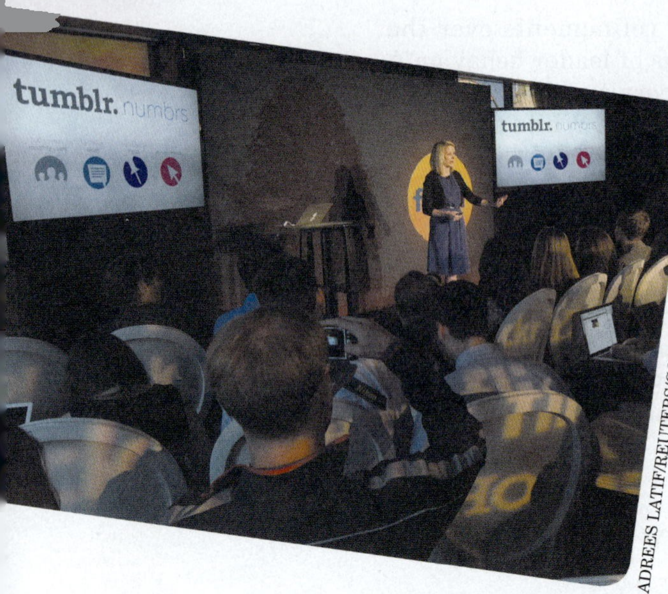

ADREES LATIF/REUTERS/CORBIS

When Marissa Mayer was lured away from Google to become CEO at Yahoo! she was hailed as a transformational leader who would, hopefully, return the firm to its earlier glory days. Thus far the results have been mixed, but she has initiated major changes at Yahoo! and restored the firm to profitability.

At the time Apple was raking in enormous profits, was becoming the most valuable company in the world, and had a strong and robust pipeline of new products and technologies in development. Hence, Cook saw little need for dramatic change. While he has changed a few things, such as paying shareholder dividends for the first time in years, Apple today is essentially the same as it was during Jobs' tenure. On the other hand, when Marissa Mayer was recruited from Google to lead Yahoo!, the need for dramatic change was obvious. While Yahoo! had once been as successful as other technology firms like Google, Microsoft, Apple, and Facebook, it was falling behind these and other high-tech giants and headed toward irrelevance. Consequently, she embarked on a series of major strategic initiatives in an attempt to revitalize the firm.

Leaders may also find it necessary to transition from either transformational or transactional leadership to the other. For instance, when Alan Mulally assumed the leadership role at Ford Motor, the firm was in desperate straits. Its production facilities were outmoded, its costs were too high, and its product line was stale and had a reputation for poor quality. Using dramatic transformational leadership, Mulally managed to completely overhaul the firm, revitalizing it along every major dimension and transforming it into the healthiest of the Big Three U.S. automakers. Indeed, while General Motors and Chrysler needed federal bailout funds during the recent recession, Ford was able to maintain operations on its own without government assistance and quickly became very profitable. After the transformation was complete, Mulally transitioned to a transactional role and continued to lead the firm toward higher revenues, market share, and profits.[9] Our *Case Study* examines another transformational leadership example.

Charismatic Leadership

Perspectives based on charismatic leadership, like the trait concepts discussed in Chapter 11, assume that charisma is an individual characteristic of the leader. ***Charisma*** is a form of interpersonal attraction that inspires support and acceptance. The *Understand Yourself* feature can give you insights into how much charisma you may have.

charisma
A form of interpersonal attraction that inspires support and acceptance

charismatic leadership
A type of influence based on the leader's personal charisma

Charismatic leadership is accordingly a type of influence based on the leader's personal charisma. All else being equal, someone with charisma is more likely to be able to influence others than someone without charisma. For example, a highly charismatic supervisor will be more successful in influencing subordinate behavior than a supervisor who lacks charisma. Thus, influence is again a fundamental element of this perspective.[10]

CASE STUDY Leading a Police Force Transformation

When Melvin Wearing obtained the Chief of Police in New Haven, Connecticut, the position he had been dreaming of for 28 years, he stepped into a huge challenge. His predecessor had undermined the department's credibility. Morale was terrible, and communication between the chief's office and the officers was often through union grievances.

Wearing had previously been an assistant chief, and the other officers respected him and called him "compassionate," "humanistic," and "a source of inspiration and pride." On his first day, Wearing visited each of the day's four line-ups (the roll call of officers that begins each shift), wearing his dress blues for the occasion. He wanted to show his pride in police work and support of the officers. He also clearly communicated to his officers that he did not want them to even *think* about messing around. This was not just a matter of restoring the force's credibility; as the department's first African American chief, he knew that he would be under special scrutiny. He quickly moved to upgrade the department's technology, installed air conditioning and laptops in cruisers, and upgraded office equipment.

Wearing also raised standards in the training academy and increased the department's diversity. By 2002, women and minorities made up 51 percent of New Haven's sworn personnel, up from 24 percent in 1990. In 1997, New Haven logged 13,950 major crimes; in 2001, the city had only 9,322. The department has even earned four national and international awards for community policing. Chief Wearing understands that he has to keep making an impact: "The real challenge for me is to sustain this over a long period of time."[11]

Questions:

1. Explain how Chief Wearing can exhibit a transformational leadership style in his role as police chief.
2. Describe the environment facing Chief Wearing in terms of leader-member relations, task structure, and position power. Using Fiedler's model, what leadership style do you think is most appropriate given the situation you just described? Does this style match Chief Wearing's?
3. If you were Chief Wearing, how might you use the information you learned in this chapter to enhance the diversity of the police force?

Robert House first proposed a theory of charismatic leadership based on research findings from a variety of social science disciplines.[12] His theory suggests that charismatic leaders are likely to have a lot of self-confidence, firm confidence in their beliefs and ideals, and a strong need to influence people. They also tend to communicate high expectations about follower performance and to express confidence in their followers. Herb Kelleher, legendary CEO of Southwest Airlines (now retired), is an excellent example of a charismatic leader. Kelleher skillfully blended a unique combination of executive skill, honesty, and playfulness. These qualities attracted a group of followers at Southwest who were willing to follow his lead without question and to dedicate themselves to carrying out his decisions and policies with unceasing passion.[13]

Other individuals who are or were seen as charismatic leaders include Mary Kay Ash, Steve Jobs, Martin Luther King, Jr., Pope John Paul II, Condoleezza Rice, and Ted Turner. Unfortunately, however, charisma can also empower leaders in other directions. Adolf Hitler had strong charismatic qualities that appealed to some followers, for instance, as did Osama bin Laden.

Figure 12.3 portrays the three elements of charismatic leadership in organizations that most experts acknowledge today.[14] First, charismatic leaders

UNDERSTAND YOURSELF

HOW CHARISMATIC ARE YOU?

Charismatic leaders seem to be able to influence others with ease. They articulate a vision, show concern for others, have high expectations, and create high-performing groups and/or organizations. This self-assessment provides an indication of your charismatic potential.

Instructions: The following statements refer to characteristics which you may have. Please read each statement carefully and decide the extent to which it applies to you. Then enter that number in the space provided.

Rating Scale

5 To a Very Great Extent
4 To a Considerable Extent
3 To a Moderate Extent
2 To a Slight Extent
1 To Little or No Extent

___ 1. My friends say I should be an actor.
___ 2. I am confident in my job and social situations.
___ 3. I love the stage.
___ 4. When I hear music, I start to keep time with the beat.
___ 5. I am often the center of attention at social functions.
___ 6. I generally try to dress to make an impact or create a favorable impression.
___ 7. When talking to close friends, I may hug or touch them.
___ 8. I am open and curious, interested in many things.
___ 9. My friends tell me their problems and ask for my advice.
___ 10. I am generally assertive.
___ 11. I tend to be socially free and authentic.
___ 12. My friends expect me to take the lead in most situations.
___ 13. I try to understand others' points of view and behavior rather than criticizing them.
___ 14. I try not to speak in a way that hurts others.
___ 15. I can easily interact with people of all ages and sexes.
___ 16. I have a good sense of humor.
___ 17. I am noted for quick humorous responses.
___ 18. I smile easily and a lot.

Interpretation: Calculate your scores by adding the numbers you assigned to each statement. If your total score is between 72 and 90 you may have a relatively high level of charisma. If your total score is between 18 and 36 you may have relatively little charisma. If your total score is between 37 and 71 you may have a moderate level of charisma.

are able to envision likely future trends and patterns, to set high expectations for themselves and for others, and to model behaviors consistent with meeting those expectations. Next, charismatic leaders are able to energize others by demonstrating personal excitement, personal confidence, and consistent patterns of success. Finally, charismatic leaders enable others by supporting them, empathizing with them, and expressing confidence in them.[15]

Charismatic leadership ideas are quite popular among managers today and are the subject of numerous books and articles.[16] Unfortunately, few studies have specifically attempted to test the meaning and impact of charismatic leadership. Lingering ethical concerns about charismatic leadership also trouble some people.

Charismatic leadership is a form of interpersonal attraction that inspires support and acceptance. Dr. Martin Luther King, Jr. was considered to be a charismatic leader during the fight for civil rights.

Figure 12.3

The Charismatic Leader

The Charismatic Leader		
Envisioning	*Energizing*	*Enabling*
Articulating a compelling vision Setting high expectations Modeling consistent behaviors	Demonstrating personal excitement Expressing personal confidence Seeking, finding, and using success	Expressing personal support Empathizing Expressing confidence in people

The charismatic leader is characterized by three fundamental attributes. As illustrated here, these are behaviors resulting in envisioning, energizing, and enabling. Charismatic leaders can be a powerful force in any organizational setting.

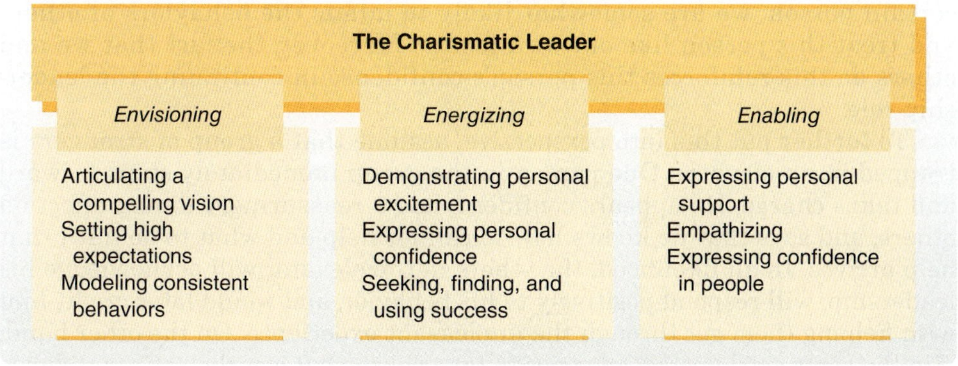

Sources: Nadler, D. A., & Tushman, M. L. (1990, Winter). Beyond the Charismatic Leader: Leadership and Organizational Change. *California Management Review*, 70–97.

They stem from the fact that some charismatic leaders inspire such blind faith in their followers that they may engage in inappropriate, unethical, or even illegal behaviors just because the leader instructed them to do so. This tendency likely played a role in the unwinding of both Enron and Arthur Andersen as people followed orders from their charismatic bosses to hide information, shred documents, and mislead investigators. Taking over a leadership role from someone with substantial personal charisma is also a challenge. For instance, the immediate successors to very successful charismatic football coaches like Vince Lombardi (Green Bay Packers), Urban Meyer (University of Florida), and Tom Osborne (University of Nebraska) each failed to measure up to his predecessor's legacy and was subsequently fired.

Attribution and Leadership

We discussed attribution theory back in Chapter 4 and noted then that people tend to observe behavior and then attribute causes (and hence meaning) to it. There are clear implications for attribution theory and leadership, especially when leadership is framed through the eyes of followers. Basically, then, the ***attribution perspective*** holds that when behaviors are observed in a context associated with leadership, different people may attribute varying levels of leadership ability or power to the person displaying those behaviors.

attribution perspective on leadership
Holds that when behaviors are observed in a context associated with leadership, different people may attribute varying levels of leadership ability or power to the person displaying those behaviors

For example, suppose we observe an individual behaving confidently and decisively; we also observe that others are paying close attention to what this person says and does and that they seem to defer to and/or consult with her on various things. We might subsequently conclude that this individual is a leader because of both her behavior and the behaviors of others. However, in a different setting we observe that a person seems to not be especially confident or decisive; we also observe that others seem relatively indifferent to what she has to say and that she is not routinely consulted about things. In this case we are more likely to assume that this person is not really a leader.

The attributions we make subsequently affect both our own behavior and the actual capacity of an individual to behave like a leader. For instance, suppose after observing the first group described above we then become a member of that group; since we have attributed leadership qualities to a certain person, we are somewhat likely to mimic the behaviors of others and treat this person like our own leader. Moreover, the fact that we and others do this reinforces this person's confidence in continuing the leadership role.

To further put this into perspective, assume that a group of strangers is trapped in an elevator. One person in the group immediately steps forward and takes charge. He appears confident, has a reassuring, calming effect on others, and says that he knows how to call for help and what to do until that help arrives. In all likelihood, the others in the elevator will acknowledge his leadership, will respond positively to his behavior, and would later credit him with helping them get through the unpleasant experience. On the other hand, if in the same setting someone tries to take charge but clearly lacks confidence and/or clearly exhibits ignorance of what to do, others will quickly pick up on this, pay little attention to what the person subsequently says, and perhaps look to someone else for leadership.

The attribution perspective on leadership is especially clear during presidential campaigns. Candidates and their handlers strive to make sure that they are always shown in the best possible light—demonstrating confidence, being sympathetic, knowing what to do, looking poised and well-groomed, and so forth. One context in which followers pay especially close attention to a leader's behavior is during a time of crisis, particularly if followers perceive that their own best interests are directly at stake. Our *Global Issues* feature looks at universal versus culturally contingent interpretations of different leadership attributes.

EFFECT OF CULTURE ON PERCEPTIONS OF LEADERS' ATTRIBUTES

Universal* Positive *Leader Attributes	***Universal* Negative *Leader Attributes***	**Culturally Contingent *Leader Attributes***
Trustworthy	Irritable	Cunning
Dependable	Dictatorial	Sensitive
Excellence-oriented	Uncooperative	Evasive
Honest	Ruthless	Risk taker
Motivating	Egocentric	Ruler

Source: Based on House, R. J., Hanges, P. J., Javidan, M., Dorfman, P. W., & Gupta, V. (2004). *Culture, Leadership, and Organizations: The GLOBE Study of 62 Societies.* London: Sage Publications; Avolio, B. J., & Dodge, G. E. (2000). E-Leadership: Implications for theory, research, and practice. *Leadership Quarterly. 11*(4), 615–668.

Leadership substitutes can facilitate performance regardless of whether or not a leader is present. For example, when this emergency vehicle pulled up to the hospital emergency room, doctors and EMT professionals knew what to do without being told. Their training and professionalism served as substitutes for leadership.

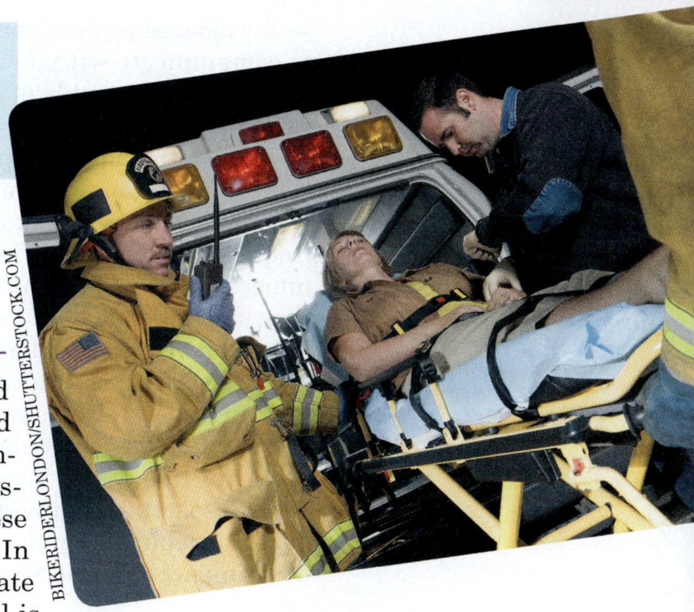
BIKERIDERLONDON/SHUTTERSTOCK.COM

ALTERNATIVES TO LEADERSHIP

Another perspective on leadership that has received considerable attention in recent years has focused on alternatives to leadership. In some cases, circumstances may exist that render leadership unnecessary or irrelevant. The factors that contribute to these circumstances are called leadership substitutes. In other cases, factors may exist that neutralize or negate the influence of a leader even when that individual is attempting to exercise leadership.

Leadership Substitutes

Leadership substitutes are individual, task, and organizational characteristics that tend to outweigh the leader's ability to affect subordinates' satisfaction and performance.[17] In other words, if certain factors are present, the employee will perform his or her job capably without the direction of a leader. Unlike traditional theories, which assume that hierarchical leadership in one form or another is always important, the premise of the leadership substitutes perspective is that leader behaviors may be irrelevant in some situations. Several basic leadership substitutes are identified in Table 12.1.

leadership substitutes
Individual, task, and organizational characteristics that tend to outweigh the leader's ability to affect subordinates' satisfaction and performance

Consider, for example, what happens when an ambulance with a critically injured victim screeches to the door of a hospital emergency room. Do the ER employees stand around waiting for someone to take control and instruct them on what to do? The answer is obviously no—they are highly trained and

Table 12.1

Substitutes and Neutralizers for Leadership

Individual	**Group**
Individual professionalism	Group norms
Motivation	Group cohesiveness
Experience and training	
Indifference to rewards	
Job	**Organization**
Structured/automated	Rigid procedures and rules
Highly controlled	Explicit goals and objectives
Intrinsically satisfying	Rigid reward system
Embedded feedback	

well-prepared professionals who know how to respond, who to depend on, who to communicate with, how to work together as a team, and so forth. In short, they are fully capable of carrying out their jobs without someone playing the role of leader.

Individual ability, experience, training, knowledge, motivation, and professional orientation are among the characteristics that may substitute for leadership. Similarly, a task characterized by routine, a high degree of structure, frequent feedback, and intrinsic satisfaction may also render leader behavior unnecessary. Thus, if the task gives the subordinate enough intrinsic satisfaction, she or he may not need support from a leader.

Explicit plans and goals, rules and procedures, cohesive work groups, a rigid reward structure, and physical distance between supervisor and subordinate are organizational characteristics that may substitute for leadership. For example, if job goals are explicit, and there are many rules and procedures for task performance, a leader providing directions may not be necessary. Research has provided support for the concept of leadership substitutes, but additional research is needed to identify other potential substitutes and their impact on leadership effectiveness.[18]

Leadership Neutralizers

leadership neutralizers
Factors that render ineffective a leader's attempts to engage in various leadership behaviors

In other situations, even if a leader is present and attempts to engage in various leadership behaviors, those behaviors may be rendered ineffective—neutralized—by various factors. These factors are referred to as ***leadership neutralizers***. Suppose, for example, that a relatively new and inexperienced leader is assigned to a workgroup comprised of very experienced employees with long-standing performance norms and a high level of group cohesiveness. The norms and cohesiveness of the group may be so strong that there is nothing the new leader can do to change things. Of course, this pattern may also work in several different ways. The norms may dictate acceptable but not high performance, and the leader may be powerless to improve things because the group is so cohesive. Or the norms may call for very high performance, such that even a bungling and ineffective leader cannot cause any damage. In both cases, however, the process is the same—the leader's ability to alter the situation is neutralized by elements in that situation.

In addition to group factors, elements of the job itself may also limit a leader's ability to "make a difference." Consider, for example, employees working on a moving assembly line. Employees may only be able to work at the pace of the moving line, so performance quantity is constrained by the speed of the line. Moreover, if performance quality is also constrained (say, by simple tasks and/or tight quality control procedures), the leader may again be powerless to influence individual work behaviors.

Finally, organizational factors can also neutralize at least some forms of leader behavior. Suppose a new leader is accustomed to using merit pay increases as a way to motivate people. But in her or his new job, pay increases are dictated by union contracts and are based primarily on employee seniority and cost of living. Or suppose that an employee is already at the top of the pay grade for his or her job. In either case, the leader's previous approach to motivating people has been neutralized and so new approaches will have to be identified.

THE CHANGING NATURE OF LEADERSHIP

Various alternatives to leadership aside, though, many settings still call for at least some degree of leadership, although the nature of that leadership continues to evolve.[19] Among the recent changes in leadership that managers should recognize are the increasing role of leaders as coaches and gender and cross-cultural patterns of leader behavior.

Leaders as Coaches

We noted in Chapter 7 that many organizations today are using teams. And many other organizations are attempting to become less hierarchical—that is, to eliminate the old-fashioned command-and-control mentality often inherent in bureaucratic organizations and to motivate and empower individuals to work independently. In each case, the role of leaders is also changing. Whereas leaders were once expected to control situations, direct work, supervise people, closely monitor performance, make decisions, and structure activities, many leaders today are being asked to change how they manage people. Perhaps the best description of this new role is that the leader is becoming a *coach* instead of an overseer or supervisor.[20]

Consider the metaphor from the standpoint of the coach of an athletic team. The coach plays a role in selecting the players for the team and deciding on the general direction to take (such as emphasizing offense versus defense). The coach also helps develop player talent and teaches them how to execute specific plays. But at game time, the coach stays on the sidelines; it's up to the players themselves to execute plays and get the job done. And while the coach may get some of the credit for the victory, he or she didn't actually score any of the points.

Likewise, then, from the standpoint of an organizational leader, a coaching perspective would call for the leader to help select team members and other new employees, to provide some general direction, to help train and develop the team and the skills of its members, and to help the team get the information and other resources it needs. The leader may also have to help resolve conflict among team members and mediate other disputes that arise. And coaches from different teams may need to play important roles in linking the activities and functions of their respective teams. But beyond these activities, the leader keeps a low profile and lets the group get its work done with little or no direct oversight from the leader.

Of course, some managers long accustomed to the traditional approach may have trouble changing to a coaching role. But others seem to make the transition with little or no difficulty. Moreover, companies such as Texas Instruments,

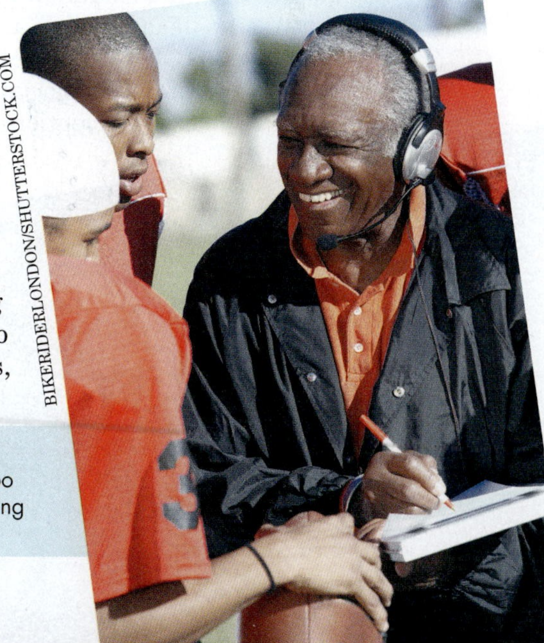
BIKERIDERLONDON/SHUTTERSTOCK.COM

Leaders are increasingly being called upon to serve as coaches rather than supervisors. Just as this football coach is giving direction to his players, so too are managers facilitating the work of their subordinates rather than supervising and controlling their performance.

Halliburton, and Yum! Brands have developed very successful training programs to help their managers learn how to become better coaches. Within the coaching role, some leaders have also excelled at taking on more responsibilities as a ***mentor***—the role of helping a less experienced person learn the ropes to better prepare himself or herself to advance within the organization. Texas Instruments has maintained a very successful mentoring program for years.

mentor
Role of helping a less experienced person learn the ropes to better prepare for career success

Gender and Leadership

Another factor that is clearly changing the nature of leadership is the growing number of women advancing to higher levels in organizations. Given that most leadership theories and research studies have focused on male leaders, developing a better understanding of how females lead is clearly an important next step. For example, do women and men tend to lead differently? Some early research suggests that there are indeed fundamental differences in leadership as practiced by women and men.[21]

For instance, in contrast to original stereotypes, female leaders are not necessarily more nurturing or supportive than are male leaders. Likewise, male leaders are not systematically more harsh, controlling, or task focused than are female leaders. The one difference that does seem to arise in some cases is that women have a tendency to be slightly more democratic in making decisions, whereas men have a similar tendency to be somewhat more autocratic.[22]

There are two possible explanations for this pattern. One possibility is that women may tend to have stronger interpersonal skills than men and are hence better able to effectively involve others in making decisions. Men, on the other hand, may have weaker interpersonal skills and thus have a tendency to rely on their own judgment. The other possible explanation is that women may encounter more stereotypic resistance to their occupying senior roles. If this is the case, they may actively work to involve others in making decisions so as to help minimize any hostility or conflict. Clearly, however, much more work needs to be done in order to better understand the dynamics of gender and leadership. It is obvious, of course, that high-profile and successful female leaders such as Hillary Clinton (former Secretary of State), Marissa Mayer (CEO of Yahoo!), Indra Nooyi (CEO of PepsiCo), are Sheryl Sandberg (COO of Facebook), are demonstrating the effectiveness with which women can be truly exceptional leaders.

Cross-Cultural Leadership

Another changing perspective on leadership relates to cross-cultural issues. In this context, culture is used as a broad concept to encompass both

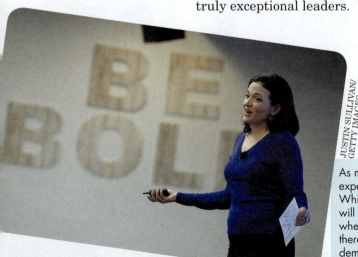

JUSTIN SULLIVAN/ GETTY IMAGES

As more and more women assume high-profile leadership positions experts have asked whether women lead differently than do men. While few meaningful differences have been identified, this question will undoubtedly continue to be raised. The issue, of course, is not whether one gender leads "better" than the other, but simply if there are differences. Sheryl Sandberg, COO of Facebook, has demonstrated high levels of leadership effectiveness.

international differences and diversity-based differences within a single culture. However, we will examine international differences in the next section, so at this point we focus first on intra-country cultural issues. And actually, given our previous discussions of diversity, social interactions, and so forth, the extension of these topics to cross-cultural leadership should be obvious.

For instance, cross-cultural factors clearly play a growing role in organizations as their workforces become more and more diverse. Most leadership research, for instance, has been conducted on samples or case studies involving white male leaders. But as African Americans, Asian Americans, Hispanics, and members of other ethnic groups achieve more and more leadership positions, it may be necessary to reassess how applicable current theories and models of leadership are when applied to an increasingly diverse pool of leaders.

Religion is also a potential issue in leadership. A Jewish or Christian leader, for example, leading a group with Islamist members may face a variety of complex issues; and, of course, those issues would also exist if the roles were reversed. There are cross-cultural issues even when leaders and followers have less visible indicators of diversity. A manager who has spent his or her entire career in, say, Texas or Alabama will likely face some adjustment issues if promoted to a leadership position in New York or San Francisco.

International Leadership and Project GLOBE

Cross-cultural issues are also obvious in international contexts. For instance, when a Japanese firm sends an executive to head up the firm's operation in the United States, that person will likely need to become acclimated to the cultural differences that exist between the two countries and consider adjusting his or her leadership style accordingly. Japan is generally characterized by collectivism, while the United States is based more on individualism. The Japanese executive, then, will find it necessary to recognize the importance of individual contributions and rewards and the differences in individual and group roles that exist in Japanese and U.S. businesses. And, obviously, similar issues will result if an American leader is posted to Asia.

To learn more about international leadership, a global team of researchers has been working on a series of studies under the general heading of Project GLOBE (Global Leadership and Organizational Behavior Research Project). GLOBE was initiated by Robert House, and research is still being conducted under its auspices.[23] GLOBE identified six leader behaviors that can be observed and assessed across a variety of cultures. These behaviors are:

- *Charismatic / value-based leadership:* the ability to inspire, to motivate, and to promote high performance; includes being visionary, self-sacrificing, trustworthy, decisive, and performance oriented.
- *Team-oriented leadership:* emphasizes team building and creating a sense of common purpose; includes being collaborative, diplomatic, and administratively competent.
- *Participative leadership:* the extent to which leaders involve others in making decisions; being participative and nonautocratic.
- *Humane-oriented leadership:* being supportive, considerate, compassionate, and generous; displaying modesty and sensitivity.
- *Autonomous leadership:* refers to being independent and individualist; being autonomous and unique.

MICHAELJUNG/GETTY IMAGES

International leadership is becoming more and more important. This Saudi Arabian manager has just been promoted to lead a new team. Both he and his team members will need to be aware of cultural differences both among team members and between team members and their new leader.

- *Self-protective leadership:* includes behaviors intending to ensure the safety and security of the leader and the group; includes being self-centered, status conscious, conflict inducing, and face saving.

These behaviors have been—and are being—studied in 62 global societies. These societies are mostly separate countries, but when there are markedly different societies with a country (such as black and white South Africa), each is examined separately. Based on the preliminary results, the original 62 societies were condensed into 10 cultural clusters—societies that yielded highly similar results to one another. For instance, the Nordic Europe cluster includes Finland, Sweden, Denmark, and Norway, and the Southern Asia cluster consists of India, Indonesia, Malaysia, Thailand, and Iran.

In general, the findings of GLOBE suggest that within any cultural cluster, followers react in similar ways to various leader behaviors. For example, employees in Nordic Europe generally want their leaders to be inspiring and to involve others in decision making but are less concerned with status and similar self-centered attributes. Therefore, charismatic/value-based and participative leadership are most important and humane-oriented and self-protective leadership are least important. In Southern Asia, however, most employees want their leaders to be collaborative, sensitive to other people's needs, and concerned with status and face saving. Consequently, self-protective and charismatic/value-based leadership are most important in these countries, while autonomous and participative leadership are least important.[24] Of course, as noted earlier, this research is still ongoing, and it would be premature to draw overly strong generalizations at this point.

EMERGING ISSUES IN LEADERSHIP

Finally, there are also three emerging issues in leadership that warrant discussion. These issues are strategic leadership, ethical leadership, and virtual leadership.

Strategic Leadership

strategic leadership
The capability to understand the complexities of both the organization and its environment and to lead change in the organization so as to achieve and maintain a superior alignment between the organization and its environment

Strategic leadership is a new concept that explicitly relates leadership to the role of top management.[25] We will define ***strategic leadership*** as the capability to understand the complexities of both the organization and its environment and to lead change in the organization so as to achieve and maintain a superior alignment between the organization and its environment. In some ways, then, strategic leadership may be seen as an extension of the transformational leadership role discussed earlier. However, this recent focus has more explicitly acknowledged and incorporated the importance of strategy and strategic decision making. That is, while both transformational and strategic leadership include the concept of change, transformational leadership implicitly emphasizes the ability to lead change as the central focus. Strategic leadership, on the other hand, puts greater weight on the leader's ability to think and function strategically.

To be effective in this role, a manager needs to have a thorough and complete understanding of the organization—its history, its culture, its strengths, and its weaknesses. In addition, the leader needs a firm grasp of the organization's environment. This understanding must encompass current conditions and circumstances as well as significant trends and issues on the horizon. The strategic leader also needs to recognize how the firm is currently aligned with its environment—where it relates effectively with that environment, and where it relates less effectively. Finally, looking at environmental trends and issues, the strategic leader works to improve not only the current alignment but also the future alignment.

Marissa Mayer (CEO of Yahoo!), A. G. Lafley (retired CEO of Procter & Gamble), and Howard Schultz (CEO of Starbucks), have all been recognized as strong strategic leaders. Reflecting on the dramatic turnaround he led at Procter & Gamble, for instance, Lafley commented, "I have made a lot of symbolic, very physical changes so people understand we are in the business of leading change." On the other hand, Raymond Gilmartin (former CEO of Merck), Scott Livengood (former CEO of Krispy Kreme), and Jürgen Schrempp (former CEO of DaimlerChrysler), have been singled out for their poor strategic leadership (and note the consistent description of "former"!).

Ethical Leadership

Most people have long assumed that top managers are ethical people. But in the wake of recent corporate scandals at firms such as Lehman Brothers, Toyota, BP, and Goldman Sachs, faith in top managers has been shaken. Hence, perhaps now more than ever, high standards of ethical conduct are being held up as a prerequisite for effective leadership. More specifically, top managers are being called upon to maintain high ethical standards for their own conduct, to unfailingly exhibit ethical behavior, and to hold others in their organizations to the same standards. ***Ethical leadership***, then, is the process of leading based on consistent principles of ethical conduct.

ethical leadership
The process of leading based on consistent principles of ethical conduct

The behaviors of top leaders are being scrutinized more than ever, and those responsible for hiring new leaders for a business are looking more and more closely at the backgrounds of those being considered. The emerging pressures for stronger corporate governance models are likely to further increase the commitment to select only those individuals with high ethical standards for leadership positions in business, and to hold them more accountable than in the past for both their actions and the consequences of those actions.[26]

IMPROVE YOUR SKILLS

NETIQUETTE TIPS FOR MANAGERS

Virtual leadership is becoming increasingly prevalent today. But leaders should still adhere to certain rules of communication even if electronic media are available. Here are a few suggested tips:

- Never use email to fire employees or deliver bad news. Because it contains no body language, facial expression, and intonation, email is the worst way to deliver bad news to employees. A one-on-one meeting is better.
- Do not use email to discuss an employee's performance with other managers. Hold these discussions privately.
- Be careful when writing email messages. Like written performance reviews and other documents, emails can be subject to discovery and subpoena. Email is also not always secure, and sometimes unintended readers receive confidential information.
- Do not rely on email to the exclusion of personal contact. Even in the age of IT, relationship skills are the heart of long-term business success. Supplement your emails with periodic face-to-face staff, customer, and supplier meetings, even if they must occur through videoconferencing.
- Do not use email when there is any chance of the message being misunderstood. Use a telephone call or a face-to-face meeting if a message is complex, technical, or in any danger of being misinterpreted.

Source: Flynn, N. (2001). The E-policy Handbook: Designing and Implementing Effective E-mail, Internet, and Software Policies.

Virtual Leadership

virtual leadership *Leadership via distance technologies*

Finally, ***virtual leadership*** is also emerging as an important issue for organizations. In earlier times, leaders and their employees worked together in the same physical location and engaged in personal (i.e., face-to-face) interactions on a regular basis. But in today's world, both leaders and their employees may work in locations that are far from one another. Such arrangements might include people who telecommute from a home office one or two days a week and people who actually live and work far from company headquarters and see one another in person only very infrequently. Virtual leadership, therefore, is leadership via various forms of distance technologies.

How, then, do managers carry out leadership when they do not have regular personal contact with their followers? And how do they help mentor and develop others? Communication between leaders and their subordinates will still occur, of course, but it may be largely by telephone, texting, and email. Hence, one implication may be that leaders in these situations simply need to work harder at creating and maintaining relationships with their employees that go beyond simply words on a computer screen. While nonverbal communication such as smiles and handshakes may not be possible online, managers can instead make a point of adding a few personal words in an email (whenever appropriate) to convey appreciation, reinforcement, or constructive feedback. Building on this, managers should then also take advantage of every single opportunity whenever they are in face-to-face situations to go further than they might have done under different circumstances to develop a strong relationship.

Beyond these simple prescriptions, there is no theory or research to guide managers functioning in a virtual world. Hence, as electronic communications continue to pervade the workplace, researchers and managers alike need to work together to help frame the appropriate issues and questions regarding virtual leadership, and then collaborate to help address those issues and answer those questions.[27]

SUMMARY AND APPLICATIONS

The leader-member exchange model (LMX) of leadership stresses the importance of variable relationships between supervisors and each of their subordinates. Each superior-subordinate pair is referred to as a "vertical dyad." The Hersey and Blanchard model argues that appropriate leader behavior depends on the subordinate's degree of motivation, competence, experience, and interest in accepting responsibility. In addition to these somewhat newer models, the three dominant situational theories have also continued to undergo various refinements and revisions.

There are three primary approaches to leadership through the eyes of followers. Transformational leadership focuses on the basic distinction between leading for change and leading for stability. Perspectives based on charismatic leadership assume that charisma is an individual characteristic of the leader. Charisma is a form of interpersonal attraction that inspires support and acceptance. The attribution perspective holds that when behaviors are

LOSKUTNIKOV/SHUTTERSTOCK.COM

REAL WORLD RESPONSE

ETHICAL LEADERSHIP AT COSTCO

Costco's founder and former CEO Jim Sinegal still plays a role in managing the company and often consults with other businesses. He responds to the criticisms of Wall Street analysts that Costco pays employees too much and keeps them too long by saying that keeping good employees is strategic for Costco's long-term success and growth. He backs up this claim with per-employee sales that are notably higher than those found at rivals such as Sam's Club.

To keep his employees happy and productive, Sinegal tried not to distance himself from his employees. Sinegal asked his employees to refer to him as "Jim, the CEO." He wore a name tag that simply says "Jim." When touring stores, he could easily be mistaken for a stock clerk. From the very beginning he wanted to create a company in which everyone is on a first-name basis.

The culture of the company flowed downward from Sinegal, who maintained an open-door policy at Costco headquarters. It was actually more of a no-door policy, since he had an entire wall removed from his office when Costco moved into a new office building.

(*Continued*)

Costco regularly improves its product mix due to alert employees in the warehouses who feed the latest information up to headquarters. Costco enjoys an extremely low turnover rate of below 6 percent among employees who have been there at least a year and has some of the lowest shrinkage (unexplained disappearances of merchandise) in the industry at one-tenth of 1 percent.

Sinegal believes the leaders should model what is expected from employees. When he went to a Costco store and took the time to pick up a piece of trash on the ground, employees immediately knew it is important and therefore did it themselves. He liked to visit as many of the stores as he could every year and liked employees to think that he might show up anytime. When Sinegal walked into one of his stores, he was treated like a celebrity. He said, "The employees know that I want to say hello to them, because I like them.... No manager and no staff in any business feels very good if the boss is not interested enough to come and see them."[28]

Sinegal also got a compensation package far below what most CEOs receive, with a combined salary and bonus of less than $600,000 in his last year (plus stock options, but even so his total compensation is low compared with peers). "I figured that if I was making something like twelve times more than the typical person working on the floor, that that was a fair salary," he said.[29] An expert on corporate governance was shocked to discover that Sinegal's employment contract was only a page long. She says, "Of the 2,000 companies in our database, he has the single shortest CEO employment contract. And the only one which specifically says he can be—believe it or not—'terminated for cause.' If he doesn't do his job, he is out the door."[30]

As Costco continues to grow internationally, Sinegal keeps watch and continues following his code of ethics. He says, "Our code of ethics says we have to obey the law. We have to take care of our customers, take care of our people. And if we do those things, we think that we'll reward our shareholders."[31]

---

observed in a context associated with leadership, others may attribute varying levels of leadership ability or power to the person displaying those behaviors.

Another perspective on leadership that has received considerable attention in recent years has focused on alternatives to leadership. In some cases, circumstances may exist that render leadership unnecessary or irrelevant. The factors that contribute to these circumstances are called leadership substitutes. In other cases, factors may exist that neutralize or negate the influence of a leader even when that individual is attempting to exercise leadership.

The nature of leadership continues to evolve. Among recent changes in leadership that managers should recognize is the increasing role of leaders as coaches. The most frequent instance of this arrangement is when an organization uses self-managing teams. Gender differences in leader behavior are also becoming more important, especially given the increasing numbers of women advancing up the organizational ladder. Cross-cultural patterns of leadership both between and within national boundaries are also taking on growing importance. Project GLOBE is shedding new light on international leadership.

Finally, there are three emerging issues in leadership. Strategic leadership is a new concept that explicitly relates leadership to the role of top management. In addition, leaders in all organizations are being called upon to maintain high ethical standards for their own conduct, to unfailingly exhibit ethical behavior, and to hold others in their organizations to the same standards. The growing importance of virtual leadership needs to be further studied.

DISCUSSION QUESTIONS

1. Compare and contrast the leader-member exchange and the Hersey and Blanchard models of leadership.
2. Are you now or have you ever been a member of an in-group? An out-group? If so, in what ways did your experiences differ?
3. Which of the three traditional situational theories discussed in Chapter 12 is most similar to the leader-member exchange model? To the Hersey and Blanchard model?
4. Identify an individual who could serve as an example of a transformational leader. How successful or unsuccessful has this person been?
5. Name the three people today whom you consider to be the most charismatic. How well do they or might they function as leaders?
6. In your opinion, is it possible for someone with little or no charisma to become charismatic? If so, how? If not, why?
7. Have you ever made direct leadership attributions about someone based on the context in which you observed them?
8. What are some of the substitutes and neutralizers to leadership that might exist in your classroom?
9. Do you believe that men and women differ in how they lead? If so, what are some of the factors that might account for the differences?
10. In what ways does strategic leadership differ from "non-strategic" leadership?
11. Some people have held that highly successful managers and leaders all face situations in which they cannot be entirely truthful and still succeed. For instance, a politician who personally believes that a tax increase is inevitable may feel that to fully disclose this belief will result in a significant loss of votes. Do you agree or disagree with the idea that sometimes people cannot be entirely truthful and still succeed?

DEVELOP YOUR SKILLS EXERCISE

Understanding Leadership Substitutes and Neutralizers

1. Identify four jobs, two that appear to be relatively simple (perhaps a custodian or a fast food cook) and two that appear to be much more complex (such as an airline pilot or software engineer).
2. For each job, identify as many potential leadership substitutes and neutralizers as possible.

3. Now, consider these questions:
   - To what extent did your own experiences affect how you performed this exercise?
   - Are there some jobs for which there are no substitutes for leadership? Provide examples.
   - Should managers actively seek substitutes for leadership? Why or why not?

GROUP EXERCISE

Who Are The Leaders?

This exercise offers you an opportunity to compare your concepts with those of others in your class about who leaders are.

Your Assignment

1. Make a list of ten very effective leaders—individuals whom most everyone would recognize as leaders.
2. In small groups share and discuss your lists.
   (A) Were the same leaders on more than one student's list?
   (B) What, if anything, do these individuals have in common—education, industry, type of jobs held, family history, etc.?
3. Have each group agree on a list of ten leaders and share those group lists with the entire class. What, if anything, do the leaders on the various group lists have in common? If any leader appears to be radically different from the others, discuss what sets that person apart from other leaders and yet makes them one of the best-known leaders.

Try repeating the exercise with the possibilities narrowed; e.g., females, Native Americans, minorities, managers/executives, politicians, religious leaders, international, or from a particular industry. What additional information do you learn from this?

VIDEO EXERCISE

Numi Organic Tea: Danielle Oviedo

When Danielle Oviedo showed up for her first day as the manager of the Distribution Center at Numi Organic Tea in Oakland, California, her new direct reports were not happy about the change. They loved Oviedo's predecessor, who was more like a friend than a boss to them. But Numi's director of operations, Brian Durkee, was looking for someone with specific skills and experience when he hired Danielle, and popularity wasn't on the list. Durkee hired Danielle because of her effectiveness and success as a manager in previous positions. She also had experience leading much big teams in similar departments.

Prior to Danielle's arrival, lead times for Numi's customer orders were not competitive. Although Numi's loyal food service customers were happy with Numi products, some customers were considering taking their business elsewhere because deliveries were unpredictable. Upon her arrival at Numi, Danielle identified the problem: employees were performing tasks in isolation with little attention to anything else.

To solve the issue, Danielle trained the Distribution Center employees in every critical task and process, explaining how all the pieces fit together. Going forward, her staff would perform multiple tasks depending on what pressing deadlines loomed. Importantly, Danielle helped her team understand their jobs on a conceptual level so they could see how their work linked directly to Numi's larger goals. With newfound effectiveness aided by Danielle's planning and organizing, the team cut lead times for international orders by about 75 percent.

Numi's customer service manager, Cindy Graffort, is thrilled about Danielle's achievements and said none of these changes were possible before Danielle arrived. According to Cindy, the dramatic changes were a direct result of Danielle's ability to come up with innovative solutions to problems plaguing the Distribution Center.

When asked for specific insight into Danielle's managerial success, Cindy highlighted her impressive human skills. Unlike old-school managers who hide in their offices and manage employees from afar, Danielle is out on the floor working with teammates, ensuring they understand the process, and being supportive.

Discussion Questions

1. How would you describe Danielle Oviedo's approach to leadership?
2. What would you predict about Danielle's future success as a leader? Why
3. In what ways, if any, does Danielle function as a coach?

Now What?

VIDEO CASE

PERCOM/SHUTTERSTOCK.COM

Imagine that your boss is delegating parts of a project to you and to another team member. Because the other team member has a longer work history with the boss and is highly trusted, you are assigned the unchallenging portions of the project. *What do you say or do?* How can you improve your relationship with your boss to get more challenging assignments and eventually earn a promotion? Go to this chapter's "Now What?" video, watch the challenge video, and choose a response. Be sure to also view the outcomes of the two responses you didn't choose.

Discussion Questions

1. In terms of LMX, what type of relationship is exhibited in the challenge video?
2. In the challenge video, according to the Hersey Blanchard model, how does Amy perceive Alex?
3. Which other aspects of leadership discussed in this chapter are illustrated in these videos? Explain your answer.
4. If this were you, what would you do to improve your relationship with your boss to get assignments that are more challenging and eventually earn a promotion?

ENDNOTES

[1]Career Opportunities for You. Costco.com. 2015. Available at: http://www.costco.com/jobs.html; Machan, D. (2008, March 27). CEO Interview: Costco's James Sinegal. SmartMoney. https://nonbreakingnews.files.wordpress.com/2008/10/ceo-interview_-costcos-james-sinegal.pdf; Chu, J., & Rockwood, K. (2008, October 13). CEO Interview: Costco's Jim Sinegal. Fast Company. Available at: http://www.fastcompany.com/ magazine/130/thinking-outside-the-big-box.html?page=0%2C2; Goldberg, A. B., & Ritter, B. (2006, August 2). Costco CEO Finds Pro-Worker Means Profitability. ABC News 20/20. Available at: http://abcnews.go.com/2020/Business/story?id=1362779; Wadhwa, V. (2009, August 17). Why Be an Ethical Company? They're Stronger and Last Longer. BusinessWeek. Available at: http://www.businessweek.com/stories/2009-08-17/whybe-an-ethical-company-theyre-stronger-and-last-longerbusinessweek-business-news-stock-market-and-financial-advice.

[2]Graen, G. & Cashman, J. F. (1975). A Role-Making Model of Leadership in Formal Organizations: A Developmental Approach. In *Leadership Frontiers*, eds. J. G. Hunt & L. L. Larson (pp. 143–165). Kent, OH: Kent State University Press; Dansereau, F., Graen, G. & Haga, W. J. (1975). A Vertical Dyad Linkage Approach to Leadership Within Formal Organizations: A Longitudinal Investigation of the Role-Making Process *Organizational Behavior and Human Performance, 15*, 46–78; see also Barling, J., Christie, A., & Hoption, C. (2010). Leadership. In *Handbook of Industrial and Organizational Psychology*, ed. S. Zedeck (pp. 183–240). Washington, DC: American Psychological Association.

[3]Gerstner, C. R., & Day, D. V. (1997). Meta-Analytic Review of Leader-Member Exchange Theory: Correlates and Construct Issues. *Journal of Applied Psychology, 82*(6), 827–844; Maslyn, J., & Uhl-Bien, M. (2001). Leader-Member Exchange and Its Dimensions: Effects of Self-Effort and Others' Effort on Relationship Quality. *Journal of Applied Psychology, 86*(4), 697–708.

[4]Hersey, P. & Blanchard, K. H. (1977). *Management of Organizational Behavior: Utilizing Human Resources* (3rd ed.). Englewood Cliffs, NJ: Prentice Hall.

[5]Fiedler, F., & Garcia, J. (1987). *New Approaches to Effective Leadership: Cognitive Resources and Organizational Performance*. New York: John Wiley and Sons.

[6]Burns, J. M. (1978). *Leadership*. New York: Harper & Row; Kuhnert, K. W., & Lewis, P. (1987, October). Transactional and Transformational Leadership: A Constructive/ Developmental Analysis. *Academy of Management Review*, 648–657; see also Turner, N., Barling, J., Epitropaki, O., Butcher, V., & Milner, C. (2002). Transformational Leadership and Moral Reasoning. *Journal of Applied Psychology, 87*(2), 304–311.

[7]Yammarino, F. J., & Dubinsky, A. J. (1994). Transformational Leadership Theory: Using Levels of Analysis to Determine Boundary Conditions. *Personnel Psychology, 47*, 787–800. See also Pieterse, A. N., van Knippenberg, D., Schippers, M., & Stam, D. (2010, May). Transformational and Transactional Leadership and Innovative Behavior: The Role of Psychological Empowerment. *Journal of Organizational Behavior*, 609–623.

[8]Goodwin, V., Wofford, J. C., & Whittington, J. L. (2001). A Theoretical and Empirical Extension to the Transformational Leadership Construct. *Journal of Organizational Behavior, 22*, 759–774; see also Colbert, A., Kristof-Brown, A., Bradley, B., & Barrick, M. (2008). CEO Transformational Leadership: The Role of Goal Congruence in Top Management Teams. *Academy of Management Journal, 51*(1), 81–96.

[9]*Hoover's Handbook of American Business 2015* (pp. 340–341). Austin, TX: Hoover's Business Press.

[10]Pastor, J.-C., Meindl, J., & Mayo, M. (2002). A Network Effects Model of Charisma Attributions. *Academy of Management Journal, 45*(2), 410–420.

[11]Tischler, L. (2002, September). Sudden Impact. *Fast Company, 62*, 106.

[12]House, R. J. (1977). A 1976 Theory of Charismatic Leadership. In *Leadership: The Cutting Edge*, eds. J. G. Hunt & L. L. Larson (pp. 189–207). Carbondale, IL: Southern Illinois University Press; see also Conger, J. A., & Kanungo, R. N. (1987, October). Toward a Behavioral Theory of Charismatic Leadership in Organizational Settings. *Academy of Management Review*, 637–647.

[13]Play Hard, Fly Right. *Time, Bonus Section: Inside Business*, June 2002, Y15–Y22.

[14]Nadler, D. A., & Tushman, M. L. (1990, Winter). Beyond the Charismatic Leader: Leadership and Organizational Change. *California Management Review*, 77–97.

[15]Waldman, D. A., & Yammarino, F. J. (1999). CEO Charismatic Leadership: Levels-of-Management and Levels-of-Analysis Effects. *Academy of Management Review, 24*(2), 266–285.

[16]Howell, J., & Shamir, B. (2005, January). The Role of Followers in the Charismatic Leadership Process: Relationships and Their Consequences. *Academy of Management Review*, 96–112.

[17]Kerr, S., & Jermier, J. M. (1978). Substitutes for Leadership: Their Meaning and Measurement. *Organizational Behavior and Human Performance, 22*, 375–403. See also Manz, C. C., & Sims, H. P., Jr. (1987, March). Leading Workers to Lead Themselves: The External Leadership of Self-Managing Work Teams. *Administrative Science Quarterly*, 106–129.

[18]Howell, J. P., Bowen, D. E., Dorfman, P. W., Kerr, S., & Podsakoff, P. M. (1990, Summer). Substitutes for Leadership: Effective Alternatives to Ineffective Leadership. *Organizational Dynamics*, 20–38; see also Podsakoff, P. M., Mackenzie, S. B., & Bommer, W. H. (1996). Transformational Leader Behaviors and Substitutes for Leadership as Determinants of Employee Satisfaction, Commitment, Trust, and Organizational Citizenship Behaviors. *Journal of Management, 22*(2), 259–298.

[19]Erickson, T. (2010, May). The Leaders We Need Now. *Harvard Business Review*, 62–67.

[20]Hackman, J. R., & Wageman, R. (2005, April). A Theory of Team Coaching. *Academy of Management Review*, 269–287; see also Peterson, D. B. (2010). Executive Coaching: A Critical Review and Recommendations for Advancing the Practice. In *Handbook of Industrial and Organizational Psychology*, ed. S. Zedeck (pp. 527–566). Washington, DC: American Psychological Association.

[21]Kent, R. L., & Moss, S. E. (1994). Effects of Sex and Gender Role on Leader Emergence. *Academy of Management Journal, 37*(5), 1335–1346.

[22]Eagly, A. H., Makhijani, M. G., & Klonsky, R. G. (1992). Gender and the Evaluation of Leaders: A Meta-Analysis. *Psychological Bulletin, 111*, 3–22.

[23]House, R. J., et al. (Eds.) (2004). *Culture, Leadership, and Organizations: The GLOBE Study of 62 Societies*. London: Sage Publications.

[24]For more details, see Chhokar, J. S., Brodbek, F. C., & House, R. J. (Eds.), (2008). *Culture and Leadership Across the World*. Hillsdale, NJ: Lawrence Erlbaum Associates; and Gupta, V., Hanges, P. J., & Dorfman, P. (2002). Cultural Clusters: Methodology and Findings. *Journal of World Business, 37*, 11–15; see also Leung, K., & Peterson, M. F. (2010). Managing a Globally Distributed Workforce: Social and Interpersonal Issues. In *Handbook of Industrial and Organizational Psychology*, ed. S. Zedeck (pp. 771–805). Washington, DC: American Psychological Association.

[25]Montgomery, C. (2008, January). Putting Leadership Back Into Strategy. *Harvard Business Review*, 54–61.

[26]Dirks, K., & Ferrin, D. (2002). Trust in Leadership. *Journal of Applied Psychology, 87*(4), 611–628; see also Meyer, C., & Kirby, J. (2010, April). Leadership in the Age of Transparency. *Harvard Business Review*, 38–46.

[27]Cordery, J., Soo, C., Kirkman, B., Rosen, B., & Mathieu, J. (2009, July–September). Leading Parallel Global Virtual Teams. *Organizational Dynamics*, 204–216.

[28]Goldberg, A. B., & Ritter, B. (2006, August 2). Costco CEO Finds Pro-Worker Means Profitability. ABC News 20/20. Available at: http://abcnews.go.com/2020/Business/story?id=1362779.

[29]Goldberg, A. B., & Ritter, B. (2006, August 2). Costco CEO Finds Pro-Worker Means Profitability. ABC News 20/20. Available at: http://abcnews.go.com/2020/Business/story?id=1362779.

[30]Goldberg, A. B., & Ritter, B. (2006, August 2). Costco CEO Finds Pro-Worker Means Profitability. ABC News 20/20. Available at: http://abcnews.go.com/2020/Business/story?id=1362779.

[31]Goldberg, A. B., & Ritter, B. (2006, August 2). Costco CEO Finds Pro-Worker Means Profitability. ABC News 20/20. Available at: http://abcnews.go.com/2020/Business/story?id=1362779.

LOSKUTNIKOV/SHUTTERSTOCK.COM

CHAPTER 13

POWER, INFLUENCE, AND POLITICS

CHAPTER OUTLINE

LEARNING OUTCOMES

After studying this chapter, you should be able to:

1. Identify and describe different kinds of position and personal power.
2. Discuss how individuals and groups obtain and use power.
3. Discuss influence and describe which influence tactics are the most and least effective.
4. Describe some of the factors that influence political behavior in organizations and the role of impression management in power and influence.

LOSKUTNIKOV/SHUTTERSTOCK.COM

—REAL WORLD CHALLENGE—

INFLUENCING ACCEPTANCE OF CHANGE AT CHURCH & DWIGHT[1]

The Church & Dwight Company is a leading consumer packaged goods company Church & Dwight's brands include Arm & Hammer, Trojan, and OxiClean. After a corporate review of its business, company leaders realized that without new successful product launches, the company would lack organic growth. To spur the creation of new products and to effectively market them the company created a new strategic plan focused on generating consistent organic growth.

One key part of the new strategy was splitting the marketing department into two parallel marketing organizations. One marketing group would now focus on new products and the other would focus on the base marketing of the company's current brands to best execute the company's new strategy.

Although Church & Dwight's leaders knew that this was the right strategy an important obstacle remained. Most marketing employees felt that the most exciting part of their job was new product development. The company's marketing professionals enjoyed doing market research, spending time with consumers, and working on new product ideas. Under the new structure, base marketing employees would have to give this up and become responsible for what many saw as the more mundane, tactical execution of base marketing. Church & Dwight knew that its marketing talent drives the company's performance, and wanted to keep them engaged.

Church & Dwight's leaders ask you for advice on how to best influence its key marketing talent to support the new strategy and embrace their new responsibilities. After reading this chapter, you should have some good ideas.

JASON KEMPIN/GETTY IMAGES

The word *power* often conjures up a variety of thoughts, both good and bad. When used effectively, power and influence are essential to every manager's performance. When used inappropriately, power can result in unethical behavior and be damaging to employees and organizations. Effectively using power and influence is a skill, and misusing either can quickly derail your career. Conflict in organizations is often about power and influence, and the way power is manifested in the organization and across workgroups. Understanding what power and influence are and how to effectively use them will enhance your success in any organization.

Politics is closely related to power and influence. In addition to impacting your own success as a manager, politics is important to understand due to its negative effects on firm performance.[2] In this chapter, we discuss the nature of power, influence, and politics. After reading this chapter, you should have a good idea of how to effectively use them in advancing your career and managing more effectively.

POWER IN ORGANIZATIONS

power
A person or group's potential to influence another person's or group's behavior

Power refers to a person or group's potential to influence another person or group to do something that would not otherwise have been done.[3] Power is held by individuals as well as by groups. People tend to respond differently when they gain power. Although some people use power altruistically, others use it for more selfish motives.[4]

need for power
Wanting to control and influence others, or to be responsible for others

leadership motive pattern
A high need for power (with high impulse control) and a low need for affiliation

Noted scholar David McClelland initially expected effective leadership to be grounded in the need to achieve, but he found that the real driver of a leader's performance was the leader's ***need for power***,[5] or the desire to control and influence others or to be responsible for others (recall that we introduced and discussed the need for power in Chapter 5). He found that an individual's power need could be directed positively if the leader could postpone immediate gratification and not act impulsively. He later called this the ***leadership motive pattern***: a high need for power (with high impulse control) and a low need for affiliation.[6] The leadership motive pattern is grounded in a need for power, and is generally associated with high managerial performance.[7]

Most experts agree that there are seven types of power. These are summarized in Table 13.1. Legitimate, reward, and coercive powers come from the position one holds in an organization. The levels of these powers are greater for employees in higher organizational levels. Expert, informational, referent, and persuasive powers are types of personal powers. The levels of these powers depend on characteristics unique to each person. We next discuss these sources of position and personal power in greater detail, and provide tips on using them most effectively.

Position Power

position power
Based on one's position in the organization influence tactics

Managers' power stems in part from organizational authority. Managers typically have formal authority because of their position, which gives them a legitimate right to ask employees to do things that are part of their job descriptions. Organizational authority gives a manager ***position power***, which is power based on one's position in the organization. For example, the president of a

Table 13.1

Types of Power

Legitimate	Power due to the position of authority held
Reward	Power due to control over rewards
Coercive	Power due to control over punishments
Expert	Power due to control because of knowledge, skills, or expertise
Informational	Power due to control over information
Referent	Power due to control because subordinates respect, admire, and identify with the leader
Persuasive	Power due to the ability to use logic and facts to persuade

company, dean of a school, or manager of a sports team has certain forms of control that come with each position. We next discuss the three types of position power: power due to one's job, power due to control over rewards, and power due to control over punishments.

Legitimate Power

Legitimate power is a form of position power based on a person's holding a managerial position rather than anything the manager is or does as a person.[8] Legitimate power is the formal authority the firm gives a manager to hire new employees, assign work, monitor employees' work, and enforce organizational rules. Subordinates comply because they believe that the managerial position gives the manager the right to make certain requests of them. For example, nurses will show up for their shifts as assigned by a supervisor, even if those shifts are not those they prefer. Because the scheduling manager has the legitimate power to assign shifts, employees accept the final work schedule.

legitimate power
A position power based on a person's holding of the managerial position rather than anything the manager is or does as a person

In using legitimate power effectively, it is important to follow the proper channels of communication and to be responsive to subordinates' concerns. Your requests should be made politely but confidently, and your authority to make the request should be clearly communicated.

Reward Power

Reward power is position power that involves the use of both tangible (e.g., pay raises or preferred work assignments) and intangible (e.g., praise) rewards to influence and motivate

reward power
A position power that involves the use of rewards to influence and motivate followers

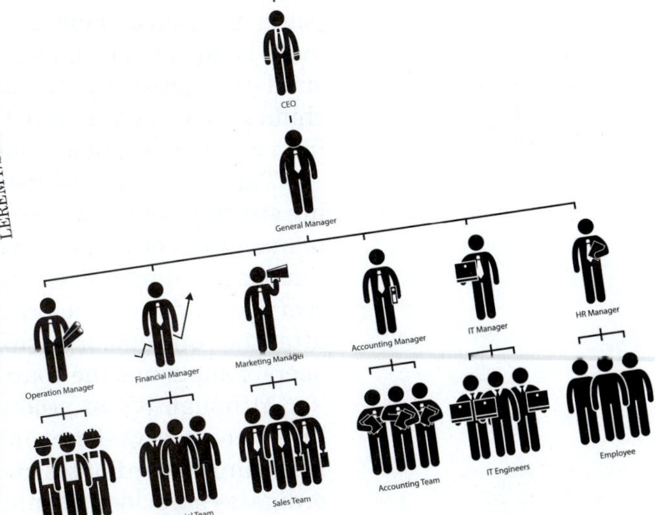

LEREMY/SHUTTERSTOCK.COM

Legitimate power is a form of position power based on a person's holding a managerial position rather than anything the manager is or does as a person. For instance, in this organizational chart the Marketing Manager has legitimate power over the Sales Team and the Accounting Manager has legitimate power over the Accounting Team. The General Manager, in turn, has legitimate power over the Marketing Manager and the Accounting Manager and, by extension, over the Sales Team and the Accounting Team.

WAVEBREAKMEDIA/SHUTTERSTOCK.COM

Reward power involves the use of rewards to influence and motivate followers. This manager is using reward power to give a subordinate a prize for being a top performer.

followers.[9] Students comply with instructor instructions and deadlines because they want to receive the reward of a good grade. Rewards are one of the strongest tools used by managers to inspire high performance. This chapter's *Real World Response* describes how Church & Dwight used reward power to influence its marketing talent to embrace the changes made to their job responsibilities.

Because rewards are such strong motivators, it is important to monitor the positive and negative impacts they have on employee behavior. For example, the manager of a hair salon wanted to motivate his stylists to sell more beauty products. The manager began offering a monthly prize to the stylist who sold the most products. Because one stylist's customers always tended to buy more products than did the other stylists' customers, the other stylists felt that there was no way they could win the prize. Rather than trying harder to sell products, they stopped trying at all, and overall product sales and revenues fell. Clearly, if rewards are improperly used, they can decrease the motivation of employees who do not expect to receive them. To effectively use your reward power, offer attractive rewards (which may differ across employees), make reasonable requests, and ensure that the rewards you offer are viewed as ethical and not as bribes.

Coercive Power

If a manager has the ability to punish subordinates, she or he can use position power to "coerce" subordinates to comply out of fear or because people want to avoid being punished. This is ***coercive power***.[10] Punishment could be any undesired or negative consequence, including a reduction in work hours, undesirable shifts, or a written or verbal reprimand. If an instructor threatens to deduct points from a paper assignment for poor grammar, this is the use of coercive power.

coercive power
A position power based on fear or a desire to avoid punishment

Threatening punishment can have negative side effects on employees, including stress, resentment, decreased morale, and retaliation[11] and can even cost the manager his or her job. William J. Fife, former CEO of Giddings and Lewis, a company that manufactures factory equipment, was fired because of his abuse of coercive power. Fife destructively used punishments such as verbally criticizing, attacking, and embarrassing top managers in meetings. After investigating managers' complaints, the board of directors asked Fife to resign.[12]

Although it can produce behavior change, use coercion only when absolutely necessary—for example, if an employee is engaging in unsafe behaviors. Informing subordinates about rules and punishments for violations, giving subordinates sufficient warning prior to the punishment and giving them a chance

Coercive power is based on fear or a desire to avoid punishment. It is often displayed by managers who yell at or berate their subordinates. This senior manager is using coercive power to criticize one of his subordinates, but everyone in the room seems to be affected by it.

PETER BERNIK /SHUTTERSTOCK.COM

to improve, and using punishment only when you are certain of a violation helps to decrease employee resentment and retaliation. To most effectively use coercive power, it is also important to administer appropriate punishment promptly and consistently, avoid appearing hostile, and give warnings and punishment notifications in private.

Personal Power

Position power does not guarantee that employees will fully cooperate with you. For example, employees of an unpopular supervisor may do the minimum amount possible to meet the requirements of their jobs. A manager's ability to influence others to give their full effort depends on the power or capability she or he has to influence other people's behavior or attitudes. Personal influence gives a manager ***personal power***, which is based on the characteristics of that individual and stays with the individual regardless of where that person works.

personal power
Based on the person's individual characteristics; stays with a person regardless of his or her job or organization

We next discuss the four types of personal power that are based on a person's unique characteristics and that are independent of one's formal position in an organization: power based on an individual's expertise, power due to control over information, power based on the respect of others, and power due to the ability to persuade.

Expert Power

Expert power is based on an individual's expertise in some area.[13] When Warren Buffet, nicknamed the "Sage of Omaha," speaks on the economy, for example, many people listen intently to what he has to say. People respond to expert power because of their belief in the person's knowledge, skills, or expertise. For example, some sales managers may have specialized knowledge of certain market segments or customers, giving them expert power among other managers and employees.

expert power
A personal power based on an individual's knowledge or expertise

Because an individuals' knowledge is the foundation of expert power, it is a personal power and can exist at any level in

AUREMAR/ SHUTTERSTOCK.COM

Expert power is based on an individual's knowledge or expertise. This manager is showing a colleague how to perform a task. The knowledge that he possesses about how to perform this task gives him expert power. Of course, once the colleague learns how to perform the task, the expert power of the first manager is diminished.

an organization. To enhance your own expert power, try to identify the technical expertise that is important in your organization. Then enhance your own expertise in this area through formal training or on-the-job learning. Become an expert in your company's industry, products, services, and systems. Maintaining credibility by telling the truth, acting confident, and staying current in your field will also enhance others' perceptions of your expert power.

Informational Power

informational power
Power derived from control over information

Control over information is ***informational power***. In addition to experts with specialized knowledge, some people in an organization have or are able to control access to important information. These *gatekeepers* are able to exert power over others by providing or withholding information that others need. For example, managers with extensive personal networks may have access to information few others have. Once shared, however, the informational power that information provided is lost. Managers who depend on informational power must therefore continually replenish their supply of hard-to-get information.

Referent Power

referent power
A personal power based on a manager's charisma or attractiveness to others

Referent power is another type of personal power based on a manager's charisma or attractiveness to others. Subordinates see the manager as a role model and comply out of respect, admiration, and liking. They behave as the manager does and wants because they seek his or her approval.[14] Consistent ethical behavior can increase your reputation and thus your referent power.

Referent power is not limited to high-visibility leaders. All managers can use referent power effectively by displaying respect for subordinates, modeling behaviors consistent with the organization's culture, and being effective role models. By consistently "walking the walk" and "talking the talk," managers can use their referent power to promote the attitudes and behaviors they desire in employees. For example, when Walmart founder Sam Walton was worth more than $25 billion, he still drove his own old pickup truck to work. His modeling of frugality permeated the company and promoted the behaviors and values that helped make Walmart consistently profitable.[15]

Persuasive Power

persuasive power
Power due to the ability to use logic and facts to persuade

Persuasive power is due to the ability to use logic and facts to persuade others to adopt one's ideas or perspectives. Good listening skills and identifying and appealing to the goals and motivations of the other person can enhance your persuasive power.

USING POWER

It is important to adjust your use of power to the situation and person you are trying to influence. Because the effects of referent and expert power rely on the employee's *internal motivation* and voluntary compliance, they are always appropriate. However, these types of power are not always effective—if they do not motivate employee behavior, then either legitimate or reward organizational power might be appropriate. Although you may lack some types of power, you should assess what types of power you do have and strategically choose which to assert in a particular situation.

Legitimate, reward, and coercive power rely on *external motivation* and obligatory obedience. Legitimate and reward power are frequently employed as methods of influence by managers, but coercive power is rarely appropriate and should be reserved for only the most extreme situations. Effective leaders tend to rely on expert and referent power more than legitimate, reward, or coercive power.[16] Using legitimate, reward, and coercive powers to influence others is using power rather than leadership. Leadership is more effective to the degree that followers' behaviors toward the leader's goals are voluntary and not coerced.

Through your speech and actions, you can use your power to motivate subordinates by arousing appropriate motives in them. For example, when competitive follower behavior is required, you might arouse followers' need for power. When you want to inspire exceptional efforts to attain difficult goals, you might arouse followers' need for achievement.[17]

Acquiring and Using Power

So how can you increase your power in your organization? How can you get a good raise and a promotion? How can you avoid abusing your power? This section will help to answer these questions and give you some ideas about how you might best acquire and use power in your own career.

Acquiring Power

It is important to recognize that you have different levels of each type of power, and to understand when each type of power is appropriate to use. Your power is greater if the things you control are important, rare, and cannot be substituted for by something else.[18] If you have expertise that is important to your company, that not many other people in your field have, and that cannot be substituted for by something else, then you will have more power than if you could be easily replaced and do not contribute much value to your workgroup or organization. Table 13.2 gives you the opportunity to understand the amount of power you hold in your own organization.

Developing your expertise and performing well can increase your power. In addition to technical expertise, becoming an expert on your own company can make you a valuable and powerful employee. Learn your company's history, strategy, and what is on its website. Learn how each department contributes to other departments and to the company as a whole. Identify emerging trends that will influence your industry or the economy as a whole. Persuade management to let you present these important issues to key people elsewhere in the company. Be sure that your work is relevant to important organizational problems and that you and your work are visible to the people who control raises and promotions. Network inside and outside your organization to develop positive relationships with people who can be helpful to you throughout your career.[19]

Table 13.2

Are You Powerful?

As you have learned in this chapter, power is greater among individuals who control scarce resources that are important to others. This assessment measures the importance and scarcity of your contributions to your supervisors and coworkers. Use the following scale to respond to the questions below.

___ 1. I do not think that my department/area would function well if my job was not done properly.
___ 2. If I were to leave, my manager would have a difficult time finding someone with my skills and abilities as a replacement.
___ 3. It seems that a lot of other people in this department/area depend on me to do my job well.
___ 4. My manager knows that I do things in my job that not very many other people can do.
___ 5. My manager depends on me a lot.
___ 6. My manager is aware that I have pretty unique job-related skills and abilities.

Scoring: To calculate your perceived power in your organization, add up your answers to the six questions. Your total should be between 6 and 30. Place your score on this continuum:

5——10——15——20——25——30

Low perceived power High perceived power

Interpretation: The higher your perceived power, the more successful your influence attempts are likely to be. You can rely on your expert, referent, and informational power to increase the success of your influence attempts. If you have low power and would like to increase it, try to identify ways you can develop skills and expertise that would be useful to your workgroup and that other group members do not already have. You might also try to develop your listening and persuasion skills.

Source: Boss, R. W. (2000). Hospital Professionals' Use of Upward Influence Tactics. *Journal of Managerial Issues 7*, 92–108.

Abuse of Power

abuse of power
Using any type of power to demean, exploit, or take advantage of another or influencing someone to do something the person later regrets

Power in an absolute sense is neither good nor bad—what matters is how the power is used. An important point to make about power is the potential for its abuse. The ***abuse of power*** is using any type of power to demean, exploit, or take advantage of another or influencing someone to do something the person later regrets. Disrespecting individual dignity and interference with job performance or deserved rewards are abuses of power.[20] It is easy to think of news stories where people have abused their power. In addition to financial damage, the results of the abuse of power may include decreased employee satisfaction and helping behaviors,[21] increased employee deviance,[22] and increased turnover.

It is important to remember that having power does not mean that you must use it. Being able to fire a subordinate if he does not follow formal work rules does not mean that you have to do so. Having power also does not guarantee that using it will be effective in influencing desired behavior.

If you have the power to punish a subordinate if she does not work a particular shift, the subordinate can still refuse the extra shift and quit. The greater the importance that others place on the resources or outcomes that you control, the greater the power you have in that relationship. If you do not have something that another person wants, you have no power over him or her.

Unchecked authority can result in the abuse of power. Managers should not have free rein to do whatever they want—managers' power should match their responsibilities. For example, a manager responsible for subordinates' performance should possess some sort of reward power such as allocating merit pay awards. But the power given to a manager should generally not exceed what is required to do his or her job. Regularly reviewing managers' behaviors and performance and holding them accountable for their actions is important. Even CEOs report to a board of directors, and legislation like the Sarbanes-Oxley Act of 2002 limits the unchecked authority of CEOs.

Perhaps the best known types of power abuse are bullying, abusive supervision, and sexual harassment (involving unwanted advances, requests, communication, or contact with the threat of punishment for noncompliance). When managers do not know how to persuade or influence through more effective tactics, they may resort to the use of fear, threats, and intimidation because that is all they know how to do.[23]

Mark Cuban, owner of the Mavericks NBA basketball team, is a good example of how power alone is insufficient in securing desired outcomes. Cuban has position power as the owner of five businesses, and many people look up to him due to his referent power. He has coercive power, which he used in firing the Mavericks' coach, and is considered an expert in business. He is well connected with other influential people, and has high information power. Nonetheless, Cuban's behavior has cost him respect as well as a lot of money. He has stormed into locker rooms and cursed players when his team lost, and he has berated referees. Although he would like to own more professional sports teams, he has stated that he knows other sports leagues might not consider his bids for ownership due to his poor NBA behavior.[24]

Empowerment

The degree to which power is shared and an employee has the authority to make and implement at least some decisions is ***empowerment***.[25] Empowerment may be organization-wide and embedded in an organization's culture, or it may be something created by individual managers. Empowering employees to improve quality, cut costs, and improve their work efficiency is becoming more common in organizations as computerized technologies increasingly give employees the feedback they need to manage themselves. If trained employees have important, accurate, and timely information, they can often handle situations and spot opportunities without a manager's intervention. This can increase the flexibility and responsiveness of organizations.

empowerment
Sharing power with employees and giving them the authority to make and implement at least some decisions

Essentially, empowerment requires two things: (1) that managers allow those beneath them to have more power and control over their work, and (2) that managers provide training, resources, and coaching to give them the skills and confidence to act empowered. Just telling an employee that he or she is empowered is not enough. Employees must have the skills to do what they are empowered to do and believe that they can successfully do it. The authors saw this when consulting for a manufacturing facility. Newly empowered employee teams had the authority to spend up to $500 to improve their teams' processes without having to consult with a manager. At first, none of the teams were willing to spend anything, fearing that they would make a bad choice. Not until the teams went through a hands-on training program teaching decision making, communication, and problem-solving skills did they have the confidence to act empowered.

Because your good reputation for ethical behavior decreases a supervisor's concern that you might behave inappropriately, it also can increase your supervisor's willingness to give you more responsibility and empowerment. A reputation for ethical behavior increases the influence you are given because you are not seen as someone trying to advance a personal agenda.[26]

Being an ethical leader is a source of power because it eliminates hidden agendas and builds trust. Ethics also increases our resistance to attempts by others to influence us because it keeps us focused, thus decreasing the power others have over us.[27]

Technology can empower employees to solve problems themselves. For example, knowing that to receive her quarterly bonus she must consistently meet call volume targets, Pat uses the digital dashboard to check her performance. The color-coded display shows that she is below target. She knows that she has been getting to work on time and that she is productive. So why is her performance below her target? Pat sees that her call volume has been consistently low for the last month, always just after lunch. This reveals the root cause of the problem. Her afternoon shift starts at exactly the time her lunch break ends, and although she hurries through lunch, she is getting back from lunch ten minutes after her scheduled start each afternoon. Pat requests a minor schedule change that gives her ten more minutes to get from the cafeteria to her workstation.[28] The digital dashboard helped to empower Pat to solve her performance problem without needing the help of a supervisor, other than for approval of the minor schedule change.

How Subunits Obtain Power

We now shift our attention away from individual power to how subunits acquire the power that allows them greater influence in organizational decisions. A workgroup's, department's, or subunit's power is derived either from its control of resources or through its strategic power.[29] The more desirable and important the resources controlled by a group (e.g., budget, space), the greater the group's *resource power*. Groups that occupy a central role in decision making wield greater *strategic power* by influencing higher-level decisions. Key subunits that influence the performance of other subunits have greater power. We next discuss several conditions that enhance a subunit's power.

Resource Scarcity

When resources are scarce, power differences across subunits are likely to be magnified. Power is greater for subunits that control scarce resources that are vital to the organization as a whole. When resources are plentiful, subunit power differences are often reduced.

Centrality

A subunit's activities are central to the extent that they influence the work of many other subunits (e.g., budget approval power), when their impact is more immediate (e.g., a performance decline in that unit would be felt faster by the organization as a whole), and when the subunit has a critical impact on the firm's key product or service. This is one reason why production and marketing departments tend to have greater power than human resource departments.

Substitutability

A subunit's power is reduced to the extent that others inside or outside of the organization can also perform its responsibilities. The labor market has a big influence on substitutability—when a subunit's skills become scarce in the labor market, the power of that subunit increases. If a subunit's work can be outsourced, that unit's power decreases because the threat of outsourcing can counter its influence attempts.

Uncertainty

Organizations do not like surprises or uncertainties. Accurate planning, financing, budgeting, and staffing all depend on a reasonably predictable future. The subunits most capable of coping with uncertainty or of guiding the organization through a period of increased uncertainty tend to have greater power.

INFLUENCE IN ORGANIZATONS

Influential people have power, but not all powerful people have influence. For example, employees are often more responsive to the social influence of their peers than to the control and incentives of management.[30] Leadership is in large part an influence process that involves the use of various powers or interpersonal styles to affect the behaviors and attitudes of others. But whether a leader's use of power to influence someone will be successful depends on whether the other person allows him- or herself to be influenced. How much formal power or authority a manager has is not nearly as important as the amount of influence the manager has over subordinates. If you lack the respect of subordinates because of unethical behavior or perceptions that you are unqualified, you will not effectively motivate your subordinates to work their hardest toward the firm's goals.

Influence Tactics

People apply their power to influence the behavior of others through ***influence tactics***. Influence tactics increase the likelihood that others will respond favorably to your requests. What might be different for you at work if you had a greater ability to influence your bosses and coworkers? What might be different for you at school if you were better able to influence your classmates and instructors?

influence tactics
How people translate their power to affect the behavior of others

Influence tactics should be matched to the situation and to the person being influenced, and can be learned with practice.[31] Responses to influence attempts are not always positive, however. Table 13.3 summarizes some influence tactics along with the possible responses to them.

Table 13.3

Influence Tactics and Responses to Them

Influence Tactics	
Coalition tactics	Engaging the help of others to persuade someone to do something; referring to the support of others to convince someone to agree to a proposal or to change his or her attitude toward something
Consultation	Requesting someone's advice to solve a problem or mutually setting goals to increase a follower's commitment to the leader's decision; being willing to modify the goals or solution based on the person's concerns and suggestions to sustain commitment
Exchange	Offering to exchange something of value now or in the future for someone's cooperation; usually used after other tactics have failed due to the higher cost
Ingratiation	Flattering or praising someone to put them in a good mood or to make them more likely to want to help (e.g., complimenting your manager's outfit before asking for additional project funding), or using humor;[32] seen as more credible when used early rather than after other influence attempts have failed
Inspirational appeals	Appealing to someone's aspirations, values, and ideals to gain his or her commitment, or increasing people's confidence that they can do something in order to increase motivation; for example, Wayne Hale, Chairman of NASA's Space Shuttle Mission Management Team during the space shuttle *Discovery's* Return to Flight mission, stated, "So the fundamental question remains, do we have those qualities that made our ancestors successful? Do we have the judgment to weigh it all in the balance? Do we have the character to dare great deeds? History is watching."[33]
Legitimating tactics	Enhancing one's formal authority to make a certain request by referring to rules, precedents, or official documents; should be used early if doubts about the request's legitimacy are expected
Personal appeals	Asking someone to do something "because we're friends" or asking for a personal favor
Pressure	Using coercion or persistent follow-up or reminders to gain influence; risks undesirable side effects such as resentment
Rational persuasion (or reason)	Using logic and facts to persuade someone
Responses to Influence Attempts	
Commitment	Endorsing and becoming an actively involved participant as a result of the influence attempt
Compliance	Going along with what the influencer wants without being personally committed
Passive resistance	Rejecting the influence attempt but not getting in the way of what the influencer is trying to do
Active resistance	Rejecting the influence attempt and actively trying to stop the influencer from doing what she or he is trying to do, or trying to change the influencer's attitudes

Source: Yukl, G. A. *Leadership in Organizations.* (7th ed., p. 172, Table 6.8). Upper Saddle River, NJ: Pearson Education. © 2010.

Of the various influence tactics, rational persuasion, inspirational appeals, and consultation have been found to be the most effective, and pressure is the least effective.[34] Using more than one influence tactic at the same time can increase your effectiveness as long as the tactics are compatible.[35] For example, ingratiation could enhance the effectiveness of a personal appeal. Rational persuasion can be combined with any of the other tactics. Pressure, on the other hand, undermines the feelings of friendship that are the foundation of personal appeals and ingratiation.

Influence tactics are most effective when they are compatible with the influencer's power relative to the target person and with the interpersonal relationship between the two people. When the influencer and target person have mutual trust and shared objectives, rational persuasion, consultation, and collaboration are often effective. A moderate degree of friendship is usually necessary for personal appeals to work. Assertiveness is not likely to be effective with a superior.

Influence attempts are often unsuccessful on the first try and require the skilled use of a sequence of tactics over time. Initial influence attempts with subordinates or peers often begin with a simple request or with a weak form of rational persuasion because these techniques are easy and relatively low in personal cost (such as a weakened friendship). Anticipated resistance may be met with a stronger form of rational persuasion and softer tactics including consultation, personal appeals, inspirational appeals, and collaboration. Continued resistance is then countered with harder tactics or abandoning the effort if the request does not warrant the risks of escalation.[36] This chapter's *Case Study* feature illustrates the use of different influence tactics among employees trying to influence a leader's decision.

LOSKUTNIKOV/SHUTTERSTOCK.COM

CASE STUDY Influencing Decisions

Imagine that you are a manager responsible for choosing which new project to support. Your budget is limited, and you can support only one new project. You must make a decision by tomorrow morning. Your staff just finished presenting their ideas to you, and you are finding it difficult to choose. Each project has merit, and you feel that they all have an equal chance of success. As the meeting comes to a close, your team members each make a last-minute appeal to win your support.

Jose: "You are a great leader and have always made great decisions for the team. I'm sure you'll choose the best one this time, too!"

Kira: "You've always said we should aim high. I think my idea will help our company reach new markets and raise us to the next level."

John: "I think my idea has the highest chance for a good return on our investment with the least risk. My market research is solid, and I think my idea is our best choice."

Sandy: "I talked to the folks in marketing and they said that we were really onto something with my idea. I think they really support this project and hope you choose it."

Questions:

1. What influence tactics did each staff member use?
2. Which influence tactic do you think would best persuade you to choose that person's idea? Why?
3. Which influence tactic do you think would be least effective in persuading you to choose that person's idea? Why?

PHANT/SHUTTERSTOCK.COM

Role of National Culture in Influence Effectiveness

Your ability to effectively influence others is enhanced by high cultural intelligence, or your ability to function effectively in culturally diverse environments. Understanding diverse cultures, values, and perspectives enhances your sensitivity to what is important to others and how to best influence them.

Influence tactics are also most effective when they are consistent with the social values in the national and organizational cultures. For example, consultation is likely to be a more effective influence tactic in a country with strong democratic traditions than in a country in which obedience to leaders is a strongly held cultural value.[37] This chapter's *Global Issues* feature describes the importance of understanding the appropriateness of using different influence tactics in different national cultures.

Persuasion Skills

Influencing others often requires persuading them to do or to believe something. Because persuasion gets people to do things differently because they want to, not because they have been ordered to, it is a more effective way to lead. The manager who wants more resources, the supervisor who wants to keep a key employee from leaving, and the company president who wants to sell her idea to the board of directors all need to be persuasive. Because most people are resistant to altering their habits, managers need to use persuasion skills whenever they need to create change.[38]

BALDYRGAN/SHUTTERSTOCK.COM

EFFECTIVENESS OF DIFFERENT INFLUENCE TACTICS DEPENDS ON NATIONAL CULTURE

Although rational persuasion and consultation have been found to be effective influence tactics in many countries,[39] national culture can affect the appropriateness of different influence tactics.[40] For example, consider Hong Kong and Taiwanese managers. Managers from both cultures believe that exchange and rational persuasion are the most effective influence tactics. However, Taiwanese managers tend to use inspirational appeals and ingratiation more than do Hong Kong managers, who feel that pressure is a more effective tactic.[41] Direct, task-oriented influence tactics are seen as more effective by western managers than by Chinese managers, who prefer tactics involving personal relations, avoidance, or an informal approach.[42] Understanding these differences is important to employees working as expatriates as well as to anyone who works in a multicultural workplace.

Matching your influence technique to the context and to the person you are trying to influence is important for upward as well as downward influence. One study found that host-country managers who demonstrate upward influence tactics that are culturally appropriate to the parent company's national culture will be more promotable than those who do not. Exchanging benefits and coalition are more likely to be associated with promotability in German firms than in domestic Ecuadorian firms.[43] Upward-appeal assertiveness is more likely to be associated with promotability in American firms than in domestic Ecuadorian firms.[44] Being aware not only of your sources of power, but also of the receptiveness of the other person to different influence tactics will improve your effectiveness as a manager.

Persuasion requires thorough and careful preparation, the compelling framing of arguments, the presentation of vivid supporting evidence, and finding the correct emotional match with the audience. It is much more than a sales skill. As one expert says, "Many businesspeople misunderstand persuasion, and more still underutilize it."

Here are some recommendations for being more persuasive:[45]

- *Build credibility* based on both your skills and your relationships. Using good posture and an appropriate tone of voice, and showing a sense of confidence will increase the chances that others will quickly see you as credible.[46]
- *Do not begin with a hard sell*. This gives potential opponents something to resist and fight against.[47]
- *Search for shared ground and be willing to compromise*. Every audience is different, and it is important not to come across as if you have already made up your mind. Communicate in words the audience easily understands and relates to, and incorporate values and beliefs they share.[48]
- *Develop compelling positions* based on only a few convincing arguments, rather than overwhelming people with facts and information.
- *Connect with people emotionally* rather than relying solely on logical arguments.
- *Create a continuous feedback loop* from the audience to yourself. Incorporate the audience's perspective back into your own arguments.[49]
- *Be patient*—people are rarely persuaded on the first try.[50]

Upward Influence

In addition to using influence to guide the behavior of subordinates, ***upward influence*** can also be used to influence superiors. When Jack Welch was the CEO of General Electric, he realized that the web was going to transform business. He recognized that GE's younger, "webified" employees had better Internet skills and e-business knowledge than did GE's older and higher-ranking executives. He decided to pair Internet-savvy employees with GE's 600 worldwide executives to share their expertise about the new technology. In addition to building the e-business capabilities of his managers, this unique "mentoring up" program made managers at all levels more comfortable with upward influence in the company.[51]

upward influence *Influencing superiors*

Upward influence is an important aspect of influence and contributes substantially to individual effectiveness in organizations.[52] There are six primary upward influence tactics:[53]

1. *Ingratiation*: using flattery and acting polite, friendly, or humble to put the supervisor in a good mood

MONKEY BUSINESS IMAGES/SHUTTERSTOCK.COM

There are several ways in which upward influence can occur in an organization. Take this young manager, for example. He is demonstrating some new software capabilities to his boss. His willingness and ability to do this, combined with his sincere pleasure in doing so, is influencing how he is perceived by his boss.

2. *Exchange*: offering to trade favors or rewards for compliance
3. *Rationality*: using logic, planning, reason, and compromise
4. *Assertiveness*: using aggression, nagging, and verbal confrontations or giving orders
5. *Coalition formation*: seeking the support of other organization members to show a united front
6. *Upward appeals*: making informal or formal appeals to organizational superiors for intervention

Your source(s) of power generally determines which upward influence tactics you tend to use. An employee with referent power might use integration, for example, and someone with expert power might prefer rationality. It is also important to adjust your influence tactic to suit the boss you are trying to influence.[54] The self-assessment in this chapter's *Understand Yourself* feature gives you the opportunity to learn more about your preferred upward influence tactics.

upward influence styles
Combinations of upward influence tactics that tend to be used together

The six upward influence tactics can be used alone, but are often used in combination with each other in what are called ***upward influence styles***. People tend to have a preferred upward influence style that they use when trying to influence their managers. The four upward influence styles are:[55]

1. *Shotgun*: This style uses the most influence and emphasizes assertiveness and bargaining. Shotgun managers tend to have less job tenure and the greatest needs to obtain personal benefits and "sell" their ideas about how the work should be done.[56] Shotgun managers attempt to obtain what they want by using many different tactics.[57] This style is associated with the highest levels of job tension and personal stress.[58]
2. *Tactician*: This style uses an average amount of influence and emphasizes reason. Tactician managers tend to direct organizational subunits involved in nonroutine work that gives them a skill and knowledge power base. Tacticians tend to have considerable influence in their organizations over budgets, policy, and personnel and rely heavily on reason and logic to gain compliance. This style is associated with the lowest levels of job tension and personal stress[59] and with more favorable individual outcomes than the more forceful shotgun style.
3. *Bystander*: This style uses little influence with superiors. Bystander managers tend to direct organizational units doing routine work and generally have little organizational power (i.e., little control over budgets, policy, or personnel matters). Because they also tend to have few personal or organizational objectives that require compliance from others, they generally exert little influence.[60] Between 30 and 40 percent of managers are classified as bystanders.[61]
4. *Ingratiator*: This style primarily uses a friendliness strategy but also uses the other influence strategies to some extent. The name of this style reflects the dominant mode by which these managers exercise influence.[62] Research has found that top managers who use ingratiation behaviors toward their CEO, including flattery, expressing confirming opinions, and performing favors, are more likely to receive board appointments at firms where their CEO is either a director or knows members of the board.[63]

UNDERSTAND YOURSELF

UPWARD INFLUENCE SCALE

People use a variety of tactics when attempting to influence their bosses. Please use the following scale to record how often you engage in each of the following behaviors when influencing your boss. Be honest—there are no right or wrong answers.

Never		Occasionally		Frequently		Almost always
1	2	3	4	5	6	7

___ 1. Act very humbly while making my request.
___ 2. Make my boss feel good about me before making my request.
___ 3. Act in a friendly manner before making my request.
___ 4. Remind my boss of past favors I have done for him/her.
___ 5. Offer an exchange (e.g., if you do this for me, I will do something for you).
___ 6. Offer to make a personal sacrifice (e.g., work late) if he/she will do what I want.
___ 7. Use logic to convince him/her.
___ 8. Explain the reasons for my request.
___ 9. Present my boss with information supporting my point of view.
___ 10. Have a showdown in which I confront my boss face-to-face.
___ 11. Express my anger verbally.
___ 12. Use a forceful manner: try things like making demands, setting deadlines, and expressing strong emotion.
___ 13. Obtain the support of coworkers to back up my request.
___ 14. Obtain the support of my subordinates to back up my request.
___ 15. Mobilize other people in the organization to help me in influencing my boss.
___ 16. Obtain the informal support of higher-ups.
___ 17. Make a formal appeal to higher levels to back up my request.
___ 18. Rely on the chain of command—on people higher up in the organization who have power over my boss.

Scoring:

Ingratiation: Add up your scores to statements 1–3 ___
Exchange: Add up your scores to statements 4–6 ___
Rationality: Add up your scores to statements 7–9 ___
Assertiveness: Add up your scores to statements 10–12 ___
Coalitions: Add up your scores to statements 13–15 ___
Upward appeal: Add up your scores to statements 16–18 ___

Interpretation: Rank the upward influence tactics from highest to lowest based on your scores. The tactics with the highest scores are your preferred influence tactics. Do you agree with the ranking? Which other tactics do you think you should try using more frequently in the future? Why?

Sources: Table 4 (adapted) from Kipnis, D., Schmidt, S. M., and Wilkinson, I. (1980). Intraorganizational influence tactics: Explorations in getting one's way. *Journal of Applied Psychology, 65*(4), 440–452. Text excerpts (adapted scale items), from Schriesheim, C. A., & Hinkin, T. R. (1990). Influence tactics used by subordinates: A theoretical and empirical analysis and refinement of the Kipnis, Schmidt, and Wilkinson subscales. *Journal of Applied Psychology, 75*(3), 246–257.

ORGANIZATIONAL POLITICS

In organizations, people differ in their ability to influence others and influence work processes. Accordingly, people differ in what they can do to protect and promote their own interests. ***Organizational politics*** are social influence attempts directed at people who can provide rewards that will help promote or protect the self-interests of the actor.[64] At some point everyone needs

organizational politics
Social influence attempts directed at those who can provide rewards that will help promote or protect the self-interests of the actor

Organizational politics are social influence attempts directed at people who can provide rewards that will help promote or protect the self-interests of the actor. These two individuals are sharing confidential information in an attempt to influence their colleagues in a meeting. Therefore, they are engaging in organizational politics.

to influence others to follow their ideas or preferred courses of action, and doing that requires the use of politics. Effectively influencing others through persuasion, generating support, and inspiring trust are the core of effective politics.

Politics are a fact of life in work organizations—virtually every employee in America can describe a political incident in which he or she was directly or indirectly involved.[65] Employees who have been negatively affected by politics tend to perceive politics to be a negative influence in organizations, whereas those whose interests were advanced through political means tend to view it as a useful tool.[66] Because employees act based on their perceptions, recognizing and understanding employees' perceptions of politics is important to managing effectively.[67]

Organizational politics are the result of both individual employees and the culture of the organization.[68] Some cultures permit and even promote certain types of political behaviors. Political behaviors are most likely to occur when there is a reasonably high degree of ambiguity or uncertainty in the work environment.[69] Some organizations proactively seek to eliminate political behavior. For example, new hires at the software company Success Factors agree in writing to fourteen "rules of engagement." Rule 14 starts out, "I will be a good person to work with—not territorial, not be a jerk." One of the company's founding principles is that "our organization will consist only of people who absolutely love what we do, with a white-hot passion. We will have utmost respect for the individual in a collaborative, egalitarian, and meritocratic environment—no blind copying, no politics, no parochialism, no silos, no games—just being good!" Employees are not expected to be perfect, but when they lose their cool or belittle colleagues, inadvertently or not, they are expected to apologize.[70]

Eugene McKenna identified these common political tactics in organizations:[71]

1. *Controlling information*: restricting information to certain people
2. *Controlling lines of communication*: establishing gatekeepers to restrict access to information
3. *Using outside experts*: outside consultants may seem neutral, but are paid and directed by management to "do their bidding"
4. *Controlling the agenda*: to ensure only certain topics are discussed
5. *Game playing*: leaking information, getting only friends to provide feedback, and so on
6. *Image building*: enlisting "spin doctors" to project a desirable image
7. *Building coalitions*: befriending powerful others or starting small subgroups to promote specific aims

8. *Controlling decision parameters*: trying to influence decisions before they are made
9. *Eliminating political rivals*: this may even mean getting them promoted to get them out of the way

When politics are constructive rather than destructive, they are unnoticeable. When politics are used to advance self-serving causes, employees tend to perceive the workplace as more highly political. The more political employees perceive a work environment to be, the greater their job anxiety and intentions to leave, and the lower their job and supervisor satisfaction and organizational commitment.[72] Individuals' perceptions about the political nature of their work environment impact employees' productivity[73] and how political the environment will actually be. Employees who perceive that others get ahead by acting politically engage in more political behaviors themselves.[74] Organizational culture is thus influenced by the perceived degree of political activity and how the employees in that organization react to these perceptions.[75]

Political skill involves having interpersonal influence as well as social astuteness, which involves showing respect for others' ways of thinking. Developing a strong network and being perceived by others as sincere also reflects high political skill.[76] Political skill has been found to be positively related to job performance.[77] The self-assessment in Table 13.4 gives you the chance to better understand your political skill.

Causes of Political Behavior

Conflict is at the core of organizational politics.[78] Because political behavior is self-serving, it has the potential to threaten the self-interests of others. When a perceived threat is followed by retaliation, conflict arises.[79] Uncertainty increases political behavior. Lacking specific rules and policies for guidance, employees develop their own rules for acceptable behavior that are often self-serving. Decisions made under uncertainty are particularly susceptible to political influence.[80]

Scarcity of valued resources (e.g., transfers, raises, office space, budgets) also promotes political behavior. Jockeying for a position to receive a valued but scarce resource is classic political behavior.[81] This is why organizations with limited resources tend to have more political environments. Understanding why resources are limited can help to predict who is likely to be the target of the political activities, as well as how strong the political behavior is likely to be. Anyone who controls critical resources that cannot be secured elsewhere is a probable target of political influence tactics.[82]

Some individuals desire to avoid conflict, and therefore tend not to resist others' influence attempts. Although this may appear to be nonpolitical, it is actually a form of political behavior. It has been suggested that the distinction between political and nonpolitical behavior in organizations can be made on the basis of intent.[83] That is, if a behavior is enacted specifically to advance one's own self-interests (including conflict avoidance), then the individual is acting politically.[84] Because employees who "don't rock the boat" are not viewed as threatening opponents, they may be welcomed into the "in-group" and receive valued outcomes simply for not interfering with a politically acting individual's or group's agenda. Inaction, or going along to get ahead, can

Table 13.4

Political Skill Inventory

This self-assessment gives you the opportunity to better understand your political skill. Be honest in responding to the statements below using the following scale:

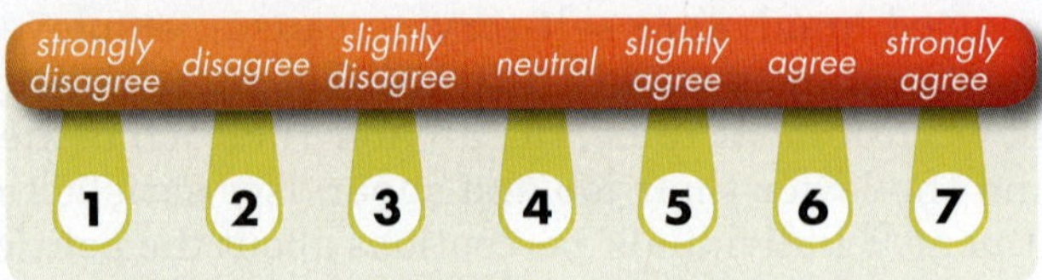

___ 1. I spend a lot of time and effort at work networking with others.
___ 2. I am able to make most people feel comfortable and at ease around me.
___ 3. I am able to communicate easily and effectively with others.
___ 4. It is easy for me to develop good rapport with most people.
___ 5. I understand people very well.
___ 6. I am good at building relationships with influential people at work.
___ 7. I am particularly good at sensing the motivations and hidden agendas of others.
___ 8. When communicating with others, I try to be genuine in what I say and do.
___ 9. I have developed a large network of colleagues and associates at work whom I can call on for support when I really need to get things done.
___ 10. At work, I know a lot of important people and am well connected.
___ 11. I spend a lot of time at work developing connections with others.
___ 12. I am good at getting people to like me.
___ 13. It is important that people believe I am sincere in what I say and do.
___ 14. I try to show a genuine interest in other people.
___ 15. I am good at using my connections and network to make things happen at work.
___ 16. I have good intuition and am savvy about how to present myself to others.
___ 17. I always seem to instinctively know the right things to say or do to influence others.
___ 18. I pay close attention to people's facial expressions.

Scoring: Add up your responses to the eighteen statements. This is your overall political skill score. Scores *over 72* are considered high and scores *below 36* are considered low. To calculate your score for the four dimensions of political skill, add up your responses to the following subsets of statements:

Social astuteness	**Interpersonal influence**	**Networking ability**	**Apparent sincerity**
5 ___	2 ___	1 ___	8 ___
7 ___	3 ___	6 ___	13 ___
16 ___	4 ___	9 ___	14 ___
17 ___	12 ___	10 ___	
18 ___		11 ___	
		15 ___	

Total Score: ___ /126
Subset Scores:
Social Astuteness: ___ /35 Interpersonal Influence: ___ /28
Networking Ability: ___ /42 Apparent Sincerity: ___ /21

Interpretation: The higher your score, the stronger your political skill in that area

Source: Ferris, G. R., Davidson, S. L., Perrewé, P. L. (2005). *Political Skill at Work: Impact on Work Effectiveness* (p. 23). Mountain View, CA: Davies-Black.

be a reasonable and profitable approach to take in order to advance one's own self-interests when working in a political environment.[85]

Organizational policies sometimes reward and perpetuate political behavior.[86] In particular, compensation policies may inadvertently reward individuals who engage in influence behaviors and penalize those who do not. Individually oriented rewards induce individually oriented behavior, which is often self-interested and political in nature. When this type of behavior is rewarded or reinforced, the tactics used to secure the reward will likely be repeated. This can lead to cultures that foster and reward political behavior. Rewarding political behavior can induce those who have not acted politically in the past to do so in the future. Individuals who perceive themselves as inequitably rewarded relative to others who engage in organizational politics may begin engaging in political behaviors to increase their own rewards.[87] This chapter's *Improve Your Skills* feature lets you hone your ability to assess the degree to which politics is a factor in your organization.

Managing Organizational Politics

Centuries ago, the philosopher Plato knew the importance of managing politics. He advised, "Those who are too smart to engage in politics are punished

IMPROVE YOUR SKILLS

RECOGNIZING POLITICS

Political behavior can be placed in three main categories: general political behavior, which includes the behaviors of individuals who act in a self-serving manner to obtain valued outcomes; going along to get ahead, which consists of a lack of action by individuals (e.g., remaining silent) in order to secure valued outcomes; and pay and promotion policies, which involve the organization behaving politically through the policies it enacts.[88] Rating the following set of statements based on the scale shown below will help you to assess the political environment that exists in your organization.

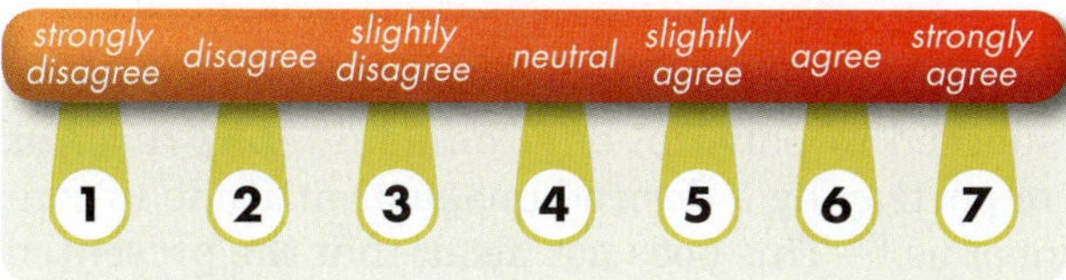

___ 1. People in this organization attempt to build themselves up by tearing others down.
___ 2. There has always been an influential group in this department that no one ever crosses.
___ 3. Agreeing with powerful others is the best alternative in this organization.
___ 4. It is best not to rock the boat in this organization.
___ 5. Sometimes it is easier to remain quiet than to fight the system.
___ 6. Telling others what they want to hear is sometimes better than telling the truth.
___ 7. It is safer to think what you are told than to make up your own mind.
___ 8. None of the raises I have received are consistent with the policies on how raises should be determined.
___ 9. When it comes to pay raise and promotion decisions, policies are irrelevant.
___ 10. Promotions around here are not valued much because how they are determined is so political.

Scoring: Add up the numbers you assigned to the ten statements. Your total should be between 10 and 70. Place your score on this continuum:

10——20——30——40——50——60——70
Not Political Extremely Political

Sources: Adapted from: Kacmar, K. M. and Ferris, G. R. (1991), Perceptions of Organizational Politics Scale (POPS): Development and Construct Validation. *Educational and Psychological Measurement, 51*, 193–205; Kacmar, K. M. & Carlson, D. S. (1997), Further Validation of the Perceptions of Politics Scale (POPS): A Multiple Sample Investigation. *Journal of Management, 23*, 627–658.

by being governed by those who are dumber." A modern expert advises, "Even if you are a person who takes no active part in [office] politics, knowing how the game is played means that you stand a good chance of surviving the depredations of those who undertake the lifestyle of cubicle warfare."[89] A survey of 150 executives of major U.S. companies found that they waste 19 percent of their time—at least one day per week—dealing with company politics.[90] The executives surveyed said they spent a bulk of that time dealing with internal conflicts, rivalry disputes, and other volatile situations at work. Because politics is pervasive and because political skill has been found to decrease job stress[91] it is worth developing your skills in this area.

Because political behaviors are enhanced by organizational factors including scarce resources, ambiguous roles and goals, centralization,[92] and complexity,[93] formal rules and procedures can help to reduce the occurrence of political behavior.[94] Clarifying job expectations; opening the communication process; confronting employees acting inefficiently, unethically, or irresponsibly; and serving as a good role model can all decrease political behavior.[95]

Keeping the number of employees assigned to each manager at a reasonable level is another way to decrease political behavior. In large workgroups, the amount of attention a supervisor is able to devote to each employee decreases. This can increase ambiguity and uncertainty, promoting a more political environment.[96]

Managing politics is about managing power. As one expert states, "Being a good office politician means that you know how to turn individual agendas into common goals."[97] If you understand the motivations and aspirations of your subordinates, you can help them to attain what they most want without resorting to politics or the inappropriate use of power. Building trust and openness to allow employees to freely discuss their feelings, fears, and opinions without fear of retaliation decreases the need for political behavior.[98]

To reduce political behavior and promote creativity at the innovation factory IDEO, company leaders have created an idea-friendly environment that minimizes the amount of corporate posturing associated with trying to guess what answer the boss is hoping for. As a result, IDEO employees tend to speak their minds, regardless of whether a "boss" is in the room.[99]

IMPRESSION MANAGEMENT

impression management
The process of portraying a desired image or attitude to control the impression others form of us

self-monitoring
Having a high concern with others' perceptions of us and adjusting our behavior to fit the situation

Being perceived positively by others is related to greater power and influence. It may also help employees succeed in political environments. ***Impression management*** is the process of portraying a desired image or attitude to control the impression others form of us.[100] This does not mean that the presented image is accurate, although misrepresenting your image can backfire if others later learn that the image is false.

Impression management is not inherently a bad thing[101]—in fact, most people regularly engage in some form of interpersonal deception. Research has found that 61.5 percent of people's natural conversation involves some form of deception,[102] and people tend to average sixteen white lies over a two-week period.[103]

People who are higher in the personality trait of ***self-monitoring***, which reflects having a high concern with others' perceptions of us and adjusting our

Impression management is the process of portraying a desired image or attitude to control the impression that others form of us. This man is checking his appearance before an important meeting. There is nothing wrong with wanting to make a "good impression," of course, as long as the impression being created is valid.

INNERVISIONART/SHUTTERSTOCK.COM

behavior to fit the situation,[104] are more likely to engage in impression management behaviors.[105] High self-monitors are good at reading situations and adjusting their behavior accordingly to maintain their desired image. Low self-monitors tend to present consistent images of themselves regardless of the situation.

People who engage in impression management often take great care to be perceived in a positive light.[106] Impression management techniques are commonly used by job applicants in interviews with positive results.[107] In particular, impression management techniques related to self-promotion[108] and ingratiation[109] tend to work well in job interviews. Self-promotion may not work as well on the job, however, because the supervisor has a better opportunity to observe what you can really do. In fact, self-promotion is related to lower performance evaluations.[110]

As a manager, being able to detect others' impression management and deception is obviously useful. Because nonverbal cues are most indicative of deception, focusing on the person's body language is particularly helpful.[111] Table 13.5 presents some tips for detecting impression management and deception on the part of others.

Table 13.5

Detecting Impression Management Behaviors

Although it can take a lot of experience and practice to be able to interpret them correctly, individuals engaging in impression management often display the following involuntary cues resulting from the emotions and cognitive effort required to manage their self-presentation:

1. *Elevated speaking pitch:* speaking at a higher pitch as compared to someone telling the truth[112]
2. *Speech errors:* interspersing words with uh, ah, or um[113]
3. *Speech pauses:* allowing greater periods of silence while engaged in a conversation[114]
4. *Negative statements:* using words like *no, not, can't,* and *won't*[115]
5. *Eye shifting;* looking away rather than at the person to whom they are speaking[116]
6. *Increased pupil dilation:* pupils tend to widen as they would in dim lighting[117]
7. *Blinking:* more frequent blinking[118]
8. *Tactile manipulation:* fondling or manipulating objects with the hands[119]
9. *Leg fidgeting:* leg twitches, foot tapping, and swiveling or rocking when sitting[120]
10. *Less hand gesturing:* "speaking" less with the hands and keeping the head relatively still[121]

SUMMARY AND APPLICATION

When used properly, power, influence, and politics are essential tools for managerial success. When used improperly, power, influence, and politics can undermine trust, result in unethical behavior, and create a toxic organization. Understanding these tools and how to use them effectively will help you to be a more successful manager.

Position power (legitimate, reward, and coercive powers) is derived from the position one holds in an organization. Personal power (expert, informational, referent, and persuasive powers) comes from the unique characteristics of individuals regardless of their position in the organization. Because leadership is more effective to the degree that followers' behaviors toward the leader's

LOSKUTNIKOV/SHUTTERSTOCK.COM

REAL WORLD RESPONSE

INFLUENCING ACCEPTANCE OF CHANGE AT CHURCH & DWIGHT

Church & Dwight knew that its marketing talent was likely to resist the change to two parallel marketing organizations, one focused on current brands and one focused on new product development. To keep its marketing talent engaged, the company ensured that its current brand team would still be involved in new product development even though the new product development team would run it and be accountable for it. The company also applied rational persuasion and showed the current brand team that the new arrangement would give them dedicated resources to use to do more with their own brands. The current brand team saw the logic of having dedicated resources to innovation and subsequent organic growth.

As expected, there was some resistance at beginning when the company carved some of the marketing people out and moved them into the new roles. To maintain job excitement, management used inspirational appeals linking the new structure and strategy to the company's success. Church & Dwight leaders also used legitimating tactics by making it clear that the change would happen and needed to happen quickly. Reward power also was used when all incentives were aligned around the new structure and objectives. This exchange of rewards for cooperation reflected the exchange influence tactic as well.

Church & Dwight's Executive Vice President of Global New Products Innovation, Steve Cugine, said that the results of the change "have been remarkable." Within three years the organic growth rate from new product development doubled to nearly 6 percent. The effectiveness of current brand marketing also increased, helping the company to achieve record organic growth of close to 10 percent for the consumer domestic U.S. business. The change has been so successful that Church & Dwight is expanding the new structure to the rest of its global locations.

Sources: This real world response is based on a telephone interview with Steve Cugine, Executive Vice President of Global New Products Innovation, Church & Dwight Co., October 2, 2009.

goals are voluntary and not coerced, effective leaders tend to rely on expert and referent power more than legitimate, reward, or coercive power.

Involvement gives subordinates influence in the decision being made; empowerment gives subordinates the ability and authority to make the decision themselves. Organizational subunits are more powerful when they control resources that are important but scarce, when they are central to the organization, when they cannot be substituted for, and when they help the organization successfully manage uncertainty.

Rational persuasion, inspirational appeals, and consultation are the most effective influence tactics, and pressure is the least effective. The six primary upward influence tactics are ingratiation, exchange, rationality, assertiveness, coalition formation, and upward appeals.

Uncertainty, scarcity of valued resources, and organizational policies can influence political behavior. Impression management involves the communication of a desired image or attitude to influence the image others form of us. Being perceived positively by others is related to greater power and influence. It may also help employees succeed in political environments.

DISCUSSION QUESTIONS

1. What power(s) does your instructor have?
2. What influence tactics does your instructor use to motivate you to learn?
3. Describe a time in the last week that someone influenced you to do something you would not otherwise have done. What influence tactic(s) did she or he use?
4. Is another person's ethics important to you in your decision to allow that person to influence you? Why or why not?
5. How can you ethically use power, influence, and politics to get a promotion?
6. Have you ever tried to influence your boss to do something? What upward influence tactics did you try? Were you successful? Why or why not?
7. Are office politics bad? Why or why not?
8. How do you use impression management at work?

DEVELOP YOUR SKILLS EXERCISE

Influencing an Ethical Decision

Read the following scenario and complete the assignment that follows it:

Soon after you begin a new job, you receive a troubling report from the company's new 401(k) provider. Several social security numbers do not match the names of the employees who provided them, which suggests that these individuals may be illegal aliens and ineligible to work in the United States. You begin an investigation, but your boss quickly orders you to stop, explaining that the company cannot afford to terminate those employees even if they are illegals because that would leave the company shorthanded. When you express your concern about this deliberate violation of federal immigration laws, the company's leadership is unworried. They have reasoned that the Immigration and Naturalization Service has bigger fish to fry, and that even if they are caught, the fine would be an acceptable business expense, since the company is making huge profits due to the cheap labor.

Assignment: Using what you have learned in this chapter, describe what you would do to change the company's policy toward employing illegal workers. How effective do you think you would be? Why?

GROUP EXERCISE

Influencing Your Instructor

Form groups of four to six students and identify your group's spokesperson. Using what you learned in this chapter, come up with a strategy to influence your instructor to change the evaluation criteria for this course (although it is likely too late in the semester for any changes to actually be made). Identify the influence tactics you will use, as well as the sources of power you will draw from. Now make a brief presentation to the class and instructor. The class will vote on which group is the most persuasive.

VIDEO EXERCISE

Numi Organic Tea: Value Chain, IT, and E-Business

Numi is the tea maker of choice for high-end restaurants, hotel chains, colleges, and cruise lines. As pioneer of green marketing, the organic beverage company is dedicated to sustainability, fair trade, and a small carbon footprint. Unlike most businesses, Numi has a three-fold bottom line of "people, planet, and profit," which requires managers to evaluate performance on a range of criteria, including the overall "greenness" of supply chain operations.

But maintaining an eco-friendly business isn't easy. Many international businesses don't share Numi's perspectives on social responsibility, waste management, and workers' rights. Some don't even speak the same ethical language. While some disagreements are acceptable, others require shrewd political calculation and pressure to resolve.

Fortunately for Numi, the technical side of managing partnerships has become easier through information technology. Whether the task involves inventory, packaging, or transport, Numi's high-tech enterprise resource planning system (ERP) enables efficient coordination with strategic partners around the globe. An ERP is a computer system that processes vast organization data and provides real time information on specific companywide operations. Since members of Numi's supply chain—mostly growers, mills, and factories—are linked to the same computer system, the tea maker is able to monitor global operations from its headquarters in Oakland, California. "We're managing our inventories in multiple countries through the same software program," says Brian Durkee, director of operations. "All we do now is simply go into the system and push a button to say we want to make a particular product, and the system pulls all the lots and materials for us and allocates the inventory."

Despite the cultural and ethical differences between Numi and certain overseas partners, managers are committed to achieving a common vision through a variety of tactics, both political and technological. The tea maker's pursuit of an ethical and sustainable supply chain reduces waste in energy and natural resources. As a result, Numi's organic tea products not only taste great, but they are good for the planet as well.

Discussion Questions

1. Describe the power relationship between Numi and its supply chain partners.
2. In the video, what issues with China-based suppliers require Numi's managers to use influence and persuasion tactics?
3. How does Numi get suppliers to comply with its policies?

Now What?

VIDEO CASE

PERCOM/SHUTTERSTOCK.COM

Imagine learning that your boss is trying unsuccessfully to influence a peer of yours to organize the company picnic again this year. When you are asked to try to influence the stubborn subordinate to agree to plan the picnic, *what do you say or do?* Go to this chapter's "Now What?" video, watch the challenge video, and choose a response. Be sure to also view the outcomes of the two responses you didn't choose.

Discussion Questions

1. Which influence tactics do you think were the most effective and why would they work?
2. If you were to use power to try to get the subordinate to do the task, which forms of power would work best and why? Which would be ineffective and why?
3. Did you detect any organizational politics, and if so, what types?
4. How else might you persuade your coworker to organize the picnic using power and influence?

ENDNOTES

[1]This vignette is based on a telephone interview with Steve Cugine, Executive Vice President of Global New Products Innovation, Church & Dwight Co., October 2, 2009.

[2]Eisenhardt, K., & Bourgeois, L. J. (1988). Politics of Strategic Decision Making in High Velocity Environments: Toward a Mid-Range Theory. *Academy of Management Journal, 31*, 737–770.

[3]Cartwright, D., & Zander, A. (1968). *Group Dynamics*. New York: Harper & Row; Richmond, V. P., McCroskey, J. C., Davis, L. M., & Koontz, K. A. (1980). Management Communication Style and Employee Satisfaction: A Preliminary Investigation. *Communication Quarterly, 28*, 37–46.

[4]For a more detailed discussion of power and influence, see Schriesheim, C., & Neider, L. (2006). *Power and Influence in Organizations: New Empirical and Theoretical Perspectives* (Vol. 5). Greenwich, CT: Information Age Publishing.

[5]McClelland, D. C. (1975). *Power: The Inner Experience*. New York: Irvington.

[6]McClelland, D. C., & Boyatzis, R. E. (1982). Leadership Motive Pattern and Long Term Success in Management. *Journal of Applied Psychology, 6*, 737–743.

[7]McClelland, D. C. (1975). *Power: The Inner Experience*. New York: Irvington.

[8]French, J. R. P., Jr., & Raven, B. H. (1968). The Bases of Social Power. In *Studies of Social Power*, ed. D. Cartwright. Ann Arbor, MI: Institute for Social Research.

[9]French, J. R. P., Jr., & Raven, B.H. (1968). The Bases of Social Power. In *Studies of Social Power*, ed. D. Cartwright. Ann Arbor, MI: Institute for Social Research.

[10]French, J. R. P., Jr., & Raven, B. H. (1968). The Bases of Social Power. In *Studies of Social Power*, ed. D. Cartwright. Ann Arbor, MI: Institute for Social Research.

[11]Inness, M., Barling, J., & Turner, N. (2005). Understanding Supervisor-Targeted Aggression: A Within-Person, Between-Jobs Design. *Journal of Applied Psychology, 90*(4), 731–739; Zellars, K. L., Tepper, B. J., & Duffy, M. K. (2002). Abusive Supervision and Subordinates' Organizational Citizenship Behavior. *Journal of Applied Psychology, 87*, 1368–1376; Williams, S. (1998). A Meta-Analysis of the Relationship Between Organizational Punishment and Employee Performance/Satisfaction. *Research and Practice in Human Resource Management, 6*, 51–64.

[12]Rose, R. L. (1993, June 22). After Turning Around Giddings and Lewis, Fife Is Turned Out Himself. *The Wall Street Journal*, A1.

[13]French, J. R. P., Jr., & Raven, B. H. (1968). The Bases of Social Power. In *Studies of Social Power*, ed. D. Cartwright. Ann Arbor, MI: Institute for Social Research.

[14]French, J. R. P., Jr., & Raven, B. H. (1968). The Bases of Social Power. In *Studies of Social Power*, ed. D. Cartwright. Ann Arbor, MI: Institute for Social Research.

[15]Tracy, B. (2005, November 21). Seven Keys to Growing Your Business. Entrepreneur.com. Available at: http://www.entrepreneur.com/article/81128.

[16]Yukl, G. (1998). *Leadership in Organizations* (4th ed.). Englewood Cliffs, NJ: Prentice Hall.

[17]House, R. J. (1977). A 1976 Theory of Charismatic Leadership. In *Leadership: The Cutting Edge*, eds. J. G. Hunt & L. L. Larson (pp. 189–207). Carbondale, IL: Southern Illinois University Press; Shamir, B., House, R. J., & Arthur, M. B. (1993). The Motivational Effects of Charismatic Leadership: A Self-Concept Based Theory. *Organization Science, 4*, 577–594.

[18]Emerson, R. M. (1962). Power-Dependence Relations. *American Sociological Review, 27*, 31–41.

[19]McIntosh, P. & Luecke, R. A. (2011). *Increase Your Influence at Work*. New York: American Management Association.

[20]Vredenburgh, D., & Brender, Y. (1998). The Hierarchical Abuse of Power in Work Organizations. *Journal of Business Ethics, 17*, 1337–1347.

[21]Zellars, K. L., Tepper, B. J., & Duffy, M. K. (2002). Abusive Supervision and Subordinates' Organizational Citizenship Behavior. *Journal of Applied Psychology, 87*, 1368–1376.

[22]Tepper, B. J., Henle, C. A., Lambert, L. S., Giacalone, R. A., & Duffy, M. K. (2008). Abusive Supervision and Subordinates' Organization Deviance. *Journal of Applied Psychology, 93*, 721–732.

[23]Furnham, A. (2005). *The Psychology of Behaviour at Work: The Individual in the Organization*. New York: Psychology Press.

[24]Lussier, R. N., & Achua, C. F. (2009). *Leadership: Theory, Application, & Skill Development* (4th ed.). Mason, OH: South-Western.

[25]Conger, J. A. (1989). Leadership: The Art of Empowering Others. *Academy of Management Executive, 3*, 17–24; Conger, J. A., & Kanungo, R. N. (1988). The Empowerment Process: Integrating Theory and Practice. *Academy of Management Review, 13*, 471–482.

[26]Deluca, J. M. (1999). *Political Savvy: Systematic Approaches to Leadership Behind the Scenes*. Berwyn, PA: EBG.

[27]Deluca, J. M. (1999). *Political Savvy: Systematic Approaches to Leadership Behind the Scenes*. Berwyn, PA: Evergreen Business Group.

[28]Based on An Analytical Approach to Workforce Management. *CRM Today*. Available at: http://www.crm2day.com/content/t6_librarynews_1.php?id=EplVpulFAusyoHEmpq.

[29]Greenberg, J., & Baron, R. A. (2003). *Behavior in Organizations* (8th ed.). Upper Saddle River, NJ: Prentice Hall.

[30]Henslin, J. M. (2008). *Sociology: A Down to Earth Approach* (9th ed.). Upper Saddle River, NJ: Pearson.

[31]Lewis-Duarte, M. & Bligh, M.C. (2012). Agents of "Influence": Exploring the Usage, Timing, and Outcomes of Executive Coaching Tactics, *Leadership & Organization Development Journal, 33*(3), 255–281.

[32]Cooper, C. (2005). Just Joking Around? Employee Humor Expression as an Ingratiatory Behavior. *Academy of Management Review, 30*, 765–776.

[33]Hale, W. (2005, April 3). NASA Internal Memo from Wayne Hale: What I Learned at ISOS. Available at: http://www.spaceref.com/news/viewsr.html?pid=16028.

[34]Yukl, G. (2002). *Leadership in Organizations* (5th ed., pp. 141–174). Upper Saddle River, NJ: Prentice Hall; Higgins, C. A., Judge, T. A., & Ferris, G. R. (2003). Influence Tactics and Work Outcomes: A Meta-Analysis. *Journal of Organizational Behavior, 24*, 89–136.

[35]Falbe, C. M., & Yukl, G. (1992). Consequences for Managers of Using Single Influence Tactics and Combinations of Tactics. *Academy of Management Journal, 35*, 638–653.

[36]Conger, J. A., & Riggio, R. E. (2006). *The Practice of Leadership: Developing the Next Generation of Leaders*. New York: Jossey-Bass.

[37]Conger, J. A., & Riggio, R. E. (2006). *The Practice of Leadership: Developing the Next Generation of Leaders*. San Francisco: Jossey-Bass.

[38]Garvin, D. A., & Roberto, M. A. (2005, February). Change Through Persuasion. *Harvard Business Review*, 134–112.

[39]Kennedy, J. C., Fu, P. P., & Yukl, G. (2003). Influence Tactics Across Twelve Cultures. *Advances in Global Leadership, 3*, 127–147.

[40]Duyar, I., Aydin, I., & Pehlivan, Z. (2009). Analyzing Principal Influence Tactics from a Cross-Cultural Perspective: Do Preferred Influence Tactics and Targeted Goals Differ by National Culture? *International Perspectives on Education and Society, 11*, 191–220.

[41]Fu, P. P., Peng, T. K., Kennedy, J. C., & Yukl, G. (2004, February). A Comparison of Chinese Managers in Hong Kong, Taiwan, and Mainland China. *Organizational Dynamics*, 32–46.

[42]Yukl, G. A., Fu, P. P., & McDonald, R. (2003). Cross-Cultural Differences in Perceived Effectiveness of Influence Tactics for Initiating or Resisting Change. *Applied Psychology: An International Review, 52*, 68–82.

[43]Herrmann, P., & Werbel, J. D. (2007). Promotability of Host-Country Nationals: A Cross-Sectional Study. *British Journal of Management, 18*, 281–293.

[44]Herrmann, P., & Werbel, J. D. (2007). Promotability of Host-Country Nationals: A Cross-Sectional Study. *British Journal of Management, 18*, 281–293.

[45]Conger, J. A. (1998, May–June). The Necessary Art of Persuasion. *Harvard Business Review*, 85–95.

[46]Conger, J. (1998). *Winning 'Em Over: A New Model for Management in the Age of Persuasion*. New York: Simon & Schuster.

[47]Conger, J. A. (1998, May–June). The Necessary Art of Persuasion. *Harvard Business Review*, 85–95.

[48]Conger, J. (1998). *Winning 'Em Over: A New Model for Management in the Age of Persuasion*. New York: Simon & Schuster.

[49]Conger, J. (1998). *Winning 'Em Over: A New Model for Management in the Age of Persuasion*. New York: Simon & Schuster.

[50]Conger, J. A. (1998, May–June). The Necessary Art of Persuasion. *Harvard Business Review*, 85–95.

[51]Breen, B. (2001, November). Trickle-Up Leadership. *Fast Company*, 52, 70.

[52]Pelz, D. (1952). Influence: A Key to Effective Leadership in the First Line Supervisor. *Personnel, 29*, 3–11; Kanter, R. M. (1977). *Men and Women of the Corporation*. New York: Basic Books.

[53]Kipnis, D., Schmidt, S. M., & Wilkinson, I. (1980). Intra-Organizational Influence Tactics: Explorations of Getting One's Way. *Journal of Applied Psychology, 65*, 440–452.

[54]Botero, I. C., Foste, E. A., & Pace, K. M. (In press). Exploring Differences and Similarities in Predictors and Use of Upward Influence Strategies in Two Countries. *Journal of Cross-Cultural Psychology, 43*(4).

[55]Kipnis, D., & Schmidt, S. M. (1988). Upward-Influence Styles: Relationship with Performance, Evaluations, Salary, and Stress. *Administrative Science Quarterly*, 33, 528–542.

[56]Schriesheim, C. A., & Hinkin, T. R. (1990). Influence Tactics Used by Subordinates: A Theoretical and Empirical Analysis and Refinement of the Kipnis, Schmidt, and Wilkinson Subscales. *Journal of Applied Psychology, 75*, 246–257.

[57]Kipnis, D., & Schmidt, S. (1983). An Influence Perspective on Bargaining. In *Negotiating in Organizations*, eds. M. Bazerman & R. Lewicki (pp. 303–319). Beverly Hills, CA: Sage Publications.

[58]Kipnis, D., & Schmidt, S. M. (1988). Upward-Influence Styles: Relationship with Performance, Evaluations, Salary, and Stress. *Administrative Science Quarterly, 33*, 528–542.

[59]Kipnis, D., & Schmidt, S. (1983). An Influence Perspective on Bargaining. In *Negotiating in Organizations*, eds. M. Bazerman & R. Lewicki (pp. 303–319). Beverly Hills, CA: Sage Publications.

[60]Kipnis, D., & Schmidt, S. (1983). An Influence Perspective on Bargaining. In *Negotiating in Organizations*, eds. M. Bazerman & R. Lewicki (pp. 303–319). Beverly Hills, CA: Sage Publications.

[61]Kipnis, D., & Schmidt, S. M. (1988). Upward-Influence Styles: Relationship with Performance, Evaluations, Salary, and Stress. *Administrative Science Quarterly, 33*, 528–542.

[62]Kipnis, D., & Schmidt, S. M. (1988). Upward-Influence Styles: Relationship with Performance, Evaluations, Salary, and Stress. *Administrative Science Quarterly, 33*, 528–542.

[63]Westphal, J. D., & Stern, I. (2006). The Other Pathway to the Boardroom: Interpersonal Influence Behavior as a Substitute for Elite Credentials and Majority Status in Obtaining Board Appointments. *Administrative Science Quarterly, 51*, 1–28.

[64]Cropanzano, R. S., Kacmar, K. M., & Bozeman, D. P. (1995). Organizational Politics, Justice, and Support: Their Differences and Similarities. In *Organizational Politics, Justice and Support: Managing Social Climate at Work*, eds. R. S. Cropanzano & K. M. Kacmar (pp. 1–18). Westport, CT: Quorum Books.

[65]Kacmar, K. M., & Carlson, D. S. (1997). Further Validation of the Perceptions of Politics Scale (POPS): A Multiple Sample Investigation. *Journal of Management, 23*, 627–658.

[66]Ferris, G. R., & Kacmar, K. M. (1992). Perceptions of Organizational Politics. *Journal of Management, 18*, 93–116.

[67]Lewin, K. (1936). *Principles of Topological Psychology*. New York: McGraw-Hill; Porter, L. W. (1976). Organizations as Political Animals. Presidential address, Division of Industrial-Organizational Psychology, 84th Annual Meeting of the American Psychological Association, Washington, DC.

[68]For a more detailed discussion of organizational politics, see Vredenburgh, D. J., & Maurer, J. G. (1984). A Process Framework of Organizational Politics. *Human Relations, 37*, 47–65.

[69]Ferris, G. R., Fedor, D. B., Chachere, J. G., & Pondy, L. R. (1989). Myths and Politics in Organizational Contexts. *Group & Organization Studies, 14*, 83–133; Fandt, P. M., & Ferris, G. R. (1990). The Management of Information and Impressions: When Employees Behave Opportunistically. *Organizational Behavior and Human Decision Processes, 45*, 140–158.

[70]Sutton, R. (2007, May). Building the Civilized Workplace. *The McKinsey Quarterly*, (2), 30–39.

[71]McKenna, E. F. (2000). *Business Psychology and Organisational Behavior: A Student's Handbook*. Hove, UK: Psychology Press.

[72]Chang, C. S., Rosen, C. C., & Levy, P. E. (2009). The Relationship Between Perceptions of Organizational Politics and Employee Attitudes, Strain, and Behavior: A Meta-Analytic Examination. *Academy of Management Journal, 52*, 779–801; Anderson, T. P. (1994). Creating Measures of Dysfunctional Office and Organizational Politics: The DOOP and Short Form DOOP Scales. *Psychology, 31*, 24–34; Croponzano, R. S., Howes, J. C., Grandey, A. A., & Toth, P. (1997). The Relationship of Organizational Politics and Support to Work Behaviors, Attitudes, and Stress. *Journal of Organizational Behavior, 18*, 159–181.

[73]Ferris, G. R., & Kacmar, M. K. (1992). Perceptions of Organizational Politics. *Journal of Management, 18*, 93–116.

[74]Ferris, G. R., Fedor, D., Chachere, J. G., & Pondy, L. (1989). Myths and Politics in Organizational Contexts. *Group & Organizational Studies, 14*, 88–133.

[75]Kacmar, K. M., & Carlson, D. S. (1997). Further Validation of the Perceptions of Politics Scale (POPS): A Multiple Sample Investigation. *Journal of Management, 23*, 627–658.

[76]Ferris, G. R., Treadway, D. C., Perrewé, P. L., Brouer, R. L., Douglas, C., & Lux, S. (2007). Political Skill in Organizations. *Journal of Management, 33*, 290–320.

[77]Kapoutsis, I., Papalexandris, A., Nikolopoulos, A., Hochwarter, W.A., & Ferris, G.R. (2011). Politics Perceptions as Moderator of the Political Skill-Job Performance Relationship: A Two-Study, Cross-National, Constructive Replication, *Journal of Vocational Behavior, 78*(1), 123–135.

[78]Drory, A., & Romm, T. (1990). The Definition of Organizational Politics: A Review. *Human Relations, 43*, 1133–1154.

[79]Porter, L. W., Allen, R. W., & Angle, H. L. (1981). The Politics of Upward Influence in Organizations (pp. 139–149). In *Research in Organizational Behavior*, eds. L. L. Cummings & B. M. Staw (Vol. 3). Greenwich, CT: JAI Press.

[80]Drory, A., & Romm, T. (1990). The Definition of Organizational Politics: A Review. *Human Relations, 43*, 1133–1154.

[81]Farrell, D., & Peterson, J. C. (1982). Patterns of Political Behavior in Organizations. *Academy of Management Review, 45*, 403–412; Kumar, P., & Ghadially, R. (1989). Organizational Politics and Its Effect on Members of Organizations. *Human Relations, 42*, 305–314.

[82]Frost, P. J. (1987). Power, Politics, and Influence. In *Handbook of Organizational Communication*, eds. F. Jablin, L. Putnam, K. Roberts, & L. Porter. Beverly Hills, CA: Sage Publications.

[83]Drory, A., & Romm, T. (1990). The Definition of Organizational Politics: A Review. *Human Relations, 43*, 1133–1154.

[84]Frost, P. J. (1987). Power, Politics, and Influence. In *Handbook of Organizational Communication*, eds. F. Jablin, L. Putnam, K. Roberts, & L. Porter. Beverly Hills, CA: Sage Publications.

[85]Kacmar, K. M., & Ferris, G. R. (1991). Perceptions of Organizational Politics Scale (POPS): Development and Construct Validation. *Educational and Psychological Measurement, 51*, 193–205. Shortened in Kacmar, K. M., & Carlson, D. S. (1997). Further Validation of the Perceptions of Politics Scale (POPS): A Multiple Sample Investigation. *Journal of Management, 23*, 627–658.

[86]Ferris, G. R., Fedor, D., Chachere, J. G., & Pondy, L. (1989). Myths and Politics in Organizational Contexts. *Group & Organizational Studies, 14*, 88–133; Ferris, G. R., & King, T. R. (1991). Politics in Human Resource Decisions: A Walk on the Dark Side. *Organizational Dynamics, 20*, 59–71; Kacmar, K. M., & Ferris, G. R. (1993). Politics at Work: Sharpening the Focus of Political Behavior in Organizations. *Business Horizons, 36*, 70–74.

[87]Ferris, G. R., Russ, G. S., & Fandt, P. M. (1989). Politics in Organizations. In *Impression Management in the Organization*, eds. R. A. Giacalone & P. Rosenfeld (pp. 143–170). Hillsdale, NJ: Lawrence Erlbaum Associates; Kacmar, K. M., & Ferris, G. R. (1993). Politics at Work: Sharpening the Focus of Political Behavior in Organizations. *Business Horizons, 36*, 70–74.

[88]Kacmar, K. M., & Carlson, D. S. (1997). Further Validation of the Perceptions of Politics Scale (POPS): A Multiple Sample Investigation. *Journal of Management, 23*, 627–658.

[89]In Martinez, M. N. (2009). Politics Come with the Office. Graduating Engineer. Available at: http://www.graduatingengineer.com/articles/20010928/Politics-Come-With-the-Office.

[90]In Martinez, M. N. (2009). Politics Come with the Office. Graduating Engineer. Available at : http://www.graduatingengineer.com/articles/20010928/Politics-Come-With-the-Office.

[91]Jam, F. A., Khan, T. I., Zaidi, B. H., & Muzaffar, S. M. (2011). Political Skills Moderates the Relationship between

Perception of Organizational Politics and Job Outcomes, *Journal of Educational and Social Research, 1*(4), 57–70.

[92]Eisenhardt, K. M., & Bourgeois, L. J. (1988). Politics of Strategic Decision Making in High Velocity Environments: Toward a Midrange Theory. *Academy of Management Journal, 31*, 737–770.

[93]Greenberg, J., & Baron, R. A. (2003). *Behavior in Organizations* (8th ed.). Englewood Cliffs, NJ: Prentice Hall.

[94]Mintzberg. H. (1979). Organizational Power and Goals: A Skeletal Theory. In *Strategic Management: A New View of Business Policy and Planning*, eds. D. Schendel & C. Hofer (pp. 143–171). Boston: Little, Brown.

[95]Greenberg, J., & Baron, R. A. (2003). *Behavior in Organizations* (8th ed.). Englewood Cliffs, NJ: Prentice Hall.

[96]Ferris, G. R., & Kacmar, M. K. (1992). Perceptions of Organizational Politics. *Journal of Management, 18*, 93–116.

[97]In Martinez, M. N. (2009). Politics Come with the Office. Graduating Engineer. Available at: http://www.graduatingengineer.com/articles/20010928/Politics-Come-With-the-Office.

[98]Cohen, A., & Bradford, D. L. (2005). Influence Without Authority (2nd ed.). New York: John Wiley and Sons.

[99]Wiscombe, J. (2007, January). IDEO: The Innovation Factory. *Workforce Management Online*. Available at: http://www.workforce.com/section/09/feature/24/73/71/index.html.

[100]Schlenker, B. R. (2003). Self-Presentation. In *Handbook of Self and Identity*, eds. M. R. Leary & J. P. Tangney (pp. 492–518). New York: Guilford.

[101]Bolino, M. C., Kacmar, K. M., Turnley, W. H., & Gilstrap, J. B. (2008). A Multi-Level Review of Impression Management Motives and Behaviors. *Journal of Management, 34*, 1080–1109.

[102]Turner, R. E., Edgley, C., & Olmstead, G. (1975). Information Control in Conversations: Honesty Is Not Always the Best Policy. *Kansas Journal of Sociology, 11*, 69–89.

[103]Camden, C., Motley, M. T., & Wilson, A. (1984). White Lies in Interpersonal Communication: A Taxonomy and Preliminary Investigation of Social Motivations. *Western Journal of Speech Communication, 48*, 309–325.

[104]Snyder, M. (1974). Self-Monitoring of Expressive Behaviour. *Journal of Personality and Social Psychology, 30*, 526–537.

[105]Turnley, W. H., & Bolino, M. C. (2001). Achieving Desired Images While Avoiding Undesired Images: Exploring the Role of Self-Monitoring in Impression Management. *Journal of Applied Psychology, 86*, 351–360.

[106]Stevens, C. K., & Kristof, A. L. (1995). Making the Right Impression: A Field Study of Applicant Impression Management During Job Interviews. *Journal of Applied Psychology, 80*,587–606.

[107]Higgins, C. A., & Judge, T. A. (2004). The Effect of Applicant Influence Tactics on Recruiter Perceptions of Fit and Hiring Recommendations: A Field Study. *Journal of Applied Psychology, 89*, 622–632.

[108]Stevens, C. K., & Kristof, A. L. (1995). Making the Right Impression: A Field Study of Applicant Impression Management During Job Interviews. *Journal of Applied Psychology, 80*, 587–606.

[109]Higgins, C. A., Judge, T. A., & Ferris, G. R. (2003). Influence Tactics and Work Outcomes: A Meta-Analysis. *Journal of Organizational Behavior, 24*, 89–136.

[110]Higgins, C. A., Judge, T. A., & Ferris, G. R. (2003). Influence Tactics and Work Outcomes: A Meta-Analysis. *Journal of Organizational Behavior, 24*, 89–136.

[111]Forrest, J. A., & Feldman, R. S. (2000). Detecting Deception and Judge's Involvement: Lower Task Involvement Leads to Better Lie Detection. *Personality and Social Psychology Bulletin, 26*, 118–125.

[112]Streeter, L. A., Krauss, R. M., Geller, V., Olson, C., & Apple, W. (1977). Pitch Changes During Attempted Deception. *Journal of Personality and Social Psychology, 35*, 345–350.

[113]Cody, M. J., Marston, P. J., & Foster, M. (1984). Deception: Paralinguistic and Verbal Leakage. In *Communication Yearbook*, eds. R. N. Bostrom & B. H. Westley (pp. 464–490). Beverly Hills, CA: Sage Publications; deTurck, M. A., & Miller, G. R. (1985). Deception and Arousal: Isolating the Behavioral Correlates of Deception. *Human Communication Research, 12*, 181–201.

[114]Cody, M. J., Marston, P. J., & Foster, M. (1984). Deception: Paralinguistic and Verbal Leakage. In *Communication Yearbook*, eds. R. N. Bostrom & B. H. Westley (pp. 464–490). Beverly Hills, CA: Sage Publications.

[115]Mehrabian, A. (1967). Orientation Behaviors and Nonverbal Attitude Communication. *Journal of Communication, 17*, 324–332; Wiener, M., & Mehrabian, A. (1968). *Language Within Language: Immediacy, a Channel in Verbal Communication*. Englewood Cliffs, NJ: Prentice Hall.

[116]Hocking, J. E., Bauchner, J. E., Kaminski, E. P., & Miller, G. R. (1979). Detecting Deceptive Communication from Verbal, Visual and Paralinguistic Cues. *Human Communication Research, 6*, 33–46.

[117]O'Hair, H. D., Cody, M. J., & McLaughlin, M. L. (1981). Prepared Lies, Spontaneous Lies, Machiavellianism, and Nonverbal Communication. *Human Communication Research, 7*, 325–339.

[118]Ekman, P., Friesen, W. V., O'Sullivan, M., & Scherer, K. R. (1980). Relative Importance of Face, Body, and Speech in Judgments of Personality and Affect. *Journal of Personality and Social Psychology, 38*, 270–277; Riggio, R. E., & Friedman, H. S. (1983). Individual Differences and Cues to Deception. *Journal of Personality and Social Psychology, 45*, 899–915.

[119]Ekman, P., & Friesen, W. V. (1972). Hand Movements. *Journal of Communication, 22*, 353–374; McClintock, C. C., & Hunt, R. G. (1975). Nonverbal Indicators of Affect and Deception in an Interview Setting. *Journal of Applied Social Psychology, 5*, 54–67.

[120]Buller, D. B., & Aune, R. K. (1987). Nonverbal Cues to Deception Among Intimates, Friends and Strangers. *Journal of Nonverbal Behavior, 11*, 269–290.

[121]Ekman, P., & Friesen, W. V. (1974). Detecting Deception from the Body or Face. *Journal of Personality and Social Psychology, 29*, 288–298.

PART 5 ORGANIZATIONAL PROCESSES AND CHARACTERISTICS

In Part 4 we continued to learn about how managers can enhance the performance behaviors, organizational commitment, and engagement of their employees in order to build organizational effectiveness and competitiveness. In particular, we examined the question of why leadership matters. In Chapter 11 we introduced traditional leadership approaches, and in Chapter 12 we learned more about modern leadership approaches. The related topics of power, influence, and politics in organizations were covered in Chapter 13.

In our final part we focus a bit more broadly on how organizational characteristics influence managerial and organizational effectiveness. In Chapter 14 we investigate organizational structure and design. Chapter 15 focuses on organizational culture. We conclude with a discussion of change management in Chapter 16. In many ways change management is a logical concluding topic for discussion in that it can be focused on any of the areas covered in our previous parts—individual behavior, group and team behavior, leadership behavior, and organizational change.

LOSKUTNIKOV/SHUTTERSTOCK.COM

CHAPTER

14 ORGANIZATIONAL STRUCTURE AND DESIGN

CHAPTER OUTLINE

LEARNING OUTCOMES

After studying this chapter you should be able to:

1. Identify the elements of organizational structure and describe mechanistic and organic structures.
2. Explain what influences an organization's structure.
3. Describe the basic types of organizational structures.
4. Identify and discuss four contemporary issues in organizational structure.

LOSKUTNIKOV/SHUTTERSTOCK.COM

—REAL WORLD CHALLENGE—

BUILDING A TREEHOUSE[1]

Ryan Carson and Alan Johnson founded Treehouse in 2011 as an online interactive education platform. Treehouse produces courses in web development and programming and business education. Or, as one business journalist puts it, Treehouse is "an online trade school whose mission is to get students jobs" without having to spend years pursuing expensive college degrees.

Fueled by $12.6 million in venture capital, Treehouse became the largest computer science school in the world within less than three years. It wasn't long, however, before Carson and Johnson were hearing rumblings of discontent. "By 2013," recalls Carson, "we had grown to 60 people with seven managers and four executives. As we added more people to the team, we noticed something disconcerting: rumors, politics, and complaints started appearing." Putting their joint ears to the ground, the cofounders learned that some front-line employees felt that their input was being ignored. The news was disturbing because Carson and Johnson believed that it was important for employees to be involved in the decision-making process.

"If they're feeling disempowered at the bottom," suggested Carson, "maybe we have too many managers." Seven managers didn't exactly seem like an army of overseers, but it did amount to more than 10 percent of the workforce. Eventually, the conversation reached a certain logical plateau: "What if we removed all management and simply empowered everyone to choose what they do every day? We laughed at first and then the conversation turned serious. We had hired talented and motivated people. Did they *need* managers?"

Carson and Johnson have asked for your advice. After reading this chapter, you should have some good ideas about what to tell them.

PROSTOCKSTUDIO/SHUTTERSTOCK.COM

In this section of the book we shift our attention to organizational design, organizational change, and managing your career. Once an organization decides how it wants its members to behave, what attitudes it wants to encourage, and what it wants its members to accomplish, it can then design an appropriate structure and develop appropriate supporting cultural values and norms. The right organizational structure can give an organization a competitive advantage by enabling it to best execute its business strategy.[2]

An organization's structure affects its performance by influencing how it operates.[3] The wrong organizational structure can hamper communication and slow work processes. Effective organizational structures improve the working efficiency of the organization, motivate employees rather than frustrate them, and facilitate working relationships among employees and across organizational units. An organization's structure also influences how it operates, how employees communicate, and how they are expected to behave.

Effective organizational structures improve efficiency and facilitate positive working relationships. Ineffective organizational structures block communication and cooperation, and drain employee motivation. Organizational structure is related to employee satisfaction, commitment,[4] and turnover.[5]

In this chapter we first discuss organizational structure and organizational charts. After discussing factors that influence organizational structure, we identify different types of structures and when they are most appropriate. We also discuss virtual organizations and ways of integrating employees in any organizational structure to enhance collaboration and knowledge transfer. After studying this chapter, you should have a good understanding of how to use organizational design to support a firm's business strategy and encourage desired employee behaviors.

organizational design
The process of selecting and managing aspects of organizational structure and culture to enable the organization to achieve its goals

organizational structure
The formal system of task, power, and reporting relationships

ORGANIZATIONAL STRUCTURE

Organizational design is the process of selecting and managing aspects of organizational structure and culture to enable the organization to achieve its goals. Designing and redesigning the organization in response to internal and external changes is a key managerial function.

One of the most important outcomes of organizational design is ***organizational structure***, or the formal system of task, power, and reporting relationships. Organizational structure is the core of what coordinates, controls, and motivates employees to cooperate toward the attainment of organizational goals. When the organizational structure is aligned with organizational needs, it results in greater organizational efficiencies and less conflict.

Organizational structures influence employee behavior by enabling or restricting

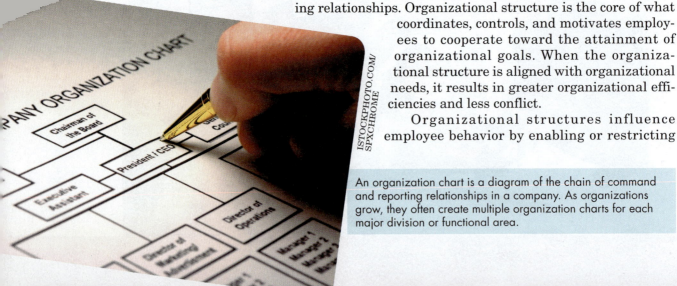

ISTOCKPHOTO.COM/SPXCHROME

An organization chart is a diagram of the chain of command and reporting relationships in a company. As organizations grow, they often create multiple organization charts for each major division or functional area.

communication, teamwork, and cooperation as well as intergroup relationships. Imagine the difference between working in an organization comprised of independent work teams given the authority to make their own decisions compared to a highly centralized bureaucratic organization in which decisions are made solely by the CEO. Your autonomy, influence, and work variety would differ greatly in each firm. Each type of structure can be effective depending on the nature of the organization and its environment, but each creates very different patterns of communication and levels of individual responsibility.

Imagine that you start a business selling homemade chocolates. You start by yourself, and your business quickly takes off. You land some big contracts and realize that there is just too much work for you to do alone. So you hire people to help you make, market, sell, and ship your candy. When they all report for their first day of work, what do you do next? You organize them to best get the work done in the way you want and need it done. You may even create an ***organizational chart*** like the one shown in Figure 14.1 to illustrate the chain of command and reporting relationships in your company. Higher levels in an organizational chart supervise and are responsible for the activities and performance of the levels beneath them.

organizational chart
Diagram of the chain of command and reporting relationships in a company

It is a common mistake to believe that a person's location in the organizational chart reflects their importance to the company and its performance. What usually matters most is what each person contributes, and people at all levels of an organization can make meaningful contributions. Think of the salespeople at a retail chain like The Gap. They may be low on the organizational chart, but imagine what would happen to The Gap's performance if its salespeople were poorly trained, poorly motivated, and poorly managed. Salespeople have a huge impact on The Gap's performance despite their position at the bottom of the organizational chart. As an executive vice president for global shipper FedEx said of its drivers, "If I don't come to work, we're OK. If they don't come to work, we're ... out of luck."[6]

Figure 14.1

Organizational Chart—Narrow Span of Control

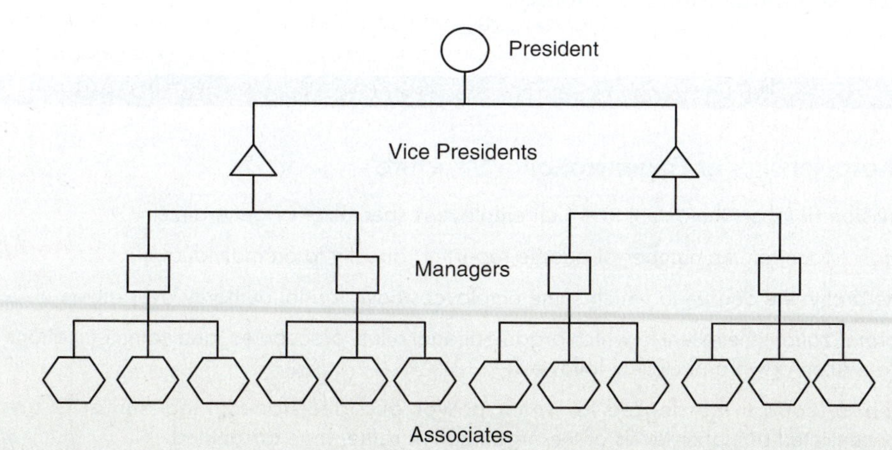

An organizational chart illustrates the chain of command and reporting relationships in a company. If the span of control in an organization is relatively narrow, as shown here, the organization tends to have more levels. That is, it is relatively "tall."

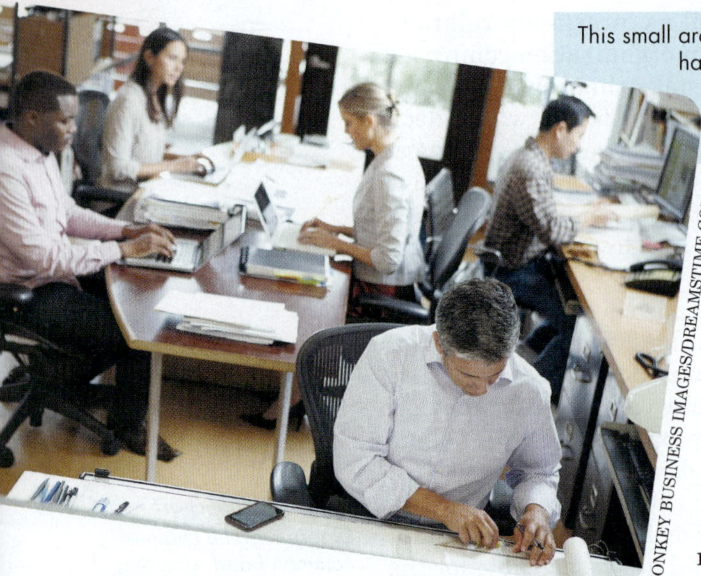

This small architectural firm is highly specialized because each employee has a set of defined tasks. The employee pictured in the front is the lead architect. The employee featured in the far right handles accounting, while the woman in the far left handles marketing.

MONKEY BUSINESS IMAGES/DREAMSTIME.COM

Characteristics of Organizational Structure

Organizational structures reflect the company's division of labor, span of control, hierarchy, formalization, and centralization. Different structures have different levels of each of these characteristics. Table 14.1 summarizes these characteristics.

Division of Labor

division of labor
The degree to which employees specialize or perform a variety of tasks as generalists

In addition to illustrating the chain of command, organizational charts show the ***division of labor***, which reflects the degree to which employees specialize or perform a variety of tasks as generalists. Highly specialized firms have a greater proportion of "specialists" who focus their attention on a well-defined set of tasks (e.g., market research, pricing, accounting). Lower levels in an organization tend to be more specialized than higher levels. The division of labor is reflected in the number of job titles in an organization,[7] or by the extent to which specialist roles exist within each functional area.[8]

Dividing work into specialized jobs increases work efficiency.[9] Specialized employees can learn their jobs faster and with less training, and because their jobs are focused they waste little time changing tasks. Division of labor also makes it easier to assess job candidates for the specific talents needed to do each job. Because specialists are experts, they often have greater autonomy and decision-making authority, which increases the firm's ability to respond quickly to environmental changes.

On the downside, employees tend to be more isolated when division of labor is high. This can make it difficult for different divisions in the company to understand each other's priorities and needs, and can increase the potential for conflict. The increased specialization of employees in each division also decreases organizational flexibility.

Table 14.1

Characteristics of Organizational Structure

Division of labor: the extent to which employees specialize or generalize

Span of control: the number of people reporting directly to an individual

Hierarchy: the degree to which some employees have formal authority over others

Formalization: the extent to which organizational rules, procedures, and communications are written down and closely followed

Centralization: the degree to which power and decision-making authority are concentrated at higher levels of the organization rather than distributed

DMITRY KALINOVSKY/SHUTTERSTOCK.COM

The span of control refers to the number of people who report directly to a manager. This manager is directing the work of three people. Of course, she likely has other people who also report to her. A number of different factors impact the extent to which a span of control should be relatively wide or narrow.

Because generalists are often less expensive than specialists, organizations employing a greater proportion of generalists may be able to reduce costs. Because they are not experts, however, generalists often need more time to make decisions and to respond to environmental changes because they need to do additional research.

Span of control

The number of people reporting directly to an individual is that person's ***span of control*** (some experts call this the *span of management*). Figure 14.2 illustrates a flatter organizational structure with a wider span of control than the structure shown earlier in Figure 14.1. The lowest-level supervisor in Figure 14.2 supervises seven rather than the three employees in the taller struc- ture in Figure 14.1. Clearly, narrow spans of control are more costly, but they also provide closer supervision and more coaching. Narrower spans of control are necessary for novel and complex tasks. Wider spans of control give subordinates greater autonomy and responsibility for self-management, and are best for routine, production-type work.

span of control
The number of people reporting directly to an individual

There is no consensus on the ideal span of control, although having more than nine direct reports is often considered too many to effectively manage. Wider spans of control are possible when technology (such as an assembly line or computerized call center management technology) substitutes for close supervision, when subordinates need less direction and control, and when the jobs being supervised are similar.

Figure 14.2

Organizational Chart—Wide Span of Control

When an organization uses a relatively wider span of control, such as the organization illustrated here, its structure has fewer levels and it tends to be somewhat "flat."

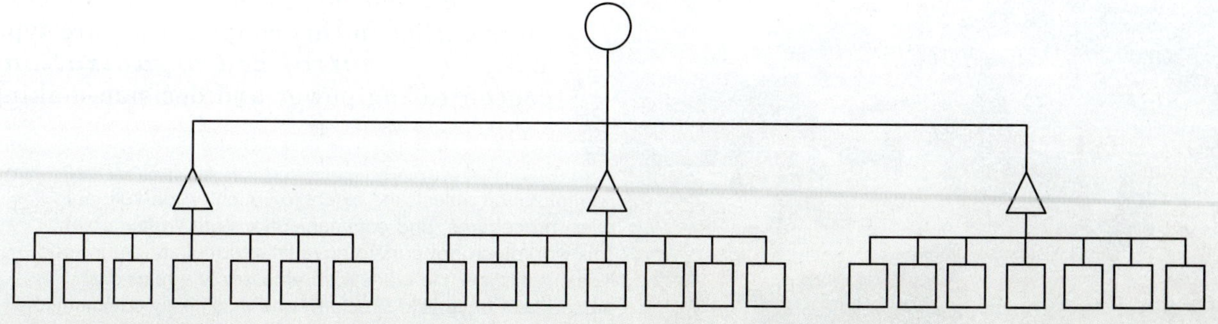

Source: Phillips/Gulley 465

Hierarchy

hierarchy
The degree to which some employees have formal authority over others

When an organization creates a ***hierarchy***, it outlines supervision relationships by giving some employees authority over others. Hierarchy establishes the "tallness" or "flatness" of an organizational chart. For example, Figure 14.1 shows four hierarchical layers, and Figure 14.2 shows a flatter three-layer firm. The more layers in an organization, the greater its hierarchy.

Although hierarchy can facilitate the coordination of different departments, organizations clearly should not have more hierarchical levels than are necessary. Not having enough levels can also create problems—when work activities require control and coordination, middle management layers can facilitate work processes. Hierarchy can give too much power to a few people at the top of the organization, which can increase the risk of unethical behavior. Because hierarchy creates a clear chain of command, it can also restrict the interaction and communication among employees.

To better compete in a fast-changing, global marketplace, organizations are increasingly restructuring to reduce their hierarchy and improve speed and efficiency. Revlon recently delayered, or flattened, its organizational structure to increase its performance. This change improved its effectiveness and removed several layers of management.[10]

Grouping employees into self-managed work teams decreases hierarchy because the teams incorporate some of the roles previously held by higher layers of management. Even in this case, though, managers are important. Although Hewlett-Packard is considered a high employee-involvement organization with minimal hierarchy, it still has eight organizational levels that coordinate its tens of thousands of employees.[11]

Formalization

Formalization reflects the extent to which organizational rules, procedures, and communications are written down.[12] In highly formalized firms, little flexibility exists in making decisions, and both procedures and rewards follow explicit rules. Formalization is not necessary for high performance—Google and Internet shoe retailer Zappos are known for having low formalization. Because formalization increases job and role clarity, it can increase employee commitment.[13] Without role clarity, dissatisfaction, anxiety, and lower performance can result.[14] If employees perceive that organizational rewards are consistently allocated based on formal rules and procedures, their confidence that they are being compensated appropriately is increased.

centralized organizations
Concentrate power and decision-making authority at higher levels of the organization

MONKEY BUSINESS IMAGES/SHUTTERSTOCK.COM

Formalization reflects the extent to which organizational rules, procedures, and communications are written down. This workplace appears to have little formalization. Instead, it seems that people work with relatively few rules and procedures, have little structure, and most likely communicate by simply talking.

Centralization

When organizations are first formed, including your hypothetical chocolate business earlier in this chapter, they are typically very ***centralized organizations*** concentrating power and decision-making authority at high levels of the organization. The two subcomponents of centralization are participation in decision making and hierarchy of authority.[15] When you first started your chocolate company, you made all the decisions and did a variety of tasks. Centralization creates clear lines of communication and responsibility, and the implementation of decisions tends to be straightforward. Centralization is best in noncomplex, stable environments.

Whereas centralized organizations concentrate authority at high levels of the organization, flatter, ***decentralized organizations*** give lower levels more authority and autonomy for making decisions.[16] Decentralized organizations tend to have flatter structures than centralized organizations because employees' greater autonomy decreases the need for middle management. Flatter structures promote innovation and increase the speed of decision making, and can save money as a result of fewer management layers. Decentralization is best when the organization performs nonroutine tasks in complex environments because it empowers the managers closest to the environment to make decisions and quickly implement them.

decentralized organizations
The authority for making decisions affecting an organization is distributed

If employees have appropriate information and are allowed to make decisions relevant to their task, there are often benefits for both the organization and the employees.[17] Employee involvement and participation (traits of decentralization) are important managerial tools in achieving increased organizational effectiveness and positive employee attitudes.[18] Decentralization increases organizational commitment through greater involvement in the organization and identification with the organization's mission and values.[19]

Organizations do not have to be fully centralized or decentralized. Centralization is best thought of as a continuum, and different functions in a company can have different degrees of centralization. When Lou Gerstner led IBM's turnaround in the 1990s, he said, "Let's decentralize decision making wherever possible, but … we must balance decentralized decision making with central strategy and common customer focus."[20]

Centralizing authority can lead many managers to feel that they are solely responsible for completing their job tasks and responsibilities. In reality, you are setting yourself up to fail if you hold onto the belief that you must do everything yourself. As Andrew Carnegie said, "No person will make a great business who wants to do it all himself or get all the credit." Delegating tasks to others not only frees you to focus on more important tasks, but also develops skills in the recipient, increases trust, and can even lead to a higher-quality product. This chapter's *Improve Your Skills* feature gives you some tips for delegating more effectively.

Mechanistic and Organic Structures

mechanistic organizations
Rigid, traditional bureaucracies with centralized power and hierarchical communications

Organizational structures can be thought of as being either more mechanical and machine-like or more biological and organic. ***Mechanistic organizations*** are rigid, traditional bureaucracies with centralized power and hierarchical communications. Job descriptions are uniform, and formal rules and regulations guide decision making. More mechanistic organizations may minimize costs, but fit best with a relatively stable or slow-changing environment. When new opportunities present themselves, mechanistic organizations usually move too slowly to capitalize on them.

organic organizations
Flexible, decentralized structures with less clear lines of authority, decentralized power, open communication channels, and a focus on adaptability in helping employees accomplish goals

In contrast, ***organic organizations*** are flexible, decentralized organizations with unclear lines of authority; they have decentralized power, open communication

IMPROVE YOUR SKILLS

DELEGATION SKILLS

In any organizational structure, it is important to occasionally relinquish control and delegate tasks and responsibilities to others. If you consistently work longer hours than other employees and have trouble completing your primary responsibilities, it may help to reflect on how much (or how little) you are delegating. It is often difficult for managers to relinquish control over tasks, but doing so is essential to managerial performance. Here are some tips to help you delegate more effectively:

1. *Delegate only when appropriate*: If recipients lack the skills, capability, and information to complete a task, then they are unlikely to successfully complete it; if the task is critical to long-term success (e.g., hiring), you should probably stay involved—you are still responsible for the final product.
2. *Provide a thorough explanation and expectation*: Explain what you are asking the recipients to do and why it is important; be clear about what is expected as a final product.
3. *Delegate the authority to complete the task*: If you want people to do a job, you must give them the authority to get it done; do not micromanage.
4. *Provide the necessary tools and information*: Without the needed resources and information, recipients are just being set up to fail.
5. *Try to create a win-win situation*: Delegate in a way that recipients can get some benefit from the delegated task; for example, assign the task to someone who can learn new skills by doing it.
6. *Respect recipients' workload*: You are not the only busy person—be sure recipients' workload enables them to take on the extra work.

channels, and a focus on adaptability in helping employees accomplish their goals.[21] Organic organizations benefit from faster awareness of and response to market and competitive changes, better customer service, and faster decision making. Organic forms like teams and other flatter structures have typically been associated with increased job satisfaction,[22] affective commitment,[23] and learning.[24]

For many years Nordstrom's extremely organic structure was reflected in its employee handbook, shown in Figure 14.3. For years new employees received

Figure 14.3

Nordstrom's Employee Handbook[25]

Nordstrom's has long been a pioneer in retailing. For years its new employees received a "handbook" consisting of a simple gray card containing 75 words.

Welcome to Nordstrom

We're glad to have you with our Company. Our number one goal is to provide outstanding customer service. Set both your personal and professional goals high. We have great confidence in your ability to achieve them.

Nordstrom Rules: Rule #1: Use good judgment in all situations. There will be no additional rules.

Please feel free to ask your department manager, store manager, or division general manager any question at any time.

Source: Spector, R. (2000). Lessons from the Nordstrom Way: How Companies Are Emulating the #1 Customer Service Company. NewYork: John Wiley

a simple gray card with these seventy-five words on it. Although employees now receive additional material summarizing more specific rules and legal regulations, Nordstrom's low formality and high emphasis on customer service continues.

Note that mechanistic and organic structures represent ends of a continuum, not a dichotomy.[26] No organization is perfectly organic or completely mechanistic. Firms usually display some characteristics of both forms along a mechanistic/organic continuum, as shown in Figure 14.4. This chapter's *Understand Yourself* feature gives you the opportunity to identify whether you prefer to work in a more organic or mechanistic organizational structure.

Figure 14.4

Mechanistic/Organic Continuum[27]

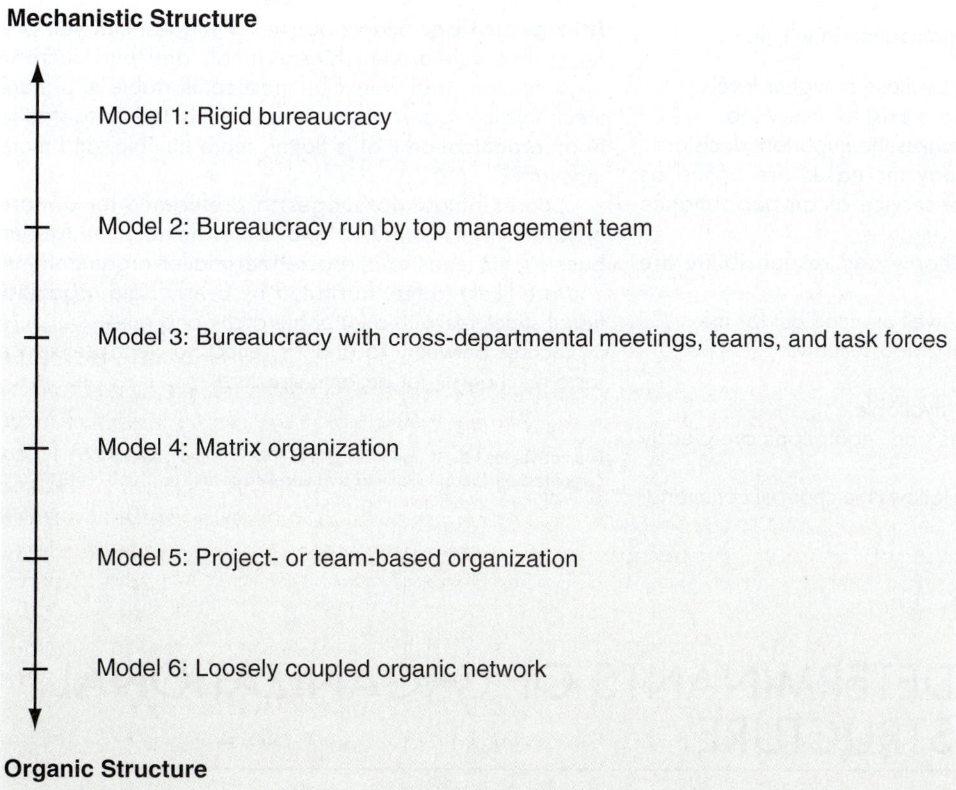

Mechanistic Structure

Model 1: Rigid bureaucracy

Model 2: Bureaucracy run by top management team

Model 3: Bureaucracy with cross-departmental meetings, teams, and task forces

Model 4: Matrix organization

Model 5: Project- or team-based organization

Model 6: Loosely coupled organic network

Organic Structure

While it is useful to describe mechanistic and organic forms of organizational structure, in reality all organizations fall somewhere between these two extreme forms. Indeed, as shown here, we can think of mechanistic and organic characteristics as anchoring a continuum.

UNDERSTAND YOURSELF

WHAT IS YOUR PREFERRED TYPE OF ORGANIZATIONAL STRUCTURE?

People differ in their preference for different types of organizational structures. This self-assessment will give you some insight into your preferred structure. Rate the fifteen statements using the scale below, and then follow the scoring instructions.

strongly disagree	disagree	slightly disagree	neutral	slightly agree	agree	strongly agree
1	2	3	4	5	6	7

I prefer to work in an organization in which:

___ 1. Goals are defined by those at higher levels.
___ 2. Clear job descriptions exist for every job.
___ 3. Top management makes the important decisions.
___ 4. Promotions and pay increases are based as much on length of service as on performance level.
___ 5. Clear lines of authority and responsibility are established.
___ 6. My career is pretty well planned out for me.
___ 7. I have a great deal of job security.
___ 8. I can specialize.
___ 9. My boss is readily available.
___ 10. Organization rules and regulations are clearly specified.
___ 11. Information rigidly follows the chain of command.
___ 12. There is a minimal number of new tasks for me to learn.
___ 13. Workgroups incur little member turnover.
___ 14. People accept the authority of a leader's position.
___ 15. I am part of a group whose members' training and skills are similar to mine.

Scoring: Add up your responses to all fifteen items. Remember that this assessment enables you to better understand your work preferences and is not an evaluation of yourself.

Interpretation: Scores above 75 suggest that you prefer stable, rule-driven, hierarchical, and bureaucratic organizations and would be most comfortable in a more mechanistic organization. You are likely to feel frustrated in an organization that is flatter, more flexible, and more innovative.

Scores below 45 suggest a preference for a more organic structure that is innovative, flexible, and team-based. This tends to characterize smaller organizations. You are likely to feel frustrated by overly rigid organizational structures with a lot of hierarchy and rules.

Scores between 45 and 75 reflect no clear preference for a mechanistic or organic structure.

Source: Veiga, J. F., & Yanouzas, J. N. (1979). *The Dynamics of Organization Theory: Gaining a Macro Perspective* (pp. 158–160). St. Paul, MN: West Publishing.

DETERMINANTS OF ORGANIZATIONAL STRUCTURE

The most appropriate structure for an organization depends on many things, as summarized in Table 14.2. Let's discuss each influence in more detail.

Business Strategy

One of the most important factors influencing the appropriateness of different organizational structures is the business strategy.[28] Simple designs are

Table 14.2

What Influences Organizational Structure?

Influence	Example
Business strategy	Being a low-cost producer would require a more hierarchical, rigid structure than would pursuing an innovation strategy.
External environment	A rapidly changing environment requires a more flexible structure than a more stable environment.
Nature of the organization's talent	If workers have professional skills (e.g., lawyers, scientists) and need to work together, then a flatter, team-based structure would be more appropriate than a taller, bureaucratic structure.
Organizational size	Larger organizations tend to have greater specialization, greater hierarchy, and more rules than do smaller firms.
Expectations of how employees should behave	If employees are expected to follow explicit rules and procedures, a hierarchical, centralized structure would be called for.
Organization's production technology	If the firm uses unit production and makes custom products, a flat structure with a low managerial span of control is most appropriate.
Organizational change	As the environment and business strategies change, organizational structures change too.

appropriate for simple strategies, and more complex designs are necessary when strategies require more complex processes and interactions. Matching organizational structure to the business strategy leads to higher firm performance.[29] For example, an innovation strategy is best supported by low formalization and centralization and high specialization. A low-cost strategy would be best executed in a structure with moderate formalization, centralization, and specialization.

External Environment

Another important factor is the company's external environment. Rapidly changing environments require more flexible structures to deal effectively with the constant changes. This usually means that authority needs to be decentralized in some way to process relevant information and adjust to the changing environment.

Firms facing a highly differentiated environment usually create different business units to best serve each market segment. For example, because consumer preferences for cars differ around the world, car manufacturers including Honda often create different business units to serve each market segment. Organizations are also sometimes able to impose elements of organizational structure on their suppliers. Walmart and General Motors impose accounting systems and cost controls on their suppliers.

Organizational Talent

A third factor influencing organizational structure is the nature of the organization's talent. For example, a flexible structure is more appropriate if highly skilled workers, who often have professional norms guiding their behavior and decisions (e.g., doctors or lawyers), need to work in flat, team-based structures to get the work done most effectively. Advertising and marketing firms are often organized into teams.

Organizational Size

An organization's size also influences its structure.[30] Smaller organizations tend to be less bureaucratic than larger firms. Larger organizations tend to have greater specialization and departmentalization, greater hierarchy, and more rules than do smaller firms. Larger firms also benefit from lower costs due to economies of scale. The larger an organization and its subunits, the taller the hierarchy, the greater the centralization, and the more bureaucratically it operates, and the greater the chances of conflict between managers and employees.[31]

It is impossible to identify an optimal organizational size. Many firms tend to start with a more organic form, but after a firm employs about 1,000 people, it usually adopts many mechanistic features to manage its increasing coordination and communication needs. As organizations grow larger, they become more bureaucratic and are often seen as less personable and harder to identify with, decreasing employee commitment.[32] Nonetheless, even some large firms including Google manage to retain elements of more organic structures.

To capitalize on the flexibility, adaptability, and decision-making speed of smaller sizes and the economies of scale of larger sizes, many firms including Johnson and Johnson—whose slogan is "small-company environment, big-company impact"—strive to create smaller units within the larger organization.

Behavioral Expectations

A fourth important factor influencing organizational structure is the organization's expectations of how employees should behave, and what attitudes it wants to encourage or suppress. This decision is based in part on the company's values. If employees are to be encouraged to make decisions and work collaboratively, a decentralized and flat structure is appropriate. If employees are expected to follow explicit rules and procedures, a more hierarchical,

An organization's size affects its structure. A smaller organization, for instance, tends to be less bureaucratic than a larger one. This two-person design firm, for example, most likely has little formal structure. Only if and when the firm grows to include more designers and other staff will it start establishing a formal structure.

A firm using unit production produces small batches or custom one-of-a-kind products. This custom apparel shop, for instance, has a flat structure with few rules and procedures.

FOTOTIP/SHUTTERSTOCK.COM

centralized structure would be called for. Because power plants and pharmaceutical manufacturing facilities need employees to follow explicit rules and procedures, they tend to be very centralized and hierarchical.

Production Technology

A fifth factor influencing organizational structure is the organization's technology, or primary production system. When a firm uses ***unit production***, it produces in small batches or makes one-of-a-kind custom products. Employees' talents are more important than the machines being used, and it is difficult to specify rules and procedures in advance. In this case, a flat structure with a low managerial span of control is most appropriate. Advertising agencies and consulting firms typically use unit production.

unit production
Producing in small batches or making one-of-a-kind custom products

When a firm uses ***mass production***, it makes large volumes of identical products, typically using assembly lines and machines. In this case, a tall, bureaucratic structure with a large managerial span of control would be appropriate. Hershey and Sam Adams Brewery are examples of companies that use mass production.

mass production
Producing large volumes of identical products

When a firm uses ***continuous production***, machines constantly make the product and employees monitor the machines and plan changes. At the bottom of the organization, continuous production requires a mechanistic structure and low levels of supervision because machines do most of the work. The structure of a firm using continuous production is often tall and thin, or even an inverted pyramid. Dow Chemical and Exxon Mobil use continuous production.

continuous production
Machines constantly make the product

Organizational Change

As organizations change their strategies and adapt to changing environments, they often modify and change their structures to support the changes. Samsung recently adopted a more centralized structure than

ISTOCKPHOTO.COM/EDSTOCK

A divisional structure is a collection of functions organized around a geographic area, product or service, or market. Pepsico uses a divisional structure. One major division is responsible for the firm's beverage products such as Pepsi Cola. Another handles Pepsico's snack businesses such as Fritos corn chips and Lay's potato chips.

previously and created a new chief operating officer position to expedite decision making and improve efficiency.[33] Avaya's CEO appointed a chief restructuring officer to lead their restructuring to support its new business strategy.[34]

TYPES OF ORGANIZATIONAL STRUCTURES

In new or young organizations, the entrepreneur or founding group makes the decisions, and most communication is one-on-one because of the small organization size. This type of early organizational structure is called ***prebureaucratic*** and is highly centralized and lacking task standardization. This type of structure is best for simple tasks and entrepreneurial organizations as the founder is able to control the organization's decisions and growth.

prebureaucratic structure
Smaller organizations with low standardization, total centralization, and mostly one-on-one communication

The founder's personal characteristics and values drive many of a company's prestructural characteristics, which often stay with the firm as it grows.[35] Indeed, other things being equal, it is the founder's personality that determines organizational structure and strategy.[36] Bill Gore's values and beliefs influenced the structure at W. L. Gore, the $2.4 billion high-tech materials company that manufactures Gore-Tex fabric.[37]

As small companies grow, they typically adopt greater standardization and taller structures and develop a ***bureaucratic structure*** with greater standardization. In a bureaucratic structure, there is a formal division of labor, hierarchy, and standardization of work procedures, and employee behaviors follow written rules.[38] The greater importance placed on employees higher in the structure is reflected in centralized decision making and a strict chain of command. Bureaucracies are most appropriate in large organizations when work tasks are well-understood and it is possible to specify the best way to execute them.

bureaucratic structure
An organizational structure with formal division of labor, hierarchy, and standardization of work procedures

As they grow, organizations must decide how to carve employees into subunits. This usually means grouping people in a way that somehow relates to the tasks they perform. Here are six common bases for grouping employees:

1. *Employee knowledge and skills*: Employees are grouped by what they know; for example, pharmaceutical organizations have departments like oncology and genetics.
2. *Business function*: Employees are grouped by business function; for example, many organizations have departments of human resources, marketing, and research and development.
3. *Work process*: Employees are grouped based on the activities they do; for example, a retailer may have different retail store and online departments reflecting two different sales processes.
4. *Output*: Employees are grouped based on the products or services they work on; for example, Colgate-Palmolive has two business divisions: One division includes oral, personal, and home care products and the other focuses on pet nutrition.
5. *Client*: Employees are grouped based on the type of clients they serve; for example, Dell Computer has different departments supporting home, medium and small business, the public sector, and large business customers.

6. *Location*: Employees are grouped based on the geographical areas they serve; for example, many retailers including Lowe's Home Improvement divide employees by regions.

Now let's discuss some of the structures that arise from these different groupings.

Functional Structure

A ***functional structure*** groups people with the same skills, or who use similar tools or work processes, together into departments. For example, a marketing department is staffed solely with marketing professionals. When Cisco Systems changed from a decentralized structure to a functional structure, it decreased the duplication and greater standardization of its products and process designs and reduced costs.[39]

functional structure
An organizational structure that groups people with the same skills, or who use similar tools or work processes, together into departments

Functional structures tend to work well for organizations in stable environments selling only a few products or services because of the increased economies of scale. Career paths within each function are clear, and employee skill development tends to be in-depth but focused on a particular function. The possible disadvantages of a functional structure include poor coordination and communication across functions and a lack of clear responsibility for the delivery of a product or service. There is also an increased risk of conflict if employees develop a narrow perspective relevant to their function and not the organization as a whole.

Divisional Structure

A ***division*** is a collection of functions organized around a particular geographic area (geographic structure), product or service (product structure), or market (market structure). Divisional structures are common among organizations with many products or services, geographic areas, and customers.

division
A collection of functions organized around a particular geographic area, product or service, or market

When companies are global, they might put different divisions in charge of different geographic regions. Alternatively, if similar products are sold in different geographic regions, the firm might keep most of the functional work at home but set up divisions in different regions to market the product. This chapter's *Global Issues* feature discusses some of the organizational structures used by multinational organizations.

AMNARJ TANONGRATTANA/ SHUTTERSTOCK.COM

A matrix organization is created by combining a functional structure with a project or product team structure. Ford Motor Company often uses a matrix structure to design and engineer automobiles such as the newest version of the Ford Mustang.

MULTINATIONAL ORGANIZATIONAL STRUCTURES

Multinational organizations have additional challenges in creating an effective structure to support their business strategies. There are four primary organizational structures that support global business:

1. *Global product division structure* (e.g., McDonald's): All functional activities are controlled by a product group at headquarters; local managers do not usually provide input into product decisions and are involved only in local administrative, legal, and financial affairs. This structure is appropriate when the benefits of global integration are large and local differences are small.
2. *Global area division structure* (e.g., Frito Lay): Regional and/or country managers are given substantial autonomy to adapt strategies to fit local situations. This structure is appropriate when local differences are large and the benefits of global integration are small.
3. *Global transnational division structure* (e.g., Kraft Foods[40]): A balanced, matrixed relationship between local managers and headquarters with a two-way flow of ideas, resources, and employees between the two locations. This structure works best when both global integration and local responsiveness are needed.
4. *Regional headquarters structure* (e.g., Coca-Cola and Sony): A regional headquarters is established in major geographical areas (often North America, Asia, Latin America, and Europe) that works collaboratively with the product divisions to give the local units clearer operational goals and directions than typically happens under the global transnational division matrix structure. This structure is best when a balance of global integration and local responsiveness is needed.

Divisional structures improve coordination across functions and enable flexibility in responding to environmental changes because employees' expertise is focused on specific products, customers, and/or geographic regions. These structures can also help organizations grow or downsize as needed because divisions can be added or deleted as required. The possible disadvantages of a divisional structure are that rivalries and conflict might emerge across divisions, economies of scale are reduced because resources and skills are duplicated across divisions, and employees may become focused on divisional rather than organizational goals.

Matrix Structure

matrix structure
Employees report to both a project or product team and to a functional manager

Can you imagine having two bosses at the same time? When employees report to both a project or product team and to a functional manager, they are working in a ***matrix structure***.[41] Employees represent their function in their work team, which allows the team to house all of the skills and expertise it needs to perform effectively and make good decisions. Project managers coordinate the different functional contributions to the project and are held accountable for the team's performance. An organizational chart for a matrix structure is shown in Figure 14.5.

Matrix structures generate complex reporting relationships because a matrixed employee essentially has two bosses: the project or product boss and

Figure 14.5

Organizational Chart—Matrix Structure

A matrix structure is created by combining a functional structure with a project or product team structure. In a matrix structure individuals usually report to more than one boss at the same time—their functional supervisor and a project or product team leader.

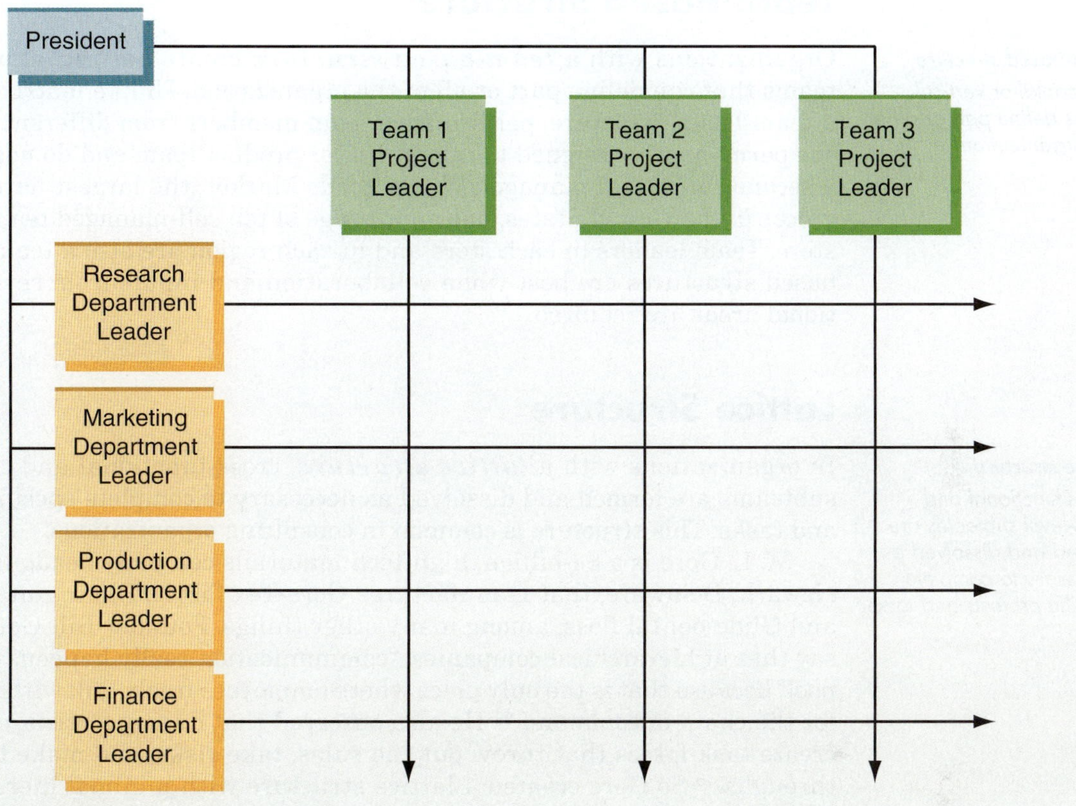

Source: Phillips/Gulley 474

his or her functional manager. Adjusting to a dual reporting relationship can be challenging, but as long as communication is open and expectations and goals are shared, the problems can be minimized. Costs tend to be higher due to the addition of program managers in addition to the functional managers, and power struggles may result from the two-boss system.

Matrix organizations are good at providing quality customer service, are very flexible, and can respond quickly to changes because the work units contain all of the needed functional expertise to make decisions. They are best suited to complex activities in uncertain environments, and work well when one affiliation is permanent (typically functional) and the other is temporary, such as a specific project—for example, assigning a production specialist in your chocolate company to a Valentine's Day project for three months and then to a Six Flags project for four months.

If project managers share organizational financial and human resources and cooperate, the matrix structure is more effective.[42] The distributed expertise, enhanced communication, and faster decision making enabled by a matrix structure decrease employees' protectionism of their functions, enabling more collaboration and more effective decision making.

Team-Based Structure

team-based structure
Horizontal or vertical teams define part or all of the organization

Organizations with a ***team-based structure*** create horizontal or vertical teams that can define part or all of the organization. Unlike matrix teams, in a team-based structure, performance team members from different functions are permanently assigned to the project or product team and do not report to a second functional manager. Whole Foods Market, the largest natural-foods grocer in the United States, has an average of ten self-managed teams in each store. Team leaders in each store and in each region are also a team.[43] Team-based structures are best when collaboration and inputs from several functional areas are required.

Lattice Structure

lattice structure
Cross-functional and cross-level subteams are formed and dissolved as necessary to complete specific projects and tasks

In organizations with a ***lattice structure***, cross-functional and cross-level subteams are formed and dissolved as necessary to complete specific projects and tasks. This structure is common in consulting organizations.

W. L. Gore is a $3-billion, high-tech materials company headquartered in Newark, Delaware, that manufactures Gore-Tex fabric, Elixir guitar strings, and Glide dental floss, among many other things. Founder Bill Gore liked to say that at hierarchical companies, "communication really happens in the car pool" because that is the only place where employees freely talk without regard for the chain of command.[44] He also observed that during a crisis, companies create task forces that throw out the rules, take risks, and make big breakthroughs.[45] So Gore created a lattice structure with minimal hierarchy and few rules, organizing the company as if it were a bunch of small task forces. He insisted on direct, one-on-one communication where any associate (the Gore term for employees) can talk to any other. Gore does have a president and CEO, divisions, and business units, but there is no organizational chart, there is minimal hierarchy, and there are sponsors rather than bosses. There is no fixed or assigned authority. Goals are set by the same people who are accountable for making them happen, and tasks and functions are organized through a system of commitments. This allows employees to create roles for themselves that leverage their talents and interests rather than be assigned formal jobs. The lattice structure of tomato processing company Morning Star is featured in this chapter's *Case Study*.

Network Organization

network organization
A collection of autonomous units or firms that act as a single larger entity, using social mechanisms for coordination and control

A ***network organization*** is a collection of autonomous units or firms that act as a single larger entity, using social mechanisms for coordination and control. Because network organizations contract out any function that can be done better or more cheaply by outside firms (e.g., marketing and payroll), managers

LOSKUTNIKOV/SHUTTERSTOCK.COM

PHANT/SHUTTERSTOCK.COM

CASE STUDY The Morning Star's Lattice Structure

The Morning Star Company, a highly successful and growing $700 million California tomato-processing company, was founded on a philosophy of self-management. The company envisions "an organization of self-managing professionals who initiate communication and coordination of their activities with fellow colleagues, customers, suppliers, and fellow industry participants, absent directives from others."[46] The core of the company's management philosophy is freedom, which is seen as important to effective coordination. The company believes that freedom allows employees to be drawn to what they really like as opposed to having to do what they're told, increasing both enthusiasm and performance. Extensive applicant screening for fit with the company's philosophy and new hire training on self-management helps employees adapt to the autonomy and responsibility of working without a formal boss.

The company's lattice structure requires a high degree of self-management. Each year every employee writes a personal mission statement that identifies how he or she will contribute to Morning Star's overall objective of "producing tomato products and services which consistently achieve the quality and service expectations of our customers." Every employee also negotiates a Colleague Letter of Understanding (CLOU) with the associates most affected by his or her work. The letter creates an operating plan for each employee, spelling out the relevant performance metrics for as many thirty activities. Employees are also personally responsible for acquiring the training, resources, and cooperation necessary to fulfill their role.[47]

As in any organization, disputes arise between employees that must be settled. If an employee believes that someone has not lived up to his or her CLOU commitments, the two meet to discuss the issue. If they cannot resolve the matter they choose a trusted internal mediator to hear their views. If the losing party objects to the proposed remedy, a panel of six colleagues assembles and either endorses the mediator's recommendation or proposes an alternative solution. If that is not accepted, the president brings both employees together and makes a binding decision. Reflecting employees' commitment to self-management, employee disputes rarely make it to the president.[48]

Questions:

1. How would working for Morning Star be different from working at a traditional, bureaucratic company? What would be the most positive and negative aspects of the experience?
2. Do you think the lattice structure is best for Morning Star? Can you identify another structure that might be more appropriate for the company's culture of empowerment and self-management?
3. Where do you think this type of lattice structure would be ineffective? What would make this type of structure inappropriate or difficult to implement?

spend a lot of time coordinating and controlling the network of contractors and strategic alliances.

Clothing retailer H&M has a team of 100 in-house designers who work with buyers to develop its clothing, which is then outsourced to a network of 700 suppliers.[49] This allows H&M to be more flexible than many of its competitors and to keep its costs down.

Network organizations are best for functions that do not require frequent exchanges, do not suffer from supply uncertainty, and do not require customization. In this case, the costs of making and monitoring the transactions will not prevent the organization from hiring specialists to do the job. These specialist firms can often deliver a higher-quality product more cheaply because of the volume they do.

Because a network organization does not have a system of direct supervision or standardized rules and procedures, it must coordinate and control the participants in some other way. Some of the ways this is done are through joint payoffs and restricted access:

- *Joint payoffs:* Because networks are organized around specific products or projects, payments are arranged based on the final product, so that if the product does not make it, no firm makes a profit. This motivates everyone to do their best.
- *Restricted access:* By restricting their exchanges to just a few long-term partners, networked organizations are more dependent on each other. By increasing their chances for future business, long-term relationships decrease the incentive for one organization to take advantage of another because they will get kicked out of the network and lose the opportunity to have future work.

CONTEMPORARY ISSUES IN ORGANIZATIONAL STRUCTURE

In this final section we will examine four emerging issues that relate to organizational structure. These are virtual organizations, mechanisms for integrating employees, communities of practice, and the effects of restructuring on performance.

Virtual Organizations

virtual organization
An organization that contracts out almost all of its functions except for the company name and managing the coordination among the contractors

A ***virtual organization*** is one that contracts out almost all of its functions except for the company name and managing the coordination among the contractors. A virtual organization may not even have a permanent office. Virtual organizations often use virtual teams linked by technology, although employees may still meet face-to-face.

Virtual organizations tend to be very complex. The loss of control over the outsourced functions creates many challenges, including communication, ambiguity over organizational membership and career paths, and skills for managing at a distance. Nonetheless, the reduced costs and increased flexibility from being virtual create a competitive advantage for many firms.

Sigma is a German training and consulting company whose freelancing consultants and trainers build small or large teams as needed to work on projects. Sigma partners work from their home offices, some full-time for Sigma, and others temporarily if their competencies are needed on a project. Project managers find new partners through recommendations from current Sigma partners. An information technology system called SigSys enables communication.[50]

Integrating Employees

Segmenting employees into divisions, functional areas, or groups requires additional integrating mechanisms that facilitate coordination and communication among employees and groups. These mechanisms can be as simple as getting managers from different units to communicate and work together to coordinate or to identify and solve shared problems. When done informally, this is simply called ***direct contact***.

Alternatively, a manager or team member can be assigned a ***liaison role*** and held formally accountable for communicating and coordinating with other groups. When a specific project or problem needs to be addressed, organizations often create a temporary committee called a ***task force***. When integration needs are permanent and more complex, a ***cross-functional team*** is created. Cross-functional teams are like permanent task forces created to address specific problems or recurring needs.

direct contact
Managers from different units informally work together to coordinate or to identify and solve shared problems

liaison role
A manager or team member is held formally accountable for communicating and coordinating with other groups

task force
A temporary committee formed to address a specific project or problem

cross-functional team
A permanent task force created to address specific problems or recurring needs

communities of practice
Groups of people whose shared expertise and interest in a joint enterprise informally binds them together

Communities of Practice

Communities of practice can also help to integrate employees and create the informal structure that nearly every business needs, regardless of its formal structure. ***Communities of practice*** are groups of people whose shared expertise and interest in a joint enterprise informally binds them together. Examples include consultants who specialize in designing training systems or environmental engineers willing to share their knowledge and insights with other environmental engineers. A community of practice may or may not meet regularly or even in person, and can be located in a single company or span companies. The people involved in a community of practice share their knowledge and experiences in open, creative ways that can create new solutions and approaches to problems.[51] In this way, the company intranet can cultivate a sense of community and employee loyalty.

Most companies have communities of practice, which often span across company boundaries. Field technicians share experiences and help each another troubleshoot problems, and researchers developing new products reach around the world to tap experts with specialized knowledge. Although these communities rarely show up on organizational charts and may not even be formally recognized by executive leadership, companies recognize their benefits and are increasingly promoting and enabling them.[52]

The Chevron Corporation has more than 100 "operational excellence" communities in place. One of those networks saved an estimated $30 million in damages by rapidly sharing information about the potential hazards of a gas-drilling technique that had caused problems in one location. Caterpillar has established more than 2,700 communities with more than 37,000 registered participants: employees, dealers, customers, and suppliers. The resulting quality and productivity improvements among dealers and suppliers have been enough to justify the investment seven times over.[53]

Managers cannot create effective communities of practice, only the conditions necessary for them to exist. A "command and control" management style is unlikely to foster successful communities of practice. Successful managers cultivate communities of practice by identifying and bringing the right people together, building trust, and providing an appropriate infrastructure.[54] Dictating goals and applying individual performance metrics can disintegrate communities of practice, and indiscriminately throwing money (or collaboration software) at them without a clear set of priorities can be equally wasteful.[55]

A relatively simple way to improve interconnectedness among community members is to develop a searchable database that identifies each community member's areas of expertise to help members quickly identify appropriate experts. Including some personal information in the database can help—knowing that the person you are contacting shares a hobby or alma mater can help break the ice.[56] The heart of a community of practice is the web of relationships among community members. Every email, wiki posting, and phone call strengthens members' relationships and builds the community.

As a manager, how can you create the conditions that enable communities of practice to flourish? Here are some experts' tips:[57]

1. *Start with a clear area of business need:* Build communities that help the company work more effectively. For example, Hewlett Packard's Work Innovation Networks are a means of focusing effort on developing a creative approach to a current problem.[58]
2. *Start small:* Test ideas and try several formats to see what employees like and what works best. For example, any Hewlett Packard business can create a network by announcing itself as the host for a series of presentations, conferences, and seminars on a topic it is currently striving to understand. An invitation is broadcast to the rest of the company, and if the "market" responds, then the subject area takes on a life of its own in a community of practice.[59]
3. *Recruit management involvement:* If lower-level employees see their bosses actively participating in the community, they are more likely to participate as well.
4. *Use technology that supports the community's needs and that community members are able to use and are comfortable using:* Some training in using wikis, portals, and other technologies may be necessary. Some companies, including Ford Motor Company and Delta Airlines, have even provided home computers and Internet connections for employees for a very low price.
5. *Respect and build on informal employee initiatives already underway:* Employees may have already created a type of community of practice to help them do their jobs better—determine what is already in place and working, and build on it. Employees will already be somewhat familiar with the community's processes and practices, and more willing to use it.
6. *Celebrate contributions and build on small successes:* Building a community of practice takes time and requires employees to behave in new ways. Highlight on the company intranet or in the company newsletter ways the community has solved business problems and recognize employees who have meaningfully contributed.

A reason many companies invest in communities of practice is the ability of these communities to transfer knowledge among people. Organizations such as IBM, HP, and Unisys even prefer to call them "knowledge networks." In the knowledge economy, organizations need their employees to become "knowledge workers" who constantly draw on their expertise to respond to a rapidly changing market. Employees need to be able to participate in a flow of knowledge that consists of not only written and online information sources, but also the active exchange of ideas with others who have related experience and skills.[60] This also helps transfer knowledge from senior to more junior employees, ensuring that key knowledge is not lost when some employees leave or retire.

Effects of Restructuring on Performance

The turnover of a CEO is frequently followed by corporate restructuring.[61] Struggling organizations often look to restructuring as a way to improve their performance.[62] Although restructuring can certainly address some issues, it is not a panacea[63] and can lead to unintended consequences.[64]

The restructuring process is stressful and can decrease employee motivation if the changes are poorly communicated. High performers often leave if the change is chaotic or if their future with the firm is ambiguous. When the new structure requires fewer employees, the survivors of the resulting downsizing can suffer stress, decreased commitment, and higher turnover intentions.[65]

Restructuring efforts must focus on positioning the organization for the future.[66] Restructuring also must address the real cause of whatever the organization wants to change.[67] For example, if a performance problem is due to low employee motivation due to poor supervisors, reorganizing the structure is not likely to fix this core problem. Restructurings should take place as infrequently as possible to create stability, enhance performance, and minimize employee stress and confusion.

SUMMARY AND APPLICATION

Organizational design is the process of selecting and managing aspects of organizational structure and culture to enable the organization to achieve its goals. Organizational structure is the formal system of task, power, and reporting relationships in an organization. Organizational charts are diagrams of the reporting relationships and chain of command in a company.

Division of labor is the degree to which employees specialize or generalize. Span of control is the number of people reporting directly to an individual. Hierarchy is the degree to which some employees have formal authority over others. Centralization is the degree to which power and decision-making authority are concentrated at high levels of the organization rather than distributed. Delegation frees manager to focus on more important tasks, develops others' skills, increases trust, and can lead to a higher-quality product.

An organization's structure is influenced by its business strategy, external environment, talent, size, expectations of how employees should behave, production technology, and organizational change. Prebureaucratic structures are most common in newer and smaller organizations. They are characterized by low standardization and total centralization, and most communication is one-on-one. Bureaucratic structures have more formal division of labor, greater hierarchy, and more standardization of work procedures.

Network organizations are best for functions that do not require frequent exchanges, do not suffer from supply uncertainty, and do not require customization. In this case, the costs of making and monitoring transactions will not prevent the organization from hiring specialists to do the job. Mechanistic organizations are rigid, traditional bureaucracies with centralized power and hierarchical communications. Organic structures are flexible, decentralized structures without clear lines of authority, with decentralized power, open communication channels, and a focus on adaptability in helping employees accomplish goals.

REAL WORLD RESPONSE

BUILDING A TREEHOUSE

As we saw earlier, Treehouse owners were deliberating their dilemma of whether or not they needed managers. Having reached a logical jumping-off point in their meditations about management, Carson and Johnson took the next logical step: They wrote up a "manifesto" about how the company would work without managers, posted it on an internal forum, and invited everyone to "discuss" the matter. "The company ground to a halt for two days," reports Carson, while the workforce generated 447 comments. When the proposal was put to a vote, 90 percent of Treehouse employees endorsed a bossless workplace.

So, in mid-2013, says Carson, "we removed all managers.... We changed the way the company operated and gave all employees 100 percent control of their time and let them decide what they work on each day. From then on, no one would tell anyone what to do, not even the CEO." The result? At first, Carson admits, "it was total chaos," but Carson and Johnson quickly realized that much of a manager's job involves *communication* and that subordinates mostly need managers because they need *information*.

In short, even if you've addressed the problem of over-managing, running an organization is basically a matter of *coordination*. "The chaos," contends Carson, came from the fact that ... non-managers aren't used to the level of communication needed to coordinate with other teams and projects, so there's often not enough proactive communication and coordination. We don't have managers to coordinate across projects, so it's up to individuals to take time to communicate what's happening on their projects and how it affects other people.

Thus, one of the first corrective measures taken by the two (former) top managers was building a new internal-information tool called Canopy, a sort of open-source email account that gives everyone the capability to access and contribute to company-wide communications. Not surprisingly, shared information is also crucial to the process of getting along without bosses. Projects are proposed by employees, who use Canopy to circulate the information needed to get other employees interested. If a proposal attracts sufficient interest, it moves forward, with the employees who've chosen to get involved selecting a manager for the project. "There are still going to be managers at Treehouse," explains Carson. "There just aren't titles. The only way you can be a leader is if you lead and people want to follow."

The system, of course, has its drawbacks. For one thing, says Carson, "I can't make people do things.... I've even had people tell me they don't have time or aren't interested in my ideas. It sucks, but it's part of

(*Continued*)

running a no-manager company." Needless to say, Carson is also frustrated by the fact that "I can't make things happen very fast. There are many times I just want to say, 'Do this right now,' but I can't. It's basically against the rules." More important, it can often take quite a while to get projects off the ground. According to Treehouse rules, "you have to propose a project, explain it thoroughly, and convince people to join. The process," Carson admits, "can take weeks or months."

Perhaps the biggest problem, however, is still ahead. "We have 70 employees now," says Carson, "and for a company our size, this model works. However, it's probably going to start showing serious signs of trouble at around 150 people. "But then again, we'll figure it out."

Communities of practice are groups of people whose shared expertise and interest in a joint enterprise informally binds them together. They help organizations share knowledge internally as well as across organizational boundaries.

DISCUSSION QUESTIONS

1. How do you think your career path might differ in a hierarchical versus a flat organization?
2. Why do you think companies are moving toward flatter, more organic structures? Do you think this is appropriate?
3. What areas of an organization (e.g., what functions) do you think are the best to centralize? Which are the best to decentralize?
4. What keeps you from delegating more? How can you overcome these obstacles?
5. If you started your own company selling iPhone applications, what organizational structure would you create? Why?
6. If you wanted employees to work collaboratively and minimize conflict, what organizational structures would you consider adopting? Why? Which structures would you avoid? Why?
7. What type of person would be a good fit with Nordstrom's extremely organic and informal structure? Why?
8. What would you do during a corporate restructuring to ensure that your best employees did not leave?

DEVELOP YOUR SKILLS EXERCISE

Am I an Effective Delegator?

As you learned in this chapter, delegation is an important managerial skill in every organizational structure. This exercise gives you the chance to assess your delegation habits.

___ 1. I'd delegate more, but the jobs I delegate never seem to get done the way I want them to be done.
___ 2. I don't feel I have the time to delegate properly.
___ 3. I carefully check on subordinates' work without letting them know I'm doing it, so I can correct their mistakes if necessary before they cause too many problems.
___ 4. I delegate the whole job—giving the opportunity for the subordinate to complete it without any of my involvement. Then I review the end result.
___ 5. When I have given clear instructions and the job isn't done right, I get upset.
___ 6. I feel the staff lacks the commitment that I have. So any job I delegate won't get done as well as I'd do it.
___ 7. I'd delegate more, but I feel I can do the task better than the person I might delegate it to.
___ 8. I'd delegate more, but if the individual I delegate the task to does an incompetent job, I'll be severely criticized.
___ 9. If I were to delegate the task, my job wouldn't be nearly as much fun.
___ 10. When I delegate a job, I often find that the outcome is such that I end up doing the job over again myself.
___ 11. I have not really found that delegation saves any time.
___ 12. I delegate a task clearly and concisely, explaining exactly how it should be accomplished.
___ 13. I can't delegate as much as I'd like to because my subordinates lack the necessary experience.
___ 14. I feel that when I delegate I lose control.
___ 15. I would delegate more but I'm pretty much a perfectionist.
___ 16. I work longer hours than I should.
___ 17. I can give subordinates the routine tasks, but I feel I must keep non-routine tasks myself.
___ 18. My own boss expects me to keep very close to all details of my work.

Scoring: Add up your responses to the eighteen statements to calculate your delegating habits score.

Interpretation: If your score is over 72, you may be seriously failing to utilize the talents of your staff and should try to delegate more.

If your score is between 36 and 71, your delegating habits could probably be improved.

If your score is below 35, you are probably an effective delegator.

Review the statements to which you responded with a 4 or 5. This will give you some insights into the obstacles and excuses that might be keeping you from delegating more.

To improve your delegation skills, imagine that you must travel to an island and will not be able to contact anyone off the island for a week. Identify what you need to accomplish in the next week, and think about how you would delegate it to get it all done. Then start delegating some tasks and responsibilities and see if you are not surprised at the results!

Source: Management review by T. J. Krein. Copyright 1982 by American Management Association.

GROUP EXERCISE

To Matrix or Not to Matrix, That is the Question

The Situation

Platinum Resorts is a chain of all-inclusive luxury resorts, with locations in Playa Del Carmen, Mexico; Negril, Jamaica; Freeport, Bahamas; and Key West, Florida. Some customers return to the same location year after year, and others enjoy trying out different locations in the group. However, recent reports indicate that sales are down and customer complaints are up. Resort managers are pointing fingers and insisting that the middle managers at each location (front desk, food service, housekeeping, and maintenance) are not upholding company standards. Currently, the company has adopted a divisional structure, with a vice-president for each of the four resorts.

The Decision

Frustrated by inconsistent service and weak sales, Platinum Resorts has enlisted the services of a consultant. After visiting each of the resorts and speaking with employees and guests, the consultant is recommending that the company move from its current divisional structure to a matrix organization. The consultant explains that a matrix organization is used by many innovative organizations, such as NASA, to achieve functional and divisional control. Although some managers think that this is a great idea, others are concerned that their authority and control may be undermined by this new organizational structure. Platinum Resorts knows that something has to change, but you are unsure if this is the right solution.

Team Activity

Form a group of four students and assign each group member to one of the following roles:

- President of Platinum Resorts
- Sales manager for the Playa Del Carmen, Mexico resort
- Housekeeper at the Key West, Florida resort
- Guest at the Negril, Jamaica resort

Exercise Activities

1. Without consulting other members of the team, and from the perspective of your assigned role, do you think that Platinum Resorts should adopt a matrix structure?
2. Assemble your group and have each member present the potential pros and cons of organizing as a matrix organization.

3. As a group, develop an organizational chart for the company in its current divisional structure and the proposed matrix structure.
4. Develop a list of alternatives to converting to a matrix structure.
5. Considering all perspectives, what is the best decision of Platimum Resorts?

VIDEO EXERCISE

Honest Tea: Organizational Structure

Honest Tea (U.S.) is a bottled organic tea company based in Bethesda, Maryland. It was founded in 1998 by Seth Goldman and Barry Nalebuff. The company is a wholly owned subsidiary of the Coca-Cola Company. Coca-Cola invested 40% in 2008 and bought the rest of the company in 2011. Honest Tea is known for its organic and fair trade products and is one of the fastest growing private companies.

Honest Tea started off with a handful of employees bringing out five products, three of which are still in the market. As Honest Tea began to grow, it became necessary to have workers specialized in different tasks so that they ultimately function as a single unit. Today the company has over 35 package varieties of not only tea but other beverages as well.

Honest Tea caters to a group of customers that prefer organic or low calorie beverages over other types of beverages. The advantage here is that Honest Tea is able to use skilled specialists to deal with this unique customer base. Honest Tea came into this category of customers as a challenger. The whole process of sourcing material, production, marketing, and sales was different since it catered to a different group of customer.

Honest Tea finds that it must continually adapt to changing circumstances and environments. Initially organic or low calorie tea was the only product, but the firm has expanded to various other beverages. Bringing out new and innovative beverages is something that Honest Tea continues to do. Honest Tea follows a very transparent work culture which has helped them to avoid some of the problems that typical growing organizations face. Honest Tea believes that growth is continuous; the firm should never consider that they have finished achieving what they set out to accomplish.

Discussion Questions

1. Describe the role of division of labor and hierarchy ay Honest Tea.
2. In what ways has business strategy and organizational size impacted Honest Tea. How might this change in the future?
3. Does Honest Tea have more of an organic or mechanistic structure? How can you tell?

VIDEO CASE

Now What?

Imagine being part of a group with the boss and another coworker in which you are discussing how you were recently beat to market by a competitor's new toy line. The boss asks the group what the company could do to prevent something similar from happening again. *What do you say or do?* Go to this chapter's "Now What?" video, watch the challenge video, and choose a response. Be sure to also view the outcomes of the two responses you didn't choose.

Discussion Questions

1. Which organizational structures are illustrated in these videos and how do they influence strategic execution? Explain.
2. How do these videos illustrate the influence of the external environment on organizational design?
3. Based on this chapter, what other ideas do you have to help Happy Time Toys to develop and manufacture new toys more rapidly and to be faster in responding to the environment?

ENDNOTES

[1]Rogoway, M. (2013, December). Portland Startup Treehouse Eliminates the Boss, Tells Workers to Manage Themselves. *OregonLive*. Available at: http://www.oregonlive.com/silicon-forest/index.ssf/2013/12/portland_startup_treehouse_eli.html; Carson, R. (2013, September 17). No Managers: Why We Removed Managers at Treehouse. *The Naive Optimist*. Available at: http://ryancarson.com/post/61562761297/no-managers-why-we-removed-bosses-at-treehouse; Treehouse Receives $7 Million in Series B Financing Led by Kaplan Ventures. Treehouse Island Inc. press release, April 9, 2013; Bryant, A. (2014, June 5). Ryan Carson of Treehouse, on When Titles Get in the Way. *NYTimes.com*. Available at: http://www.nytimes.com/2014/06/06/business/ryan-carson-of-treehouse-on-killing-all-the-titles.html?_r=0; Spencer, M. (2014, October 9). Five Things I Learned from One of Portland's Most Bustling Startups. *Portland* (Oregon) *Business Journal*. Available at: http://www.bizjournals.com/portland/blog/2014/10/5-things-i-learned-from-one-of-portlands-most.html; Carson, R. (2014, January17). The Negative Side of #NoManager Companies. *The Naive Optimist*. Available at: http://ryancarson.com/post/73639971628/the-negative-side-of-nomanager-companies.

[2]Ketchen, D. J., Jr., Combs, J. G., Russell C. R., Shook, C., Dean, M. A., Runge, J., Lohrke, F. T., Naumann, S. E., Haptonstahl, D. E., Baker, R., Beckstein, B. A., Handler, C., Honig, H., & Lamoureux, S. (1997). Organizational Configurations and Performance: A Meta-Analysis. *Academy of Management Journal, 40*, 223–240.

[3]Covin, J. G., & Slevin, D. P. (1989). Strategic Management of Small Firms in Hostile and Benign Environments. *Strategic Management Journal, 10*, 75–87; Jennings, D. F., & Seaman, S. L. (1990). Aggressiveness of Response to New Business Opportunities Following Deregulation: An Empirical Study of Established Financial Firms. *Journal of Business Venturing, 5*, 177–189.

[4]Morris, J. H., & Steers, R. M. (1980). Structural Influences on Organizational Commitment. *Journal of Vocational Behavior, 17*, 50–57.

[5]Pugh, D. S., Hickson, D. J., Hinings, C. R., & Turner, C. (1968). Dimensions of Organizational Structure. *Administrative Science Quarterly, 13*, 65–105.

[6]Katz, J. (2010). The Soul of Memphis. *Smithsonian*, 71.

[7]Blau, P. M., & Schoenherr, R. A. (1971). *The Structure of Organizations*. New York: Basic Books.

[8]Pugh, D. S., Hickson, D. J., Hinings, C. R., & Turner, C. (1969). Dimensions of Organizational Structure. *Administrative Science Quarterly, 13*, 65–105.

[9]Campion, M. A. (1989). Ability Requirement Implications of Job Design: An Interdisciplinary Perspective. *Personnel Psychology, 42*, 1–24.

[10]Revlon Implements Worldwide Organizational Restructuring. (2009, June 1). *GCImagazine.com*. Available at: http://www.gcimagazine.com/business/marketers/announcements/46625697.html.

[11]Lashinsky, A., Burker, D., & Kaufman, S. (2006, April 17). The Hurd Way. *Fortune*, 92.

[12]Pugh, D. S., Hickson, D. J., Hinings, C. R., & Turner, C. (1969). Dimensions of Organizational Structure. *Administrative Science Quarterly, 13*, 65–105.

[13]Morris, J. H., & Steers, R. M. (1980). Structural Influences on Organizational Commitment. *Journal of Vocational Behavior, 17*, 50–57.

[14]Hartenian, L. S, Hadaway, F. J., & Badovick, G. J. (1994). Antecedents and Consequences of Role Perceptions: A Path Analytic Approach. *Journal of Applied Business Research, 10*, 40–52.

[15]Hage, J., & Aiken, M. (1969). Routine Technology, Social Structure, and Organizational Goals. *Administrative Science Quarterly, 14*, 366–376.

[16]Pugh, D. S., Hickson, D. J., Hinings, C. R., & Turner, C. (1968). Dimensions of Organizational Structure. *Administrative Science Quarterly, 13*, 65–105.

[17]Glew, D. J., O Leary-Kelly, A. M., Griffin, R. W., & Van Fleet, D. D. (1995). Participation in Organizations: A Preview of the Issues and Proposed Framework for Future Analysis. *Journal of Management, 21*, 395–421.

[18]Shadur, M. A., Kienzle, R., & Rodwel, J. J. (1999). The Relationship Between Organizational Climate and Employee Perceptions of Involvement. *Group & Organization Management, 24*, 479–503.

[19]Meyer, J., & Allen, N. (1991). A Three-Component Conceptualization of Organizational Commitment. *Human Resource*

Management Review, 1, 69–89; Herscovitch, L., & Meyer, J. P. (2002). Commitment to Organizational Change: Extension of a Three Component Model. *Journal of Applied Psychology, 87*, 474–487.

[20]Gerstner, L. V., Jr., (2002). *Who Says Elephants Can't Dance? Inside IBM's Historic Turnaround* (p. 22). New York: HarperBusiness.

[21]Burns, T., & Stalker, G. M. (1961). *The Management of Innovation*. London: Tavistock; Lawrence, P. R., & Lorsch, J. W. (1967). *Organization and Environment*. Homewood, IL: Irwin.

[22]Rahman, M., & Zanzi, A. (1995). A Comparison of Organizational Structure, Job Stress, and Satisfaction in Audit and Management Advisory Services (MAS) in CPA Firms. *Journal of Managerial Issues, 7*, 290–305.

[23]Meyer, J. P., & Allen, N. J. (1997). *Commitment in the Work Place: Theory Research and Application*. London: Sage Publications.

[24]Covin, J. G., & Slevin, D. P. (1989). Strategic Management of Small Firms in Hostile and Benign Environments. *Strategic Management Journal, 10*, 75–87.

[25]Spector, R. (2000). *Lessons from the Nordstrom Way: How Companies Are Emulating the #1 Customer Service Company.* New York: John Wiley.

[26]Burns, T., & Stalker, G. M. (1961). *The Management of Innovation*. London: Tavistock; Lawrence, P. R., & Lorsch, J. W. (1967). *Organization and Environment*. Homewood, IL: Irwin.

[27]Based on Burns, T., & Stalker, G. M. (1961). *The Management of Innovation*. London: Tavistock; Lawrence, P. R., & Lorsch, J. W. (1967). *Organization and environment*. Homewood, IL: Irwin.

[28]Chenhall, R.H., Kallunki, J.P., & Silvola, H. (2011). Exploring the Relationships Between Strategy, Innovation and Management Control Systems: The Roles of Social Networking, Organic Innovative Culture and Formal Controls, *Journal of Management Accounting Research, 23*(1), 99–128.

[29]Olson, E. M., Slater, S. F., & Hult, G. T. (2005). The Importance of Structure and Process to Strategy Implementation. *Business Horizons, 48*, 47–54.

[30]Gooding, R. Z., & Wagner, III, J. A. (1985, December). A Meta-Analytic Review of the Relationship Between Size and Performance: The Productivity and Efficiency of Organizations and Their Subunits. *Administrative Science Quarterly*, 462–481; Bluedorn, A. C. (1993, Summer). Pilgrim's Progress: Trends and Convergence in Research on Organizational Size and Environments. *Journal of Management*, 163–192.

[31]Harrison, F. L., & Lock, D. (2004). *Advanced Project Management: A Structured Approach* (4th ed.). Burlington, VT: Gower.

[32]Mathieu, J. E., & Zajac, D. M. (1990). A Review and Meta-Analysis of the Antecedents, Correlates, and Consequences of Organizational Commitment. *Psychological Bulletin 108*, 171–194.

[33]Samsung (2010). About Samsung Electronics. Available at: http://www.samsung.com/us/aboutsamsung/sustainability/sustainabilityreports/download/2009/2009%20About% 20 Samsung%20Electronics.pdf.

[34]Greene, T. (2009, March 26). Avaya's New CEO Sets Three Top Goals for Company. *Network World*. Available at: http://www.techpub.com/voip/avayas-new-ceo-sets-three-top-goals-for-company/.

[35]Hambrick, D., & Mason, P. (1984). Upper Echelons: The Organization as a Reflection of Its Top Managers. *Academy of Management Review*, 193–206; Lewin, A. Y., & Stephens, C. U. (1994). CEO Attitudes as Determinants of Organization Design: An Integrated Model. *Organization Studies, 15*, 183–212.

[36]Miller, D., & Droge, C. (1986). Psychological and Traditional Determinants of Structure. *Administrative Science Quarterly, 31*, 539–560.

[37]Deutschman, A. (2004, December). The Fabric of Creativity. *Fast Company, 89*, 54.

[38]Gerth, H. H., & Mills, C. W. (1958). From *Max Weber: Essays in Sociology*. New York: Oxford University Press; Walton, E. (2005). The Persistence of Bureaucracy: A Meta-Analysis of Weber's Model of Bureaucratic Control. *Organization Studies, 26*, 569–600.

[39]Galbraith, J. (2009, August). How Do You Manage in a Downturn? *Talent Management Magazine*, 44–46.

[40]Kraft Foods Announces New Global Organizational Structure. (2004, August 1). *The Moodie Report*. Available at: http://www.moodiereport.com/document.php?c_id=1178&doc_id=2628.

[41]Kolodny, H. F. (1979). Evolution to a Matrix Organization. *Academy of Management Review, 4*, 543–544.

[42]Davidovitch, L., Parush, A., & Shtub, A. (2010). Simulator-Based Team Training to Share Resources in a Matrix Structure Organization, *IEEE Transactions on Engineering Management, 57*(2), 288–300.

[43]Fishman, C. (1996, April 30). Whole Foods Is All Teams. *Fast Company*. Available at: http://www.fastcompany.com/magazine/02/team1.html?page=0%2C0.

[44]Deutschman, A. (2004, December). The Fabric of Creativity. *Fast Company, 89*, 54.

[45]Deutschman, A. (2004, December). The Fabric of Creativity. *Fast Company, 89*, 54.

[46]The Morning Star Company (2012). Self-Management. Available at: http://www.morningstarco.com/index.cgi?Page=Self-Management.

[47]Flegal, S. (2012, January 18). 1 Company Thrives With No Managers. *The Telegraph*. Available at: http://www.nashuatelegraph.com/business/946895-192/1-company-thrives-with-no-managers.html.

[48]Hamel, G. (2011). First, Let's Fire All the Managers, *Harvard Business Review, 89*(12), 48–59.

[49]Capell, K. (2008, September 3). H&M Defies Retail Gloom. *BusinessWeek*. Available at: http://www.businessweek.com/globalbiz/content/sep2008/gb2008093_150758.htm.

[50]Jacobsen, K. (2004, Fall). *A Study of Virtual Organizations* (p. 36). Norwegian University of Science and Technology Department of Computer and Information Science. Available at: http://www.idi.ntnu.no/grupper/su/fordypningsprosjekt-2004 /Jacobsen2004.pdf.

[51]Wenger, E. C., & Snyder, W. M. (2000, January–February). Communities of Practice: The Organizational Frontier. *Harvard Business Review*, 139–145.

[52]Laseter, T., & Cross, R. (2007, January 31). The Craft of Connection. Strategy + Business. Available at: http://www.strategy-business.com/article/06302?gko=ee374.

[53]Laseter, T., & Cross, R. (2007, January 31). The Craft of Connection. Strategy + Business. Available at: http://www.strategy-business.com/article/06302?gko=ee374.

[54]Wenger, E. C., & Snyder, W. M. (2000, January–February). Communities of Practice: The Organizational Frontier. *Harvard Business Review*, 139–145.

[55]Laseter, T., & Cross, R. (2007, January 31). The Craft of Connection. Strategy + Business. Available at: http://www.strategy-business.com/article/06302?gko=ee374.

[56]Laseter, T., & Cross, R. (2007, January 31). The Craft of Connection. Strategy + Business. Available at: http://www.strategy-business.com/article/06302?gko=ee374.

[57]Based on Stuckey, B., & Smith, J. D. (2004). Building Sustainable Communities of Practice. In *Knowledge Networks: Innovation Through Communities of Practice*, eds. P. M. Hildreth & C. Kimple (pp. 150–164). Hershey, PA: Idea Group; Vestal, W. C., & Lopez, K. (2004). Best Practices: Developing Communities That Provide Business Value. Building Sustainable Communities of Practice. In *Knowledge Networks: Innovation Through Communities of Practice*, eds. P. M. Hildreth & C. Kimple (pp. 142–149). Hershey, PA: Idea Group; Ambrozek, J., & Ambrozek, L. B. (2002, December). Building Business Value Through Communities of Practice. *Workforce Online*; Weigner, E. (2002). *Cultivating Communities of Practice*. Boston: Harvard Business School Press.

[58]Stewart, T. A. (1997). *Intellectual Capital: The New Wealth of Organizations*. New York: Doubleday.

[59]Stewart, T. A. (1997). *Intellectual Capital: The New Wealth of Organizations*. New York: Doubleday.

[60]Gongla, P., & Rizzuto, C. (2001). Evolving Communities of Practice: IBM Global Services Experience. *IBM Systems Journal, 40*(4), 842–862.

[61]Perry, T., & Shivdasani, A. (2005). Do Boards Affect Performance? Evidence from Corporate Restructuring. *Journal of Business, 78*(4), 1403–1432.

[62]Denis, D. J., & Kruse, T. A. (2000). Managerial Discipline and Corporate Restructuring Following Performance Declines. *Journal of Financial Economics, 55*, 391–424.

[63]Fraser, C. H., & Strickland, W. L. (2006, February). When Organization Isn't Enough. *McKinsey Quarterly, 1*.

[64]Bowman, E. H., & Singh, H. (1993). Corporate Restructuring: Reconfiguring the Firm. *Strategic Management Journal, 14*, 5–14.

[65]Probst, T. M. (2003). Exploring Employee Outcomes of Organizational Restructuring. *Group & Organization Management, 28*, 416–439.

[66]Marshall, R., & Yorks, L. (1994). Planning for a Restructured, Revitalized Organization. *MIT Sloan Management Review, 35*(4), 81–91.

[67]Carter, L., Ulrich, D., & Goldsmith, M. (2005). *Best Practices in Leadership Development and Organization Change: How the Best Companies Ensure Meaningful Change and Sustainable Leadership*. San Francisco, CA: John Wiley and Sons.

LOSKUTNIKOV/SHUTTERSTOCK.COM

CHAPTER 15

ORGANIZATIONAL CULTURE

CHAPTER OUTLINE

LEARNING OUTCOMES

After studying this chapter you should be able to:

1. Describe the meaning, importance, and origins of organizational culture.
2. Discuss cultures of conflict and cultures of inclusion.
3. Identify and discuss how technology and innovation affect organizational culture.
4. Describe how effective organizations manage their culture.

—REAL WORLD CHALLENGE—

CULTURE CHANGE AT AVAYA

LOSKUTNIKOV/SHUTTERSTOCK.COM

Avaya is a global business communications company that was spun off from Lucent. Seven years later, the company was taken private by two private equity firms. This transition accelerated Avaya's strategy to become a business collaborator and provider of unified communications including web conferencing rather than just voice telephony. The change highlighted a need for a new culture that better supported its new business strategy.[1]

Avaya's bureaucratic culture reflected the strong influence of both AT&T and Lucent.[2] Avaya knew that this culture would not support its new business strategy. The company wanted to change Avaya's culture to better support creativity and collaboration. What advice would you give Avaya in making this organizational culture change? After reading this chapter, you should have some good ideas.

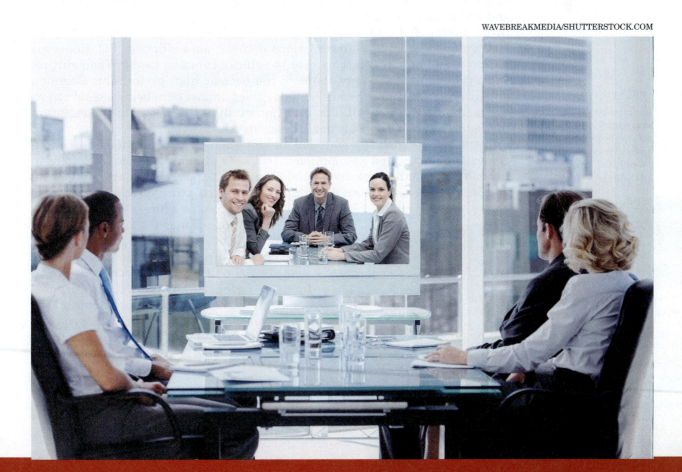

WAVEBREAKMEDIA/SHUTTERSTOCK.COM

Organizational culture is essential to organizational performance. Not only does it influence the decisions and behaviors of employees, but it also explains what is happening in an organization and why it is happening. Just as organizational structure can be thought of as an organization's skeleton, organizational culture can be thought of as its personality because it influences the way employees behave. Understanding and managing organizational culture is an important management role that can improve your own and your organization's performance. After reading this chapter, you should better understand organizational culture and how to manage it.

THE MEANING AND DETERMINANTS OF ORGANIZATIONAL CULTURE

organizational culture
A system of shared values, norms, and assumptions that guide members' attitudes and behaviors

When we say that an organization has a certain type of culture, what do we mean? ***Organizational culture*** is a system of shared values, norms, and assumptions that guides members' attitudes and behaviors[3] and influences how they perceive and react to their environment. These assumptions are usually taken for granted by organizational members, and are taught to new members as they are socialized into the group.

An organization's culture is reflected in how it gets work done and how employees interact with each other. It takes a long time for a culture to evolve, and a long time to change it. Trust is the foundation of culture, and is earned through repeated interactions over time. When a positive culture becomes strong enough, employee interactions become more efficient. Relationships improve, and employees cooperate to achieve common goals. When culture supports business strategy, the firm can become high performing. Common organizational culture themes include ethics, innovation, being casual or formal, and collaboration.[4] Of course, as important as it is to create and maintain the right culture, doing so is not necessarily easy.

artifacts
The physical manifestation of the culture including open offices, awards, ceremonies, and formal lists of values

Cultures are made up of formal and informal practices, artifacts, espoused values and norms, and assumptions. ***Artifacts*** are physical manifestations of the culture including the myths and stories told about the organization or its founder, awards, ceremonies and rituals, decorations, office space allocations, the dress code, how people address each other, published lists of organizational values, and so on.

When Lou Gerstner wanted to reinforce his culture change efforts at IBM, he abolished the firm's famous white shirt and tie dress code.[5] Steelmaker Nucor Corporation lists every single employee's name on the front cover of its annual report as a symbolic gesture to build and reinforce its team culture.[6]

BLAZ KURE/ SHUTTERSTOCK.COM

Culture is the shared values, norms, and assumptions that guide behaviors in an organization. Artifacts are the physical manifestations of culture. This office setting, for example, has numerous artifacts that suggest a culture of openness, informality, and an appreciation of the environment.

Espoused values and norms are those that are explicitly stated by the organization. For example, an organization might state that ethical behavior is a preferred value and norm, and it might hang signs in the office stating that ethical behavior is a driving principle of the company as an artifact of that cultural component. Nokia communicates its espoused values through videos, its intranet, and in its communications on company strategy.[7]

espoused values and norms
The preferred values and norms explicitly stated by the organization

Enacted values and norms are those that employees exhibit based on their observations of what actually goes on in the organization. If a company's top managers engage in illegal or unethical behavior, these are the enacted values and norms of the firm no matter what its formally stated ethics values are. If the company has the espoused value that ethics are important, the difference between that espoused value and its enacted values creates a gap that can negatively affect employee attitudes and company performance.[8] Performance management, feedback, and compensation systems all help align espoused and enacted values and norms.

enacted values and norms
Values and norms that employees exhibit based on their observations of what actually goes on in the organization

Assumptions are those organizational values that have become so taken for granted over time that they become the core of the company's culture.[9] These basic assumptions are highly resistant to change, and guide organizational behavior. For example, outdoor clothing company Patagonia is noted for its social responsibility and environmental awareness.[10] Patagonia employees would be stunned to see their managers engage in environmentally irresponsible behavior. Figure 15.1 illustrates these four levels of culture.[11]

assumptions
Those organizational values that have become so taken for granted over time that they become the core of the company's culture

Formal practices that influence culture include compensation strategies like profit sharing, benefits, training and development programs, and even the use of teleconferencing to enable some employees to work from home. Informal practices include "open-door management" to promote upward communication and the sharing of ideas, employees helping each other, and employees of different ranks eating lunch together to share ideas.

Figure 15.1

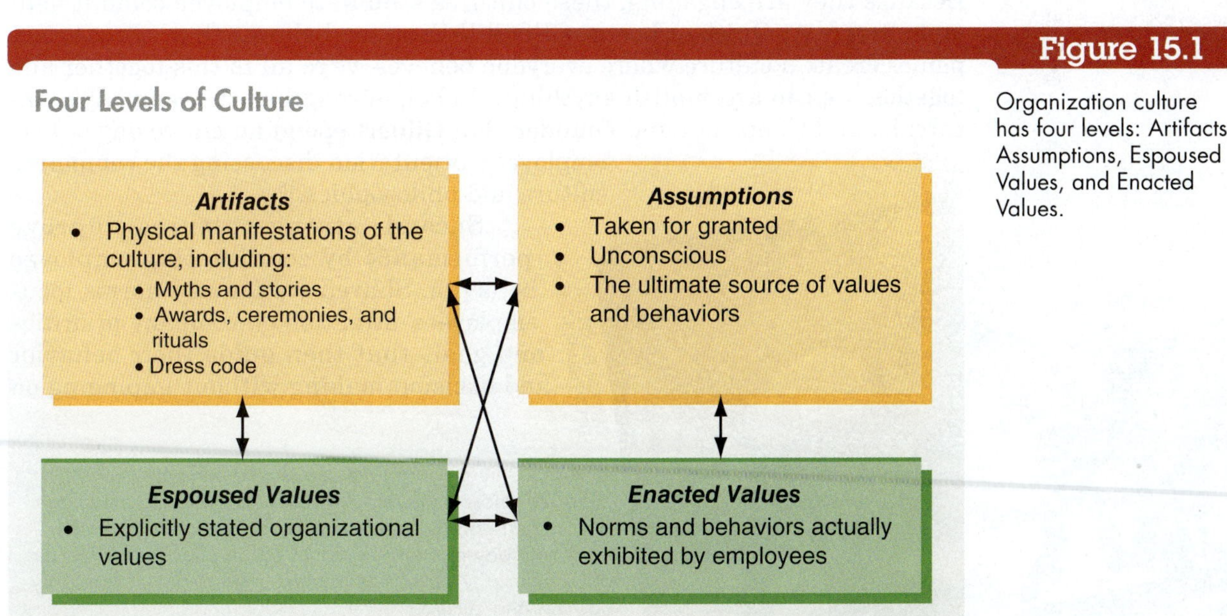

Organization culture has four levels: Artifacts, Assumptions, Espoused Values, and Enacted Values.

Does Culture Matter?

Does culture matter? One expert believes that "Organizational culture is the key to organizational excellence ... and the function of leadership is the creation and management of culture."[12] Research has shown that by actively managing culture, your organization and its employees will be more likely to deliver on strategic objectives over the long run. In particular, culture boosts organizational performance when it (1) is strategically relevant, (2) is strong, and (3) emphasizes innovation and change to adapt to a changing environment.[13] The effects of culture on a firm's effectiveness are even stronger when employees have positive attitudes.[14] A company's culture should reinforce its business strategy, and can give a firm a competitive advantage. If a business strategy and corporate culture are pulling in two different directions, the culture will win no matter how good the strategy is.[15]

Culture is a source of competitive advantage. Creating a culture that supports sharing and helping other employees can have positive performance results. Technology can make a sharing culture possible. For example, Xerox gave its 25,000 field-service engineers access to a knowledge-sharing system that they can consult during sales calls. The system led to a nearly 10 percent savings on parts and labor, worth $15 to $20 million per year. Dan Holtshouse, director of knowledge initiatives, is proud of "the 50,000 solution tips that have been entered into the knowledge base, all on a purely voluntary basis, in exchange for contributors being recognized. What we have learned is the importance of creating a work environment with a culture and incentives that are conducive to sharing, and to support that environment with improved work processes and strong technology."[16]

Organizational cultures can be strong or weak. Strong cultures clarify appropriate behavior, are widely shared, and are internally consistent. Strong cultures can enhance organizational performance in two ways. First, they improve performance by energizing employees—appealing to their higher ideals and values, and rallying them around a set of meaningful, unified goals. Because they are engaging, these cultures stimulate employee commitment and effort.[17] At Quicken Loans, CEO Bill Emerson believes that, "Great companies create a culture where everyone believes we're all in this together and together we can accomplish anything." To help strengthen the company's culture, he and Chairman and Founder Dan Gilbert spend an entire day of new employees' orientation discussing the company's culture and philosophies.[18]

Second, strong cultures improve performance by coordinating employee behavior. Shared values and norms focus employees' attention on company priorities and goals that then guide their behavior and decision making without impinging on

WAVEBREAKMEDIA/ SHUTTERSTOCK.COM

A strong culture coordinates employee behavior and energizes those same employees to rally around meaningful and unified goals. These employees are working together on a Saturday morning to plant trees in a local park as part of a community service campaign. Their organization likely has a strong culture.

employee autonomy like formal control systems do. This makes strong cultures particularly helpful for dealing with changing environments.[19]

Strong cultures are not always better than weak cultures, however—whether the culture is positive or negative also matters. A strong positive culture promotes employee commitment to the firm's value system and helps to align employee and company values. An example of employee behaviors in a strong positive culture would be employees' reaction to the arrival of the plant manager: "We're proud to have our plant manager come onto the production floor to observe our ethical, high-performance, high-quality work behaviors. We work this way whether the manager is here or not." In a strong negative culture, which means that employees have shared norms and values that are not consistent with what the organization wants or values, employee reactions to the plant manager's arrival would be: "Heads up! The plant manager is coming onto the production floor—look busy!"

Because strong cultures create stable and consistent employee values and behaviors, they are slow to change. If a company needs to change its culture to adapt to changing competition or a new business strategy, a strong culture can create difficulty in its ability to evolve. A company with a weaker culture (but not *too* weak) should be able to more quickly adapt to different circumstances. Culture is like the glue that holds things together in an organization—if it is too weak, it does not effectively guide employees. Research has found that long-term financial performance is highest for organizations with an adaptive culture receptive to change and innovation.[20]

When a culture is strong, it pushes employees to engage in behaviors that reinforce the firm's values and culture, whether good or bad. Strong ethical cultures are known to influence employees' ethical behavior and commitment through formal and informal organizational structures and systems.[21] An overall ethical environment that includes leadership, communication, reward systems, and a formal ethical behavior code of conduct decreases employees' unethical conduct.[22]

What ruined Enron? Unethical conduct and misleading accounting are the easy answers. But underlying many of its problems was a culture that pushed for visible results and individual performance above all else. An emphasis on consistent earnings growth and individual initiative, combined with the absence of the usual corporate checks and balances, tipped the culture to one that reinforced unethical corner cutting.[23] During the housing crisis, rampant unethical corporate behavior led FBI Director Robert Mueller to call for a "culture of integrity" to combat the rampant mortgage fraud and other white-collar crime.[24]

A good example of how a company's culture influences employee behaviors is seen in the way Acadian Ambulance Service in New Orleans responded after hurricane Katrina hit in the fall of 2005. Employees from medics to mechanics, some of whom had lost their homes, quickly began delivering supplies, cooking, and keeping generators working. By the weekend, more than 5,000 patients and about 11,000 hospital staff and family members were evacuated. Ross Judice, M.D., Acadian Ambulance Service's medical director, said, "Acadian's culture has always been to 'Get the job done.' … Things happen because you have good people wanting to do good things who have the leadership and the motivation to do it. We saw a need and stepped up. That happened over and over again."[25]

Culture matters to organizations because it influences employees' discretionary behaviors, including what they do in situations when the rules and expectations are unclear or when there is no direct supervision. This is critical because organizations cannot create procedures or policies covering every possible situation. One of the most important sources of employee motivation is the firm's culture.

Understanding your corporate culture can create a personal competitive advantage by reducing the chances of your offending superiors or making a social blunder. Phrasing your ideas in ways consistent with actual company values and with the way top management views the world also increases your influence.

How Leaders Create and Maintain Culture

An organization's culture is influenced in part by its industry. Different industries develop different cultures. For example, nuclear power plants have a very different culture than do Internet or biotech firms. Organizational culture is also influenced by the national culture in which the organization is embedded. Russian, Chinese, and American companies tend to differ due to the national cultures in which they are embedded. Company founders and leaders also influence a firm's culture.

Most managers' training prepares them well to set the business strategy and ensure that the organization's capabilities are in line with this strategy. Shaping an organization's culture is harder to learn in school and takes personal involvement. A leader has to define the culture to support the business strategy, consistently behave in ways that demonstrate the culture, explain the culture to employees so they understand why it is critical, and then hold him- or herself and others accountable for maintaining it. It can be very time-consuming to create and maintain an organizational culture. Nevertheless, organizations like Nordstrom, Southwest Airlines, and Nike did not earn their success by letting their cultures develop accidentally.

An organization's founder and early management team shape a firm's culture, which is then reinforced by management's philosophy, values, vision, and goals. These cultural choices then influence the company's structure, compensation system, customer relations policies, human resources policies, and individual behavior and motivation, which reinforce the culture.

When beverage giant Molson Coors' new CEO Peter Swinburn took the reins after a series of ten acquisitions and joint ventures created a mishmash of workforces, he made it his top priority to forge a cohesive corporate culture.[26] As Swinburn says, "If you spend five years developing a brand, why shouldn't you spend five years developing a culture?"[27] So how can leaders create, maintain, or change an organization's culture? Table 15.1 highlights some tactics several experts recommend.[28]

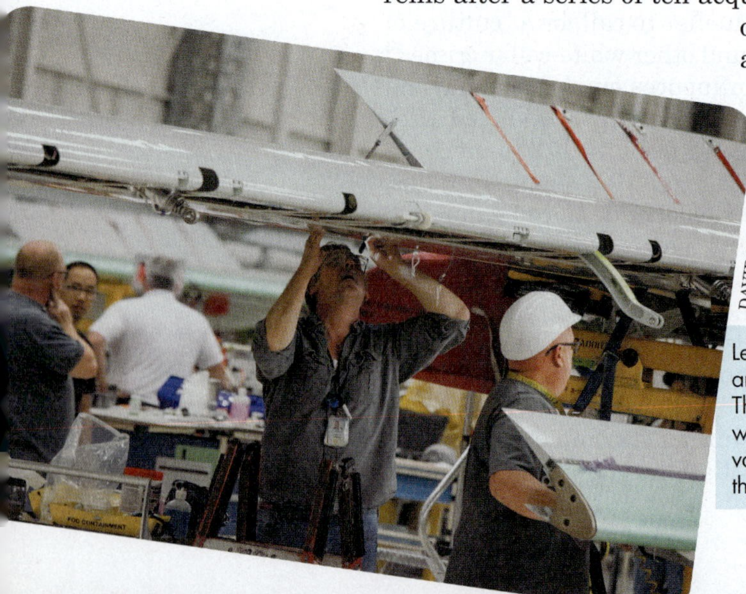

DAVID RYDER/BLOOMBERG/ GETTY IMAGES

Leaders at Southwest Airlines have worked consistently to build and maintain a culture centered around fun and teamwork. These Southwest maintenance employees are effectively working together as a team to perform maintenance work on various airplane parts. The company's strong culture helps them carry this work out quickly and effectively.

Table 15.1

How Leaders Can Influence an Organization's Culture

- Develop a clear sense of mission and values about what the company should be, and communicate it to employees through what you pay attention to, measure, and control.
- Select employees who can share, express, and reinforce the desired values in order to help build the desired culture. Furniture retailer IKEA hires employees based on their attitudes, values, and fit with the company culture as much as for their qualifications. Steelmaker Nucor Corporation protects its culture by making cultural compatibility a key issue in acquiring other companies. In visiting companies it is interested in acquiring, Nucor pays careful attention to how plant managers and employees interact.[29]
- Use daily routines and concrete actions and behaviors to demonstrate and exemplify appropriate values and beliefs. For example, Walmart employees are constantly reminded of the company's cost-control culture. Reinforcing the company's thrift, a Walmart vice president responsible for billions of dollars' worth of business has his visitors sit in mismatched, cast-off lawn chairs likely left behind as free samples during a sales call.[30]
- Consistently role-model behaviors that reinforce the culture. Walmart CEO Lee Scott and Chief Financial Officer Tom Schoewe each earn millions of dollars a year, but on business trips, the two regularly share a modest hotel room. "Sharing rooms is a very symbolic part of what we do," Scott says. "It's also an equalizer. If I'm asking the district managers to share a room, but I won't share a room with Schoewe, then what am I saying? There are two different standards here? The customer is the most important thing for all of you, but for me I think I'll run a different standard."[31] Leaders set the culture, and employees learn what behaviors and attitudes are appropriate from their leaders' behaviors.
- Make your human resource management procedures and criteria consistent. Communicate your priorities in the way you reward employees. Linking raises and promotions to specific behaviors communicates leaders' priorities. When Lou Gerstner took the lead at IBM, he reinforced his performance focus with new performance appraisal and compensation systems.
- Nurture traditions and rituals that express, define, and reinforce the culture. Awards and recognition ceremonies, having the CEO address new employees during their orientations, and reciting stories of past company successes can all define and reinforce a firm's culture.

Employment and staffing service provider Randstad wanted its new hire training program to include information about the company's culture. What started as a one-week on-site course for new hires has grown into a sixteen-week program that combines e-learning, in-class training, on-the-job learning, and mentoring. During their first week at Randstad, new hires receive a virtual call in which executives welcome them to the company. Participants then take an e-learning course about the culture and the history of the organization and receive classroom training from their district managers on the culture and values of the company. Randstad believes that the training helps the business run more smoothly and gives employees a sense of having a career, not just a job.[32]

Changes in strategy, technology, and organizational structure all trigger a need for changes in employees' attitudes, behaviors, values, and skills.

This can require changes in the organization's culture to reinforce these new employee behaviors and values. To assess important dimensions of their culture, companies like Coca-Cola use surveys and focus groups to regularly evaluate employees' perceptions of the company's support for diversity.[33]

Organizational culture has many layers. Outer layers of the culture, such as marketing strategies and customer service perceptions, can change fairly quickly. Inner layers, including fundamental values and ideologies, are much slower to change.

Organizations can also have different cultures in different areas. Different business units or subgroups of organizations can develop unique cultures supporting their unique business needs. This can actually mean that employees who belong to multiple subgroups simultaneously participate in several different organizational cultures.

CULTURES OF CONFLICT AND CULTURES OF INCLUSION

conflict culture
Shared norms for managing conflict

active conflict management norms
Resolve conflict openly

passive conflict management norms
Avoid addressing conflict

agreeable conflict management norms
Resolve conflict in a cooperative manner

disagreeable conflict management norms
Resolve conflict competitively

To better understand organizational culture, let's now discuss two specific types of culture: cultures of conflict and cultures of inclusion.

Cultures of Conflict

Conflict cultures are one example of a specific type of culture. Firms develop distinct ***conflict cultures***, or shared norms for managing conflict, which reflect different degrees of active versus passive and agreeable versus disagreeable conflict management norms.[34] ***Active conflict management norms*** resolve conflict openly, whereas ***passive conflict management norms*** tend to avoid addressing conflict. ***Agreeable conflict management norms*** resolve conflict in a cooperative manner, whereas ***disagreeable conflict management norms*** resolve conflict competitively. This results in four types of conflict cultures: dominating, collaborative, avoidant, and passive-aggressive, as shown in Figure 15.2.[35]

Figure 15.2

There are four kinds of cultures of conflict. These vary based on active or passive norms and agreeable or disagreeable norms.

Cultures for Managing Conflict

	Disagreeable	Agreeable
Active	Dominating	Collaborative
Passive	Passive-Aggressive	Avoidant

Source: Gelfand, M.J., Leslie, L.M., & Keller, K.M. (2008). On the etiology of conflict cultures, Research in Organizational, Behavior, 28, 137–166.

Dominating Conflict Cultures

Dominating conflict cultures are active and disagreeable—open confrontations are accepted as well as heated arguments and threats.[36] The Digital Equipment Corporation had a dominating conflict culture as described by a former employee:

> People at Digital seemed to fight a lot with one another. Shouting matches were a frequent occurrence, and I came to conclude that Digital people didn't like one another. I was subsequently told by more senior members that it was okay to disagree with someone, because truth would ultimately prevail.... After one of these exchanges, one in which I almost came to blows with one of my peers, I was called in by my manager the next morning. Sensing that this time I had really exceeded the bounds of propriety, I thought about updating my resume. It was with great and pleasant surprise that I was told that my behavior the previous day had been admirable.[37]

Collaborative Conflict Cultures

Collaborative conflict cultures are active and agreeable. Employees actively manage and resolve conflicts cooperatively to find the best solution for all involved parties.[38] Southwest Airlines has a collaborative conflict culture, as described by a chief pilot:

> Pilots and flight attendants—sometimes an interaction didn't go right between them. [If] they are upset, then we get them together and work it out, in a teamwork approach. If you have a problem, the best thing is to deal with it yourself. If you can't, then we take it to the next step—we call a meeting of all the parties.[39]

Avoidant Conflict Cultures

Avoidant conflict cultures are passive and agreeable. This type of culture strives to preserve order and control and/or to maintain harmony and interpersonal relationships.[40] Typical behaviors include accommodating or giving in to the other's point of view, changing the subject, or evading open discussion of the conflict issue.

Avoidant conflict norms often start at the top. At Wang Laboratories, a once-successful computer company that eventually went bankrupt, the founder and director developed and sustained a conflict avoidant culture by sending a strong message that he did not want to hear any conflicts or disagreements with his policies and practices. Although he acted in ways he believed would benefit the entire organization, which worked for a while, everyone prospered only as long as his instincts and actions were correct.[41]

Passive-Aggressive Conflict Cultures

Passive-aggressive conflict cultures are both passive and disagreeable. Rather than dealing openly with conflict, this culture develops norms to handle it via passive resistance such as refusing to participate in conflict-related discussions, giving the silent treatment, withholding information, or withdrawing from work and from interactions with coworkers.[42] Hospitals often have passive-aggressive conflict cultures due to the many layers of authority and strong bureaucracy.[43]

National and regional culture can influence which type of conflict culture develops in an organization. This chapter's *Global Issues* feature describes some of the cross-cultural influences on conflict cultures.

GLOBAL ISSUES

CROSS-CULTURAL INFLUENCES ON CONFLICT CULTURES

Societal culture influences aspects of an organization's culture, including its conflict culture. Dominating conflict cultures may occur more often in national cultures emphasizing individualism, as in the United States. In the U.S. media and institutions, for example, conflict is often referred to adversarially as "a war" or something that should be "won."[44]

Collaborative conflict cultures may be more common in more egalitarian and collectivistic cultures and those that value cooperation over competition, such as The Netherlands.[45]

Conflict avoidant cultures may occur more often in cultures higher in uncertainty avoidance and collectivism, where people are motivated to submit to authorities and maintain group harmony, as is the case in many Asian cultures.[46]

Passive-aggressive conflict cultures may be more likely in societal cultures with higher power distance, or where less powerful members of society and organizations expect and accept unequal power distribution.[47] Passive-aggressive cultures may also be more prevalent in societies where there are abusive leaders.[48]

Cultures of Inclusion

Organizational culture is an important part of effective diversity management. An organization's values and culture interact with its demographic composition to influence social interaction, conflict, productivity, and creativity.[49] Organizations that focus on collective interests better capitalize on the potential benefits of demographic diversity. Research has supported the idea that pro-diversity cultures are related to lower turnover among blacks, whites, and Hispanics.[50] Perceiving that the organization values diversity is also related to reduced absenteeism among black employees.[51]

culture of inclusion
The extent to which majority members value efforts to increase minority representation, and whether the qualifications and abilities of minority members are questioned

An organization's ***culture of inclusion*** reflects the extent to which majority members value efforts to increase minority representation, and whether the qualifications and abilities of minority members are questioned.[52] These perceptions may be affected by the firm's diversity actions as well as by the extent to which diversity is salient to a particular individual.[53]

When home finance company Fannie Mae wanted a corporate culture that values and retains employees, they asked employees, "From your own perspective, what could we do to improve the culture here?" They learned that Jewish, Muslim, and Hindu groups felt that the company always acknowledged Christmas, but never acknowledged Rosh Hashanah, Ramadan, or Diwali. The issue came up again when Fannie Mae was rushing to complete a financial restatement. Working twelve-hour days, six days a week cut into some people's religious observances. As a result, the company created a multicultural calendar noting religious celebrations throughout the year. When holidays approach, an article about the holiday's meaning and history written by an employee group is then posted on the company intranet; a note at the bottom directs managers on how to accommodate employees celebrating the holiday.[54] This chapter's *Case Study* feature describes how Whirlpool built an inclusive culture. Our *Improve Your Skills* feature also gives you some tips to better assess a company's culture.

CASE STUDY Building a Culture for Inclusion at Whirlpool

Approximately 60 percent of the employees of Michigan-based Whirlpool Corporation, the world's largest manufacturer of home appliances, are located outside of North America. Even within North America, the company has a rich multicultural mix of employees.[55] Diversity and inclusion are central to Whirlpool Corporation's goal of placing its appliances in "every home, everywhere"—a vision that guides its employees around the world.[56] Whirlpool believes that acknowledging its diversity and practicing inclusiveness allows it to utilize all employees' unique strengths to increase Whirlpool's productivity, profit, and performance.

"At Whirlpool, we best serve the unique needs of our customers through diverse, inclusive and engaged employees who truly reflect our global customer base," says Jeff Fettig, chairman and CEO.[57] Because diverse employees help provide a keen understanding of its diverse global customers' needs, diversity and inclusion are encouraged throughout the organization. Whirlpool views diversity as about being different, and inclusion as the respectful involvement of all people and making use of everyone's talents. Whirlpool believes that differences create value, and they practice inclusion because it enables the company to best respond to the needs of its diverse customers.[58]

Senior leaders make inclusion a top priority. A diversity council oversees the efforts of the corporate diversity network, and a diversity network mentoring program addresses the needs of new hires. The company also hosted a diversity summit to discuss building a culture of inclusion.[59]

Whirlpool understands that its leaders must first show an understanding of and interest in diversity before it can become part of the company culture. To involve busy senior leadership and middle management in the company's diversity efforts, it creates short five- to ten-minute podcasts that report on the company's diversity initiatives, and gives iPod Shuffles to upper management so that they can listen to these programs while on the go. Executives can also print them out as short, two-page papers. A diversity and inclusion "lunch and learn" series, hosted by the employee-based diversity networks, offers a comfortable environment to generate discussion among peers. The engagement of Whirlpool's leaders has stimulated positive change throughout the organization.[60]

Whirlpool integrated diversity and inclusion into its business in three phases:[61]

1. *Awareness building*: Whirlpool began by building the business case for diversity in a changing consumer marketplace, and then delivered that message along with diversity training to the company's approximately 18,000 employees.
2. *Building competency and capacity*: Next, it developed tools to enable senior managers to effectively manage a global workforce and build employee engagement.
3. *Embedding best practices*: After training managers and employees, Whirlpool wove best practices into the fabric of the organization. It began by previewing the company's diversity strategy for new employees and continued through the development of an educational development curriculum that prepares senior managers to effectively manage a multicultural workforce.

Whirlpool's slogan even reflects its culture of diversity: "The only thing more diverse than our products ... Are the people who create them."[62] Whirlpool was among Diversity Inc's Top 50 Companies for Diversity in 2011. In addition, Whirlpool has received a 100 percent rating in the Human Rights Campaign Corporate Equality Index.[63]

Questions:

1. Do you agree that Whirlpool can realize a competitive advantage through its diverse employees?
2. How else can technology be used to enhance Whirlpool's culture of inclusion?
3. Do you feel that Whirlpool's efforts to create a culture of inclusion are worthwhile? Explain your answer.

ILDOGESTO/SHUTTERSTOCK.COM

IMPROVE YOUR SKILLS

ASSESSING CULTURE

To be a successful and happy employee, it is important to match your values, preferences, and goals to the corporate culture. But how can you identify what a company's culture is before you become an employee? Here are some experts' suggestions:[64]

1. *Observe the physical surroundings.* Pay attention to how employees are dressed, how open the offices are, what type of furniture is used, and what is displayed on the walls. Signs warning of prohibited activities can also provide insights.
2. *Ask open-ended questions about the culture.* Ask several employees, "How would you describe your organization's culture?" and listen closely to their responses. Do they agree? Do they seem positive and enthusiastic?
3. *Check out the website.* How does the company choose to present itself? Do employee testimonials seem scripted or authentic?
4. *Listen to the language.* Do you hear a lot of talk about "customer service" and "ethics" or do you hear more emphasis on "making our numbers"?
5. *Note to whom you are introduced and how they act.* Are the people you meet formal or casual, serious or laid-back? Do you feel you are being introduced to everyone in the unit or only to a few select employees?
6. *Get the views of outsiders, including vendors, customers, and former employees.* Do these sources of information consistently describe the company in terms such as "bureaucratic," "frustrating to deal with," "open and flexible," or "a positive and engaging place to work"?

EFFECTS OF TECHNOLOGY AND INNOVATION ON CULTURE

Creating and maintaining a desired culture can be facilitated by technology, but at the same time can be made more difficult by the consequences of using technology to work remotely. Innovation and culture also have major impacts on each other.

Using Intranets to Build and Maintain Culture

By building and fostering a sense of community among employees, intranets can help reinforce an organization's culture. An organization's culture can vary across divisions and even across managers. Ask people who work in different parts of a large company to describe its culture and you are likely to get different answers. Because workgroups develop their own subcultures,

RAWPIXEL LTD/ GETTY IMAGES

Intranets build a common cultural foundation that aims to bring together employees in various units and locations. They help employees maintain connectivity to the organization as a whole.

intranets can be used to build a common cultural foundation that can help unify employees in different units and locations around common company values. This keeps people connected to the broader organization and also promotes consistency in how employees behave and make decisions.

The key issue for organizations is not about using the latest information technologies, but about leveraging the right technologies for creating and maintaining a culture of trust, openness, relationship building, and information sharing. Each intranet design reflects a different type of organizational culture, and in turn reinforces the firm's culture by controlling the flow of information and establishing norms of behavior. Following are some of the ways intranets can both reflect and influence organizational culture:

1. *Their scope*. Intranets with a narrow scope can reinforce a culture of secrecy and information hoarding. Intranets that contain information on a variety of topics and links to other useful sites such as human resources, company and industry news, blogs, wikis, interviews with company leaders, and performance indicators reflect a culture of openness and teamwork.
2. *Their openness to employee feedback and contributions*. Intranets that contain "like it or not?" feedback tools and features that allow employees to contribute reflect a participative culture that values employee contributions. A more centralized, heavily edited and filtered site reflects a culture in which information flows less freely and employee contributions are less valued.
3. *The frequency with which they are updated*. Intranets that are rarely updated are not likely to influence the company's culture and can reflect a culture that does not value employee contributions, has poor internal communication, and has poor attention to detail. Lucent updates its intranet multiple times a day if appropriate. It also posts two weekly feature articles that reinforce the strategic vision and positioning of the company to entice employees to visit multiple times each week.
4. *The number of intranets*. This refers to whether there is just one company intranet, or several, each serving different groups of employees. For example, some organizations have one intranet for the sales force and another, completely different looking one, for the R&D group.
5. *The use of symbols, stories, and ceremonies*. Because these express a company's culture, intranets can convey such information via news of events affecting the organization, messages from CEOs, and announcements of employees' awards programs of importance to the organization.

Building and Maintaining Culture with Remote Employees

Being virtual challenges an organization's identity and culture, particularly when the company relies on free agents or alliances with other firms that have their own cultures. Because they spend little time face-to-face with coworkers, it is harder for virtual employees to become familiar with an organization's culture. It is also harder for the organization to reinforce its cultural values among remote employees. This has important implications for employee identification with the organization and for the management of employee behaviors.[65]

GPOINTSTUDIO/SHUTTERSTOCK.COM

Organizations face special challenges in building and maintaining a culture that effectively includes employees who work remotely. This manager, for instance, may be performing her work at a very high level from her home office. At the same time, though, she may also not be as fully integrated into the firm's culture as she would like to be.

Because they are not able to see and experience the culture firsthand, acclimating teleworking employees to a corporate culture can be challenging. Business research firm Dun & Bradstreet's formal telework program requires employees to put in at least three months in an office before working remotely. This office time lets managers assess employees' strengths, weaknesses, and work habits in person. Employees also experience the company's unique corporate culture and work ethic firsthand. Working in the same place also allows team members to get to know one another before embarking on an email and phone-based relationship.[66]

Innovation and Culture

innovation
The process of creating and doing new things that are introduced into the marketplace as products, processes, or services

Innovation is the process of creating and doing new things that are introduced into the marketplace as products, processes, or services. Innovation involves every aspect of the organization, from research through development, manufacturing, and marketing. One of the organization's biggest challenges is to bring innovative technology to the needs of the marketplace in the most cost-effective manner possible.[67] Note that innovation does not just involve the technology to create new products: true organizational innovation is pervasive throughout the organization. According to *Fortune* magazine, the most admired organizations are those that are the most innovative.[68] Those companies are innovative in every way—staffing, strategy, research, and business processes. 3M has long been one of those companies known for its creativity and innovation.

Many risks are associated with being an innovative company. The most basic is the risk that decisions about new technology or innovation will backfire. As research proceeds, and engineers and scientists continue to develop new ideas or solutions to problems, there is always the possibility that innovations will fail to perform as expected. For this reason, organizations commit considerable resources to testing innovations.[69] A second risk is the possibility that a competitor will make decisions enabling it to get an innovation to the market first. The marketplace has become a breeding ground for continuous innovation.

In all fairness, some authors have suggested that the term, "innovation," has become a cliché from overuse by companies and consultants. As companies create positions, such as chief innovation officer, and consultants sell their services for hundreds of thousands of dollars, some claim that creating new products barely different from old ones or increasing production by small

In 2015, Research in Motion (RIM) released its BlackBerry Leap smartphone. While it was once a leader in the cell phone and email device market, it now sits near the bottom in this sector. Its failure to innovate led to its gradual demise.

SVETLANA DIKHTYAREVA/SHUTTERSTOCK.COM

percentages may not deserve to be called innovations. They call for the term to be reserved for major disruptive or radical shifts in products, services, or processes.[70]

While these criticisms may have some merit, organizations still need to be wary of simply maintaining the status quo and risk getting surpassed by more innovative practices by their competition or by new technological breakthroughs. For evidence, one needs only to examine the demise of the BlackBerry by Research in Motion (RIM), which dominated the market for cell phone and email devices from 2003 to 2009. Apple's iPhone and the Google Android devices, initially introduced in 2007 and 2008 and refined several times since then, along with thousands of applications (apps), have pushed RIM to the brink of collapse.[71]

Types of Innovation

Innovation can be radical, systems, or incremental. A ***radical innovation*** (sometimes called disruptive innovation) is a major breakthrough that changes or creates whole industries. Examples include xerography (which was invented by Chester Carlson in 1935 and became the hallmark of Xerox Corporation), steam engines, and the internal combustion engine (which paved the way for today's automobile industry). ***Systems innovation*** creates a new functionality by assembling parts in new ways. For example, the gasoline engine began as a radical innovation and became a systems innovation when it was combined with bicycle and carriage technology to create automobiles. ***Incremental innovation*** continues the technical improvement and extends the applications of radical and systems innovations. There are many more incremental innovations than there are radical and systems innovations. In fact, several incremental innovations are often necessary to make radical and systems innovations work properly. Incremental innovations force organizations to continuously improve their products and keep abreast or ahead of the competition.

radical innovation (sometimes called disruptive innovation)
A major breakthrough that changes or creates whole industries

systems innovation
Creates a new functionality by assembling parts in new ways

incremental innovation
Continues the technical improvement and extends the applications of radical and systems innovations

New Ventures

New ventures based on innovations require entrepreneurship and good management to work. The profile of the entrepreneur typically includes a need for achievement, a desire to assume responsibility, a willingness to take risks, and a focus on concrete results. Entrepreneurship can occur inside or outside large organizations. Outside entrepreneurship requires all of the complex aspects of the innovation process. Inside entrepreneurship occurs within a system that usually discourages chaotic activity.

Large organizations typically do not accept entrepreneurial types of activities. Thus, for a large organization to be innovative and develop new ventures, it must actively encourage entrepreneurial activity within the organization.

intrapreneurship
Entrepreneurial activity that takes place within the context of a large corporation

This form of activity, often called ***intrapreneurship***, usually is most effective when it is a part of everyday life in the organization and occurs throughout the organization rather than in the research and development department alone.

Corporate Research

The most common means of developing innovation in the traditional organization is through corporate research, or research and development. Corporate research is usually set up to support existing businesses, provide incremental innovations in the organization's businesses, and explore potential new technology bases. It often takes place in a laboratory, either on the site of the main corporate facility or some distance away from normal operations.

Corporate researchers are responsible for keeping the company's products and processes technologically advanced. Product life cycles vary a great deal, depending on how fast products become obsolete and whether substitutes for the product are developed.

Obviously, if a product becomes obsolete or some other product can be substituted for it, the profits from its sales will decrease. The job of corporate research is to prevent this from happening by keeping the company's products current.

The corporate culture can be instrumental in fostering an environment in which creativity and innovation occur. For example, 3M is a company known for its innovation. Its scientists developed masking tape, Scotch tape, Scotchguard fabric protector, Post-it Notes, Thinsulate material, and literally thousands of other innovative products. The company once allowed employees to spend up to 15 percent of their paid time on any projects they chose. Several years ago, though, innovation at 3M had slowed to the point that it was taking years for new products to come to market, manufacturing was inefficient, and profits were almost nonexistent. A new CEO, Jim McNerney, was brought onboard; his new initiatives included Six Sigma quality training, forced performance rankings, and cost efficiency measures throughout the company. Problems soon arose: the new approach reduced not just costs but innovation as well and the number of new products on the market slowed even more. McNerney left the company and was replaced by George Buckley. Buckley immediately increased the research and development budget by 20 percent, but his most important task was to restore the innovative culture that is the company's heritage.[72] He succeeded in doing this, fortunately, and 3M has again come to be known as a highly innovative company.

MANAGING ORGANIZATION CULTURE

Earlier we discussed how leaders create organizational culture. In this section we look more closely at how existing cultures are managed. The three elements of managing organization culture are (1) taking advantage of the existing culture, (2) teaching the organization culture, and (3) changing the organization culture.

Taking Advantage of the Existing Culture

Most managers are not in a position to create an organization culture; rather, they work in organizations that already have cultural values. For these managers, the central issue in managing culture is how best to use the existing cultural system. It may be easier and faster to alter employee behaviors within the culture in place than it is to change the history, traditions, and values that already exist.[73]

To take advantage of an existing cultural system, managers must first be fully aware of the culture's values and what behaviors or actions those values support. Becoming fully aware of an organization's values usually is not easy, however. It involves more than reading a pamphlet about what the company believes in. Managers must develop a deep understanding of how organizational values operate in the firm—an understanding that usually comes only through experience.

This understanding, once achieved, can be used to evaluate the performances of others in the firm. Articulating organizational values can be useful in managing others' behaviors. For example, suppose a subordinate in a firm with a strong cultural value of "sticking to its knitting" develops a business strategy that involves moving into a new industry. Rather than attempting to argue that this business strategy is economically flawed or conceptually weak, the manager who understands the corporate culture can point to the company's organizational value: "In this firm, we believe in sticking to our knitting."

Senior managers who understand their organization's culture can communicate that understanding to lower-level individuals. Over time, as these lower-level managers begin to understand and accept the firm's culture, they will require less direct supervision. Their understanding of corporate values will guide their decision making.

Teaching the Organization Culture: Socialization

socialization *The process through which individuals become social beings*

organizational socialization *The process through which employees learn about the firm's culture and pass their knowledge and understanding on to others*

Socialization is the process through which individuals become social beings.[74] As studied by psychologists, it is the process through which children learn to become adults in a society—how they learn what is acceptable and polite behavior and what is not, how they learn to communicate, how they learn to interact with others, and so on. In complex societies, the socialization process takes many years.

Organizational socialization is the process through which employees learn about their organization's culture and pass their knowledge and understanding on to others. Employees are socialized into organizations, just as people are socialized into societies; that is, they come to know over time what is acceptable in the organization and what is not, how to communicate their feelings, and how to interact with others. They learn both through observation and through efforts by managers to communicate this information to them.

PIXELPETER/SHUTTERSTOCK.COM

Organizations use a variety of methods to socialize new employees and teach them about the organization's culture. These new employees are going through orientation together and learning about their new employer.

Research into the process of socialization indicates that for many employees, socialization programs do not necessarily change their values, but instead they make employees more aware of the differences between personal and organization values and help them develop ways to cope with the differences.[75]

A variety of organizational mechanisms can affect the socialization of workers in organizations. Probably the most important are the examples that new employees see in the behavior of experienced people. Through observing examples, new employees develop a repertoire of stories they can use to guide their actions. When a decision needs to be made, new employees can ask, "What would my boss do in this situation?" This is not to suggest that formal training, corporate pamphlets, and corporate statements about organization culture are unimportant in the socialization process. However, these factors tend to support the socialization process based on people's close observations of the actions of others.

In some organizations, the culture described in pamphlets and presented in formal training sessions conflicts with the values of the organization as they are expressed in the actions of its people. For example, a firm may say that employees are its most important asset but treat employees badly. In this setting, new employees quickly learn that the rhetoric of the pamphlets and formal training sessions has little to do with the real organization culture. Employees who are socialized into this system usually come to accept the actual cultural values rather than those formally espoused. Our *Understand Yourself* feature can give you some insights into your own ability to understand the culture of an organization.

Changing the Organization Culture

Much of our discussion to this point has assumed that an organization's culture enhances its performance. When this is the case, learning what an organization's cultural values are and using those values to help socialize new workers and managers is very important, for such actions help the organization succeed. But not all firms have cultural values that are consistent with high performance. Research suggests that while some firms have performance-enhancing values, others have performance-reducing values. What should a manager who works in a company with performance-reducing values do?

The answer to this question is, of course, that top managers in such firms should try to change their organization's culture. However, this is a difficult thing to do.[76] Organization culture resists change for all the reasons that it is a powerful influence on behavior—it embodies the firm's basic values, it is often taken for granted, and it is typically most effectively communicated through stories or other symbols. When managers attempt to change organization culture, they are attempting to change people's basic assumptions about what is and is not appropriate behavior in the organization. Changing from a traditional organization to a team-based organization is one example of an organization culture change. Another is the attempt by 3M to change from its low-cost and efficiency culture to return to its roots as an innovative culture.[77]

Despite these difficulties, some organizations have changed their cultures from performance-reducing to performance-enhancing.[78] This change process

UNDERSTAND YOURSELF

REFINING YOUR SENSE OF CULTURE

This exercise is designed to help you assess what you now know about organization culture. The ten statements in the following table reflect certain opinions about the nature of work performed in the context of organization culture. Indicate the extent to which you agree or disagree with each opinion by circling the number in the appropriate column.

Statement of Opinion	*Strongly agree*				*Strongly disagree*
1. If a person can do well in one organization, he or she can do well in any organization.	1	2	3	4	5
2. Skills and experience are all that really matter; how a job candidate will "fit in" is not an important factor in hiring.	1	2	3	4	5
3. Members of an organization explicitly tell people how to adhere to its culture.	1	2	3	4	5
4. After appropriate study, astute managers can fairly quickly change a corporate culture.	1	2	3	4	5
5. A common culture is important for unifying employees but does not necessarily affect the firm's financial health.	1	2	3	4	5
6. Conscientious workers are not really influenced by an organization's culture.	1	2	3	4	5
7. Strong organization cultures are not necessarily associated with high organization performance.	1	2	3	4	5
8. Members of a subculture share the common values of the subculture but not those of the dominant organization culture.	1	2	3	4	5
9. Job candidates seeking to understand a prospective employer's culture can do so by just asking the people who interview them.	1	2	3	4	5
Your Total Score					

How to score: To get your total score, add up the values of the numbers that you have circled. You can then interpret your score as follows:

Your Score	
35–45	You have excellent instincts about organization cultures and how people respond to them.
25–34	You show average or above-average awareness of the principles of organization culture.
15–24	You have some sense of how cultures affect workers, but you need to improve your knowledge.
0–14	You definitely need to bolster your knowledge before thinking further about assessing or modifying an organization culture.

Source: Hunsaker, P. L. (2005). *Management: A Skills Approach* (2nd ed.). Upper Saddle River, NJ: Pearson Education. © 2005. Reprinted by permission of Pearson Education, Inc.

is described in more detail in Chapter 16. The earlier section on creating organization culture describes the importance of linking the strategic values and the cultural values in creating a new organization culture. We briefly discuss other important elements of the cultural change process in the following sections.

Managing Symbols

Research suggests that organization culture is understood and communicated through the use of stories and other symbolic media. If this is correct, managers interested in changing cultures should attempt to substitute stories and myths that support new cultural values for those that support old ones. They can do so by creating situations that give rise to new stories.

Suppose an organization traditionally has held the value "employee opinions are not important." When management meets in this company, the ideas and opinions of lower-level people—when discussed at all—are normally rejected as foolish and irrelevant. The stories that support this cultural value tell about subordinate managers who tried to make a constructive point only to have that point lost in personal attacks from superiors.

An upper-level manager interested in creating a new story, one that shows lower-level managers that their ideas are valuable, might ask a subordinate to prepare to lead a discussion in a meeting and follow through by asking the subordinate to take the lead when the topic arises. The subordinate's success in the meeting will become a new story, one that may displace some of the many stories suggesting that the opinions of lower-level managers do not matter.

The Difficulty of Change

Changing a firm's culture is a long and difficult process. A primary problem is that upper-level managers, no matter how dedicated they are to implementing some new cultural value, may sometimes inadvertently revert to old patterns of behavior. This happens, for example, when a manager dedicated to implementing the value that lower-level employees' ideas are important vehemently attacks a subordinate's ideas.

This mistake generates a story that supports old values and beliefs. After such an incident, lower-level managers may believe that although the boss seems to want employee input and ideas, in fact, nothing could be further from the truth. No matter what the boss says or how consistent his or her behavior is in the future, some credibility has been lost, and cultural change has been made more difficult.

The Stability of Change

The processes of changing a firm's culture start with a need for change and move through a transition period in which efforts are made to adopt new values and beliefs. In the long run, a firm that successfully changes its culture will find that the new values and beliefs are just as stable and influential as the old ones. Value systems tend to be self-reinforcing. Once they are in place, changing them requires an enormous effort. Thus, if a firm can change its culture from performance-reducing to performance-enhancing, the new values are likely to remain in place for a long time. Again, these issues are revisited in our discussions of organizational change and change management in Chapter 16.

SUMMARY AND APPLICATION

Organizational culture is a system of shared values, norms, and assumptions that guides members' attitudes and behaviors and influences how they perceive and react to their environment. Cultures are made up of formal and informal practices, artifacts, espoused values and norms, and assumptions. Artifacts are physical manifestations of the culture. Espoused values and norms are those that are explicitly stated by the organization. Enacted values and norms are those that employees exhibit based on their observations of what actually goes on in the organization. Assumptions are those organizational values that have become so taken for granted over time that they become the core of the company's culture.

Creating and maintaining a desired culture can be facilitated by technology, but at the same time can be made more difficult by the consequences of using technology to work remotely. Innovation and culture also have major impacts on each other. By building and fostering a sense of community among employees, intranets can help reinforce an organization's culture. The key issue for organizations is not about using the latest information technologies, but about leveraging the right technologies for creating and maintaining a culture of trust, openness, relationship building, and information sharing.

LOSKUTNIKOV/SHUTTERSTOCK.COM

REAL WORLD RESPONSE

CULTURE CHANGE AT AVAYA

Avaya began its culture change initiative by identifying its desired culture and comparing it to its current culture. Marketing-style focus groups, interviews with departing employees, and conversations with the executive team helped the company identify what it needed to change and become.[79] Avaya learned that loyalty, integrity, and trust were a strong part of its culture, and that innovation was truly valued by employees. They also learned that employees were averse to taking risks, feeling that they needed to ask permission before making decisions, and that numerous restructurings and changes over the years had created a mentality that employees needed to keep their heads down to survive. Avaya's change leaders realized that no one "owned" the culture and no one had taken the initiative to manage it during Avaya's formative years.[80]

Core values and beliefs were identified that Avaya needed to reinforce throughout the organization. "Success profiles" describing what employees at each organizational level would need to know and do to support the business strategy and desired culture were identified and communicated. Performance management, employee development, and pay-for-performance plans were put in place to support the desired employee behaviours.[81]

Avaya is now making big strides toward changing its culture[82] despite numerous challenges including a global recession.

Innovation is the process of creating and doing new things that are introduced into the marketplace as products, processes, or services. Innovation involves every aspect of the organization, from research through development, manufacturing, and marketing. Innovation can be radical, systems, or incremental. A radical innovation (sometimes called disruptive innovation) is a major breakthrough that changes or creates whole industries. Systems innovation creates a new functionality by assembling parts in new ways. Incremental innovation continues the technical improvement and extends the applications of radical and systems innovations.

The three elements of managing organization culture are (1) taking advantage of the existing culture, (2) teaching the organization culture, and (3) changing the organization culture. To take advantage of an existing cultural system, managers must first be fully aware of the culture's values and what behaviors or actions those values support. Organizational socialization is the process through which employees learn about their organization's culture and pass their knowledge and understanding on to others. Research suggests that while some firms have performance-enhancing values, others have performance-reducing values. In this case managers should try to change their organization's culture. However, this is a difficult thing to do.

DISCUSSION QUESTIONS

1. Describe three different types of organizational cultures. When would each be most and least effective for a research and development company dependent on employee innovation?
2. Do you think that culture is important to organizational performance? Why or why not?
3. How do you learn about prospective employers' cultures? How important is a company's culture to you when you decide to apply or to accept a job offer?
4. Which of the four conflict management cultures would be the best fit for you? Why?
5. What can companies do to create and reinforce a culture of inclusion?
6. In what ways can the influence of the founder of an organization be assessed after that founder is no longer a part of the organization?
7. How are technology and innovation interrelated?
8. What current examples can you identify to reflect radical, systems, and incremental innovations?
9. Describe how you might go about taking advantage of an existing organizational culture.

DEVELOP YOUR SKILLS EXERCISE

Performance Improvement Through Culture Change

Imagine that you have just accepted a leadership position with Pirate Cove, an Internet retail company focused on a wide variety of pirate-themed products.

The organization's financial performance has been worsening and its market share slipping, which is why the company hired you to come in and make some changes. You have been given the authority to do whatever you need to do to improve the company's performance.

After collecting a lot of information and speaking with a wide variety of employees, you have determined that the biggest cause of the company's underperformance is that its culture is too complex and consensus-oriented, which makes decision making too slow. The first thing you decide to do is to change the culture. What type of culture do you want to adopt? How will you change the culture? What will you do to reinforce the changes you suggest (e.g., staffing, rewards, performance feedback)? You will have twenty minutes to work alone or in a small group. Be prepared to share your insights with the rest of the class.

GROUP EXERCISE

Culture of the Classroom

The class will divide into groups of four to six. Each group will analyze the organization culture of a college class. Students in most classes that use this book will have taken many courses at the college they attend and therefore should have several classes in common. Form groups on the basis of classes you have had in common.

1. Each group should first decide which class it will analyze. Each person in the group must have attended the class.
2. Each group should list the cultural factors to be discussed. Items to be covered should include
   a. Stories about the professor
   b. Stories about the exams
   c. Stories about the grading
   d. Stories about other students
   e. The use of symbols that indicate the students' values
   f. The use of symbols that indicate the instructor's values
3. Students should carefully analyze the stories and symbols to discover their underlying meanings. They should seek stories from other members of the group to ensure that all aspects of the class culture are covered. Students should take notes as these items are discussed.
4. After twenty to thirty minutes of work in groups, the instructor will reconvene the entire class and ask each group to share its analysis with the rest of the class.

Follow-Up Questions

1. What was the most difficult part of this exercise? Did other groups experience the same difficulty?
2. How did your group overcome this difficulty? How did other groups overcome it?
3. Do you believe your group's analysis accurately describes the culture of the class you selected? Could other students who analyzed the culture of

the same class come up with a very different result? How could that happen?

4. If the instructor wanted to try to change the culture in the class you analyzed, what steps would you recommend that he or she take?

VIDEO EXERCISE

The Environment and Corporate Culture at Recycline

Ever since green became the new black, U.S. companies have been scrambling to change their products, packaging, and energy consumption to stay in the game. Thanks to Eric Hudson's perceptive scanning of the external environment in the mid-1990s, recycled products firm Recycline discovered an opportunity others missed.

Hudson broke into the natural product arena with an innovative toothbrush made from recycled materials—a bold decision in 1996. Hudson named his first product the Preserve Toothbrush, and Recycline was born. The toothbrush, with its nylon bristles and ergonomically curved handle made of 100 percent recycled material, was a hit with eco-conscious consumers. New converts flocked to it, and Hudson gradually added personal care and kitchenware items to his line of recycled products. Today, Preserve products can be found at top retail chains including Target, Whole Foods, and Wal-Mart.

For environmentally sensitive consumers, integrity is everything. Recycline believes that customers are getting wise to the "green-washing effect" in which businesses cultivate a superficial green image without the substance to back it up. A close look at Recycline's internal culture confirms that Hudson's company is authentically green. First, as Preserve's cultural leader, Hudson practices what he preaches; When he isn't pedaling twenty-two miles to and from work on his bicycle, he's cruising in a Volkswagen that has been converted to run on french-fry grease—an emerging symbol of the modern-day eco-hero. Additionally, everyone at Preserve tries to do right by the natural environment, whether it's composting, conserving energy, or using eco-friendly cleaning products.

But Recycline's organizational culture isn't just green—it's effective. Because of Recycline's small size, anyone interested in taking on a new initiative is encouraged to do so, regardless of position. The vice president of sales, John Turcott, believes that Preserve's size is critical for rapid response: "Our decision-making process is quicker. We pull together the resources we need to solve a problem, we get it done and move on to the next thing." Since everything at Preserve happens at high-speed, everyone has to be driven, creative, and adaptable.

Discussion Questions

1. What are some visible aspects of Recycline's culture that reflect the company's values and commitment to green issues?
2. What role do leaders play in shaping Recycline's organizational culture? Explain.
3. Could Recycline easily change its organizational culture if the green products market encounters a backlash? How would management know if a permanent change in culture has occurred?

Now What?

VIDEO CASE

PERCOM/SHUTTERSTOCK.COM

Imagine attending a meeting with your boss and two coworkers to discuss declining sales for a previously popular product. A competitor introduced a similar but better product that has been taking your market share. The company knew about the competitor's product, but underestimated the threat. Happy Time Toys wants to make sure it recognizes potential threats faster in the future. *What do you say or do?* Go to this chapter's "Now What?" video, watch the challenge video, and choose a response. Be sure to also view the outcomes of the two responses you didn't choose. One of the stated solutions is to conduct a competitor analysis and an after action review (AAR). This is a structured review or debriefing process that is used to analyze positive and negative outcomes of an action. The steps include analyzing: (a) what should have happened; (b) what actually happened; and (c) how the systems or process can be improved. A competitor analysis is related but focuses on an assessment of the strengths and weaknesses of current and potential competitors.

Discussion Questions

1. In what ways might culture influence how responsive Happy Time Toys is to competitor threats?
2. How are ethics illustrated in these videos? What is the best way to ensure decisions are made ethically?
3. Based on the chapter, what other suggestions would you make to change the culture to enhance responsiveness to the environment and why would you suggest them?

ENDNOTES

[1]Gaston, R. & Fitzgerald, S. (2010). Culture Change at Avaya. Denison Consulting. Available at: http://www.denisonconsulting.com/docs/Culture%20Change%20At%20Avaya.pdf.

[2]Denison Consulting (2011). Avaya: Culture Transformation through Alignment, *Denison, 6*(2), 1–4.

[3]O'Reilly, C. A., & Chatman, J. A. (1996). Cultures as Social Control: Corporations, Cults, and Commitment. In *Research in Organizational Behavior*, eds. L. Cummings & B. M. Staw (Vol. 18, pp. 157–200, p. 166). Greenwich, CT: JAI Press.

[4]Chatman, J. A., & Jehn, K. A. (1994). Assessing the Relationship Between Industry Characteristics and Organizational Culture: How Different Can You Be? *Academy of Management Journal, 37*, 522–553.

[5]Gerstner, L. V., II (2002). *Who Says Elephants Can't Dance? Inside IBM's Historic Turnaround*. New York: HarperCollins.

[6]Byrnes, N. (2006, May 1). The Art of Motivation. *BusinessWeek*, 56–62.

[7]Our Culture and Values. (2015). Nokia.com. http://networks.nokia.com/about-us/sustainability/employees/our-culture-and-values.

[8]For an example, see Clarke, S. (1999, March). Perceptions of Organizational Safety: Implications for the Development of Safety Culture. *Journal of Organizational Behavior*, 185–198.

[9]Schein, E. (1985). *Organizational Culture and Leadership*. San Francisco, CA: Jossey-Bass.

[10]Gardiner, L. (2010). From Synchilla to School Support. Markkula Center for Applied Ethics. Available at: http://www.scu.edu/ethics/publications/iie/v8n1/synchilla.html.

[11]Note: Three levels, combining espoused and enacted values, are referred to in Schein, E. (1992). *Organizational Culture and Leadership* (2nd ed.). San Francisco, CA: Jossey-Bass.

[12]Schein, E. (1992). *Organizational Culture and Leadership* (2nd ed.). San Francisco, CA: Jossey-Bass.

[13]Chatman, J. A., & Cha, S. E. (2003). Leading by Leveraging Culture. *California Management Review, 45*, 20–34.

[14]Gregory, B. T., Harris, S. G., Armenakis, A. A., & Shook, C. L. (2009). Organizational Culture and Effectiveness: A Study of Values, Attitudes, and Organizational Outcomes. *Journal of Business Research, 62*, 673–679.

[15]Neuhauser, P. C., Bender, R., & Stromberg, K. L. (2000). *Culture.com: Building Corporate Culture in the Connected Workplace*. New York: John Wiley and Sons.

[16]Ambrozek, J., & Ambrozek, L. B. (2002, November 28). Building Business Values Through Online Knowledge. *Workforce.com*. Available at: http://www.workforce.com/articles/building-business-values-through-online-knowledge.

[17]Walton, R. E. (1980). Establishing and Maintaining High Commitment Work Systems. In *The Organizational Life Cycle: Issues in the Creation, Transformation and Decline of Organizations*, eds. J. R. Kimberly & R. H. Miles, & Associates (pp. 208–290). San Francisco, CA: Jossey-Bass.

[18]Quicken Loans Named to *Fortune*'s "100 Best Companies to Work For" List for Third Consecutive Year. (2006). Quicken Loans press release. Available at: http://www.quickenloans.com/press-room/2006/01/09/quicken-loans-named-fortune-100-companies-work-list-consecutive-year/

[19]Tushman, M. L., & O'Reilly, C. A. (1997). *Winning Through Innovation: A Practical Guide to Leading Organizational Change and Renewal*. Boston: Harvard Business School Press.

[20]Kotter, J. P., & Heskett, J. L. (1992). *Corporate Culture and Performance*. New York: Free Press.

[21]Treviño, L. K., Weaver, G. R., & Reynolds, S. J. (2006). Behavioral Ethics in Organizations: A Review. *Journal of Management, 32*, 951–990.

[22]Treviño, L. K. (1990). A Cultural Perspective on Changing and Developing Organizational Ethics. In *Research in Organizational Change and Development*, eds. R. Woodman and W. Passmore (Vol. 4, pp. 195–230). Greenwich, CT: JAI Press.

[23]Byrne, J. A., France, M., & Zellner, W. (2002, February 24). At Enron, the Environment Was Ripe for Abuse. *BusinessWeek*. Available at: http://www.bloomberg.com/bw/stories/2002-02-24/at-enron-the-environment-was-ripe-for-abuse.

[24]FBI: Beware of Mortgage Fraud. (2008, May 13). Money.CNN.com. Available at: http://money.cnn.com/2008/05/13/real_estate/mortgage_fraud/.

[25]Robyn, K. (2005, December 1). Acadian Ambulance Got It Done. *Emergency Medical Services*. Available at: http://www.emsmagazine.com/publication/article.jsp?pubId=1&id=2613.

[26]MacMillan, D. (2010, March 1). Survivor: CEO Edition, Bloomberg. *BusinessWeek*, 32–38.

[27]MacMillan, D. (2010, March 1). Survivor: CEO Edition, Bloomberg. *BusinessWeek*, 38.

[28]Brief, A. P., Schneider, B., & Guzzo, R. A. (1996). Creating a Climate and Culture for Sustainable Organizational Change. *Organizational Dynamics, 24*(4), 7–19; Schein, E. (1985). *Organizational Culture and Leadership* (pp. 224–237). San Francisco, CA: Jossey-Bass; Deal, T. E., & Peterson, K. D. (1998). *Shaping School Culture: The Heart of Leadership*. San Francisco, CA: Jossey-Bass.

[29]Byrnes, N. (2006, May 1). The Art of Motivation. *BusinessWeek*, 56–62.

[30]Fishman, C. (2006, January). The Man Who Said No to Wal-Mart. *Fast Company, 102*, 66.

[31]Faber, D. (2004). The Age of Wal-Mart: Inside America's Most Powerful Company. Digital Films. Available at: http://digital.films.com/play/UPAK6H#.

[32]Marquez, J. (2006, March 13). Randstad North America: Optimas Award Winner for Competitive Advantage. *Workforce Management*, 18.

[33]Lundquist, K. K. (2008). Coca-Cola Measures Progress on Diversity Journey. Talent Management, January, 21.

[34]Gelfand, M. J., Leslie, L. M., & Keller, K. M. (2008). On the Etiology of Conflict Cultures. *Research in Organizational Behavior, 28*, 137–166.

[35]Gelfand, M. J., Leslie, L. M., & Keller, K. M. (2008). On the Etiology of Conflict Cultures. *Research in Organizational Behavior, 28*, 137–166.

[36]Gelfand, M. J., Leslie, L. M., & Keller, K. M. (2008). On the Etiology of Conflict Cultures. *Research in Organizational Behavior, 28*, 137–166.

[37]DeLisi, P. S. (1998). A Modern-Day Tragedy. *Journal of Management Inquiry, 7*, 120.

[38]Gelfand, M. J., Leslie, L. M., & Keller, K. M. (2008). On the Etiology of Conflict Cultures. *Research in Organizational Behavior, 28*, 137–166.

[39]Gittell, J. H. (2003). *The Southwest Airlines Way: Using the Power of Relationships to Achieve High Performance*. New York: McGraw-Hill.

[40]Gelfand, M. J., Leslie, L. M., & Keller, K. M. (2008). On the Etiology of Conflict Cultures. *Research in Organizational Behavior, 28*, 137–166.

[41]Finkelstein, S. (2005). When Bad Things Happen to Good Companies: Strategy Failure and Flawed Executives. *Journal of Business Strategy, 26*, 19–28.

[42]Baron, R., & Neuman, J. (1996). Workplace Violence and Workplace Aggression: Evidence on Their Relative Frequency and Potential Causes. *Aggressive Behavior, 22*, 161–173; Geddes, D., & Baron, R. A. (1997). Workplace Aggression as a Consequence of Negative Performance Feedback. *Management Communication Quarterly, 10*, 433–454.

[43]Musiker, H. R., & Norton, R. G. (1983). The Medical System: A Complex Arena for the Exhibition of Passive-Aggressiveness. In *Passive-Aggressiveness: Theory and Practice*, eds. R. D. Parsons & R. J. Wicks (pp. 194–212). New York: Brunner/Mazel.

[44]Gelfand, M. J., Nishii, L. H., & Raver, J. L. (2006). On the Nature and Importance of Cultural Tightness-Looseness. *Journal of Applied Psychology, 91*, 1225–1244.

[45]Sigler, T., & Pearson, C. (2000). Creating and Empowering Culture: Examining the Relationship Between Organizational Culture and Perceptions of Empowerment. *Journal of Quality Management, 5*, 27–52; Leung, K., Bond, M. H., Carment, D. W., & Krishnan, L. (1990). Effects of Cultural Femininity on Preferences for Methods of Conflict Processing: A Cross Cultural Study. *Journal of Experimental Social Psychology, 26*, 373–388.

[46]Triandis, H. C., & Gelfand, M. J. (1998). Converging Measurement of Horizontal and Vertical Individualism and Collectivism. *Journal of Personality and Social Psychology, 74*, 118–128.

[47]Gelfand, M. J., Nishii, L. H., & Raver, J. L. (2006). On the Nature and Importance of Cultural Tightness-Looseness. *Journal of Applied Psychology, 91*, 1225–1244.

[48]Gelfand, M. J., Leslie, L. M., & Keller, K. M. (2008). On the Etiology of Conflict Cultures. *Research in Organizational Behavior, 28*, 137–166.

[49]Chatman, J. A., Polzer, J. T., Barsade, S. G., & Neale, M. A. (1998). Being Different Yet Feeling Similar: The Influence of

Demographic Composition and Organizational Culture on Work Processes and Outcomes. *Administrative Science Quarterly, 43*, 749–780.

[50]McKay, P. F., Avery, D. R., Tonidandel, S., Morris, M. A., Hernandez, M., & Hebl, M. R. (2007). Racial Differences in Employee Retention: Are Diversity Climate Perceptions the Key? *Personnel Psychology, 60*, 35–62.

[51]Avery, D. R., McKay, P. F. Wilson, D. C., & Tonidandel, S. (2007). Unequal Attendance: The Relationships Between Race, Organizational Diversity Cues, and Absenteeism. *Personnel Psychology, 60*, 875–902.

[52]Kossek, E. E., & Zonia, S. C. (1993). Assessing Diversity Climate: A Field Study of Reactions to Employer Efforts to Promote Diversity. *Journal of Organizational Behavior, 14*, 61–81.

[53]Mor Barak, M. E., Cherin, D. A., & Berkman, S. (1998). Organizational and Personal Dimensions in Diversity Climate: Ethnic and Gender Differences in Employee Perceptions. *Journal of Applied Behavioral Science, 34*, 82–104.

[54]Toppling a Taboo: Businesses Go "Faith-Friendly." (2007, January 24). Knowledge @ Wharton. Available at: http://knowledge.wharton.upenn.edu/article.cfm?articleid=1644&CFID=15563496&CFTOKEN=55015521&jsessionid=a8307d84d98967424b15.

[55]Whirlpool. (2015). Employees. Available at: http://www.whirlpoolcorp.com/diversity-inclusion/.

[56]Whirlpool (2015). About Whirlpool. Available at: http://www.whirlpoolcorp.com/about/.

[57]Diversity and Inclusion at Whirlpool. (2008, March). Diversityinc.com. Available at: http://www.diversityinc.com/pdf/specialsections/michigan-sect-march2008.pdfl

[58]Whirlpool (2015). Employees. Available at: http://www.whirlpoolcorp.com/diversity-inclusion/.

[59]Henneman, T. (2004, MAy 29). Diversity Training Addresses Sexual Orientation. Workforce Management Online. Available at: http://www.workforce.com/articles/diversity-training-addresses-sexual-orientation.

[60]Diversity Best Practices. (2007, April). White Male Engagement: Inclusion Is Key. *CDO Insights 1*, 21–24.

[61]Diversity and Inclusion at Whirlpool. (2008, March). Diversityinc.com, 60.

[62]http://www.whirlpoolcorp.com.

[63]Whirlpool (2015). Awards and Recognition. Available at: http://www.whirlpoolcorp.com/awards-and-recognition/.

[64]Based on Hunsaker, P. (2001). *Training in Management Skills* (p. 323). Upper Saddle River, NJ: Prentice Hall; Seidel, H. (2005). Assessing an Organization's Culture—Before You Join. Jobfind.com; Paulson, C. (2009, September 14). How to Spot the Corporate Culture. Boston.com. Available at: http://www.boston.com/jobs/bighelp2009/september/articles/how_to_evaluate_corporate_culture/.

[65]Rousseau, D. M. (1998) Why Workers Still Identify with Organizations. *Journal of Organizational Behavior, 19*, 217–233; Pratt, M. G., & Foreman, P. O. (2000). Classifying Managerial Responses to Multiple Organizational Identities. *Academy of Management Review, 25*, 18–42.

[66]Mayor, T. (2001, April 1). Remote (Worker) Control. *CIO Magazine*. Available online: http://www.cio.com/article/30100/Management_Remote_Worker_Control.

[67]Humphrey, W. S. (1987). *Managing for Innovation: Leading Technical People*. Englewood Cliffs, NJ: Prentice Hall, 1987.

[68]O'Reilly, B. (1997, March 3). Secrets of the Most Admired Corporations: New Ideas and New Products. *Fortune*, 60–64.

[69]Lewis, L. K., & Seibold, D. R. (1993, April). Innovation Modification During Intraorganizational Adoption. *Academy of Management Review, 10*(2), 322–354.

[70]Kwoh, L. (2012, May 23). You Call That Innovation? *Wall Street Journal*, B1.

[71]Tobak, S. (2012, April 2). Leadership Lessons from BlackBerry's Demise. *CBS MoneyWatch*. Available at: http://www.cbsnews.com/8301-505125_162-57407782/leadership-lessons-from-blackberrysdemise/.

[72]Hindo, B. (2007, June 11). 3M's Culture of Innovation. *Business Week*. Available at: http://www.bloomberg.com/ss/07/05/0530_3m_products/source/1.htm; Hindo, B. (2007, June 10). At 3M, a Struggle Between Efficiency and Creativity. *Business Week*. Available at: http://www.bloomberg.com/bw/stories/2007-06-10/at-3m-a-struggle-between-efficiency-and-creativity; Hindo, B. (2007, June 10). 3M Chief Plants a Money Tree. *Business Week*. Available at: http://www.bloomberg.com/bw/stories/2007-06-10/online-extra-3m-chief-plants-a-money-tree.

[73]Wilhelm, W. (1992, November). Changing Corporate Culture—Or Corporate Behavior? How to Change Your Company. *Academy of Management Executive*, 72–77.

[74]"Socialization" has also been defined as "the process by which culture is transmitted from one generation to the next." See Whiting, J. W. M. (1968). Socialization: Anthropological Aspects. In *International Encyclopedia of the Social Sciences*, ed. D. Sils (Vol. 14, p. 545). New York: Free Press.

[75]Hebden, J. E. (1986, Summer). Adopting an Organization's Culture: The Socialization of Graduate Trainees. *Organizational Dynamics*, 54–72.

[76]Barney, J. B. (1986, July). Organizational Culture: Can It Be a Source of Sustained Competitive Advantage? *Academy of Management Review*, 656–665.

[77]Hindo, B. (2007, June 11). 3M's Culture of Innovation. *Business Week*. Available at: http://www.bloomberg.com/ss/07/05/0530_3m_products/source/1.htm.

[78]Norman, J. R. (1993, September 27). A New Teledyne," *Forbes*, 44–45.

[79]Denison (2011). Avaya: Culture Transformation through Alignment, *Denison, 6*(2), 14.

[80]Gaston, R. & Fitzgerald, S. (2010). Culture Change at Avaya. Denison Consulting. Available at: http://www.denisonconsulting.com/docs/Culture%20Change%20At%20Avaya.pdf.

[81]Denison Consulting (2011). Avaya: Culture Transformation through Alignment, *Denison, 6*(2), 1–4.

[82]Avaya (2015). Our Culture. Available online: http://www.avaya.com/usa/about-avaya/our-company/our-culture/our-culture.

LOSKUTNIKOV/SHUTTERSTOCK.COM

CHAPTER 16

ORGANIZATION CHANGE AND CHANGE MANAGEMENT

CHAPTER OUTLINE

LEARNING OUTCOMES

After studying this chapter, you should be able to:

1 Summarize the dominant forces for change in organizations and describe the process of planned organization change.

2 Discuss several approaches to organization development.

3 Explain resistance to change.

4 Identify the keys to managing successful organization change and development and describe organizational learning.

LOSKUTNIKOV/SHUTTERSTOCK.COM

REAL WORLD CHALLENGE

MISMANAGED CHANGE AT KODAK[1]

As recently as 1994 Eastman Kodak was among the top 20 companies in the *Fortune 500*. In 1996, the renowned manufacturer of photographic film and equipment employed 145,000 workers and enjoyed revenues of more than $13 billion. As of 2005, the workforce had been trimmed to 51,000 but revenues topped $14 billion. By 2015, Kodak was reporting revenues of $2.5 billion and its workforce had been reduced to 13,000.

What had happened to the onetime corporate giant? Or, more to the point, what changed everything and reduced a blue-chip corporation to a shadow of itself in just a couple of decades? Most analysts approach this question by citing the advent of digital technology—the capacity to store and process data as computerized bits and bytes rather than as streams of electronic signals loaded onto such physical materials as magnetic tape or silver halide film (known as analog technology). The so-called Digital Revolution—the widespread transition from analog to digital—took off in the 1980s and 1990s, as cellphones became ubiquitous and the Internet became a fixture in business operations. A former Kodak executive now working for a different company has asked for your thoughts on why Kodak failed to adapt. After reading this chapter you should have some good ideas to share with your colleague.

OLYA STECKEL/SHUTTERSTOCK.COM

Companies that change appropriately can continue as viable businesses. Those that do not make the right changes, like Kodak, lose their ability to compete, cease to exist by going out of business, or get gobbled up by a more successful organization. This chapter is about how organizations need to face the prospect of change and develop processes to ensure their viability in a complex, ever-changing global environment. The chapter begins with a discussion of some of the forces that create pressures for change followed by a detailed explanation of the complex change process. Then we describe organization development and sources of resistance to change, finishing with a summary view of how to manage change in organizations.

FORCES FOR CHANGE

An organization is subject to pressures for change from far more sources than can be discussed here. Moreover, it is difficult to predict what types of pressures for change will be most significant in the next decade because the complexity of events and the rapidity of change are increasing. However, it is possible—and important—to discuss the broad categories of pressures that probably will have major effects on organizations. The four areas in which the pressures for change appear most powerful involve people, technology, information processing and communication, and competition. Table 16.1 gives examples of each of these categories.

People

Approximately 76 million people were born in the United States between 1946 and 1964. As we discussed in Chapter 2, these baby boomers differed significantly from previous generations with respect to education, expectations, and value systems. As this group has aged, the median age of the U.S. population has gradually increased, passing 32 for the first time in 1988 and further increasing to 37.3 in 2011. The special characteristics of baby boomers show up in distinct purchasing patterns that affect product and service innovation, technological change, and marketing and promotional activities. Employment practices, compensation systems, promotion and managerial succession systems, and the entire concept of human resource management are also affected.

Other population-related pressures for change involve the generations that sandwich the baby boomers: the increasing numbers of

RAWPIXEL/SHUTTERSTOCK.COM

There are many different forces for change that affect organizations. One major force is people. As shown here, diversity has increased substantially in the labor force and therefore in most organizations as well. Organizations can leverage diversity to enhance creativity and performance but must also change in order to accommodate diverse needs, preferences, and expectations.

Table 16.1

Pressures for Organization Change

Category	Examples	Type of Pressure for Change
People	Generation X, Y, Millennials Global labor supplies Senior citizens Workforce diversity	Demands for different training, benefits, workplace arrangements, and compensation systems
Technology	Manufacturing in space Internet Global design teams	More education and training for workers at all levels, more new products, products move faster to market
Information Processing and Communication	Computer, satellite communications Global sourcing Videoconferencing Social networking	Faster reaction times, immediate responses to questions, new products, different office arrangements, telecommuting, marketing, advertising, recruiting on social networking sites
Competition	Global markets International trade agreements Emerging nations	Global competition, more competing products with more features and options, lower costs, higher quality

senior citizens and those born after 1960. The parents of the baby boomers are living longer, healthier lives than previous generations, and today they expect to live the "good life" that they missed when they were raising their children. The impact of the large number of senior citizens is already evident in part-time employment practices, in the marketing of everything from hamburgers to packaged tours of Asia, and in service areas such as health care, recreation, and financial services. The post-1960 generation of workers who entered the job market in the 1980s—often called generation X—was different from the baby boom generation. Sociologists and psychologists have identified another group, often called millennials, born from roughly between 1980 and 2000 (experts differ on start and end dates from as early as 1977 to as late as 2002), who seem to be experiencing a distinct and separate life stage in between adolescence and adulthood in which young people may jump from job to job and relationship to relationship, often living at home with few responsibilities and experimenting with life. Millennials are putting off marriage, childbearing, home purchases, and most adult responsibilities.[2] However, they seem to be much more group oriented, to celebrate diversity, are optimistic, and they assimilate technology very fast.[3] On the job, millennials seem to prefer positive reinforcement, like clarity in job assignments, want more flexibility in how to do their jobs, and want to be treated as different individuals rather than everyone being treated the same.[4] These changes in demographics extend to the composition of the workforce, family lifestyles, and purchasing patterns worldwide.

The increasing diversity of the workforce in coming years will mean significant changes for organizations. This increasing diversity was discussed in some detail in Chapter 2. In addition, employees are facing a different work environment in the twenty-first century. The most descriptive word for this new work environment is "change." Employees must be prepared for constant change. Change is occurring in organizations' cultures, structures, work relationships, and customer relationships, as well as in the actual jobs that people do. People will have to be completely adaptable to new situations while maintaining productivity under the existing system.[5] Our *Understand Yourself* feature will give you some insights into your own readiness for change.

UNDERSTAND YOURSELF

WHAT IS YOUR TOLERANCE FOR AMBIGUITY?

This feature gives you an opportunity to better understand your tolerance for ambiguity. Please respond to the following statements as honestly as possible using the following scale:

strongly disagree	somewhat disagree	neutral	somewhat agree	strongly agree
1	2	3	4	5

___ 1. I do not like to get started in group projects unless I feel assured that the project will be successful.

___ 2. In a decision-making situation where there is not enough information to process the problem, I feel very uncomfortable.

___ 3. I do not like to work on a problem unless there is a possibility of coming out with a clear-cut and unambiguous answer.

___ 4. I function poorly whenever there is a serious lack of communication in a job situation.

___ 5. In a situation in which other people evaluate me, I feel a great need for clear and explicit evaluations.

___ 6. If I am uncertain about the responsibility of a job, I get very anxious.

___ 7. A problem has very little attraction for me if I don't think it has a solution.

___ 8. It's satisfying to know pretty much what is going to happen on the job from day to day.

___ 9. The most interesting life is one that is lived under rapidly changing conditions.

___ 10. When planning a vacation, a person should have a schedule to follow if he or she is really going to enjoy it.

___ 11. Adventurous and exploratory people go farther in this world than do systematic and orderly people.

___ 12. Doing the same things in the same places for long periods of time makes for a happy life.

___ 13. I don't tolerate ambiguous situations well.

___ 14. I find it difficult to respond when faced with an unexpected event.

___ 15. I am good at managing unpredictable situations.

___ 16. I prefer familiar situations to new ones.

___ 17. I enjoy tackling problems that are complex enough to be ambiguous.

___ 18. I prefer a situation in which there is some ambiguity.

Scoring: For statements 1 through 8, 10, 12, 13, 14, and 16, subtract your score from 6 and replace your initial score with this new number (high scores should become low, and low scores should become high). Then add up your scores for all eighteen statements to calculate your tolerance for ambiguity score.

Interpretation: Possible scores range from 18 to 90. The higher your score, the greater your tolerance for ambiguity. Higher scores mean that you are more comfortable with change and are less likely to interfere with change efforts. Scores above 72 reflect a particularly high tolerance for ambiguity. If you have a lower score, you are less comfortable with uncertainty and with change. To increase your ambiguity tolerance, try to recognize why you are not more comfortable with ambiguity and work on developing the confidence that you can successfully handle ambiguous situations.

Sources: Gupta, A. K., & Govindarajan, V. (1984). Business Unit Strategy, Managerial Characteristics, and Business Unit Effectiveness at Strategy Implementation. *Academy of Management Journal, 27,* 25–41; Lorsch, J. W., & Morse, J. J. (1974). *Organizations and Their Members: A Contingency Approach. New York:* Harper & Row; Norton, R. W. (1975). Measurement of Ambiguity Tolerance. *Journal of Personality Assessment, 39,* 607–619.

Technology is a major driver of organization change. Just as one simple example, ancient businesses used hand methods to calculate profits, expenses and so forth. In succession, though, hand methods gave way to mechanical adding machines and then to electronic calculators. Now many different digital devices can perform the same functions.

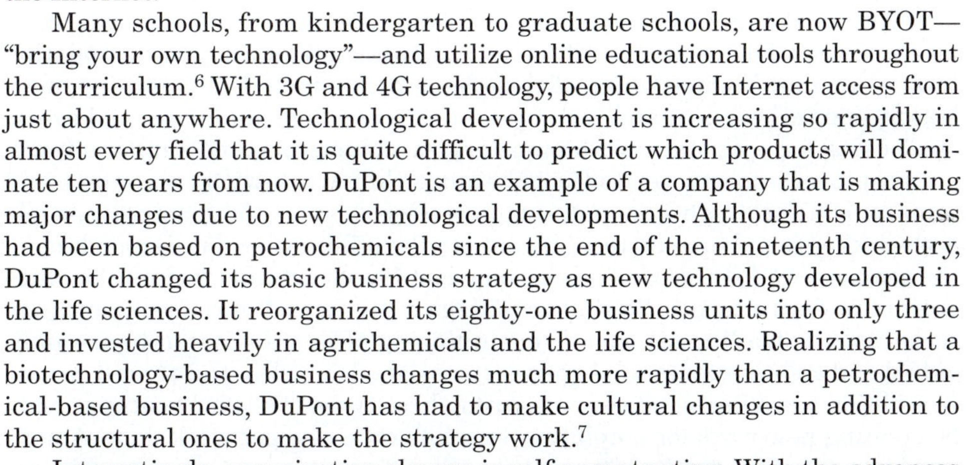
AE.PANUWAT STUDIO/SHUTTERSTOCK.COM

Technology

Not only is technology changing, but the rate of technological change is also increasing. In 1970, for example, all engineering students owned computational devices known as "slide rules" and used them in almost every class. By 1976, slide rules had given way to portable electronic calculators. In 1993, the Scholastic Aptitude Test (SAT), which many college-bound students take to get into college, allowed calculators to be used during the test. Today students cannot make it through the university without owning or at least having ready access to a digital device of some sort—a laptop or notebook computer or iPad, for instance. Entire campuses at most universities are wired for direct computer access for email and class assignments and for connection to the Internet.

Many schools, from kindergarten to graduate schools, are now BYOT—"bring your own technology"—and utilize online educational tools throughout the curriculum.[6] With 3G and 4G technology, people have Internet access from just about anywhere. Technological development is increasing so rapidly in almost every field that it is quite difficult to predict which products will dominate ten years from now. DuPont is an example of a company that is making major changes due to new technological developments. Although its business had been based on petrochemicals since the end of the nineteenth century, DuPont changed its basic business strategy as new technology developed in the life sciences. It reorganized its eighty-one business units into only three and invested heavily in agrichemicals and the life sciences. Realizing that a biotechnology-based business changes much more rapidly than a petrochemical-based business, DuPont has had to make cultural changes in addition to the structural ones to make the strategy work.[7]

Interestingly, organization change is self-perpetuating. With the advances in information technology, organizations generate more information, and it circulates faster. Consequently, employees can respond more quickly to problems, so the organization can respond more quickly to demands from other organizations, customers, and competitors. Honda, long known as a leader in developing and using new technologies in its plants, has introduced hyper-efficient robots in its efforts to improve productivity, reduce costs and pioneer new manufacturing technologies.[8]

New technology will affect organizations in ways we cannot yet predict. Gesture technology may eliminate all controls in your home, from your AV system remote to your thermostat, and replace them with your own gestures with your hands and fingers. HP's TouchSmart technology allows people to touch things without actually touching them, and could drive innovations in medicine and education within a decade. Sensawaft technology will allow people to control devices such as smartphones and ATMs using exhaled breath—which could dramatically increase mobility and control for people with limited mobility.[9]

Several companies are developing systems to manufacture chemicals and exotic electronic components in space. The Internet, the World Wide Web, and cloud computing are changing the way companies and individuals communicate, market, buy, and distribute faster than organizations can respond. Thus, as organizations react more quickly to change, change occurs more rapidly, which in turn necessitates more rapid responses.

Information Processing and Communication

Advances in information processing and communication have paralleled each other. A new generation of computers, which will mark another major increase in processing power, is being designed. Satellite systems for data transmission are already in use. Today people carry a device in their pocket that serves as their portable computer, e-reader, pocket-size television, camera, video recorder, music player, and personal communication device (telephone), all in one device. And they work all over the world.

Social networking may be the most radical and fastest growing aspect of the advances in information processing and communication so far. Through such sites as Facebook, Twitter, LinkedIn, Ning, Yammer, Bebo, Viadeo, Skype, FaceTime, and many others, people are networking with others exploring common interests. People are spending hours reading about others and updating their own sites. Business uses of this phenomenon include advertising, marketing, market research and test marketing, recruiting, and more. And everyone looking for a job starts with Monster.com, Jobing.com, and similar sites.[10]

Employees do not need offices because they work with computers and communicate through new data transmission devices. Increasingly, people are working from home instead of going to the office every day. Depending on the company and the type of work, some employees actually go into the office only a few days a month. Taking advantage of this trend, some companies are reconfiguring traditional space by minimizing offices dedicated to one individual and creating communal spaces, unassigned cubicles, and shared spaces. In addition to saving on office space costs, these types of shared spaces seem to be creating new ways for employees to collaborate and get work done. American Express estimates that 20 percent of their five-thousand-person workforce are in the office at their headquarters in New York more than a few days a week. GlaxoSmithKline estimates it is saving almost $10 million a year in real estate costs by using unassigned seating that is made possible by having more and more employees who work somewhere other than the traditional office.[11]

Flexible work stations, both inside and outside of offices, are more electronic than paper and pencil. For years, the capability has existed to generate, manipulate, store, and transmit more data than managers could use, but the benefits were not fully realized. Now the time has come to utilize all of that information-processing potential, and companies are making the most of it. Typically, companies received orders by mail in the 1970s, by toll-free telephone numbers in the 1980s, by fax machine in the late 1980s and early 1990s, and by electronic data exchange in the mid-1990s. Orders used to take a week; now they are placed instantaneously, and companies can and must be able to respond immediately, all because of changes in information processing and communication.[12] Zappos.com can ship a pair of shoes in as little as eight minutes from receiving an order.[13] Suppliers and end users in some industries now have the parts systems integrated so closely that new parts shipments sometimes are not even ordered—they just show up at the receiving dock when they are needed.

Competition

Although competition is not a new force for change, competition today has some significant new twists. First, most markets are global because of decreasing transportation and communication costs and the increasing export orientation of business.[14] The adoption of trade agreements such as the North American Free Trade Agreement (NAFTA) and the presence of the World Trade Organization (WTO) have changed the way business operates. In the future, competition from industrialized countries such as Japan and Germany will take a back seat to competition from the booming industries of developing nations such as China and India. The Internet is creating new competitors overnight in ways that could not have been imagined five years ago. Companies in developing nations may soon offer different, newer, cheaper, or higher quality products while enjoying the benefits of low labor costs, abundant supplies of raw materials, expertise in certain areas of production, and financial protection from their own governments that may not be available to firms in older industrialized states.

Consider, for example, the market for cell phones or smartphones. Once consumers simply compared calling plans and phone costs and chose a phone available from a provider with the best deal and coverage in their primary area of usage. Currently, the choices are far more complex: we now have platforms in addition to manufacturers and carriers or service providers. Manufacturers include Apple, Blackberry, Motorola, Samsung, Sony, HTC, LG, Nokia, Toshiba, and others. Carriers include Verizon, T-Mobile, AT&T, Sprint, Virgin Mobile, China Telecom, Bell, Orange, O2, Vodafone, and others. Platforms include Android, iOS, Windows Phone, BlackBerry, Firefox OS, Sailfish OS, Tizen, Ubuntu Touch, and others. For consumers the choices are seemingly endless and extremely confusing. Manufacturers have to develop new equipment and software combinations to work on various platforms for a variety of carriers. Carriers must decide which instruments and platform combinations to offer to subscribers. And platform developers must show their platform can do more things, simpler and with fewer errors, with maximum flexibility. And every month there are new combinations of all three to further confuse consumers and industry experts. The global environment of business also compounds these challenges for managers. Our *Global Issues* feature provides more detail about change in international organizations.

97/GETTY IMAGES

Competition can cause organizations to change in different ways. Take the market for cell phones, for example. Every cell phone manufacturer has had to change how it does research, how it judges customer demand, how it manufactures and distributes products, and how it selects and compensates its employees, all due to changes in technology.

THE ADDED COMPLEXITY OF GLOBAL CHANGE

Imagine the challenges faced by a manager planning and implementing an organizational change in facilities located in Fresno, Dallas, and Miami. Now take those challenges and multiple them by 100. This might come close to assessing the additional complexity of change in a multinational corporation. Consider just a few points of change, for instance, related to organization design, leadership and motivation, and organizational control.

Managers in international businesses must attend to a variety of organizing issues. For example, General Electric has operations scattered around the globe. The firm has made the decision to give local managers a great deal of responsibility for how they run their business. In contrast, many Japanese firms give managers of their foreign operations relatively little responsibility. As a result, those managers must frequently travel back to Japan to present problems or get decisions approved. Managers in an international business must address the basic issues of organization structure and design, and dealing with human resources. Strategically, too, organizing decisions can be used to help promote everything from organizational flexibility to the development of expatriate managers. So, obviously, change focused on any of these areas will pose challenges.

Individual managers must also be prepared to deal with various cultural factors as they manage change involving people from different cultural backgrounds. Managers must understand how cultural factors affect individuals, how motivational processes vary across cultures, how the role of leadership changes in different cultures, how communication varies across cultures, and how interpersonal and group processes depend on cultural background.

Managers in international organizations must also be concerned with control. Distances, time zone differences, and cultural factors also play a role in control. For example, in some cultures close supervision is seen as being appropriate, whereas in other cultures it is not. Likewise, executives in the United States and China may find it difficult to communicate vital information to one another because of the time zone differences. Basic control issues for the international manager revolve around operations management, productivity, quality, technology, and information systems. Clearly, then, managing change in a multinational organization is no small task!

PROCESSES FOR PLANNED ORGANIZATION CHANGE

External forces may impose change on an organization. Ideally, however, the organization will not only respond to change but will also anticipate it, prepare for it through planning, and incorporate it in the organization strategy. Organization change can be viewed from a static point of view, such as that of Lewin (see next section), or from a dynamic perspective.

Lewin's Process Model

Planned organization change requires a systematic process of movement from one condition to another. Kurt Lewin suggested that efforts to bring about planned change in organizations should approach change as a multistage process.[15] His model of planned change is made up of three steps—unfreezing, change, and refreezing—as shown in Figure 16.1.

unfreezing
The process by which people become aware of the need for change

Unfreezing is the process by which people become aware of the need for change. If people are satisfied with current practices and procedures, they may

Figure 16.1

Lewin's Process of Organization Structure

In Lewin's three-step model, change is a systematic process of transition from an old way of doing things to a new way. Inclusion of an "unfreezing" stage indicates the importance of preparing for the change. The "refreezing" stage reflects the importance of following up on the change to make it permanent.

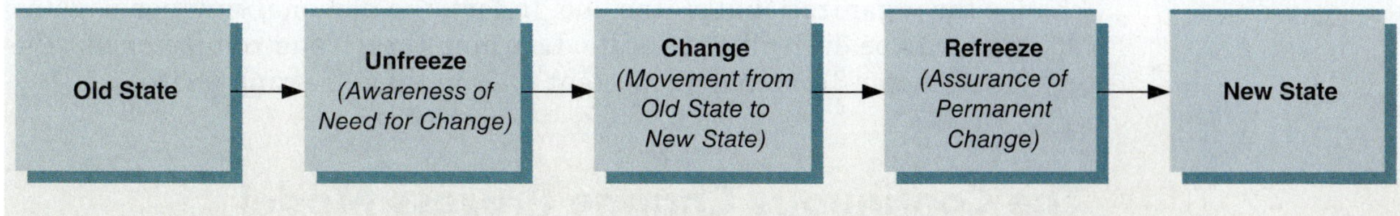

have little or no interest in making changes. The key factor in unfreezing is making employees understand the importance of a change and how their jobs will be affected by it. The employees who will be most affected by the change must be made aware of why it is needed, which in effect makes them dissatisfied enough with current operations to be motivated to change. Creating in employees the awareness of the need for change is the responsibility of the leadership of the organization.[16]

Following the recent deep recession with the high number of downsizings, layoffs, restructurings, and takeovers, employees may be weary of the constant pressure and uncertainties of their position and/or organization. Top managers and change agents are urged to make the effort to empathize with employees, acknowledge the difficulties of the past and uncertainties of the present, and provide forums for employees to vent a little, followed up with workshops for information sharing and training. After making the emotional connection with employees, top management can make the intellectual connection and make the business case by sharing economic and marketing data and the short- and long-term visions for the organization, and by involving employees at all levels in translating organizational goals into division, department, and work unit goals.[17]

refreezing
The process of making new behaviors relatively permanent and resistant to further change

Change itself is the movement from the old way of doing things to a new way. Change may entail installing new equipment, restructuring the organization, or implementing a new performance appraisal system—anything that alters existing relationships or activities.

Refreezing makes new behaviors relatively permanent and resistant to further change. Examples of refreezing techniques include repeating newly learned skills in a training

Refreezing helps to make a change more permanent and resistant to further change. This work group has just gone though a significant change. The leader is explaining to the rest of the team that it will be necessary for each of them to follow the new procedures.

session and then role playing to teach how the new skill can be used in a real-life work situation. Refreezing is necessary because without it, the old ways of doing things might soon reassert themselves while the new ways are forgotten. For example, many employees who attend special training sessions apply themselves diligently and resolve to change things in their organizations. But when they return to the workplace, they find it easier to conform to the old ways than to make waves. There usually are few, if any, rewards for trying to change the organizational status quo. In fact, the personal sanctions against doing so may be difficult to tolerate. Learning theory and reinforcement theory (see Chapter 3) can play important roles in the refreezing phase.

The Continuous Change Process Model

Perhaps because Lewin's model is very simple and straightforward, virtually all models of organization change start with his approach. However, it does not deal with several important issues. A more complex, and more helpful, approach is illustrated in Figure 16.2. This approach treats planned change from the perspective of top management and indicates that change is continuous. Although we discuss each step as if it were separate and distinct from the others, it is important to note that as change becomes continuous in organizations, different steps are probably occurring simultaneously throughout the organization. The model incorporates Lewin's concept into the implementation phase.

In this approach, top management perceives that certain forces or trends call for change, and the issue is subjected to the organization's usual problem-solving and decision-making processes. Usually, top management defines its goals in terms of what the organization or certain processes or outputs will be like after the change. Alternatives for change are generated and evaluated, and an acceptable one is selected.

Figure 16.2

The continuous change process model incorporates the forces for change, a problem-solving process, a change agent, and transition management. It takes a top-management perspective and highlights the fact that in organizations today, change is a continuous process.

Continuous Change Process Model of Organization Change

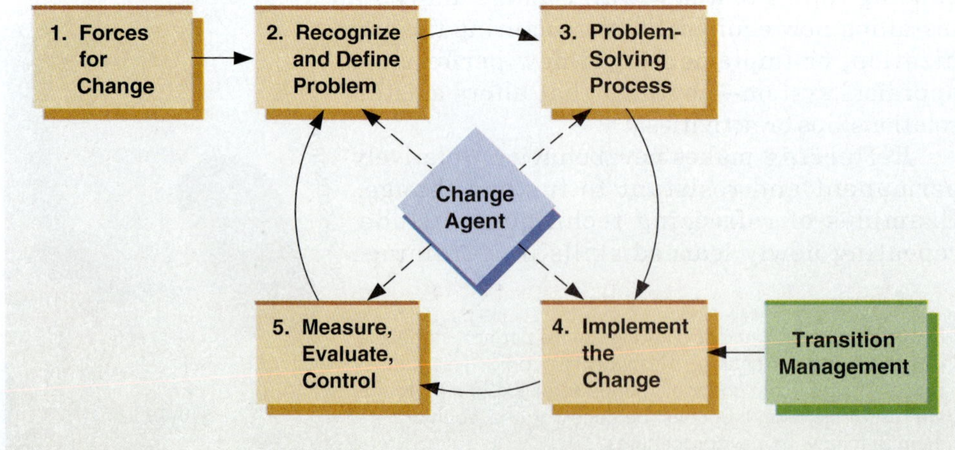

Early in the process, the organization may seek the assistance of a ***change agent***—a person who will be responsible for managing the change effort. The change agent may also help management recognize and define the problem or the need for the change and may be involved in generating and evaluating potential plans of action. The change agent may be a member of the organization, an outsider such as a consultant, or even someone from headquarters whom employees view as an outsider. An internal change agent is likely to know the organization's people, tasks, and political situations, which may be helpful in interpreting data and understanding the system; but an insider may also be too close to the situation to view it objectively. (In addition, a regular employee would have to be removed from his or her regular duties to concentrate on the transition.) An outsider, then, is often received better by all parties because of his or her assumed impartiality. Under the direction and management of the change agent, the organization implements the change through Lewin's unfreeze, change, and refreeze process.

change agent
A person responsible for managing a change effort

The final step is measurement, evaluation, and control. The change agent and the top management group assess the degree to which the change is having the desired effect; that is, they measure progress toward the goals of the change and make appropriate changes if necessary. The more closely the change agent is involved in the change process, the less distinct the steps become. The change agent becomes a "collaborator" or "helper" to the organization as she or he is immersed in defining and solving the problem with members of the organization. When this happens, the change agent may be working with many individuals, groups, and departments within the organization on different phases of the change process. When the change process is moving along from one stage to another, it may not be readily observable because of the total involvement of the change agent in every phase of the project. Throughout the process, however, the change agent brings in new ideas and viewpoints that help members look at old problems in new ways. Change often arises from the conflict that results when the change agent challenges the organization's assumptions and generally accepted patterns of operation.

Through the measurement, evaluation, and control phase, top management determines the effectiveness of the change process by evaluating various indicators of organizational productivity and effectiveness or employee morale. It is expected the organization will be better after the change than before. However, the uncertainties and rapid changes in all sectors of the environment make constant organization change a given for most organizations.

Transition management is the process of systematically planning, organizing, and implementing change, from the disassembly of the current state to the realization of a fully functional future state within an organization.[18] No matter how much planning precedes the change and how well it is implemented, because people are involved there will always be unanticipated and unpredictable things that happen along the way.[19] One key role of transition management is to deal with these unintended consequences. Once change begins, the organization is in neither the old state nor the new state, yet business must go on. Transition management also ensures that business continues while the change is occurring; therefore, it must begin before the change occurs. The members of the regular management team must take on the role of transition managers and coordinate organizational activities with the change agent. An interim management structure or interim positions may be created to ensure continuity and control of the business during the transition.

transition management
The process of systematically planning, organizing, and implementing change

CASE STUDY Flexibility at KPMG

Accounting firm KPMG's UK offices wanted to decrease payroll costs while maintaining the company's commitment to its employees. So KPMG gave its UK-based employees the choice of either volunteering for a four-day workweek at 90 percent of their salary (80 percent if fewer than 75 percent of employees signed up); a four- to twelve-week sabbatical at 30 percent of their base pay; either or both; or neither. Volunteering for the program, called Flexible Futures, triggered an eighteen-month change in the employee's employment contract giving KMPG the right to exercise the chosen option if and when it needed to. This allowed the company to reduce employee hours and pay on short notice and reduce the need for large-scale staff reductions if economic challenges arose.

To educate employees about their options, KPMG held conference calls, trained managers to answer potential questions, and posted a long list of questions and answers on a dedicated Flexible Futures page on its intranet. The website also included a calculator to enable employees to easily calculate what their take-home pay would be under any of the options. A link to KPMG's corporate responsibility website helped connect employees interested in sabbaticals with nonprofit organizations that needed accounting expertise.

Flexible Futures gives employees greater job security and control over their own destiny. This has allowed them to worry less about their jobs and focus more on their clients. More than 85 percent of KPMG employees signed up for at least one of the options. KPMG expects this to save the company up to 15 percent of payroll costs and to boost employee morale.

Questions:

1. How does this program help KPMG?
2. How does this program help KPMG's employees?
3. If you were employed by KPMG, would this program appeal to you? Why or why not?

Sources: Campbell, R., & Payne, T. (2012, February). The Future is Flexible. KPMG; KPMG Asks Staff to Accept Temporary Flexible Contracts if the Need Arises (2009, January 29). *People Management Magazine*, 8; Hewlett, S. A. (2010, January); KPMG's Flexible Futures. Talent Management, 22; Huber, N. (2009, February 12). Huge Demand for Flexible Working at KPMG. *Accountancy Age*. Available at: http://www.accountancyage.com/accountancyage/news/2236299/huge-demand-flexible-working-4476838.

Communication about the changes to all involved, from employees to customers and suppliers, plays a key role in transition management.[20] This chapter's *Case Study* details a very effective change that was implemented using the continuous change model.

ORGANIZATION DEVELOPMENT

On one level, organization development is simply the way organizations change and evolve. Organization change can involve personnel, technology, competition, and other areas. Employee learning and formal training, transfers, promotions, terminations, and retirements are all examples of personnel-related changes. Thus, in the broadest sense, organization development means organization change.[21] The term as used here, however, means something more specific. Over the past forty years, organization development has emerged as a distinct field of study and practice. Experts now substantially agree as to what constitutes organization development in general, although arguments about details continue.[22] Our definition of organization development is an attempt to describe a very complex process in a simple manner. It is also an attempt to capture the best points of several definitions offered by writers in the field.

Organization Development Defined

"***Organization development*** (OD) is a system-wide application of behavioral science knowledge to the planned development and reinforcement of organizational strategies, structures, and processes for improving an organization's effectiveness."[23] Three points in this definition make it simple to remember and use. First, organization development involves attempts to plan organization changes, which excludes spontaneous, haphazard initiatives. Second, the specific intention of organization development is to improve organization effectiveness. This point excludes changes that merely imitate those of another organization, are forced on the organization by external pressures, or are undertaken merely for the sake of changing. Third, the planned improvement must be based on knowledge of the behavioral sciences such as organizational behavior, psychology, sociology, cultural anthropology, and related fields of study rather than on financial or technological considerations.

organization development
A system-wide application of behavioral science knowledge to the planned development and reinforcement of organizational strategies, structures, and processes for improving organizational effectiveness

Under this definition, the replacement of manual personnel records with a computerized system would not be considered an instance of organization development. Although such a change has behavioral effects, it is a technology-driven reform rather than a behavioral one. Likewise, alterations in record keeping necessary to support new government-mandated reporting requirements are not a part of organization development because the change is obligatory and the result of an external force. The three most basic types of techniques for implementing organization development are system-wide, task and technological, and group and individual.

Organization development was initially treated as a field of study and practiced by specially trained OD professionals. However, as organization change became the order of the day in progressive organizations around the world, it became clear that all organizational leaders needed to become leaders and teachers of change throughout their organizations if their organizations were going to survive. Excellent examples of organizations that have embraced OD are the U.S. Army, General Electric, and Royal Dutch Shell.[24]

System-Wide Organization Development

The most comprehensive type of organization change involves a major reorientation or reorganization—usually referred to as a ***structural change*** or a system-wide rearrangement of task division and authority and reporting relationships. A structural change affects performance appraisal and rewards, decision making, and communication and information-processing systems. Reengineering and rethinking the organization are two contemporary approaches to system-wide structural change. Reengineering can be a difficult process, but it has great potential for organizational improvement. It requires that managers challenge long-held assumptions about everything they do and set outrageous goals and expect that they will be met. An organization may change the way it divides tasks into jobs, combines jobs

structural change
A system-wide organization development involving a major restructuring of the organization or instituting programs such as quality of work life

Most forms of organization change that are implemented though organization development require the use of a coach or facilitator. This manager is playing this role as he explains to everyone how they will now become an integrated team rather than a collection of individual performers.

RAWPIXEL/SHUTTERSTOCK.COM

into departments and divisions, and arranges authority and reporting relationships among positions. It may move from functional departmentalization to a system based on products or geography, for example, or from a conventional linear design to a matrix or a team-based design. Other changes may include dividing large groups into smaller ones or merging small groups into larger ones. In addition, the degree to which rules and procedures are written down and enforced, as well as the locus of decision-making authority, may be altered. Supervisors may become "coaches" or "facilitators" in a team-based organization. The organization will have transformed both the configurational and the operational aspects of its structure if all of these changes are made.

No system-wide structural change is simple.[25] A company president cannot just issue a memo notifying company personnel that on a certain date they will report to a different supervisor and be responsible for new tasks and expect everything to change overnight. Employees have months, years, and sometimes decades of experience in dealing with people and tasks in certain ways. When these patterns are disrupted, employees need time to learn the new tasks and to settle into the new relationships. Moreover, they may resist the change for a number of reasons; we discuss resistance to change later in this chapter. Therefore, organizations must manage the change process.

Ford Motor Company is pretty typical of organizations that have had to make major organization-wide and worldwide changes. Over the years, Ford had developed several regional fiefdoms, such as Ford of Europe, Ford United States, and Ford Australia, which all operated relatively independently. When Jacques Nasser was named CEO, he set out to tear down those regionally based organizations and to create a truly globally integrated car manufacturer. As his plan was unfolding, however, Ford continued to lose market share, so, Nasser was replaced as CEO by Ford family member William Clay (Bill) Ford Jr. Ford eventually turned over the reins to Alan Mulally, who oversaw Ford and made a stunning turnaround.[26] Now Mulally has stepped aside and former COO Mark Fields is running the company. Each of these successive leaders made major organization-wide and worldwide changes.

quality-of-work-life
The extent to which workers can satisfy important personal needs through their experiences in the organization

Another system-wide change is the introduction of ***quality-of-work-life*** programs, defined as the degree to which members of a work organization are able to satisfy important personal needs through their experiences in the organization.[27] Quality-of-work-life programs focus strongly on providing a work environment conducive to satisfying individual needs. The emphasis on improving life at work developed during the 1970s, a period of increasing inflation and deepening recession. The development was rather surprising because an expanding economy and substantially increased resources are the conditions that usually induce top management to begin people-oriented programs. However, top management viewed improving life at work as a means of improving productivity.

Any movement with broad and ambiguous goals tends to spawn diverse programs, each claiming to be based on the movement's goals, and the quality-of-work-life movement is no exception. These programs vary substantially, although most espouse a goal of "humanizing the workplace." Richard Walton divided them into the eight categories shown in Figure 16.3.[28] Obviously, many types of programs can be accommodated by the categories, from changing the pay system to establishing an employee bill of rights that guarantees workers the rights to privacy, free speech, due process, and fair and equitable treatment. The Defense Information Systems Agency (DISA) has a QWL program that includes options for a compressed work schedule, in which employees can work eighty hours in nine workdays over a two-week period, and a "telework" option in which eligible employees may telework at an alternative worksite such as a telework center, at home, or at a satellite office, on a regular and recurring schedule for a maximum of three days per week. The program is designed to promote a more beneficial lifestyle for employees both personally and professionally.[29]

Figure 16.3

Walton's Categorization of Quality-of-Work-Life Programs

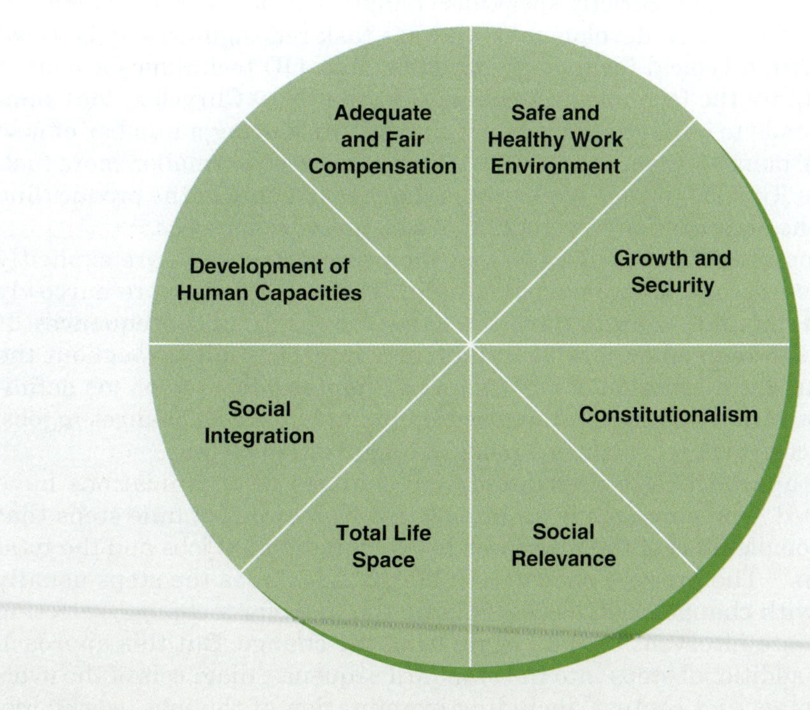

Quality-of-work-life programs can be categorized into eight types. The expected benefits of these programs are increased employee morale, productivity, and organizational effectiveness.

Source: Adapted from Walton, R. E. (1973, Fall). Quality of Work Life: *What Is It? Sloan Management Review*, 11–21.

Total quality management, which was discussed in several earlier chapters, can also be viewed as a system-wide organization development program. In fact, some might consider total quality management as a broad program that includes both structural change and quality of work life. It differs from quality of work life in that it emphasizes satisfying customer needs by making quality-oriented changes rather than focusing on satisfying employee needs at work. Often, however, the employee programs are very similar to it.

The benefits gained from quality-of-work-life programs differ substantially, but generally they are of three types. A more positive attitude toward the work and the organization, or increased job satisfaction, is perhaps the most direct benefit.[30] Another is increased productivity, although it is often difficult to measure and separate the effects of the quality-of-work-life program from the effects of other organizational factors. A third benefit is increased effectiveness of the organization as measured by its profitability, goal accomplishment, shareholder wealth, or resource exchange. The third gain follows directly from the first two: if employees have more positive attitudes about the organization and their productivity increases, everything else being equal, the organization should be more effective.

Task and Technological Change

Another way to bring about system-wide organization development is through changes in the tasks involved in doing the work, the technology, or both. The direct alteration of jobs usually is called "task redesign." Changing how inputs are transformed into outputs is called "technological change" and also usually results in task changes. Strictly speaking, changing the technology is typically not part of organization development whereas task redesign usually is. However, even with a typical technology-based change, OD techniques are often used to facilitate the technological changes. At the "New Chrysler," for example, Fiat intends to enhance the product line by introducing a number of new technologies, many of them essential to the development of smaller, more fuel-efficient cars. This long-range plan entails changes not only in the product line but also in the organization's perception of consumer preferences.[31]

The structural changes discussed in the preceding section are explicitly system-wide in scope. Those we examine in this section are more narrowly focused and may not seem to have the same far-reaching consequences. It is important to remember, however, that their impact is felt throughout the organization. The discussion of job design in Chapter 6 focused on job definition and motivation and gave little attention to implementing changes in jobs. Here we discuss task redesign as a mode of organization change.

Several approaches to introducing job changes in organizations have been proposed. One approach is an integrative framework of nine steps that reflect the complexities of the interfaces between individual jobs and the total organization.[32] The process, shown in Table 16.2, includes the steps usually associated with change, such as recognizing the need for a change, selecting the appropriate intervention, and evaluating the change. But this approach inserts four additional steps into the standard sequence: diagnosis of the overall work system and context, including examination of the jobs, workforce, technology, organization design, leadership, and group dynamics; evaluating the costs and benefits of the change; formulating a redesign strategy; and implementing supplemental changes.

Table 16.2

Integrated Framework for Implementation of Task Redesign in Organizations

Step 1: Recognition of a need for a change
Step 2: Selection of task redesign as a potential intervention
Step 3: Diagnosis of the work system and context

a. Diagnosis of existing jobs
b. Diagnosis of existing workforce
c. Diagnosis of technology
d. Diagnosis of organization design
e. Diagnosis of leader behavior
f. Diagnosis of group and social processes

Step 4: Cost-benefit analysis of proposed changes
Step 5: Go/no-go decision
Step 6: Formulation of the strategy for redesign
Step 7: Implementation of the task changes
Step 8: Implementation of any supplemental changes
Step 9: Evaluation of the task redesign effort

Source: Griffin, R. W. (1982) *Task Design: An Integrative Framework* (p. 208). Glenview, IL: Scott, Foresman. Used by permission.

Diagnosis includes analysis of the total work environment within which the jobs exist. It is important to evaluate the organization structure, especially the work rules and decision-making authority within a department, when job changes are being considered.[33] For example, if jobs are to be redesigned to give employees more freedom in choosing work methods or scheduling work activities, diagnosis of the present system must determine whether the rules will allow that to happen. Diagnosis must also include evaluation of the work group and teams, as well as the intragroup dynamics. Furthermore, it must determine whether workers have or can easily obtain the new skills to perform the redesigned task.

It is extremely important to recognize the full range of potential costs and benefits associated with a job redesign effort. Some are direct and quantifiable; others are indirect and not quantifiable. Redesign may involve unexpected costs or benefits; although these cannot be predicted with certainty, they can be weighed as possibilities. Factors such as short-term role ambiguity, role conflict, and role overload can be major stumbling blocks to a job redesign effort.

Implementing a redesign scheme takes careful planning, and developing a strategy for the intervention is the final planning step. Strategy formulation is a four-part process. First, the organization must decide who will design the changes. Depending on the circumstances, the planning team may consist of only upper-level management or may include line workers and supervisors. Next, the team undertakes the actual design of the changes based on job design theory and the needs, goals, and circumstances of the organization. Third, the team decides the timing of the implementation, which may require a formal transition period during which equipment is purchased and installed, job training takes place, new physical layouts are arranged, and the bugs in the new system are worked out. Fourth, strategy planners must consider whether the job changes require adjustments and supplemental changes in other organizational components such as reporting relationships and the compensation system.

Group and Individual Change

Groups and individuals can be involved in organization change in a vast number of ways. Retraining a single employee can be considered an organization change if the training affects the way the employee does his or her job. Familiarizing managers with the leadership grid or the Vroom decision tree (as discussed in Chapters 11 and 12) in order to improve the way they lead or involve subordinate participation in decision making is an attempt at change. In the first case, the goal is to balance management concerns for production and people; in the second, the goal is to increase the participation of rank-and-file employees in the organization's decision making. In this section, we present an overview of four popular types of people-oriented change techniques: training, management development, team building, and survey feedback.

Training

Training generally is designed to improve employees' job skills. Employees may be trained to run certain machines, taught new mathematical skills, or acquainted with personal growth and development methods. Stress management programs are becoming popular for helping employees, particularly executives, understand organizational stress and develop ways to cope with it.[34] Training may also be used in conjunction with other, more comprehensive organization changes. For instance, if an organization is implementing a management-by-objectives program, training in establishing goals and reviewing goal-oriented performance is probably needed. One important type of training that is becoming increasingly more common is training people to work in other countries. Companies such as Motorola give extensive training programs to employees at all levels before they start an international assignment. Training includes intensive language courses, cultural courses, and courses for the family.

Among the many training methods, the most common are lecture, discussion, a lecture-discussion combination, experiential methods, case studies, films or videos, and online training modules. Training can take place in a standard classroom, either on company property or in a hotel, at a resort, at a conference center, or

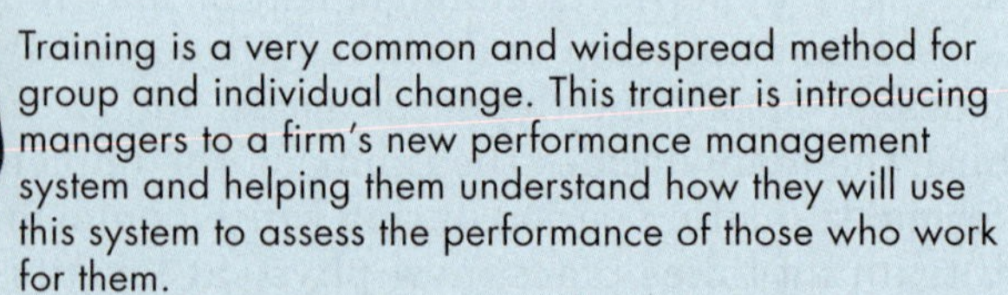

MATEJ KASTELIC/SHUTTERSTOCK.COM

Training is a very common and widespread method for group and individual change. This trainer is introducing managers to a firm's new performance management system and helping them understand how they will use this system to assess the performance of those who work for them.

online from anywhere. On-the-job training provides a different type of experience in which the trainee learns from an experienced worker. Most training programs use a combination of methods determined by the topic, the trainees, the trainer, and the organization.

A major problem of training programs is transferring employee learning to the workplace. Often an employee learns a new skill or a manager learns a new management technique, but upon returning to the normal work situation, he or she finds it easier to go back to the old way of doing things. As we discussed earlier, the process of refreezing is a vital part of the change process, and some way must be found to make the accomplishments of the training program permanent.

Management Development

Management development programs, like employee training programs, attempt to foster certain skills, abilities, and perspectives. Often, when a highly qualified technical person is promoted to manager of a work group, he or she needs training in how to manage or deal with people. In such cases, management development programs can be important to organizations, both for the new manager and for his or her subordinates.

Typically, management development programs use the lecture-discussion method to some extent but rely most heavily on participative methods such as case studies and role playing. Participative and experiential methods allow the manager to experience the problems of being a manager as well as the feelings of frustration, doubt, and success that are part of the job. The subject matter of this type of training program is problematic, however, in that management skills, including communication, problem diagnosis, problem solving, and performance appraisal, are not as easy to identify or to transfer from a classroom to the workplace as the skills required to operate a machine. In addition, rapid changes in the external environment can make certain managerial skills obsolete in a very short time. As a result, some companies are approaching the development of their management team as an ongoing, career-long process and require their managers to periodically attend refresher courses.

Jack Welch was so committed to making cultural changes within GE that he created the now famous Crotonville, New York, training facility to develop an army of change leaders. GE put more than ten thousand managers a year through a three-step workshop series called the Change Acceleration Program (CAP). Leadership was redefined as a teaching activity in which leaders taught their direct reports how to change the way they did their jobs. In order to make the system-wide changes Welch thought were needed, he turned to individual OD.[35]

As corporate America invests hundreds of millions of dollars in management development, certain guiding principles are evolving: (1) management development is a multifaceted, complex, and long-term process to which there is no quick or simple approach; (2) organizations should carefully and systematically identify their unique developmental needs and evaluate their programs accordingly; (3) management development objectives must be compatible with organizational objectives; and (4) the utility and value of management development remain more an article of faith than a proven fact.[36]

Team Building

When interaction among group members is critical to group success and effectiveness, team development, or team building, may be useful. Team building emphasizes members working together in a spirit of cooperation and generally has one or more of the following goals:

1. To set team goals and priorities
2. To analyze or allocate the way work is performed
3. To examine how a group is working—that is, to examine processes such as norms, decision making, and communications
4. To examine relationships among the people doing the work[37]

Total quality management efforts usually focus on teams, and the principles of team building must be applied to make them work. Team participation is especially important in the data-gathering and evaluation phases of team development. In data gathering, the members share information on the functioning of the group. The opinions of the group thus form the foundation of the development process. In the evaluation phase, members are the source of information about the effectiveness of the development effort.[38]

Like total quality management and many other management techniques, team building should not be thought of as a one-time experience, perhaps something undertaken on a retreat from the workplace; rather, it is a continuing process. It may take weeks, months, or years for a group to learn to pull together and function as a team. Team development can be a way to train the group to solve its own problems in the future. Research on the effectiveness of team building as an organization development tool so far is mixed and inconclusive.

Survey Feedback

Survey feedback techniques can form the basis for a change process. In this process, data are gathered, analyzed, summarized, and returned to those who generated them to identify, discuss, and solve problems. A survey feedback process is often set in motion either by the organization's top management or by a consultant to management. By providing information about employees' beliefs and attitudes, a survey can help management diagnose and solve an organization's problems. A consultant or change agent usually coordinates the process and is responsible for data gathering, analysis, and summary. The three-stage process is shown in Figure 16.4.[39]

The use of survey feedback techniques in an organization development process differs from their use in traditional attitude surveys. In an organization

Figure 16.4

The Survey Feedback Process

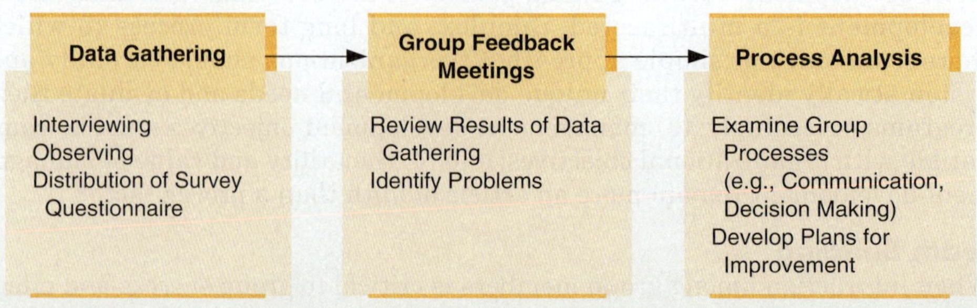

The survey feedback process has three distinct stages, which must be fully completed for the process to be most effective. As an organization development process, its purpose is to fully involve all employees in data analysis, problem identification, and development of solutions.

development process, data are (1) returned to employee groups at all levels in the organization and (2) used by all employees working together in their normal work groups to identify and solve problems. In traditional attitude surveys, top management reviews the data and may or may not initiate a new program to solve problems the survey has identified.

In the data-gathering stage, the change agent interviews selected personnel from appropriate levels to determine the key issues to be examined. Information from these interviews is used to develop a survey questionnaire, which is distributed to a large sample of employees. The questionnaire may be a standardized instrument, an instrument developed specifically for the organization, or a combination of the two. The questionnaire data are analyzed and aggregated by group or department to ensure that respondents remain anonymous.[40] Then the change agent prepares a summary of the results for the group feedback sessions. From this point on, the consultant is involved in the process as a resource person and expert.

The feedback meetings generally involve only two or three levels of management. Meetings are usually held serially, first with a meeting of the top management group, which is then followed by meetings of employees throughout the organization. The group manager rather than the change agent typically leads sessions to transfer "ownership" of the data from the change agent to the work group. The feedback consists primarily of profiles of the group's attitudes toward the organization, the work, the leadership, and other topics on the questionnaire. During the feedback sessions, participants discuss reasons for the scores and the problems that the data reveal.

In the process analysis stage, the group examines the process of making decisions, communicating, and accomplishing work, usually with the help of the consultant. Unfortunately, groups often overlook this stage as they become absorbed in the survey data and the problems revealed during the feedback sessions. Occasionally, group managers simply fail to hold feedback and process analysis sessions. Change agents should ensure that managers hold these sessions and that they are rewarded for doing so. The process analysis stage is important because its purpose is to develop action plans to make improvements. Several sessions may be required to discuss the process issues fully and to settle on a strategy for improvements. Groups often find it useful to document the plans as they are discussed and to appoint a member to follow up on implementation. Generally, the follow-up assesses whether communication and communication processes have actually been improved. A follow-up survey can be administered several months to a year later to assess how much these processes have changed since they were first reported.

The survey feedback method is probably one of the most widely used organization change and development interventions. If any of its stages are compromised or omitted, however, the technique becomes less useful. A primary responsibility of the consultant or change agent, then, is to ensure that the method is fully and faithfully carried through.

RESISTANCE TO CHANGE

Change is inevitable; so is resistance to change. Paradoxically, organizations both promote and resist change. As an agent for change, the organization asks prospective customers or clients to change their current purchasing habits by switching to the company's products or services, asks current customers to change by increasing their purchases, and asks suppliers to reduce the costs of raw materials. The organization resists change in that its structure and control systems protect the daily tasks of producing a product or service from uncertainties in the environment. The organization must have some elements of permanence to avoid mirroring the instability of the environment, yet it must also react to external shifts with internal change to maintain currency and relevance in the marketplace.

A commonly held view is that all resistance to change needs to be overcome, but that is not always the case. Resistance to change can be used for the benefit of the organization and need not be eliminated entirely. By revealing a legitimate concern that a proposed change may harm the organization or that other alternatives might be better, resistance may alert the organization to reexamine the change.[41] For example, an organization may be considering acquiring a company in a completely different industry. Resistance to such a proposal may cause the organization to examine the advantages and disadvantages of the move more carefully. Without resistance, the decision might be made before the pros and cons have been sufficiently explored. Some have suggested that change agents may contribute to resistance through their mismanagement of the change process or miscommunication throughout the process.[42]

Resistance may come from the organization, the individual, or both. Determining the ultimate source is often difficult, however, because organizations are composed of individuals. Table 16.3 summarizes various types of organizational and individual sources of resistance. Our *Improve Your Skills* feature will also help you better assess your own aptitude toward change, especially as that change relates to innovation.

Table 16.3

Organizational and Individual Sources of Resistance

Organizational Sources	**Examples**
Overdetermination	Employment system, job descriptions, evaluation and reward system, organization culture
Narrow Focus of Change	Structure changed with no concern given to other issues (e.g., jobs, people)
Group Inertia	Group norms
Threatened Expertise	People move out of area of expertise
Threatened Power	Decentralized decision making
Resource Allocation	Increased use of part-time help
Individual Sources	**Examples**
Habit	Altered tasks
Security	Altered tasks or reporting relationships
Economic Factors	Changed pay and benefits
Fear of the Unknown	New job, new boss
Lack of Awareness	Isolated groups not heeding notices
Social Factors	Group norms

IMPROVE YOUR SKILLS

INNOVATIVE ATTITUDE SCALE

Change and innovation are important to organizations. This assessment surveys your readiness to accept and participate in innovation. Indicate the extent to which each of the following statements is true of either your *actual* behavior or your *intentions* at work. That is, describe the way you are or the way you intend to be on the job. Use this scale for your responses:

Rating Scale

5 - *Almost always true*
4 - *Often true*
3 - *Not applicable*
2 - *Seldom true*
1 - *Almost never true*

___ 1. I openly discuss with my boss how to get ahead
___ 2. I try new ideas and approaches to problems.
___ 3. I take things or situations apart to find out how they work.
___ 4. I welcome uncertainty and unusual circumstances related to my tasks.
___ 5. I negotiate my salary openly with my supervisor.
___ 6. I can be counted on to find a new use for existing methods or equipment.
___ 7. Among my colleagues and coworkers, I will be the first or nearly the first to try out a new idea or method.
___ 8. I take the opportunity to translate communications from other departments for my work group.
___ 9. I demonstrate originality.
___ 10. I will work on a problem that has caused others great difficulty.
___ 11. I provide critical input toward a new solution.
___ 12. I provide written evaluations of proposed ideas.
___ 13. I develop contacts with experts outside my firm.
___ 14. I use personal contacts to maneuver myself into choice work assignments.
___ 15. I make time to pursue my own pet ideas or projects.
___ 16. I set aside resources for the pursuit of a risky project.
___ 17. I tolerate people who depart from organizational routine.
___ 18. I speak out in staff meetings.
___ 19. I work in teams to try to solve complex problems.
___ 10. If my coworkers are asked, they will say I am a wit.

Scoring: Count the number of times you circled each of the 5 responses, and then use the following table to compute your score:

Answer Scale:	# of Times Circled	×	# of Points	=	Totals
5 - Almost always true	____	×	5	=	____
4 - Often true	____	×	4	=	____
3 - Not applicable	____	×	3	=	____
2 - Seldom true	____	×	2	=	____
1 - Almost never true	____	×	1	=	____
TOTAL					____

Interpretation: The higher your total score, the more willing you are to be innovative. Your attitude toward innovation is more positive than that of people who score low. A score of 72 or greater is relatively high, while a score of 45 or less is relatively low. People who are not innovators have a tendency to maintain the status quo.

Source: Adapted Ettlie, J. E., & O'Keefe, R. D. (1982). Innovative Attitudes, Values, and Intentions in Organizations, *Journal of Management Studies, 19*, 176. ©1982 by Blackwell Publishers Ltd. Reprinted by permission of Blackwell Publishing Ltd.

Organizational Sources of Resistance

Daniel Katz and Robert Kahn have identified six major organizational sources of resistance: overdetermination, narrow focus of change, group inertia, threatened expertise, threatened power, and changes in resource allocation.[43] Of course, not every organization or every change situation displays all six sources.

Overdetermination

Organizations have several systems designed to maintain stability. For example, consider how organizations control employees' performance. Job candidates must have certain specific skills so that they can do the job the organization needs them to do. A new employee is given a job description, and the supervisor trains, coaches, and counsels the employee in job tasks. The new employee usually serves some type of probationary period that culminates in a performance review; thereafter, the employee's performance is regularly evaluated. Finally, rewards, punishment, and discipline are administered, depending on the employee's level of performance. Such a system is said to be characterized by ***overdetermination***, or ***structural inertia***,[44] in that one could probably have the same effect on employee performance with fewer procedures and safeguards. In other words, the structure of the organization produces resistance to change because it was designed to maintain stability. Another important source of overdetermination is the culture of the organization. As discussed in Chapter 15, the culture of an organization can have powerful and long-lasting effects on the behavior of its employees.

overdetermination (structural inertia)
Occurs because numerous organizational systems are in place to ensure that employees and systems behave as expected to maintain stability.

Narrow Focus of Change

Many efforts to create change in organizations adopt too narrow a focus. Any effort to force change in the tasks of individuals or groups must take into account the interdependence among organizational elements such as people, structure, tasks, and the information system. For example, some attempts at redesigning jobs fail because the organization structure within which the jobs must function is inappropriate for the redesigned jobs.[45]

Group Inertia

When an employee attempts to change his or her work behavior, the group may resist by refusing to change other behaviors that are necessary complements to the individual's altered behavior. In other words, group norms may act as a brake on individual attempts at behavior change.

Threatened Expertise

A change in the organization may threaten the specialized expertise that individuals and groups have developed over the years. A job redesign or a structural change may transfer responsibility for a specialized task from the current expert to someone else, threatening the specialist's expertise and building his or her resistance to the change.

Threatened Power

Any redistribution of decision-making authority, such as with reengineering or team-based management, may threaten an individual's power relationships with others. If an organization is decentralizing its decision making, managers who wielded their decision-making powers in return for special favors from others may resist the change because they do not want to lose their power base.

Resource Allocation

Groups that are satisfied with current resource allocation methods may resist any change they believe will threaten future allocations. Resources in this context can mean anything from monetary rewards and equipment to additional seasonal help to more computer time.

These six sources explain most types of organization-based resistance to change. All are based on people and social relationships. Many of these sources of resistance can be traced to groups or individuals who are afraid of losing something—resources, power, or comfort in a routine.

Individual Sources of Resistance

Individual sources of resistance to change are rooted in basic human characteristics such as needs and perceptions. Researchers have identified six reasons for individual resistance to change: habit, security, economic factors, fear of the unknown, lack of awareness, and social factors (see Table 16.3).[46]

Habit

It is easier to do a job the same way every day if the steps in the job are repeated over and over. Learning an entirely new set of steps makes the job more difficult. For the same amount of return (pay), most people prefer to do easier rather than harder work.

Security

Some employees like the comfort and security of doing things the same old way. They gain a feeling of constancy and safety from knowing that some things stay the same despite all the change going on around them. People who believe their security is threatened by a change are likely to resist the change.

Economic Factors

Change may threaten employees' steady paychecks. Workers may fear that change will make their jobs obsolete or reduce their opportunities for future pay increases.

Fear of the Unknown

Some people fear anything unfamiliar. Changes in reporting relationships and job duties create anxiety for such employees. Employees become familiar with their bosses and their jobs and develop relationships with others within the organization, such as contact people for various situations. These relationships and contacts help facilitate their work. Any disruption of familiar patterns

CATALIN PETOLEA/ SHUTTERSTOCK.COM

People tend to resist change for a variety of reasons. Organizations and managers who effectively overcome this resistance will likely continue to keep abreast of their competitors and remain viable organizations. But organizations and managers who do not deal with resistance may be contributing to the eventual demise of the firm.

may create fear because it can cause delays and foster the belief that nothing is getting accomplished.

Lack of Awareness

Because of perceptual limitations such as lack of attention or selective attention, a person may not recognize a change in a rule or procedure and thus may not alter his or her behavior. People may pay attention only to things that support their point of view. As an example, employees in an isolated regional sales office may not notice—or may ignore—directives from headquarters regarding a change in reporting procedures for expense accounts. They may therefore continue the current practice as long as possible.

Social Factors

People may resist change for fear of what others will think. As we mentioned before, the group can be a powerful motivator of behavior. Employees may believe change will hurt their image, result in ostracism from the group, or simply make them "different." For example, an employee who agrees to conform to work rules established by management may be ridiculed by others who openly disobey the rules.

MANAGING SUCCESSFUL ORGANIZATION CHANGE AND DEVELOPMENT

In order to increase the chances of successful organization change and development, it is useful to consider seven keys to managing change in organizations. They relate directly to the problems identified earlier and to our view of the organization as a comprehensive social system. Each can influence the elements of the social system and may help the organization avoid some of the major problems in managing the change. Table 16.4 lists the points and their potential impacts.

Consider Global Issues

One factor to consider is how global issues dictate organization change. As we have already noted, the environment is a significant factor in bringing about organization change. Given the additional environmental complexities multinational organizations face, it follows that organization change may be even more critical to them than it is to purely domestic organizations. Dell Computer, for example, owes much of its success to its original strategy of selling directly to consumers. Since 2006, however, it has expanded its distribution activities to include retail sales, and significant system-wide change has eased the company's entry into some key foreign markets.[47]

A second point to remember is that acceptance of change varies widely around the globe. Change is a normal and accepted part of organization life in some cultures. In other cultures, change causes many more problems. Managers should remember that techniques for managing change that have worked routinely back home may not work at all and may even trigger negative responses if used indiscriminately in other cultures.[48]

Table 16.4

Keys to Managing Successful Organization Change and Development

Key	Impact
Consider global issues	Keeps in touch with the latest global developments and how change is handled in different cultures
Take a holistic view of the organization	Helps anticipate the effects of change on the social system and culture
Start small	Works out details and shows the benefits of the change to those who might resist
Secure top-management support	Gets dominant coalition on the side of change: safeguards structural change, heads off problems of power and control
Encourage participation by those affected by the change	Minimizes transition problems of control, resistance, and task redefinition
Foster open communication	Minimizes transition problems of resistance and information and control systems
Reward those who contribute to change	Minimizes transition problems of resistance and control systems

Take a Holistic View

Managers must take a holistic view of the organization and the change project. A limited view can endanger the change effort because the subsystems of the organization are interdependent. A holistic view encompasses the culture and dominant coalition as well as the people, tasks, structure, and information subsystems.

Start Small

Peter Senge claims that every truly successful, system-wide change in large organizations starts small.[49] He recommends that change start with one team, usually an executive team. One team can evaluate the change, make appropriate adjustments along the way, and, most importantly, show that the new system works and gets desired results. If the change makes sense, it begins to spread to other teams, groups, and divisions throughout the system. Senge described how significant changes at Shell and Ford started small, with one or two parallel teams, and then spread as others recognized the benefits of the change. When others see the benefits, they automatically drop their inherent resistance and join in. They can voluntarily join and be committed to the success of the change effort.

Secure Top Management Support

The support of top management is essential to the success of any change effort. As the organization's probable dominant coalition, it is a powerful element of the social system, and its support is necessary to deal with control and power problems. For example, a manager who plans a change in the ways in which tasks are assigned and responsibility is delegated in his or her department must notify top management and gain its support. Complications may arise if disgruntled employees complain to high-level managers who have not been notified of the change or do not support it. The employees' complaints may jeopardize the manager's plan—and perhaps her or his job.

Encourage Participation

Problems related to resistance, control, and power can be overcome by broad participation in planning the change. Allowing people a voice in designing the change may give them a sense of power and control over their own destinies, which may help to win their support during implementation.

Foster Open Communication

Open communication is an important factor in managing resistance to change and overcoming information and control problems during transitions. Employees typically recognize the uncertainties and ambiguities that arise during a transition and seek information on the change and their place in the new system. In the absence of information, the gap may be filled with inappropriate or false information, which may endanger the change process. Rumors tend to spread through the grapevine faster than accurate information can be disseminated through official channels. A manager should always be sensitive to the effects of uncertainty on employees, especially during a period of change; any news, even bad news, seems better than no news.

Reward Contributors

Although this last point is simple, it can easily be neglected. Employees who contribute to the change in any way need to be rewarded. Too often, the only people acknowledged after a change effort are those who tried to stop it. Those who quickly grasp new work assignments, work harder to cover what otherwise might not get done during the transition, or help others adjust to changes deserve special credit—perhaps a mention in a news release or the internal company newspaper, special consideration in a performance appraisal, a merit raise, or a promotion. From a behavioral perspective, individuals need to benefit in some way if they are to willingly help change something that eliminates the old, comfortable way of doing the job.

In the current dynamic environment, managers must anticipate the need for change and satisfy it with more responsive and competitive organization systems. These seven keys to managing organization change may also serve as general guidelines for managing organizational behavior because organizations must change or face elimination.

ORGANIZATIONAL LEARNING

As American capitalist icon and philanthropist Andrew Carnegie said, "The only irreplaceable capital an organization possesses is the knowledge and ability of its people. The productivity of that capital depends on how effectively people share their competence with those who can use it." As Ray Stata, President and CEO of Analog Devices, said, "The rate at which organizations learn may become the only sustainable source of competitive advantage."[50]

A ***learning organization*** is an organization that facilitates the learning of all its members and continually transforms itself.[51] In a learning organization, continual learning and change become part of the culture. Wikis, blogs, and searchable databases are sometimes used to collect employees' knowledge and make it available to others.

learning organization
Organization that facilitates the learning of all its members and continuously transforms itself

To facilitate organizational learning, it is important that learning happen during a project and continue after the project ends. As one expert says, "You need to have some coaching or debriefing afterward, to make sure that people learn what you want them to learn. You need to get them to think through the experience. If things worked, why did they work? If they were screwed up, why did things get screwed up?" Without reflection, tasks may be completed, but learning does not occur.[52]

One of the best ways to encourage continual learning is through an *after-action review*, or a professional discussion of an event that enables discovery of what happened, why it happened, and how to sustain strengths and improve on weaknesses.[53] After-action reviews are conducted for both successes and failures and occur after any identifiable event or milestone during a project or after the project is completed. The purpose is never to assign credit or blame, but to carefully identify the circumstances that led to successful and less successful outcomes to enable learning.

Learning from an after-action review is usually by the group and for the group, although individuals can also conduct such a review. The review is usually conducted fairly quickly using a simple process. In an open and honest meeting usually lasting twenty minutes or less, everyone who participated in the event or project discusses four simple questions:

1. What was supposed to happen?
2. What actually happened?
3. Why were there differences?
4. What did we learn?

Building trust and team integrity are additional outcomes of after-action reviews.

Another factor influencing an organization's ability to learn is its approach to failure. Many organizations punish failures through lower performance evaluations, lower bonuses, or even terminations. More learning-oriented firms recognize the learning opportunities presented by "intelligent failures," that is, the failures of events or projects that had a good chance of working, did not work out, but provide a good learning opportunity. At the computer chipmaker Intel, one manager threw a big dinner every month—not for the group that had been most successful, but for the "failure of the month," to honor the group that had made a valiant effort that just did not work out. That manager communicated to his people that failures were an inevitable accompaniment of risk taking that should be talked about openly, not hidden, papered over, or blamed on others.[54] High-quality relationships in which employees feel psychologically safe enable organizational members to engage in learning from failures.[55]

SUMMARY AND APPLICATION

Change may be forced on an organization, or an organization may change in response to the environment or an internal need. Forces for change are interdependent and influence organizations in many ways. Currently, the areas in which the pressures for change seem most powerful involve people, technology, information processing and communication, competition, and social trends.

Planned organization change involves anticipating change and preparing for it. Lewin described organization change in terms of unfreezing, the change itself, and refreezing. In the continuous change process model, top management recognizes forces encouraging change, engages in a problem-solving process to design the change, and implements and evaluates the change.

Organization development is the process of planned change and improvement of organizations through the application of knowledge of the behavioral sciences. It is based on a systematic change process and focuses on managing the culture of the organization. The most comprehensive change involves altering the structure of the organization through reorganization of departments, reporting relationships, or authority systems.

Quality-of-work-life programs focus on providing a work environment in which employees can satisfy individual needs. Task and technological changes alter the way the organization accomplishes its primary tasks. Along with the steps usually associated with change, task redesign entails diagnosis, cost-benefit analysis, formulation of a redesign strategy, and implementation of supplemental changes.

Frequently used group and individual approaches to organization change are training and management development programs, team building, and survey feedback techniques. Training programs are usually designed to improve employees' job skills, to help employees adapt to other organization changes (such as a management-by-objectives program), or to develop employees' awareness and understanding of problems such as workplace safety or stress. Management development programs attempt to foster in current or future managers the skills, abilities, and perspectives important to good management. Team-building programs are designed to help a work team or group develop into a mature, functioning team by helping it define its goals or priorities, analyze its tasks and the way they are performed, and examine relationships among the people doing the work. As used in the organization development process, survey feedback techniques involve gathering data, analyzing and summarizing them, and returning them to employees and groups for discussion and to identify and solve problems.

Resistance to change may arise from several individual and organizational sources. Resistance may indicate a legitimate concern that the change is not good for the organization and may warrant a reexamination of plans. To manage change in organizations, international issues must be considered, and managers should take a holistic view of the organization and start small. Top management support is needed, and those most affected by the change must participate. Open communication is important, and those who contribute to the change effort should be rewarded.

A learning organization is an organization that facilitates the learning of all its members and continually transforms itself. In a learning organization, continual learning and change become part of the culture. To facilitate organizational learning, it is important that learning happen during a project and continue after the project ends.

LOSKUTNIKOV/SHUTTERSTOCK.COM

REAL WORLD RESPONSE

MISMANAGED CHANGE AT KODAK

According to Harvard's John Kotter, a widely acknowledged authority on organizational change, "Kodak's problem ... is that it did not move into the digital world well enough and fast enough." It's pretty much a consensus opinion, but Kotter is careful to add the qualifier "on the surface." Below the surface, suggests Kotter, where Kodak made the business decisions that led to bankruptcy, it's an opinion that needs further investigation. Kodak, for example, pioneered digital technologies throughout the 1970s and 1980s, including innovations in color digital cameras, digital print kiosks, and digital image compression.

However, says Bill Fischer, CEO of the private equity firm Manzanita Capital, Kodak "failed to take advantage of their unique perspective.... We can suspect that Kodak, while recognizing the impending threat of a digital 'something,' probably did not immediately imagine that it would be a 'telephone' that would ultimately be the most damaging agent of disruption" to its core film- and camera-making businesses."

Some of the company's critics charge that, even on the brink of bankruptcy, Kodak managers failed—or refused—to acknowledge that many of the company's products had been marginalized by digital substitutions. During the bankruptcy process, for example, Kodak management hoped to sell one of the firm's prized assets—a package of 1,100 digital-imaging patents—for as much as $2.6 billion. Ultimately, the portfolio brought in only $527 million.

Kotter agrees with the consensus opinion that Kodak's demise was a result of "strategic decisions either avoided or made poorly." He reminds us, however, that there's still an underlying question to be answered: "*Why* did Kodak managers make the poor strategic decisions they made?" His own answer is fairly simple—on the surface: "The organization," he charges, "overflowed with complacency." In particular, says Kotter, Kodak failed to recognize that digital was a "huge opportunity" only if the company acted with equally "huge urgency." As a matter of fact, Kodak had developed the first electronic photographic camera in 1975, and as of 2005, it was the number-one seller of digital cameras in the U.S. Within two years, however, it had slipped to fourth, and by 2010 it had plummeted to number seven.

DISCUSSION QUESTIONS

1. Is most organization change forced on the organization by external factors or fostered from within? Explain.
2. What broad category of pressures for organization change other than the four discussed in the chapter can you think of? Briefly describe it.
3. Which sources of resistance to change present the most problems for an internal change agent? For an external change agent?
4. Which stage of the Lewin model of change do you think is most often overlooked? Why?
5. What are the advantages and disadvantages of having an internal change agent rather than an external change agent?
6. How does organization development differ from organization change?
7. How and why would organization development differ if the elements of the social system were not interdependent?
8. Do quality-of-work-life programs rely more on individual or organizational aspects of organizational behavior? Why?
9. Describe how the job of your professor could be redesigned. Include a discussion of other subsystems that would need to be changed as a result.
10. Which of the seven keys for successfully managing an organizational change effort seem to be the most difficult to manage? Why?

DEVELOP YOUR SKILLS

You are the general manager of a hotel situated along a beautiful stretch of beach on a tropical island. One of the oldest of six large resorts in the immediate area, your hotel is owned by a group of foreign investors. For several years, it has been operated as a franchise unit of a large international hotel chain, as are all of the other hotels on the island.

For the past few years, the hotel's franchisee-owners have been taking most of the profits for themselves and putting relatively little back into the hotel. They have also let you know that their business is not in good financial health and that the revenue from the hotel is being used to offset losses incurred elsewhere. In contrast, most of the other hotels on the island have recently been refurbished, and plans for two brand new hotels have been announced for the near future.

A team of executives from franchise headquarters has just visited your hotel. They are quite disappointed in the property, particularly because it has failed to keep pace with other resorts on the island. They have informed you that if the property is not brought up to standards, the franchise agreement, which is up for review in a year, will be revoked. You realize that this move would be a potential disaster because you cannot afford to lose the franchisor's brand name or access to its reservation system.

Sitting alone in your office, you identified several seemingly viable courses of action:

1. Convince the franchisee-owners to remodel the hotel. You estimate that it will take $5 million to meet the franchisor's minimum standards and another $5 million to bring the hotel up to the standards of the top resort on the island.

2. Convince the franchisor to give you more time and more options for upgrading the facility.
3. Allow the franchise agreement to terminate and try to succeed as an independent hotel.
4. Assume that the hotel will fail and start looking for another job. You have a pretty good reputation but are not terribly happy about the possibility of having to accept a lower-level position (say, as an assistant manager) with another firm.

Having mulled over your options, do the following:

1. Rank-order your four alternatives in terms of probable success. Make any necessary assumptions.
2. Identify alternatives other than those that you have identified above.
3. Ask yourself: Can more than one alternative be pursued simultaneously? Which ones?

Develop an overall strategy for trying to save the hotel while protecting your own interests.

GROUP EXERCISE

Planning a Change at the University

This exercise will help you understand the complexities of change in organizations.
Format: Your task is to plan the implementation of a major change in an organization.

Part 1

The class will divide into five groups of approximately equal size. Your instructor will assign each group one of the following changes:

1. A change from the semester system to the quarter system (or the opposite, depending on the school's current system)
2. A requirement that all work—homework, examinations, term papers, problem sets—be done digitally on computers and submitted online
3. A requirement that all students live on campus
4. A requirement that all students have reading, writing, and speaking fluency in at least three languages, including English and Japanese, to graduate
5. A requirement that all students room with someone in the same major

First, decide what individuals and groups must be involved in the change process. Then decide how the change will be implemented using Lewin's process of organization change (Figure 16.1) as a framework. Consider how to deal with resistance to change, using Tables 16.3 and 16.4 as guides. Decide whether a change agent (internal or external) should be used. Develop a realistic timetable for full implementation of the change. Is transition management appropriate?

Part 2

Using the same groups as in Part 1, your next task is to describe the techniques you would use to implement the change described in Part 1. You may use structural changes, task and technology methods, group and individual programs, or any combination of these. You may need to go to the library to gather more information on some techniques. You should also discuss how you will utilize the seven keys to successful change management discussed at the end of the chapter.

Your instructor may make this exercise an in-class project, but it is also a good semester-ending project for groups to work on outside of class. Either way, the exercise is most beneficial when the groups report their implementation programs to the entire class. Each group should report on which change techniques are to be used, why they were selected, how they will be implemented, and how problems will be avoided.

Follow-Up Questions Part 1

1. How similar were the implementation steps for each change?
2. Were the plans for managing resistance to change realistic?
3. Do you think any of the changes could be successfully implemented at your school? Why or why not?

Part 2

1. Did various groups use the same technique in different ways or to accomplish different goals?
2. If you did outside research on organization development techniques for your project, did you find any techniques that seemed more applicable than those in this chapter? If so, describe one of them.

VIDEO EXERCISE

Mitchell Gold + Bob Williams: Organization Change and Development

When Kim Clay began answering phones as a consumer inquiry representative for Mitchell Gold + Bob Williams, she was neither particularly self-confident, nor was she certain about the direction of her career. Nevertheless, her co-workers instantly noted her positive work attitudes, and Clay eventually moved on to the Customer Care department where her good-natured personality was popular not only with customers but also with co-workers who often requested her assistance on computer issues.

In many organizations, hidden talents often remain hidden. But at Mitchell Gold + Bob Williams, managers encourage employees to discover their talents and seize new opportunities. When managers discovered Clay's knack for handling computer issues, they decided to create a new position for her: computer help desk specialist. Despite her lack of formal computer education, Clay jumped at the opportunity, and today, she is the chief of technology for MG+BW. To managers and colleagues who spotted Clay's positive work attitudes early on, the employee's rise through the ranks was no surprise. Even so, no one could have predicted the unique career path she made for herself.

Discussion Questions

1. What forces for organization change are reflected at Mitchell Gold + Bob Williams?
2. Suppose that there was a need to move Kim Clay out of her current job and into a new one. How might this change process be managed most effectively?
3. In what ways is Mitchell Gold + Bob Williams using organization development?

Now What?

VIDEO CASE

PERCOM/SHUTTERSTOCK.COM

Imagine Happy Time Toys has been making changes to both toy product lines and quality goals. You find yourself listening to a coworker exhibiting resistance to Happy Time Toys' quality and production goals for a new product line. She complains about the changes and states that the product is tricky to assemble and the goals are unrealistic. Also, because of recent changes, the coworker believes that the company is too concerned about quality at the expense of productivity. The coworker feels that the company could make a lot more money if they let some of the team's borderline products go through. The coworker is going to continue to tell the team to pass borderline products to help the team meet its production goals to earn the bonus. This would reduce the employees' stress and, after all, the products are not that bad. *What do you say or do?* Go to this chapter's "Now What?" video, watch the challenge video, and choose a response. Be sure to also view the outcomes of the two responses you didn't choose.

Discussion Questions

1. What types of resistance to change did you see in the various situations?
2. How did Alex unfreeze Allison's perspective and what impact did that have?
3. Using concepts from the chapter, what would you have done to make the transition to the new product line go more smoothly?

ENDNOTES

[1]Kotter, J. (2012, May 2). Barriers to Change: The Real Reason behind the Kodak Downfall. *Forbes*. Available at: http://www.forbes.com/sites/johnkotter/2012/05/02/barriers-to-change-the-real-reason-behind-the-kodak-downfall/; DiSalvo, D. (2011, October 2). The Fall of Kodak: A Tale of Disruptive Technology and Bad Business. *Forbes*. Available at: http://www.forbes.com/sites/daviddisalvo/2011/10/02/what-i-saw-as-kodak-crumbled/; Fischer, B. (2014, July 4). There Are No "Kodak Moments." *Forbes*. Available at: http://www.forbes.com/sites/billfischer/2014/07/04/there-are-no-kodak-moments/; Julie Creswell, J. (2013, May 3). Kodak's Fuzzy Future. *New York Times*. Available at: http://dealbook.nytimes.com/2013/05/03/after-bankruptcy-a-leaner-kodak-faces-an-uphill-battle/; Hill, A. (2012, April 5). Kodak—A Victim of Its Own Success. *Financial Times*. Available at: http://www.ft.com/cms/s/0/b2076888-7a52 11e1-839f-00144feab49a.html#axzz3e052KBe0.

[2]Grossman, L. (2005, January 24). Grow Up? Not So Fast. *Time*, 42.

[3]Thielfoldt, D. & Scheef, D. (2004, August). Generation X and the Millennials: What You Need to Know About Mentoring

the New Generations. *Law Practice Today*. Available at: http://apps.americanbar.org/lpm/lpt/articles/mgt08044.html

[4]Olguin, M. A. (2012, April 13). 5 Tips for Managing Millennial Employees. *Inc.com*. Available at: http://www.inc.com/michael-olguin/5-tips-for-managing-millennial-employees.html.

[5]Huey, J. (1993, April 5). Managing in the Midst of Chaos. *Fortune*, 38–48.

[6]Stanley, C. (2012, May 6). At one school district, the motto is BYOT—Bring Your Own Technology. *NBC News*. Available at: http://dailynightly.msnbc.msn.com/_news/2012/05/06/11567170-at-one-school-district-the-motto-is-byot-bring-your-own-technology?lite.

[7]DuPont Adopts New Direction in China. Xinhua News Agency. September 7, 1999, p.1008250h0104; Taylor, A., III (1999, April 26). Why DuPont Is Trading Oil for Corn. *Fortune*, 154–160; Palmer, J. (1998, May 11). New DuPont: For Rapid Growth, an Old-Line Company Looks to Drugs, Biotechnology. *Barron's*, 31.

[8]Greimel, H. (2013, December 1st). Honda's new plant takes manufacturing to the next level. http://www.autonews.com/article/20131201/OEM01/312029986/hondas-new-plant-takes-manufacturing-to-the-next-level. Chappell, L. (2015, August, 17th). Honda's factory fix: Robots. http://www.autonews.com/article/20150817/OEM01/308179970/hondas-factory-fix:-robots. Honda in Canada (2015, August 29th). HCM Operations. https://www.honda.ca/honda-in-canada/manufacturing/operations (accessed August 29th, 2015).

[9]Schomer, S. (2010, May). Body Language. *Fast Company*, 61–66.

[10]Tsai, E. (2010, May 20). How to Integrate Email Marketing, SEO, and Social Media. *bx.businessweek.com*. Available at: http://www.designdamage.com/how-to-integrate-email-marketing-seo-and-social-media/#axzz3e0UD0VG1.

[11]Silverman, R. E., & Sidel, R. (2012, April 18). Warming Up to the Officeless Office. *Wall Street Journal*, B1.

[12]Stewart, T. A. (1993, December 13). Welcome to the Revolution. *Fortune*, 66–80.

[13]Chafkin, M. (2009, May 1). The Zappos Way of Managing. *Inc.com*. Available at: http://www.inc.com/magazine/20090501/the-zappos-way-of-managing_pagen_6.html.

[14]For an excellent account of the impact of globalization and technology, see Friedman, T. L. (2007). *The World Is Flat 3.0: A Brief History of the Twenty-First Century*. New York: Farrar, Straus & Giroux.

[15]Lewin, K. (1951). *Field Theory in Social Science*. New York: Harper & Row.

[16]Burke, W. W. (2003). Leading Organizational Change. In *Organization 21C: Someday All Organizations Will Lead This Way*, ed. S. Chowdhury (pp. 291–310). Upper Saddle River, NJ: Financial Times Prentice Hall.

[17]Marks, M. L. (2010, May 24). In With the New. *Wall Street Journal*, B1.

[18]Ackerman, L. S. (1982, Summer). Transition Management: An In-Depth Look at Managing Complex Change. *Organizational Dynamics*, 46–66; Nadler, D. A. (1982, Summer). Managing Transitions to Uncertain Future States. *Organizational Dynamics*, 37–45.

[19]Burke, W. W. (2003). Leading Organizational Change. In *Organization 21C: Someday All Organizations Will Lead This Way*, ed. S. Chowdhury (pp. 291–310). Upper Saddle River, NJ: Financial Times Prentice Hall.

[20]Tichy, N. M., & Ulrich, D. O. (1984, Fall). The Leadership Challenge—A Call for the Transformational Leader. *Sloan Management Review*, 59–68.

[21]Burke, W. W. (1982). *Organization Development: Principles and Practices*. Boston: Little, Brown.

[22]Beer, M. (1980). *Organization Change and Development*. Santa Monica, CA: Goodyear; Burke, W. W. (1982). *Organization Development: Principles and Practices*. Boston: Little, Brown.

[23]Cummings, T. G., & Worley, C. G. (1997). *Organization Development and Change* (6th ed., p. 2). Cincinnati, OH: South-Western Publishing.

[24]Tichy, N. M., & DeRose, C. (2003). The Death and Rebirth of Organizational Development. In *Organization 21C: Someday All Organizations Will Lead This Way*, ed. S. Chowdhury (p. 155–177). Upper Saddle River, NJ: Financial Times Prentice Hall.

[25]Miller, D. & Friesen, P. H. (1982, December). Structural Change and Performance: Quantum Versus Piecemeal-Incremental Approaches. *Academy of Management Journal*, 867–892.

[26]Carty, S. S. (2005, February 27). Bill Ford Carries on Family Name with Grace. *USA Today* Available at: http://www.usatoday.com/money/autos/2005-02-27-ford-ceo-usat_x.htm; Ford Enters New Era of E-Communication: New Web Sites Connect Dealers, Consumer, Suppliers. *PR Newswire*, January 24, 2000, p. 7433; Wetlaufer, S. (1999, March–April). Driving Change. *Harvard Business Review*, 77–85; Ford's Passing Fancy, *Business Week*, March 15, 1999, 42; Saporito, B. (2010, August 9). Can Alan Mulally Keep Ford in the Fast Lane? *Time*. Available at: http://content.time.com/time/magazine/article/0,9171,2007401,00.html.

[27]Suttle, J. L. (1977). Improving Life at Work— Problems and Prospects. In *Improving Life at Work: Behavioral Science Approaches to Organizational Change*, eds. J. R. Hackman & J. L. Suttle (p. 4). Santa Monica, CA: Goodyear.

[28]Walton, R. E. (1983, Fall). Quality of Work Life: What Is It? *Sloan Management Review*, 11–21.

[29]See DISA website. Available at: http://www.disa.mil/Careers/Quality-of-Work-Life.

[30]Ondrack, D. A., & Evans, M. G. (1987, March). Job Enrichment and Job Satisfaction in Greenfield and Redesign QWL Sites. *Group & Organization Studies*, 5–22.

[31]Farmer, B. (2008, September 5). Fiat 500 Is Britain's Sexiest Car. *Telegraph*, http://www.telegraph.co.uk/motoring/news/2754447/Fiat-500-is-Britains-sexiest-car.html; Gumbel, P. Chrysler's Sergio Marchionne: The Turnaround Artista. *Time*, http://content.time.com/time/magazine/article/0,9171,1905416,00.html; Online Extra: Fiat's Sexy Designs on Success, *BusinessWeek*, January 16, 2006. Available at: http://www.bloomberg.com/bw/stories/2006-01-15/online-extra-fiats-sexy-designs-on-success; Langlois, S. (2009, December 3). Style and Substance. *MarketWatch*. Available at: http://www.marketwatch.com/story/fiats-marchionne-drives-change-2009-12-03.

[32]Griffin, R. W. (1982). *Task Design: An Integrative Framework*. Glenview, IL: Scott, Foresman.

[33]Moorhead, G. (1981, April). Organizational Analysis: An Integration of the Macro and Micro Approaches. *Journal of Management Studies*, 161–218.

[34]Quick, J. C., & Quick, J. D. (1984). *Organizational Stress and Preventive Management*. New York: McGraw-Hill.

[35]Tichy, N. M., & DeRose, C. (2003). The Death and Rebirth of Organizational Development. In *Organization 21C: Someday All Organizations Will Lead This Way*, ed. S. Chowdhury (pp. 155–177). Upper Saddle River, NJ: Financial Times Prentice Hall.

[36]Wexley, K. N., & Baldwin, T. T. (1986, Summer). Management Development. *1986 Yearly Review of Management of the Journal of Management*, *Journal of Management*, 277–294.

[37]Beckhard, R. (1972, Summer). Optimizing Team-Building Efforts. *Journal of Contemporary Business*, 23–27, 30–32.

[38]Bass, B. M. (1983, February). Issues Involved in Relations Between Methodological Rigor and Reported Outcomes in Evaluations of Organizational Development. *Journal of Applied Psychology*, 167–201; Vicars, W. M., & Hartke, D. D. (1984, June). Evaluating OD Evaluations: A Status Report. *Group & Organization Studies*, 177–188.

[39]Beer, M. (1980). *Organization Change and Development*. Santa Monica, CA: Goodyear.

[40]Franklin, J. L. (1978, May–June). Improving the Effectiveness of Survey Feedback. *Personnel*, 11–17.

[41]Lawrence, P. R. (1954, May–June). How to Deal with Resistance to Change. *Harvard Business Review*. Reprinted in *Organizational Change and Development*, eds. G. W. Dalton, P. R. Lawrence, & L. E. Greiner (pp. 181–167. Homewood, IL: Irwin.

[42]Ford, J. D., Ford, L. W., & D'Amelio, A. (2008,April). Resistance to Change: The Rest of the Story. *Academy of Management Review*, 362–377.

[43]Katz, D., & Kahn, R. L. (1978). *The Social Psychology of Organizations* (2nd ed., pp. 36–68). New York: John Wiley and Sons.

[44]For an in-depth discussion of structural inertia, see Hannah, M. T., & Freeman, J. (1984, April). Structural Inertia and Organizational Change. *American Sociological Review*, 149–164.

[45]Moorhead, G. (1981, April). Organizational Analysis: An Integration of the Macro and Micro Approaches. *Journal of Management Studies*, 161–218.

[46]Zaltman, G. & Duncan, R. (1977). *Strategies for Planned Change*. New York: John Wiley and Sons; Nadler, D. A. (1983). Concepts for the Management of Organizational Change. In *Perspectives on Behavior in Organizations*, eds. J. R. Hackman, E. E. Lawler III, & L. W. Porter (2nd ed., pp. 551–561). New York: McGraw-Hill.

[47]Dell Sees Unrivalled Opportunity in Connected Era and Fast Growing Economies," Dell Inc. press release, April 10, 2008. Available at: http://cityskywallpaper.blogspot.com/2008/09/dell-sees-unrivalled-opportunity-in.html; Ewing, J. (2007, September 27). Where Dell Sells with Brick and Mortar. *BusinessWeek*, Available at: http://www.bloomberg.com/bw/stories/2007-09-27/where-dell-sells-with-brick-and-mortarbusinessweek-business-news-stock-market-and-financial-advice; Dell Says Sales in India Grew to $700 Million. *Wall Street Journal*, March 25, 2008, B1; Einhorn, B. (2007, September 24). Dell Goes Retail in China with Gome. *BusinessWeek*. Available at: http://www.bloomberg.com/bw/stories/2007-09-24/dell-goes-retail-in-china-with-gomebusinessweek-business-news-stock-market-and-financial-advice; Microsoft Sees China PC Sales Growing 20% in 2011. *MarketWatch*, March 18, 2010.

[48]Jaeger, A. M. (1986, January). Organization Development and National Culture: Where's the Fit? *Academy of Management Review*, 178–160.

[49]Webber, A. M. (1999, May). Learning for a Change. *Fast Company*, 178–188.

[50]Senge, P. (2006). *The Fifth Discipline: The Art and Practice of the Learning Organization* (p. 349). New York: Broadway Business.

[51]Pedler, M., Burgogyne, J., & Boydell, T. (1997). *The Learning Company: A Strategy for Sustainable Development* (2nd ed., p. 1). London: McGraw-Hill.

[52]Kiger, P. J. (2007, May). Task Force Training Develops New Leaders, Solves Real Business Issues, and Helps Cut Costs. *Workforce Management Online*. Available at: http://www.workforce.com/articles/task-force-training-develops-new-leaders-solves-real-business-issues-and-helps-cut-costs.

[53]Ellis, S., Ganzach, Y., Castle, E., & Sekely, G. (2010). The Effect of Filmed Versus Personal After-Event Reviews on Task Performance: The Mediating and Moderating Role of Self-Efficacy. *Journal of Applied Psychology, 95*, 122–131.

[54]Simons, R. (2005). *Levers of Organization Design: How Managers Use Accountability Systems for Greater Performance and Commitment* (p. 184). Boston: Harvard Business School Press.

[55]Carmeli, A., & Gittell, J. H. (2008). High-Quality Relationships, Psychological Safety, and Learning from Failures in Work Organizations. *Journal of Organizational Behavior, 30*, 709–729.

NAME INDEX

Y

Z

COMPANY INDEX

SUBJECT INDEX

C

F

G

H

I

J

K

L

M

P

Q

R

S

T

U

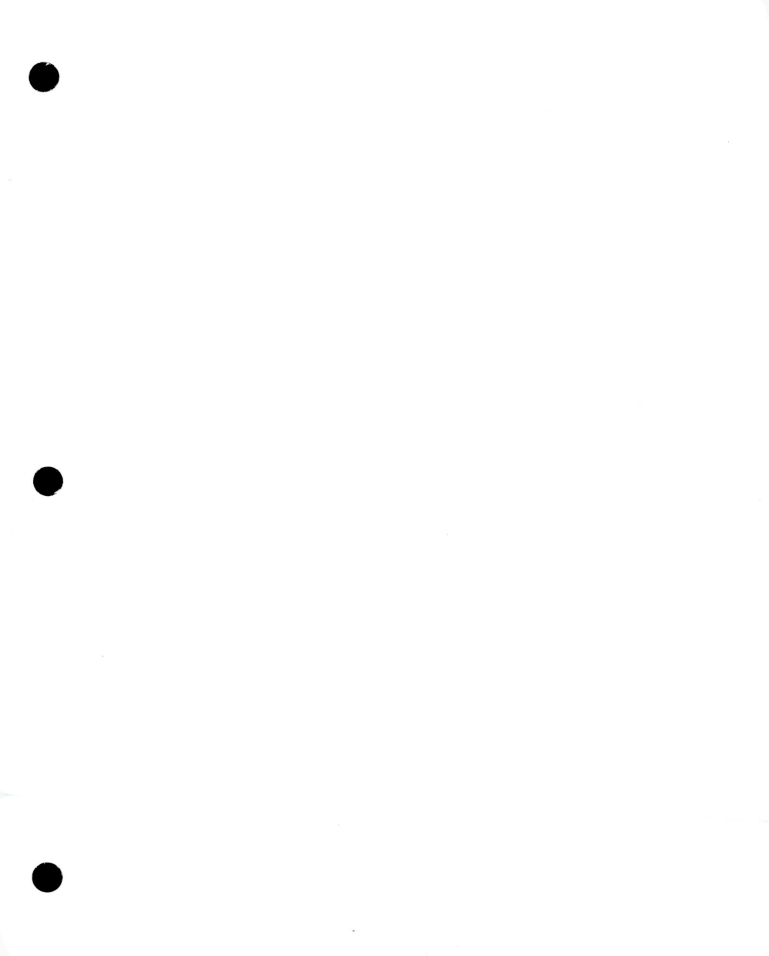